ACCA

PAPER P3

BUSINESS ANALYSIS

BPP Learning Media is an **ACCA Approved Content Provider**. This means we work closely with ACCA to ensure this Study Text contains the information you need to pass your exam.

In this Study Text, which has been reviewed by the **ACCA examination team,** we:

- Highlight the most important elements in the syllabus and the key skills you need

- Signpost how each chapter links to the syllabus and the study guide

- Provide lots of exam focus points demonstrating what is expected of you in the exam

- Emphasise key points in regular fast forward summaries

- Test your knowledge in quick quizzes

- Examine your understanding in our practice question bank

- Reference all the important topics in our full index

BPP's **Practice & Revision Kit** also supports this paper.

FOR EXAMS FROM 1 SEPTEMBER 2015 TO 31 AUGUST 2016

First edition 2007
Eighth edition April 2015

ISBN 9781 4727 2681 0
(Previous ISBN 9781 4727 1087 1)

eISBN 9781 4727 2759 6

British Library Cataloguing-in-Publication Data

A catalogue record for this book
is available from the British Library

Published by

BPP Learning Media Ltd
BPP House, Aldine Place
London W12 8AA

www.bpp.com/learningmedia

Printed in the United Kingdom by

Polestar Wheatons
Hennock Road
Marsh Barton
Exeter
EX2 8RP

Your learning materials, published by BPP Learning
Media Ltd, are printed on paper obtained from
traceable sustainable sources.

We are grateful to the Association of Chartered Certified
Accountants for permission to reproduce past
examination questions. The suggested solutions in the
practice answer bank have been prepared by BPP
Learning Media Ltd, unless otherwise stated.

BPP
LEARNING MEDIA

Contents

A note about copyright

Dear Customer

What does the little © mean and why does it matter?

Your market-leading BPP books, course materials and elearning materials do not write and update themselves. People write them: on their own behalf or as employees of an organisation that invests in this activity. Copyright law protects their livelihoods. It does so by creating rights over the use of the content.

Breach of copyright is a form of theft – as well being a criminal offence in some jurisdictions, it is potentially a serious breach of professional ethics.

With current technology, things might seem a bit hazy but, basically, without the express permission of BPP Learning Media:
- Photocopying our materials is a breach of copyright
- Scanning, ripcasting or conversion of our digital materials into different file formats, uploading them to Facebook or emailing them to your friends is a breach of copyright

You can, of course, sell your books, in the form in which you have bought them – once you have finished with them. (Is this fair to your fellow students? We update for a reason.) But the e-products are sold on a single user licence basis: we do not supply 'unlock' codes to people who have bought them second hand.

And what about outside the UK? BPP Learning Media strives to make our materials available at prices students can afford by local printing arrangements, pricing policies and partnerships which are clearly listed on our website. A tiny minority ignore this and indulge in criminal activity by illegally photocopying our material or supporting organisations that do. If they act illegally and unethically in one area, can you really trust them?

Helping you to pass

BPP Learning Media – ACCA Approved Content Provider

As an ACCA **Approved Content Provider**, BPP Learning Media gives you the **opportunity** to use study materials reviewed by the ACCA examination team. By incorporating the examination team's comments and suggestions regarding the depth and breadth of syllabus coverage, the BPP Learning Media Study Text provides excellent, **ACCA-approved** support for your studies.

The PER alert

Before you can qualify as an ACCA member, you not only have to pass all your exams but also fulfil a three year **practical experience requirement** (PER). To help you to recognise areas of the syllabus that you might be able to apply in the workplace to achieve different performance objectives, we have introduced the '**PER alert**' feature. You will find this feature throughout the Study Text to remind you that what you are **learning to pass** your ACCA exams is **equally useful to the fulfilment of the PER requirement**.

Your achievement of the PER should now be recorded in your on-line *My Experience* record.

Tackling studying

Studying can be a daunting prospect, particularly when you have lots of other commitments. The **different features** of the text, the **purposes** of which are explained fully on the **Chapter features** page, will help you whilst studying and improve your chances of **exam success**.

Developing exam awareness

Our Texts are completely **focused** on helping you pass your exam.

Our advice on **Studying P3** outlines the **content** of the paper, the **necessary skills** you are expected to be able to demonstrate and any **brought forward knowledge** you are expected to have.

Exam focus points are included within the chapters to highlight when and how specific topics were examined, or how they might be examined in the future.

Using the Syllabus and Study Guide

You can find the Syllabus and Study Guide on page xvii–xxxii of this Study Text.

Testing what you can do

Testing yourself helps you develop the skills you need to pass the exam and also confirms that you can recall what you have learnt.

We include **Questions** – lots of them – both within chapters and in the **Practice Question Bank**, as well as **Quick Quizzes** at the end of each chapter to test your knowledge of the chapter content.

Chapter features

Each chapter contains a number of helpful features to guide you through each topic.

Topic list

Topic list	Syllabus reference

What you will be studying in this chapter and the relevant section numbers, together with ACCA syllabus references.

Introduction

Puts the chapter content in the context of the syllabus as a whole.

Study Guide

Links the chapter content with ACCA guidance.

Exam Guide

Highlights how examinable the chapter content is likely to be and the ways in which it could be examined.

Knowledge brought forward from earlier studies

What you are assumed to know from previous studies/exams.

FAST FORWARD

Summarises the content of main chapter headings, allowing you to preview and review each section easily.

Examples

Demonstrate how to apply key knowledge and techniques.

Key terms

Definitions of important concepts that can often earn you easy marks in exams.

Exam focus points

When and how specific topics were examined, or how they may be examined in the future.

Formula to learn

Formulae that are not given in the exam but which have to be learnt.

Gives you a useful indication of syllabus areas that closely relate to performance objectives in your Practical Experience Requirement (PER).

 Question

Gives you essential practice of techniques covered in the chapter.

 Case Study

Real world examples of theories and techniques.

Chapter Roundup

A full list of the Fast Forwards included in the chapter, providing an easy source of review.

Quick Quiz

A quick test of your knowledge of the main topics in the chapter.

Practice Question Bank

Found at the back of the Study Text with more comprehensive chapter questions. Cross referenced for easy navigation.

BPP LEARNING MEDIA

Studying P3

Much of the P3 exam is concerned with business strategy. As a Chartered Certified Accountant you are likely to find yourself dealing with matters that are of strategic importance to your organisation. It is important, therefore, that you have an understanding of the way business strategy is conducted so that your input is appropriate and properly considered.

However, the name of P3 is **Business Analysis**, not Business Strategy. Business Analysis is wider than simply strategy and this paper will also draw from your financial and business skills gained during your studies so far. It brings these concepts together and encourages you to take a wider view of the organisations you are presented with in order to give your analysis of those organisations as a whole.

1 What P3 is about

The aim of the syllabus is to develop students' ability to **apply relevant knowledge and skills**, and exercise the **professional judgement** in assessing strategic **position**, determining strategic **choice**, and implementing strategic **action** through beneficial business process and structural change that involve people, finance and information technology.

This is an **advanced level** paper which builds on a number of the topics covered in Paper F1 Accountant in Business as well as topics you will have seen in Paper F5 Performance Management. However, as an advanced paper it tests much more than just your ability to recall models and theories. You must be able to **evaluate** data, **assess** the strategic consequences of decisions and **advise** on alternative courses of action.

The syllabus is divided into eight main sections, (although the examining team are keen that you view them as an integrated whole, rather than as a series of unrelated sections).

(a) **Strategic position**

The syllabus begins by considering the impact of the **external environment** on an organisation, and looks at the competitive forces organisations face. It then also looks at an organisation's **internal capabilities** and expectations, to see how an organisation can position itself to get the most value out of its resources.

However, an organisation also needs to consider its responsibilities to differing **stakeholder groups**, and how the expectations of stakeholders, alongside ethics and culture, help shape organisational purpose.

(b) **Strategic choice**

Once an organisation has established its current strategic position it can start thinking about the direction it wants to take in the future. This section looks at the decisions which have to be made about an organisation's future and the way an organisation can respond to the influences and pressures which it identified while assessing its strategic position.

(c) **Strategic action**

This section deals with the **implementation of strategic choices**, and the transformation of these choices into organisational action. This action takes place in a context of operational **processes** and **relationships,** which need to be managed in line with the intended strategy, and involves the effective coordination of business processes, information technology, people and finance.

You will be expected to identify problems and issues in an organisation which prevent it from achieving its strategies, and make recommendations about how these problems can be resolved.

(d) **Business and process change**

This section is the first considering how organisational elements support business strategy and it highlights that business process redesign can lead to significant organisational improvements. Again, you will be expected to identify problems or inefficiencies with existing processes and make recommendations as to how they can be made more effective.

(e) **Information technology**

The application of information technology is often one of the ways that business processes can be redesigned. This reflects the fact that many existing processes are less efficient than they could be, and that new technology and the **application of e-business models** make it possible to design those processes more efficiently.

(f) **Project management**

In (c) above we noted that effective strategic action requires the coordination of a number of operational processes. This coordination can be facilitated through effective project management.

(g) **Financial analysis**

Strategic planning and strategic implementation should be subject to financial benchmarks. Financial analysis explicitly recognises this, reminding you of the importance of focusing on key ratios and measures that can be used to assess the **viability** of a strategy and to monitor or **measure its success**.

(h) **People**

Human resource management plays a vital role in underpinning strategy. Successful strategic planning and implementation require the effective recruitment, training, and organisation of people, coupled with strong leadership.

As with so many other areas of the syllabus, it is crucial that an organisation's personnel resources are appropriate for the strategy it is pursuing.

2 Skills you have to demonstrate

- An ability to **integrate** knowledge and understanding from across the syllabus

- Application of your knowledge to the specific circumstances described by the question

- An ability to make **reasoned judgements** and give **practical, commercial advice** based on the facts presented in the question scenario

- Careful reading and analysis of the question scenarios, and the question requirements

- If you read the main capabilities listed by ACCA that students are expected to have on completion of P3, you will find continued reference to the verbs 'evaluate', 'assess', 'advise' and 'explain' – make sure you can do **all of these** in relation to the different aspects of the syllabus.

3 How to pass

- Study the **entire** syllabus – questions may span a number of syllabus areas and you must be prepared for anything!

- **Practise** as many questions as you can under **timed conditions.** This is the best way of developing good exam technique. Make use of the **Question Bank** at the back of this Study Text, and, more importantly, **BPP's Practice & Revision Kit**. The Kit contains numerous exam standard questions (many of them taken from past exam papers) as well as three mock exams for you to try.

- P3 questions will be scenario-based and all the information given in the scenarios will be relevant to the questions set. Make sure you relate your answers to the scenario rather than letting them become generic. Answers that are simply regurgitated from texts are unlikely to score well.

- Present your answers in a **professional** manner – there are marks available for coherent, well structured arguments and for making recommendations when required. You should be aiming to achieve all of these marks.

- Manage your time in the exam hall carefully. **Answer plans** will help you to focus on the requirements of the question and enable you to manage your time effectively. Also, **do not waffle**. Make your answers complete, but brief.

- Answer the question that you are most comfortable with first – it will help to settle you down if you feel you have answered the first question well.

- **Answer all parts** of the question – leaving out a five mark discursive element for example may mean the difference between a pass and a fail.

- Read the financial press and relevant web sites (for example, the BBC business website) for real life examples. The examination team is specifically looking for evidence of **wider reading**. They have repeatedly stressed the importance of reading the finance section of a **good quality newspaper** so that you can draw on real-life situations to help inform your answers.

  This does not, of course, mean you should simply quote real life examples in your exam just to show you have read widely. Instead you should use the real life examples to help inform your answers to the questions set.

- Check the P3 section of the ACCA website regularly – it often contains technical articles written either by, or on the recommendation of, the examination team which can be invaluable for future exams.

4 Answering questions

4.1 Analysing question requirements

It's particularly important to **consider the question requirements carefully** to make sure you understand exactly what the question is asking, and whether each question part has to be answered in the **context of the scenario** or is more general. You also need to be sure that you understand all the **tasks** that the question is asking you to perform.

Remember that every word will be important. If for example you are asked to:

'Explain the importance of identifying all risks that Company X is facing', then you would explain that:

- Taking risks is bound up with strategic decision-making
- Some risks may have serious consequences
- Identifying all risks means they can be prioritised and managed efficiently and effectively

You would **NOT** identify all the risks that Company X would be facing.

4.2 Understanding the question verbs

Important!

> In the report for the first P3 exam, the examination team highlighted lack of understanding of the requirements of question verbs as the most serious weakness in many candidates' scripts. The examination team will use question verbs very deliberately to signal what is required.

Verbs that are likely to be frequently used in this exam are listed below, together with their intellectual levels and guidance on their meaning.

Intellectual level		
1	Define	Give the meaning of
1	Explain	Make clear
1	Identify	Recognise or select
1	Describe	Give the key features
2	Distinguish	Define two different terms, viewpoints or concepts on the basis of the differences between them
2	Compare and contrast	Explain the similarities and differences between two different terms, viewpoints or concepts
2	Contrast	Explain the differences between two different terms, viewpoints or concepts
2	Analyse	Give reasons for the current situation or what has happened
3	Assess	Determine the strengths/weaknesses/ importance/ significance/ability to contribute
3	Examine	Critically review in detail
3	Discuss	Examine by using arguments for and against
3	Explore	Examine or discuss in a wide-ranging manner
3	Criticise	Present the weaknesses of/problems with the actions taken or viewpoint expressed, supported by evidence
3	Evaluate/critically evaluate	Determine the value of in the light of the arguments for and against (critically evaluate means weighting the answer towards criticisms/arguments against).
3	Construct the case	Present the arguments in favour or against, supported by evidence
3	Recommend	Advise the appropriate actions to pursue in terms the recipient will understand

A lower level verb such as define will require a more **descriptive answer**. A higher level verb such as evaluate will require a more **applied, critical answer**. The examination team has stressed that **higher-level requirements and verbs** will be most significant in this paper, for example critically evaluating a statement and arguing for or against a given idea or position. The examination team aims to set questions that provide evidence of student understanding.

Certain verbs have given students particular problems.

(a) **Identify and explain**

Although these verbs are both Level 1, the examination team sees them as requiring different things. You have to go into more depth if you are asked to **explain** than if you are asked to **identify**. An explanation means giving more detail about the problem or factor identified, normally meaning that you have to indicate **why** it's significant. If you were asked to:

(i) **Identify the main problem with the same person acting as chief executive and chairman**
– you would briefly say excessive power is exercised by one person.

(ii) **Explain the main problem with the same person acting as chief executive and chairman**
– you would say excessive power is exercised by one person and then go on to say it would mean that the same person was running the board and the company. As the board is meant to monitor the chief executive, it can't do this effectively if the chief executive is running the board. Also you may be asked to explain or describe something complex, abstract or philosophical in nature.

(b) **Evaluate**

Evaluate is a verb that the examination team uses frequently. Its meaning may be different from the way that you have seen it used in other exams. The examination team expects to see arguments for **and** against, or pros **and** cons for what you are asked to evaluate.

Thus for example if a question asked you to:

'Evaluate the contribution made by non-executive directors to good corporate governance in companies'

you would not only have to write about the factors that help non-executive directors make a worthwhile contribution (independent viewpoint, experience of other industries). You would also have to discuss the factors that limit or undermine the contribution non-executive directors make (lack of time, putting pressure on board unity).

If the examination team asks you to critically evaluate, you will have to consider both viewpoints. However you will concentrate on the view that you are asked to critically evaluate, as the mark scheme will be weighted towards that view.

4.3 Analysing question scenarios

When reading through the scenario you need to think widely about how the scenario relates to the underlying themes of the syllabus, and also important content from whatever areas of the syllabus the question covers:

(a) **Corporate governance**

In questions on **corporate governance**, you are likely to be looking out for **weaknesses** in the current arrangements and trying to **recommend improvements** that are line with governance best practice.

(b) **Control systems**

With **control systems** questions, you are most likely to be interested in the **design and appropriateness of the control systems**, whether there are **obvious shortcomings** with them, and also **details of the control environment**.

(c) **Culture**

If you are asked about the organisation's **culture and ethos**, you should be looking for evidence of directors' views and actions, for signs of how the tone is being set at the top of the organisation. You should also look for evidence of how the ethos is being established further down the organisation, in particular how the organisation's **culture, systems, procedures, reward mechanisms, human resource policies, training** are used to embed the tone of the organisation.

(d) **Risks**

With **risks** you are looking for the **most significant risks**. If these are not highlighted, you should look for the risks that are **connected with the organisation's strategy** or which **relate to significant changes** that the organisation and its business environment are going through, or are about to go though. You should also try to determine the extent to which **risk awareness is embedded** in the **organisation's culture**.

(e) **Risk management**

If you are asked how organisations should **respond to particular risks**, you'll need to use the scenario detail to determine how serious these risks are, and suggest **responses** that are **relevant** to **counter the risks** and are **appropriate for the organisation**. It's no use for example suggesting that the organisation sets up a large risk management function if it is not big enough to warrant one.

(f)   **Ethics**

With **ethical issues** you are not just looking to determine not only the **ethical issues at stake**. You also need to consider the **ethical position of the organisation** and individuals and the **factors that determine the ethical position**. These will be significant when you think about solutions to the ethical problems.

(g)   **Framework**

Look out in any question scenarios or frameworks for hints that you may have to provide a critique of the **overall framework or model** that is being operated. If you're basing your answer on content from corporate governance or ethical codes, will you have to criticise the principles or rules on which they are founded. If you have to make recommendations that benefit shareholders, is the shareholders' viewpoint the most valid or should other stakeholders' interests be taken into account.

4.4 Consider the moral and ethical frameworks

The examination team has stressed that these will affect the judgements you make when answering questions as they do in real-life. In particular the stakeholders **affected** by **business and strategic decisions** and whether some stakeholders are being favoured over others need to be considered.

Remember the exam is designed to make you take a questioning approach to wide issues, and this may mean having to argue in favour of a viewpoint with which you don't agree.

4.5 Content of answers

Well-judged, clear recommendations grounded in the scenario will always score well as markers for this paper have a wide remit to reward good answers. You need to be **selective**. As we've said, lists of points memorised from texts and reproduced without any thought won't score well.

Important!

> The examination team identified lack of application skills as a serious weakness in many student answers. What constitutes good application will vary question by question but is likely to include:
>
> - Only including technical knowledge that is **relevant** to the scenario. For example, although the SPAMSOAP mnemonic can be a useful memory aid, you shouldn't quote it in full just because the question requirements contain the word 'control'
> - Only including scenario details that **support the points** you are making, for example quoting from the scenario to explain why you're making a particular recommendation
> - **Tackling the problems** highlighted in the scenario and the question requirements
> - Explaining **why** the factors you're discussing are significant
> - Taking a **top-down strategic approach** – remember that at Professional level you're meant to be adopting the viewpoint of a partner or finance director. Excessive detail about operations is not important

5 Gaining professional marks

As P3 is a Professional level paper, 4 or 5 **professional level marks** will be awarded in the compulsory question. The examination team has stated that some marks may be available for presenting your answer in the form of a letter, presentation, memo, report, briefing notes, management reporting, narrative or press statement. You may also be able to obtain marks for the layout, logical flow and presentation of your answer. You should also make sure that you provide the points required by the question.

Important!

> Whatever the form of communication requested, you will **not** gain professional marks if you fail to follow the basics of good communication. Keep an eye on your **spelling and grammar**. Also think carefully, am I saying things that are **appropriate in a business communication**?

6 Brought forward knowledge

As mentioned previously, this paper builds on knowledge brought forward from Paper F1, Accountant in Business and F5 Performance Management. If you have not studied F1 or F5, or were exempt, you should spend some time considering the syllabus and study guide to identify any gaps in your knowledge. You must ensure you cover any areas you are unsure of before your exam, so that you would be comfortable referring to them as necessary.

The syllabus information is available on the ACCA website, www.accaglobal.com.

Analysis of past papers

The table below provides details of when each element of the syllabus has been examined and the question number and section in which each element appeared. Further details can be found in the Exam Focus Points in the relevant chapters.

Covered in Text chapter		Dec 2014	June 2014	Dec 2013	June 2013	Dec 2012	June 2012	Dec 2011	June 2011	Dec 2010	June 2010	Dec 2009	June 2009	Dec 2008	June 2008	Dec 2007	Pilot Paper
	STRATEGIC POSITION																
1	Business strategy	C				O	C	C	C		C						
1	Strategy lenses				C								C	C			
2	PESTEL analysis							C	C		C			C			C
2	National competitiveness			C							O						
2	Competitive forces					O			C				C		C		C
2	Business scenario building & forecasting			O	O				O	O							O
3	Marketing and market segmentation		O	O					O								
3	Industry lifecycle																
4	Value chain; supply chain management	O					O						O			O	O
4	SWOT analysis	O	C				C	C			C		C			C	
4	Benchmarking					C											
5	Stakeholders												C				
5	Culture and the cultural web			O	C				O		O			C			
	STRATEGIC CHOICES																
6	Generic strategies														C	C	
6	Product-market strategy														O		
6	BCG	C				C											
6	Methods of growth			C		O							C	O			O
6	Corporate parents									C				O			
6	SAF	C		C													
	STRATEGIC ACTION																
7	Organisational structures									O	O						

Covered in Text chapter		Dec 2014	June 2014	Dec 2013	June 2013	Dec 2012	June 2012	Dec 2011	June 2011	Dec 2010	June 2010	Dec 2009	June 2009	Dec 2008	June 2008	Dec 2007	Pilot Paper
8	Managing strategic change		C			C				C					O		
	BUSINESS AND PROCESS CHANGE																
9	Process-strategy matrix				O		O	O				O			O		
9	Outsourcing	O							C		O				O		
9	Business process redesign	O					O		O	C			C				
10	Managing risk					O											
	INFORMATION TECHNOLOGY																
11	E-business and upstream supply chain management							O	O							O	O
11	E-business and downstream supply chain management									O						O	O
12	E-marketing		O	O		O			O	O	C				O		
12	Customer relationship marketing				O												
	PROJECT MANAGEMENT																
13	Project management	O	O		C		O	O		O		O		O		O	
	FINANCIAL ANALYSIS																
14	Finance				O			O		O							C
	PEOPLE																
15	Leadership				O								O				
15	Job design				O												
15	Staff development																
	STRATEGIC DEVELOPMENT																
16	Developing strategies																

The exam paper

Format of the paper

		Number of marks
Section A:	One compulsory case study	50
Section B:	Choice of two from three questions, 25 marks each	50
		100

Time allowed: 3 hours (plus 15 minutes of reading and planning time)

Section A will be a compulsory case study question with several requirements relating to the same scenario information. The question will usually assess and link several subject areas from across the syllabus, and will require you to demonstrate high-level capabilities to evaluate, relate and apply the information in the scenario to the question requirements. There will always be some financial or numerical data in the scenario and marks will be available for numerical analysis which supports your written argument.

The compulsory Section A question can draw on ALL areas of the syllabus, making it imperative that you cover all areas of the syllabus in your studies.

Section B questions are more likely to examine discrete subject areas. They will be based on short scenarios, and you will be expected to apply information from the scenarios to the question requirements. Again the questions can be drawn from all area of the syllabus, and the limited extent of the choice (two from three) reinforces the importance of covering all areas of the syllabus.

P3 is designed to be a global paper, meaning that the case studies and the scenarios will focus on an **industry of global significance**, which should be known to candidates wherever they live or work. Although a lot of the examples in this text are based in the UK, they are designed to illustrate points which could apply equally in other countries. The exam will not focus specifically on UK industries, nor the UK business environment.

Questions in this exam will not require specialist knowledge of any particular industries, nor the business environment of any particular country. However, an awareness of current business issues overall will be useful in providing real-life examples to support your answers – hence the examination team's instruction that candidates should read the financial sections of a good quality newspaper or other business material regularly.

Syllabus and Study Guide

The P3 syllabus and study guide can be found below.

Business Analysis (P3) September 2015 to June 2016

This syllabus and study guide is designed to help with planning study and to provide detailed information on what could be assessed in any examination session.

THE STRUCTURE OF THE SYLLABUS AND STUDY GUIDE

Relational diagram of paper with other papers

This diagram shows direct and indirect links between this paper and other papers preceding or following it. Some papers are directly underpinned by other papers such as Advanced Performance Management by Performance Management. These links are shown as solid line arrows. Other papers only have indirect relationships with each other such as links existing between the accounting and auditing papers. The links between these are shown as dotted line arrows. This diagram indicates where you are expected to have underpinning knowledge and where it would be useful to review previous learning before undertaking study.

Overall aim of the syllabus

This explains briefly the overall objective of the paper and indicates in the broadest sense the capabilities to be developed within the paper.

Main capabilities

This paper's aim is broken down into several main capabilities which divide the syllabus and study guide into discrete sections.

Relational diagram of the main capabilities

This diagram illustrates the flows and links between the main capabilities (sections) of the syllabus and should be used as an aid to planning teaching and learning in a structured way.

Syllabus rationale

This is a narrative explaining how the syllabus is structured and how the main capabilities are linked. The rationale also explains in further detail what the examination intends to assess and why.

Detailed syllabus

This shows the breakdown of the main capabilities (sections) of the syllabus into subject areas. This is the blueprint for the detailed study guide.

Approach to examining the syllabus

This section briefly explains the structure of the examination and how it is assessed.

Study Guide

This is the main document that students, learning and content providers should use as the basis of their studies, instruction and materials. Examinations will be based on the detail of the study guide which comprehensively identifies what could be assessed in any examination session. The study guide is a precise reflection and breakdown of the syllabus. It is divided into sections based on the main capabilities identified in the syllabus. These sections are divided into subject areas which relate to the sub-capabilities included in the detailed syllabus. Subject areas are broken down into sub-headings which describe the detailed outcomes that could be assessed in examinations. These outcomes are described using verbs indicating what exams may require students to demonstrate, and the broad intellectual level at which these may need to be demonstrated (*see intellectual levels below).

Learning Materials

ACCA's Approved Content Programme is the programme through which ACCA approves learning materials from high quality content providers designed to support study towards ACCA's qualifications.

ACCA has three Approved Content Providers, Becker Professional Education, BPP Learning Media and Kaplan Publishing.

For information about ACCA's Approved Content Providers please go to ACCA's Content Provider Directory.

The Directory also lists materials by other publishers, these materials have not been quality assured by ACCA but may be helpful if used in conjunction with approved learning materials or for variant exams where no approved content is available. You will also find details of Additional Reading suggested by the examining teams and this may be a useful supplement to approved learning materials.

ACCA's Content Provider Directory can be found here –

> http://www.accaglobal.com/uk/en/student/acca-qual-student-journey/study-revision/learning-providers/alp-content.html

Relevant articles are also published in Student Accountant and available on the ACCA website.

INTELLECTUAL LEVELS

The syllabus is designed to progressively broaden and deepen the knowledge, skills and professional values demonstrated by the student on their way through the qualification.

The specific capabilities within the detailed syllabuses and study guides are assessed at one of three intellectual or cognitive levels:

Level 1: Knowledge and comprehension
Level 2: Application and analysis
Level 3: Synthesis and evaluation

Very broadly, these intellectual levels relate to the three cognitive levels at which the Knowledge module, the Skills module and the Professional level are assessed.

Each subject area in the detailed study guide included in this document is given a 1, 2, or 3 superscript, denoting intellectual level, marked at the end of each relevant line. This gives an indication of the intellectual depth at which an area could be assessed within the examination. However, while level 1 broadly equates with the Knowledge module, level 2 equates to the Skills module and

level 3 to the Professional level, some lower level skills can continue to be assessed as the student progresses through each module and level. This reflects that at each stage of study there will be a requirement to broaden, as well as deepen capabilities. It is also possible that occasionally some higher level capabilities may be assessed at lower levels.

LEARNING HOURS AND EDUCATION RECOGNITION

The ACCA qualification does not prescribe or recommend any particular number of learning hours for examinations because study and learning patterns and styles vary greatly between people and organisations. This also recognises the wide diversity of personal, professional and educational circumstances in which ACCA students find themselves.

As a member of the International Federation of Accountants, ACCA seeks to enhance the education recognition of its qualification on both national and international education frameworks, and with educational authorities and partners globally. In doing so, ACCA aims to ensure that its qualifications are recognized and valued by governments, regulatory authorities and employers across all sectors. To this end, ACCA qualifications are currently recognized on the education frameworks in several countries. Please refer to your national education framework regulator for further information.

Each syllabus contains between 23 and 35 main subject area headings depending on the nature of the subject and how these areas have been broken down.

GUIDE TO EXAM STRUCTURE

The structure of examinations varies within and between modules and levels.

The Fundamentals level examinations contain 100% compulsory questions to encourage candidates to study across the breadth of each syllabus.

The Knowledge module is assessed by equivalent two-hour paper based and computer based examinations.

The Skills module examinations F5-F9 are all paper based three-hour papers containing a mix of objective and longer type questions. The *Corporate and Business Law* (F4) paper is a two- hour computer based objective test examination which is also available as a paper based version from the December 2014 examination session.

The Professional level papers are all three-hour paper based examinations, all containing two sections. Section A is compulsory, but there will be some choice offered in Section B.

For all three hour examination papers, ACCA has introduced 15 minutes reading and planning time.

This additional time is allowed at the beginning of each three-hour examination to allow candidates to read the questions and to begin planning their answers before they start writing in their answer books. This time should be used to ensure that all the information and exam requirements are properly read and understood.

During reading and planning time candidates may only annotate their question paper. They may not write anything in their answer booklets until told to do so by the invigilator.

The Essentials module papers all have a Section A containing a major case study question with all requirements totalling 50 marks relating to this case. Section B gives students a choice of two from three 25 mark questions.

Section A of both the P4 and P5 Options papers contain one 50 mark compulsory question, and Section B will offer a choice of two from three questions each worth 25 marks each.

Section A of each of the P6 and P7 Options papers contains 60 compulsory marks from two questions; question 1 attracting 35 marks, and question 2 attracting 25 marks. Section B of both these Options papers will offer a choice of two from three questions, with each question attracting 20 marks.

All Professional level exams contain four professional marks.

The pass mark for all ACCA Qualification examination papers is 50%.

GUIDE TO EXAMINATION ASSESSMENT

ACCA reserves the right to examine anything contained within the study guide at any examination session. This includes knowledge, techniques, principles, theories, and concepts as specified.

For the financial accounting, audit and assurance, law and tax papers except where indicated otherwise, ACCA will publish *examinable documents* once a year to indicate exactly what regulations and legislation could potentially be assessed within identified examination sessions..

For paper based examinations regulation *issued* or legislation *passed* on or before 1st September annually, will be examinable from 1st September of the following year to 31st August of the year after that. Please refer to the examinable documents for the paper (where relevant) for further information.

Regulation issued or legislation passed in accordance with the above dates may be examinable even if the *effective* date is in the future.

The term issued or passed relates to when regulation or legislation has been formally approved.

The term effective relates to when regulation or legislation must be applied to an entity transactions and business practices.

The study guide offers more detailed guidance on the depth and level at which the examinable documents will be examined. The study guide should therefore be read in conjunction with the examinable documents list.

Syllabus

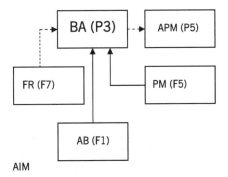

AIM

To apply relevant knowledge, skills, and exercise professional judgement in assessing strategic position, determining strategic choice, and implementing strategic action through beneficial business process and structural change; coordinating knowledge systems and information technology and by effectively managing processes, projects, and people within financial and other resource constraints.

MAIN CAPABILITIES

On successful completion of this paper, candidates should be able to:

A   Assess the strategic position of an organisation

B   Evaluate the strategic choices available to an organisation

C   Discuss how an organisation might go about its strategic implementation

D   Evaluate and redesign business processes and structures to implement and support the organisation's strategy taking account of customer and other major stakeholder requirements

E   Integrate appropriate information technology solutions to support the organisation's strategy

F   Advise on the principles of project management to enable the implementation of aspects of the organisation's strategy with the twin objectives of managing risk and ensuring benefits realisation

G   Analyse and evaluate the effectiveness of a company's strategy and the financial consequences of implementing strategic decisions

H   Assess the role of leadership and people management in formulating and implementing business strategy.

RELATIONAL DIAGRAM OF MAIN CAPABILITIES

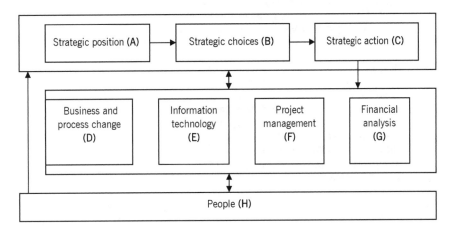

BPP LEARNING MEDIA

RATIONALE

The syllabus for Paper P3, *Business Analysis*, is primarily concerned with two issues. The first is the external forces (the behaviour of customers, the initiatives of competitors, the emergence of new laws and regulations) that shape the environment of an organisation. The second is the internal

ambitions and concerns (desire for growth, the design of processes, the competences of employees, the financial resources) that exist within an organisation. This syllabus looks at both of these perspectives, from assessing strategic position and choice to identifying and formulating strategy and strategic action. It identifies opportunities for beneficial change that involve people, finance and information technology. It examines how these opportunities may be implemented through the appropriate management of programmes and projects.

The syllabus begins with the assessment of strategic position in the present and in the future using relevant forecasting techniques, and is primarily concerned with the impact of the external environment on the business, its internal capabilities and expectations and how the organisation positions itself under these constraints. It examines how factors such as culture, leadership and stakeholder expectations shape organisational purpose. Strategic choice is concerned with decisions which have to be made about an organisation's future and the way in which it can respond to the influences and pressures identified in the assessment of its current and future strategic position.

Strategic action concerns the implementation of strategic choices and the transformation of these choices into organisational action. Such action takes place in day-to-day processes and organisational relationships and these processes and relationships need to be managed in line with the intended strategy, involving the effective coordination of information technology, people, finance and other business resources.

Companies that undertake successful business process redesign claim significant organisational improvements. This simply reflects the fact that many existing processes are less efficient than they could be and that new technology makes it possible to design more efficient processes. Strategic planning and strategy implementation has to be subject to financial benchmarks. Financial analysis explicitly recognises this, reminding candidates of the importance of focusing on the key management accounting techniques that help to determine strategic action and the financial ratios and measures that may be used to assess the viability of a strategy and to monitor and measure its success.

Throughout, the syllabus recognises that successful strategic planning and implementation requires the effective recruitment, leadership, organisation and training and development of people.

DETAILED SYLLABUS

A Strategic position

1. The need for, and purpose of, strategic and business analysis

2. Environmental issues affecting the strategic position of, and future outlook for, an organisation

3. Competitive forces affecting an organisation

4. Marketing and the value of goods and services

5. The internal resources, capabilities and competences of an organisation

6. The expectations of stakeholders and the influence of ethics and culture

B Strategic choices

1. The influence of corporate strategy on an organisation

2. Alternative approaches to achieving competitive advantage

3. Alternative directions and methods of development

C Strategic action

1. Organising and enabling success

2. Managing strategic change

3. Understanding strategy development

D Business and process change

1. Business change

2. The role of process and process change initiatives

3. Improving the processes of the organisation

4. Software solutions

E Information technology

1. Principles of information technology

2. Principles of e-business

3. E-business application: upstream supply chain management

4. E-business application: downstream supply chain management

5. E-business application: customer relationship management

F Project management

1. The nature of projects

2. Building a business case

3. Managing and leading projects

4. Planning, monitoring and controlling projects

5. Concluding a project

G Financial Analysis

1. The link between strategy and finance

2. Finance decisions to formulate and support business strategy

3. The role of cost and management accounting in strategic planning and implementation

4. Financial implications of making strategic choices and of implementing strategic actions

H People

1. Strategy and people: leadership

2. Strategy and people: job design

3. Strategy and people: staff development

APPROACH TO EXAMINING THE SYLLABUS

The syllabus is assessed by a three-hour paper-based examination.

Section A
Section A contains one multi-part question based on a case study scenario. This question is worth 50 marks.

Section B
Section B will consist of three discrete questions each worth 25 marks. Candidates must answer two questions from this section.

Total: 100 marks

Study Guide

A STRATEGIC POSITION

1. The need for, and purpose of, strategic and business analysis

a) Recognise the fundamental nature and vocabulary of strategy and strategic decisions.[2]

b) Discuss how strategy may be formulated at different levels (corporate, business level, operational) of an organisation.[2]

c) Explore the Johnson, Scholes and Whittington model for defining elements of strategic management – the strategic position, strategic choices and strategy into action.[3]

d) Analyse how strategic management is affected by different organisational contexts.[3]

e) Compare three different strategy lenses (Johnson, Scholes and Whittington) for viewing and understanding strategy and strategic management.[3]

f) Explore the scope of business analysis and its relationship to strategy and strategic management in the context of the relational diagram of this syllabus.[3]

2. Environmental issues affecting the strategic position of, and future outlook for, an organisation

a) Assess the macro-environment of an organisation using PESTEL.[3]

b) Highlight the external key drivers of change likely to affect the structure of a sector or market.[3]

c) Explore, using Porter's Diamond, the influence of national competitiveness on the strategic position of an organisation.[2]

d) Prepare scenarios reflecting different assumptions about the future environment of an organisation.[3]

e) Evaluate methods of business forecasting used when quantitatively assessing the likely outcome of different business strategies.[3]

3. Competitive forces affecting an organisation

a) Discuss the significance of industry, sector and convergence.[3]

b) Evaluate the sources of competition in an industry or sector using Porter's five forces framework.[3]

c) Assess the contribution of the lifecycle model, the cycle of competition and associated costing implications to understanding competitive behaviour.[3]

d) Analyse the influence of strategic groups and market segmentation.[3]

e) Determine the opportunities and threats posed by the environment of an organisation.[2]

4. Marketing and the value of goods and services

a) Analyse customers and markets[2]

b) Establish appropriate critical success factors (CSF) and key performance indicators (KPI) for products and services[2]

c) Explore the role of the value chain in creating and sustaining competitive advantage.[2]

d) Advise on the role and influence of value networks.[3]

e) Assess different approaches to benchmarking an organisation's performance.[3]

5. The internal resources, capabilities and competences of an organisation

a) Discriminate between strategic capability, threshold resources, threshold competences, unique resources and core competences.[3]

b) Discuss from a strategic perspective, the continuing need for effective cost management and control systems within organisations.[3]

c) Discuss the capabilities required to sustain competitive advantage.[2]

d) Explain the impact of new product, process, and service developments and innovation in supporting business strategy.[2]

e) Discuss the contribution of organisational knowledge to the strategic capability of an organisation.[2]

f) Determine the strengths and weaknesses of an organisation and formulate an appropriate SWOT analysis.[2]

6. **The expectations of stakeholders and the influence of ethics and culture**

a) Advise on the implications of corporate governance on organisational purpose and strategy.[2]

b) Evaluate, through stakeholder mapping, the relative influence of stakeholders on organisational purpose and strategy.[3]

c) Assess ethical influences on organisational purpose and strategy.[3]

d) Explore the scope of corporate social responsibility.[3]

e) Assess the impact of culture on organisational purpose and strategy.[3]

f) Prepare and evaluate a cultural web of an organisation.[2]

g) Advise on how organisations can communicate their core values and mission.[3]

h) Explain the role of integrated reporting in communicating strategy and strategic performance.[2]

B STRATEGIC CHOICES

1. **The influence of corporate strategy on an organisation**

a) Explore the relationship between a corporate parent and its business units.[2]

b) Assess the opportunities and potential problems of pursuing different corporate strategies of product/market diversification from a national, international and global perspective.[3]

c) Assess the opportunities and potential problems of pursuing a corporate strategy of international diversity, international scale operations and globalisation.[3]

d) Discuss a range of ways that the corporate parent can create and destroy organisational value.[2]

e) Explain three corporate rationales for adding value – portfolio managers, synergy managers and parental developers.[3]

f) Explain and apply the following portfolio models (the BCG growth/share matrix, public sector matrix, the parenting matrix or Ashridge Portfolio display) to assist corporate parents in managing their business portfolios.[3]

2. **Alternative approaches to achieving competitive advantage**

a) Evaluate, through the strategy clock, generic strategy options available to an organisation.[3]

b) Advise on how price-based strategies, differentiation and lock-in can help an organisation sustain its competitive advantage.[3]

c) Assess opportunities for improving competitiveness through collaboration.[3]

3. **Alternative directions and methods of development**

a) Determine generic development directions (employing an adapted Ansoff matrix and a TOWS matrix) available to an organisation.[2]

b) Assess how internal development, mergers, acquisitions, strategic alliances and franchising can be used as different methods of pursuing a chosen strategic direction.[3]

BPP
LEARNING MEDIA

c) Establish success criteria to assist in the choice of a strategic direction and method (strategic options).[2]

d) Assess the suitability of different strategic options to an organisation.[3]

e) Assess the feasibility of different strategic options to an organisation.[3]

f) Establish the acceptability of strategic options to an organisation through analysing risk and return on investment.[3]

C STRATEGIC ACTION

1. Organising and enabling success

a) Advise on how the organisation can be structured to deliver a selected strategy.[3]

b) Explore generic processes that take place within the structure, with particular emphasis on the planning process.[3]

c) Discuss how internal relationships can be organised to deliver a selected strategy.[2]

d) Discuss how organisational structure and external relationships (boundary-less organisations; hollow, modular and virtual) and strategic alliances (joint ventures, networks, franchising, licensing) and the supporting concepts of outsourcing, offshoring and shared services, can be used to deliver a selected strategy.[2]

e) Discuss how big data can be used to inform and implement business strategy.[2].

f) Explore (through Mintzberg's organisational configurations) the design of structure, processes and relationships.[3]

2. Managing strategic change

a) Explore different types of strategic change and their implications.[2]

b) Determine and diagnose the organisational context of change using Balogun and Hope Hailey's contextual features model and the cultural web.[3]

c) Establish potential blockages and levers of change.[2]

d) Advise on the style of leadership appropriate to manage strategic change.[2]

3. Understanding strategy development

a) Discriminate between the concepts of intended and emergent strategies.[3]

b) Explain how organisations attempt to put an intended strategy into place.[2]

c) Highlight how emergent strategies appear from within an organisation.[3]

d) Discuss how process redesign, and e-business can contribute to emergent strategies.[2]

e) Assess the implications of strategic drift and the demand for multiple processes of strategy development.[3]

D BUSINESS AND PROCESS CHANGE

1. Business change

a) Explain how business change projects are initiated to address strategic alignment.[2]

b) Apply the stages of the business change lifecycle (alignment, definition, design, implementation, realisation).[3]

c) Assess the value of the four view (POPIT – people, organisation, processes and information technology) model to the successful implementation of business change [3]

2. The role of process and process change initiatives

a) Advise on how an organisation can reconsider the design of its processes to deliver a selected strategy.[3]

b) Appraise business process change initiatives previously adopted by organisations.[3]

c) Establish an appropriate scope and focus for business process change using Harmon's process-strategy matrix.[3]

d) Explore the commoditisation of business processes.[3]

e) Advise on the implications of business process outsourcing.[3]

f) Recommend a business process redesign methodology for an organisation.[2]

3. Improving the processes of the organisation

a) Evaluate the effectiveness of current organisational processes.[3]

b) Describe a range of process redesign patterns.[2]

c) Establish possible redesign options for improving the current processes of an organisation.[2]

d) Assess the feasibility of possible redesign options.[3]

e) Assess the relationship between process redesign and strategy.[3]

4. Software solutions

a) Establish information system requirements required by business users.[2]

b) Assess the advantages and disadvantages of using a generic software solution to fulfil those requirements.[2]

c) Establish a process for evaluating, selecting and implementing a generic software solution.[2]

d) Explore the relationship between generic software solutions and business process redesign.[2]

E INFORMATION TECHNOLOGY

1. Principles of information technology

a) Advise on the basic hardware and software infrastructure required to support business information systems[2].

b) Identify and analyze general information technology controls and application controls required for effective accounting information systems[2].

c) Analyze the adequacy of general information technology controls and application controls for relevant application systems[3].

d) Evaluate controls over the safeguarding of information technology assets to ensure the organizational ability to meet business objectives[3].

2. Principles of e-business

a) Discuss the meaning and scope of e-business.[2]

b) Advise on the reasons for the adoption of e-business and recognise barriers to its adoption.[3]

c) Evaluate how e-business changes the relationships between organisations and their customers.[3]

d) Discuss and evaluate the main business and marketplace models for delivering e-business.[3]

3. E-business application: upstream supply chain management

a) Analyse the main elements of both the push and pull models of the supply chain.[2]

b) Discuss the relationship of the supply chain to the value chain and the value network.[2]

c) Assess the potential application of information technology to support and restructure the supply chain.[3]

d) Advise on how external relationships with suppliers and distributors can be structured to deliver a restructured supply chain.[3]

e) Discuss the methods, benefits and risks of e-procurement.[2]

f) Assess different options and models for implementing e-procurement.[2]

4. E-business application: downstream supply chain management

a) Define the scope and media of e-marketing.[2]

b) Highlight how the media of e-marketing can be used when developing an effective e-marketing plan.[2]

c) Explore the characteristics of the media of e-marketing using the '6I's of Interactivity, Intelligence, Individualisation, Integration, Industry structure and Independence of location.[2]

d) Evaluate the effect of the media of e-marketing on the traditional marketing mix of product, promotion, price, place, people, processes and physical evidence.[3]

e) Describe a process for establishing a pricing strategy for products and services that recognises both economic and non-economic factors.[2]

f) Assess the importance of on-line branding in e-marketing and compare it with traditional branding.[2]

5. E-business application: customer relationship management

a) Define the meaning and scope of customer relationship management.[2]

b) Explore different methods of acquiring customers through exploiting electronic media.[2]

c) Evaluate different buyer behaviour amongst on-line customers.[3]

d) Recommend techniques for retaining customers using electronic media.[2]

e) Recommend how electronic media may be used to increase the activity and value of established, retained customers.[2]

f) Discuss the scope of a representative software package solution designed to support customer relationship management.[2]

F PROJECT MANAGEMENT

1. The nature of projects

a) Determine the distinguishing features of projects and the constraints they operate in.[2]

b) Discuss the implications of the triple constraint of scope, time and cost.[2]

c) Discuss the relationship between organisational strategy and project management.[2]

d) Identify and plan to manage risks. [2]

e) Advise on the structures and information that have to be in place to successfully initiate a project.[3]

f) Explain the relevance of projects to process re-design and e-business systems development.[2]

2. Building the business case

a) Describe the structure and contents of a business case document.[2]

b) Analyse, describe, assess and classify benefits of a project investment.[3]

c) Analyse, describe, assess and classify the costs of a project investment[3]

d) Evaluate the costs and benefits of a business case using standard techniques

e) Establish responsibility for the delivery of benefits[2]

f) Explain the role of a benefits realisation plan[2]

3. Managing and leading projects

a) Discuss the organisation and implications of project-based team structures.[2]

b) Establish the role and responsibilities of the project manager and the project sponsor.[2]

c) Identify and describe typical problems encountered by a project manager when leading a project.[2]

d) Advise on how these typical problems might be addressed and overcome.[3]

4. Planning, monitoring and controlling projects

a) Discuss the principles of a product breakdown structure [2]

b) Assess the importance of developing a project plan and discuss the work required to produce this plan.[3]

c) Monitor the status of a project and identify project risks, issues, slippage and changes.[2]

d) Formulate responses for dealing with project risks, issues, slippage and changes.[2]

e) Discuss the role of benefits management and project gateways in project monitoring.[2]

5. Concluding a project

a) Establish mechanisms for successfully concluding a project.[2]

b) Discuss the relative meaning and benefits of a post-implementation and a post-project review.[2]

c) Discuss the meaning and value of benefits realisation.[2]

d) Evaluate how project management software may support the planning and monitoring of a project.[3]

e) Apply 'lessons learned' to future business case validation and to capital allocation decisions.[3]

G   FINANCIAL ANALYSIS

1. The link between strategy and finance

a) Explain the relationship between strategy and finance [3]
   i) Managing for value
   ii) Financial expectations of stakeholders
   iii) Funding strategies

b) Discuss how the finance function has transformed to enabling an accountant to have a key role in the decision making process from strategy formulation and implementation to its impact on business performance[2]

2. Finance decisions to formulate and support business strategy

a) Determine the overall investment requirements of the business.[2]

b) Evaluate alternative sources of finance for these investments and their associated risks.[3]

c) Efficiently and effectively manage the current and non-current assets of the business from a finance and risk perspective.[2]

3. The role of cost and management accounting in strategic planning and decision-making

a) Evaluate budgeting, standard costing and variance analysis in support of strategic planning and decision making.[3]

b) Evaluate strategic and operational decisions taking into account risk and uncertainty. (Including using decision trees).[3]

c) Evaluate the following strategic options using marginal and relevant costing techniques.[3]
   i) Make or buy decisions
   ii) Accepting or declining special contracts
   iii) Closure or continuation decisions
   iv) Effective use of scarce resources

d) Evaluate the role and limitations of cost accounting in strategy development and implementation, specifically relating to:[2]
   i) Direct and indirect costs in multi-product contexts
   ii) Overhead apportionment in full costing
   iii) Activity based costing in planning and control

4. Financial implications of making strategic choices and of implementing strategic actions

a) Apply efficiency ratios to assess how efficiently an organisation uses its current resources.[2]

b) Apply appropriate gearing ratios to assess the risks associated with financing and investment in the organisation.[2]

c) Apply appropriate liquidity ratios to assess the organisation's short-term commitments to creditors and employees.[2]

d) Apply appropriate profitability ratios to assess the viability of chosen strategies.[2]

e) Apply appropriate investment ratios to assist investors and shareholders in evaluating organisational performance and strategy.[2]

H PEOPLE

(Note that Section H of the syllabus is underpinned directly by knowledge gained in F1, *Accountant in Business*. Students are expected to be familiar with the following Study Guide subject areas from that syllabus: A1, A2, B1-B3, D1, and D4-D6)

1. **Strategy and people: leadership**

a) Explain the role of visionary leadership and identify the key leadership traits effective in the successful formulation and implementation of strategy and change management.[3]

b) Apply and compare alternative classical and modern theories of leadership in the effective implementation of strategic objectives.[3]

2. **Strategy and people: job design**

a) Assess the contribution of four different approaches to job design (scientific management, job enrichment, Japanese management and re-engineering).[3]

b) Explain the human resource implications of knowledge work and post-industrial job design.[2]

c) Discuss the tensions and potential ethical issues related to job design.[2]

d) Advise on the relationship of job design to process re-design, project management and the harnessing of e-business opportunities.[3]

3. **Strategy and people: staff development**

a) Discuss the emergence and scope of human resource development, succession planning and their relationship to the strategy of the organisation.[2]

b) Advise and suggest different methods of establishing human resource development.[3]

c) Advise on the contribution of competency frameworks to human resource development.[3]

d) Discuss the meaning and contribution of workplace learning, the learning organisation, organisation learning and knowledge management.[3]

SUMMARY OF CHANGES TO P3

ACCA annually reviews its qualification so that they fully meet the needs of stakeholders including employers, students, regulatory and advisory bodies and learning providers. The following syllabus changes are effective from September 2015 and the next update will be September 2016.

The changes are introduced to the syllabus to reflect the latest business and educational developments affecting this paper. These are summarised in the table below.

Summary of changes to P3 (Table):

Section and subject area	Syllabus content
New C1e added	Discuss how big data can be used to inform and implement business strategy.
New G1b added	Discuss how the finance function has transformed to enabling an accountant to have a key role in the decision making process from strategy formulation and implementation to its impact on business performance
G1 heading amended	Finance
G2a and b clarified	Evaluate budgeting, standard costing and variance analysis in support of strategic planning and decision making
G2c clarified	Evaluate strategic and operational decisions taking into account risk and uncertainty. (Including using decision trees).

Strategic position

Business strategy

Topic list	Syllabus reference
1 What is strategy?	A1(a), (f) A6(g)
2 Levels of strategy in an organisation	A1(b)
3 Elements of strategic management	A1(c)
4 The importance of context	A1(d)
5 The strategy lenses	A1(e)

Introduction

This Study Text concerns the ACCA examination called **Business Analysis**. Analysis, of various kinds, forms an important element of the wider activity of **strategic management**. Despite its name, your syllabus deals with the full scope of strategic management and we will provide you with complete coverage in this Text.

Section A of your syllabus is largely concerned with the analysis aspect of strategic management, but before we start to discuss that in detail, we will give you an overview of how it fits into the bigger strategic picture. This exploration of strategic management covers the material specified in the first element of syllabus Section A.

The main reference for Sections A, B and C of your syllabus is the seventh edition of *Exploring Corporate Strategy* by Johnson, Scholes and Whittington. We shall make frequent reference to this book using the abbreviation, JS&W.

Study guide

		Intellectual level
A1	**The need for, and purpose of, strategic and business analysis**	
(a)	Recognise the fundamental nature and vocabulary of strategy and strategic decisions	2
(b)	Discuss how strategy may be formulated at different levels (corporate, business level, operations) of an organisation	2
(c)	Explore the Johnson, Scholes and Whittington model for defining elements of strategic management – the strategic position, strategic choices and strategy into action	3
(d)	Analyse how strategic management is affected by different organisational contexts	3
(e)	Compare three different strategy lenses (Johnson, Scholes and Whittington) for viewing and understanding strategy and strategic management	3
(f)	Explore the scope of business analysis and its relationship to strategy and strategic management in the context of the relational diagram of this syllabus	3
A6	**The expectations of stakeholders and the influence of ethics and culture**	
(g)	Advise on how organisations can communicate their core values and mission	3

Exam guide

This chapter covers fundamental concepts that are likely to be relevant to any exam question. They could be examined directly, or they could be used in the context of a scenario. If a strategy is to be successful, it must be appropriate to the organisation or situation described in the scenario.

Models

Two models from this chapter are explicitly referenced in the Study Guide:

- Johnson, Scholes and Whittington's (JS&W's) model for defining elements of strategic management – strategic position, strategic choices and strategy into action.

- JS&W's model of the three strategy lenses.

These models could be specifically referred to in an exam question.

1 What is strategy?

FAST FORWARD

Strategy is the direction and scope of an organisation over the long term, which achieves advantage in a changing environment through its configuration of resources and competences with the aim of fulfilling stakeholder expectations. Strategic decisions are made under conditions of complexity and uncertainty; they have wide impact on the organisation and often lead to major change.

Strategy is difficult to define; it is a topic with several different aspects and the word is used to mean several different things. We are concerned with its meaning in relation to the higher management of organisations. This is a complex process, but examining some of its features will help us to develop an understanding of what is meant by strategy and strategic management.

Business strategy is as much an art as it is a science. This is because it is concerned with the **behaviour of people,** both individually and in large numbers.

Moreover, there is still vigorous debate, not only about how organisations *should* make their strategies but also about how they **actually do** make them.

As a result of this, there is rarely a single correct answer to business strategy problems.

This means that your exam is **not only about things you can learn by heart**, such as models and procedures, but it is also about selecting and **applying** ideas and theories to scenarios in order to reach sensible conclusions and make reasonable suggestions.

To be successful in the P3 exam, it is very important that you realise that models and theories are only useful to you if you apply them appropriately.

It is worth reviewing at this point the view of the relationship between strategy and accountancy taken by a former member of the examining team under the old P3 syllabus, who commented that '... accountants, with their ability to subject proposals to robust analysis (have) an active and positive role to play in resource allocation.... An accountant's realism can balance the naturally optimistic marketeer.'

1.1 Defining strategy

JS&W explore the significance of strategy by considering the subject matter of **strategic decisions**. They discern **six general areas for decision-making** that will normally be regarded as strategic.

(a) The organisation's **long-term direction**: no specific timescale is envisaged, but you should think in terms in excess of one year and more probably of about five years or more.

(b) The **scope of an organisation's activities**: this will include both the overall roles and purposes the organisation accepts for itself and the activities it undertakes in pursuit of them. Strategic planning considers the whole organisation.

(c) For commercial organisations and for many not-for-profit organisations too, strategy will be about gaining some kind of **advantage in competition**.

(d) Strategic management in some organisations will take the form of **adapting their activities to fit the business environment**. In its simplest form, this will involve adapting products and services to gradually changing **customer requirements**.

(e) A contrasting approach will be to **exploit unique resources** and the organisation's **special competences** in particular. This approach sees the business environment as **something that can be changed** by the organisations' own actions.

(f) Strategic decisions are affected by the **values and expectations** of all of the organisation's **stakeholders**. Stakeholders are people who have a legitimate interest in what the organisation does.

These six considerations lead JS&W to suggest the definition of strategy given below.

Key term

Strategy is the direction and scope of an organisation over the long term, which achieves advantage in a changing environment through its configuration of resources and competences with the aim of fulfilling stakeholder expectations.

If you look at this definition alongside the top layer of the relational diagram describing the P3 syllabus, you should get some idea of the context of strategic decisions:

Strategic position $\longrightarrow$ Strategic choices $\longrightarrow$ Strategic action

1.2 Characteristics of strategic decisions

Having defined the matters that require decisions of a strategic nature, JS&W go on to describe some **important characteristics of the strategic decisions** themselves.

(a) Decisions about strategy are likely to be **complex** since there are likely to be a number of significant factors to take into consideration and a variety of possible outcomes to balance against one another.

(b) There is likely to be a high degree of **uncertainty** surrounding a strategic decision, both about the precise nature of current circumstances and about the likely consequences of any course of action.

(c) Strategic decisions have extensive impact on **operational decision-making**; that is, decisions at lower levels in the organisation.

(d) Strategic decisions affect the organisation as a whole and require processes that cross operational and functional boundaries within it. An **integrated approach** is therefore required.

(e) Strategic decisions are likely to lead to **change** within the organisation as resource capacity is adjusted to permit new courses of action. Changes with implications for **organisational culture** are particularly complex and difficult to manage.

1.3 Mission, goals and objectives   6/12, 6/10

FAST FORWARD

Strategies are developed in order to achieve desired outcomes. These are inherent in the organisation's mission or defining purpose. Mission guides strategic decisions and provides values and a sense of direction.

The **Ashridge College model of mission** links business strategy to culture and ethics by including four separate elements in an expanded definition of mission.

(a) **Purpose**. Why does the organisation exist? Who does it exist for?

  (i) To create wealth for owners?
  (ii) To satisfy the needs of all stakeholders?
  (iii) To reach some higher goal such as the advancement of society?

(b) **Values** are the beliefs and moral principles that underlie the organisation's culture.

(c) **Strategy** provides the commercial logic for the company, and so addresses the following question: 'What is our business? What should it be?' Strategy in this sense is referred to by JS&W as a 'business model'.

(d) **Policies and standards of behaviour** provide guidance on how the organisation's business should be conducted. For example, a service company that wishes to be the best in its market must aim for standards of service, in all its operations, which are at least as good as those found at its competitors.

1.3.1 The importance of mission for corporate strategy

There are several reasons why a business should give serious consideration to establishing a clear concept of its corporate mission and values.

(a) **Values** are acknowledged as integral elements of consumers' buying decisions; this is shown by the attention paid to them in advertising, brand building and market research. Customers ask not only 'What do you sell?' but 'What do you stand for?'

(b) Studies into organisational behaviour show that **people are motivated by many things** other than money: employees are likely to be both more productive and more satisfied with their work when they feel that what they are doing has significance beyond the mere pursuit of a living.

(c) Some writers believe there is an empirical relationship between strong corporate values and profitability.

1.3.2 Mission statements

Mission statements are formal documents that state the organisation's mission. They are published within organisations to promote desired behaviour: support for strategy and purpose, adherence to core values and adoption of policies and standards of behaviour.

Some are suspicious of mission statements for the following reasons.

(a)   They can sometimes be **public relations** exercises rather than an accurate portrayal of the firm's actual values.

(b)   They can often be full of **generalisations** which are impossible to tie down to specific strategic implications.

(c)   **They may be ignored** by the people responsible for formulating or implementing strategy.

1.3.3 Mission and planning

The mission statement can play an important role in the strategic planning process.

(a)   **Inspires and informs planning**. Plans should further the organisation's goals and be consistent with its core values.

(b)   **Screening**. Mission acts as a yardstick by which plans are judged.

(c)   Mission also affects the **implementation** of a planned strategy in terms of the ways in which the firm carries out its business and the culture of the organisation.

Exam focus point

An article entitled 'Communicating core values and mission' is available in the technical articles section for P3 on the ACCA website. This article focuses on mission, mission statement and core values, and explores the importance to organisations of communicating these to stakeholders.

Requirement (b) from question 1 in the June 2012 exam asked students to advise the owners of a shoe manufacturer on the importance of mission, values and objectives in communicating the company's strategy.

1.3.4 Goals, objectives and targets

FAST FORWARD

A structure of goals and objectives derives from mission and supports it. All the parts of this structure should be mutually supportive.

Understanding the organisation's mission is invaluable for setting and controlling the overall functioning and progress of the organisation. However, an organisation can operate reasonably effectively even if most of the people within it have only a **vague understanding of its purpose**. Most people's work is defined in terms of far more specific and immediate things to be achieved: if these things are related in some way to the wider purpose, the organisation will function.

Loosely speaking, these 'things to be achieved' are the goals, objectives and targets of the various departments, offices, and individuals that make up the organisation. In more effective organisations, **goal congruence** will be achieved: all these disparate goals, objectives and targets will be consistent with one another and will operate together to support progress with the mission.

Goals can be related in several ways:

*   **Hierarchically**, as in the pyramid structure outlined below
*   **Functionally**, as when colleagues collaborate on a project
*   **Logistically**, as when resources must be shared or used in sequence
*   **In wider organisational senses**, as when senior executives make decisions about their operational priorities. For example, balancing the need to contain costs whilst increasing productivity by investing in improved plant

1.3.5 A hierarchy of objectives

A simple model of the relationship between the various goals, objectives and targets is a **pyramid** analogous to the traditional organisational hierarchy. At the top is the **overall mission**; this is supported by a small number of **wide ranging goals**, which may correspond to overall departmental or functional responsibilities. For a business, a primary, corporate objective will be the return offered to shareholders, however this is measured. There may be other primary objectives and there will certainly be supporting objectives for costs, innovation, markets, products and so on.

Each of the high level goals is supported in turn by more detailed, **subordinate goals**. These may correspond, perhaps, to the responsibilities of the senior managers in the function concerned. A more modern pattern is for the hierarchy (and indeed many other aspects of the organisation) to be based on major **value-creating processes** rather than on functional departments. We will return to this topic later in this Study Text. In any event, the pattern is continued downwards until we reach the **work targets** of individual members of the organisation.

We owe the concept of a hierarchy or cascade of objectives to the great management thinker and writer Peter Drucker, who outlined the system now known as **management by objectives** (MbO) in the middle of the twentieth century. MbO is still in use as a management tool, though no longer promoted as a universal solution. Its importance for this discussion of goals and objectives is that Drucker was the first to suggest that objectives should be SMART:

Specific   **M**easurable   **A**chievable   **R**ealistic   **T**ime-related

Today, **realistic** is often replaced with **results-focused,** for two reasons.

(a)   The current pursuit of innovation as a route to competitive advantage makes it very important that managerial attention is directed towards **achieving results** rather than just **administering established processes**.

(b)   Realistic means much the same thing as achievable, anyway.

There are other variants: **achievable** may be replaced with **attainable**, which has an almost identical meaning, and **relevant** (meaning appropriate to the group or individual concerned) has been proposed as a third option for **R**.

Functions of objectives

(a)   **Planning**: objectives define what the plan is about.

(b)   **Responsibility**: objectives define the responsibilities of managers and departments.

(c)   **Integration**: objectives should support one another and be consistent; this integrates the efforts of different departments.

(d)   **Motivation**: the first step in motivation is knowing what is to be done. Objectives must be created for all areas of performance.

(e)   **Evaluation**: performance is assessed against objectives and control exercised.

These objectives can be remembered using the acronym 'PRIME'.

1.4 The vocabulary of strategy

FAST FORWARD ▶ Strategy has its own vocabulary, though usage varies. JS&W provide a very useful list.

The field of business strategy has its own vocabulary that you must become familiar with. Unfortunately, there is no generally accepted list of definitions and you may encounter a variety of usages. The key terms box below is based on the definitions used by JS&W.

Key terms

> **Mission** is the organisation's overriding purpose; it reflects the values or expectations of stakeholders and answers the question 'what business are we in?'.
>
> **Vision or strategic intent** is the future state desired by the organisation's strategists: they aim to guide the organisation's collective aspiration towards it.
>
> A **goal** is a statement of a general aim or purpose that supports the mission. It **may** be qualitative in nature.
>
> An **objective** is a more specific aim or purpose and will probably be quantified.
>
> **Strategic capability** flows from resources and competences. **Unique resources and core competences** create **competitive advantage**. (We will define these terms more precisely later in this Study Text.)
>
> A **business model** describes the structure of product, service and information flows between the parties involved.
>
> **Strategic control** has two parts: monitoring the effectiveness of strategies and actions; and taking corrective action when required.

1.5 The business analysis syllabus

RELATIONAL DIAGRAM OF MAIN CAPABILITIES

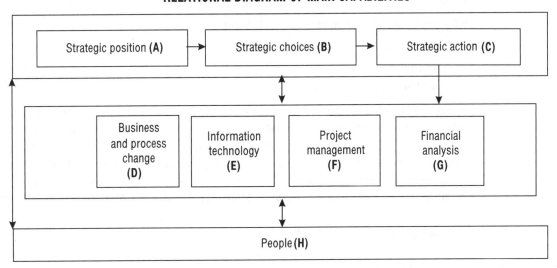

Section A1(f) of the Study Guide for your syllabus calls explicitly for an understanding of the nature and scope of business strategy, as envisioned by the syllabus and summarised in the relational diagram shown above.

This vision adopts the **systems approach** to understanding the way organisations work and therefore emphasises the importance of both the **internal linkages** between the various organisational components and the **boundary-spanning links** between the organisation and its environment. These two elements are reflected in the two main strategic issues dealt with by the syllabus: the external forces that influence the organisation's strategy and the internal forces and activities that sustain it.

The relational diagram shows the syllabus and, by extension, the nature of business strategy, as **three interconnected layers**.

The top layer is concerned with the **overall strategic perspective**, moving from the analysis of strategic position through strategic choices to strategic action.

The middle layer expands on the basic idea of strategic implementation. The focus is on **two linked aspects of business process management**.

- Process improvement
- IS and e-business

Both of these elements must be **financially feasible** and require good **project management**: project management itself can be of strategic significance, as is discussed later in Part F of this Study Text.

The middle layer is also a reminder that strategy may **emerge** from within the day-to-day activities of the organisation. Notice the double-headed arrow between the middle layer (D–G) and the top layer (A–C). This indicates that as well as strategy being translated into action through a top-down approach, the actions and processes within an organisation can also help shape its strategy (a middle-up approach).

The bottom layer of the model emphasises the importance of the **human resource** to all the other aspects and, therefore, of effective human resource management.

2 Levels of strategy in an organisation

FAST FORWARD

There are three main levels of strategy in an organisation.

- **Corporate**: the general direction of the whole organisation
- **Business**: how the organisation or its SBUs tackle particular markets
- **Operational/functional**: specific strategies for different departments of the business

Any level of the organisation can have objectives and devise strategies to achieve them. The strategic management process is multi-layered.

Hofer and Schendel refer to three levels of strategy:

(i)   **Corporate**
(ii)   **Business**
(iii)   **Functional** or **operational**

The distinction between corporate and business strategy arises because of the development of the **divisionalised** business organisation, which typically has a corporate centre and a number of **strategic business units** (SBUs) dealing with particular markets. Chandler described how four large US corporations found that the best way to divide strategic responsibility was to have the corporate HQ allocate resources and exercise overall financial control, while the SBUs were each responsible for their own product-market strategies. Operational strategies are then developed for component parts of SBUs.

2.1 Corporate strategies

Key term

> **Corporate strategy** is concerned with the overall purpose and scope of the organisation and how value will be added to the different parts (business units) of the organisation.   *JS&W*

Defining aspects of corporate strategy

Characteristic	Comment
Scope of activities	Strategy and strategic management impact upon the whole organisation: all parts of the business operation should support and further the strategic plan.
Expectations of stakeholders	There may be a mission statement, but in any case, stakeholder expectations must be prioritised and managed.
Resources	Strategy involves choices about allocating or obtaining corporate resources, now and in future.

2.2 Business-level strategy

Key term

> **Business strategy** is about how to compete successfully in particular markets.   *JS&W*

Business-level strategy is about the particular and distinct combination of products and markets dealt with by one business unit. A business unit might be a small, independent organisation or part of a larger one. In the first case, business and corporate strategy merge with one another; in the second, SBU level strategies must be co-ordinated with corporate strategy and with each other.

2.3 Operational strategies

Key term

> **Operational strategies** are concerned with how the component parts of an organisation deliver effectively the corporate- and business-level strategies in terms of resources, processes and people.   *JS&W*

Much operational strategy is created by individual business functions and delivered by them.

Functional area	Comment
Marketing	Devising products and services, pricing, promoting and distributing them, in order to satisfy customer needs at a profit. Marketing and corporate strategies are interrelated.
Production	Factory location, manufacturing techniques, outsourcing and so on.
Finance	Ensuring that the firm has enough financial resources to fund its other strategies by identifying sources of finance and using them effectively.
Human resources management	Secure personnel of the right skills in the right quantity at the right time, and to ensure that they have the right skills and values to promote the firm's overall goals.
Information systems	A firm's information systems are becoming increasingly important, as an item of expenditure, as administrative support and as a tool for competitive strength. Not all information technology applications are strategic, and the strategic value of IT will vary from case to case.
R&D	New products and techniques.

Question   Levels of strategy

Ganymede Co is a company selling widgets. The finance director says: 'We plan to issue more shares to raise money for new plant capacity – we don't want loan finance – which will enable us to compete better in the vital and growing widget markets of Latin America. After all, we've promised the shareholders 5% profit growth this year, and trading is tough.'

Identify the **corporate**, **business** and **functional** strategies in the above statement.

Answer

The corporate objective is profit growth. The corporate strategy is the decision that this will be achieved by entering new markets, rather than producing new products. The business strategy suggests that those markets include Latin America. The operational or functional strategy involves the decision to invest in new plant (the production function) which is to be financed by shares rather than loans (the finance function).

3 Elements of strategic management

JS&W suggest a three part structure for thinking about strategy.

- Strategic position
- Strategic choices
- Strategy into action

JS&W analyse strategic management into three main elements.

- **Strategic position**
- **Strategic choices**
- **Strategy into action** (implementation)

If you refer back to the diagram of the syllabus relational model shown at Section 1.5 earlier in this chapter, you will see that these three elements form its top layer.

Exam focus point

Two articles titled 'The Strategic Planning Process, Part 1 & 2' written by Sean Purcell are available in the technical articles section for P3 on the ACCA website. The articles provide a useful insight on how to apply your knowledge of management and strategy to scenario questions by considering the three key stages in the strategic planning process (analysis, choice and implementation).

A further article titled 'Strategic planning' (2008) written by David Jennings explores the main processes in strategic planning and illustrates the costs and benefits of planning. It would be worth taking the time to study these articles.

3.1 Strategic position   12/12, 6/10

The strategic managers must attempt to understand the organisation's strategic position. There are **three main groups of influences** to consider: the environment; strategic capability and the expectations of stakeholders.

3.1.1 The environment

The environment of business includes wider political, economic, social, technological, environmentally conscious and legal forces as well as the more immediate pressures of business competition. It is both **complex** and subject to constant **change**, to an extent that probably precludes **complete understanding**. However, if the more salient aspects of the environment can be identified and described, they may be diagnosed into **opportunities** and **threats**. We will look at the environment in more detail in Chapter 2.

3.1.2 Strategic capability

The organisation's **resources** and **competences** make up its strategic capability. This may be analysed into **strengths** and **weaknesses**; these influence, enable or constrain possible future strategic choices.

3.1.3 Stakeholders' expectations

Strategy is made in order to achieve the organisation's **purpose**. This may have a formal, even legal, definition and **corporate governance** may be a relevant issue. Consideration must also be given to the **expectations of stakeholder groups** that have a less formal relationship with the organisation. **Stakeholder power and interest** influence the direction in which strategy evolves, as do **ethical issues**. We will look at stakeholders in more detail in Chapter 5.

3.2 Strategic choices

Strategic choices are made at both the **corporate** and **business unit** level. At the level of the business unit, these choices are about how to achieve **competitive advantage** and are based on an understanding of

customers and markets. At the corporate level, strategy is primarily about **scope**: this is concerned with the overall product/business portfolio, the spread of markets and the relationship between business units and the corporate centre.

Strategic choices must also be made about the **direction** and **method** of development.

3.3 Strategy into action (implementation)

Strategies must be made to work in practice. Major issues here include **structuring**, **enabling** and **change**.

(a) **Structuring** includes processes, relationships, organisation structure and how these elements work together.

(b) **Enabling** is the complex two-way process by which the organisation's resources are managed to both support and to create strategies.

(c) **Change** is a very common feature of strategic development and the management of change is an important feature of strategic implementation.

Exam focus point

An article titled 'The seven deadly sins of strategy implementation' (2007) written by Martin Corboy and Diarmid Corrbui is available in the technical articles section for P3 on the ACCA website. The article explores the main pitfalls of successful strategy implementation. It would be worth taking the time to study this article.

3.3.1 A rational model

JS&W's model for thinking about strategy is a **rational model**, as illustrated below.

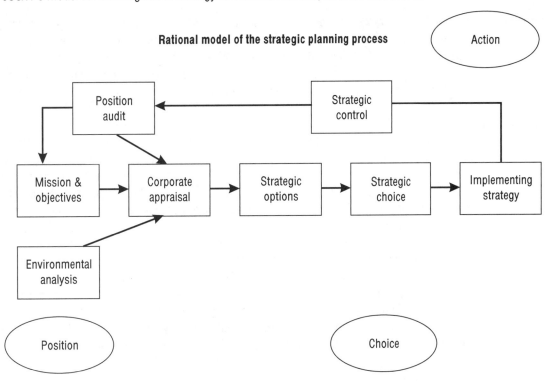

Rational model of the strategic planning process

However, whereas the **rational model** is usually presented as a **linear model**, JS&W also recognise the **interdependencies** between analysis, choice and implementation.

JS&W represent these interdependencies as a Venn diagram as illustrated below:

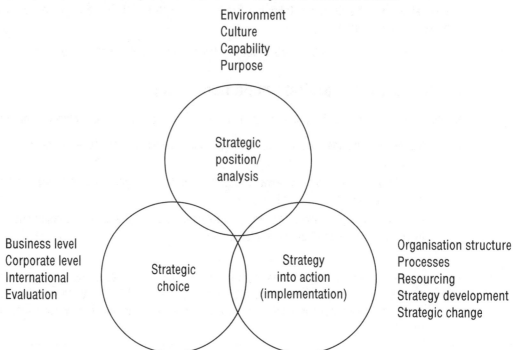

4 The importance of context

FAST FORWARD

The **context of strategy** is the organisational setting in which it is developed. **Small businesses** tend to have limited resources and strong competition; **multinationals** are more concerned with problems of structure, resource allocation and logistics. **Public sector** and **not-for-profit** organisations are influenced by ideology, politics, and the influence of a range of stakeholders. Intangible aspects have become very important for companies dealing in physical products.

Exam focus point

Context is particularly important to you as a candidate for the P3 exam, since question settings will nearly always provide detailed contexts for the problems they feature. You must always consider the question context and make your answer clearly relevant to it. For example, if the scenario describes a small company, this must be recognised in your answer, and you should not suggest strategies which would only be appropriate for a large company, such as raising money for expansion through a share issue on the stock exchange.

Strategic management has many aspects and the relative importance of each of these aspects for individual organisations may vary considerably. For example, an organisation heavily influenced by national political activity, such as the UK National Health Service, is likely to find the management of conflicting stakeholder expectations of far greater significance than might a privately owned distributor of standard electrical components. Even within a single company, differences of industry and market are likely to require different business units to take different approaches to strategy.

4.1 Small businesses

Characteristic	Effect on strategic processes
Limited range of products in a limited market	Few problems of scope
Limited planning resources; ownership interest among managers	Strategy based on values and experience

Characteristic	Effect on strategic processes
Significant pressure from competitors	Exploitation of competences and resources, choice of competitive strategy and knowledge of market and competition all very important
Limited financial resources	Constant attention to building relationship with providers of funds, especially bankers

4.2 Multinationals

Characteristic	Effect on strategic processes
Diverse products, processes and markets	Problems of relationships, structure and control
Significant resources of all kinds	Allocation and co-ordination of resources
Multiple markets, operations and facilities	Great importance of logistics of manufacturing and supply

4.3 The public sector

The public sector has distinct strategic characteristics.

(a)   Influence of **ideology** on strategy

(b)   **External influence** and even control, especially by government

(c)   **Political constraints on funding and strategic choice** even for state-owned organisations with a commercial role

(d)   Requirement to provide a **universal service**

(e)   **Competition for resource inputs** within a political arena for non-commercial organisations

(f)   Need to demonstrate **best value** in outputs

(g)   Increasing need to demonstrate **improvement in social outcomes**

4.4 Not-for-profit organisations

Not-for-profit organisations also have their particular features.

(a)   Importance of underlying **values and purposes**

(b)   **Diverse sources of funds** that may have to be competed for

(c)   Potential for conflict between stakeholders and need for transparency of governance may require **centralised decision-making**

Exam focus point

The not-for-profit sector is an important part of the economy, and charities and other not-for-profit organisations have featured several times in recent P3 exams. The compulsory question in June 2010, and a Section B question in December 2009 both centred around charitable organisations.

The following two articles written by Robert Souster were published in *Student Accountant*, and are available on the ACCA website:

'Not-for-profit organisations' (Sept 2009) and 'Not-for-profit organisations – part 2' (Oct 2009) It would be worth taking the time to study both of these articles.

4.5 Intangible products

There has been an element of strategic convergence between companies supplying **manufactured goods**, on the one hand and those supplying **services,** on the other. While the nature of the physical product is still strategically important for the manufacturer, it has become common for competitive advantage to depend as much on the customer's perception of the **intangibles** that are included in the complete market offering. Factors such as product information, after-sales service and brand values have become as

strategically important to manufacturers as intangibles, such as staff competence and manner, have always been to providers of services.

5 The strategy lenses

FAST FORWARD

The study of business strategy is fairly new and opinion as to its nature and content is only just beginning to settle. The breadth of opinion about it can be analysed into three different approaches or 'lenses' for looking at individual strategies. These lenses are **strategy as design**, **strategy as experience** and **strategy as ideas**.

5.1 A brief history of the study of business strategy

In the 1960s and extending into the 1970s, the highly rational **corporate planning approach** was popular. This incorporated operational research ideas and highly systematised analysis of the influences on the organisation's operations. At the same time, writers such as Simon and Lindblom were challenging rational decision models as unrealistic because of the impossibility of carrying out the full analysis of relevant factors that such models demanded. However, the planning model was popular and corporate planning departments were common in large organisations. In JS&W's terms, this approach sees **strategy as design**.

Subsequently, there was considerable **empirical research** aimed at establishing evidence for the likely outcomes of business decisions about products, markets and structures. At the same time, writers such as Quinn and Mintzberg argued that the sheer **complexity of the world severely limited the usefulness of the analytic approach**. These writers argued that strategic decisions were heavily influenced by experience, politics, culture and history and, as a result, tended to be sub-optimal. This is **strategy as experience**.

In the 1980s, economic thinking led to the influential work of Porter on **competitive advantage** and the emergence of the **resource-based** view of the firm.

More recent ideas have focussed on the concept of the organisation as an organism, adapting to environmental forces through processes of **social interaction** that promote **innovation and change**.

5.2 The strategy lenses   6/13, 6/09

Each of the approaches briefly outlined above has something to offer in understanding of what strategy is and what it is for. JS&W suggest that they can be summarised into **three lenses** through which strategy may be examined.

- Strategy as **design**
- Strategy as **experience**
- Strategy as **ideas**

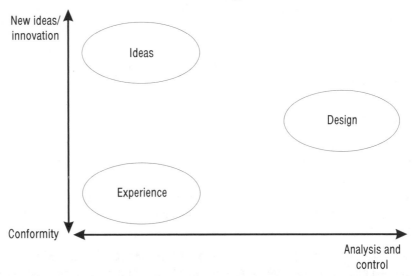

The strategy lenses

New ideas/innovation

Ideas

Design

Experience

Conformity

Analysis and control

Exam focus point

In the post-exam report on the June 2013 exam, the examining team noted that students did not appear to have understood the three strategic lenses when asked to apply these to a public sector organisation. This model had been tested in earlier examinations but students appeared to have not spent sufficient time learning it. This is an important model which is explicitly mentioned in the study guide learning objectives.

5.2.1 Strategy as design

There is a widely held view of strategy as a **rational, top-down** process by which senior managers analyse and evaluate strategic constraints and forces in order to establish a clear and rational course of strategic action. This is a traditional view and one that appeals to managers: it is orthodox, logical and supportive of their own view of their role. It also appeals to stakeholders such as shareholders, banks, many employees and public servants.

However, this view makes a number of important assumptions that might be subject to debate. Some of these are given below.

(a)   Managers are **rational decision-makers** and the strategic problems facing the organisation are susceptible to **rational analysis**.

(b)   There are clear and explicit **objectives**.

(c)   The organisation is a hierarchy in which strategy is an **exclusively management responsibility**.

(d)   The organisation is also a **rational, almost engineered, system** that is capable of putting management's plans into effect.

The view of strategy as design is useful since it leads to the use of a number of tools and techniques that are both logical and practical. However, it does not describe the whole of strategic management.

5.2.2 Strategy as experience

This view sees strategy as an adaptation and extension of **what has worked in the past**. It is firmly based in the **experience** and **assumptions** of influential figures in the organisation and the ways of doing things approved by the organisation's cultural norms. We will discuss the idea of cultural norms later in this Study Text when we consider the **paradigm**.

Managers tend to **simplify** the complexity they face in order to be able to deal with it, selecting and using the elements of their knowledge and understanding that seem most relevant or important. This process is related to the habit of **exemplifying complex forces** in the form of their most important elements.

Thus, where there is an identifiable main competitor, this entity may come to represent competition in general. The problem here is that this may blind managers to emerging competitors that have the potential to dislocate the existing market structure.

Where there are choices or disputes about strategic options, these are resolved by negotiation and bargaining. The result is decisions that **satisfice rather than optimise** and strategies that develop in an incremental and adaptive way. Another feature of this view is that strategies are as likely to **emerge** from intermediate and lower levels of the organisational hierarchy as they are to be decided at its apex. *Mintzberg* described an **emergent strategy** as one 'where patterns developed in the absence of intentions, or despite them'.

5.2.3 Strategy as ideas

This approach to strategy emphasises **innovation** and the need for **diversity of ideas** in the organisation: strategy can emerge from the way the people within the organisation handle and respond to the changing forces present, both in the organisation and in the environment. Supporters of this view argue partly by analogy with evolutionary theory, suggesting that where there is diversity of approach, a change in environmental conditions is likely to be accommodated by one of the various methods, products or systems already in existence.

The role of senior managers is to create the **context and conditions** in which new ideas can emerge and the best ones survive and thrive. An important feature of this role is to avoid relying on either the design approach or the experience approach. The first tends to lead to an over-emphasis on control, while the second tends to develop a kind of incremental momentum. In either case, innovation is unlikely and the result is **strategic drift**. Senior managers must take care to avoid pressure for conformity, particularly in the matter of cultural assumptions.

Not all of the factors that encourage innovation are under the control of managers, or even easily influenced by them.

(a)   **Boundaries** between the organisation and the environment should be **fluid** and **permeable**. Network organisations and those that co-operate widely with others are the model here. Staff should be encouraged to be in contact with, and responsive to, the changing environment. Attention should be paid to their **intuitions**.

(b)   **Informal interaction and co-operation** can be more innovative than carefully designed official systems.

(c)   Culturally, **questioning and challenge** are more valuable than **consensus**.

(d)   There should be deliberate support for personal projects and **experimentation**.

(e)   A degree of **ambiguity** in direction sanctions freedom of thought and effort.

Despite all this, there is a need for some degree of control. The aim is to achieve an 'adaptive tension' that will keep the organisation functioning without either resorting to machine-like procedure or descending into unproductive disarray. This can be achieved by the use of **simple rules**, which are general principles, rather than detailed procedures. These rules should focus on important basic principles, such as the criteria to be used when ranking potential opportunities.

Question   Holiday

Apply the three strategic lenses to a process you are familiar with, such as choosing a holiday.

Answer

You may have come up with other ideas, but we suggest the following are relevant:

Strategy as design

- Prices
- Method of travel, distance, cost
- Quality of accommodation
- Availability of activities/things to do
- Weather
- Language

Strategy as experience

I've been to that area before, so I know it quite well and I like it there.

Strategy as ideas

Let's try something different. We've never been to xxx before, and it looks a very interesting place.

Chapter Roundup

- **Strategy** is the direction and scope of an organisation over the long term, which achieves advantage in a changing environment through its configuration of resources and competences with the aim of fulfilling stakeholder expectations. Strategic decisions are made under conditions of complexity and uncertainty; they have wide impact on the organisation and often lead to major change.

- Strategies are developed in order to achieve desired outcomes. These are inherent in the organisation's mission or defining purpose. Mission guides strategic decisions and provides values and a sense of direction.

- A structure of goals and objectives derives from mission and supports it. All the parts of this structure should be mutually supportive.

- Strategy has its own vocabulary, though usage varies. JS&W provide a very useful list.

- There are many levels of strategy in an organisation.
  - **Corporate**: the general direction of the whole organisation
  - **Business**: how the organisation or its SBUs tackle particular markets
  - **Operational/functional**: specific strategies for different departments of the business

- JS&W suggest a three part structure for thinking about strategy.
  - Strategic position
  - Strategic choices
  - Strategy into action

- The **context of strategy** is the organisational setting in which it is developed. **Small businesses** tend to have limited resources and strong competition; **multinationals** are more concerned with problems of structure, resource allocation and logistics. **Public sector** and **not-for-profit** organisations are influenced by ideology, politics, and the influence of a range of stakeholders. Intangible aspects have become very important for companies dealing in physical products.

- The study of business strategy is fairly new and opinion as to its nature and content is only just beginning to settle. The breadth of opinion about it can be analysed into three different approaches or 'lenses' for looking at individual strategies. These lenses are **strategy as design**, **strategy as experience** and **strategy as ideas**.

Quick Quiz

1   What is strategy?

2   What are the four elements of the Ashridge model of mission?

3   What are the qualities of SMART objective?

4   What are the three elements of the JS&W model of strategy?

5   What are the three strategy lenses and what are the relationships between them?

Answers to Quick Quiz

1   The JS&W definition of strategy is worth committing to memory. Essential elements are **long-term direction** and **scope**; **advantage**; **changing environment**; **resources** and **competences**; and **stakeholder expectations**.

2   Purpose; values; strategy; and policies and standards of behaviour.

3   Specific, measurable, achievable, realistic (relevant, results-focused), time-related.

4   Strategic position, strategic choices, strategy into action.

5   The **design** lens shows strategy as a rational, top-down process under careful controls. This contrasts with the **experience** lens which presents strategy as an extension of what has worked in the past. The **ideas** lens suggests that strategy is formed by diversity of ideas, which leads to innovation. The ideas lens fills a gap left by the design and experience lenses and emphasises that much strategy is not dependent on managerial decisions.

Now try the question below from the Practice Question Bank

Number	Level	Marks	Time
Q1	Preparation	n/a	20 mins

Environmental issues

Topic list	Syllabus reference
1 The organisation in its environment	A2
2 The macro-environment	A2(a)
3 Key drivers of environmental change	A2(b)
4 The competitive advantage of nations	A2(c)
5 The environment in the future	A2(d), (e)
6 Industry and sector	A3(a)
7 Competitive forces	A3(b)

Introduction

The changing environment is one of the essential elements of JS&W's definition of strategy and analysis of the environment is a fundamental part of the process of developing strategy. Traditionally, strategy in business has been seen as a process of adapting the firm to its environment: the importance of environmental analysis in this approach is obvious. Other views of strategy have emerged that place less emphasis on adaptation, but even when a firm sets out to dominate its environment, it must have a full knowledge of the nature of that environment.

Study guide

		Intellectual level
A2	**Environmental issues affecting the strategic position of, and future outlook for, an organisation**	
(a)	Assess the macro-environment of an organisation using PESTEL	3
(b)	Highlight the external key drivers of change likely to affect the structure of a sector or market	3
(c)	Explore, using Porter's Diamond, the influence of national competitiveness on the strategic position of an organisation	2
(d)	Prepare scenarios reflecting different assumptions about the future environment of an organisation	3
(e)	Evaluate methods of business forecasting used when quantitatively assessing the likely outcome of different business strategies	3
A3	**Competitive forces affecting an organisation**	
(a)	Discuss the significance of industry, sector and convergence	3
(b)	Evaluate the sources of competition in an industry or sector using Porter's five forces framework	3

Exam guide

This chapter, like the previous one, deals with wide topics that may be relevant to almost any exam question. However, it also covers some key models, such as **PESTEL** and **Porter's five forces**, that you must study in detail. Environmental analysis is a well-established aspect of the theory of business strategy and the examining team find it an easy topic to introduce into questions. It will be unusual to come across a question that deals exclusively with the environment, but it is common in this field for the examining team to give a fair amount of environmental detail. Make sure you read question scenarios carefully and note the potential implications of the environmental background.

Models

Three models covered in this chapter are explicitly referenced in the Study Guide and so could be specifically required in a question:

- PESTEL
- Porter's Diamond
- Porter's five forces framework

Exam focus point	A technical article in the P3 section of the ACCA website titled 'The adaptability of strategic models' (2007) written by Malcolm Eva explores the importance of understanding models such as those listed above and illustrates how they can be used to identify and analyse strategic issues. Eva highlights that often the key to using such models lies in the flexibility of their application to different scenarios. It would be worth taking the time to study this article.

1 The organisation in its environment

All organisations are open systems: they exist within a complex environment and have a variety of interchanges with that environment, both receiving inputs from it and providing outputs to it. Organisations try to control the nature of their **outputs**, but very few of them can control more than a few of the **inputs** they receive. Understanding the nature of the business environment and the changes taking place within it is therefore a vital part of business analysis.

1.1 Analysing the environment

The environment may be divided for convenience into three concentric layers: the macro-environment; the industry or sector; and competitors and markets. The layers and the elements within them all interact with one another.

We will divide the environment into a variety of components in order to explain it. However, you should be aware that the environmental influences affecting an organisation do not come in neatly labelled packages; there are complex interactions between the elements we will discuss and you must always try to understand the broader picture when you are thinking about the environment.

Following JS&W, we will start our analysis of the environment by dividing it into three parts, each of which has its own particular tools or theories that provide a basis for thinking about it.

Environmental element	Basis of analysis
Macro-environment	PESTEL Key drivers of change Scenarios
Industry or sector	Five forces Cycles of competition
Competitors and markets	Strategic groups Market segments Critical success factors

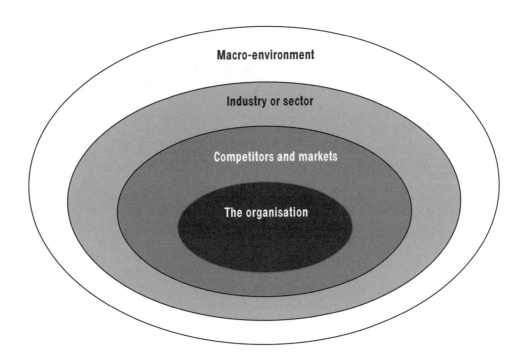

1.2 Environmental uncertainty

Environmental uncertainty depends on the degree of **complexity** and the degree of **stability** present.

A large part of business strategy consists of making the organisation's interaction with its environment as efficient as possible. In the context of strategic management, therefore, the degree of **uncertainty** in the environment is of great importance. The greater the uncertainty, the greater the strategic challenge.

Uncertainty depends on **complexity** and **stability**: the more complex or dynamic the environment is, the more uncertain it is.

(a)   An uncomplicated, stable environment can be dealt with as a matter of routine. The security and efficiency of a mechanistic or bureaucratic approach to management can be exploited. Since the future is likely to resemble the past, extrapolation from history is a satisfactory way of preparing for future events.

(b)   Where the environment is dynamic, the management approach must emphasise response to rapid change. Scenario planning, intuition and a learning approach are all valid features of such a response.

(c)   Complexity makes an environment difficult to understand. Diversity of operations and technological advances contribute to complexity. Complexity is difficult to analyse. It may be that it is best dealt with by a combination of experience and extensive decentralisation.

2 The macro-environment   12/11, 6/11, 12/10, 6/10

The macro-environment may be analysed into six segments using the PESTEL framework.

Analysis of the macro-environment is commonly based on breaking it down into a handful of major aspects. Your syllabus requires you to be familiar with the PESTEL framework, which is based on six segments.

- **P**olitical
- **E**conomic
- **S**ocio-cultural
- **T**echnological
- **E**nvironmental
- **L**egal

Macro-environmental influences

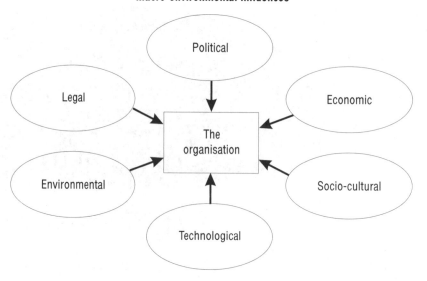

PESTEL is a useful checklist for general environmental factors, but remember, in the real world, these factors are often **interlinked**. Any single environmental development can have implications for all six PESTEL aspects. In particular, political, social and economic affairs tend to be closely related. Do not spend too much time in the exam trying to categorise whether a factor is political, social, economic or so on. The important thing is that you recognise the relevant factors, not whether you get them in the right category.

Note. The acronym **PESTEL** is sometimes replaced by **SLEPT**, in which the environmental protection aspect is folded into the other five, or even by **STEEPLE**, where the extra E stands for **ethics**.

An exam question may not refer to the PESTEL framework directly. Instead it may ask you for an 'environmental analysis' or an 'analysis of the macro environment'. However, you should understand from these instructions that a PESTEL analysis is required.

Remember, though, that PESTEL is only concerned with the **external** environment, not the internal capabilities of an organisation.

When required to use the PESTEL framework when answering questions, it is important to avoid commenting on the featured organisation's internal strengths and weaknesses. These are not relevant to a macro-environmental analysis, and so mentioning these issues would earn no marks.

2.1 The political environment

FAST FORWARD

Government is responsible for providing a stable framework for economic activity and, in particular, for maintaining and improving the physical, social and market infrastructure. Public policy on **competition** and **consumer protection** is particularly relevant to business strategy.

2.1.1 Government policy

Government policy affects the whole **economy**, and governments are responsible for enforcing and creating a **stable framework** in which business can be done. A report by the World Bank indicated that the quality of **government policy is important in providing** three things.

- Physical infrastructure (eg transport)
- Social infrastructure (education, a welfare safety net, law enforcement, equal opportunities)
- Market infrastructure (enforceable contracts, policing corruption)

However, it is **political change** which complicates the planning activities of many firms. Here is a checklist for case study use. It shows a sequence of considerations.

Consideration	Example
Possibility of political change	Effect on economic policies
Likely nature of impact	Change in taxes and interest rates
Consequences	Cash flow and availability of resources
Coping strategies	Cash flow planning
Influence on decision making	Lobbying and publicity

 Case Study | India's challenge to attract new investment

China's growth as an economic power has been widely reported for many years. An article titled 'India's strongman' published in the *Economist* (2014) reported, GDP per citizen has risen from $300 to $6,750 over 30 years. By contrast, India, one of the so-called 'BRIC' economies expected to achieve exponential economic growth, has struggled to achieve the same level of global dominance in international trade. In the mid-1980s India's GDP per head was the same as China's, however today it is now less than a quarter.

According to the *Economist*, India's economic failings have been largely due to a string of weak government administrations which have left the country with a vast population of people underemployed and living in poverty, and an inability to attract new investment from foreign companies.

Historically, India's system of government has deterred foreign investors, as the country is governed on a devolved regional basis, increasing the difficulty for the central administration to enact national business-friendly policies. However, some commentators are optimistic about India's future. In May 2014, Narendra Modi and his BJP party were elected as the country's new prime minister and government respectively. The challenges Mr Modi faces are vast and include, among other issues, dealing with India's debt-burdened banks, improving the tax system, reducing inflation and investing in the country's transport infrastructure.

In 2012, companies including Vodafone and Nokia made the headlines when the then Indian government changed the country's tax rules governing mergers and acquisitions. This move required Vodafone to pay tax on companies it had previously acquired, with subsidiaries of Nokia also being accused of having 'unpaid' tax liabilities.

2.1.2 Public policy on competition

In a perfect monopoly, there is only one firm that is the sole producer of a product that has no closely competing substitutes, so that the firm controls the supply of the product to the market. The definition of a monopoly in practice is wider than this, because governments seeking to control the growth of monopoly firms will probably choose to regard any firm that acquires a major share of the market as a potential monopolist.

Monopoly generally exploits customers, but it may have both economic disadvantages and economic advantages.

(a)   A **beneficial monopoly** achieves **economies of scale** in an industry where the **minimum efficient scale** is at a level of production that would mean having to achieve a large share of the total market supply. In these circumstances, monopoly may be tolerated but is likely to be regulated or even taken into government ownership. Many utilities, such as railways, telecommunications and power generation fall into this category.

Key term

> **Economies of scale** arise when a business grows to the extent that it is able to increase its input of all four types of productive resource: land, labour, capital and enterprise. The effect is to cause the whole structure of short-run costs to fall.

(b)   A monopoly would be detrimental to the public interest if **cost efficiencies** are not achieved. Oliver Williamson suggested that monopolies might be inefficient if 'market power provides the firm with the opportunity to pursue a variety of other-than-profit objectives'. For example, managers might instead try to maximise sales, or try to maximise their own prestige.

Consumer protection policies may be required.

(a)   Control over markets can arise by firms eliminating the opposition, either by merging with or taking over rivals or preventing other firms from entering the market. When a single firm controls a big enough share of the market, it can begin to behave as a monopolist, even though its market share is below 100%.

(b)   Several firms could behave as monopolists by agreeing with each other not to compete. This could be done in a variety of ways – for example, by exchanging information, by setting common prices or by splitting up the market into geographical areas and operating only within allocated boundaries. Such a **collusive oligopoly** is called a cartel and is illegal in most jurisdictions. For example, in 2007, British Airways was fined heavily by the US Department of Justice and the UK's Office of Fair Trading for colluding with its rival, Virgin Atlantic, in fixing how much extra to charge on passenger and cargo flights, to cover fuel costs.

The activity of the Competition and Markets Authority in the UK is a good example of the way governments may approach the problem of monopoly. The Competition and Markets Authority (CMA) has the power to investigate if it appears that competition is being prevented, distorted or restricted in a particular market. The Secretary of State may do the same if any proposed takeover or merger would create a firm that controlled 25% or more of the market and where a merger appears to lead to a substantial lessening of competition in one or more markets. The Authority will then investigate the proposed merger or takeover and recommend whether or not it should be allowed to proceed.

2.1.3 Anticipating changes in the law

- The governing party's election **manifesto** should be a guide to its political priorities, even if these are not implemented immediately.
- The government often publishes advance information about its plans for consultation purposes.

2.1.4 Political risk

The political risk in a decision is the risk that political factors will invalidate the strategy and perhaps severely damage the firm. Examples are wars, political chaos, corruption and nationalisation.

A **political risk checklist** was outlined by Jeannet and Hennessey. Companies should ask the following six questions.

1   How stable is the host country's political system?

2   How strong is the host government's commitment to specific rules of the game, such as ownership or contractual rights, given its ideology and power position?

3   How long is the government likely to remain in power?

4   If the present government is succeeded, how would the specific rules of the game change?

5   What would be the effects of any expected changes in the specific rules of the game?

6   In light of those effects, what decisions and actions should be taken now?

2.2 The economic environment

FAST FORWARD

The **economic** environment affects firms at national and international level, both at the general level of economic activity and in terms of particular variables, such as exchange rates, interest rates and inflation.

The economic environment is an important influence at **local and national level**.

Factor	Impact
Overall growth or fall in gross domestic product	Increased/decreased demand for goods (eg dishwashers) and services (eg holidays).
Local economic trends	Type of industry in the area. Office/factory rents. Labour rates. House prices.
Inflation	Low in most countries; distorts business decisions; wage inflation compensates for price inflation.
Interest rates	How much it costs to borrow money affects cash flow. Some businesses carry a high level of debt. How much customers can afford to spend is also affected as rises in interest rates affect people's mortgage payments.
Tax levels	Corporation tax affects how much firms can invest or return to shareholders. Income tax and sales tax (eg VAT) affect how much consumers have to spend, hence demand.

Factor	Impact
Government spending	Suppliers to the government (eg construction firms) are affected by spending.
The business cycle	Economic activity is always punctuated by periods of growth followed by decline, simply because of the nature of trade. The UK economy has been characterised by periods of boom and bust. Government policy can cause, exacerbate or mitigate such trends, but cannot abolish the business cycle. (Industries which prosper when others are declining are called counter-cyclical industries.)

The **forecast state of the economy** will influence the planning process for organisations which operate within it. In times of boom and increased demand and consumption, the overall planning problem will be to **identify** the demand. Conversely, in times of recession, the emphasis will be on cost-effectiveness, continuing profitability, survival and competition.

Impact of **international factors** on the economic environment

Factor	Impact
Exchange rates	Cost of imports, selling prices and value of exports; cost of hedging against fluctuations
Characteristics of overseas markets	Desirable overseas markets (demand) or sources of supply (cheap imports)
International capital markets	Generally, advanced economies accept that supply and demand set the value of their currencies, using interest rates only to control inflation.
Large multinational companies (MNCs)	MNCs have huge turnovers and significant political influence because of governments' desire to attract capital investment.
Government policy on trade/protection	Cost of barriers to trade, effect on supplier interests of free trade, erection of reciprocal barriers, possibility of dumping

Fairly obviously, there is constant and large scale interaction between government and economy through the various aspects of **government economic policy**.

2.3 The sociocultural environment

FAST FORWARD

The **social and cultural** environment features long-term social trends and people's beliefs and attitudes.

Key term

Demography is the study of human population and population trends.

Factors of importance to organisational planners

Factor	Comment
Growth	The rate of growth or decline in a national population and in regional populations.
Age	Changes in the age distribution of the population. In some countries, there may be an increasing proportion of the national population over retirement age. In others there are very large numbers of young people.
Geography	The concentration of population into certain geographical areas.
Ethnicity	A population might contain groups with different ethnic origins from the majority.
Household and family structure	A household is the basic social unit and its size might be determined by the number of children, whether elderly parents live at home and so on. In the UK, there has been an increase in single-person households and lone parent families.
Social structure	The population of a society can be broken down into a number of subgroups, with different attitudes and access to economic resources.

Factor	Comment
Employment	In part, this is related to changes in the workplace. Many people believe that there is a move to a casual flexible workforce; factories will have a group of **core employees**, supplemented by a group of insecure **peripheral employees**, on part time or temporary contracts, working as and when required. Some research indicates a 'two-tier' society split between **'work-rich'** (with two wage-earners) and **'work-poor'**. However, despite some claims, **most employees are in permanent, full-time employment**.
Wealth	Rising standards of living lead to increased demand for certain types of consumer good. This is why developing countries are attractive as markets.

Implications of demographic change

(a) **Changes in patterns of demand**: an ageing population suggests increased demand for health care services: a young growing population has a growing demand for schools, housing and work.

(b) **Location of demand**: people may be moving to the suburbs and small towns.

(c) **Recruitment policies**: there may be relatively fewer young people so firms will have to recruit from less familiar sources of labour (and the retirement age may need to be increased).

(d) **Wealth and tax**: Patterns of poverty and hence, need for welfare provisions may change. The tax base may alter.

2.3.1 Culture

Through contact with a particular culture, individuals learn a language, acquire values and learn habits of behaviour and thought.

(a) **Beliefs and values**: Beliefs are what we feel to be the case on the basis of objective and subjective information (eg people can believe the world is round or flat). **Values** are beliefs which are relatively enduring, relatively general and fairly widely accepted as a guide to culturally appropriate behaviour.

(b) **Customs**: modes of behaviour which represent culturally accepted ways of behaving in response to given situations.

(c) **Artefacts**: all the physical tools designed by human beings for their physical and psychological well-being: works of art, technology, products.

(d) **Rituals**: A ritual is a type of activity which takes on symbolic meaning, consisting of a fixed sequence of behaviour repeated over time.

The learning and sharing of culture is made possible by **language** (both written and spoken, verbal and non-verbal).

Knowledge of the culture of a society is clearly of value to businesses in a number of ways.

(a) **Culture influences tastes and lifestyles** and therefore influences the sorts of products and services a business should offer.

(b) **Marketers** can adapt their products accordingly, and be fairly sure of a sizeable market. This is particularly important in export markets.

(c) **Human resource managers** may need to tackle cultural differences in recruitment. For example, some ethnic minorities have different body language which may be hard for some interviewers to interpret.

Culture in a society can be divided into **subcultures** reflecting social differences. Most people participate in several of them.

Subculture	Comment
Class	People from different social classes might have different values reflecting their position in society.
Ethnic background	Some ethnic groups can still be considered a distinct cultural group.
Religion	Religion and ethnicity are related.
Geography or region	Distinct regional differences might be brought about by the past effects of physical geography (socio-economic differences etc). Speech accents most noticeably differ.
Age	Age subcultures vary according to the period in which individuals were socialised to an extent, because of the great shifts in social values and customs in this century. ('Youth culture'; the 'generation gap')
Sex	Some products are targeted directly to women or to men.
Work	Different organisations have different corporate cultures, in that the shared values of one workplace may be different from another.

Cultural change might have to be planned for. There has been a revolution in attitudes to female employment, despite the well-publicised problems of discrimination that still remain.

Question

Club Fun

Club Fun is a UK company that sells packaged holidays. Founded in the 1960s, it offers a standard 'cheap and cheerful' package to resorts in Spain and, more recently, to some of the Greek islands. It is particularly successful at providing holidays for the 18–30 age group.

What do you think the implications are for Club Fun of the following developments?

- A fall in the number of school leavers
- The fact that young people are more likely now than in the 1960s to go into higher education
- Holiday programmes on TV which feature a much greater variety of locations
- Greater disposable income amongst the 18–30 age group

Answer

The firm's market is shrinking. There is an absolute fall in the number of school leavers. Moreover, it is possible that the increasing proportion of school leavers going into higher education will mean there will be fewer who can afford Club Fun's packages. That said, a higher disposable income in the population at large might compensate for this trend. People might be encouraged to try destinations other than Club Fun's traditional resorts if these other destinations are publicised on television.

2.4 The technological environment

FAST FORWARD Technological developments can affect all aspects of business, not just products and services.

The word 'technology' is used to mean three rather different things.

(a) **Apparatus** or equipment such as a video camera

(b) **Technique**: for instance how to use the video camera to best effect, perhaps in conjunction with other equipment such as lights

(c) **Organisation**: for example, the grouping of camera operators into teams, to work on a particular project, for example making a film

Technology contributes to overall economic growth. The **production possibility curve** describes the total production in an economy. There are three ways in which technology can increase total output.

(a) Gains in **productivity** (more output per units of input)

(b) Reduced **costs** (eg transportation technology)

(c) New types of **product**

Effects of technological change on organisations

(a) **The type of products or services that are made and sold.**

(b) **The way in which products are made** (eg process automation, new raw materials).

(c) **The way in which goods and services are sold.** The growth of direct selling via the **internet** has had a significant impact on the implementation of business strategy

(d) **The way in which markets are identified.** Database systems make it much easier to analyse the market place.

(e) **The way in which firms are managed.** IT encourages delayering of organisational hierarchies, homeworking, and better communication. Technology has also enabled greater integration between buyers and suppliers via the use of extranets.

(f) **The means and extent of communications with external clients.** The financial sector is rapidly becoming electronic – call centres are now essential to stay in business, online banking is becoming increasingly common, and the internet and interactive TV are featuring in business plans.

We will look at **e-business and e-marketing** in more detail later in this Study Text.

The impact of recent technological change also has potentially important social consequences, which in turn, can have an impact on business.

(a) **Homeworking.** Whereas people were once collected together to work in factories, home working will become more important.

(b) **Knowledge work.** Certain sorts of skill, related to interpretation of data and information processes, are likely to become more valued than manual or physical skills.

(c) **Services.** Technology increases manufacturing productivity, releasing human resources for service jobs. These jobs require **greater interpersonal skills** (eg in dealing with customers).

PESTEL analysis is normally something an organisation carries out to help it understand its environment. However, note that one of the aspects of the ACCA Practical Experience Requirement is that you, "Recognise the political, economic, social and technological context within which the accounting function operates". You can use your understanding of PESTEL analysis to help with this.

2.5 Environmental protection

FAST FORWARD

The **physical** environment is important for logistical reasons, as a source of resources, and because of increasing regulation.

The importance of physical environmental conditions

(a) **Resource inputs.** Managing physical resources successfully (eg oil companies, mining companies) is a good source of profits.

(b) **Logistics.** The physical environment presents logistical problems or opportunities to organisations. Proximity to road and rail links can be a reason for siting a warehouse in a particular area.

(c) **Government.** The physical environment is under government influence.

(i) Local authority town planning departments can influence where a building and necessary infrastructure can be sited.

(ii) Governments can set regulations about some of the organisation's environmental interactions.

(d) **Disasters.** In some countries, the physical environment can pose a major threat to organisations. For example, a major earthquake struck the Sichuan province in China in May 2008, three months before the Beijing Olympics.

FAST FORWARD

The impact of business activity on the physical environment is now a major concern. Companies are under pressure to incorporate measures to protect the environment into their plans. This presents both challenges and opportunities, since some measures will impose costs, but others will allow significant savings. There is also a new range of markets for goods and services designed to protect or have minimum impact on the environment.

2.5.1 Environmental protection policy

Environmental protection is now a key aspect of **corporate social responsibility**. Pressure on businesses for better environmental performance is coming from many quarters.

(a) **Green pressure groups** have increased their membership and influence dramatically.

(b) **Employees** are increasing pressure on the businesses in which they work for a number of reasons – partly for their own safety, partly in order to improve the public image of the company.

(c) **Legislation** is increasing almost by the day. Growing pressure from the green or green-influenced vote has led to mainstream political parties taking these issues into their programmes, and most countries now have laws to cover land use planning, smoke emission, water pollution and the destruction of animals and natural habitats.

(d) **Environmental risk screening** has become increasingly important. Companies in the future will become responsible for the environmental impact of their activities.

Exam focus point

Here we are looking at 'environmental' awareness and policy as an important aspect of overall strategy, so be careful with terminology. The 'natural' environment has become an important part of the overall business 'environment'. But note: where your syllabus (A2) refers to 'environmental issues affecting the strategic position of an organisation,' it is referring to the overall business environment, not specifically 'green' issues. 'Green' issues should be considered as one part of the wider business environment.

2.5.2 How green issues impinge on business

Possible issues to consider are these.

- **Consumer demand** for products that appear to be environmentally friendly (eg wood from sustainable forests)
- Demand for **less pollution** from industry
- Greater **regulation** by government, such as recycling targets
- Demand that **businesses be charged** with the external cost of their activities
- **Scarcity** of non-renewable resources (eg the need to find alternative fuels to replace oil when current reserves run out)
- Opportunities to develop **products and technologies** that are environmentally friendly
- Taxes (eg landfill tax)

Martin Bennett and Peter James looked at the **ways in which a company's concern for the environment can impact on its performance**.

(a) **Short-term savings** through waste minimisation and energy efficiency schemes can be substantial.

(b) **Pressures on businesses** for environmental action are increasing.

(c) Companies with poor environmental performance may face **increased cost of capital** because investors and lenders demand a higher risk premium.

(d) There are a growing number of **energy and environmental taxes**, such as landfill tax.

(e) Accidents and long-term environmental effects can result in **large financial liabilities**.

(f) **Pressure group campaigns** can cause damage to reputation and/or additional costs.

(g) **Environmental legislation** may cause some products to be phased out, but in doing so, can provide opportunities for new products to replace them.

(h) The cost of processing input which becomes **waste** is equivalent to 5–10% of some organisation's turnover.

They go on to suggest six main ways in which business and environmental benefits can be achieved.

(a) **Integrating the environment into capital expenditure decisions** (by considering environmental opposition to projects which could affect cash flows, for example).

(b) **Understanding and managing environmental costs.** Environmental costs are often 'hidden' in overheads, and environmental and energy costs are often not allocated to the relevant budgets.

(c) **Introducing waste minimisation schemes**

(d) **Understanding and managing life cycle costs.** For many products, the greatest environmental impact occurs upstream (such as mining raw materials) or downstream from production (such as energy to operate equipment). This has led to producers being made responsible for dealing with the disposal of products such as cars, and government and third party measures to influence raw material choices. Organisations therefore need to identify, control and make provision for environmental life cycle costs and work with suppliers and customers to identify environmental cost reduction opportunities.

(e) **Measuring environmental performance.** Business is under increasing pressure to measure all aspects of environmental performance, both for statutory disclosure reasons and due to demands for more environmental data from customers.

(f) **Involving management accountants** in a strategic approach to environment-related management accounting and performance evaluation.

Such analysis and action should help organisations to better understand present and future environmental costs and benefits.

2.5.3 Renewable and non-renewable resources

Key term

> **Sustainability** involves developing strategies so that the company only uses resources at a rate that allows them to be replenished. At the same time, emissions of waste are confined to levels that do not exceed the capacity of the environment to absorb them.

Sustainability means that resources consumed are **replaced** in some way: for every tree cut down, another is planted. Some resources, however, are inherently non-renewable. For example, oil will eventually run out, even though governments and oil firms have consistently underestimated reserves.

(a) Metals can be recycled. Some car manufacturers are building cars with recyclable components.

(b) An argument is that as the price of resources rise, market forces will operate to make more efficient use of them or to develop alternatives. When oil becomes too expensive, solar power will become economic.

John Elkington, chairman of the think-tank SustainAbility Ltd, has said that **sustainability** now embraces not only environmental and economic questions, but also social and ethical dimensions. He writes about the **triple bottom line**, which means that business people must increasingly recognise that the challenge now is to help deliver simultaneously:

- Economic prosperity
- Environmental quality
- Social equity

Case Study

Kvaerner

Elkington quotes the example of Kvaerner, the Norwegian construction company, to show how important it is to control material and energy usage. An environmental report compiled by the company listed the following.

- A 20% cut in insurance premiums would be worth $15 million
- A 1% reduction in absence due to sick leave is worth $30 million
- A 1% reduction in material and energy consumption is worth $60 million

2.6 The legal environment

Laws come from common law, parliamentary legislation and government regulations derived from it, and obligations, for example under EU membership and other treaties.

Legal factors affecting all companies

Factor	Example
General legal framework: contract, tort, agency	Basic ways of doing business; negligence proceedings; ownership; rights and responsibilities; property
Criminal law	Theft; insider dealing; bribery; deception; industrial espionage
Company law	Directors and their duties; reporting requirements; takeover proceedings; shareholders' rights; insolvency
Employment law	Trade Union recognition; Social Chapter provisions; possible minimum wage; unfair dismissal; redundancy; maternity; Equal Opportunities
Health and Safety	Fire precautions; safety procedures
Data protection	Use of information about employees and customers
Marketing and sales	Laws to protect consumers (eg refunds and replacement, 'cooling off' period after credit agreements); what is or isn't allowed in advertising
Environment	Pollution control; waste disposal
Tax law	Corporation tax payment; Collection of income tax (PAYE) and National Insurance contributions; sales tax (VAT)
Competition law	General illegality of cartels

Some legal and regulatory factors affect **particular industries**, if the public interest is served. For example, in the UK, electricity, gas, telecommunications, water and rail transport may be subject to **regulators** who have influence over market access, competition and pricing policy (can restrict price increases).

This is for either of two reasons.

- The industries are, effectively, monopolies.
- Large sums of public money are involved (eg in subsidies to rail companies following the privatisation of the rail network in the UK).

Case Study

Gas deregulation in the UK

Government policy. Gas used to be a state monopoly in the UK. The industry was privatised as one company, British Gas. Slowly, the UK gas market was opened to competition: eventually, about 20 suppliers competed with British Gas.

Regulators. Ofgas regulates the gas industry. Ofgas has introduced a Code of Conduct requiring gas suppliers to train sales agents, allow for a cooling off period in new sales contracts and so on.

Contracts. When British Gas was privatised, it inherited 'take or pay contracts' requiring it to buy gas at a specific price from gas producers. Since that time, gas prices have fallen, and competitors have been able to benefit from this.

New markets. Government policy has also deregulated the electricity market, so that companies such as British Gas can now sell electricity.

3 Key drivers of environmental change

FAST FORWARD

Four aspects of **globalisation** are key drivers of change.

- Market globalisation grows as tastes converge and communications improve.
- Cost globalisation spreads as trade barriers fall and economies of scale and experience grow.
- Governments promote free trade and international standards.
- International competition promotes further trade and interaction.

In the previous section, we looked at environmental factors which can have an impact on an organisation's strategy. However, it is important to realise that these environmental factors are not static, but rather that they change over time. In this section, we will look at some of the key drivers of environmental change.

JS&W, following Yip, identify four aspects of **globalisation** as **key drivers of change** in the macro-environment.

- Market globalisation
- Cost globalisation
- Government activity and policy
- Global competition

3.1 Market globalisation

Gradual **globalisation of markets** is taking place because of the interplay of a number of forces. It is impossible to isolate a simple chain of causation here.

(a) **Consumer tastes** are becoming more homogeneous in such matters as clothes and entertainment.

(b) As markets globalise, firms supplying them become **global customers** for their own inputs and seek **global suppliers**.

(c) **Improvements in global communications and logistics** reduce costs, make globalisation easier and allow the creation of global brands. The latter feeds back to the homogenisation of taste.

3.2 Cost globalisation

(a) **Economies of scale** are a major source of cost advantage: companies in some industries, such as some electronics manufacture, can continue to gain such economies even as they (the companies) expand up to global size.

(b) **Experience effects** can continue to drive down costs in the same way. An organisation undertaking any activity learns to do it more efficiently over time, as it gains more experience of carrying out that activity. This increased efficiency reduces unit costs.

(c) **Sourcing efficiencies** may be achieved by central procurement from global lowest-cost suppliers.

(d) Country-specific cost advantages, such as low labour costs or a favourable exchange rate, encourage purchasers to search globally for suppliers.

(e) **High costs of product development** can be spread over longer production runs if products are standardised and sold globally.

3.3 Government policy

The climate of government opinion has been increasingly sympathetic to **free trade**, though producer special interests and popular discontent continue to hamper it. **Technical standardisation** in both manufacturing and services has also encouraged increased trade, while some governments have been active in seeking foreign direct investment.

3.4 Global competition

Competitive forces seem to have had global effects:

(a)   Existing high levels of international trade encourage further interaction between competitors as a matter of routine.

(b)   The existence of global competitors and global customers in an industry prompts purely national firms to start trading globally so as to be able to compete on an even footing.

4 The competitive advantage of nations   12/13, 6/10

FAST FORWARD

Porter identifies four principal determinants of national competitive advantage.

- **Factor conditions**
- **Firm strategy structure and rivalry**
- **Demand conditions**
- **Related and supporting industries**

Exam focus point

Porter's diamond is a very important model. In the December 2013 exam, students were expected to apply the model to assess the attractiveness of a foreign country. The examining team noted that although most students appeared to be aware of the diamond and its constituent parts, many were not clear on their meaning.

A significant number of students confused the diamond model with Porter's Five Forces (see later in the Study Text) and therefore answered the question incorrectly. The examining team noted that many candidates commented that the absence of competition in the foreign country was a 'good thing' for the featured organisation. From the perspective of 'competitive rivalry' which is a key part of Porter's Five Forces framework, this assertion would be correct. However, in the context of the diamond this could be interpreted as a weakness, because a strong, vigorous rivalry is required to produce and retain a nation's competitive advantage in an industry. It is critical that you understand both models and are confident in applying them to a scenario.

Michael Porter's *The Competitive Advantage Of Nations,* suggests that some nations' industries are more internationally competitive than others. For example, UK leadership in many heavy industries, such as ship-building, has been overtaken by Japan and Korea.

Porter does not believe that countries or nations as such are competitive, but rather that the **conditions within a country may help firms to compete**.

The original explanation for **national** success was the theory of **comparative advantage**. This held that **relative opportunity costs** determined the appropriateness of particular economic activities in relation to other countries. (Opportunity cost is defined as the value of that which must be given up in order to acquire or achieve something.)

Porter argues that comparative advantage is **too general a concept** to explain the success of individual companies and industries. He suggests that industries that require **high technology** and **highly skilled employees** are less affected than low technology industries by the relative costs of their inputs of raw materials and basic labour, as determined by the national endowment of factors of production.

We must therefore look elsewhere for the determinants of national competitive advantage.

Porter identifies four principal factors, which are outlined in the diagram below. Porter refers to this as the **diamond**.

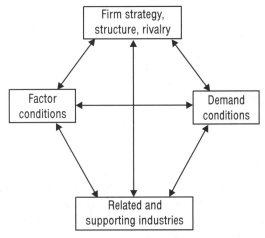

Porter's Diamond

4.1 Analysing the diamond

4.1.1 Factor conditions

Factor conditions are a country's endowment of inputs to production.

- Human resources (skills, price, motivation, industrial relations)
- Physical resources (land, minerals, climate, location relative to other nations)
- Knowledge (scientific and technical know-how, educational institutions)
- Capital (amounts available for investment, how it is deployed)
- Infrastructure (transport, communications, housing)

Porter distinguishes between **basic** and **advanced** factors.

(a)   **Basic factors** are natural resources, climate, semiskilled and unskilled labour. They are inherent, or at best their creation involves little investment. They are **unsustainable** as a source of national competitive advantage, since they are widely available. For example, the wages of unskilled workers in industrial countries are undermined by even lower wages elsewhere.

(b)   **Advanced factors** are associated with a well-developed scientific and technological infrastructure and include modern digital communications infrastructure, highly educated people (eg computer scientists), university research laboratories and so on. They are necessary to achieve high order competitive advantages such as differentiated products and proprietary production technology.

An abundance of factors is not enough. It is the efficiency with which they are deployed that matters. The former USSR had an abundance of natural resources and a fairly well educated workforce, but was an economic catastrophe.

Porter also notes that **generalised factors**, such as transport infrastructure do not provide as decisive and sustainable bases for competitive advantage as **do specialised factors**. These are factors that are relevant to a limited range of industries, such as knowledge bases in particular fields and logistic systems developed for particular goods or raw materials. Such factors are integral to innovation and very difficult to move to other countries.

4.1.2 Demand conditions: the home market

The **home market determines how firms perceive, interpret and respond to buyer needs.** This information puts pressure on firms to innovate and provides a launch pad for global ambitions.

(a)   There are **no cultural impediments** to communication.

(b)   The **segmentation** of the home market shapes a firm's priorities: companies will be successful globally in segments which are similar to the home market.

(c) **Sophisticated and demanding buyers** set standards. If the home market sets high standards, achieving these high standards will put a firm in a strong position to be competitive on the international market.

(d) **Anticipation of buyer needs:** if consumer needs are expressed in the home market earlier than in the world market, the firm benefits from experience.

(e) The **rate of growth**. Slow growing home markets do not encourage the adoption of state of the art technology.

(f) **Early saturation** of the home market will encourage a firm to export.

4.1.3 Related and supporting industries

Competitive success in one industry is linked to success in related industries. Domestic suppliers are preferable to foreign suppliers, as they offer continuing close co-operation and co-ordination. The process of innovation is also enhanced when suppliers are of high quality, since information is transmitted rapidly and problems are solved by joint effort.

4.1.4 Firm strategy, structure and rivalry

Management style and industrial structure. Nations are likely to display competitive advantage in industries that are culturally suited to their normal management practices and industrial structures. For example, German managers tend to have a strong bias towards engineering and are best at products demanding careful development and complex manufacturing processes. They are less successful in industries based on intangibles such as fashion and entertainment.

Strategy. Industries in different countries have different **time horizons**, funding needs and so forth.

(a) **National capital markets** set different goals for performance. In Germany and Switzerland, banks are the main source of capital, not equity shareholders. Short-term fluctuations in share prices are not regarded as of great importance as funds are invested for the long term. In the US, most shares are held by financial institutions whose own performance indicators emphasise short-term earnings growth.

(b) **National attitudes to wealth** are important. The egalitarian Swedes are rarely successful in industries that have the potential to create individual fortunes but depend on new start-ups.

(c) **National culture** affects industrial priorities through the relative prestige it allots to various industries and their leaders. Italy values fashion and furnishings, for instance, while in Israel the most prestigious industries are agriculture and those related to defence.

Domestic rivalry is important for several reasons.

- There can be no special pleading about unfair foreign competition.
- With little domestic rivalry, firms are happy to rely on the home market.
- Tough domestic rivals teach a firm about competitive success.
- Domestic rivalry forces firms to compete on grounds other than basic factors.
- Each rival can try a different strategic approach.

The promotion by government of one or two **'national champions'** who can reap major economies of scale in the domestic market is undermined by the vigorous domestic competition among high-performing global companies. Examples are the Swiss pharmaceutical industry and the US IT industry.

4.2 Influencing the diamond

A nation's competitive industries tend to be **clustered**. Porter believes **clustering** to be a key to national competitive advantage. A cluster is a linking of industries through relationships that are either vertical (buyer-supplier) or horizontal (common customers, technology, skills). For example, the UK financial services industry is clustered in London, the US hi-tech electronics industry is clustered in Silicon Valley.

No part of the Basque country's rich industrial heritage can rival its €10bn annual turnover car industry as the driving force of the region's economy.

Generating 18 per cent of the region's gross domestic product, the sector and its associated companies employ more than 76,000 people globally, and account for almost 40 per cent of all car parts exported from Spain.

The Basque car sector has grown over several decades to such an extent that a region of less than 7,800 square kilometres is home to every part of the car production process, from steel factories to engineering companies and technical universities.

More than 30 multinational companies connected to the automotive industry have factories and offices in the region. They include Michelin, the tyre manufacturer, Valeo, the components manufacturer, and Daimler, which has a production plant in Vitoria.

Other companies involved in different stages of the car production chain include ArcelorMittal, the steelmaker, which has six production sites and a research centre in the Basque country, and Saint-Gobain, the French construction materials company.

Exemplifying this integrated approach is the Automotive Intelligence Centre, a business and development hub for the sector located outside Bilbao. The wavy-roofed steel and glass building opened just over three years ago and contains numerous companies, both Basque and foreign, that have operations in the region.

Serving as a research and development centre, industry infrastructure and training site, among other functions, the AIC is aimed at forging collaboration between the numerous companies related to the Basque automotive sector to increase their international competitiveness.

"We felt the industry was very vertically oriented, from the final clients downwards," says Inés Anitua, managing director of the AIC and of ACICAE, the Basque country's automotive industry cluster.

"We wanted to start working more horizontally, to think differently. In Europe we have a strong knowledge [base] and the car industry was born here, so it is important we can sustain that knowledge."

Originally thought up in 2006, the AIC was funded at first by the local administration and the European Union, but is now sustained by contributions from its industry members.

The industry in the region is very close-knit, with an interesting mix of companies, says Ms Anitua. More than 30 foreign groups have invested in the region, which has its own "global players", she adds.

Mondragon Automoción, part of the Mondragon co-operative group, supplies parts to Honda, Ford and Renault-Nissan, among others, and is one example of a local company with a wide international footprint, with production plants in Brazil, Mexico and China.

Another is CIE Automotive, which is one of the companies with a base in the AIC and is quoted on the Madrid and São Paulo stock exchanges.

"We have many [opportunities] to work with other companies in our sector on different projects," says Iñigo Loizaga, a technical operator with CIE Automotive at the AIC. "We can also work together on certain commercial needs, demonstrate what we do together to clients and look at international expansion more efficiently. There are many synergies," he says.

Oriel Saperas, director of the AIC's competitive intelligence department, produces sweeping opinion pieces on important developments in the sector, as well as confidential intelligence reports commissioned by members and companies outside the cluster.

"People receive a lot of information. We can organise this into something to suit the strategic objectives of companies, using a global view," he says.

This collection of companies, a mix of foreign multinationals and indigenous manufacturers, allows the different parts of the production process to be in proximity to each other, and reduces the risk of one part suffering if a large component maker were to close down.

"The mix we have here is quite unique. Other regions may have a vehicle manufacturer, then foreign parts manufacturers. But if the big brand decides to close, the others will then move. We are not as dependent, as we export 80 per cent of production," says Mr Saperas.

The steps taken by the Basque car industry to internationalise in recent years have produced impressive results.

Now, 80 per cent of total sales are to outside Spain, with a rising proportion derived from countries beyond Europe, and this is expected to result in record total sales for this year.

Sales outside the EU more than doubled between 2006 and 2009 from 14.6 per cent of the total to 32.5 per cent, while sales within the EU, excluding Spain, fell over the same period from 56.6 per cent to 46.2 per cent.

"In the past, we used to talk about exporting by selling to France or Germany. Now, you have to prove you can sell parts to many parts of the world to be able to survive. We have done that, and that is why some of our members have not only survived but have grown," says Mr Saperas.

During the economic crisis, sales fell in 2010 to €10bn, compared with the €11bn generated in 2009, but the AIC expects an increase in international sales to help total revenues for 2011 come in above, or at least match, the 2009 figure once final numbers are calculated.

"This structure has enabled us to grow together at all levels," says Ms Anitua. "We have achieved something unique here that will keep the sector strong."

(Financial Times, 27 March 2012)

How does a country create a diamond of competitive advantage? Governments cannot compete; only firms can do that. Governments can influence the **context** in which an industry operates and can create opportunities and pressures for innovation.

(a) Factors of production provide the seed corn. Eg A large endowment of easily mined iron ore would suggest metal-working industries.

(b) Related and supporting industries can also be a foundation, if the competences within them can be configured in a new way.

(c) **Government policy** should support cluster development and promote high standards of education, research and commercially relevant technologies. Although, government is not one of the four primary factors on the diamond, **governments** can play a crucial role in developing national competitive advantage. For example, governments can help shape levels of infrastructure and education in a country, and can directly affect a country's attractiveness as an investment location through their tax policies.

(d) Extraordinary demand in the **home market** based on national peculiarities and conditions can set the demand conditions determinant in the diamond.

It must be remembered that the creation of competitive advantage can take many years.

However, while Porter's theory suggests that clustering will help international competitiveness, the cluster approach is not guaranteed to be successful.

If a firm wishes to compete in an industry in which there is no national competitive advantage, it can take a number of steps to succeed.

(a) **Compete in the most challenging market,** to emulate domestic rivalry and to obtain information. If a firm can compete successfully in such a market, even if this only means carving out a small niche, it should do well elsewhere.

(b) **Spread research and development** activities to countries where there is an established research base or industry cluster already.

(c) Be prepared to **invest heavily in innovation**.

(d) **Invest in human resources**, both in the firm and the industry as a whole. This might mean investing in training programmes.

(e) **Look out for new technologies** which will change the rules of the industry. The UK, with its large efficient research base, should have some creative ideas.

(f) **Collaborate with foreign companies.** American motor companies, successfully learned Japanese production techniques.

(g) **Supply overseas companies**. Japanese car plants in the UK have encouraged greater quality in UK components suppliers. Inward investment provides important **learning opportunities** for domestic companies.

(h) **Source components from overseas**. In the UK crystal glass industry, many firms buy crystal glass from the Czech Republic, and do the cutting and design work themselves. Conversely, firms can sell more abroad.

(i) **Exert pressure on politicians** and opinion formers to create better conditions for the diamond to develop (eg in education).

Exam focus point

The examining team frequently stress the importance of ensuring that any models used must be relevant in answering the question. Students often seem to attempt to use too many models, apparently in the hope that merely displaying their knowledge of the models will gain extra credit. This is not the case though: marks will only be awarded for referring to theories or models which are relevant to the question set. In addition, the examining team has highlighted that students who perform best in the P3 exam tend to 'only use more than one framework where a further framework gives an insight or provides a suggestion that the initial framework has failed to provide'.

5 The environment in the future

FAST FORWARD

The past is not necessarily a good guide to the future. It may be so in simple static conditions, but more complex or dynamic environments require sophisticated techniques such as the use of leading indicators and scenarios.

Exam focus point

An article titled 'Business forecasting and strategy' (January 2011) written by Ken Garrett was published in *Student Accountant*, and is available in the technical articles section for P3 on the ACCA website. It would be worth taking the time to study this article.

5.1 Scenario building   6/13

Macro scenarios are used to consider possible future environmental conditions overall. **Industry scenarios** deal with an individual industry in more detail.

Because the environment is so complex, it is easy to become overwhelmed by the many factors. Firms therefore try to model the future and this technique is called **scenario building**.

Key term

A **scenario** is a detailed and consistent view of how the business environment of an organisation might develop in the future.   *JS&W*

Scenarios are built with reference to key influences and change drivers in the environment. They inevitably deal with conditions of high uncertainty, so they are not forecasts; they are, rather, internally consistent views of potential future conditions.

5.1.1 Macro scenarios

Macro scenarios use macro-economic or political factors, creating alternative views of the future environment (eg global economic growth, political changes, interest rates).

5.1.2 Building scenarios

Keeping the scenario process simple is the way to get the most out of scenario building.

(a)   Normally a team is selected to develop scenarios, preferably of people from diverse backgrounds. The team should include 'dissidents' who challenge the consensus and some reference outsiders to offer different perspectives.

(b)   Most participants in the team draw on both general reading and specialist knowledge.

Steps in scenario planning (Mercer).

Step 1   **Decide on the drivers for change**

- Environmental analysis helps determine key factors.

- At least a ten year time horizon is needed, to avoid simply extrapolating from the present.

- Identify and select the important issues and degree of certainty required.

Step 2   **Bring drivers together into a viable framework**

- This relies almost on an intuitive ability to make patterns out of 'soft' data, so is the hardest part of the process.

- Items identified can be brought together as mini-scenarios.

- There might be many trends, but these can be grouped together.

- It is inappropriate to attempt to allocate probabilities

Step 3   **Produce seven to nine mini-scenarios**. The underlying logic of the connections between the items can be explored.

Step 4   **Group mini-scenarios into two or three larger scenarios** containing all topics.

- This generates most debate and is likely to highlight fundamental issues.
- More than three scenarios will confuse people.

- The scenarios should be complementary, not opposite. They should be equally likely. There is no 'good' or 'bad' scenario.

- The scenarios should be tested to ensure they hang together. If not, go back to Step 1.

Step 5   **Write the scenarios**

- The scenarios should be written up in the form most suitable for managers taking decisions based on them.

- Most scenarios are qualitative rather than quantitative in nature.

Step 6   **Identify issues arising**

- Determine the most critical outcomes, or branching points which are critical to the long term survival of the organisation.

- Role play can be used to test what the scenarios mean to key actors in the future of the business.

5.1.3 Industry scenarios

Porter believes that the most appropriate use for scenario analysis is if it is restricted to an industry. An **industry scenario** is an internally consistent view of an **industry's** future structure. It is not a forecast, but a possibility. A set of scenarios would reflect the possible future implications of current uncertainties. Different competitive strategies may be appropriate to different scenarios.

Using scenarios to formulate competitive strategy

(a)   A strategy built in response to only one scenario is **risky**, whereas one supposed to cope with them all might be **expensive**.

(b)   Choosing scenarios as a basis for decisions about competitive strategy.

Approach	Comment
Assume the most probable	This choice puts too much faith in the scenario process and guesswork. A less probable scenario may be one whose **failure** to occur would have the **worst** consequences for the firm.
Hope for the best	A firm designs a strategy based on the scenario most attractive to the firm: this is wishful thinking.
Hedge	The firm chooses the strategy that produces **satisfactory** results under **all** scenarios. **Hedging, however, is not optimal**. The **low risk** is paid for by a **low reward**.
Flexibility	A firm taking this approach plays a 'wait and see' game. It is safer, but sacrifices first-mover advantages.
Influence	A firm will try and influence the future, for example, by influencing demand for related products in order that its favoured scenario will be realised in events as they unfold.

Exam focus point

A question in the June 2013 exam required students to discuss the potential use of scenarios by a company's management team when considering whether to enter an overseas market. The examining team noted that a significant number of students appeared to be unfamiliar with the use of scenarios, even though the terms such as 'best-case' and 'worst-case' scenario are often used in the business world.

 Case Study   Leading through uncertainty

In December 2008, *The McKinsey Quarterly* published an online article called 'Leading through uncertainty'.

This article argued that the economic downturn in 2008 required executives to find new ways of operating that were suited to the uncertain business environment. 'They need greater flexibility to create strategic and tactical options they can use defensively or offensively as conditions change. They need a sharper awareness of their own and their competitors' positions.'

The article argued that instead of focusing on quarterly performance, companies should take a more flexible approach to planning, and should develop several coherent, multipronged strategic action plans.

These plans shouldn't be just academic exercises. Executives must be ready to pursue them as the future unfolds. Which acquisitions could be attractive, and on what terms? How much capital or management capabilities would be required? What new products would best fit different scenarios? If one or more major competitors falter, how will the company react? In which markets can it gain market share? If one or more major suppliers falter, how will the company react?

The problems in the global credit markets in 2008 created volatility and destroyed existing business models. This highlighted the need for organisations to understand how their revenues, costs, profits, and cash flows will fare under different scenarios, and identify the risks that they face. This information will

help executives plan for the future. Is the firm prepared for the bankruptcy of major customers? Could it halve capital spending quickly if necessary?

The value of asking these questions is that it should help organisations be better prepared and to recognise as early as possible which scenario is developing. Such knowledge is critical in a crisis, when lead times disappear quickly, and organisations can only seize the initiative if they act before everyone else understands the probable outcome.

Business intelligence is also vital, because it promotes faster, more effective decision making. Organisations can often gain insights into the potential moves of competitors by analysing news reports about their activities, reviewing stock market analysts reports. They can also gather information by talking to customers and suppliers. All of this information is important. In difficult economic conditions, it can make the difference between missing opportunities to buy distressed assets and leaping in to catch them. And it can also make the difference between rushing in to buy what appeared a bargain but was actually a business which should have been avoided at all costs.

> Adapted from an article, 'Leading through uncertainty' by Lowell Bryan and Diana Farrell, *McKinsey Quarterly*, December 2008
>
> www.mckinseyquarterly.com/strategy/

5.2 Forecasts

Forecasting attempts to reduce the uncertainty managers face, by predicting what is likely to happen. Virtually every form of decision making and planning activity faced by organisations will involve some form of forecasting. In **simple and static conditions, the past is a relatively good guide** to the future, but the past is not such a good guide when conditions are dynamic, volatile and going through substantial change.

Forecasting can be carried out using both qualitative and quantitative techniques. **Quantitative techniques** use historical data as a basis for predicting the future. **Qualitative techniques** make much more use of judgement about changing conditions and are more appropriate when the past should not be used as a guide for the future.

5.2.1 Qualitative forecasting methods

Qualitative techniques include the Delphi technique, sales force opinions, executive opinions and market research.

(a) The **Delphi technique** involves selecting a panel of experts, each of which are asked to produce an independent forecast. These forecasts are shared, and each then goes on to produce a revised forecast. The process continues until they are in agreement and a definitive forecast is produced.

(b) **Sales force opinions** involve a sales manager gathering input from the sales team and collating their opinions into an aggregate forecast.

(c) **Executive opinions** arise from meetings of high level managers during which they develop forecasts based on their knowledge of their own individual areas of responsibility.

(d) **Market research** involves the use of customer surveys to evaluate potential demand.

Qualitative techniques, such as those described above, are generally much more subjective than quantitative techniques.

5.2.2 Quantitative forecasting techniques: linear regression analysis   12/13, 12/11

Quantitative techniques are based on the use of historical data to predict the future. They involve the identification of patterns and variations between variables.

A commonly-used forecasting method is the linear regression method, also known as the **least squares technique**. This method uses historical data to predict a linear relationship between an independent

variable, x, and a dependent variable, y. Changes in the value of y are predicted from changes in the value of x, based on the linear relationship that is calculated.

Linear regression analysis therefore uses historical data to establish a formula:

$y = a + bx$ where

      y is the dependent variable, its value is determined by the value of x

      x is the independent variable, whose value helps to determine the value of y

      a is the intercept of the line on the y axis: this is the value of y when $x = 0$

      ib the gradient of the line: this is the amount of the predicted change in the value of y for each change in the value of x by 1.

When linear regression analysis is used to predict the value of y in a future time period, the independent variable x is time, and successive time periods are converted into numerical values 1, 2, 3, 4 and so on. For example, if we are trying to forecast future sales from historical sales figures and we assume that sales are rising or falling in a straight-line trend, x (the independent variable) would be time and y (the dependent variable, whose value depends on changes in the value of x) would be sales in each time period.

Linear regression analysis is called the least squares method because the 'line of best fit' that is calculated from the historical data is a straight line that minimises the total of the differences squared between the actual values of y in the historical data, and the predicted values of y that would be calculated using the line of best fit.

Exam focus point

> In the exam, you may be required to analyse and comment on forecasts that are made using linear regression analysis.
>
> A question in the December 2013 exam required students to consider least squares regression and time series analysis approaches to forecasting. The examining team noted that a significant number of students missed obvious points, such as explaining the meaning of the correlation coefficient, and thereby failed to achieve the easy marks on offer.
>
> When attempting questions which require calculations, it is important that you interpret the figures you calculate. This is a skill which often lets students down. Interpreting figures is your opportunity to show that you understand the meaning behind the numbers. For example, if you calculate the correlation coefficient between two variables and this generates a low figure, you should go on to highlight what this means. In this case, a low correlation figure indicates a weak connection between the two variables.

5.2.3 Example: linear regression analysis

Units of sales of a product Z for the eight-year period 2004 – 2011 were as follows:

Year	x =	Sales (y)
		units
2004	1	500
2005	2	525
2006	3	541
2007	4	562
2008	5	589
2009	6	600
2010	7	624
2011	8	620

A line of best fit (with values rounded) calculated using linear regression analysis is:

$y = 488 + 18 x$

Required

Calculate the forecast sales for 2012 and 2013.

Solution

We can forecast 2012 and 2013 sales as follows:

2012: x = 9   forecast sales = 488 + (18 * 9) = 650

2013: x = 10   forecast sales = 488 + (18 * 10) = 668.

5.2.4 Correlation

It is important to assess the extent to which forecasts based on a line of best fit can be relied upon. Correlation refers to the extent to which the values of x and y are related to each other. In other words, to what extent are changes in the value of y correlated to changes in the value of x?

Correlation does not necessarily mean a cause-and-effect relationship. Changes in the value of y may be caused by changes in the value of y. On the other hand, changes in the value of y may be related to changes in the value of x without changes in x being the cause of changes in y. Sales of ice cream and of sunglasses are well correlated, not because of a direct causal link, but because the weather influences both variables.

Having said this, it is of course possible that where two variables are correlated, there is a direct causal link to be found.

The correlation between changes on the value of y and x can be measured statistically, by a coefficient of correlation r and a coefficient of determination r^2.

(a)   The **coefficient of correlation r** has a value between - 1 and + 1. A value of - 1 indicates that there is perfect negative correlation between y and x. This means that as the value of x increases, the value of y falls (the line of best fit is downward-sloping) and there are no variations at all between actual values of y and predicted values of y using the line of best fit. A value of + 1 indicates that there is perfect positive correlation between y and x. This means that as the value of x increases, the value of y also increases (the line of best fit is upward-sloping) and there are no variations at all between actual values of y and predicted values of y using the line of best fit. When r is 0 there is no observable correlation at all. The closer the value of r to – 1 or + 1, the closer the correlation between values of y and x.

(b) The **coefficient of determination r^2** is the square of the coefficient of correlation. It measures the proportion of the total variation in the value of y that can be explained by variations in the value of x. For example, if r is −0.992, then r^2 is 0.984. This means that over 98% of variations in y can be explained by variations in x, and less than 2% of the variations would be explained by other variables.

In the previous example, it could be calculated that the coefficient of correlation between sales of Product Z and time is + 0.986, and r^2 is 0.972, indicating that over 97% of variations in annual sales of Product Z can be explained by the passage of time.

5.2.5 Problems with least squares regression analysis

There are several major problems with using linear regression analysis for forecasting:

(a) It assumes that historical data can be used to forecast what will happen in the future, which may not be appropriate. In the previous example, there was a fall in sales between Year 7 and Year 8, which might indicate that sales of Product Z may be going into decline and the historical growth pattern of the past may not continue into the future.

(b) It assumes a linear relationship between changes in the value of y and changes in the value of x, which may also be an incorrect assumption.

(c) When the value of r is low, the reliability of a line of best fit must be questionable. For example, if r = + 0.60, only 36% of variations in y could be explained by changes in the value of x, leaving 64% of variations in y to be attributable to other factors.

(d) It assumes that the value of one variable, y, can be predicted or estimated from the value of one other variable, x. In reality the value of y might depend on several other variables, or a common external factor, not just x.

(e) As with any forecasting process, the amount of data available is very important. Even if correlation is high, if the analysis is based on no more than about ten pairs of values, we must regard any forecast as being somewhat unreliable.

Exam focus point

The December 2011 exam included a Section B question which asked candidates to evaluate linear regression and correlation data for use in the pricing decision for an e-learning product, particularly highlighting any limitations in using such data. This question was an unpopular choice and a general lack of knowledge in this area was evident in many of those who did attempt it.

5.2.6 Least squares regression analysis for other dependent relationships

The example of least squares regression analysis for forecasting is an example of time series analysis, and forecasting future values of y from a trend line over time. The same technique may be used to predict a relationship between other independent and dependent variables.

For example, it may be possible to predict the amount of a household's monthly spending (dependent variable) from the amount of monthly income that members of the household earn. Historical data could be used to calculate a linear relationship between the two variables, and the coefficients of correlation and determination could be used to measure the strength of the connection between them.

The only requirements for estimating dependent relationships and values are that:

(a) An independent and a dependent variable should be identified

(b) Each of them should be measurable quantitatively, in pairs of data (values for x and corresponding values for y).

5.2.7 Time series analysis with seasonal or cyclical variations

Forecasting future values over time (time series analysis) from historical data can be complicated by the existence of seasonal variations or cyclical variations in the value of in the dependent variable y. For example, forecasting future sales in each month from historical sales data may be complicated by the fact that there are regular seasonal variations in monthly sales, with higher sales in some months and lower sales in others.

Moving averages can be used to:

(a)   Calculate a historical trend line, from which it is possible to establish a trend line of best fit, using linear regression analysis (or another forecasting method), and measure the correlation between time and the dependent variable (using r or r^2)

(b)   Estimate the amount of seasonal variation for each 'season' (day of the week, or month or quarter of the year)

(c)   Combine forecasts using the line of best fit and the estimated seasonal variation to forecast future seasonal sales in the future.

5.2.8 Example: trend line and seasonal variations

Sales of Product x (in units) in each quarter for the years 2008 – 2011 were as follows.

	Quarter 1	Quarter 2	Quarter 3	Quarter 4
2008	94	111	124	106
2009	102	117	135	118
2010	109	127	142	122
2011	110	135	152	128

Management are assuming that sales are on a linear rising trend, but with seasonal variations in sales in each quarter.

Required

(a)   What is a suitable estimate of seasonal variations in sales each quarter?

(b)   If the trend line estimate for sales in the four quarters of 2012 is 136, 138, 140 and 142 in quarters 1, 2, 3 and 4 respectively, what will the forecast of sales be in each quarter of 2012?

Solution

(a)   The first step is to calculate a trend line and seasonal variations from the trend in each quarter. The trend line is calculated as a moving average. Since there are four quarters in each year, a moving average would be calculated as the average of sales over a cycle of four quarters. However, the average of quarters 1, 2, 3 and 4 is quarter 2.5, and the average of quarters 2, 3, 4 and 5 is quarter 3.5. To obtain a moving average for quarter 3, we must therefore calculate the moving average of quarters 1 – 4 and quarters 2 – 5, and then calculate the average of these.

In the table below, the column for the moving total for 2008 Quarter 3 is the sum of sales in time periods (1 – 4) + (2 – 5). Similarly the moving total for 2008 Quarter 4 is the sum of sales in time periods (2 – 5) + (3 – 6) , and so on. The trend line is calculated by dividing the moving total by 8 (8 quarters in the total) and the total variation for the quarter is the difference between actual sales and trend line sales in the quarter.

Year	Qtr	Time period	Sales	Moving total	Trend	Variation	Seasonal variation	Residual
2008	1	1	94					
	2	2	111					
	3	3	124	878	109.75	+ 14.25	+ 15.9	− 1.65
	4	4	106	892	111.50	−5.50	− 4.0	− 1.50
2009	1	5	102	909	113.63	− 11.63	− 14.6	+ 2.97
	2	6	117	932	116.50	+ 0.50	+ 2.7	− 2.2
	3	7	135	951	118.88	+ 16.12	+ 15.9	+ 0.22
	4	8	118	968	121.00	− 3.00	− 4.0	+ 1.0
2010	1	9	109	985	123.13	− 14.13	− 14.6	+ 0.47
	2	10	127	996	124.50	+ 2.50	+ 2.7	− 0.20
	3	11	142	1,001	125.13	+ 16.87	+ 15.9	+ 0.97
	4	12	122	1,010	126.25	− 4.25	− 4.0	− 0.25
2011	1	13	110	1,028	128.50	− 18.50	− 14.6	− 3.90
	2	14	135	1,044	130.50	+ 4.50	+ 2.7	+ 1.80
	3	15	152					
	4	16	128					

The seasonal variation for each quarter is calculated as the average of the variations for the quarter, as shown below. Adjustments are made so that the total of seasonal variations from the trend line each year add up to 0, and there is some rounding of the figures to limit the seasonal variations to one decimal place.

	Q1	Q2	Q3	Q4	Total
2008			+ 14.25	− 5.50	
2009	− 11.63	+ 0.50	+16.12	− 3.00	
2010	− 14.13	+ 2.50	+ 16.87	− 4.25	
2011	− 18.50	+ 4.50			
Total	− 44.26	+ 7.50	+ 47.24	− 12.75	
Average	− 14.75	+ 2.50	+ 15.75	− 4.25	− 0.75
Reduce to 0	+ 0.19	+ 0.19	+0.19	+ 0.19	+ 0.75
Adjusted	− 14.56	+ 2.69	+ 15.94	− 4.06	
Round	− 14.6	+ 2.7	+ 15.9	− 4.0	0

The seasonal variations are shown in the large table, and the residual is the difference between the actual variation in each quarter (difference between actual sales and the trend line) and the estimated seasonal variation.

When the residual is large, the accuracy of either the trend line or the seasonal variation estimates would be called into question.

(b) Given the estimates for the trend line of sales in 2012, the forecast of sales in each quarter can now be calculated.

2012	Trend line	Seasonal variation	Sales forecast
Q1	136	− 14.6	121.4
Q2	138	+ 2.7	140.7
Q3	140	+ 15.9	155.9
Q4	142	− 4.0	138.0

The figures can be rounded to the nearest whole number if required.

5.2.9 Limitations of moving averages and seasonal variations

Forecasting with moving averages and seasonal variations has several limitations.

(a) The use of a trend line assumes that future sales growth (or decline) will follow the same trend as in the past, and that there have been no changes in the trend. This assumption may be inaccurate.

(b) It assumes that the seasonal variation for each season is the same amount in each year, which may not be correct.

5.2.10 Exponential smoothing

Linear regression analysis assumes that the trend line is rising or falling in a straight line. An alternative forecasting assumption is that the trend is getting steeper than in the past, or the trend is becoming flatter.

Exponential smoothing is a technique that can be applied to time series data in order to develop a forecast. It is commonly applied to financial market and economic data, but can be used for any forecasting.

With exponential smoothing, the forecast for the next time period s_{t+1} is:

$\alpha x_t + (1 − \alpha)s_t$

Where α is any value between 0 and 1

x_t is the actual result (say, actual sales) in time period t

s_t is the forecast that was made for time period t.

So the forecast for the next time period is based on actual results in the most recent period and the forecast that was made for the most recent period. The closer that α is to 1, the less the reliance that is placed on previous forecasts and so on actual results in previous periods.

5.2.11 Econometric models for medium term forecasting

Econometrics is the study of economic variables and their interrelationships.

(a) **Leading indicators** are indicators which change **before** market demand changes. For example, a sudden increase in the birth rate would be an indicator of future demand for children's clothes.

(b) The ability to predict the span of time between a change in the indicator and a change in market demand is important. Change in an indicator is especially useful for demand forecasting when they reach their highest or lowest points (when an increase turns into a decline or vice versa).

Exam focus point

The Pilot Paper included a 25 mark question which required candidates to explain and evaluate a forecast spreadsheet, and to then go on to analyse the performance of the organisation. The level of this Pilot Paper question provides a good pointer as to the level of knowledge required in this area of the syllabus.

6 Industry and sector

FAST FORWARD

The immediate business environment of firms producing similar goods is called the **industry**. **Sector** may be used in a similar way in public and not-for-profit services.

The macro environment provides a general background of influences on the organisation. Closer in, we find the day-to-day environment of immediate business concerns: the industry or sector, competitors and markets. Taken together, these factors are sometimes called the **task environment**.

Key term

> An **industry** is a group of firms producing the same product or products that are close substitutes for one another.

The industry concept may be extended into the arena of **public** and **not –for-profit** services, though the term **sector** is normally used rather than **industry**. The terminology is a little vague in that, for example, 'the public sector' is also used to mean **all** public services of whatever kind.

For convenience, we will use the word 'industry' as shorthand to mean 'industry or sector', unless there are considerations that require us to be more specific.

Industries tend not to be stable: such features as location, products, customers and rate of growth all tend to be more or less variable. One important feature of this instability is the way in which the **boundaries** of an industry can change. Previously distinct industries can **converge**: their technologies; activities and products start to mingle or become complementary; and their member firms start to compete or collaborate. This process can be supply-led or demand-led.

Supply-led convergence occurs where suppliers discover links with suppliers in other industries and move together to co-operate in building new markets. Such convergence is common in the public sector, where government departments are regularly merged and re-organised. Government can also promote supply-led convergence in the private sector, especially by deregulation, as has happened in the UK financial services industry. The development of e-commerce has provided manufacturers with a completely new route to consumers, eroding the boundaries of traditional retailing and distribution industries in the process.

Demand-led convergence occurs when customers treat the products of different industries as **substitutable**, as in the case of mobile and fixed line telephones, or **complementary**, as in the case of air travel and car hire.

7 Competitive forces   6/13, 12/11, 6/11, 6/10, 12/09

FAST FORWARD

The **competitive environment** is structured by five forces: **threat of new entrants; substitute products;** the bargaining power of **customers;** the bargaining power of **suppliers; competitive rivalry.**

Exam focus point

> The five forces is one of the three or four most important models in the field of strategy and is explicitly referenced in the Study Guide for P3, so could be specifically required to answer an exam question . Therefore you must study it carefully and be able to apply it. In particular, you need to be able to decide which of the five categories properly describes a given strategic problem which may be discussed in a scenario. Pay particular attention to the nature of the **substitutes**.

In discussing competition, Porter (*Competitive Strategy*) distinguishes between factors that characterise the nature of competition.

(a) **In one industry compared with another** (eg in the chemicals industry compared with the clothing retail industry), some factors make one industry as a whole potentially more profitable than another (ie yielding a bigger return on investment).

(b) Factors **within a particular industry** lead to the competitive strategies that individual firms might select.

Five **competitive forces** influence the state of competition in an industry, and collectively determine the **profit potential** of the industry as a whole. (You must learn these five factors).

- The threat of **new entrants** to the industry
- The threat of **substitute** products or services
- The bargaining power of **customers**
- The bargaining power of **suppliers**
- The **rivalry** amongst current competitors in the industry

Exam focus point

> A question in the June 2013 exam specifically required candidates to use Porter's Five Forces model to assess the attractiveness to the featured company (a fixed-price discount retailer) of entering the discount retail market in a foreign country.
>
> The June 2008 exam asked candidates to use an appropriate model to analyse the competitive environment of a mobile telephone company. The case study scenario highlighted barriers to entry very clearly, and described industry competitors. This should have indicated to candidates that the Five Forces model was an appropriate model to use.

7.1 The threat of new entrants (and barriers to entry to keep them out)

A new entrant into an industry will bring extra capacity and more competition (and so could, in turn, drive down profits). The strength of this threat is likely to vary from industry to industry and depends on two things.

- The strength of the **barriers to entry**. Barriers to entry discourage new entrants.
- The likely **response of existing competitors** to the new entrant.

Barriers to entry

(a) **Scale economies**. High fixed costs often imply a high breakeven point, and a high breakeven point depends on a large volume of sales. If the market as a whole is not growing, the new entrant has to capture a large slice of the market from existing competitors. This is expensive (although Japanese companies have done this in some cases).

(b) **Product differentiation**. Existing firms in an industry may have built up a good brand image and strong customer loyalty over a long period of time. A few firms may promote a large number of brands to crowd out the competition.

(c) **Capital requirements**. When capital investment requirements are high, the barrier against new entrants will be strong, particularly when the investment would possibly be high-risk.

(d) **Knowledge requirements**. As well as high capital requirements, knowledge and know-how are also a barrier to entry. It is much more difficult to enter an industry which requires significant specialist knowledge and skills, than an industry where no specialist skills are required.

(e) **Switching costs**. Switching costs refer to the costs (time, money, convenience) that a customer would have to incur by switching from one supplier's products to another's. Although it might cost a **consumer** nothing to switch from one brand of frozen peas to another, the potential costs for the **retailer or distributor** might be high.

(f) **Access to distribution channels**. Distribution channels carry a manufacturer's products to the end-buyer. New distribution channels are difficult to establish; and existing distribution channels, hard to gain access to.

(g) **Cost advantages of existing producers, independent of economies of scale** include:

  (i) Patent rights
  (ii) Experience and know-how
  (iii) Government subsidies and regulations
  (iv) Favoured access to raw materials

 **Case Study**   **Japanese firms**

Thirty years ago, it was assumed that, following the success of Japanese firms worldwide in motor vehicles (Nissan, Honda, Toyota) and consumer electronics (eg Sony, JVC, Matsushita), no Western companies were safe from Japanese competition. Kao (household goods), Suntory (drinks), Nomura (banking and securities) were seen as successors to firms such as Procter and Gamble and Heineken.

This has not happened, however. For example, Japanese pharmaceutical firms, such as Green Cross, have not achieved the world domination they were expected to in the 1980's. US and European firms are still dominant in this industry.

Perhaps cars and consumer electronics are the exception rather than the rule. The reason for this might be distribution. Normally, outsiders do not find it easy to break into established distribution patterns. However, distribution channels in cars and consumer electronics offered outsiders an easy way in.

(a) The car industry is vertically integrated, with a network of exclusive dealerships. Given time and money, the Japanese firms could simply build their own dealerships and run them as they liked, with the help of local partners. This barrier to entry was not inherently complex.

(b) Consumer electronics

  (i) In the early years, the consumer electronics market was driven by technology, so innovative firms such as Sony and Matsushita could overcome distribution weaknesses with innovative products, as they had plenty to invest. This lowered entry barriers.

  (ii) Falling prices changed the distribution of hi-fi goods from small specialist shops to large cut-price outlets. Newcomers to a market are the natural allies of such new outlets: existing suppliers prefer to shun 'discount' retailers to protect margins in their current distribution networks.

Japanese firms have not established dominant positions in:

(a) Healthcare, where national pharmaceuticals wholesalers are active as 'gatekeepers'
(b) Household products, where there are strong supermarket chains and global brands
(c) Cosmetics, where department stores and specialist shops offer a wide choice

Entry barriers might be **lowered** by the impact of change.

• Changes in the environment
• Technological changes (including the internet)
• New distribution channels for products or services (again, including the internet)

When considering the impact of change nowadays it is impossible not to mention the impact of e-commerce and the internet, because they have enabled new business models to be established. We will look at e-business in more detail later in this Study Text.

7.2 The threat from substitute products

A **substitute product** is a goods or service produced by **another industry** which satisfies the same customer needs. Substitutes are always present, but they can be easy to overlook because they may be very different from the industry's product. For example, video conferencing could be a substitute for business travel.

Exam focus point

It is very easy to misunderstand the nature of substitute products in Porter's model: while they provide competition, they are **not** goods or services produced by competitors in the same industry.

Case Study   The Channel Tunnel

Passengers have several ways of getting from London to Paris, and the pricing policies of the various industries transporting them there reflects this.

(a)   'Le Shuttle' carries cars in the Channel Tunnel. Its main competitors come from the ferry companies, offering a substitute service. Therefore, you will find that Le Shuttle sets its prices with reference to ferry company prices, and vice versa.

(b)   Eurostar is the rail service from London to Paris/Brussels. Its main competitors are not the ferry companies but the airlines. Prices on the London-Paris air routes fell with the commencement of Eurostar services, and some airlines have curtailed the number of flights they offer.

When the threat of substitutes is high, industry profitability suffers. Substitute products or services limit an industry's profit potential by placing a ceiling on prices (because buyers will switch to the substitute if it offers a better value alternative).

The threat of a substitute is high if:

*   It offers an attractive alternative to the industry's product in terms of price and performance.
*   The buyer's cost of switching to the substitute is low.

7.3 The bargaining power of customers

Customers want better quality products and services at a lower price. Satisfying this want might force down the profitability of suppliers in the industry. Just how strong the position of customers will be depends on a number of factors.

*   How much the customer buys

*   How many buyers there are: if there are relatively few buyers but each is large relative to the supplier, then the buyers will be powerful

*   How critical the product is to the customer's own business (if the customer is completely reliant on a product, this will reduce the customer's bargaining power)

*   Switching costs (ie the cost of switching supplier)

*   Whether the products are standard items (hence, easily copied) or specialised

*   The customer's own profitability: a customer who makes low profits will be forced to insist on low prices from suppliers

*   Customer's ability to bypass the supplier (or take over the supplier)

*   The skills of the customer purchasing staff, or the price-awareness of consumers

*   When product quality is important to the customer, the customer is less likely to be price-sensitive, and so the industry might be more profitable as a consequence

7.4 The bargaining power of suppliers

Suppliers can exert pressure for higher prices. The ability of suppliers to get higher prices depends on several factors.

- Whether there are just **one or two dominant suppliers** to the industry, able to charge monopoly or oligopoly prices

- The threat of **new entrants** or substitute products to the **supplier's industry**

- Whether the suppliers have **other customers** outside the industry, and do not rely on the industry for the majority of their sales

- The **importance of the supplier's product** to the customer's business

- Whether the supplier has a **differentiated product** which buyers need to obtain

- Whether **switching costs** for customers would be high

7.5 The rivalry amongst current competitors in the industry

The **intensity of competitive rivalry** within an industry will affect the profitability of the industry as a whole. Competitive actions might take the form of price competition, advertising battles, sales promotion campaigns, introducing new products for the market, improving after sales service or providing guarantees or warranties. Competition can stimulate demand, expanding the market, or it can leave demand unchanged, in which case, individual competitors will make less money, unless they are able to cut costs.

Factors determining the intensity of competition

(a) **Market growth**. Rivalry is intensified when firms are competing for a greater market share in a total market where growth is slow or stagnant. For example, the major supermarkets (eg Tesco, Sainsbury's, Asda) in the UK are becoming increasingly competitive in their attempt to increase market share, in the context of the economic downturn which has seen shoppers become more cautious in their spending.

(b) **Cost structure**. High fixed costs are a temptation to compete on price, as in the short run any contribution from sales is better than none at all. A perishable product produces the same effect.

(c) **Switching**. Suppliers will compete if buyers can, and do, switch easily (eg Coke vs Pepsi).

(d) **Capacity**. A supplier might need to achieve a substantial increase in output capacity, in order to obtain reductions in unit costs.

(e) **Uncertainty**. When one firm is not sure what another is up to, there is a tendency to respond to the uncertainty by formulating a more competitive strategy.

(f) **Strategic importance**. If success is a prime strategic objective, firms will be likely to act very competitively to meet their targets.

(g) **Exit barriers** make it difficult for an existing supplier to leave the industry. These can take many forms.

   (i) Non-current assets with a low **break-up value** (eg there may be no other use for them, or they may be old)

   (ii) The cost of **redundancy payments** to employees

   (iii) If the firm is a division or subsidiary of a larger enterprise, the **effect of withdrawal on the other operations** within the group

   (iv) The **reluctance of managers** to admit defeat, their loyalty to employees and their fear for their own jobs

   (v) **Government pressures** on major employers not to shut down operations, especially when competition comes from foreign producers rather than other domestic producers

Question

Since the turn of the century, the global tea industry has seen a noticeable reversal in its fortunes. Between the 1970s and the early 2000s, the tea industry was characterised by oversupply, with a surplus of about 80,000 tonnes a year. However, this trend has now reversed, with demand now outstripping supply. Some reports suggest that global tea consumption has increased by nearly 60% since the early 1990s. This increase has been partially helped by a global shortage of coffee, which has led to price rises.

The surge in the demand for tea has, however, resulted in a number of challenges for growers.

The rising price of tea around the world is being driven in part by the impact of adverse weather patterns as a result of climate change which has been damaging crops. Growers have also been affected by the loss of skilled workers who are choosing to leave the industry due to the low wages on offer. Tea estates swallow capital, and the return is not as attractive as in industries such as technology or services.

Many tea-bag manufacturers own their own estates, as well as buying in tea from outside sources. In recent times, there has been an increase in the number of well known manufacturers working more closely together in a bid to make tea growing more sustainable.

Today, China and India are the two largest growers of tea in the world. Experts predict that both countries will lead a boom in the growth of the global population over the next 100 years, which in turn will put increasing strain on demand for food and drink. It is predicted that home demand in both countries for tea may reduce the quantities available for export to other tea drinking nations.

Carry out a five forces analysis of the tea growing industry.

Answer

Here are some ideas. Barriers to entry are high (eg the increasing cost of hiring skilled workers to work on tea estates coupled to the need to find areas of the world which are less susceptible to the impact of climate change). There are plenty of substitute products (most notably, coffee). Competitive rivalry is high because of the difficulty of stockpiling fresh tea. The impact of the increase in demand for tea will also drive competition among growers to obtain the best prices from large manufacturers.

Customer bargaining power is lowering as the shortage of available tea around the world means that tea-bag manufacturers have to accept the growers higher prices. By contrast, supplier power is likely to be increasing: if workers on a tea estate are classed as suppliers to the tea growing industry, then their power is gradually increasing as they can now command better wages.

7.6 The impact of information technology on the competitive forces

FAST FORWARD

IT has characteristics that can affect all five competitive forces. These characteristics generally amount to communication improvements but IT can also be a substantial product in its own right.

Barriers to entry and IT

(a) **IT can raise entry barriers** by increasing economies of scale, raising the capital cost of entry (by requiring a similar investment in IT) or effectively colonising distribution channels by tying customers and suppliers into the supply chain or distribution chain.

(b) **IT can surmount entry barriers**. The use of IT can reduce the costs of selling and distribution and even substitute for traditional methods entirely. An example is the use of internet banking, which sometimes eliminates the need to establish a branch network.

Bargaining power of suppliers and IT

(a) **Increasing the number of** accessible **suppliers.** Supplier power can derive from various factors such as geographical proximity and the fact that the organisation requires goods of a certain standard within a certain time. IT enhances supplier information available to customers.

(b) **Closer supplier relationships.** Suppliers' power can be **shared**. CAD can be used to design components in tandem with suppliers. Such relationships might be developed with a few key suppliers. The supplier and the organisation both benefit from performance improvement, but the relations are closer.

(c) **Switching costs.** Suppliers can be integrated with the firm's administrative operations, by a system of electronic data interchange.

Bargaining power of customers. IT can lock customers in.

(a) **IT can raise switching costs** by locking customers into networks.

(b) **Customer information systems** can enable a thorough analysis of marketing information so that products and services can be tailored to the needs of certain segments.

(c) Customers also have access to improved information; this can increase their bargaining power.

(d) Suppliers can gain access to larger number of customers, reducing their dependence on a few large buyers.

Substitutes. In many respects, **IT itself is the substitute product.** Here are some examples.

(a) Video-conferencing systems might substitute for air transport in providing a means by which managers from all over the world can get together in a meeting.

(b) IT is the basis for new leisure activities (eg computer games) which substitute for TV or other pursuits.

(c) Email substitutes for some postal deliveries.

IT and the state of competitive rivalry. In many industries, IT will enable newcomers to imitate existing products and services, though set up costs may limit this effect. The effect of the internet may be to expand the size of the market.

(a) IT can be used in support of a firm's **competitive** strategy of cost leadership, differentiation or focus. These are discussed later in this Text.

(b) IT can be used in a **collaborative** venture, perhaps to set up new communications networks. Some competitors in the financial services industry share the same ATM network.

7.7 Using the five forces model: a caution

The five forces model provides a comprehensive framework for analysing the competitive environment. However, it must be used with caution. Because it is comprehensive, it can encourage a feeling of that all factors have been duly considered and dealt with. Any analysis must pursue as high a degree of **objectivity** as possible. If there is too much subjectivity, unfounded complacency will result.

The effect of subjectivity appears at an early stage in any analysis using the five forces approach. It is necessary to define with great care just what **market** or **market segment** you are dealing with. For a large organisation, or one operating in a complex environment, this may be extremely difficult.

BPP's UK provision of classroom training in accountancy is a good example. BPP provides training for three main accountancy qualifications: The Association of Chartered Certified Accountants (ACCA), The Chartered Institute of Management Accountants (CIMA) and The Institute of Chartered Accountants in England and Wales (ICAEW).

The market for training for potential ICAEW accountants is subject to considerable **customer** bargaining power, since there are a few large firms that predominate. ACCA and CIMA courses, on the other hand, are

more subject to the rivalry of existing **competitors**, since, as well as other commercial training providers, universities and local technical colleges are also sources of competition.

The need for careful analysis is, perhaps, most demanding in the area of substitute products or services. It takes a particular alertness to discern potential substitutes in the early stages of their development.

7.8 Government

It is possible to view the influence of **government** as so great as to justify viewing it as a sixth force. The activities of government would normally be analysed using the PESTEL model but, as we have pointed out, the division of the general environment into these categories is arbitrary and it may be useful to reconsider government in the task environment context. There is also the consideration that competition itself is often the target of specific government policies, either to encourage it or, quite often, to restrict it.

Porter argues that the best approach is to assess the impact of government on one or more of the five forces, rather than viewing it as a separate six force.

<table>
<tr>
<td>

Exam focus point

</td>
<td>

The examining team has commented that candidates often do not appear to understand how the five forces interrelate, or how the importance of a particular force varies over time. It is crucial that you consider the forces as being dynamic rather than static.

</td>
</tr>
</table>

Chapter Roundup

- The environment may be divided for convenience into three concentric layers: the macro-environment; the industry or sector; and competitors and markets. The layers and the elements within them all interact with one another.

- Environmental uncertainty depends on the degree of **complexity** and the degree of **stability** present.

- The macro-environment may be analysed into six segments using the PESTEL framework.

- Government is responsible for providing a stable framework for economic activity and, in particular, for maintaining and improving the physical, social and market infrastructure. Public policy on **competition** and **consumer protection** is particularly relevant to business strategy.

- The **economic** environment affects firms at national and international level, both at the general level of economic activity and in terms of particular variables, such as exchange rates, interest rates and inflation.

- The **social and cultural** environment features long-term social trends and people's beliefs and attitudes.

- Technological developments can affect all aspects of business, not just product and services.

- The **physical** environment is important for logistical reasons, as a source of resources, and because of increasing regulation.

- The impact of business activity on the physical environment is now a major concern. Companies are under pressure to incorporate measures to protect the environment into their plans. This presents both challenges and opportunities, since some measures will impose costs, but others will allow significant savings. There is also a new range of markets for goods and services designed to protect or have minimum impact on the environment.

- Four aspects of globalisation are key drivers of change.

    - Market globalisation grows as tastes converge and communications improve.
    - Cost globalisation spreads as trade barriers fall and economies of scale and experience grow.
    - Governments promote free trade and international standards.
    - International competition promotes further trade and interaction.

- Porter identifies four principal determinants of national competitive advantage.

    - **Factor conditions**
    - **Firm strategy structure and rivalry**
    - **Demand conditions**
    - **Related and supporting industries**

- The past is not necessarily a good guide to the future. It may be so in simple static conditions, but more complex or dynamic environments require sophisticated techniques such as the use of leading indicators and scenarios.

- The immediate business environment of firms producing similar goods is called the **industry**. **Sector** may be used in a similar way in public and not-for-profit services.

- The **competitive environment** is structured by five forces: **threat of new entrants; substitute products**; the bargaining power of **customers**; the bargaining power of **suppliers**; **competitive rivalry**.

- IT has characteristics that can affect all five competitive forces. These characteristics generally amount to communication improvements but IT can also be a substantial product in its own right.

1   What are the three concentric layers that make up the business environment?

2   What does PESTEL stand for?

3   Which four aspects of globalisation may be regarded as key drivers of change?

4   What are the four elements of Porter's diamond?

5   What are the steps in scenario planning?

6   What are the five forces?

7   Fill in the gaps. Five competitive forces influence the state of competition in ...., and collectively determine the .... of the .... as a whole.

8   In Porter's five forces model, what is a substitute product?

Answers to Quick Quiz

1   Macro-environment; industry or sector; and competitors and markets

2   Political, economic, socio-cultural, technological, environmental protection, legal

3   Market globalisation; cost globalisation; government activity and policy; global competition

4   Firm strategy, structure and rivalry; factor conditions; demand conditions; related and supporting industries

5   The steps which Mercer suggests for scenario planning are:

- Decide on the drivers for change
- Bring drivers together into a viable framework
- Produce seven to nine mini-scenarios
- Group the mini-scenarios into two or three larger scenarios
- Write the scenarios
- Identify issues arising

6   Threat of new entrants; substitute products; bargaining power of customers; bargaining power of suppliers; competitive rivalry among existing firms

7   An industry; profit potential; industry

8   A substitute product is a good or service produced by another industry which satisfies the same customer needs. (Note: substitutes are not goods or services produced by competitors in the same industry; they are produced by another industry.)

Now try the question below from the Practice Question Bank

Number	Level	Marks	Time
Q2	Preparation	n/a	20 mins

Competitors and customers

Introduction

Competitors and markets make up the inner layer of the environmental shell. A detailed knowledge of both is essential for the development of effective strategy. In particular, customer reaction is what determines an organisation's critical success factors.

In this chapter, we start to deal with specific topics that may form the basis of exam questions.

Study guide

		Intellectual level
A3	**Competitive forces affecting an organisation**	
(c)	Assess the contribution of the lifecycle model, the cycle of competition and associated costing implications to understanding competitive behaviour	3
(d)	Analyse the influence of strategic groups and market segmentation	3
(e)	Determine the opportunities and threats posed by the environment of an organisation	2
A4	**Marketing and the value of goods and services**	
(a)	Analyse customers and markets	2
(b)	Establish appropriate critical success factors (CSF) and key performance indicators (KPI) for products and services	2

Exam guide

In this chapter, we start to look at some very specific aspects of strategy. Much of the material, such as the discussion of the nature of marketing, is still background, but the more specific topics, such as market segmentation, critical success factors and customer analysis, may have direct relevance to future examination questions.

Models

Two frameworks covered in this chapter are explicitly referenced in the Study Guide and so could be specifically required in a question:

- Cycle of competition
- Lifecycle model

The other models referred to in the chapter, for example the marketing mix, could still be important in helping you answer a question, so you should not overlook them. The marketing mix is defined later in this Study Text.

1 Competition dynamics

FAST FORWARD

The dynamic nature of competition may be considered using a variety of concepts.

- The **cycle of competition** describes the typical development of the relationship between an established firm and a new challenger.
- **Hyper-competition** is an unstable state of constantly shifting short-term advantage.
- The **industry life cycle** has four phases: inception, growth, maturity/shakeout and decline. Each phase has typical implications for customers, competitors, products and profits.
- **Strategic group analysis** examines the strategic space occupied by groups of close competitors in order to identify potential competitive advantage.

The five forces model is a very useful tool for analysing the nature of competition within an industry, but it is essentially static: it does not focus on the **dynamic nature** of the business environment. The nature of competition is that future developments are not controllable by a single firm; each competitor will exercise its own influence on what happens. The business environment is therefore subject to constant change. Strategic managers must attempt to forecast what form this change is likely to take, since it is their responsibility to make plans that will be appropriate under future conditions. JS&W, quoting D'aveni with Gunter, describe a typical **cycle of competition**.

1.1 Cycle of competition

1.1.1 The challenge

An **incumbent firm** already operating successfully in an industry improves existing **barriers to entry** and erects new ones. Any **challenger firm** wishing to enter the industry must attempt to overcome these barriers. This does not necessarily mean attacking the market leader head-on. This is a risky strategy in any case, because of the incumbent firm's resources in cash, promotion and innovation. Instead, the challenger may attack smaller regional firms or companies of similar size to itself that are vulnerable through lack of resources or poor management.

Military analogies have been used to describe the challenger's attacking options.

(a) The **head-on attack** matches the target's marketing mix in detail, product for product and so on. A limited frontal attack may concentrate on selected desirable customers.

(b) The **flank attack** is mounted upon a market segment, geographic region or area of technology that the target has neglected.

(c) The **encirclement attack** consists of as large a number of simultaneous flank attacks as possible in order to overwhelm the target.

(d) The **bypass attack** is indirect and unaggressive. It focuses on unrelated products, new geographic areas and technical leap-frogging to advance in the market.

(e) **Guerrilla attack** consists of a series of aggressive, short-term moves to demoralise, unbalance and destabilise the opponent. Tactics include drastic price cuts, poaching staff, political lobbying and short bursts of promotional activity.

1.1.2 The response

If the incumbent makes no response to the initial campaign, the challenger will widen its attack to other, related or vulnerable market segments, using similar methods to those outlined above. On the other hand, the incumbent may respond; this will often be by means that amount to reinforcing the barriers to entry, such as increasing promotional spending.

Military analogies have also been used to describe defensive strategies for market leaders.

(a) **Position defence** relies upon not changing anything. This does not work very well.

(b) **Mobile defence** uses market broadening and diversification.

(c) **Flanking defence** is needed to respond to attacks on **secondary markets** with growth potential.

(d) **Contraction defence** involves withdrawal from vulnerable markets and those with low potential. It may amount to surrender.

(e) **Pre-emptive defence** gathers information on potential attacks and then uses competitive advantage to strike first. Product innovation and aggressive promotion are important features.

A challenger faced with such moves may decide to start a **price war**. The disadvantage of this is that it will erode the company's own margins as well as those of the incumbent, but it does have the potential to reshape the market and redistribute longer-term market share.

1.1.3 Fighting back

An incumbent faced with a vigorous and resourceful challenger may decide in turn to **attack the entrant's own base**, perhaps by cutting prices in its strongest market. This may cause the challenger to move on towards entry into another attractive market as it seeks to expand.

1.1.4 Resource implications

Both attacking and defending require the deployment of cash and strategic skill. In particular, extending competition to new geographical and national markets can raise the risks and costs involved in operating to the extent that it inhibits rivalry.

1.1.5 Hypercompetition

It is possible for competition in an industry to cycle fairly slowly, with extended periods of stability. This allows the careful building of competitive advantages that are difficult to imitate. **Hypercompetition**, by contrast, is a condition of constant competitive change. It is created by frequent, boldly aggressive competitive moves. This state makes it impossible for a firm to create lasting competitive advantage; firms that accept this will deliberately disrupt any stability that develops in order to deny long-term advantage to their competitors. Under these conditions, continuing success depends on effective exploitation of a series of short-term moves.

1.2 The industry life cycle

FAST FORWARD

Industries may display a **lifecycle**: this will affect and interact with the five forces.

Later in this Study Text, we will discuss the concept of the **product life cycle**: this is a well established strategic and marketing tool. It may be possible to discern an **industry life cycle**, which will have wider implications for the nature of competition and competitive advantage. This cycle reflects **changes in demand** and the **spread of technical knowledge** among producers. Innovation creates new industry, and this is normally achieved through product innovation. Later, innovation shifts to **processes** in order to maintain margins. The overall progress of the industry lifecycle is illustrated below.

	Inception	Growth	Maturity/shakeout	Decline
Product characteristics	Basic, no standards established	Improved design and quality, differentiated	Standardised product with little differentiation	Varied quality but fairly undifferentiated
Competitors	None to few	Many entrants	Competition increases, weaker players leave	Few remain. Competition may be on price
Buyers	Early adopters, prosperous, curious must be induced	More customers attracted and aware	Mass market, brand switching common	Enthusiasts, traditionalists, sophisticates
Profits	Negative – high first mover advantage	Good, possibly starting to decline	Eroding under pressure of competition	Variable
Technology	No standards established	Technologies become more standardised	Technology is understood across the industry	Technology is understood across the industry
Production processes	Small scale batch production. Specialised distributors	Mass production. Distribution networks expanded	Long production runs. Cost efficiency critical	Overcapacity. Production is reduced

Each phase has different implications for competitive behaviour and corporate strategy eg if an industry is growing, the organisations in that industry can grow as the market develops. In a mature industry, growth can only be achieved by stealing market share from other competitors and typically the market becomes more fragmented.

Costs faced by organisations will also vary at different stages in the industry lifecycle. For example, research and development costs will be very high in the inception phase. Production costs may be low during the maturity stage as processes have been refined and contracts negotiated, but marketing expenditure may be high in order to protect market share.

Financial returns to an industry also vary according to the lifecycle stage.

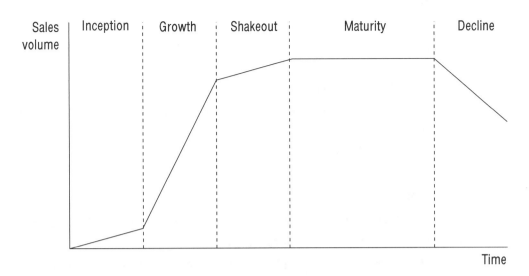

Industry lifecycle

The characteristics of the industry at the different phases of the lifecycle are shown in the table below.

	Inception	Growth	Shakeout	Maturity	Decline
Customers	Experimenters, innovators	Early adopters	Growing selectivity of purchase	Mass market, Products well known	Price competition Commodity product
R&D	High	Extend product before competition	Seek lower cost methods of supply to access new markets	Low	
Company	Early mover Production focused	React to more competitors with increased marketing mass production	Potential consolidation through taking-over rivals. Long production runs	Battles over market share. Seek cost reduction. Long production runs	Cost control or exit
Competitors	A few No major barriers to entry	More entrants to the market	Many competitors, price cutting but weeding out of weaker players	Depending on industry, a few large competitors Difficult for newcomers to dislodge entrenched companies	Price-based competition, fewer competitors
Profitability	Low or negative, as an investment	Growing	Levelling off	Stable, high or under pressure	Falling, unless cost control

The industry life cycle has strategic implications for organisations operating in that industry. Management must pursue different strategies at each stage.

Inception stage

- Attract trend-setting buyer groups by promotion of technical novelty or fashion
- Price high (skim) to cash in on novelty, or price low (penetration) to gain adoption and high initial share
- Support product despite poor current financial results
- Review investment program periodically in light of success of launch (eg delay or bring forward capacity increases)
- Build channels of distribution
- Monitor success of rival technologies and competitor products

Growth stage

- Ensure capacity expands sufficiently to meet firm's target market share objectives
- Penetrate market, possibly by reducing price
- Maintain barriers to entry (eg fight patent infringements, keep price competitive)
- High promotion of benefits to attract early majority of potential buyers
- Build brand awareness to resist impact from new entrants
- Ensure investors are aware of potential of new products to ensure support for financial strategy
- Search for additional markets and product refinements (ie market penetration)
- Consider methods of expanding and reducing costs of production (eg contract manufacturing overseas, building own factory in a low cost location)
- Product development

Shakeout phase

- Monitor industry for potential mergers and rationalisation behaviour
- Periodic review of production and financial forecasts in light of sales growth rates
- Shift business model from customer acquisition to extracting revenue from existing customers
- Seek to extend growth by finding new markets or technologies

Maturity phase

- Maximise current financial returns from product
- Defend market position by matching pricing and promotion of rivals
- Modify markets by positioning product to gain acceptance from non-buyers (eg new outlets or suggested new uses)
- Modify the product to make it cheaper or of greater benefit
- Intensify distribution
- Leverage the existing customer database to gain additional incomes
- Engage in integration activities with rivals (eg mergers, mutual agreements on competition)
- Ensure successor industries are ready for launch to pick up market

Decline phase

- Harvest cash flows by minimising spending on promotion or product refinement
- Simplify range by weeding out variations
- Narrow distribution to target loyal customers and reduce stocking costs
- Evaluate exit barriers and identify the optimum time to leave the industry (eg leases ending, need for renewal investment)
- Seek potential exit strategy (eg buyer for business, firms willing to buy licences etc)
- The response of competitors is particularly important – there may be threats as they attempt to defend their position, or opportunities, eg when a competitor leaves the market.

	Inception	Growth	Maturity	Decline
Product	• Correct any problems in product design • Improve features to develop competitive advantage	• Ensure product quality is maintained despite volume growth • Look at ways to improve quality and design to sustain competitive advantage	• Product efficiency • Cost control • Quality control (minimise defective products) • Only the most productive/ efficient firms will survive	• Assess if it is possible to modify product so that life cycle is started again
Marketing	• Establish product position and target markets • Develop product awareness (advertising; promotion)	• Market penetration • Establish market niche for product • Establish brand loyalty: heavy media use, product samples and other promotions • Establish distribution capabilities to support increased production	• Marketing aimed at maintaining customer loyalty	• Advertising and promotion is minimised
HR	• Establish staff requirements • Recruiting staff	• Training and development of staff to deal with competitive pressures as competition gets tougher	• Personnel incentives to improve productivity and efficiency	• Staff transferred to products in earlier stages of life cycle
Finance	• Arrange funding for product development and marketing • Assess capital requirements for production facilities which may be needed for increased capacity in growth phase			• Liquidation (worst case scenario)

The industry life cycle model is an important concept that may illuminate some aspects of strategic thought. Like other models, it has some value for analysis, for forecasting trends and for suggesting

possible courses of action, but it would be a mistake to attempt to apply it to all industries at all times. Proper attention must always be paid to current circumstances and options.

 **Case Study**   **The decline of the Scottish newspaper industry**

This case study illustrates the importance of adapting to environmental changes to prolong the industry lifecycle.

In August 2013, the BBC reported on the continued decline of the Scottish newspaper industry. The Audit Bureau of Circulation (ABC) confirmed that Scottish newspaper sales had fallen by 11% in the preceding 12 months. Several newspapers have seen their sales fall by more than half in the past decade.

The decline in sales of *The Scotsman* newspaper have left it classed as being a 'regional' title. Interestingly, online readership of the *Scotsman.com* has increased though. 'The free-to-access web service saw a rise in daily browsers of 13%, according to ABC, reaching 120,000. The failure to convert the increase in online readers into increased advertising revenue had led to a decline in the value of the titles owned by Johnston Press, the Edinburgh-based company which includes *The Scotsman* among more than 200 mainly local titles. Johnston Press recently announced that it is writing down the asset valuation of its newspapers by nearly £200m'.

John McLellan, of the Scottish Newspaper Society said, "some titles have been responding to changing market conditions for 20 years of the digital revolution. The truth is that while we can't deny there are challenges, so far as hard copy sales are concerned, the journalism produced by all newspaper companies is being accessed by more people than ever".

Professor Raymond Boyle, a communications expert at Glasgow University, commented on the state of the industry: "Traditionally, Scottish newspapers have been a very important part of Scottish national identity. That's changed over the past 10 to 15 years. Certain sectors remain very strong; sport, for example, and football remains an important part of Scottish newspapers and their identity. But the sense of newspapers being carriers of national identity is no longer sustainable".

Adapted from an article:

'Further decline in Scottish newspaper sales' (August 2013) published on the *BBC* website; www.bbc.co.uk

Exam focus point

> When considering an organisation's strategy, it is important to consider where its industry (or its products) are in their lifecycles. Again, context is crucial. If there is a mismatch between strategy and the position in a lifecycle, the strategy will not be successful. For example, if a company in a mature industry decides to start charging premium prices for its product, it is unlikely to be successful. By the mature phase, products will be fairly standardised and there is likely to be intense price competition in the industry. If the company increases prices, customers will simply switch and buy a competitor's product. Instead the company should be looking to make production as efficient and cost-effective as possible to preserve its margins by reducing its costs.
>
> The lifecycle model is explicitly referenced in the Study Guide so it may be specifically required in a question. Make sure you would be comfortable applying it to a scenario.

1.3 Strategic group analysis

Five forces analysis deals with the competitive environment in broad **industry-wide** terms. It is possible to refine this by considering **strategic groups**. These are made up of organisations with similar strategic characteristics, following similar strategies or competing on similar bases. Such groups arise for a variety of reasons, such as barriers to entry or the attractiveness of particular market segments.

The **strategic space** pertaining to a strategic group is defined by two or three common strategic characteristics. Here are some examples of such characteristics.

- Product diversity
- Geographical coverage
- Extent of branding
- Pricing policy
- Product quality
- Distribution method
- Target market segment

A series of 2-axis maps may be drawn up, using selected pairs of these characteristics to define both the extent of the strategic space and any unfilled gaps that exist within it. (A similar technique is used for specific products and is illustrated later in this chapter: this is **product positioning**.)

The **identification of potential competitive advantage** is the reason for analysing strategic groups. It improves knowledge of competitors and shows gaps in the organisation's current segments of operations. It may also reveal opportunities for migration to more favourable segments. Strategic problems may also be revealed.

2 The marketing mix 12/13

FAST FORWARD

The marketing function aims to satisfy customer needs profitably through an appropriate **marketing mix.**

The **marketing mix** comprises **product, price, place** and **promotion**. For **services**, this is extended to include **people**, **processes** and **physical evidence**.

Key term

Marketing mix: the set of controllable variables and their levels that the firm uses to influence the target market. These are **product**, **price**, **place** and **promotion** and are sometimes known as the four Ps.

Elements in the marketing mix **act partly as substitutes for each other** and they must be **integrated.** This is so the product can be positioned in the market to appeal to the customer. For example, a firm can raise the selling price of its products if it also raises product quality or advertising expenditure.

Exam focus point

The **marketing mix** can be useful when answering questions that require you to advise on courses of action. While it is unlikely that you will be required to discuss all of the variables, thinking about the relationship between two or three of them may give some useful insights.

A question in the December 2013 exam required students to use their understanding of the marketing mix to recommend appropriate marketing strategies for use at a visitor attraction which was experiencing financial difficulties. A significant number of students failed to apply enough elements of the model to the scenario. The examining team highlighted that students should have used the model as a framework to help come up with ideas on future marketing strategies.

2.1 Product

Key term

A **product** (goods or services) is anything that satisfies a need or want. It is not a 'thing' with 'features,' but a package of benefits.

From the firm's point of view, the product element of the marketing mix is what is being sold. From the customer's point of view, a **product is a solution to a problem or a package of benefits.** Many products might satisfy the same customer need.

Product issues in the marketing mix will include such factors as:

- Design (size, shape)
- Features
- Quality and reliability
- After-sales service (if necessary)
- Packaging

2.2 Place

Place deals with how the product is distributed, and how it reaches its customers.

(a)   **Channel**. Where are products sold?

(b)   **Logistics**. The location of warehouses and efficiency of the distribution system.

A firm can distribute the product itself (direct distribution) or through intermediary organisations such as retailers.

2.3 Promotion

Many of the practical activities of the marketing department are related to **promotion**. Promotion is the element of the mix over which the marketing department generally has most control.

Promotion in the marketing mix includes all marketing communications which let the public know of the product or service.

*   Advertising (newspapers, billboards, TV, radio, direct mail, internet)
*   Sales promotion (discounts, coupons, special displays in particular stores)
*   Direct selling by sales personnel
*   Public relations

2.4 Price

The price element of the marketing mix is the only one which brings in **revenue**. Price is influenced by many factors including economic factors (supply and demand), competitor's prices and payment terms. Pricing will be looked at in detail in Chapter 12 of this text.

2.5 The extended marketing mix

This is also known as the service marketing mix because it is specifically relevant to the marketing of **services,** rather than **physical products**. The intangible nature of services makes these extra three Ps particularly important.

2.5.1 People

Employees are particularly important in **service marketing**. Front-line staff must be selected, trained and motivated with particular attention to customer care and public relations.

In some services, the **physical presence** of people performing the service is a vital aspect of customer satisfaction. The staff involved are performing or producing a service, selling the service and also liaising with the customer to promote the service, gather information and respond to customer needs.

2.5.2 Processes

Efficient **processes** can become a marketing advantage in their own right. If an airline, for example, develops a sophisticated ticketing system, it can offer shorter waits at check-in or a wider choice of flights through allied airlines. This both increases customer satisfaction and cuts down on the time it takes to complete a sale.

2.5.3 Physical evidence

Services are **intangible:** they have no physical substance. The customer has no **evidence of ownership** and so may find it harder to perceive, evaluate and compare the qualities of service provision, and this may therefore dampen the incentive to consume.

This could be addressed through physical representation such as tickets and programs relating to entertainment, or by incorporating evidence into the design and specification of the service environment such as decor, colour scheme, noise levels, background music, fragrance and general ambience.

3 Customers and segmentation

3.1 Buyer behaviour

> The decision to make a purchase can be very simple, very complex or somewhere between the two. Buyers do not always proceed rationally, though the motivation of industrial buyers may be more logical than that of consumers.

In marketing, a market is defined in terms of its **buyers** or **potential buyers**.

- **Consumer markets** (eg for soap powder, washing machines, TV sets, clothes)
- **Industrial markets** (eg for machine tools, construction equipment)
- **Government markets** (eg for armaments, and, in the UK, medical equipment)
- **Reseller markets**
- **Export markets**

3.1.1 Consumer goods

Consumer goods are in such a form that they can be used by the consumer without the need for any further commercial processing. Consumer goods are further classified according to the method by which they are purchased.

- **Convenience goods**
- **Shopping goods**
- **Speciality goods**

If an article has close substitutes, is purchased regularly in small amounts of low unit value, and the customer insists on buying it with the minimum of inconvenience, the article is called a **convenience good**. These are everyday purchases such as toothpaste, bread or coffee, and are likely to be produced by several manufacturers. Promoting a unique image for the product, for example by **branding**, is therefore important.

Shopping goods are goods for which customers are more discriminating. They usually have a higher unit value than convenience goods and are bought less frequently, usually from a specialist outlet with a wider range on offer. **Examples** are cars, furniture, hi-fi equipment, many clothes, household appliances such as washing machines and cookers.

When a manufacturer, either by product design or advertising, has become associated in the public mind with a particular product (eg Rolls Royce cars, Wedgwood pottery) the article produced is no longer a shopping good, but a **speciality good**, possessing a unique character which will make a customer go out of their way to ask for it by name and find a dealer who sells it.

3.1.2 Industrial or business-to-business (B2B) markets

In industrial markets, the customer is another firm, such as for the sale of machine tools or consultancy advice. The industrial market, more than the consumer market, is influenced by the general state of the economy and the government's economic policy.

The demand for industrial goods and services is **derived** from the demand for the product or service to which they contribute. For example, the demand for aluminium is in part derived from the demand for cans, which might itself be derived from demand for the beer with which the cans will be filled.

Industrial buyers are more **rationally motivated** than consumers in deciding which goods to buy. Sales policy decisions by a supplier are therefore more important than sales promotion activities in an industrial market. In selling, special attention should be given to quality, price, credit, delivery dates, after-sales service, etc, and it is the importance of these rational motivations which make it difficult for an untried newcomer to break into an industrial goods market.

3.1.3 Organisational buying behaviour

The organisational buying behaviour process has some similarities with consumer buyer behaviour, but is supposedly more rational.

- How are needs recognised in a company?
- What is the type of buying situation?
- How is a supplier selected?
- How will performance be reviewed after purchase?

Supply selection and supplier performance are important aspects of supply chain management which we will return to later in this Study Text, particularly in the context of how technology can shape relationships with suppliers.

3.1.4 The decision-making unit

The **decision-making unit** (DMU) is a term used to describe the person or people who actually take the decision to buy a particular good or service. The marketing manager needs to know who in each organisation makes the effective buying decisions and how decisions are made: the DMU might act with formal authority, or as an informal group reaching a joint decision. Many large organisations employ specialist purchasing departments or 'buyers' – but the independence of the buyers will vary from situation to situation.

3.1.5 Factors in the motivation mix of business or government buyers

Business or government buyers are motivated as follows.

(a) **Quality**.

(b) **Price**. Where profit margins in the final market are under pressure, the buyer of industrial goods will probably make price the main purchasing motivation.

(c) **Budgetary control** may encourage the buying department to look further afield for potential suppliers to obtain a better price or quality of goods.

(d) **Fear of breakdown**. Where a customer has a highly organised and costly production system, they will clearly want to avoid a breakdown in the system, due to a faulty machine or running out of stocks of materials.

(e) **Credit**. The importance of credit could vary with the financial size of the buyer.

3.2 Market segmentation

Segments are groups of customers with similar needs that can be **targeted** with a distinctively **positioned** marketing **mix**. Both consumer and industrial markets can usefully be segmented and several bases exist for the process. The aim is to identify a coherent segment that is both **valid** and **attractive**.

Much marketing planning is based on the concepts of **segmentation and product positioning.** The purpose of segmentation is to identify target markets in which the firm can take a position. A market is not a mass, homogeneous group of customers, each wanting an identical product. Every market consists of potential buyers with different **needs** and different **buying behaviour**. These different customers may be **grouped into segments**. A different marketing approach will be taken by an organisation for each market segment.

Note: As with so many other aspects of business, access to customers and markets has increased with the growth of the internet and e-business. Therefore, the ideas we are discussing here will also link into the chapters of e-business and e-marketing later in this Study Text.

Key term

Market segmentation is 'the subdividing of a market into distinct and increasingly homogeneous subgroups of customers, where any subgroup can conceivably be selected as a target market to be met with a distinct marketing mix'.

Kotler

There are two important elements in this definition of market segmentation.

(a) Although the total market consists of widely different groups of consumers, each group consists of people (or organisations) with **common needs and preferences**, who perhaps react to 'market stimuli' in much the same way.

(b) Each market segment can become a **target market for a firm**, and would require a unique marketing mix if the firm is to exploit it successfully.

Reasons for segmenting markets

Reason	Comment
Better satisfaction of customer needs	One solution will not satisfy all customers
Growth in profits	Some customers will pay more for certain benefits
Revenue growth	Segmentation means that more customers may be attracted by what is on offer, in preference to competing products
Customer retention	By targeting customers, a number of different products can be offered to them
Targeted communications	Segmentation enables clear communications as people in the target audience share common needs
Innovation	By identifying unmet needs, companies can innovate to satisfy them

3.3 Identifying segments

An important initial marketing task is the **identification of segments** within the market. Segmentation applies more obviously to the consumer market, but it can also be applied to an **industrial market**.

(a) One basis will not be appropriate in every market, and sometimes two or more bases might be valid at the same time.

(b) One basis or segmentation variable might be superior to another in a hierarchy of variables. There are thus **primary and secondary segmentation variables.**

3.4 The bases for segmentation

Segmentation variables fall into a small number of categories.

3.4.1 Geographical segmentation

Geographical segmentation is very simple, but useful, especially in business-to-business marketing, which relies heavily on personal selling. It can be combined with socio-demographic segmentation (see below).

3.4.2 Psychographic or lifestyle segmentation

Psychographic segmentation is not based on objective data so much as how people see themselves and their **subjective** feelings and attitudes towards a particular product or service, or towards life in general. It makes use of variables such as interests, activities, personality and opinions. This is very useful for many consumer goods, since they can be designed and promoted to appeal on the basis of such variables.

3.4.3 Behavioural segmentation

The behavioural approach segments buyers into groups based on their attitudes to and use of the product, and the **benefits** they expect to receive. It uses such variables as usage rate, impulse purchase, brand loyalty and sensitivity to marketing mix variables such as price, quality and promotion.

The table below illustrates an example of market segmentation where marketers have noticed people can be categorised by which toothpaste they use.

Benefit segmentation of the toothpaste market						
Segment name	Principal benefit sought	Demographic strengths	Special behavioural characteristics	Brands dis-proportionately favoured	Personality character-istics	Lifestyle characteristics
The sensory segment	Flavour, product appearance	Children	Users of spearmint flavoured toothpaste	Colgate, Stripe	High self-involvement	Hedonistic
The Sociables	Brightness of teeth	Teens, young people	Smokers	Macleans, Ultra-Brite	High sociability	Active
The Worriers	Decay prevention	Large families	Heavy users	Crest	High hypochon-driasis	Conservative
The Independent Segment	Price	Men	Heavy users	Brands on sale	High autonomy	Value oriented

3.4.4 Socio-demographic segmentation

Socio-demographic segmentation is based on social, economic and demographic variables such as those below.

- Age
- Sex
- Income
- Occupation
- Education

- Religion
- Ethnicity/national origin
- Social class
- Family size

3.5 Segmentation of the industrial market

Industrial markets can be segmented with many of the bases used in consumer markets such as geography, usage rate and benefits sought. Additional, more traditional bases include customer type, product/technology, customer size and purchasing procedures.

(a) **Geographic location**. Some industries and related industries are clustered in particular areas. Firms selling services to the banking sector might be interested in the City of London.

(b) **Type of business** (eg service, manufacturing).

    (i) **Type of organisation.** Organisations in an industry as a whole may have certain needs in common. Employment agencies offering business services to publishers, say, must offer their clients personnel with experience in particular desk top publishing packages. Suitable temporary staff offered to legal firms can be more effective if used to legal jargon. Each different type of firm can be offered a tailored product or service.

    (ii) **Components manufacturers specialise in the industries of the firms to which they supply components**.

(c) **Use of the product.** In the UK, many new cars are sold to businesses, as benefit cars. Although this practice is changing with the viability of a 'cash alternative' to a company car, the varying levels of specification are developed with the business buyer in mind (eg junior salesperson gets a Ford Fiesta, Regional Manager gets a Ford Mondeo).

(d) **Size of organisation**. Large organisations may have elaborate purchasing procedures, and may do many things in-house. Small organisations may be more likely to subcontract certain specialist services.

3.6 Segment validity

A market segment will only **be valid if it is worth designing and developing a unique** marketing mix for that specific segment. The following questions are commonly asked to decide whether or not the segment can be used for developing marketing plans.

Criteria	Comment
Can the segment be measured?	It might be possible to conceive of a market segment, but it is not necessarily easy to measure it. For example, for a segment based on people with a conservative outlook to life, can conservatism of outlook be measured by market research?
Is the segment big enough?	There has to be a large enough potential market to be profitable.
Can the segment be reached?	There has to be a way of getting to the potential customers via the organisation's promotion and distribution channels.
Do segments respond differently?	If two or more segments are identified by marketing planners but each segment responds in the same way to a marketing mix, the segments are effectively one and the same and there is no point in distinguishing them from each other.
Can the segment be reached profitably?	Do the identified customer needs cost less to satisfy than the revenue they earn?
Is the segment suitably stable?	The stability of the segment is important, if the organisation is to commit huge production and marketing resources to serve it. The firm does not want the segment to 'disappear' next year. Of course, this may not matter in some industries.

3.7 Segment attractiveness

A segment might be valid and potentially profitable, but is it potentially **attractive?** For example, a segment that has **high barriers to entry** might cost more to enter but will be less **vulnerable to competitors.** The most attractive segments will be those whose needs can be met by building on the company's strengths and where forecasts for demand, sales profitability and **growth** are favourable.

3.8 Target markets

FAST FORWARD

Companies select particularly attractive segments and approach them with a carefully designed marketing mix. This **concentrated** marketing approach is more effective than the **undifferentiated**, mass marketing method when customers are likely to exercise careful choice.

Because of limited resources, competition and large markets, organisations are not usually able to sell with equal efficiency and success to every market segment. It is necessary to select **target markets**. A target market is a particularly attractive segment that will be served with a distinct marketing mix. The marketing management of a company may choose one of the following policy options.

Key terms

Undifferentiated marketing: this policy is to produce a single product and hope to get as many customers as possible to buy it; that is, ignore segmentation entirely.

Concentrated marketing: the company attempts to produce the ideal product for a single segment of the market (eg Rolls Royce cars for the wealthy).

Differentiated marketing: the company attempts to introduce several product versions, each aimed at a different market segment. For example, manufacturers of soap powder make a number of different brands, marketed to different segments.

It is important to assess company strengths when evaluating attractiveness and targeting a market. This can help determine the appropriate strategy, because once the attractiveness of each identified segment

has been assessed, it can be considered along with relative strengths to determine the potential advantages the organisation would have. In this way, preferred segments can be targeted.

The major **disadvantage of differentiated marketing** is the additional costs of marketing and production (more product design and development costs, the loss of economies of scale in production and storage, additional promotion costs and administrative costs etc). When the **costs of further differentiation of the market exceed the benefits** from further segmentation and **target marketing**, a firm is said to have **over-differentiated**.

The major **disadvantage of concentrated marketing** is the business risk of relying on a single segment of a single market. On the other hand, specialisation in a particular market segment can give a firm a profitable, although perhaps temporary, competitive edge over rival firms.

The choice between undifferentiated, differentiated or concentrated marketing as a marketing strategy will depend on the following factors.

(a) The extent to which the product and/or the market may be considered **homogeneous**. **Mass marketing** may be 'sufficient' if the market is largely homogeneous (for example, for safety matches).

(b) The **company's resources** must not be over extended by differentiated marketing. Small firms may succeed better by concentrating on one segment only.

(c) The product must be sufficiently **advanced in its life cycle** to have attracted a substantial total market; otherwise segmentation and target marketing is unlikely to be profitable, because each segment would be too small in size.

3.9 Product positioning

FAST FORWARD

A product's **positioning** defines how it is intended to be perceived by customers and how it differs from current and potential competing products.

It is not always possible to identify a market segment where there is no direct competitor, and a marketing problem for the firm will be the creation of some form of **product differentiation** (real or imagined) in the marketing mix of the product. The aim is to make the customer perceive the product as different from its competitors.

A perceptual map of product positioning can be used to identify **gaps in the market**. This example might suggest that there could be potential in the market for a low-price high-quality bargain brand. A company that carries out such an analysis might decide to conduct further research to find out whether there is scope in the market for a new product which would be targeted at a market position where there are few or no rivals. (A firm successfully pursuing **cost leadership** might be in a good position to offer a **bargain brand**.)

Perceptual map of product positioning

Similar matrices to explore possible product positions in terms of, for instance, attributes, applications, users, occasions for use and specific aspects of quality may be drawn to refine knowledge of product position.

4 Understanding the customer

4.1 The strategic customer

The **strategic customer** is the entity that decides to make the purchase, not the end user.

Many goods and services are purchased, not by their end users but by intermediaries such as retailers, sales agents and procurement department staff. Where this pattern applies, the supplier has to take account of the influence of the intermediary; indeed, **the intermediary is the strategic customer**, not the end user, and it is the intermediary's requirements that are of primary strategic importance. The requirements of the end user are important, but subordinate in many cases to those of the intermediary.

4.2 What customers value – critical success factors   12/11

Critical success factors are product features that are **particularly valued by customers**.

Customers purchase products and services because they value the things the products and services provide them with. This may be a relatively simple satisfaction, as when motorists buy petrol, or it may include a wide range of **both tangible and intangible benefits**. Many products are, in fact, **complex packages of features** that their producers have worked hard to assemble. The intangibles among these features are often collectively referred to as **brand values**.

Consider a wristwatch, for example. It would be a mistake to imagine that most wristwatches are bought because they tell the time. They also reflect the taste, self-image and status of the purchaser.

There is likely to be a wide range of opinion among customers as to the features of a product that provide them with the greatest satisfaction, but, equally, it is also likely that **some features will be widely regarded as particularly important**. These features, the satisfactions they provide and the demands they make on the organisation's way of doing business constitute **critical success factors**: the organisation must get these things right if it is to be successful in what it does.

Thus, for a producer of luxury goods, manufacturing quality would undoubtedly be a critical success factor, but ensuring that an air of luxury pervaded its retail outlets would be just as important.

Key term

> **Critical success factors (CSFs)** are those product features that are particularly valued by a group of customers and, therefore, where the organisation must excel to outperform competitors.   *JS&W*

Exam focus point

> An article titled 'Defining manager's information requirements' (2006) written by Jim Stone provides an in-depth look at the role of critical success factors in business strategy. This is available in the technical articles section for P3 on the ACCA website. It would be worth taking the time to study this article.

There are important messages connected with this concept. First, value must be assessed **through the eyes of the customer**, not those of the designer or professional specialist. Second, **resources** should be deployed so as to achieve high performance in critical success factors.

This also illustrates the importance of aligning external forces (customer desires) with internal factors (resources).

An organisation can measure how well it is achieving the critical success factors through the use of **key performance indicators (KPIs).** CSFs represent 'what' an organisation needs to do in order to be successful. KPIs are the **measures** then used to assess whether or not the CSFs are being achieved.

> **Key performance indicators (KPIs)** are quantifiable measurements that management can use to monitor and control progress towards achieving its critical success factors.

In practice, the term KPI tends to be overused and can describe almost any kind of measurement. However, in order to be useful they should clearly identify the information needs required to demonstrate how well the organisation is doing in achieving its overall strategy. They should:

- Reflect the performance and progress of the organisation

- Be measurable

- Be comparable – ie can be compared to a standard such as budgeted figures, or prior year data

- Be usable – ie provide data that can be acted upon

For example, an organisation may have a critical success factor of providing the highest level of customer service. Appropriate KPIs may relate to the speed of the delivery time, the number of repeat business transactions from existing customers, or the scores achieved in customer satisfaction surveys.

Exam focus point

> The compulsory question in the December 2011 exam included a 10 mark requirement in which students were required to explain and discuss the concepts of CSFs and KPIs within the context of the scenario. This was the first time that CSFs and KPIs had been specifically examined and this was problematic for some students. If faced with such a question, the balanced scorecard can be a useful basis for generating ideas but don't lose sight of the organisation in question and remember to relate your answer specifically back to the given scenario.

4.3 Reviewing the customer portfolio

FAST FORWARD

> The **customer base** is an asset to be invested in, as future benefits will come from existing customers, but not all customers are as important as others. It will help you in evaluating the customer portfolio if you consider the customer base as an asset worth investing in.

Case Study

Customer portfolio

(a) Coca-Cola paid $200m to Pernod of France, which, under contract, had effectively built a customer base for Coca-Cola, as well as building up a distribution network. Coca-Cola wanted to take charge of the marketing of Coke in France.

(b) Supermarket loyalty cards reward customers with bonus points, saving them money, or allowing them to redeem points for products according to how much they spend.

(c) Many banks lose money on student accounts, in the hope that they will earn it back later in the customer's life cycle.

As already mentioned, a **marketing audit** involves a review of an organisation's products and markets, the marketing environment, and its marketing system and operations. The profitability of each product and each market should be assessed, and the costs of different marketing activities established.

Information obtained about markets

(a) **Size of the customer base**. Does the organisation sell to a large number of small customers or a small number of big customers?

(b) **Size of individual orders**. The organisation might sell its products in many small orders, or it might have large individual orders. Delivery costs can be compared with order sizes.

(c) **Sales revenue and profitability.** The performance of individual products can be compared. An imbalance between sales and profits over various product ranges can be potentially dangerous.

(d) **Segments.** An analysis of sales and profitability into export markets and domestic markets.

(e) **Market share.** Estimated share of the market obtained by each product group.

(f) **Growth.** Sales growth and contribution growth over the previous four years or so, for each product group.

(g) Whether the **demand** for certain products is **growing, stable or likely to decline.**

(h) Whether **demand is price sensitive** or not.

(i) Whether there is a growing tendency for the market to become **fragmented**, with more specialist and 'custom-made' products.

Information about current marketing activities

- Comparative pricing
- Advertising effectiveness
- Effectiveness of distribution network
- Attitudes to the product, in comparison with competitors

4.4 Customer analysis

Key customer analysis calls for six main areas of investigation into customers. A firm might wish to identify which customers offer most profit.

Area	Detail
Key customer identity	<ul><li>Name of each key customer</li><li>Location</li><li>Status in market</li><li>Products they make and sell</li><li>Size of firm (capital employed, turnover, number of employees)</li></ul>
Customer history	<ul><li>First purchase date.</li><li>Who makes the buying decision in the customer's organisation?</li><li>What is the average order size, by product?</li><li>What is the regularity/periodicity of the order, by product?</li><li>What is the trend in size of orders?</li><li>What is the motive in purchasing?</li><li>What does the customer know about the firm's and competitors' products?</li><li>On what basis does the customer reorder?</li><li>How is the useful life of the product judged?</li><li>Were there any lost or cancelled orders? For what reason?</li></ul>
Relationship of customer to product	<ul><li>What does the customer use the product for?</li><li>Do the products form part of the customer's own service/product?</li></ul>
Relationship of customer to potential market	<ul><li>What is the size of the customer in relation to the total end-market?</li><li>Is the customer likely to expand, or not? Diversify? Integrate?</li></ul>
Customer attitudes and behaviour	<ul><li>What interpersonal factors exist which could affect sales by the firm and by competitors?</li><li>Does the customer also buy competitors' products?</li><li>To what extent may purchases be postponed?</li></ul>
The financial performance of the customer	<ul><li>How successful is the customer?</li></ul>

Notice that customer analysis allows a firm to find out information about its customers. Some of this information can then be used to help build up a relationship with the customer. This forms the basis of

customer relationship management which we will look at in the e-marketing chapter later in this Study Text.

4.5 Customer profitability analysis (customer account profitability)

FAST FORWARD

Customer profitability analysis is an analysis of the total sales revenue generated from a customer or customer group, less all the costs that are incurred in servicing that customer group.

Key term

> **Customer profitability analysis (CPA)** is an analysis of the revenue streams and service costs associated with specific customers or customer groups to identify the profitability of servicing those customers.

'An immediate impact of introducing any level of strategic management accounting into virtually every organisation is to destroy totally any illusion that the same level of profit is derived from all customers'.

(Ward, *Strategic Management Accounting*)

Different customer costs can arise out of the following.

- Order size
- Sales mix
- Order processing
- Transport costs (eg if a just in time (JIT) production system requires frequent deliveries)
- Management time
- Cash flow problems (eg increased overdraft interest) caused by slow payers
- Order complexity (eg if the order has to be sent out in several stages)
- Inventory holding costs can relate to specify customers
- The customer's negotiating strength

The total costs of servicing customers can vary depending on how customers are serviced.

(a) **Volume discounts**. A customer who places one large order is given a discount, presumably because it benefits the supplier to do so (eg savings on administrative overhead in processing the orders – as identified by an activity based costing system).

(b) **Different rates** charged by power companies to domestic as opposed to business users. This in part reflects the administrative overhead of dealing with individual customers. In practice, many domestic consumers benefit from cross-subsidy.

Remember

> Customer profitability is the 'total sales revenue generated from a customer or customer group, less all the costs that are incurred in servicing that customer or customer group.'

It is possible to analyse customer profitability over a single period but more useful to look at a longer time scale. Such a multi period approach fits in with the idea of **relationship marketing**, with its emphasis on customer retention for the longer term.

Customer profitability analysis focuses on profits generated by customers and suggests that **profit does not automatically increase with sales revenue**. CPA can benefit a company in the following ways.

- It enables a company to **focus resources** on the most profitable areas

- It identifies unexpected **differences in profitability** between customers

- It helps quantify the **financial impact** of proposed changes

- It helps highlight the **cost** of obtaining **new** customers and the **benefit** of retaining existing customers

- It helps to highlight whether **product** development or **market** development is to be preferred

- An appreciation of the costs of servicing clients assists in **negotiations** with customers

4.6 The customer lifecycle

The **customer lifecycle** concept is less developed than the equivalent product and industry lifecycle models, but it can be useful to consider the following matters.

(a) **Promotional expense** relating to a single customer is likely to be heavily **front-loaded**: it is much cheaper to retain a customer than to attract one.

(b) It is likely that **sales** to a customer will start at a low level and increase to a higher level as the customer gains confidence, though this is not certain and will vary from industry to industry.

(c) A customer who purchases a basic or commodity product initially may move on to **more differentiated products** later.

(d) In consumer markets, career progression is likely to provide the individual with steadily increasing amounts of disposable income, while the **family lifecycle** will indicate the ranging nature of likely purchases as time passes.

Any attempt to estimate lifecycle costs and revenues should also consider existing and potential **environmental impacts**, including, in particular, the likely actions of competitors and the potential for product and process innovation.

5 Opportunities and threats

The strategic influence of the environment may be summarised into lists of **opportunities** and **threats**.

It is important to remember the purpose of all environmental analysis ideas is to provide input into the process of designing a **practical business strategy**.

One very useful way of thinking about the implications of environmental information is to consider it in terms of **opportunities and threats**.

5.1 Threats

For a commercial organisation, the most urgent threats are likely to emerge from within the immediate industry arena. The **five forces** model provides a good summary of the threats inherent here, supplemented by strategic group analysis. Recognising threats in the wider PESTEL environment is, perhaps, more difficult, since it covers such an enormous range of factors.

5.2 Opportunities

Opportunities may take the form of **strategic gaps**: these are potentially profitable aspects of the competitive environment that are not being exploited by rivals. JS&W give several examples of how these might arise.

(a) Potential **substitutes** for existing products might be created. This is largely a technology-based opportunity, but an important route to the development of substitutes is the imaginative development of new uses for existing products and methods.

(b) Other **strategic groups** may present opportunities, especially if there are changes in the macro-environment, such as deregulation or opening of new markets in developing countries.

(c) It may be possible to target **different strategic customers**. In the case of consumer goods, the development of internet selling means that the ultimate user is displacing the distributor as the strategic customer.

(d) There may be potential to market **complementary products**. For example, capital goods manufacturers routinely offer credit services to assist the customer to buy.

(e) New **market segments** may have potential, though there may be a need to adapt the product.

All of the environmental factors affecting an organisation can be summarised as either opportunities or threats. The diagram below illustrates this.

External forces

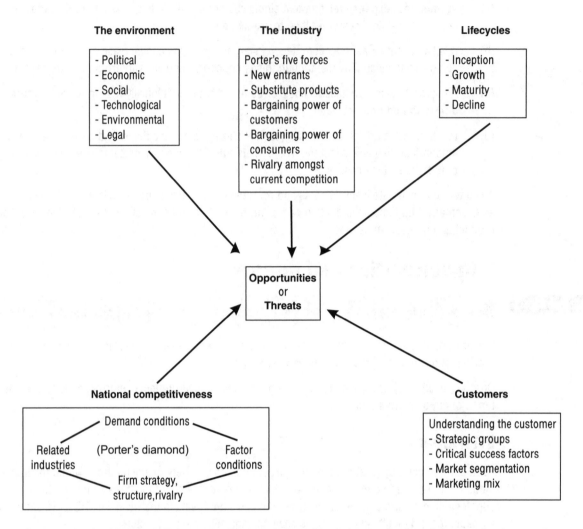

However, having identified all the external factors influencing their organisation, the strategist then needs to work out how best to align them to the internal strengths and weaknesses of an organisation.

We will now move on to look at the internal resources of organisations in the next chapter of this Study Text.

Chapter Roundup

- The dynamic nature of competition may be considered using a variety of concepts.

    - The **cycle of competition** describes the typical development of the relationship between an established firm and a new challenger.

    - **Hyper-competition** is an unstable state of constantly shifting short-term advantage.

    - The **industry life cycle** has four phases: inception, growth, maturity/shakeout and decline. Each phase has typical implications for customers, competitors, products and profits.

    - **Strategic group analysis** examines the strategic space occupied by groups of close competitors in order to identify potential competitive advantage.

- Industries may display a **lifecycle**: this will affect, and interact with, the five forces.

- The marketing function aims to satisfy customer needs profitably through an appropriate **marketing mix.**

- The **marketing mix** comprises **product**, **price**, **place** and **promotion**. For **services**, this is extended to include **people**, **processes** and **physical evidence**.

- The decision to make a purchase can be very simple, very complex or somewhere in between the two. Buyers do not always proceed rationally, though the motivation of industrial buyers may be more logical than that of consumers.

- **Segments** are groups of customers with similar needs that can be **targeted** with a distinctively **positioned** marketing **mix**. Both consumer and industrial markets can usefully be segmented and several bases exist for the process. The aim is to identify a coherent segment that is both **valid** and **attractive**.

- Companies select particularly attractive segments and approach them with a carefully designed marketing mix. This **concentrated** marketing approach is more effective than the **undifferentiated**, mass marketing method when customers are likely to exercise careful choice.

- A product's **positioning** defines how it is intended to be perceived by customers and how it differs from current and potential competing products.

- The **strategic customer** is the entity that decides to make the purchase, not the end user.

- **Critical success factors** are product features that are **particularly valued by customers**.

- The **customer base** is an asset to be invested in, as future benefits will come from existing customers, but not all customers are as important as others. It will help you in evaluating the customer portfolio if you consider the customer base as an asset worth investing in.

- **Customer profitability analysis** is an analysis of the total sales revenue generated from a customer or customer group, less all the costs that are incurred in servicing that customer group.

- The strategic influence of the environment may be summarised into lists of **opportunities** and **threats**.

Quick Quiz

1   What is hypercompetition?

2   What are the four stages of the industry life cycle?

3   What is a strategic group?

4   What are the seven elements of the extended marketing mix for services?

5   What is the main behavioural difference between consumers and industrial buyers?

6   What bases might be used to segment an industrial market?

7   What is meant by 'the strategic customer'?

8   What are critical success factors?

Answers to Quick Quiz

1   A condition of constant competitive change typified by frequent aggressive moves to establish temporary competitive advantage.

2   Inception; growth; maturity/shakeout; and decline.

3   A group of businesses with similar strategic characteristics, following similar strategies or competing on similar bases.

4   Product, place, price, promotion, people, processes and physical evidence.

5   Generally, industrial buyers will approach purchase decisions in an entirely rational manner; this is frequently not the case with consumers, whose behaviour is influenced by emotional responses.

6   Geography, business type, product usage, organisation size.

7   The actual purchaser of output, not the eventual end user further down the supply chain.

8   Product features that are particularly valued by a group of customers and where the organisation must excel to outperform competitors.

Now try the question below from the Practice Question Bank

Number	Level	Marks	Time
Q4	Exam	25	45 mins

Strategic capability

4

Introduction

In this chapter, we move deeper into highly examinable territory. It is a long chapter and contains a number of very important ideas and models. You should work through it with care. When you reach the last section, do not be tempted to dismiss the content as a simple mnemonic: both SWOT and TOWS have important things to say about potential strategic choices.

Study guide

		Intellectual level
A4	**Marketing and the value of goods and services**	
(c)	Explore the role of the value chain in creating and sustaining competitive advantage	2
(d)	Advise on the role and influence of value networks	3
(e)	Assess different approaches to benchmarking an organisation's performance	3
A5	**The internal resources, capabilities and competences of an organisation**	
(a)	Discriminate between strategic capability, threshold resources, threshold competences, unique resources and core competences	3
(b)	Discuss from a strategic perspective, the continuing need for effective cost management and control systems within organisations	3
(c)	Discuss the capabilities required to sustain competitive advantage	2
(d)	Explain the impact of new product, process and service developments and innovation in supporting business strategy	2
(e)	Discuss the contribution of organisational knowledge to the strategic capability of an organisation	2
(f)	Determine the strengths and weaknesses of an organisation and formulate an appropriate SWOT analysis	2
B3	**Alternative directions and methods of development**	
(a)	Determine generic development directions (employing an adapted Ansoff matrix and a TOWS matrix) available to an organisation.	2

Exam guide

In this chapter, we introduce some specific models that you must become very familiar with.
They are useful both for analysing data and structuring answers. The most important, by far, is the **value chain**: you must have this model at your fingertips.

Models and frameworks

Three frameworks covered in this chapter are explicitly referenced in the Study Guide and so could be specifically required in a question:

*   Porter's Value Chain
*   SWOT analysis
*   TOWS Matrix

The Ansoff Matrix referred to at B3(a) in the Study Guide is covered in further detail in Chapter 6.

1 The organisation's resources

A **position audit** is undertaken in order to give strategic managers a clear understanding of the organisation's **strategic capability**; that is, its resources, competences and the constraints that limit their use.

1.1 Strategic capability

Managers responsible for an organisation's strategy need a clear and detailed knowledge of its **strategic capability**.

Key term

> An organisation's ability to survive and prosper depends on its **strategic capability**; this is defined by the adequacy and suitability of its resources and competences.

The process of analysing and assessing the organisation's resources and competences is called **position audit**.

Key term

> **Position audit** is the part of the planning process that examines the current state of the business entity's strategic capability.

Much of the rest of this chapter is concerned with the tools and methods that can be used to carry out the task of position audit. However, we must first discuss **resource-based strategy** and look more closely at resources and competences.

Exam focus point

> An article titled 'Position based and resource based strategies' (October 2010) written by Ken Garrett was published in *Student Accountant*, and is available in the Technical Articles section for P3 on the ACCA website. It would be worth taking the time to study this article.

1.2 Resources and limiting factors

FAST FORWARD

Resource audits identify human, financial and material resources and how they are deployed.

A **resource audit** is a review of all aspects of the resources the organisation uses. The **Ms model** categorises the factors as follows.

Resource	Example
Machinery	Age. Condition. Utilisation rate. Value. Replacement cost.
Make-up	Culture and structure. Patents. Goodwill. Brands.
Management	Size. Skills. Loyalty. Career progression. Structure.
Management information	Ability to generate and disseminate ideas. Innovation. Information systems.
Markets	Products and customers. Specialised or general. Regional, national, international.
Materials	Source. Suppliers and partnering. Waste. New materials. Cost. Availability. Future provision.
Men and women	Number. Skills. Efficiency. Industrial relations. Adaptability. Innovatory capacity. Wage costs. Labour turnover.
Methods	How are activities carried out? Outsourcing, quality.
Money	Credit and turnover periods. Cash surpluses/deficits. Short term and long term finance. Gearing levels. Debts.

Unique resources are particularly valuable and an important source of competitive advantage.

Key term

> A **unique resource** is one which is both better than its equivalent employed by competitors and difficult to imitate.

Resources are of no value unless they are organised into systems, and so a resource audit should go on to consider how well or how badly resources have been utilised, and whether the organisation's systems are effective and efficient.

1.3 Limiting factors

Every organisation operates under resource **constraints**.

Key term

> A **limiting factor** or **key factor** is 'a factor which at any time or over a period may limit the activity of an entity, often one where there is shortage or difficulty of supply.'

1.3.1 Examples

- A shortage of production capacity
- A limited number of key personnel, such as salespeople with technical knowledge
- A restricted distribution network
- Too few managers with knowledge about finance, or overseas markets
- Inadequate research design resources to develop new products or services
- A poor system of strategic intelligence
- Lack of money
- A lack of adequately trained staff

Once the limiting factor has been identified, the planners should do two things.

- In the short term, make best use of the resources available
- Try to reduce the limitation in the long term

1.4 Resource-based strategy

FAST FORWARD

The resource-based approach to strategy starts from a consideration of capabilities and, in particular, of distinctive **competences** and **resources**.

There are two fundamentally different approaches to strategy: position-based strategy, and resource-based strategy.

Position-based strategy seeks to develop competitive advantage in a way that responds to the **nature of the competitive environment**: the firm **positions** its offering in response to the external opportunities or threats it discerns, and develops the appropriate competences and resources it needs to compete.

The contrasting **resource-based strategy** was developed in response to two problems with the position-based strategy.

(a) Many environments are **too complex and dynamic** to permit continuing effective analysis and response.

(b) Once an opportunity is discerned and an offering made, it is very easy for competitors to make similar offerings, thus rapidly eroding competitive advantage.

Blackberry

The following case study highlights the perils organisations face when pursuing a position-based strategy. This case study focuses on the problems that Blackberry encountered by failing to understand changes that occurred in the mobile phone market.

By the mid 2000s Blackberry had established itself as the mobile phone of choice among users, finding popularity among business professionals. Blackberry's popularity was driven in part by the ability of users to access their emails on the go, while the device's QWERTY key pad resembled the keyboard many users were familiar with using in the workplace. At its peak the company even developed a celebrity following with many celebrities claiming to own a Blackberry.

However, in 2007 Blackberry's dominance came under threat when Apple unveiled its first iPhone device. Apple's offering with its innovative touchscreen technology made the Blackberry appear dated. The iPhone's advanced iOS (operating system) meant users could experience high quality graphics and a new range of applications available for download through the Apple App store. By contrast, Blackberry's operating system was principally engineered as a communication tool. Senior management at Blackberry were convinced that the popularity among business professionals would be sufficient to help reduce the threat posed by the iPhone.

However, by 2013 Blackberry's fortunes had drastically changed. The iPhone had become the number one selling mobile device. Blackberry had overestimated the appeal of its own offering and its ability to continue to attract members of its target market, with many professionals switching allegiance to the iPhone. In response Blackberry switched its focus towards people using their phones for social and private use, rather than business use and unveiled its own touchscreen smartphone, producing the Blackberry Z10.

In a bid to rival the iPhone, the Z10 provided users with the ability to access popular integrated apps such as Facebook and Twitter. The development of the Z10 took a number of years and resulted in significant expenditure on developing the technology to produce a functioning touchscreen mobile device, as Blackberry struggled to make-up the ground lost to Apple.

The introduction of the Z10 did little to reverse Blackberry's fortunes, as the device failed to take off as anticipated. The launch of the Z10 was hit with reports that stockists were unable to obtain sufficient inventory of the device. Blackberry's problems were further compounded when the Z10's operating system required an urgent 'fix' prior to its full launch. In September 2013, Blackberry reported a significant fall in sales which triggered a drop in the company's share price and left the company's shares trading at a fraction of their 2007 value. Following the announcement the company declared that it was shedding 4,500 workers (40% of the workforce).

The resource-based view is that sustainable competitive advantage is only attained as a result of the **possession of distinctive resources**. These may be **physical resources**, such as the effective monopolisation of diamonds by De Beers, or, more typically in today's service economies, they may be **competences**. So resource-based strategy focuses **internally,** rather than externally.

JS&W argue that a resource-based strategy is the more appropriate approach for most organisations to take because it is the better way of achieving a sustainable advantage, as it enables organisations to have **control** over the means of obtaining advantages (ie their resources).

1.5 Terminology

As is so often the case, the terminology used in the literature of resource-based strategy is not standardised. JS&W use their own very clear and specific set of terms when discussing resources and competences and your syllabus requires that you should understand and use these terms also.

BPP LEARNING MEDIA

Part A Strategic position | **4: Strategic capability** **95**

Strategic capability is the adequacy and suitability of the resources and competences of an organisation for it to survive and prosper.

Tangible resources are the physical assets of an organisation, such as plant, labour and finance.

Intangible resources are non-physical assets such as information, reputation and knowledge.

Competences are the activities and processes through which an organisation deploys its resources effectively.

Threshold capabilities are essential for the organisation to be able to compete in a given market.

Threshold resources and **threshold competences** are needed to meet customers' minimum requirements and therefore for the organisation to continue to exist.

Unique resources and **core competences** underpin competitive advantage and are difficult for competitors to imitate or obtain.

This analysis requires some discussion.

(a) Note the way that JS&W use the word **capabilities** to denote a useful overall category that contains both resources and competences.

(b) Look carefully at the definitions of **tangible** and **intangible resources**. These are not the tangible and intangible *assets* you are familiar with as an accountant: the inclusion of labour and finance under tangible resources, for example, demonstrates this.

(c) A connected point is the definition of **competences**; make sure you appreciate the difference between a **competence** and an **intangible resource**. We might say that the relationship between the two is that a competence might well create, use or exploit an intangible resource (or a tangible one, for that matter). Thus, information is an **intangible resource**; the ability to make good use of it is a **competence**.

(d) We have said that **capabilities** consist of **resources** and **competences**. As you can see, this means that JS&W effectively give a choice of definition for **threshold resources** and **threshold competences**. Each has its own specific definition, but since each qualifies as a **threshold capability**, we could, presumably, also use that definition.

(e) JS&W do not provide a term to mean **unique resources** and **core competences** taken together as a class: we might speculate that **unique capabilities** or **core capabilities** could be used in this way, but it would probably be unwise to do this in the exam.

To some extent, the resource-based approach is the opposite to the marketing concept since, instead of approaching strategy on the basis of giving customers what they want, it concentrates on exploiting what the business already has to offer.

In fact, this distinction is largely theoretical, but it leads to some important ideas that you could use in the exam.

(a) Where the marketing concept is adopted, it will still be necessary to deploy threshold capabilities in all critical areas and the possession of unique resources and core competences will enhance the market offering.

(b) Conversely, where strategy is built on unique resources and core competences, marketing activities must be carried out with at least threshold competence if the customer is to be satisfied.

2 Cost efficiency

FAST FORWARD

Cost efficiency is fundamental to strategic capability: the public sector demands value for money, while in the private sector, price competition makes cost efficiency fundamental to survival. Cost efficiency is achieved in four main ways.

- Exploitation of **scale economies**
- Control of the cost of **incoming supplies**
- **Careful design** of products and processes
- Exploitation of **experience effects**

2.1 The importance of cost efficiency

Cost efficiency is a fundamental aspect of strategic capability. It requires both the possession and efficient use of **appropriate resources** and the ability to **manage costs** so that they are under constant downward pressure. The requirement for cost efficiency applies equally in the public and private sectors.

(a) In the **public sector**, cost efficiency is demanded by the political imperative to provide improved and extended levels of service while containing or reducing the cost to the public finances.

(b) For a **commercial organisation**, cost efficiency permits the firm to offer extended benefits at the same price, the same benefits at a lower price, or a combination of the two.

In the private sector, a sufficient degree of cost efficiency might constitute a **core competence** in that it might enable a firm to achieve competitive advantage. Nevertheless, for many firms, cost efficiency is merely a **threshold competence**: it is required for mere survival and does not form the basis of advantage. There are two reasons for this.

(a) **Customers are sensitive to price**: when making their buying decision, they will seek a balance between the desirability of the product's features and the sacrifice involved in paying for it. This means that whatever the features of their particular product offerings, all suppliers must strive to provide proper **value for money**. Failure to do this is an invitation to the customer to go elsewhere.

(b) All firms operating in a given market will seek to drive down their costs in order to offer better value to the customer; the search for cost efficiency is a fundamental aspect of **competitive rivalry**.

2.2 Sources of cost efficiency

JS&W identify four main sources of cost efficiency.

2.2.1 Economies of scale

The effect of economies of scale is to reduce costs per unit as the scale of operations increases. They arise for a range of reasons, including the efficiencies generated by increased **specialisation** and the **spreading of fixed elements of cost** over a greater number of units of output. Some industries possess more of the features that lead to their occurrence than do others. The high costs of plant in the motor vehicle and chemicals industries have made scale of output important, while other industries, such as tobacco and drinks have benefited from economies of scale in marketing and distribution. In other industries, such as textiles, economies of scale have been less important.

2.2.2 Supply costs

The prices paid for inputs from suppliers have an obvious effect on cost structures. Two important influences are transport costs and, therefore, proximity to sources of supply; and relationships with suppliers, including the ability to negotiate good prices. The second factor is greatly influenced by quantity purchased over time and is thus a further example of **scale economy**.

Supply costs are particularly important for firms that have little opportunity to add value. These include trading intermediaries and processors of commodities, such as some chemicals manufacturers. For many

intermediaries, **market intelligence** is a key resource; knowledge of who needs to buy what, when and at which price, enables profitable trading. In obtaining this resource, personal contact and networking are being superseded by IT systems, whose effective use therefore becomes a threshold competence.

2.2.3 Design of products and processes

Well-designed and operated **business processes** can be a source of cost efficiency, minimising both direct and indirect costs. Examples include obvious matters such as labour productivity, materials yield and the careful control of working capital. JS&W also mention the **management of capacity-fill**. This problem is typical of service sectors such as transport or live entertainment, where there is no possibility of storing unfilled seats. This is, in fact, yet another kind of scale economy and is known in economic theory as the **utilisation of indivisibilities**.

We will look at business processes and aspects of improving processes in more detail later in this Study Text.

Product design also affects the cost base and can have impact on costs beyond those of supplies and the production process. Aircraft, for example, are now commonly designed so as to minimise **lifetime costs**, with ease of servicing and repair built in.

2.2.4 Experience

You are probably familiar with the way the **learning curve** effect has been used for many years as a means of estimating the future manufacturing costs of existing products. (The learning curve illustrates that as workers become more familiar with their jobs, they learn to do them more efficiently. As a process is repeated, it is expected that costs will be reduced due to this increased efficiency.)

The principle can be extended to activities other than manufacturing, to the extent that the passage of time should allow any organisation to improve the cost efficiency of any of its activities and thus experience a continuing decline in real unit costs. This can be seen in the **experience curve**: as output increases, the cost per unit of output falls. This wider experience curve effect holds out the possibility of developing core competences through the acquisition of experience, though the probability that this will happen is low. There are other important considerations.

(a) There should be an advantage in being the **first mover** in a new market, in that it should give an opportunity to create an experience-based cost advantage lead over later-entering rivals.

(b) **Outsourcing** may allow an organisation to benefit from the experience of suppliers. Outsourcing is discussed in more detail later in this Study Text.

(c) Since **competitive rivalry** prompts all the firms in an industry to seek cost advantage, as mentioned earlier, so it follows that they will all seek the experience advantages that come with growth. This will be particularly apparent during the growth phase of the industry lifecycle.

3 Strategic capability and sustainable competitive advantage

If strategy is to be based on strategic capabilities, those capabilities must have four qualities.

- **Value to buyers**
- **Rarity**
- **Robustness** (difficult for competitors to imitate)
- **Non-substitutability**

Under conditions of **hyper-competition**, organisations must possess **dynamic capabilities**: the ability to develop and adjust competences to cope with rapidly changing environmental pressures.

Even if we do not entirely accept the resource-based view of strategy, it is clear that unique resources and core competences are of great importance in creating and sustaining competitive advantage. JS&W

suggest that if competitive advantage is to be based on strategic capabilities, they must have four qualities:

- They must produce effects that are **valuable to buyers**
- They must be **rare**
- They must be **robust**
- They must be **non-substitutable**

The first of these points is almost self-evident, but it must not be overlooked. The remaining three relate to the definition of unique resources and core competences as being **difficult for competitors to imitate or obtain**.

We must now consider these aspects of strategic capability more closely.

3.1 The importance of customer needs

Strategic capability only exists to the extent that it contributes to the organisation's ability to **satisfy its customers' needs**. No matter how rare a resource or how well developed a competence is, it cannot create competitive advantage if customers do not value it or the things it enables the organisation to do.

3.2 Rarity

A single **unique resource** *may* have the potential to create competitive advantage by itself. Here are some examples.

(a)   A unique **tangible resource** in the form of ownership of extraction rights to an easily worked deposit of a scarce and valuable mineral

(b)   A unique **intangible resource** in the form of ownership of the copyright of a best-selling novel

(c)   A **core competence** in a dangerous and demanding process such as extinguishing oil well fires

The importance of rarity is that if a resource or competence is generally available (ie not rare) then an organisation's competitions will have access to it in the same way as the organisation does. In which case, the resource or competence does not confer any advantage to the organisation compared to its rivals.

3.3 Robustness

Robustness is the term JS&W use to mean that a resource is difficult for competitors to imitate. They point out that, generally, it is difficult to base competitive advantage simply on possession of tangible resources, since they can often be imitated or simply bought in. Robustness most frequently resides in the **competences** involved in linking activities and processes in ways that both satisfy the critical success factors defined by customer priorities, and which are difficult for competitors to imitate.

There are three main aspects of a **competence** that tend to make it **robust**.

(a)   **Complexity** arises from the linkages between the activities the organisation undertakes and the way it organises them. It also appears when organisations develop **complex links with their customers**.

(b)   The **culture and history** of the organisation provided tacit knowledge (see below) and capability in the form of an accepted, if ill-defined, way of doing things.

(c)   **Causal ambiguity** occurs when the processes and linkages that produce the organisation's competences are difficult to discern and so competitors are **uncertain about how to imitate** them.

3.4 Non-substitutability

Substitutability of strategic capability has two forms and managers must be alert to the emergence of either, since both are a threat to even a competence that possesses the other three vital qualities.

(a)   The substitute **product** you are familiar with from our earlier discussion of the **five forces**

(b) The substitute **competence**: an example is the deployment of expert systems as substitutes for expensive professional advisers.

3.5 Hypercompetition and dynamic capabilities

The nature of the strategic capabilities, as we have discussed them so far, is that they are **long-term phenomena**: tangible and intangible resources will be more valuable if they can be counted on to last a long time, while the development of core competences might well be expected to be a fairly protracted process.

Under conditions of **hypercompetition**, described earlier in this Study Text, strategic capability takes a different form. In order to deal with the rapid market changes seen under conditions of hypercompetition, firms must possess **dynamic capabilities**.

> **Dynamic capabilities** are an organisation's abilities to develop and change competences to meet the needs of rapidly changing environments. *JS&W*

Such capabilities demand the ability to change, to innovate and to learn. They can take many forms and may include such things as systems for new product development or the acquisition of market intelligence and the absorption of new skills and products acquired by merger or acquisition. Indeed, we might regard the ability to 'develop and change competences' as a competence in its own right a higher-order competence, perhaps.

4 Knowledge

The aim of **knowledge management** is to capture, organise and make widely available all the knowledge the organisation possesses, whether **explicit** (in recorded form) or **tacit** (in people's heads).

Knowledge management is a relatively new concept in business theory. It is connected with the theory of the **learning organisation** and founded on the idea that knowledge is a major source of competitive advantage in business.

Studies have indicated that 20 to 30 percent of company resources are wasted because organisations are not aware of what knowledge they already possess. Lew Platt, Ex-Chief Executive of Hewlett Packard, has articulated this, saying 'If only HP knew what HP knows, we would be three times as profitable'.

Knowledge is thus seen as an important **resource** and may in itself constitute a **competence**: it can certainly **underpin** many competences.

> **Organisational knowledge** is the collective and shared experience accumulated through systems, routines and activities of sharing across the organisation. *JS&W*

4.1 Organisational learning

Organisational learning is particularly important in the increasing number of task environments that are both complex and dynamic. It becomes necessary for strategic managers to promote and foster a **culture that values intuition**, argument from **conflicting views** and **experimentation**. A willingness to back ideas that are not guaranteed to succeed is another aspect of this culture: there must be freedom to make mistakes.

The aim of **knowledge management** is to exploit existing knowledge and to create new knowledge so that it may be exploited in turn. This is not easy. All organisations possess a great deal of data, but it tends to be unorganised and inaccessible. It is often locked up inside the memories of people who do not realise the value of what they know. This is what Nonaka calls **tacit knowledge**. Even when it is made **explicit**, by being recorded in some way, it may be difficult and time consuming to get at, as is the case with most paper archives. This is where knowledge management technology (discussed below) can be useful.

Another important consideration is that tacit knowledge is inherently more **robust** (in the sense explained in Section 3.3 above) than explicit knowledge.

Exam focus point

An article titled 'The learning organisation' written by Fearghal McHugh is available in the technical articles section for P3 on the ACCA website. It would be worth taking the time to study this article.

4.2 Managing explicit knowledge

4.2.1 Data, information and knowledge

FAST FORWARD

Data are simple facts that can be organised in a way that creates **information**. **Knowledge** is patterns of information that are strategically useful and context independent.

There is an important conceptual hierarchy underpinning knowledge management. This distinguishes between **data, information** and **knowledge**. The distinctions are not clear-cut and, to some extent, are differences of degree rather than kind. An understanding of the terms is best approached by considering the relationships between them.

Data

Data typically consists of individual facts, but in a business context may include more complex items such as opinions, reactions and beliefs. A quantity of data, no matter how large, does not constitute **information**.

Information

Information is data that is **organised** in some useful way. For instance, an individual credit sale will produce a single invoice identifying the goods, the price, the customer, the date of the sale and so on. These things are data: their usefulness does not extend beyond the purpose of the invoice, which is to collect the sum due. Even if we possess a copy of every invoice raised during a financial year, we still only have data.

However, if we **process that data we start to create information**. For instance, a simple combination of analysis and arithmetic enables us to state total sales for the year, to break that down into sales for each product and to each customer, to identify major customers and so on. These are pieces of information: they are useful for the **management** of the business, rather than just inputs into its administrative systems.

Nevertheless, we still have not really produced any **knowledge**. Information may be said to consist of the **relationships between** items of data, as when we combine turnover with customer details to discover which accounts are currently important and which are not. We need to go beyond this in order to create knowledge.

Difference between information and knowledge

The conceptual difference between data and information is fairly easy to grasp: it lies chiefly in the **processes** that produce the one from the other. The difference between information and knowledge is more complex and varies from setting to setting. This is not surprising, since knowledge itself is more complex than the information it derives from.

A good starting point for understanding the difference is an appreciation of the importance of pattern: knowledge tends to originate in the **discovery of trends or patterns in information**. To return to our invoicing example, suppose we found that certain combinations of goods purchased were typical of certain customers. We could then build up some interesting customer profiles that would enhance our market segmentation and this in turn might influence our overall strategy, since we could identify likely prospects for cross-selling effort.

Another important aspect of the differences between data, information and knowledge is the relevance of **context**. Our sales invoice is meaningless outside its context; if you, as a marketing person, found an invoice in the office corridor, it would be little more than waste paper to you, though no doubt, the

accounts people would like it back. However, if you found a list of customers in order of annual turnover, that would be rather more interesting from a marketing point of view. The information is **useful outside of its original context** of the accounts office.

This idea also applies to the difference between information and knowledge. If you were a visitor to a company and found a copy of the turnover listing, it would really only be useful to you if you were trying to sell the same sort of thing to the same customers. Its value outside its context would be small. However, if you found a marketing report that suggested, based on evidence, that customers were becoming more interested in quality and less interested in price, that would be applicable to a wide range of businesses, and possibly of strategic importance.

Here are a table and a diagram that summarise the progression from data to knowledge.

	Data	Information	Knowledge
Nature	Facts	Relationships between processed facts	Patterns discerned in information
Importance of context	Total	Some	Context independent
Importance to business	Mundane	Probably useful for management	May be strategically useful

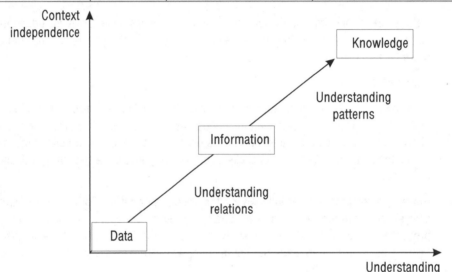

Progression from data to knowledge

There is one final important point to note here and that is that the **progression** from data to knowledge is not the same in all circumstances. The scale is moveable and depends on the general complexity of the setting. Something may be **information** within its own context. Something similar may be **knowledge** in a different context. The difference will often be associated with the scale of operations.

Take the example of a customer going into insolvent liquidation with $200,000 outstanding on its account. For a small supplier with an annual turnover of, say, $10 million, a bad debt of this size would be of strategic importance and might constitute a threat to its continued existence. Advance notice of the possibility would be valuable **knowledge**. However, for a company operating on a global scale, the bad debt write-off would be annoying but still only one item in a list of bad debts – **data**, in other words.

4.2.2 Other ideas about knowledge

Individuals acquire knowledge in a variety of ways including those listed below:

- Education and training
- Experience of work
- Observation of others
- Informal exchanges such as coaching and brain storming

Davenport and Pansak echo our earlier description of the relationship between data, information and knowledge and suggest that people **create knowledge from information by four processes**:

- **Comparison** with earlier experience
- **Consequences**: the implication of information
- **Connections**: relationships between items
- **Conversation**: discussion with others

4.2.3 Knowledge management

Exam focus point

An article titled 'Knowledge management' written by Fearghal McHugh is available in the technical articles section for P3 on the ACCA website. It would be worth taking the time to study this article.

Knowledge management is the process by which organisations generate value from their intellectual and knowledge-based assets. This involves:

- Discovering or identifying knowledge
- Capturing knowledge
- Sharing knowledge
- Distributing knowledge
- Using knowledge
- Maintaining knowledge

In effect, knowledge management has three phases: capture, record and disseminate.

Knowledge management is becoming increasingly important in helping organisations sustain competitive advantage.

As organisations become more complex, there is more knowledge to manage. Moreover, the importance of capturing and sharing it is increased as job mobility increases. If staff leave, there is a danger knowledge could leave with them, if it has not been properly managed within the organisation.

Also organisations' external environments – technology, competitors, markets – are changing rapidly so organisations need to ensure they have up-to-date knowledge about these external factors to take account of the opportunities and threats they represent.

 Case Study   **Knowledge management**

How to facilitate knowledge sharing

An article by Forbes (2012) highlighted that 'scientists have worked out exactly how much data is sent to a typical person in the course of a year – the equivalent of every person in the world reading 174 newspapers every single day'. To combat the perils of data overload many companies actively attempt to manage knowledge throughout the organisation. The article argues that good knowledge management systems are central to success by helping to:

- Facilitate decision-making
- Build the learning organisation
- Stimulate cultural change and innovation

Facilitates decision-making

Companies that have cultures that encourage knowledge sharing can unlock the rich stores of knowledge within each employee: sharing promotes overall knowledge, and facilitates further creativity. World class companies are innovatively implementing best practice sharing to shake them out of the rut of 'the way it's always been done.' Programs such as General Electric's Corporate Executive Council (CEC) provide the company's executives with the opportunity to cut out so-called 'noise' (being unnecessary data).

Forbes highlights that 'the CEC is composed of the heads of GE's 14 major businesses and the two-day sessions are forums for sharing best practices, accelerating progress, and discussing successes, failures, and experiences'. Equally, Wal-Mart's famous Saturday meetings help employees challenge conventions and suggest creative new ideas that drive process improvement, increased efficiency, and overall, a stronger bottom line.

Build learning organisations

The fundamental goal of knowledge management is to capture and disseminate knowledge across an increasingly global enterprise, enabling individuals to avoid repeating mistakes and to operate more intelligently – striving to create an entire learning organisation that works as efficiently as its most seasoned experts.

Forbes highlights the words of David Garvin who notes that 'to move ahead, one must often first look behind'. 'The US Army's After Action Reviews (AAR's) are an example of a knowledge management system that has helped build the Army into a learning organisation by making learning routine...After every important activity or event, Army teams review assignments, identify successes and failures, and seek ways to perform better the next time.'

Stimulates cultural change and innovation

Positive management of knowledge may help organisations to stimulate innovation through the free flow of ideas. Best Practices LLC's (research and consulting firm) report, *Knowledge Management of Internal Best Practices*, profiles innovative methods used by world-class companies to improve internal communication. The study provides recommendations on how to create a culture which shares best practice through all levels of the organisation, how to use both external and internal sources to find best practices and how to capture that knowledge and communicate it to all employees.

Best Practices LLC, contacted over 50 leading companies at the vanguard of knowledge management to compile its report. Some of the vital issues these thought leaders addressed include measurement and management of intellectual assets, best practice identification and recognition systems, best practice prioritisation systems, communication of best practices, and knowledge sharing through technology. For example, in the area of best practice communications, the report examines how General Electric spreads best practices with regular job rotations.

Fortune notes that 'Fortune 500 companies lose roughly $31.5bn a year by failing to share knowledge.'

Source: Adapted from 'Why knowledge management is important to the success of your company', written by Lisa Quast, August 2012, *Forbes* [online]

4.2.4 Knowledge management (KM) systems

FAST FORWARD

> Knowledge must be managed in a way that makes it easily available. Systems include office automation, groupware, intranets, extranets, expert systems and data mining.

Recognition of the value of knowledge and understanding of the need to organise data and make it accessible have provoked the development of sophisticated IT systems. Such systems deal, by definition with **explicit knowledge**: that is, knowledge that is widely distributed. **Tacit knowledge** exists within individuals' brains and is not readily available, especially when its possession enhances power and status. Tacit knowledge only becomes available to the KM System when conscious decisions are taken to share it.

(a) **Office automation systems** are IT applications that improve productivity in an office. These include word processing and voice messaging systems.

(b) **Groupware**, such as **Lotus Notes** provides functions for collaborative work groups. In a sales context, for instance, it would provide a facility for recording and retrieving all the information relevant to individual customers, including notes of visits, notes of telephone calls and basic data like address, credit terms and contact name. These items could be updated by anyone who had contact with a customer and would then be available to all sales people.

Groupware also provides such facilities as messaging, appointment scheduling, to-do lists, and jotters.

(c) An **intranet** is an internal network used to share information using internet technology and protocols. The **firewall** surrounding an intranet fends off unauthorised access from outside the organisation. Each employee has a browser, used to access a server computer that holds corporate

information on a wide variety of topics, and in some cases also offers access to the internet. Applications include company newspapers, induction material, procedure and policy manuals and internal databases.

(i) Savings accrue from the **elimination of storage**, **printing** and **distribution of documents** that can be made available to employees online.

(ii) Documents online are often **more widely used** than those that are kept filed away, especially if the document is bulky (eg manuals) and needs to be searched. This means that there are improvements in productivity and efficiency.

(iii) It is much easier to **update information in electronic form**.

When access to an intranet is extended to trusted external agencies, such as suppliers and customers, it becomes an **extranet**. Security is a major issue for extranets and may require firewalls, server management, encryption and the issue of digital certificates.

(d) An **expert system** is a computer program that captures **human expertise** in a limited domain of knowledge. Such software uses a knowledge base that consists of facts, concepts and the relationships between them and uses pattern-matching techniques to solve problems. For example, many financial institutions now use expert systems to process straightforward loan applications. The user enters certain key facts into the system such as the loan applicant's name and most recent addresses, their income and monthly outgoings, and details of other loans. The system will then:

(i) Check the facts given against its **database** to see whether the applicant has a good previous credit record.

(ii) Perform **calculations** to see whether the applicant can afford to repay the loan.

(iii) Make a **judgement** as to what extent the loan applicant fits the lender's profile of a good risk (based on the lender's previous experience).

(iv) **A decision is then suggested**, based on the results of this processing.

(e) IT systems can be used to store vast amounts of data in accessible form. A **data warehouse** receives data from operational systems, such as a sales order processing system, and stores them in its most fundamental form, without any summarisation of transactions. Analytical and query software is provided so that reports can be produced at any level of summarisation and incorporating any comparisons or relationships desired.

(f) The value of a data warehouse is enhanced when **data mining** software is used. True data mining software **discovers previously unknown relationships** and provides insights that cannot be obtained through ordinary summary reports. These hidden patterns and relationships constitute **knowledge**, as defined above, and can be used to guide decision making and to predict future behaviour. Data mining is thus a contribution to organisational learning.

Note these systems are all primarily designed with an **internal focus** – allowing organisations to share and distribute knowledge more easily. However, do not forget organisations also use IT applications to enhance the service they provide their customers. We will look in more detail at the range of IT applications an organisation can draw on in the eBusiness chapter later in this Study Text.

Case Study
Wal-Mart

The American retailer Wal-Mart discovered an unexpected relationship between the sale of nappies and beer! Wal-Mart found that both tended to sell at the same time, just after working hours, and concluded that men with small children stopped off to buy nappies on their way home, and bought beer at the same time. Logically, therefore, if the two items were put in the same shopping aisle, sales of both should increase. Wal-Mart tried this and it worked.

Here is an amended version of our earlier table. This one includes the relevant IT systems.

	Data	Information	Knowledge
Nature	Facts	Relationships between processed facts	Patterns discerned in information
Importance of context	Total	Some	Context independent
Importance to business	Mundane	Probably useful for management	May be strategically useful
Relevant IT systems	Office automation Data warehouse	Groupware Expert systems Report writing software Intranet	Data mining Intranet Expert systems

Note that knowledge management is also important to you as an accountant. One of the Practical Experience Requirements you need to be able to demonstrate for your ACCA qualification is that you can 'Apply information systems and knowledge management to implement and support business functions and strategic objectives.'

5 Converting resources: the value chain

FAST FORWARD

The **value chain** describes those activities of the organisation that add value to purchased inputs. Primary activities are involved in the production of goods and services. Support activities provide necessary assistance. **Linkages** are the relationships between activities.

The **value chain** model of corporate activities offers a bird's eye view of the firm and what it does. Competitive advantage arises out of the way in which firms organise and perform **activities** to add value.

5.1 Value activities

Key term

Value activities are the means by which a firm creates value in its products.

Activities incur costs, and, in combination with other activities, provide a product or service which earns revenue.

5.2 Example

Let us explain this point by using the example of a **restaurant**. A restaurant's activities can be divided into buying food, cooking it, and serving it (to customers). There is no reason, in theory, why the customers should not do all these things themselves, at home. The customer however, is not only prepared to **pay for someone else** to do all this but also **pays more than the cost of** the resources (food, wages and so on). The ultimate value a firm creates is measured by the amount customers are willing to pay for its products or services above the cost of carrying out value activities. A firm is profitable if the realised value to customers exceeds the collective cost of performing the activities.

(a)   Customers **purchase value**, which they measure by comparing a firm's products and services with similar offerings by competitors.

(b)   The business **creates value** by carrying out its activities either more efficiently than other businesses, or by combining them in such a way as to provide a unique product or service.

Outline different ways in which the restaurant can create value.

Answer

Here are some ideas. Each of these options is a way of organising the activities of buying, cooking and serving food in a way that customers will value.

(a)   It can become more efficient, by automating the production of food, as in a fast food chain.

(b)   The chef can develop commercial relationships with growers, so he or she can obtain the best quality fresh produce.

(c)   The chef can specialise in a particular type of cuisine (eg Nepalese, Korean).

(d)   The restaurant can be sumptuously decorated for those customers who value atmosphere and a sense of occasion, in addition to a restaurant's purely gastronomic pleasures.

(e)   The restaurant can serve a particular type of customer (eg students).

5.3 The value chain   6/12, 12/09

Porter (in *Competitive Advantage*) grouped the various activities of an organisation into a **value chain**. Here is a diagram.

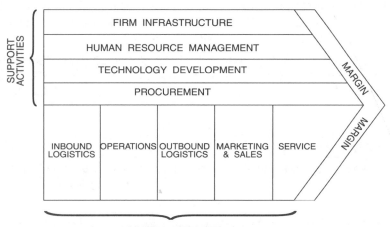

Porter's value chain model

The **margin** is the excess the customer is prepared to **pay** over the **cost** to the firm of obtaining resource inputs and providing value activities. It represents the **value created** by the **value activities** themselves and by the **management of the linkages** between them.

Exam focus point

> The Value Chain is explicitly referenced in the Study Guide and so could be specifically examined in your exam. Make sure you know all the activities in the chain.
>
> The value chain diagram is also worth **committing to memory** since it is an excellent basic description of how an organisation works. It is not only suitable for answering questions that require analysis of how an organisation works, but is also very useful as a kind of checklist for brainstorming a wide range of questions that require you to make suggestions for dealing with business problems. Work your way through the various activities asking yourself what the organisation could do about each one, if anything.
>
> The Value Chain was specifically examined in December 2009, where one of the 25 mark questions related entirely to the Value Chain. In part (a), worth 10 marks, candidates were required to analyse the primary activities of the value chain of the products in question. Part (b), worth 15 marks, asked candidates to suggest changes that could be made to the primary activities in order to improve the competitiveness of the organisation (a charity).

The Value Chain was also examined in December 2010 as part of a Section B question. For 12 marks candidates were required to analyse the Value Chain activities of the featured company, which specialised in the production of bespoke sofas and chairs. Candidates were required to use this analysis to highlight areas of weakness at the company.

Primary activities are directly related to production, sales, marketing, delivery and service.

	Comment
Inbound logistics	Receiving, handling and storing inputs to the production system: warehousing, transport, inventory control and so on.
Operations	Converting resource inputs into a final product: resource inputs are not only materials. People are a resource, especially in service industries.
Outbound logistics	Storing the product and its distribution to customers: packaging, testing, delivery and so on; for service industries, this activity may be more concerned with bringing customers to the place where the service is available; an example would be front of house management in a theatre.
Marketing and sales	Informing customers about the product, persuading them to buy it, and enabling them to do so: advertising, promotion and so on.
After sales service	Installing products, repairing them, upgrading them, providing spare parts and so forth.

Support activities provide purchased inputs, human resources, technology and infrastructural functions **to support the primary activities**. It may seem an obvious point that support activities need to support the primary activities, but do not overlook it. For example, staff recruitment and training need to be appropriate for the item being produced in the operations.

Activity	Comment
Procurement	All of the processes involved in acquiring the resource inputs to the primary activities (eg purchase of materials, subcomponents equipment).
Technology development	Product design, improving processes and resource utilisation.
Human resource management	Recruiting, training, managing, developing and rewarding people; this activity takes place in all parts of the organisation, not just in the HRM department.
Firm infrastructure	Planning, finance, quality control, the structures and routines that make up the organisation's culture.

Linkages connect the activities of the value chain:

(a) **Activities in the value chain affect one another**. For example, more costly product design or better quality production might reduce the need for after-sales service.

(b) **Linkages require co-ordination**. For example, Just In Time requires smooth functioning of operations, outbound logistics and service activities such as installation.

The value chain concept is an important tool in analysing the organisation's strategic capability, since it focuses on the overall means by which value is created, rather than on structural functions or departments. There are two important, connected aspects to this analysis:

(a) It enables managers to establish the **activities** that are particularly important in **providing customers with the value they want**: this leads on to a consideration of where management attention and other resources are best applied, either to improve weakness or to further exploit strength. A further possible consequence would be decisions about outsourcing.

(b) This analysis can be extended to include an assessment of the **costs and benefits** associated with the various value activities.

5.4 The value chain, core competencies and outsourcing

Core competences are the basis for the creation of value; activities from which the organisation does not derive significant value may be outsourced.

The purpose of value chain analysis is to understand how the company creates value. It is unlikely that any business has more than a handful of activities in which it outperforms its competitors. There is a clear link here with the idea of **core competences**: a core competence will enable the company to create value in a way that its competitors cannot imitate. These **value activities** are the basis of the company's unique offering.

There is a strong case for examining the possibilities of **outsourcing** non-core activities so that management can concentrate on what the company does best.

5.5 The value network

The value network joins the organisation's value chain to those of its suppliers and customers.

Activities and linkages that add value do not stop at the organisation's **boundaries**. For example, when a restaurant serves a meal, the quality of the ingredients – although they are chosen by the cook – is determined by the grower. The grower has added value, and the grower's success in growing produce of good quality is as important to the customer's ultimate satisfaction as the skills of the chef.

Similarly, the value received by a person buying a new car has been created by a **complex system** that includes several organisations' value chains. These would include the nominal manufacturer, their suppliers of parts and subsystems, *their* suppliers in turn, the retailer, the transport companies that delivered the car to the showroom and possibly others as well. A firm's value chain is connected to other value chains in what JS&W call a **value network**. (Porter used the term **value system**; value network is a better term since it emphasises the **interconnectedness of separate organisations**.)

Key term

> The value network is the set of inter-organisational links and relationships that are necessary to create a product or service. *JS&W*

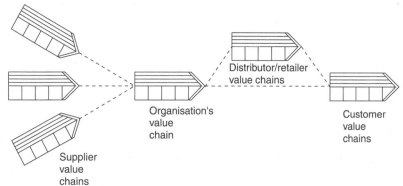

Value network

The diagram illustrates the similarities between the value network and a supply chain. However, whereas a supply chain shows the system of organisations, people, technology or activities involved in transforming a product or service from its raw materials to a finished product to be delivered to the end user customer, the value network places an emphasis on the value-creating capability within the supply chain processes.

In this respect, understanding value networks can be helpful when looking at supply chain management.

It may be possible to capture the benefit of some of the value generated both upstream and downstream in the value network. An obvious way to do this is by **vertical integration** through the acquisition of suppliers and customers. This aspect of strategy is dealt with in more detail later in this Study Text.

It is possible for large and powerful companies to exercise less formal power over suppliers and customers by using their **bargaining power** to achieve purchase and selling prices that are biased in their favour.

A more subtle advantage is gained by fostering good relationships that can promote **innovation** and the **creation of knowledge**.

Case Study   Toyota

Toyota is well-known for close involvement with its suppliers. The company works with suppliers to improve their methods and the quality of their output; and to develop new, improved materials and components for input into its own operations. The relationship has benefits for all parties, but tends to be unequal, with Toyota dominating the operations of a large number of semi-captive suppliers.

Li & Fung aim for more equal relationships with the large number of clothing manufacturers they deal with. It guarantees to take at least 30% of a supplier's output in order to build a close relationship and improve innovation and learning. But it also tries to limit its purchases to no more than 70% of a supplier's output in order to avoid creating a dependent organisation whose managers are influenced more by fear than by trust.

Using the value chain. A firm can secure competitive advantage in several ways:

- Invent new or better ways to do activities
- Combine activities in new or better ways
- Manage the linkages in its own value chain
- Manage the linkages in the value network

Question   Value chain

Sana Sounds is a small record company. Representatives from Sana Sounds scour music clubs for new bands to promote. Once a band has signed a contract (with Sana Sounds) it makes a recording. The recording process is subcontracted to one of a number of recording studio firms which Sana Sounds uses regularly. (At the moment, Sana Sounds is not large enough to invest in its own equipment and studios.) Sana Sounds also subcontracts the production of CDs to a number of manufacturing companies. Sana Sounds then distributes the disks to selected stores, and engages in any promotional activities required.

What would you say were the activities in Sana Sounds' value chain?

Answer

Sana Sounds is involved in the record industry from start to finish. Although recording and CD manufacture are contracted out to external suppliers, this makes no difference to the fact that these activities are part of Sana Sounds' own value chain. Sana Sounds earns its money by managing the whole set of activities. If the company grows, then perhaps it will acquire its own recording studios.

5.6 Section summary

- The value chain models how activities can be deployed to add value for the customer
- Value chains are part of a value network
- Firms can benefit by performing activities in a unique way and/or exploiting linkages

An article titled 'Value chains, value networks and supply chain management' written by Ken Garrett is available in the Technical Articles section for P3 on the ACCA website. The article focuses on the role of the value chain in creating value for customers and considers different types of supply chain models. You are strongly advised to read this article.

6 Outputs: the product portfolio

Many firms make a number of different products or services. Each product or service has its own financial, marketing and risk characteristics. The combination of products or services influences the attractiveness and profitability of the firm.

6.1 The product life cycle   6/09

FAST FORWARD

The **product life cycle** concept holds that products have a life cycle, and that a product demonstrates different characteristics of profit and investment at each stage in its life cycle. The life cycle concept is a model, not a prediction. (Not all products pass through each stage of the life cycle.) It enables a firm to examine its portfolio of goods and services as a whole.

The profitability and sales of a product can be expected to change over time. The **product life cycle** is an attempt to recognise distinct stages in a product's sales history. Marketing managers distinguish between different aspects of the product.

(a)   **Product class:** this is a broad category of product, such as cars, washing machines, newspapers also referred to as the **generic product**.

(b)   **Product form:** within a product class there are different forms that the product can take, for example, five-door hatchback cars or two-seater sports cars; twin tub or front loading automatic washing machines; national daily newspapers or weekly local papers and so on.

(c)   **Brand:** the particular type of the product form (for example, for cars – Volkswagen Golf, Vauxhall Astra; or for newspapers – *Financial Times*, *Daily Mail*, *Sun*).

The product life cycle applies in differing degrees to each of the three cases. A product-class (eg cars) may have a long maturity stage, and a particular make or brand might have an erratic life cycle (eg Rolls Royce) or not. Product forms, however, tend to conform to the classic life cycle pattern.

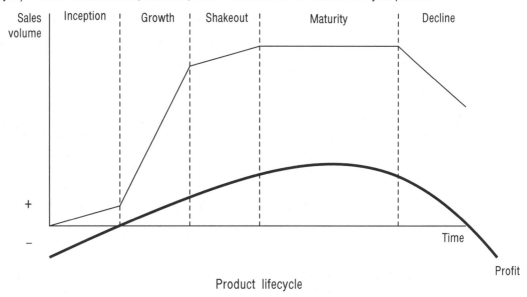

Product lifecycle

6.1.1 Inception

- A new product takes time to find acceptance by would-be purchasers and there is a slow growth in sales. Unit costs are high because of low output and expensive sales promotion.

- There will be high marketing costs in order to get the product recognised by customers.

- There may be early teething troubles with production technology.

- The product for the time being is a loss-maker.

- The product has few competitors (because they are not willing to take similar risks).

6.1.2 Growth

- If the new product gains market acceptance, sales will eventually rise more sharply and the product will start to make profits.

- Capital investments are needed to fulfil the level of demand, meaning cash flow remains lower than profit. Cash flow is likely to remain negative.

- Competitors are attracted. As sales and production rise, unit costs fall.

- Need to add additional features to differentiate from competitors, so product complexity likely to rise. Costs involved in developing this could be high. Alternatively, could chose to lower price and compete on price grounds.

- Continued marketing expenditure required to differentiate the firm's product from competitors' offerings.

- Growth is sustained by attracting new types of customers.

6.1.3 Maturity

- The market is no longer growing. Purchases are now based on repeat or replacement purchases, rather than new customers.

- The rate of sales growth slows down and the product reaches a period of maturity, which is probably the longest period of a successful product's life. Most products on the market will be at the mature stage of their life.

- Profits remain good, and levels of investment are low, meaning cash flow is also positive.

- Prices start to decline, as firms compete with one another to try to increase their share of a fixed-size market.

- Firms try to capitalise on a brand name by launching spin off products under the same name.

- The number of firms in industry reduces, due to consolidation in the industry in an attempt to restore profitability.

6.1.4 Decline

Eventually, sales will begin to decline so that there is over-capacity of production in the industry. Severe competition occurs, profits fall and some producers leave the market. The remaining producers seek means of prolonging the product life by modifying it and searching for new market segments. Many producers are reluctant to leave the market, although some inevitably do because of falling profits.

6.1.5 The relevance of the product life cycle to strategic planning

In reviewing outputs, planners should assess products in three ways:

(a) The **stage of its life cycle** that any product has reached.
(b) The **product's remaining life**, ie how much longer the product will contribute to profits.
(c) How **urgent is the need to innovate**, to develop new and improved products?

Case Study
Apple and portfolio management

American technology giant Apple, maker of the iPhone and iPad, actively manages its product portfolio in order to keep ahead of the competition. In March 2014, a report in the *Wall Street Journal* highlighted that the company had taken to hiring engineers from competing technology companies, including HTC. Apple's recruitment push has been largely driven by the need to produce new products faster in response to growing demand for the latest iPhone and iPad devices.

The lifecycle of many of Apple's products has reduced in recent years as competitors such as Samsung have been increasing the speed at which it develops its own range of mobile devices. To date, Apple has taken to releasing a new iPhone nearly every year to replace older models which are nearing the end of their lifecycle.

Case Study
Television

Over time, the design and specification of television sets has changed. Black and white screens have been superceded by colour; cathode ray tubes have been superceded by flat screens and plasma screens, and manufacturers have developed home cinema systems.

However, the switch to online distribution methods of video content has also had a significant impact on the television set industry. Online TV, mobile and tablet TV, and free TV catch up services offered by the major channels give viewers much greater choice, allowing them to watch programmes at their own convenience.

To prevent decline, the TV industry has had to adapt to cope with these changes, and internet-enabled television has emerged. 3D televisions have also been developed to differentiate television from internet viewing and to capitalise on the changes in the cinema industry.

6.1.6 Difficulties of the product life cycle concept

(a) **Recognition**. How can managers recognise where a product stands in its life cycle?

(b) **Not always true**. The theoretical curve of a product life cycle does not always occur in practice. Some products have no maturity phase, and go straight from growth to decline. Some never decline if they are marketed competitively.

(c) **Changeable**. Strategic decisions can change or extend a product's life cycle.

(d) **Competition varies** in different industries. The financial markets are an example of markets where there is a tendency for competitors to copy the leader very quickly, so that competition has built up well ahead of demand.

6.2 Product portfolio models

Exam focus point

It has been common to analyse product portfolios using models such as the Boston Consulting Group (BCG) matrix. You will learn about such models in a later chapter. JS&W do not recommend their use in relation to portfolios of individual products, restricting them to the analysis of strategic business unit portfolios.

This means that where a question calls for some kind of product portfolio analysis, you should initially think in terms of the product life cycle. Nevertheless, there may be advantages in then considering the use of techniques such as the BCG matrix, but if you do so, you must also indicate that you know of JS&W's opinion.

7 New products and innovation

7.1 Innovation

> **Innovation** can be a major source of competitive advantage but brings a burden of cost and uncertainty. To avoid waste, there should be a programme of assessment for major product development. The firm must decide whether to be a leader or a follower.

7.1.1 Innovation and competitive advantage

For many organisations, product innovation and being the **first mover** may be a major source of competitive advantage.

(a) A reputation for innovation will attract **early adopters**, though it depends in part on promotional effort.

(b) Customers may find they are locked in to innovative suppliers by unacceptable **costs of switching** to competitors.

(c) The **learning** (or experience) **curve** effect may bring cost advantages.

(d) The first mover may be able to **define the industry standard**.

(e) A **price skimming** strategy can bring early profits that will be denied to later entrants.

(f) L**egal protection,** such as patents, for intellectual property may bring important revenue advantages. This is particularly important in the pharmaceutical industry.

However, the first mover also has particular problems:

- Gaining regulatory approval where required
- Uncertain demand
- High levels of R&D costs
- Lower cost imitators
- Costs of introduction such as training sales staff and educating customers

Key term

> **PIMS** stands for Profit Impact of Marketing Strategy. The concept originated in a 1960s General Electric project to compare the profitability of GE SBUs. An extensive PIMS database of strategic actions and results is now administered by the American Strategic Planning Institute.

PIMS data indicate that there is a **negative correlation** between **profitability** and a high level of expenditure on **R&D**, perhaps because of the costs associated with these problems.

7.1.2 Technology and the value chain

Porter points out in *Competitive Advantage* that 'every value activity uses some technology to combine purchased inputs and human resources to produce some output.' He goes on to discuss the varied role of **information technology** and emphasises the often-overlooked importance of **administrative** or **office technology**. The significance of this for strategy lies in the area of **core competences**. Just as **R&D** is as much concerned with processes as with products, so improvement in the linkages of the value chain will enhance competitive advantage.

7.2 New product strategies

The development of new products might be considered an important aspect of a firm's competitive and marketing strategies.

(a) New and innovative products can lower **entry barriers** to existing industries and markets, if new technology is involved.

(b)   The interests of the company are best met with a balanced product portfolio. Managers therefore must plan when to introduce new products, how best to extend the life of mature ones and when to abandon those in decline.

A strategic issue managers must consider is their approach to new product development.

(a)   **Leader strategy**. Do they intend to gain competitive advantage by operating at the leading edge of new developments? There are significant implications for the R&D activity and the likely length of product life cycles within the portfolio if this strategy is adopted. Also, **R&D costs** are likely to be heavy, with a significant reduction in potential profitability as a result.

(b)   **Follower strategy**. Alternatively, they can be more pro-active, adopt a follower strategy, which involves lower costs and less emphasis on the R&D activity. It sacrifices early rewards of innovation, but avoids its risks. A follower might have to license certain technologies from a leader (as is the case with many consumer electronics companies). However, research indicates that this can be a **more profitable strategy** than being an innovator, especially when the follower is able to learn from the leader's mistakes.

A matrix of new **product strategies** and new **market strategies** can be set out as follows.

| | Product | | |
	No technological change	Improved technology	New technology
Market unchanged	–	**Reformulation** A new balance between price/quality has to be formulated	**Replacement** The new technology replaces the old
Market strengthened (ie new demand from same customers)	**Remerchandising** The product is sold in a new way – eg by re-packaging	**Improved product** Sales growth to existing customers sought on the strength of product improvements	**Product line extension** The new product is added to the existing product line to increase total demand
New market	**New use** By finding a new use for the existing product, new customers are found	**Market extension** New customers sought on the strength of product improvements	**Diversification**

7.3 Types of 'new' products

Booz, Allen and Hamilton identified the following categories of 'new' products based on a survey of 700 firms:

	%
• New to the world	10
• New product lines	20
• Additions to product line	26
• Repositionings	7
• Improvements/revisions	26
• Cost reductions	11

7.4 Research and development

Research may be **pure**, **applied** or **development**. It may be intended to improve **products** or **processes**. New product development should be controlled by requiring strategic approval at key points of development.

R&D should support the organisation's strategy and be closely co-ordinated with marketing. There are distinct problems to managing R&D.

Here are some definitions to start with:

Pure research is original research to obtain new scientific or technical knowledge or understanding. There is no obvious commercial or practical end in view.

Applied research is also original research work like pure researchabove, but it has a specific practical aim or application (eg research on improvements in the effectiveness of medicines etc).

Development is the use of existing scientific and technical knowledge to produce new (or substantially improved) products or systems, prior to starting commercial production operations.

Many organisations employ **specialist staff** to conduct research and development (R&D). They may be organised in a separate functional department of their own. In an organisation run on a product division basis, R&D staff may be employed by each division.

7.5 Product and process research

There are two categories of R&D.

Product research is based on creating new products and developing existing ones, in other words the organisation's 'offer' to the market.

Process research is based on improving the way in which those products or services are made or delivered, or the efficiency with which they are made or delivered.

Product research – new product development

The new product development process must be carefully controlled; new products are a major source of competitive advantage but can cost a great deal of money to bring to market. A screening process is necessary to ensure that resources are concentrated on projects with a high probability of success and not wasted on those that have poor prospects.

Cooper describes a typical modern product innovation screening process that he calls **Stage-Gate**™. This emphasises a cross-functional, prioritised, quality managed, project management approach consisting, typically, of five stages. We look at project management as a whole in more detail later in this Study Text, but this early reference is an indication of the importance of managing projects effectively.

In Cooper's model, each stage begins with a **gate**; that is, a review meeting of managers who have the power either to kill the project or to allocate the resources necessary for it to progress to the next gate.

7.6 Process research

Process research involves attention to how the goods/services are produced. Process research has these aspects.

(a)   **Processes** are crucial in service industries (eg fast food), where processes are part of the services sold.

(b)   **Productivity**. Efficient processes save money and time.

(c)   **Planning**. If you know how long certain stages in a project are likely to take, you can plan the most efficient sequence.

(d)   **Quality management** for enhanced quality.

We will have a lot more to say about process development later in this Study Text, but these early references should alert you to the fact that they are important considerations in business strategy.

An important aspect of process research is that advances are much more difficult to imitate than product developments. Competitors can purchase and **reverse engineer** new products. With good physical security in place, they will find it much more difficult to imitate new processes.

The strategic role of R&D. R&D should support the organisation's chosen strategy. To take a simple example, if a strategy based on high quality and luxury has been adopted, it would be inappropriate to expend much effort on researching ways of minimising costs. If the company has a competence in R&D,

this may form the basis for a strategy of product innovation. Conversely, where product lifecycles are short, as in consumer electronics, product development is fundamental to strategy.

7.7 Problems with R&D

(a) **Organisational**. Problems of authority relationships and integration arise with the management of R&D. The function will have to liaise closely with marketing and with production, as well as with senior management responsible for corporate planning: its role is both strategic and technical.

(b) **Financial**. R&D is by nature not easily planned in advance, and financial performance targets are not easily set. Budgeting for long-term, complex development projects with uncertain returns can be a nightmare for management accountants.

(c) **Evaluation and control**. Pure research or even applied research may not have an obvious pay off in the short term. Evaluation could be based on successful application of new ideas, such as patents obtained and the commercial viability of new products.

(d) **Staff problems**. Research staff are usually highly qualified and profession-orientated, with consequences for the style of supervision and level of remuneration offered to them.

(e) **Cultural problems**. Encouraging innovation means trial and error, flexibility, tolerance of mistakes in the interests of experimentation, high incentives etc. If this is merely a subculture in an essentially bureaucratic organisation, it will not only be difficult to sustain, but will become a source of immense 'political' conflict. The R&D department may have an 'academic' or university atmosphere, as opposed to a commercial one.

7.8 R&D and marketing

(a) Customer needs, as identified by marketers, should be a vital input to new product developments.

(b) The R&D department might identify possible changes to product specifications so that a variety of marketing mixes can be tried out and screened.

7.8.1 Intrapreneurship

FAST FORWARD

Intrapreneurship is entrepreneurship carried on at intermediate levels within the organisation.

The encouragement of intrapreneurship is an important way of promoting innovation. Such encouragement has many aspects:

(a) Encouragement for individuals to achieve results in their own way without the need for constant supervision.

(b) A culture of risk-taking and tolerance of mistakes.

(c) A flexible approach to organisation that facilitates the formation of project teams.

(d) Willingness and ability to devote resources to trying out new ideas.

(e) Incentives and rewards policy that support intrapreneurial activity.

7.8.2 Market pull and technology push

Marketers would have us believe that the best way to competitive advantage is to find out what the market wants and give it to them. We might call this approach, when applied to innovation, **market pull**. Unfortunately, it tends merely to produce better versions of products that already exist. A more fruitful approach may be the 'product orientation', disdained by the marketing fraternity: the world is full of products that noone asked for, including post-it notes and mobile phones that are also cameras. This approach we might call **technology push**.

Perhaps the most fruitful approach would be a combination of the two, where technologists try to solve customers' problems and marketers try to find applications for new and emerging technologies. Many new developments are, in fact, the result of **collaboration between suppliers and customers**.

 **Case Study**   **Microsoft Xbox One**

A company's policy on innovation will be linked to its assessment of how the product lifecycle concept applies to its portfolio.

In late 2013, Microsoft launched its next generation games console: Xbox One. The launch of the Xbox One followed the introduction of Sony's Playstation 4 earlier that year.

The BBC's technology reporter, Leo Kelion, pointed out at the time that Microsoft's Xbox One 'will be more expensive, but includes a higher resolution body-movement sensor in the Kinnect; better voice recognition; and a more ambitious bid to take charge of your living room thanks to its ability to control satellite and cable TV set top boxes'.

Gaming expert Brian Crecente told the BBC 'Where Sony's PlayStation 4 delivers an intensely focused gaming machine, Microsoft's Xbox One promises an entertainment hub, a system just as capable of controlling your cable box as it is delivering a new game for you to play'.

In recent years, there has been an interesting evolution in the relationship between gaming console manufacturers and their customers. Users of game consoles and mobile technologies have in turn become suppliers of content for others to enjoy.

Recognising this, Microsoft announced its intention that in the future, every standard Xbox One will work as a development kit, allowing developers to develop and self-publish games digitally on the Xbox One. This move follows Google Play and Apple's App Store which have created open markets for all kinds of developers.

Microsoft's decision to introduce the Xbox One was made having acknowledged that its earlier console, the Xbox 360 (which had been introduced in 2005) was nearing the end of its lifecycle. In 2011, *Computer and Video Games.com* highlighted comments made by Microsoft Vice president Chris Lewis who stated that 'Xbox 360 was halfway through its lifecycle'.

Adapted from two articles:

1) 'Playstation 4 v Xbox One' by Leo Kelion (November 2013) published on the *BBC* website; www.bbc.co.uk

2) 'Xbox 360: about halfway through its lifecycle' (June 2011) published by *Computer and Video Games.com:* www.computer andvideogames.com

8 Benchmarking   *12/12*

FAST FORWARD

Benchmarking enables a firm to meet industry standards by copying others, but it is perhaps less valuable as a source of innovation. It is a good way to challenge existing ways of doing things.

Key term

Benchmarking is the process of gathering data about targets and comparators, that permit current levels of performance to be identified and evaluated against best practice. Adoption of identified best practices should improve performance.

There are a number of different types of benchmarking. JS&W propose the following categories:

Historical benchmarking is an internal comparison of current against past performance. This is unsatisfactory, since it can induce complacency; comparison with competitors is the real test of performance.

Industry/sector benchmarking compares like with like across the industry or similar providers in the public service. In the UK public sector, league tables are an obvious example of this approach. The limitation of this method is that the whole industry may be under-performing and in danger from substitute products provided by other industries.

Best-in-class benchmarking looks for best practice wherever it can be found. This involves making comparisons with similar features or processes in other industries. JS&W suggest that this approach can have a shock effect on complacent managers and lead to dramatic performance improvements.

8.1 The benchmarking process

Benchmarking can be divided into stages.

Stage 1 The first stage is to **ensure senior management commitment** to the benchmarking process. This will only be genuinely available when the senior managers have a full appreciation of what is involved: senior people are quite capable of changing their minds when it becomes apparent that they did not anticipate the actual levels of cost or inconvenience, for example.

Stage 2 **The areas to be benchmarked should be determined and objectives should be set**. Note that here, the objectives will not be in the form of targets for improvement to specific processes and practices, but more in the nature of stating the extent and depth of the enquiry. For example, if a charity is undertaking a benchmarking exercise in respect of fundraising, it might be decided to look specifically at the security of cash collections.

Stage 3 **Key performance measures must be established**. This will require an understanding of the systems involved. This, in turn, will require discussion with key stakeholders and observation of the way work is carried out. For example, in a university, where research funding is important, this stage could be carried out by examining the processes for assessing applications for research grants.

Stage 4 **Select organisations to benchmark against**. Internal benchmarking may be possible where divisions in the same organisation operate similar processes. Where internal departments have little in common, comparisons must be made against other organisations or equivalent parts of other organisations. The aim will be to find an organisation that does similar things (industrial benchmarking) or one which is recognised as having the most efficient practices (best-in-class benchmarking).

Stage 5 **Measure own and others' performance**. Negotiation should take place to establish just who does the measurement: ideally, a joint team should do it, but there may be issues of **confidentiality** or **convenience** that mean each organisation does its own measuring.

Stage 6 **Compare performance**. Raw data must be carefully analysed if appropriate conclusions are to be drawn. It will be appropriate to discuss initial findings with the **stakeholders** concerned: they are likely both to have useful comments to offer and to be anxious about the possibility of adverse reflection upon them. It is important that managers and staff do not view benchmarking as something designed to criticise their performance, but rather as a way of improving performance.

Stage 7 **Design and implement improvement programmes**. It may be possible to import complete systems; alternatively, it may be appropriate to move towards a synthesis that combines various elements of best practice. Sometimes, improvements require extensive **reorganisation** and **restructuring**. In any event, there is likely to be a requirement for **training**. Improvements in administrative systems often call for investment in new equipment, particularly in IT systems.

Stage 8 **Monitor improvements**. The continuing effectiveness of improvements must be monitored. At the same time, it must be understood that **improvements are not once and for all** and that further adjustments may be beneficial.

8.2 Using benchmarking

JS&W set out questions that should be asked when carrying out a benchmarking exercise as part of a wider strategic review:

- **Why** are these products or services provided at all?
- Why are they provided **in that particular way**?
- What are the examples of **best practice** elsewhere?
- How should activities be **reshaped** in the light of these comparisons?

They see three levels of benchmarking.

Level of benchmarking	Through	Examples of measures
Resources	Resource audit	Quantity of resources • Revenue/employee • Capital intensity Quality of resources • Qualifications of employees • Age of machinery • Uniqueness (eg patents)
Competences in separate activities	Analysing activities	Sales calls per salesperson Output per employee Materials wastage
Competences in linked activities	Analysing overall performances	Market share Profitability Productivity

When selecting an appropriate **benchmark basis**, companies should ask themselves the following questions:

(a) Is it possible and easy to obtain reliable competitor information?

(b) Is there any wide discrepancy between different internal divisions?

(c) Can similar processes be identified in non-competing environments and are these non-competing companies willing to co-operate?

(d) Is best practice operating in a similar environmental setting?

(e) What is our timescale?

(f) Do the chosen companies have similar objectives and strategies?

8.3 Reasons for undertaking benchmarking

Benchmarking has the following advantages:

(a) **Position audit**. Benchmarking can assess a firm's existing position, and provide a basis for establishing standards of performance.

(b) The comparisons are **carried out by the managers** who have to live with any changes implemented as a result of the exercise.

(c) Benchmarking **focuses** on improvement in key areas and sets targets which are challenging but evidently achievable.

(d) The sharing of information can be a **spur to innovation**.

(e) The result should be **improved performance**, particularly in cost control and delivering value.

8.4 Drawbacks of benchmarking

Many companies have gained significant benefits from benchmarking, but it is worth pointing out a number of possible dangers:

(a) It can cloud perception of strategic purpose by attracting too much attention to the detail of what is measured, since it concentres on **doing things right** rather than **doing the right thing**: the difference between **efficiency** and **effectiveness**. A process can be efficient but its output may not be useful.

A linked point is that the benchmark may be **yesterday's solution to tomorrow's problem**. For example, a cross-channel ferry company might benchmark its activities (eg speed of turnaround at Dover and Calais, cleanliness on ship) against another ferry company, whereas the real competitor is the Channel Tunnel.

(b) Benchmarking does not identify the **reasons** why performance is at a particular level, whether good or bad.

(c) It is a **catching-up exercise,** rather than the development of anything distinctive. After the benchmarking exercise, the competitor might improve performance in a different way.

(d) It depends on **accurate** information about comparator companies.

(e) It is not cost-free and can divert management attention.

(f) It can become a hindrance and even a threat: sharing information with other companies can be a burden and a security risk.

Exam focus point

> An article titled 'Benchmarking' can be found in the Technical Articles section for P3 on ACCA's website. The article explores how benchmarking can be applied at key stages in the rational planning approach to strategy setting. It would be worth taking the time to study this article.
>
> In the December 2012 exam, part of a question required students to discuss the advantages and disadvantages of benchmarking in the context of a company which offered outsourced IT solutions to a city council.

9 Managing strategic capability

FAST FORWARD

> Managers must take great care not to disrupt strategic capability that arises from flexible, informal practices by trying to systematise and improve them. However, a policy of gradual extension and improvement of desirable activities may be useful and may be combined with culling of superfluous ones. Also, since much strategic capability is traceable to individual skill and ability, good HRM practice can help to create and improve it.

So far in this chapter we have concentrated on the analysis of strategic capability. We must now turn our attention to the problems of managing and improving it.

9.1 Limitation on the management of strategic capability

There is an important problem in the management of strategic capability, in that it can be very difficult to **understand** it properly. Quite often, core competences derive from **informal and flexible activities and processes** that are not subject to management from above: they simply exist. Sometimes, managers do not appreciate that these competences exist; where they do, they may or may not understand them or value them. Where managers recognise such competences, it is very important that they take great care with attempts to improve or even to formalise them. The former can be highly **disruptive**, while the latter can **eliminate the inherent flexibility** such competences tend to display.

9.2 Improving strategic capability

Despite the limitation discussed above, there may be opportunities to stretch existing capabilities and to add new ones.

(a) **Competences can be extended**. Competences that support existing business may be equally relevant to new activities.

(b) **Non-essential activities can cease**. It may be possible to make significant cost savings by abolishing, minimising or outsourcing current activities that do not support critical success factors.

(c) **Best practice can be extended**. Strategic capability identified in one part of the organisation might be introduced in other parts; though the difficulties associated with the management of change can make this very difficult.

(d) **Activities can be added and existing ones improved** in order to better support critical success factors.

(e) **Activities can be re-structured**. System overlaps and inconsistencies may require attention, particularly when there are marked differences between the requirements of the various market segments served.

(f) **Weaknesses can be remedied**. Known weaknesses in resources or activities might have the potential to create competitive advantage if suitable market opportunities exist. Such weaknesses must then be remedied by suitable investment and management activity.

(g) **External capability can be introduced** by acquisition and through alliances and joint ventures.

9.3 Developing competences through the human resource

Since much strategic capability resides in the organisation's staff in the form of their abilities and skills, human resource development can be particularly important in building that capability.

(a) **Recruitment and selection** practice can be designed to emphasise the need for particular aptitudes, such as leadership or innovation.

(b) **Training and development** can be targeted at specific requirements rather than generic skills.

(c) **Individual strategic awareness** can be developed so that staff understand how their activities enhance strategic capability.

10 SWOT analysis   6/14, 6/11, 6/10, 6/09

FAST FORWARD

> The **SWOT analysis** combines the results of the environmental analysis and the internal appraisal into one framework for assessing the firm's current and future strategic fit, or lack of it, with the environment. It is an analysis of the organisation's strengths and weaknesses, and the opportunities and threats offered by the environment. Weirich's TOWS matrix emphasises the importance of threats and opportunities.

We examined the way in which **opportunities and threats** in the environment are detected and analysed in the previous chapters. In this chapter, we have discussed the analysis of the organisation's strategic capability; that is to say, its **strengths and weaknesses**. A complete awareness of the organisation's environment and its internal capacities is *necessary* for a rational consideration of future strategy, but it is not *sufficient*. The threads must be drawn together so that potential strategies may be developed and assessed. This is done by combining the internal and external analyses into a **SWOT analysis** or **corporate appraisal**.

Key term

> **SWOT analysis** summarises the key issues from the business environment and the strategic capability of an organisation that are most likely to impact on strategy development.   *JS&W*

It is crucial that you understand that opportunities and threats are **external** factors while strengths and weaknesses are **internal** factors.

An exam question may ask you for a full SWOT analysis, or may focus on either internal or external factors. It is important that you understand what the question is asking for, and answer accordingly. The December 2007 exam asked candidates to evaluate the strengths and weaknesses of an airline company, but the examining team noted some candidates still described SWOT analysis overall. This was not required. More importantly, points made about opportunities and threats would have gained no marks, because the questions specifically asked for strengths and weaknesses rather than for a full strategic appraisal (SWOT).

A case study scenario in the June 2011 exam featured a car manufacturer. The company's management had identified three organisational weaknesses, focusing on a lack of control and co-ordination, research and development and succession planning. Candidates had to analyse the weaknesses and then recommend how they could be addressed.

Question 1 in June 2014 asked candidates to undertake a SWOT analysis of the featured company as part of a report to potential investors. The examining team noted that a significant number of students misclassified weaknesses as threats. As previously highlighted, it is critical that you remember that opportunities and threats represent external factors, and that strengths and weaknesses are internally focused. As the examining team highlighted, 'misclassified answers were given some credit, but in SWOT analysis classification is important, otherwise the analysis is just an unstructured list'.

10.1 The SWOT analysis

Effective SWOT analysis does not simply require a categorisation of information, it also requires some **evaluation of the relative importance** of the various factors under consideration.

(a) These features are only of relevance if they are **perceived to exist by the consumers.** Listing corporate features that internal personnel regard as strengths/weaknesses is of little relevance if they are not perceived as such by the organisation's consumers.

(b) In the same vein, threats and opportunities are conditions presented by the external environment and they should be independent of the firm.

The SWOT can now be used guiding strategy formulation.

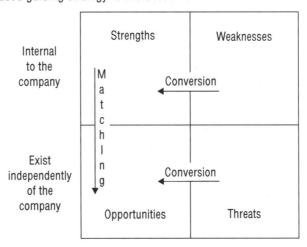

SWOT analysis model

(a) **Match strengths with market opportunities**
Strengths that do not match any available opportunity are of limited use while opportunities which do not have any matching strengths are of little immediate value.

(b) **Conversion**
This requires the development of strategies that will convert weaknesses into strengths in order to take advantage of some particular opportunity, or converting threats into opportunities which can then be matched by existing strengths.

The SWOT technique can also be used for specific areas of strategy such as IT and marketing.

10.2 Weirich's TOWS matrix   6/14, 6/12

Exam focus point

In the June 2014 exam, the compulsory question required students to recommend strategic options for each quadrant of a TOWS matrix applied to the company featured in the scenario. This requirement followed on from the preparation of a SWOT analysis. This requirement was not well answered. The examining team noted that some candidates got the quadrants of the matrix wrong, for example, by trying to find strengths to overcome weaknesses. As a result very few answers focused on strategic options.

Weirich, one of the earliest writers on corporate appraisal, originally spoke in terms of a **TOWS matrix** in order to emphasise the **importance of threats and opportunities**. This is therefore an inherently **positioning** approach to strategy. A further important element of Weirich's discussion was his categorisation of **strategic options** :

- SO strategies employ strengths to seize opportunities
- ST strategies employ strengths to counter or avoid threats
- WO strategies address weaknesses so as to be able to exploit opportunities
- WT strategies are defensive, aiming to avoid threats and the impact of weaknesses

One useful impact of this analysis is that **the four groups of strategies tend to relate well to different time horizons**. SO strategies may be expected to produce good short-term results, while WO strategies are likely to take much longer to show results. ST and WT strategies are more probably relevant to the medium term.

This consideration of time horizon may be linked to the **overall resource picture**: SO strategies can be profitable in the short term, generating the cash needed for investment in WO strategies, improving current areas of weakness so that further opportunities may be seized. ST and WT strategies are likely to be more or less resource-neutral, but care must be taken to achieve an overall balance.

It is important to remember the TOWS matrix when considering the strategic options available to an organisation. We will look at these strategic options later in this Study Text.

Exam focus point

Both SWOT analysis and the TOWS matrix are explicitly stated in the Study Guide, and so may be specifically required in an exam question.

Chapter Roundup

- A **position audit** is undertaken in order to give strategic managers a clear understanding of the organisation's **strategic capability**; that is, its resources, competences and the constraints that limit their use.

- **Resource audits** identify human, financial and material resources and how they are deployed.

- The resource-based approach to strategy starts from a consideration of capabilities and, in particular, of distinctive **competences** and **resources**.

- **Cost efficiency** is fundamental to strategic capability: the public sector demands value for money, while in the private sector, price competition makes cost efficiency fundamental to survival. Cost efficiency is achieved in four main ways.

    - Exploitation of **scale economies**
    - Control of the cost of **incoming supplies**
    - **Careful design** of products and processes
    - Exploitation of **experience effects**

- If strategy is to be based on strategic capabilities, those capabilities must have four qualities.

    - **Value to buyers**
    - **Rarity**
    - **Robustness** (difficult for competitors to imitate)
    - **Non-substitutability**

    Under conditions of **hyper-competition**, organisations must possess **dynamic capabilities:** the ability to develop and adjust competences to cope with rapidly changing environmental pressures.

- The aim of **knowledge management** is to capture, organise and make widely available all the knowledge the organisation possesses, whether **explicit** (in recorded form) or **tacit** (in people's heads).

- **Data** are simple facts that can be organised in a way that creates **information**. **Knowledge** is patterns of information that are strategically useful and context independent.

- Knowledge must be managed in a way that makes it easily available. Systems include office automation, groupware, intranets, extranets, expert systems and data mining.

- The **value chain** describes those activities of the organisation that add value to purchased inputs. Primary activities are involved in the production of goods and services. Support activities provide necessary assistance. **Linkages** are the relationships between activities.

- Core competences are the basis for the creation of value; activities from which the organisation does not derive significant value may be outsourced.

- The value network joins the organisation's value chain to those of its suppliers and customers.

- The **product life cycle** concept holds that products have a life cycle, and that a product demonstrates different characteristics of profit and investment at each stage in its life cycle. The life cycle concept is a model, not a prediction. (Not all products pass through each stage of the life cycle.) It enables a firm to examine its portfolio of goods and services as a whole.

- **Innovation** can be a major source of competitive advantage but brings a burden of cost and uncertainty. To avoid waste, there should be a programme of assessment for major product development. The firm must decide whether to be a leader or a follower.

- Research may be **pure, applied** or **development**. It may be intended to improve **products** or **processes**. New product development should be controlled by requiring strategic approval at key points of development.

Chapter Roundup (cont'd)

- R&D should support the organisation's strategy and be closely co-ordinated with marketing. There are distinct problems to managing R&D.

- **Intrapreneurship** is entrepreneurship carried on at intermediate levels within the organisation.

- **Benchmarking** enables a firm to meet industry standards by copying others, but it is perhaps less valuable as a source of innovation. It is a good way to challenge existing ways of doing things.

- Managers must take great care not to disrupt strategic capability that arises from flexible, informal practices by trying to systematise and improve them. However, a policy of gradual extension and improvement of desirable activities may be useful and may be combined with culling of superfluous ones. Also, since much strategic capability is traceable to individual skill and ability, good HRM practice can help to create and improve it.

- The **SWOT analysis** combines the results of the environmental analysis and the internal appraisal into one framework for assessing the firm's current and future strategic fit, or lack of it, with the environment. It is an analysis of the organisation's strengths and weaknesses, and the opportunities and threats offered by the environment. Weirich's TOWS matrix emphasises the importance of treats and opportunities.

Quick Quiz

1   What are the nine categories of resources described by the Ms Model?

2   What are core competences?

3   What four qualities enable a capability to form the basis of competitive advantage?

4   What is the difference between tacit and explicit knowledge?

5   What is a data warehouse?

6   Draw a value chain diagram.

7   What does the value chain illustrate?

8   List the stages of the product life cycle.

9   What are the three types of benchmarking described by *Johnson, Scholes and Whittington*?

10   What are the four types of strategy described by Weirich and based on the TOWS matrix?

1
- Machinery
- Make-up
- Management
- Management information
- Markets
- Materials
- Men and women
- Methods
- Money

2   Competences that underpin competitive advantage and that are difficult to imitate.

3   Value to buyers; rarity; robustness (difficulty of imitation); non-substitutability

4   Tacit knowledge exists only inside people's heads; explicit knowledge is recorded in some way.

5   A data warehouse receives data from operational systems and stores them in their most fundamental form, without any summarisation of transactions

6

SUPPORT ACTIVITIES	FIRM INFRASTRUCTURE					MARGIN
	HUMAN RESOURCE MANAGEMENT					
	TECHNOLOGY DEVELOPMENT					
	PROCUREMENT					
	INBOUND LOGISTICS	OPERATIONS	OUTBOUND LOGISTICS	MARKETING & SALES	SERVICE	MARGIN

PRIMARY ACTIVITIES

7   The value chain illustrates how value is created by value activities and the linkages between them, and that the customer is prepared to pay for that value. (Ultimately the value is created for the customer.)

8   Inception, growth, shakeout, maturity, decline

9   Historical; Industry/Sector; Best-in-class.

10   SO   Strategies employ strengths to seize opportunities.
     ST   Strategies employ strengths to counter or avoid threats.
     WO   Strategies address weaknesses so as to be able to exploit opportunities.
     WT   Strategies are defensive, aiming to avoid threats and the impact of weaknesses.

Now try the question below from the Practice Question Bank

Number	Level	Marks	Time
Q5	Exam	20	36 mins

Stakeholders, ethics, culture and integrated reporting

Topic list	Syllabus reference
1 Ethics and the organisation	A6(c)
2 Social responsibility	A6(b), (d)
3 Corporate governance	A6(a)
4 The role of culture	A6(e), (f)
5 Integrated reporting	A6 (h)

Introduction

Organisations are part of society and, like individual people, are subject to rules that govern their conduct towards others. Some of these rules are **law** and enforced by legal sanction. Other rules fall into the realm of **ethics** or morality and are enforced only by the strength of society's approval or disapproval. The first section of this chapter is concerned with the strategic impact of ethical ideas on organisations.

The behaviour of organisations may also be considered in the light of notions of **corporate social responsibility**. This is a rather poorly defined concept. However, there does now seem to be widespread acceptance that commercial organisations should devote some of their resources to the promotion of wider social aims that are not necessarily mandated by either law or the rules of ethics.

The third section of this chapter is concerned with **corporate governance** and the mechanisms that may be installed to promote fair and honest behaviour at the strategic apex.

The fourth section discusses the influence of culture on the organisation and its people. Finally, we conclude the chapter with a discussion of integrated reporting.

Study guide

		Intellectual level
A6	**The expectations of stakeholders and the influence of ethics and culture**	
(a)	Advise on the implications of corporate governance on organisational purpose and strategy	2
(b)	Evaluate, through stakeholder mapping, the relative influence of stakeholders on organisational purpose and strategy	3
(c)	Assess ethical influences on organisational purpose and strategy	3
(d)	Explore the scope of corporate social responsibility	3
(e)	Assess the impact of culture on organisational purpose and strategy	3
(f)	Prepare and evaluate a cultural web of an organisation	2
(h)	Explain the role of integrated reporting in communicating strategy and strategic performance	2

Exam guide

The importance of the topics covered in this chapter is indicated by the emphasis laid on them by all professional bodies. Ethics and social responsibility are things that are relevant to all behaviour, so could be included in a question on any topic.

In particular, there are likely to be stakeholder, ethical or cultural issues in most case studies.

Models and frameworks

This chapter refers to a number of models and frameworks. However, in your P3 exam, you will not be examined specifically on a single theory or model unless it is explicitly referenced in the Study Guide. You can see from the Study Guide (above) that you need to have a general understanding of these issues rather than learning the ideas of specific theorists in detail. However, because the Study Guide refers explicitly to the **cultural web** you may get a question which specifically requires you to use this model (which is covered in Section 4.3 of this Chapter).

The role of integrated reporting in communicating strategy is a new addition to the Study Guide. Since integrated reporting is mentioned explicitly in the Study Guide, it could be examined directly in an exam question, so you need to ensure you have a good understanding of it. Integrated reporting is covered in Section 5 of this chapter.

1 Ethics and the organisation

Knowledge brought forward from earlier studies

The syllabus for Paper F1 *Accountant in Business* includes sections on ethics, governance and social responsibility. You should already be familiar with many of the basic ideas underpinning this chapter. Also, if you have already studied Paper P1 *Governance, Risk & Ethics* you will have a detailed knowledge of these matters. Our coverage here is intended to provide a minimum of essential revision and new material relevant to the Business Analysis syllabus. However, if you do not feel comfortable with the underlying material here, you would be well advised to look back at your F1 Text.

FAST FORWARD

Ethics is about right and wrong but it is not the same thing as law or the rules of religion. Cognitive approaches to ethics assume that objective moral truths can be established.

1.1 Ethics and business

Ethics is concerned with right and wrong and how conduct should be judged to be good or bad. It is about how we should live our lives and, in particular, how we should behave towards other people. Business life is a fruitful source of ethical dilemmas because its whole purpose is material gain, the making of profit. Success in business requires a constant, avid search for potential advantage over others and business people are under pressure to do whatever yields such advantage.

1.2 Non-cognitivism, ethical relativism and intuitionism

The approach called **non-cognitivism** suggests that all moral statements are essentially subjective and arise from the culture, belief or emotion of the speaker.

Non-cognitivism recognises the differences that exist between the rules of behaviour prevailing in different cultures. The view that right and wrong are culturally determined is called **ethical relativism** or **moral relativism**. This is clearly a matter of significance in the context of **international business**. Managers encountering cultural norms of behaviour that differ significantly from their own may be puzzled to know what rules to follow.

1.3 Cognitivism

Cognitivist approaches to ethics are built on the principle that objective, universally applicable moral truths exist and can be known. There are four important cognitivist theories to consider after we have looked at **law** and **religion** in relation to ethics.

(a) Religions are based on the concept of universally applicable principles but they cannot be regarded as reliable guides to ethical conduct since they differ so much between themselves, forming, in fact the basis of the moral relativist approach. This problem may be approached by asking how does God decide what is right and what is wrong? Presumably, it is not mere whim and **moral principles** are involved. The implication is that it is proper to seek to understand these reasons for ourselves and to use them as the basis of our moral code.

(b) Cognitivist ethics and law can be seen as parallel and connected systems of rules for **regulating conduct**. Both are concerned with right conduct and the principles that define it. However, **ethics and law are not the same thing**. Law must be free from ambiguity. However, unlike law, ethics can quite reasonably be an arena for debate, about both the principles involved and their application in specific rules. The law must be certain and therefore finds it difficult to deal with problems of conduct that are subject to opinion and debate. Another difference is that many legal rules are only very remotely connected with ethics, if at all, and some laws in some countries have been of debateable moral stature, to say the least.

1.4 Consequentialist ethics: utilitarianism

FAST FORWARD

Consequentialist ethics judges actions by their outcomes; deontology assumes the existence of absolute moral principles and ignores outcomes. Natural law is about rights and duties, while virtue ethics is based on moderation in behaviour and the idea of leading a harmonious life.

Ethical theory is not integrated: consequentialist, deontological and natural law based rules are capable of pointing to different conclusions. Partly as a result of this, **ethical dilemmas** can exist at all levels in the organisation.

The **consequentialist** approach to ethics is to make moral judgements about courses of action by reference to their outcomes or consequences. Right or wrong becomes a question of benefit or harm.

Utilitarianism is the best-known formulation of this approach and can be summed up in the '**greatest good**' principle. This says that when deciding on a course of action we should choose the one that is likely to result in the greatest good for the greatest number of people.

There is an immediate problem here, which is how we are to define what is good for people.

The utilitarian approach may also be questioned for its potential effect upon minorities. A situation in which a large majority achieved great happiness at the expense of creating misery among a small minority would satisfy the 'greatest good' principle. It could not, however, be regarded as ethically desirable.

However, utilitarianism can be a useful guide to conduct. It has been used to derive wide ranging rules and can be applied to help us make judgements about individual, unique problems.

1.5 Deontological ethics

Deontology is concerned with the application of universal ethical principles in order to arrive at rules of conduct, the word deontology being derived from the Greek for 'duty'. Whereas the consequentialist approach judges actions by their outcomes, deontology lays down *a priori* criteria by which they may be judged in advance. The definitive treatment of deontological ethics is found in the work of Immanuel Kant.

Kant suggested that if we make moral judgements about facts, the criteria by which we judge are separate from the facts themselves: the criteria come from within ourselves and are based on an intuitive awareness of the nature of good.

For Kant, moral conduct is defined by categorical imperatives. A **categorical imperative**, however, defines a course of action without reference to outcomes. We must act in certain ways because it is right to do so – **right conduct is an end in itself**.

Kant arrived at two formulations of the categorical imperative with which we should be familiar:

(a)   Never act in a way that you would condemn in others.

(b)   Do not treat people simply as a means to an end. (Note that this does not preclude us from using people as a means to an end as long as we, at the same time, recognise their right to be treated as autonomous beings. Clearly, organisations and even society itself could not function if we could not make use of other people's services.)

1.6 Natural law

Natural law approaches to ethics are based on the idea that a set of objective or 'natural' moral rules exists and we can come to know what these rules are. In terms of business ethics, the natural law approach deals mostly with rights and duties. Where there is a right, there is also a duty to respect that right.

Unfortunately, the implications about duties can only be as clear as the rights themselves and there are wide areas in which disagreement about rights persists.

1.7 Duty and consequences

In their pure form, neither the duties of natural law nor Kant's categorical imperative will admit consideration of the consequences of our actions: we act in a certain way because we are obeying inflexible moral rules.

Unfortunately, such an approach can have undesirable results. If people have absolute rights that we must respect whatever the circumstances, we may find that our actions in doing so harm the common good. An example is the accused person who commits an offence while on bail. The potential threat to public safety has to be balanced against the right of the individual to liberty. There is thus a great potential for conflict between courses of action based on the consequentialist approach and those based on deontology or natural law.

While individual cases are bound to provoke debate, it would be reasonable to suggest that an inflexible approach to rules of conduct is likely to produce ethical dilemmas. Deciding what to do when the arguments point in opposite directions is always going to be difficult. However, generally we do not have the option of doing nothing, and this is particularly true of business.

1.8 Virtue ethics

The virtue ethics approach consists of pursuing a harmonious or virtuous life and a rational judgement about what constitutes good. To some extent, this consists of avoiding extremes of any kind. For example, courage lies between cowardice at one end of the scale and foolhardiness at the other. The cultivation of appropriate virtues has been proposed as a route to ethical behaviour in business. For example, managers might cultivate a range of virtues such as honesty, courage, fairness and firmness.

1.9 Ethics and strategy

In this Study Text we have emphasised that what the organisation wishes to achieve – its **mission** – is fundamental to any focussed control of its activities. When we discussed the concept of mission, we made passing reference to **policies and standards of behaviour**.

It is important to understand that if ethics is applicable to corporate behaviour at all, it must therefore be a fundamental aspect of **mission**, since everything the organisation does flows from that. Managers responsible for strategic decision making cannot avoid responsibility for their organisation's ethical standing. They should consciously apply ethical rules to all of their decisions in order to filter out potentially undesirable developments.

An understanding of the everyday ethical dilemmas that you may face in your career is outlined in the next section. It is worth taking the time to read this carefully as it provides some useful background reading before attempting the professional ethics module.

1.10 Ethical dilemmas

There are a number of areas in which the various approaches to ethics and conflicting views of business responsibility can create **ethical dilemmas** for managers. These can impact at the highest level, affecting the development of policy, or lower down the hierarchy, especially if policy is unclear and guidance from more senior people is unavailable.

Dealing with **unpleasantly authoritarian governments** can be supported on the grounds that it contributes to economic growth and prosperity and all the benefits they bring to society in both countries concerned. This is a consequentialist argument. It can also be opposed on consequentialist grounds as contributing to the continuation of the regime, and on deontological grounds as fundamentally repugnant.

Honesty in advertising is an important problem. Many products are promoted exclusively on image. Deliberately creating the impression that purchasing a particular product will enhance the happiness, success and sex-appeal of the buyer can be attacked as dishonest. It can be defended on the grounds that the supplier is actually selling a fantasy or dream, rather than a physical article.

Dealings with **employees** are coloured by the opposing views of corporate responsibility and individual rights. The idea of a job as property to be defended has now disappeared from UK labour relations, but there is no doubt that corporate decisions that lead to redundancies are still deplored. This is because of the obvious impact of sudden unemployment on aspirations and living standards, even when the employment market is buoyant. Nevertheless, it is only proper for businesses to consider the cost of employing labour as well as its productive capacity. Even employers who accept that their employees' skills are their most important source of competitive advantage can be reduced to cost cutting in order to survive in lean times.

Another ethical problem concerns **payments by companies to officials** who have power to help or hinder the payers' operations. In *The Ethics of Corporate Conduct,* Clarence Walton discusses the fine distinctions which exist in this area.

(a) **Extortion**. Foreign officials have been known to threaten companies with the complete closure of their local operations unless suitable payments are made.

(b) **Bribery**. This is payments for services to which a company is not legally entitled. There are some fine distinctions to be drawn; for example, some managers regard political contributions as bribery.

(c)   **Grease money**. Multinational companies are sometimes unable to obtain services to which they are legally entitled because of deliberate stalling by local officials. Cash payments to the right people may then be enough to oil the machinery of bureaucracy.

(d)   **Gifts**. In some cultures (such as Japan) gifts are regarded as an essential part of civilised negotiation, even in circumstances where to Western eyes they might appear ethically dubious. Managers operating in such a culture may feel at liberty to adopt the local customs.

Business ethics are also relevant to competitive behaviour. This is because a market can only be free if competition is, in some basic respects, fair. There is a distinction between competing aggressively and competing unethically.

1.11 The scope of corporate ethics

FAST FORWARD

Corporate ethics has three contexts.

- Interaction with national and international society
- Effects of routine operations
- Behaviour of individuals

If constructed with care, a corporate ethical code can be valuable.

Corporate ethics may be considered in three contexts.

- The organisation's interaction with **national** and **international society**
- The effects of the organisation's **routine operations**
- The behaviour of **individual members** of staff

Influencing society. The organisation operates within and interacts with the political, economic and social framework of wider society. It is both inevitable and proper that it will both influence and be influenced by that wider framework. Governments, individual politicians and pressure groups will all make demands on such matters as employment prospects and executive pay. Conversely, organisations themselves will find that they need to make their own representations on such matters as monetary policy and the burden of regulation. International variation in such matters and in the framework of **corporate governance** will affect organisations that operate in more than one country. It is appropriate that the organisation develops and promotes its own policy on such matters.

Corporate behaviour. The organisation should establish **corporate policies** for those issues over which it has direct control. Examples of matters that should be covered by policy include health, safety, labelling, equal opportunities, environmental effects, political activity, bribery and support for cultural activities.

Individual behaviour. Policies to guide the behaviour of individuals are likely to flow from the corporate stance on the matters discussed above. The organisation must decide on the extent to which it considers it appropriate to attempt to influence individual behaviour. Some aspects of such behaviour may be of strategic importance, especially when managers can be seen as representing or embodying the organisation's standards. Matters of financial rectitude and equal treatment of minorities are good examples here.

Corporate ethical codes. Organisations often publish corporate codes of ethical standards. Fundamentally, this is a good idea and can be a useful way of disseminating the specific policies we have discussed above. However, care must be taken over such a document.

(a)   It should not be over-prescriptive or over-detailed, since this encourages a legalistic approach to interpretation and a desire to seek loopholes in order to justify previously chosen courses of action.

(b)   It will only have influence if senior management adhere to it consistently in their own decisions and actions.

Ethical codes and policies on behaviour can, of course, be linked to and summarised in the **mission statement**.

It is important to note, however, that managers need not be corrupt in order to fail in their responsibilities or duties to their organisations. The CEO who sets in motion a takeover bid that will enhance his prestige, the head of department who 'empire builds', and the IT manager who buys an unnecessarily sophisticated system are all failing in their responsibilities to the owners of the company (usually, the shareholders) even though they have not acted illegally or received any material benefit themselves.

 Case Study

Bonus culture in the banking industry

The former bosses of the two biggest casualties of the 2008 banking crisis in the UK have apologised 'profoundly and unreservedly' for their banks' failure.

Former Royal Bank of Scotland (RBS) chief executive Sir Fred Goodwin told MPs on the Treasury Committee that he 'could not be more sorry' for what happened. He also admitted that the bonus culture in banks had contributed to the crisis and needed to be reviewed.

But he added if bankers felt they were not paid enough, they would leave.

Andy Hornby, former CEO of HBOS, also conceded that the culture of cash bonuses needed looking at. 'The bonus system has proved to be wrong. Substantial cash bonuses do not reward the right kind of behaviour,' he said.

However, when he was asked whether the bonus culture encouraged excessive risk taking and had exacerbated the banking crisis, Sir Fred Goodwin argued that traders were trading within set limits, and were simply doing 'what they were authorised to do.'

However, a rather different picture is emerging from HBOS. It has emerged that a senior HBOS employee was sacked in 2004 for warning that the bank's risky sales culture could 'lead to disaster.' Paul Moore – who was head of group regulatory risk – was dismissed for pointing out that the bank was ignoring checks and balances. He argued that 'anyone whose eyes were not blinded by money, power and pride' would have realised that problems were building up for HBOS and other banks.

Mr Moore also insisted that the subsequent banking crisis could have been avoided if there were adequate systems to hold bank chiefs to account. The real problem, and the cause of this crisis, was that people were too afraid to speak up, and the balance of power was weighted far too much in favour of the executive.

Nonetheless, bonuses and poor internal controls were not the only cause of the bank's problems.

Sir Fred Goodwin oversaw a number of acquisitions that made RBS one of the world's biggest banks. But his takeover of Dutch rival ABN Amro late in 2007 is now seen as ill-timed and a deal too far, in the light of RBS's inability to survive the credit crunch without a massive injection of Government funds.

Sir Fred admitted that the deal to buy ABN was 'a big mistake'. 'We bought it at the top of the market, and anything we paid was an error. We are sorry we bought ABN Amro,' he added.

Adapted from an online article:

'Former banking bosses say sorry' (February 2011) published on the *BBC website*; www.bbc.co.uk

2 Social responsibility

FAST FORWARD

There is a fundamental split of views about the organisation's relationship with its stakeholders and the nature of corporate responsibility.

- The **strong view** that a range of goals should be pursued
- The **weak view** that the business organisation is a purely **economic force**, subject to law

2.1 Stakeholders

Knowledge brought forward from earlier studies

The syllabus for Paper F1 *Accountant in Business* includes material on stakeholders. You should, therefore, be familiar with many of the ideas in this section. The coverage here is intended to provide a minimum of essential revision coupled with new material relevant to the P3 syllabus. If you do not feel comfortable with the underlying material here, you should look back at your F1 Text.

FAST FORWARD

Stakeholders have an interest in what the organisation does.

Key term

Stakeholders: groups or individuals whose interests are directly affected by the activities of a firm or organisation

Here are some stakeholder groups:

Stakeholder group	Members
• Internal stakeholders	Employees, management
• Connected	Shareholders, customers, suppliers, lenders
• External	The government, local government, the public

Stakeholder groups can exert influence on strategy. The greater the power of a stakeholder group, the greater its influence will be. Each stakeholder group has different expectations about what it wants, and the expectations of the various groups will conflict. To some extent, the expectations of stakeholders will influence the organisation's mission.

2.1.1 Stakeholders' objectives

Here is a checklist of stakeholders' objectives. It is not comprehensive.

(a) **Employees and managers**

    (i)   Job security (over and above legal protection)
    (ii)   Good conditions of work (above minimum safety standards)
    (iii) Job satisfaction
    (iv) Career development and relevant training

(b) **Customers**

    (i)   Products of a certain quality at a reasonable price
    (ii)   Products that should last a certain number of years
    (iii) A product or service that meets customer needs.

(c) **Suppliers**: regular orders in return for reliable delivery and good service

(d) **Shareholders**: long-term wealth

(e) **Providers of loan capital (stock holders):** reliable payment of interest due and maintenance of the value of any security.

(f) **Society as a whole**

    (i)   Control pollution
    (ii)   Financial assistance to charities, sports and community activities
    (iii) Co-operate with government in identifying and preventing health hazards

2.1.2 Competitors

Competitors can be stakeholders. You may find this easier to understand if you think of all the competitors in a given industry as stakeholders in that industry's overall status and the public's perception.

2.1.3 Stakeholder risks

Stakeholder	Interests to defend	Response to risk
Internal Managers and employees (eg restructuring, relocation)	• Jobs/careers • Money • Promotion • Benefits • Satisfaction	• Pursuit of systems goals rather than shareholder interests • Industrial action • Negative power to impede implementation • Refusal to relocate • Resignation
Connected Shareholders (corporate strategy)	• Increase in shareholder wealth, measured by profitability, P/E ratios, market capitalisation, dividends and yield • Risk	• Sell shares (eg to predator) or replace management
Bankers (cash flows)	• Security of loan • Adherence to loan agreements	• Denial of credit • Higher interest charges • Receivership
Suppliers (purchase strategy)	• Profitable sales • Payment for goods • Long-term relationship	• Refusal of credit • Court action • Wind down relationships
Customers (product market strategy)	• Goods as promised • Future benefits	• Buy elsewhere • Complain • Sue
External Government	• Jobs, training, tax	• Tax increases • Regulation • Legal action
Interest/pressure groups	• Pollution • Rights • Other	• Publicity • Direct action • Sabotage • Pressure on government

How stakeholders relate to the management of the company depends very much on what **type of stakeholder** they are – internal, connected or external – and on the **level in the management hierarchy** at which they are able to apply pressure. Clearly a company's management will respond differently to the demands of, say, its shareholders and the community at large.

2.2 Balancing priorities

Cyert and March suggest that a business is actually run in the interests of an **organisational coalition** of stakeholders. Political processes managed by the strategic apex lead to a compromise on what the company's goals actually are. This usually results in a satisficing approach to balance the various priorities.

2.3 Stakeholder theory

We may discern two extreme approaches to stakeholder theory for profit-orientated business organisations.

Strong view	Weak view
Each stakeholder in the business has a legitimate claim on management attention. Management's job is to balance stakeholder demands.	Satisfying stakeholders such as customers is a good thing – but only because it enables the business to satisfy its primary purpose, the long-term growth in owner wealth.

2.3.1 Problems with the strong stakeholder view

(a) Managers who are accountable to everyone are, in fact, accountable to no one.

(b) If managers are required to balance different stakeholders' interests, there is a danger that they will favour their own interests.

(c) It confuses a stakeholder's interest in a firm with a person's citizenship of a state.

(d) People have interests, but this does not give them rights.

2.4 Managing stakeholders   12/09

FAST FORWARD

An organisation's stakeholder relationships must be managed in accordance with their bargaining strength, influence, power and degree of interest. *Mendelow* summarises the possibilities in his stakeholder map. Stakeholders have three options: loyalty, exit and voice.

The way in which the relationship between company and stakeholders is conducted is a function of the parties' **relative bargaining strength** and the philosophy underlying **each party's objectives**. This can be shown by means of a spectrum.

2.4.1 Stakeholder mapping

Mendelow classifies stakeholders on a matrix whose axes are power held and likelihood of showing an interest in the organisation's activities. These factors will help define the type of relationship the organisation should seek with its stakeholders.

Level of interest

	Low	High
Low	A	B
Power		
High	C	D

Mendelow's matrix

(a) **Key players** are found in segment D: strategy must be *acceptable* to them, at least. An example would be a major customer.

(b) Stakeholders in segment C must be treated with care. While often passive, they are capable of moving to segment D. They should, therefore be **kept satisfied.** Large institutional shareholders might fall into segment C.

(c) Stakeholders in segment B do not have great ability to influence strategy, but their views can be important in influencing more powerful stakeholders, perhaps by lobbying. They should therefore be **kept informed.** Community representatives and charities might fall into segment B.

(d) Minimal effort is expended on segment A.

Stakeholder mapping is used to assess the significance of stakeholder groups. This, in turn, has implications for the organisation.

(a) The framework of **corporate governance** should recognise stakeholders' levels of interest and power.

(b) It may be appropriate to seek to **reposition** certain stakeholders and discourage others from repositioning themselves, depending on their attitudes.

(c) Key **blockers** and **facilitators** of change must be identified.

Stakeholder mapping can also be used to establish **political priorities**. A map of the current position can be compared with a map of a desired future state. This will indicate critical shifts that must be pursued.

Exam focus point

Stakeholders and their influence are regular features of business strategy exam questions.

Mendelow's Matrix is not mentioned explicitly in the P3 Study Guide, so you will not have a question specifically about it.

However, the Study Guide does state that you need to be able to 'Evaluate, through stakeholder mapping, the relative influence of stakeholders on organisational purpose and strategy'. Mendelow's Matrix would be a very useful framework for any such stakeholder mapping.

2.4.2 The internal and external coalitions

In *Power In and Around Organisations*, Mintzberg identifies groups that not only have an **interest** in an organisation but **power** over it:

The external coalition	The internal coalition
• Owners (who hold legal title)	• The chief executive and board at the strategic apex
• Associates (suppliers, customers, trading partners)	• Line managers
• Employee associations (unions, professional bodies)	• Operators
	• The technostructure
• Public (government, media)	• Support staff
	• Ideology (ie culture)

Each of these groups has three basic choices:

(a) **Loyalty**. They can do as they are told.

(b) **Exit**. For example by selling their shares, or getting a new job.

(c) **Voice**. They can stay and try to change the system. Those who choose **voice** are those who can, to varying degrees, influence the organisation. Influence implies a degree of power and willingness to exercise it.

Existing **structures and systems** can **channel stakeholder influence.**

(a) They are the **location of power**, giving groups of people varying degrees of influence over strategic choices.

(b) They are **conduits of information**, which shape strategic decisions.

(c) They **limit choices** or give some options priority over others. These may be physical or ethical constraints over what is possible.

(d) They **embody culture**.

(e) They **determine the successful implementation** of strategy.

(f) The **firm has different degrees of dependency** on various stakeholder groups. A company with a cash flow crisis will be more beholden to its bankers than one with regular cash surpluses.

Different stakeholders will have their own views as to strategy. As some stakeholders have **negative power**, in other words power to impede or disrupt the decision, their likely response might be considered.

2.5 Corporate social responsibility

FAST FORWARD

> The extent to which an organisation recognises obligations to society in general is as much subject to debate as its relationships with stakeholder groups.

Businesses, particularly large ones, are subject to increasing expectations that they will exercise **social responsibility**. This is an ill-defined concept, but appears to focus on the provision of **specific benefits to society in general**, such as charitable donations, the creation or preservation of employment, and spending on environmental improvement or maintenance. A great deal of the pressure is created by the activity of minority action groups and is aimed at businesses because they are perceived to possess extensive resources.

The momentum of such arguments is now so great that the notion of social responsibility has become almost inextricably confused with the matter of ethics. It is important to remember the distinction. **Social responsibility** and **ethical behaviour** are **not the same thing**.

In this context, you should remember that a business managed with the sole objective of maximising shareholder wealth can be run in just as ethical a fashion as one in which far wider stakeholder responsibility is assumed. On the other hand, there is no doubt that many large businesses have behaved irresponsibly in the past and some continue to do so.

2.6 Against corporate social responsibility

Milton Friedman argued against corporate social responsibility along the following lines.

(a) Businesses do not have responsibilities, only people have responsibilities. Managers in charge of corporations are responsible to the owners of the business, by whom they are employed.

(b) These employers may have charity as their aim, but 'generally [their aim] will be to make as much money as possible while conforming to the basic rules of the society, both those embodied in law and those embodied in ethical custom.'

(c) If the statement that a manager has social responsibilities is to have any meaning, 'it must mean that he is to act in some way that is not in the interest of his employers.'

(d) If managers do this, they are, generally speaking, spending the owners' money for purposes other than those they have authorised; sometimes it is the money of customers or suppliers that is spent and, on occasion, the money of employees. By doing this, the manager is, in effect, both raising taxes and deciding how they should be spent, which are functions of government, not of business. There are two objections to this:

   (i) Managers have not been democratically elected (or selected in any other way) to exercise government power.

   (ii) Managers are not experts in government policy and cannot foresee the detailed effect of such social responsibility spending.

Friedman argues that the social responsibility model is politically **collectivist** in nature and deplores the possibility that collectivism should be extended any further than absolutely necessary in a free society.

A second argument against the assumption of corporate social responsibility is that the **maximisation of wealth is the best way that society can benefit from businessactivities**.

(a) Maximising wealth has the effect of increasing the tax revenues available to the state to disburse on socially desirable objectives.

(b) Maximising shareholder value has a 'trickle down' effect on other disadvantaged members of society.

(c) Many company shares are owned by pension funds, whose ultimate beneficiaries may not be the wealthy anyway.

2.7 The stakeholder approach to corporate social responsibility

The **stakeholder approach is based on the premise** that many groups have a stake in what the organisation does. This is particularly important in the business context, where shareholders own the business but employees, customers and government also have particularly strong claims to having their interests considered. This is fundamentally an argument derived from **natural law theory** and is based on the notion of individual and collective **rights**.

It is suggested that modern corporations are so powerful socially, economically and politically, that **unrestrained use of their power will inevitably damage other people's rights**. For example, they may blight an entire community by closing a major facility, thus enforcing long-term unemployment on a large proportion of the local workforce. Similarly, they may damage people's quality of life by polluting the environment. They may use their purchasing power or market share to impose unequal contracts on suppliers and customers alike. They may also exercise undesirable influence over government through their investment decisions. Under this approach, the exercise of corporate social responsibility constrains the corporation to act at all times as a good citizen.

Another argument points out that corporations exist within society and are **dependent upon it for the resources they use**. Some of these resources are obtained by direct contracts with suppliers but others are not, being provided by **government expenditure**. Examples are such things as transport infrastructure,

technical research and education for the workforce. Clearly, corporations contribute to the taxes that pay for these things, but the relationship is rather tenuous and the tax burden can be minimised by careful management. The implication is that corporations should recognise and pay for the facilities that society provides by means of socially responsible policies and actions.

Henry Mintzberg (in *Power In and Around Organisations*) suggests that simply viewing organisations as vehicles for shareholder investment is inadequate.

(a) In practice, he says, organisations are rarely controlled effectively by shareholders. Most shareholders are passive investors.

(b) Large corporations can manipulate markets. Social responsibility, forced or voluntary, is a way of recognising this.

(c) Moreover, as mentioned above, businesses do receive a lot of government support. The public pays for roads, infrastructure, education and health, all of which benefits businesses. Although businesses pay tax, the public ultimately pays, perhaps through higher prices.

(d) Strategic decisions by businesses always have wider social consequences. In other words, says Mintzberg, the firm produces two kinds of outputs: **goods and services** and the **social consequences of its activities** (eg pollution).

2.8 Externalities

FAST FORWARD

There is particular concern over **externalities**, or the social and environmental costs of corporate activities.

If it is accepted that businesses do not bear the **total social cost of their activities**, then the exercise of social responsibility is a way of compensating for this. An example is given by the environment. Industrial pollution is injurious to health: if someone is made ill by industrial pollution, then arguably the polluter should pay the sick person, as damages or in compensation, in the same way as if a construction company had accidentally bulldozed somebody's house.

In practice, of course, while it is relatively easy to identify statistical relationships between pollution levels and certain illnesses, mapping out the chain of cause and effect from an individual's wheezing cough to the dust particles emitted by Factory X, as opposed to Factory Y, is quite a different matter.

Of course, it could be argued that these external costs are met out of general taxation: but this has the effect of spreading the cost amongst other individuals and businesses. Moreover, the tax revenue may be spent on curing the disease, rather than stopping it at its source. Pollution control equipment may be the fairest way of dealing with this problem. Thus advocates of social responsibility in business would argue that responsibilities of business then do not rest with paying taxes.

Is there any justification for social responsibility outside remedying the effects of a business's direct activities? For example, should businesses give to charity or sponsor the arts? Several arguments have been advanced suggesting that they should.

(a) If the **stakeholder concept** of a business is held, then the public is a stakeholder in the business. A business only succeeds because it is part of a wider society. Giving to charity is one way of encouraging a relationship.

(b) Charitable donations and artistic sponsorship are a useful medium of **public relations** and can reflect well on the business. It can be regarded, then, as another form of promotion, which like advertising, serves to enhance consumer awareness of the business, while not encouraging the sale of a particular brand.

The arguments for and against social responsibility are complex ones. However, ultimately they can be traced to **different assumptions about society** and the relationships between the individuals and organisations within it.

2.9 The ethical stance

FAST FORWARD

An organisation's **ethical stance** is the extent to which it will exceed its minimum obligations to stakeholders. There are four typical stances.

- Short-term shareholder interest
- Long-term shareholder interest
- Multiple stakeholder obligations
- Shaper of society

Key term

An organisation's **ethical stance** is defined by JS&W as the extent to which it will exceed its minimum obligation to stakeholders and society at large.

JS&W illustrate the range of possible ethical stances by giving four illustrations.

- **Short-term shareholder interest**
- **Long-term shareholder interest**
- **Multiple stakeholder obligations**
- **Shaper of society**

2.9.1 Short-term shareholder interest

An organisation might limit its ethical stance to taking responsibility for **short-term shareholder interest** on the grounds that it is for **government** alone to impose wider constraints on corporate governance. This minimalist approach would accept a duty of obedience to the demands of the law, but would not undertake to comply with any less substantial rules of conduct. This stance can be justified on the grounds that going beyond it can **challenge government authority**; this is an important consideration for organisations operating in developing countries.

2.9.2 Long-term shareholder interest

There are two reasons why an organisation might take a wider view of ethical responsibilities when considering the **longer-term interest of shareholders**.

(a)   The organisation's **corporate image** may be enhanced by an assumption of wider responsibilities. The cost of undertaking such responsibilities may be justified as essentially promotional expenditure.

(b)   The responsible exercise of corporate power may prevent a build-up of social and political **pressure for legal regulation**. Freedom of action may be preserved and the burden of regulation lightened by acceptance of ethical responsibilities.

2.9.3 Multiple stakeholder obligations

An organisation might accept the **legitimacy of the expectations of stakeholders other than shareholders** and build those expectations into its stated purposes. This would be because, without appropriate relationships with groups such as suppliers, employers and customers, the organisation would not be able to function.

A distinction can be drawn between **rights** and **expectations**. The *Concise Oxford Dictionary* defines a right as 'a legal or moral entitlement'. One is on fairly safe interpretative ground with legal rights, since their basis is usually clearly established, though subject to development and adjustment. The concept of **moral** entitlement is much less well defined and subject to partisan argument, as discussed above in the context of **natural law**. There is, for instance, an understandable tendency for those who feel themselves aggrieved to declare that their **rights** have been infringed. Whether or not this is the case is often a matter of opinion. For example, in the UK, there is often talk of a 'right to work' when redundancies occur. No such right exists in UK law, nor is it widely accepted that there is a moral basis for such a right. However, there is a widespread acceptance that governments should make the prevention of large-scale unemployment a high priority.

Clearly, organisations have a duty to respect the **legal rights** of stakeholders other than shareholders. These are extensive in the UK, including wide-ranging **employment law** and **consumer protection law**, as well as the more basic legislation relating to such matters as contract and property. Where **moral entitlements** are concerned, organisations need to be practical: they should take care to establish just what **expectations** they are prepared to treat as **obligations**, bearing in mind their general ethical stance and degree of concern about bad publicity.

Acceptance of obligations to stakeholders implies that **measurement of the organisation's performance** must give due weight to these extra imperatives. For instance, as is widely known, the late Anita Roddick did not care to have the performance of Body Shop assessed in purely financial terms. Instead, she wanted performance to be measured in terms of addressing climate change through reducing energy usage, defending human rights by improving the working conditions in their suppliers' organisations, and upholding animal rights by ensuring that no animals were used in the testing of toiletries or cosmetics.

2.9.4 Shaper of society

It is difficult enough for a commercial organisation to accept wide responsibility to stakeholders. The role of **shaper of society** is even more demanding and largely the province of public sector organisations and charities, though some well-funded private organisations might act in this way. The legitimacy of this approach depends on the framework of corporate governance and accountability. Where organisations are clearly set up for such a role, either by government or by private sponsors, they may pursue it. However, they must also satisfy whatever requirements for financial viability are established for them.

3 Corporate governance

Corporate governance is the conduct of the organisation's senior officers. Abuses have led to a range of measures to improve corporate governance. Non-executive directors have a particular role to play.

Key term

The conduct of an organisation's senior officers constitutes its **corporate governance**.

3.1 The governance framework

JS&W say that the most fundamental expectations of organisations concern who they should serve and how their direction and purposes should be determined. This is the province of corporate governance, which is also concerned with the supervision and accountability of executives.

Key term

The **governance framework** describes whom the organisation is there to serve and how the purposes and priorities of the organisation should be decided.

JS&W

3.1.1 The governance chain

Where the management of a business is separated from its ownership by the employment of professional managers, the managers may be considered to be the agents of the owners. **Agency theory** is concerned with adverse selection and moral hazard, the problems that arise as a result of the separation of ownership and control. In many organisations, corporate governance takes the form of a chain of responsibility and accountability.

Few large businesses are directly managed by their owners. In the case of larger companies, the shareholders may be numerous and unlikely to wish to take part in the management of the company, viewing it simply as a vehicle for investment. Even where ownership is concentrated, large companies tend to be managed mostly by professional managers who have little ownership interest, if any.

In most large commercial organisations, the situation is even more complex in that governance is exercised through many links in a chain. Managers are accountable to more senior managers and so on, up to the board of directors. The directors enjoy an element of autonomy, but in many cases, they will effectively be accountable to the representatives of a few large institutional shareholders or perhaps those of a single venture capital company. The chain of accountability may then continue, with those representatives themselves accountable ultimately to the individual savers and investors that provide their funds.

This **separation of ownership from control** has been a feature of business for over a century and brings with it a recurring problem: the business should be managed so as to promote the economic interest of the shareholders as a body, but the power to manage lies in the hands of people who may use it to promote their own interests. How may such **conflicts of interest** be resolved and managers be made to favour the interest of the owners, rather than their own?

This problem is not confined to the management of companies: it is the general problem of the **agency relationship** and occurs whenever one person (the **principal**) gives another (the **agent**) power to deal with his or her affairs. The relationship between principal and agent has been subjected to some quite abstruse economic and mathematical analysis; this area of study is called **agency theory**. It proceeds on the basis that principals and agents are rational utility maximisers.

Two important concepts are used to explain the things that can go wrong in the agency relationship: **adverse selection** and **moral hazard**.

> **Adverse selection** is the making of poor choices. It occurs perhaps most often because the chooser lacks the information necessary to make a good choice.

Adverse selection can be exacerbated in the agency relationship when the agent has an incentive to withhold information from the principal, thus creating **information asymmetry**. We see this in two important instances:

(a) **Appointment of the agent**: the principal attempts to appoint a competent and trustworthy agent, but potential agents thus have an incentive to conceal any evidence there may be that they are incompetent or untrustworthy.

(b) **Assessing the agent's performance**: the principal desires to reward the agent according to the standard of their performance, but the agent controls or is able to influence the information the principal uses to assess that performance.

Disclosure is thus a major theme in corporate governance.

> **Moral hazard** arises whenever people are protected from the adverse consequences of their actions; they have no incentive to exercise correct judgement and are free to act in an irresponsible manner.

To protect a person from the adverse consequences of their behaviour is to encourage irresponsibility, hence the moral dimension of the concept.

Moral hazard is not confined to principal-agent relationships. It occurs in banking, for example, when government guarantee schemes allow bankers to make injudicious loans.

In the agency relationship, we are concerned with the use the agent makes of the authority with which they have been entrusted. Moral hazard will exist unless at least part of the agent's remuneration is contingent upon them making responsible use of their authority.

Agency theory is clearly relevant to the modern business organisation. The directors are the agents of the shareholders, employed to manage the business in the shareholders' interest. To do this they are given considerable power over the resources of the business. How can the shareholders be sure that they will not abuse this trust?

To a lesser extent, agency theory also applies within the organisation. The directors cannot do everything: as we have said, they must employ subordinate managers to put their plans into action. How can the directors be sure that those subordinates are not abusing their trust?

They rely to an increasing extent on the initiative, skills, creativity and enthusiasm of quite junior members of the organisation, since this is what creates competitive advantage. They also depend on both motivating and empowering these employees. Therefore, the issue of trust comes to prominence.

Agency theory is thus very relevant to the fields of both performance measurement and executive compensation. **Moral hazard** can be reduced by making the rewards paid to the directors and managers contingent upon their satisfactory performance: the information asymmetry that leads to **adverse selection** can be reduced by making proper information about that performance available to the shareholders (in the case of the directors) and to the directors (in the case of the subordinate managers).

3.1.2 The board of directors

FAST FORWARD

There are four models of governance:

1   The Anglo-Saxon model is fast in action but may be short-termist and unresponsive to external criticism.
2   The Rhine model has more robust governance and takes a long view of investment.
3   The Japanese model values consensus, takes a very long view and makes decisions slowly. Accountability and governance may be poor.
4   The Latin model emphasises the role of the state: investment is likely to be for the very long-term but governance may suffer from political activity.

Most organisations will have some kind of governing body. In the private sector, we are used to the concept of the board of directors; not-for-profit organisations are likely to have a board of trustees and, possibly, an executive committee of professional managers as well; while public sector organisations will usually have a similar body in overall charge.

The characteristics, role and functioning of boards of directors vary across the world: Michel Albert distinguishes three typical forms of corporate governance: the **Anglo-Saxon**, the **Rhine** and the **Japanese**. The first differs from the other two in that shares in such companies tend to be widely held in small quantities, which tends to permit significant autonomy to a small number of senior managers. In the other two models, top management is more **collective** in nature involving a larger team, and is responsible to a more stable body representing outside interests, such as founding family shareholders and trade unions in the Rhine model; and large institutions, in the Japanese models.

JS&W discuss a fourth model: this is the **Latin**, typical of France, Spain and Italy.

The Anglo-Saxon model

The Anglo-Saxon model is found in the UK, the US and Australasia. There is a single level of board membership, which includes both executive and non-executive directors. The effectiveness of the non-executive directors in curbing the power of the executives varies. The wide spread of shareholding found in many large companies tends to limit the power of individual shareholders, though major institutional shareholders such as pension funds are becoming more assertive.

Corporate finance emphasises the dominant position of equity and relationships with banks tend to be contractually-based. This can lead to difficulties, since banks' own commercial considerations may lead them to withdraw funds. Shareholders thus assume most of the burden of financial risk and limit the extent of gearing as a result.

This kind of company tends to be very market-oriented, internationalised and able to raise and use large amounts of capital. However, it has been criticised for being unstable, for taking a short-term view of strategy and for poor standards of corporate governance.

The Rhine model

The Rhine model is found in such countries as Germany, the Netherlands and Switzerland; and, to some extent, in France. The two-tier board is common (and may be mandatory), with strong employee representation on the supervisory board and an emphasis on co-determination, or joint decision-making.

There are robust procedures for corporate governance. The supervisory board restrains the autonomy of the managerial professionals on the lower tier board.

Such companies have a long-term strategy with stable capital investment policies. However, they tend to be inflexible and slow to invest in new industries and international projects.

The Japanese model

Japanese business culture is respectful of consensus and rather patriarchal. Promotion to the board is decided by the Chairman after consultation, often with interested external parties such as bankers. Directors are expected to promote the interests of employees as a matter of course. Governance procedures tend to be secretive and can be corrupt, with weak accountability. A very long view is taken of industrial strategy and capital investment is stable, though there can be an element of financial speculation. Decision-making can be very slow.

Banks have extensive shareholdings as well as making loans and take a close interest in the management of the companies they finance. In times of difficulty, they are more likely to promote change, rather than simply withdrawing funds.

The Latin model

The Latin model features heavy state involvement in business and industrial strategy, with consistency between political, economic and administrative goals. Investment is very stable. However, government involvement can lead to over-emphasis on political priorities and over-intimate relations between directors, politicians and civil servants.

3.1.3 Governance and strategy

FAST FORWARD ▶▶

The board must decide the extent of its involvement in the strategic process. If it decides on a stewardship role, it must ensure that the organisation's activity is not directed to management's own ends, rather than those of legitimate stakeholders. If it engages in the strategic process, it must act independently of management and in a competent fashion.

Directors' involvement in the making of strategy may be limited to a stewardship role in which the board delegates the process to full-time executives, retaining only a final approval role. When this is done, the board must take steps to prevent the executives from pursuing their own interest, rather than those of legitimate stakeholders.

There are a number of ways in which the board can engage in the strategic process: some of these are discussed elsewhere in this Study Text. Directors who take part in the making of strategy must be competent and have sufficient time to do so. They must ensure that they act independently in the interests of stakeholders and pay proper attention to personal and collective accountability and performance assessment.

3.2 The driving forces of governance development

Corporate governance issues came to prominence in the US during the 1970s; and in the UK and Europe, from the late 1980s. There were several reasons why this happened.

(a) **Increasing internationalisation and globalisation** meant that investors, and institutional investors in particular, began to invest outside their home countries. This lead to calls for companies to operate in an acceptable fashion and to report corporate performance fairly.

(b) Issues concerning **financial reporting** were raised by many investors and were the focus of much debate and litigation. Shareholder confidence in many instances was eroded and, while focus solely on accounting and reporting issues is inadequate, the regulation of practices such as off-balance sheet financing has led to greater transparency and a reduction in risks faced by investors.

(c) An increasing number of **high profile corporate scandals** and collapses including Polly Peck International, BCCI, and Maxwell Communications Corporation prompted the development of

governance codes in the early 1990s. However, the scandals since then such as Enron, Parmalat and WorldCom have raised questions about further measures that may be necessary.

The speed and severity of the downturn in the global financial system in 2008-09 also suggest that more stringent controls and regulation over the global banking system are required.

3.3 Features of poor corporate governance

The scandals over the last 25 years have highlighted the need for guidance to tackle the various risks and problems that can arise in organisational systems of governance.

3.3.1 Domination by a single individual

A feature of many corporate governance scandals has been boards dominated by a single senior executive with other board members merely acting as a rubber stamp. Sometimes the single individual may bypass the board to action their own interests. For example, a company director may pay themselves a significant reward without consulting the other directors.

3.3.2 Lack of involvement of board

Boards that meet irregularly or fail to consider systematically the organisation's activities and risks are clearly weak. Sometimes the failure to carry out proper oversight is due to a **lack of information** being provided.

3.3.3 Lack of adequate control function

An obvious weakness is a **lack of internal audit.**

Another important control is **lack of adequate technical knowledge** in key roles, for example, in the audit committee or in senior compliance positions. A rapid turnover of staff involved in accounting or control may suggest inadequate resourcing, and will make control more difficult because of lack of continuity.

3.3.4 Lack of supervision

Employees who are not properly supervised can create large losses for the organisation through their own incompetence, negligence or fraudulent activity. The behaviour of Nick Leeson, the employee who caused the collapse of Barings bank was not challenged because he appeared to be successful, whereas he was using unauthorised accounts to cover up his large trading losses. Leeson was able to do this because he was in charge of both dealing and settlement, a systems weakness or **lack of segregation of key roles** that featured in other financial frauds.

3.3.5 Lack of independent scrutiny

External auditors may not carry out the necessary questioning of senior management because of fears of losing the audit, and internal audit do not ask awkward questions because the chief financial officer determines their employment prospects. Often corporate collapses are followed by criticisms of external auditors, such as the Barlow Clowes affair, where poorly planned and focused audit work failed to identify illegal use of client monies.

3.3.6 Lack of contact with shareholders

Often board members may have grown up with the company but lose touch with the interests and views of shareholders. One possible symptom of this is the payment of remuneration packages that do not appear to be warranted by results.

3.3.7 Emphasis on short-term profitability

Emphasis on short-term results can lead to the **concealment of problems or errors,** or **manipulation of accounts** to **achieve desired results**.

3.3.8 Misleading accounts and information

Often misleading figures are symptomatic of other problems (or are designed to conceal other problems) but in many cases, poor quality accounting information is a major problem if markets are trying to make a fair assessment of the company's value. Giving out misleading information was a major issue in the UK's Equitable Life scandal where the company gave contradictory information to savers, independent advisers, media and regulators.

3.4 Risks of poor corporate governance

Clearly, the ultimate risk is of the organisation **making such large losses** that **bankruptcy** becomes inevitable. The organisation may also be closed down as a result of **serious regulatory breaches,** for example, misapplying investors' monies.

4 The role of culture

FAST FORWARD

Culture is important, both in organisations and in the wider world. It is the knowledge, beliefs, customs and attitudes which people adhere to. In wider society, it is affected by factors such as age, class, race and religion, while in organisations it is defined by assumptions, beliefs and artefacts. These, in turn, are influenced by history, management, structure and systems. The organisational iceberg concept shows how culture relates to other aspects of the organisation. The **paradigm** is the common, basic assumptions and beliefs held by an organisation's decision-makers. Combined with the physical manifestations of culture, it makes up the **cultural web**.

4.1 Organisational culture   6/12

Key term

The word, **culture** is used by sociologists and anthropologists to encompass the sum total of the beliefs, knowledge, attitudes of mind and customs to which people are exposed in their social conditioning.'

Exam focus point

An article titled 'Culture and configuration' written by Ken Garrett is available in the Technical Articles section for P3 on the ACCA website. The article focuses on key models of organisational culture, which is assumed knowledge brought forward from paper F1. Consideration is given to the interaction between organisational configuration and culture. Henry Mintzberg's theory of organisational configuration is covered later in this study text.

The compulsory question in the June 2013 exam focused on how an understanding of organisational culture would have helped the newly appointed CEO of a hospital manage change. The CEO had joined the hospital from a commercial organisation and didn't appear to appreciate the extent of the cultural differences between the two organisations.

Through contact with a particular culture, individuals learn a language, acquire values and learn **habits of behaviour and thought**.

(a)   **Beliefs and values**. Beliefs are what we feel to be the case on the basis of objective and subjective information (eg people can believe the world is round or flat). Values are beliefs which are relatively enduring, relatively general and fairly widely accepted as a guide to culturally appropriate behaviour.

(b)   **Customs.** Customs are modes of behaviour which represent culturally accepted ways of behaving in response to given situations.

(c)   **Artefacts.** Artefacts are all the physical tools designed by human beings for their physical and psychological well-being, including works of art, technology, products.

(d)   **Rituals.** A ritual is a type of activity which takes on symbolic meaning; it consists of a fixed sequence of behaviour repeated over time.

The learning and sharing of culture is made possible by **language** (both written and spoken, verbal and non-verbal).

Knowledge of the culture of a society is clearly of value to businesses in a number of ways.

(a) **Marketers** can adapt their products accordingly, and be fairly sure of a sizeable market. This is particularly important in export markets.

(b) **Human resource managers** may need to tackle cultural differences in recruitment. For example, some ethnic minorities have a different body language from the majority, which may be hard for some interviewers to interpret.

Culture in a society can be divided into **subcultures** reflecting social differences. Most people participate in several of them.

<table>
<tr><td>Key term</td><td>Organisational culture consists of the beliefs, attitudes, practices and customs to which people are exposed during their interaction with the organisation.</td></tr>
</table>

Culture is both internal to an organisation and external to it. The culture of an organisation is embedded in the culture of the wider society. Its importance to strategy is that it can predispose the organisation towards, or away from, a particular course of action.

All organisations will generate their own cultures, whether spontaneously or under the guidance of positive managerial strategy. Schein suggests that three aspects of culture can be distinguished in organisations.

(a) **Basic, underlying assumptions** which guide the behaviour of the individuals and groups in the organisation. These may include customer orientation, or belief in quality, trust in the organisation to provide rewards, freedom to make decisions, freedom to make mistakes and the value of innovation and initiative at all levels.

(b) **Overt beliefs** expressed by the organisation and its members, which can be used to condition the assumptions mentioned above. These beliefs and values may emerge as sayings, slogans and mottoes, such as IBM's motto, 'Think'. They may emerge in a rich mythology of jokes and stories about past successes and heroic failures.

(c) **Visible artefacts** – the style of the offices or other premises, dress rules, visible structures or processes, the degree of informality between superiors and subordinates and so on.

Management can encourage this by selling a sense of the corporate mission, or by promoting the corporate image. It can reward the right attitudes and punish (or simply not employ) those who are not prepared to commit themselves to the culture.

An organisation's culture is influenced by many factors.

(a) **The organisation's founder**. A strong set of values and assumptions is set up by the organisation's founder, and even after he or she has retired, these values have their own momentum. Or, to put it another way, an organisation might find it hard to shake off its original culture. Peters and Waterman believed that 'excellent' companies began with strong leaders.

(b) **The organisation's history**. Johnson, Scholes and Whittington state that the way an organisation works reflects the era when it was founded. Farming, for example, sometimes has a craft element to it. The effect of history can be determined by stories, rituals and symbolic behaviour. They legitimise behaviour and promote priorities. (In some organisations, certain positions are regarded as intrinsically more 'heroic' than others.)

(c) **Leadership and management style**. An organisation with a strong culture recruits managers who naturally conform to it.

(d) **Structure and systems** affect culture as well as strategy.

4.2 The organisational iceberg

French and Bell described the **organisational iceberg** in which formal aspects are **overt** and informal aspects are **covert** or hidden, rather as the bulk of an iceberg is underwater.

Formal aspects

- Goals
- Terminology
- Structure
- Policies and procedures
- Products
- Financial resources

Informal aspects

- Beliefs and assumptions
- Perceptions, attitudes and feelings about the formal systems
- Values
- Informal interactions
- Group norms

4.3 The paradigm and the cultural web

Exam focus point

> The Study Guide – A6(f) – requires you to be able to prepare and evaluate a cultural web of an organisation. Section C2(b) also requires you to be able to determine and diagnose the organisational context of change using the cultural web.
>
> A question in the December 2011 exam required students to analyse the culture of the organisation described in the case study scenario. ACCA's answer draws on the cultural web model covered in the next section. The cultural web provides a useful framework when analysing organisational culture, as its component parts can be used as headings which help to structure your answer when applying it to the scenario.
>
> The examining team reported that the cultural web was an area of the syllabus that students appeared to be familiar with. However, when attempting questions which require the application of a model to a scenario, is important to avoid spending too much time purely describing the theory. Applying your knowledge directly to the question scenario is crucial for passing paper P3. Sadly, as the examining team highlighted, too many answers focused too much on description with limited analysis, and therefore students gained few marks.

4.3.1 The paradigm

The word **paradigm** was first used outside its original context by *Kuhn* and defined by him as 'an entire constellation of beliefs, values and techniques, and so on, shared by the members of a given community'. In a business context, it may be used to signify the **basic assumptions and beliefs** that an organisation's decision-makers **hold in common** and **take for granted**. Note that this is a slightly different concept from **culture**. The paradigm represents **collective experience** and is used to make sense of a given situation; it is thus essentially conservative and inhibiting to innovation, while an innovative **culture** is entirely feasible.

4.3.2 The cultural web   12/11, 12/10

Johnson, Scholes and Whittington use the term **cultural web** to mean a combination of the assumptions that make up the **paradigm**, together with the **physical manifestations** of culture.

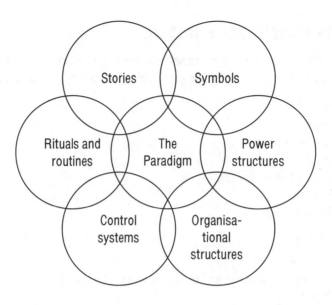

The cultural web

The cultural web model may be used to gain an understanding of an organisation's culture and thence the way its members **behave** and how its strategy develops. JS&W suggest that careful examination of each aspect of the web may lead to a brief summary of an organisation in cultural terms. Culture tends to be fairly simple, though manifested in complex ways: different but consistent elements may be discerned by investigating each constituent of the cultural web.

Let us look at the six physical manifestations of culture which make up the web in more detail.

1   **Stories** – The stories concern past events and people talked about inside and outside the company. 'Who' and 'what' is talked about most in these stories can often illustrate the behaviour the organisation encourages, and the sorts of things it values.

2   **Symbols** – The visual representations of an organisation, including logos, premises, and dress can illustrate the nature of that organisation. Also, verbal representations like language and titles can symbolise the nature of an organisation.

3   **Power structures** – Who has the real power in the organisation? This may be held by one or two key senior executives, a whole group of executives, or even a department. The key is that these people have the greatest amount of influence on decisions, operations, and the strategic direction of an organisation.

4   **Organisational structures** – This includes both the formal structure defined by the organisation chart, and the unwritten lines of power and influence that indicate whose contributions are most valued. Structure is likely to reflect power.

5   **Control systems** – These concern the ways the organisation is controlled. They include financial systems, quality systems, and rewards (including the way they are measured and distributed within the organisation.) Looking at the areas which are controlled most closely can indicate what is seen as most important to an organisation, and where most attention is focused.

6   **Rituals and routines** – The daily behaviour and actions of people signal what is considered acceptable in an organisation. This determines what is expected to happen in given situations, and what is valued by management.

4.3.3 Example of the cultural web

The table below illustrates some of the questions which the cultural web prompts us to ask about an organisation. It also gives some examples of the expressions of culture that could be generated by the web. The example below is based on the cultural web for a car repair workshop.

Cultural web	Examples (based on car repair workshop)
Stories	
What stories do people tell about the organisation?	They're always the cheapest on the market; they do things the cheapest way they can.
What do these stories say about the values of the organisation?	
What reputation is communicated among customers and other stakeholders?	They are known for having high numbers of customer complaints, and for low quality workmanship.
What do employees talk about when they think of the history of the organisation?	The founder started the company himself with a loan from a friend.
Rituals and routines	
What do employees expect when they come to work?	Employees have to sign in, and are then given a job sheet by the boss showing their jobs for the day.
What do customers expect when they walk in?	Customers expect to hear the radio playing and to be given a mug of coffee while they wait to collect cars.
What would be immediately obvious if it changed?	Workshop repainted and new machinery installed
What behaviour do the routines encourage?	Lots of talk about money-saving, and especially how to cut costs
Symbols	
What language and jargon is used? Is it well known and usable by all?	Mechanics use jargon which customers don't understand to describe parts and problems
What aspects of strategy are highlighted in publicity?	Adverts and leaflets say they won't be beaten on price
Are there any status symbols?	No, the boss wears an overall, like the staff
Organisational structure	
Is the structure formal or informal? Flat or hierarchical?	Flat structure: Owner, Mechanics, Receptionist.
What are the formal lines of authority?	The mechanics report to the owner (who is also a mechanic by trade)
Are there any informal lines of authority?	The receptionist is the owner's wife so she discusses customer complains directly with him
Do structures encourage cooperation and collaboration?	Each mechanic looks after himself. There is no sharing of tools or jobs.

Cultural web	Examples (based on car repair workshop)
Control systems	
What process has the strongest controls?	Costs are very tightly controlled. Customers are billed for all parts used.
What process has the weakest controls?	Quality is not seen as important. Getting work done as cheaply as possible is emphasised ahead of quality.
Is emphasis on rewarding good work or penalising poor work?	In their pay review, employees are judged on the actual costs of their jobs compared to their job quotes. Staff whose actual costs exceed quotes tend to get smaller pay rises than those whose job costs are lower than their quotes.
Power structures	
Who has the real power in the organisation?	The owner
How strongly held are the beliefs of the people with power?	The owner believes strongly in a low cost model, and is prepared to lose repeat customers in order to keep costs down.
How is power used or abused?	Knowing that their pay reviews are dependent on cost control keeps mechanics working to this low cost model.
What are the main blockages to change?	The owner insists that his low cost model is the best way to run the business and won't invest in any new equipment if it will cost lots of money to do so.

4.3.4 The cultural web and business strategy

The importance of the cultural web for business strategy is that it provides a means of looking at cultural assumptions and practices, to make sure that organisational elements are aligned with one another, and with an organisation's strategy.

If an organisation is not delivering the results its management wants, management can use the web to help diagnose whether the organisation's culture is contributing to the underperformance.

There are three phases to such analysis. First, management can look at organisational culture as it is now. Second they can to look at how they want the culture to be, and third they can identify the differences between the two. These differences indicate the changes which will need to be made to achieve the high-performance culture that they are seeking.

In this way, the cultural web can play a significant role in change management, and changing organisational culture.

5 Integrated reporting

Exam focus point

The role of integrated reporting in communicating strategy is an important part of the P3 syllabus. It is important that you are familiar with integrated reporting as exam questions may require an explanation of how it can be used by a company featured in a question. You may also be required to comment on the implications of introducing integrated reporting.

FAST FORWARD

Integrated reporting is concerned with conveying a wider message on organisational performance. It is fundamentally concerned with reporting on the value created by the organisation's resources. Resources are referred to as 'capitals', and value is created or lost through the way in which capitals interact with one another. The aim of integrated reporting is to encourage a holistic view when assessing organisational performance.

5.1 Rise of integrated reporting

In recent years, there has been increasing demand for the senior management in large organisations to provide greater detail on how they use the resources at their disposal to create value. Traditional corporate reporting which focuses on financial performance is said to only tell part of the story.

Integrated reporting is concerned with conveying a wider message on an entity's performance. It is not solely centred on profit, or the organisation's financial position, but details how its activities interact to create value over the short, medium and long term.

5.1.1 Value creation

In 2013, the International Integrated Reporting Council (IIRC) introduced the integrated reporting framework. The framework refers to an organisation's resources as 'capitals'. Capitals are used to assess value creation. Increases or decreases in these capitals indicate the level of value created or lost over a period. Capitals cover various types of resources found in a standard organisation. Integrated reporting refers to six different types of capital.

5.1.2 Types of capital

The integrated reporting framework classifies the capitals as:

Capital	Comment
Financial capital	The pool of funds that is: • Available to an organisation for use in the production of goods or the provision of services • Obtained through financing, such as debt, equity or grants, or generated through operations or investments
Manufactured capital	Manufactured physical objects (as distinct from natural physical objects) that are available to an organisation for use in the production of goods or the provision of services, including: • Buildings • Equipment Infrastructure (such as roads, ports, bridges and waste and water treatment plants) Manufactured capital is often created by other organisations, but includes assets manufactured by the reporting organisation for sale or when they are retained for its own use.
Intellectual capital	Organisational knowledge-based intangibles, including: • Intellectual property, such as patents, copyrights, software, rights and licences • 'Organisational capital' such as tacit knowledge, systems, procedures and protocols

Capital	Comment
Human capital	People's competencies, capabilities and experience, and their motivations to innovate, including their: • Alignment with, and support for, an organisation's governance framework, risk management approach and ethical values • Ability to understand, develop and implement an organisation's strategy • Loyalties and motivations for improving processes, goods and services, including their ability to lead, manage and collaborate
Social and relationship capital	The institutions and the relationships within and between communities, groups of stakeholders and other networks, and the ability to share information to enhance individual and collective well-being. Social and relationship capital includes: • Shared norms and common values and behaviours • Key stakeholder relationships and the trust and willingness to engage that an organisation developed and strives to build and protect with external stakeholders • Intangibles associated with the brand and reputation that an organisation has developed • An organisation's social licence to operate
Natural capital	All renewable and non-renewable environmental resources and processes that provide goods or services that support the past, current or future prosperity of an organisation. It includes: • Air, water, land, minerals and forests • Biodiversity and eco-system health

Source: The International Integrated Reporting Framework, *www.theiirc.org*

5.1.3 Interaction of capitals

Capitals continually interact with one another: an increase in one may result in a decrease another. For example, a decision to purchase a new IT system would improve an entity's 'manufactured' capital while decreasing its financial capital in the form of its cash reserves.

5.1.4 Short-term v long-term

Integrated reporting forces management to balance the organisation's short-term objectives against its longer term plans. Business decisions which are solely dedicated to the pursuit of increasing profit (financial capital) at the expense of building good relations with key stakeholders such as customers (social capital) are likely to hinder value creation in the longer term. It is thought that producing a holistic view of organisational performance will lead to improved management decision making, ensuring that decisions are not taken in isolation.

5.1.5 The Guiding Principles of Integrated Reporting

The International Integrated Reporting Council identified seven Guiding Principles which support the preparation of an integrated report:

(a) Strategic focus and future orientation
(b) Connectivity of information
(c) Stakeholder relationships
(d) Materiality
(e) Conciseness
(f) Reliability and completeness
(g) Consistency and comparability

Strategic focus and future orientation

A good integrated report should help users understand the organisation's strategy with particular emphasis on how value can be created over the short, medium and long term. To convey this message, the integrated report is likely to set out the significant risks and external opportunities available to the organisation, with the associated detail of how such issues can be reduced or exploited.

The board of directors can also use the report to communicate how the organisation's current strategy has been shaped by past experiences. A focus on future oriented information allows the board to highlight any prospective legal and/or regulatory matters which may impact the organisations ability to achieve its objectives.

Connectivity of information

A key part of integrated reporting focuses on the interrelatedness or 'connectivity of information' throughout the organisation. The IIRC highlight that integrated reporting is aimed at joining up the flow of information to allow users of integrated reports to better understand how resources (capitals) are being used in the pursuit of the organisation's strategic aims and to show how the entity's strategy is adapted to reflect 'real world' changes in the external environment.

It is important to note that integrated reporting is not aimed at attaching a monetary value to every aspect of the organisation's operations. It is fundamentally concerned with letting stakeholders evaluate value creation, and it does this by communicating a range of qualitative and quantitative performance measures. Key performance indicators are effective in communicating performance.

For example, when providing detail on customer satisfaction, this can be communicated as the number of customers retained compared to the previous year. Best practice in integrated reporting requires organisations to report on both positive and negative movements in 'capital' to avoid only providing half the story.

Stakeholder relationships

Integrated reporting highlights the importance of stakeholder relationships. An Integrated Report should highlight how the organisation interacts with key stakeholder groups. This provides the board with the opportunity to show that it understands the interests of different groups and sets out the organisation's approach to responding to stakeholder needs. Proponents of integrated reporting argue that a stronger emphasis on the importance of stakeholders is central to improving the transparency and accountability of organisational reporting.

Materiality

One of the Guiding Principles of integrated reporting requires management to disclose matters which are likely to impact on an organisation's ability to create value. Internal weaknesses and external threats regarded as being materially important are evaluated and quantified (where possible). This provides users with an indication of how management intend to combat risks, should they materialise.

Conciseness

The IIRC recognises that a good Integrated Report should be concise and to the point. Users of the report are likely to want sufficient detail to help them understand the organisation's performance and future strategic direction, without the need to be presented with irrelevant information.

Reliability and completeness

As discussed earlier in respect of materiality, an Integrated Report requires a balanced presentation of both positive and negative information. IIRC highlight that reliable information needs to be 'free from material error' if it is to be useful to interested parties. This requires the organisation to have in place a sound system of internal reporting. Furthermore, to be effective, an integrated report should be complete, meaning that certain matters must not be omitted simply because they relate to unfavourable movements in 'capitals'.

Consistency and comparability

A good integrated report should communicate the same type of information from period to period, eg reporting the same KPIs year on year. To support user understanding when there have been significant movements between periods, the Guiding Principles highlight the need for organisations to provide an explanation for the change and to quantify this if possible.

The principle of comparability requires integrated reports to be presented to allow for easier comparison with similar entities. Comparability in integrated reporting is particularly difficult to achieve as every organisation is unique and will create value differently. The IIRC highlights that comparability in information can be improved in reporting through the use of benchmarking an entity's performance against industry metrics (KPIs) and ratios eg the percentage movement in staff training and development programmes compared to the industry average.

The issue of comparability is further complicated as, at present, there is no compulsory requirement for organisations to adopt integrated reporting at all.

5.1.6 Implications of introducing integrated reporting

Implications	Comment
IT costs	The introduction of integrated reporting will most likely require significant upgrades to be made to the organisation's IT and information system infrastructure. Such developments will be needed to capture KPI data. Due to the broad range of business activities reported on using integrated reporting (customer, supplier relations, finance and human resources) it is likely the costs of improving the infrastructure will be significant.
Time/staff costs	The process of gathering and collating the data for inclusion in the report is likely to require a significant amount of staff time. This may serve to decrease staff morale if they are expected to undertake this work in addition to existing duties. This may require additional staff to be employed.
Consultancy costs	Organisations producing their first integrated report may seek external guidance from an organisation which provides specialist consultancy on integrated reporting. Consultancy fees are likely to be significant.
Disclosure	There is a danger that organisations may volunteer more information about their operational performance than intended. Disclosure of planned strategies and key performance measures are likely to be picked up by competitors.

The ACCA produced its first integrated report in 2011/2012, this formed part of the ACCA's annual report. It was prepared following the guidelines of the International Integrated Reporting Council's framework. Since this time, ACCA has continued to report on performance using the principles of integrated reporting. In 2013/14 the ACCA produced it's third 'annual integrated report'.

The intentions of ACCA's first integrated report were made clear at the outset, 'we are aiming to tell a clear and coherent story about the ACCA's strategic performance and future prospects. Most importantly, we are using this report to explain how we create value for our stakeholders – primarily our members – and the place we occupy in society'.

The following section illustrates some of the key features from ACCA's integrated reports between 2011/12 and 2013/14.

Key elements from ACCA's 2011-2014 integrated reports

Key achievements

ACCA annually publishes its key achievements in pursuit of its objectives. ACCA's performance against its objectives is measured through the use of a number of key performance indicators. The commentary gives some detail as to the targets achieved and those not met.

The following extract has been amended to include ACCA's result's against it's targets since 2011/12.

Our 2015 strategic objective	How we measure this	Targets for 2011-2012	What was delivered in 2011-12	Targets for 2012-2013	What was delivered in 2012-13	Targets for 2013-2014	What was delivered in 2013-14
To be the leading global professional accountancy body in reputation, influence and size	Number of members	154,700 members	Not achieved: 154,337 members at 31.03.12.	162,015 members	Not achieved: 161,943 members at 31.03.13	170,650 Members	Not achieved: 169,602 members at 31.03.14
To lead and shape the agenda of the profession	% of employees who consider that ACCA's public positions on the agenda of the profession promote public value	47%	Achieved: 53.7%	57.7%	Not achieved: 42.2%	44.4%	Not achieved: 43.1%
To recruit and retain our membership base	Number of ACCA Qualification students	363,350 ACCA Qualification students	Achieved: 368,145 ACCA Qualification students at 31.03.12.	380,000 ACCA Qualification students	Not achieved: 372,248 ACCA Qualification students at 31.03.13	381,000 ACCA Qualification students	Achieved: 384,287 ACCA Qualification students at 31.03.14

Stakeholders

The ACCA acknowledges its obligations to its key stakeholders. In it's integrated reports ACCA highlight how it engages with a number of groups including, members, students and employers. The 2013/14 report notes that 'one of the integrated reporting principles we have found particularly helpful is that of stakeholder engagement. Since we moved to an integrated reporting approach, we have consulted with a range of stakeholders on every report, asking whether it meets their needs and refining our reporting in response to their feedback.'

Strategic focus and risk

ACCA's 2011/12 report placed a strong focus on the steps the ACCA had been taking to achieve its vision up to 2015. This theme is continued in the 2013/14 report which introduces ACCA's new organisational strategy up to 2020. Those factors likely to impact on ACCA's ability to achieve its objectives are covered in a section designated to risk management.

Value creation

In addition to the traditional reporting of financial performance, the integrated reports also detail those 'capitals' regarded as being important in creating value over the long term. One capital mentioned focuses on the role of people in the organisation.

The ACCA regard having the right people with the right skills and capabilities as being critical in being able to deliver its strategy. Over the year, the ACCA enhanced its people capital through investments in staff development and training programmes.

Source: The ACCA's first integrated report and subsequent annual reports can be found at: www.accaglobal.com

5.2 Section summary

This chapter brings us to the end of Section A of the P3 syllabus, 'Strategic position'. In the next chapter, we will start looking at the 'Strategic choices' available to an organisation. These choices obviously depend on its current position and the various internal and external factors affecting it, which we have looked at in Section A. The diagram below summarises these factors which shape strategic position:

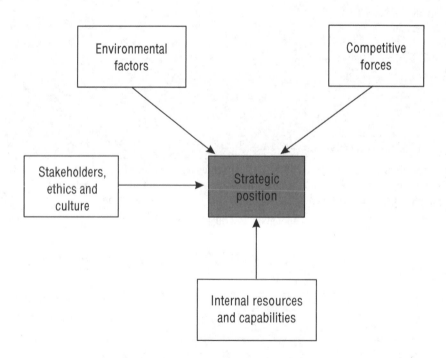

Chapter Roundup

- Ethics is about right and wrong but it is not the same thing as law or the rules of religion. Cognitive approaches to ethics assume that objective moral truths can be established.

- Consequentialist ethics judges actions by their outcomes; deontology assumes the existence of absolute moral principles and ignores outcomes. Natural law is about rights and duties, while virtue ethics is based on moderation in behaviour and the idea of leading a harmonious life.

  Ethical theory is not integrated: consequentialist, deontological and natural law based rules are capable of pointing to different conclusions. Partly as a result of this, **ethical dilemmas** can exist at all levels in the organisation.

- Corporate ethics has three contexts.

  - Interaction with national and international society
  - Effects of routine operations
  - Behaviour of individuals

  If constructed with care, a corporate ethical code can be valuable.

- There is a fundamental split of views about the organisation's relationship with its stakeholders and the nature of corporate responsibility.

  - The **strong view** that a range of goals should be pursued
  - The **weak view** that the business organisation is a purely **economic force**, subject to law

- Stakeholders have an interest in what the organisation does.

- An organisation's stakeholder relationships must be managed in accordance with their bargaining strength, influence, power and degree of interest. *Mendelow* summarises the possibilities in his stakeholder map. Stakeholders have three options: loyalty, exit and voice.

- The extent to which an organisation recognises obligations to society in general is as much subject to debate as its relationships with stakeholder groups.

- There is particular concern over **externalities**, or the social and environmental costs of corporate activities.

- An organisation's **ethical stance** is the extent to which it will exceed its minimum obligations to stakeholders. There are four typical stances.

  - Short-term shareholder interest   – Multiple stakeholder obligations
  - Long-term shareholder interest   – Shaper of society

- **Corporate governance** is the conduct of the organisation's senior officers. Abuses have led to a range of measures to improve corporate governance. Non-executive directors have a particular role to play.

- Where the management of a business is separated from its ownership by the employment of professional managers, the managers may be considered to be the agents of the owners. **Agency theory** is concerned with adverse selection and moral hazard, the problems that arise as a result of the separation of ownership and control. In many organisations, corporate governance takes the form of a chain of responsibility and accountability.

- There are four models of governance.

  1. The Anglo-Saxon model is fast in action but may be short-termist and unresponsive to external criticism.
  2. The Rhine model has more robust governance and takes a long view of investment.
  3. The Japanese model values consensus, takes a very long view and makes decisions slowly. Accountability and governance may be poor.
  4. The Latin model emphasises the role of the state: investment is likely to be for the very long term but governance may suffer from political activity.

Chapter Roundup (cont'd)

- The board must decide the extent of its involvement in the strategic process. If it decides on a stewardship role, it must ensure that the organisation's activity is not directed to management's own ends, rather than those of legitimate stakeholders. If it engages in the strategic process, it must act independently of management and in a competent fashion.

- Culture is important, both in organisations and in the wider world. It is the knowledge, beliefs, customs and attitudes which people adhere to. In wider society, it is affected by factors such as age, class, race and religion, while in organisations, it is defined by assumptions, beliefs and artefacts. These, in turn, are influenced by history, management, structure and systems. The organisational iceberg concept shows how culture relates to other aspects of the organisation. The **paradigm** is the common, basic assumptions and beliefs held by an organisation's decision-makers. Combined with the physical manifestations of culture, it makes up the **cultural web**.

- Integrated reporting is concerned with conveying a wider message on organisational performance. It is fundamentally concerned with reporting on the value created by the organisation's resources. Resources are referred to as 'capitals', and value is created or lost through the way in which capitals interact with one another. The aim of integrated reporting is to encourage a holistic view when assessing organisational performance.

Quick Quiz

1   What is an organisation's ethical stance?

2   Stakeholders can be classified into three broad groups. What are they?

3   A stakeholder group has high interest in, but low powers over, an organisation's activities. How should the organisation deal with that stakeholder group?

    A   Make sure its strategies are acceptable to it
    B   Make sure it is kept satisfied
    C   Make sure it is kept informed
    D   Do nothing

4   When should ethical considerations be included in performance measures?

5   What is corporate governance?

6   What is an externality?

7   What are the six physical manifestations of culture that make up the cultural web?

8   What is the paradigm, in JS&W's terms?

1   The extent to which it will exceed its minimum obligation to shareholders

2   Internal; connected; external stakeholders.

3   C   A stakeholder group with high interest but low power does not have much ability to influence strategy on its own, but it may be able to influence other more powerful stakeholders. It should therefore be **kept informed**.

4   When moral expectations are accepted as obligations

5   The conduct of the organisation's senior officers

6   A social or environmental cost of the organisation's activities not borne by the organisation

7   Stories; symbols; power structures; organisational structures; control systems; rituals and routines

8   The common, basic assumptions and beliefs held by an organisation's decision-makers

Now try the question below from the Practice Question Bank

Number	Level	Marks	Time
Q6	Examination	20	36 mins

Strategic choices

Strategic choices

Topic list	Syllabus reference
1 Corporate strategy	B1(a)
2 Diversity of products and markets	B1(b), (c)
3 International diversification	B1(b), (c)
4 The corporate parent and value creation	B1(d), (e)
5 The corporate portfolio	B1(f)
6 Business unit strategy: generic strategies	B2(a)
7 Sustaining competitive advantage	B2(b), (c)
8 Using the value chain in competitive strategy	B2
9 Product-market strategy: direction of growth	B3(a)
10 Method of growth	B3(b)
11 Strategy and market position	B2
12 Success criteria	B3(c), (d), (e), (f)

Introduction

In this chapter, we will examine the various strategic choices that present themselves to the organisation. The process of selecting from these choices should, of course, be illuminated by the analyses of environmental and internal factors that we have already discussed.

There are two main areas to cover in our examination of strategic choices: these are, first, the role of the corporate headquarters of an organisation that is made up of a number of business units; and, second, the strategies available to the business units themselves in their own separate industries and sectors. The second area is equally applicable to smaller organisations that are, effectively, independent businesses operating on their own account and not subject to any form of hierarchical supervision.

Study guide

		Intellectual level
B1	**The influence of corporate strategy on an organisation**	
(a)	Explore the relationship between a corporate parent and its business units	2
(b)	Assess the opportunities and potential problems of pursuing different corporate strategies of product/market diversification from a national, international and global perspective	3
(c)	Assess the opportunities and potential problems of pursuing a corporate strategy of international diversity, international scale operations and globalisation	3
(d)	Discuss a range of ways that the corporate parent can create and destroy organisational value	2
(e)	Explain three corporate rationales for adding value – portfolio managers, synergy managers and parental developers	3
(f)	Explain and apply the following portfolio models (the BCG growth/share matrix, public sector matrix, the parenting matrix or Ashridge Portfolio display) to assist corporate parents in managing their business portfolios.	3
B2	**Alternative approaches to achieving competitive advantage**	
(a)	Evaluate, through the strategy clock, generic strategy options available to an organisation	3
(b)	Advise on how price-based strategies, differentiation and lock-in can help an organisation sustain its competitive advantage	3
(c)	Assess opportunities for improving competitiveness through collaboration	3
B3	**Alternative directions and methods of development**	
(a)	Determine generic development directions (employing an adapted Ansoff matrix and a TOWS matrix) available to an organisation	2
(b)	Assess how internal development, mergers, acquisitions, strategic alliances, and franchising can be used as different methods of pursuing a chosen strategic direction	3
(c)	Establish success criteria to assist in the choice of a strategic direction and method (strategic options)	2
(d)	Assess the suitability of different strategic options to an organisation	3
(e)	Assess the feasibility of different strategic options to an organisation	3
(f)	Establish the acceptability of strategic options to an organisation through analysing risk and return on investment	3

Exam guide

This is another chapter that is packed with highly examinable material. In particular, it is very common in business strategy exams to be confronted with a complex scenario and be required to suggest sensible courses of action, with reasonable justification. It is very important, therefore, to understand the general circumstances in which a particular strategic option is appropriate. It is not sufficient to be able to describe the options without understanding when they are to be recommended. A strategy must be appropriate to its context, and therefore any strategy you recommend in an exam answer must be appropriate to the scenario described in the question.

The chapter concludes with a discussion of success criteria: these are the criteria against which possible courses of action are judged and they draw together the threads of choice we emphasise above. Pay careful attention to the nature of these criteria: they are not as simple as they might seem to be.

Models and theories

This chapter covers a number of models which are explicitly referenced in the Study Guide, and so could be specifically required in a question.

The models referenced in the Study Guide are as follows:

- JS&W's three strategic rationales for corporate parents
- BCG Matrix
- Public sector portfolio matrix
- Ashridge portfolio display
- The strategy clock
- TOWS Matrix
- Ansoff's Matrix (product market mix)

Do not overlook the other models and ideas in this chapter because they could be useful in supporting your answer. However, they will not be specifically required by a question.

1 Corporate strategy

FAST FORWARD

> Many large businesses consist of a corporate parent and a number of SBUs. The defining characteristic of the corporate parent is that it has no direct contact with the buyers or competitors, its role being to manage the overall scope of the organisation in terms of diversity of products, markets and international operations.

Many organisations consist, essentially, of a number of strategic business units (SBUs) and a **corporate parent**. Each SBU has its own products, with which it serves its own market sector, and its managers are, to a greater or lesser extent, responsible for its overall success (or failure). In very large organisations, SBUs may be grouped into **divisions**, with divisional managers providing an intermediate level of management between the SBU and the corporate parent.

The defining feature of the **corporate parent** is that it has no direct contact with buyers and competitors. Its role is generally to manage the **scope of the organisation**. There are two main, linked subjects for decisions about scope.

- Diversity of products and markets
- International and geographic diversity

The processes involved in making and implementing these decisions are complex and the role of the corporate parent is of very great importance to the success or failure of the organisation. In our consideration of the corporate centre we will also, therefore, examine the ways in which it can **create or destroy value**.

Exam focus point

Your syllabus is very clear in its separate treatment of the corporate parent and its SBUs, and this is also apparent in Johnson, Scholes & Whittington's *Exploring Corporate Strategy*, upon which much of the syllabus is based. You must therefore understand the differences between these two aspects of strategy and be able to recognise which is required by question scenarios. The picture will, of course, be complicated by the examining team possibly by presenting questions about companies that consist of a single business unit. In this case, the strategic managers will have to develop both corporate and business-level strategies.

2 Diversity of products and markets

FAST FORWARD

Diversity of products and markets may be advantageous for three reasons.

- **Economies of scope** may arise in several forms of **synergy**.
- **Corporate management skills** may be extendible.
- **Cross-subsidy** may enhance **market power**.

Related diversification, whether horizontal or vertical, usually works better than conglomerate, or unrelated, diversification.

The corporate parent controls the extent of product and market **diversification** undertaken by the organisation as a whole. JS&W suggest three reasons why diversification may be advantageous.

(a) **Economies of scope** (as opposed to economies of scale) may result from the **greater use of under-utilised resources**. These benefits are often referred to as **synergy** and can take several forms:

    (i) **Marketing synergy** is achieved by extending the use of marketing facilities such as distribution channels; sales staff and administration; and warehousing. For example, the UK Automobile Association, which is primarily a provider of breakdown services for motorists, now offers loans to customers as well as breakdown services.

    (ii) **Operating synergy** arises from the better use of operational facilities and personnel, bulk purchasing, and a greater spread of fixed costs whereby the firm's competence can be transferred to making new products. For example, although there is very little in common between sausages and ice cream, both depend on a competence of refrigeration.

    (iii) **Investment synergy** comes from the wider use of a common investment in non-current assets, working capital or research, such as the joint use of plant, common raw material inventory and transfer of research and development from one product to another.

    (iv) **Management synergy** is the advantage to be gained where management skills concerning current operations are easily transferred to new operations because of the similarity of problems in the two industries.

(b) **Corporate management skills** may be extendible across a range of unrelated businesses. In a way this is also a kind of synergy, in which the corporate parent represents the resource that can be more intensively utilised. This kind of approach is commonly seen in consumer goods groups that deploy brand management skills across a diverse range of products and markets. Virgin is a good example.

(c) Diversification can increase **market power** *via* cross-subsidisation. A high margin business can subsidise a low margin one, enabling it to create a price advantage over its rivals and building market share. Eventually, it may achieve a dominant position that enables it to increase its prices and recoup earlier group losses.

JS&W also discuss **three questionable reasons** that may be advanced to justify a policy of diversification.

(a) **Response to environmental change** can be justified as a reason to diversify if it is undertaken in order to protect existing shareholder value by, for example, responding to the emergence of new and threatening technology developments. However, the environmental change reasoning is sometimes used as a cover for what is actually a move to protect the interests of top management; typically, this will lead to ill-considered acquisitions that destroy value.

(b) **Risk spreading** can be a valid reason for an owner-managed business to diversify, but modern financial theory suggests that shareholders in large corporations can manage their risk exposure better themselves by diversifying their own portfolios.

(c) The **expectations of powerful stakeholders** can lead to inappropriate strategies generally. JS&W give the example of Enron, whose strategic managers were under pressure from the stock market to deliver continuing growth in revenues and responded with ill-considered diversification.

2.1 Related diversification

Key term

> **Related diversification** is development beyond current products and markets but within the capabilities or value network of the organisation. *JS&W*

The **argument of synergy** is often used to justify related diversification. However, achieving synergy can be difficult and requires considerable strategic skill, both to recognise synergistic potential and to achieve it in practice. Simply undertaking more and more value activities is not necessarily a route to improved performance: each activity undertaken must be **managed in a skilful and appropriate manner**. A number of very large corporations have actually de-merged with success. Also, the **management of external relationships** with suppliers, customers and collaborators is emerging as an effective alternative to expansion.

Horizontal integration makes use of current capabilities by development into activities that are competitive with, or directly **complementary** to, a company's present activities. An example would be a TV company that moved into film production.

Vertical integration occurs when a company expands backwards or forwards within its existing value network and thus becomes its own supplier or distributor. For example, **backward integration** would occur if a milk processing business acquired its own dairy farms, rather than buying raw milk from independent farmers. If a cloth manufacturer began to produce shirts instead of selling all of its cloth to other shirt manufacturers, that would be **forward integration**.

Vertical integration has its greatest potential for success when **the final customer's needs are not being properly satisfied**. If there is potential for improving the satisfaction of the end user by improving the links in the value network, then an integration strategy may succeed. Examples would be where there is a premium on speed, as in the marketing of fresh foodstuffs, or when complex technical features require great attention to quality procedures.

2.1.1 Advantages of vertical integration

- A **secure supply of components** or **materials,** hence lower supplier bargaining power
- **Stronger relationships** with the final consumer of the product
- A share of the **profits** at all stages of the value network
- More effective pursuit of a **differentiation strategy**
- Creation of **barriers to entry**

Note that vertical integration could have significant benefits for supply chain management. We will look at supply chain management in more detail later in this Study Text.

 Case Study   **Vertical integration in Japan**

Kumio Nakamura, president of Matsushita has said that, 'the vertical integration of Japanese manufacturers is a huge advantage because it enables us to move from development to production in a short time.'

2.1.2 Disadvantages of vertical integration

(a) **Overconcentration.** A company places 'more eggs in the same end-market basket' (Ansoff). Such a policy is fairly inflexible, more sensitive to instabilities and increases the firm's dependence on a particular aspect of economic demand.

(b) The firm **fails to benefit from any economies of scale or technical advances** in the industry into which it has diversified. This is why, in the publishing industry, most printing is subcontracted to specialist printing firms, who can work machinery to capacity by doing work for many firms.

(a)   **Horizontal integration**. The Walt Disney Company is an American entertainment and media organisation. In 1923, the company began trading under the name of the 'Disney Brothers Studio', producing animated cartoons and introducing the now well known Mickey Mouse cartoon character. In the 1950's using the financial reserves and film production expertise gained from producing children's cartoons, the company moved into the 'live-action' movie market, releasing its first full feature film 'Treasure Island' in 1950.

(b)   **Vertical integration**. Before privatisation, the UK electricity industry was a state-owned monopoly, vertically integrated from power generation to distribution. Privatisation effectively split up these two businesses, to introduce competition in power generation, so that the regional distribution companies could buy from a number of suppliers. However, the power distribution companies sought to buy a regional distribution company, giving them a captive market: National Power was set to buy Southern Electric, but the bid was blocked by the government on the grounds that it would inhibit competition.

2.2 Unrelated diversification

Key term

> **Unrelated diversification** is the development of products or services beyond the current capabilities or value network.   *JS&W*

Unrelated diversification produces the type of company known as a **conglomerate**. Conglomerate diversification has been a key strategy for companies in Asia, particularly South Korea, where the *chaebol*, as they are known, have provided better markets for capital and managerial skills than were available in the economy generally. Conglomerate diversification can also succeed when managed by particularly talented strategic leaders who deploy an effective **dominant logic;** dominant logic is the term used by Prahalad and Bettis to signify a cognitive orientation or world view based on sound judgement and experience.

Potential advantages of conglomerate diversification

Bear in mind our discussion of questionable reasons for diversification when considering these points.

(a)   **Risk-spreading.** Entering new products into new markets can compensate for the failure of current products and markets.

(b)   **Improved profit opportunities**. An improvement of the **overall profitability and flexibility** of the firm may arise through acquisition in industries with better prospects than those of the acquiring firms.

(c)   **Escape** from a declining market.

(d)   **Use a company's image and reputation** in one market to develop into another where corporate image and reputation could be vital ingredients for success.

Potential disadvantages of conglomerate diversification

(a)   The **dilution of shareholders' earnings** if diversification is into growth industries with high P/E ratios.

(b)   **Lack of a common identity and purpose** in a conglomerate organisation. A conglomerate will only be successful if it has a high quality of management and financial ability at central headquarters, where the diverse operations are brought together.

(c)   **Failure in one of the businesses will drag down the rest**, as it will eat up resources.

(d)   **Lack of management experience**. Japanese steel companies have diversified into areas completely unrelated to steel such as personal computers, with limited success.

2.3 Diversity and strategic success

JS&W's summary of the results of research into the impact of diversification on strategic performance tells us that organisations undertaking a **limited degree of related diversification are likely to perform better** than those that remain undiversified. However, as the degree of diversification **increases**, the rate of performance improvement is likely to **reduce** and may then become negative as the organisation becomes extensively diversified into unrelated fields.

3 International diversification

FAST FORWARD

Despite wide-ranging measures to liberalise trade and the resulting major growth in world trade, there has been little globalisation of services. Language differences and restrictions on population movement hamper the growth of international markets for labour, even when it is highly skilled.

3.1 Globalisation

Since 1945, the volume of world trade has increased. There have been several factors at work.

(a) **Import substitution.** A country aims to produce manufactured goods which it previously imported, by protecting local producers. This has had limited success.

(b) **Export-led growth.** The success of this particular strategy has depended on the existence of open markets elsewhere. Japan, South Korea and the other Asian 'tiger' economies (eg Taiwan) have chosen this route.

(c) **Market convergence**. Transnational market segments have developed whose characteristics are more homogeneous than the different segments within a given geographic market. **Youth culture** is an important influence here.

(d) **Increase in internet usage.** The growth in internet usage has resulted in cheaper, faster and easier means of global communication. This development has played a significant role in the widespread use of e-commerce by organisations and individuals in breaking down traditional trading barriers.

This has meant a proliferation of suppliers exporting to, or trading in, a wider variety of places. In many domestic markets, it is now likely that the same international companies will be competing with one another. However, the existence of global markets should not be taken for granted in terms of **all** products and services, or indeed in **all** territories.

(a) Some **services** are still subject to managed trade (for example, some countries prohibit firms from other countries from selling insurance). Trade in services has been liberalised under the auspices of the World Trade Organisation.

(b) **Immigration.** There is unlikely ever to be a global market for labour, given the disparity in skills between different countries and restrictions on immigration.

(c) The market for some goods is much more globalised than for others.

  (i) Upmarket luxury goods may not be required or afforded by people in developing nations.

  (ii) Some goods can be sold almost anywhere, but to limited degrees. Television sets are consumer durables in some countries, but still luxury or relatively expensive items in other ones.

  (iii) Other goods are needed almost everywhere. In oil, a truly global industry exists in both production (eg North Sea, Venezuela, Russia, Azerbaijan, Gulf states) and consumption (any country using cars and buses, not to mention those with chemical industries based on oil).

3.2 Management orientation

FAST FORWARD

Perlmutter identifies four orientations in the management of international business.

- **Ethnocentrism** is a home country orientation
- **Polycentrism** adapts totally to local environments
- **Geocentrism** adapts only to add value. It 'thinks globally, acts locally'
- **Regiocentrism** recognises regional differences

3.2.1 Ethnocentrism

Key term

> **Ethnocentrism** is a **home country orientation**. The company focuses on its domestic market and sees exports as secondary to domestic marketing.

This approach simply ignores any inter-country differences which exist. Ethnocentric companies will tend to market the same products with the same marketing programmes in overseas countries as at home. Marketing management is centralised in the home country and the marketing mix is standardised. There is no local market research or adaptation of promotion. As a result, market opportunities may not be fully exploited and foreign customers may be alienated by the approach.

 Case Study   Pepsi

Pepsi experienced customer alienation when it attempted to mechanically import its global younger challenger to Coke's image into Russia. It lost ground to an obscure Swiss rival, Herschi, which used Russian sports stars and celebrities in its campaign.

3.2.2 Polycentrism

Key term

> With **polycentrism**, objectives are formulated on the assumption that it is necessary to adapt almost totally the product and the marketing programme to each local environment. Thus, the various country subsidiaries of a multinational corporation are free to formulate their own objectives and plans.

The polycentric company believes that each country is unique. It therefore establishes largely independent local subsidiaries and decentralises its marketing management. This can produce major increases in turnover but the loss of economies of scale can seriously damage profitability. Such companies tend to

think of themselves as **multinationals**. (Later in this chapter, we introduce a slightly different polycentric company: the **transnational**.)

3.2.3 Geocentrism and regiocentrism

Key term

Geocentrism and **regiocentrism** are syntheses of the two previous orientations. They are based on the assumption that there are both similarities and differences between countries that can be incorporated into regional or world objectives and strategies.

Geocentrism and **regiocentrism** differ only in geographical terms: the first deals with the world as a unity, while the second considers that there are differences between regions. Bearing this in mind, we will speak in terms of geocentrism only, for simplicity.

Geocentrism treats the issues of standardisation and adaptation on their merits so as to formulate objectives and strategies that exploit markets fully while minimising company costs. The aim is to create a global strategy that is fully responsive to local market differences. This has been summed up as: 'think globally, act locally'.

Geocentric companies use an integrated approach to marketing management. Each country's conditions are given due consideration, but no one country dominates. A great deal of experience and commitment are required to make this approach work. A strong, globally recognised brand is a major aspect of the marketing approach. Geocentrically oriented companies both promote and benefit from **market convergence**.

3.3 Developing the global business

FAST FORWARD

Ohmae describes five stages in the evolution of a global business.

- **Exporting** is an extension of home sales, using foreign intermediaries. It is low risk and **ethnocentric**.
- **Overseas branches** arise when turnover is large enough. It requires greater investment and is still **ethnocentric**.
- **Overseas production** exploits cheap labour and reduces exporting costs. The orientation is still **ethnocentric** and the business is still largely run from its HQ.
- **Insiderisation** is a shift to **polycentrism**, with fully functional organisations being set up overseas. This reduces exchange rate and political risk but economies of scale may be lost and there may be problems of co-ordination. The company is a **multinational**.
- **The global company** takes a world view while recognising total differences: it has a **geocentric** orientation. It integrates learning, skills and competences to achieve global efficiencies while retaining local responsiveness.

Ohmae offers five reasons for globalisation.

- **Customer:** market convergence
- **Company:** economies of scale
- **Competition:** keeping up
- **Currency:** exchange rate risk
- **Country:** absolute and comparative advantage; local orientation

Following *Ohmae*, we may describe five stages in the evolution of global business operations. These may be related to Perlmutter's classification of orientations:

(a) **Exporting.** The product is saleable in overseas markets and they are exploited by means of foreign intermediaries such as agents and distributors. Foreign sales are a profitable extension of domestic operations. Little or no adjustment is made to the product in order to reap economies of scale. This is a low risk strategy, since there is little financial commitment, but the company is very much dependent on the effort and motivation of its foreign intermediaries. The management orientation is **ethnocentric**.

(b)   **Overseas branches**. Existing and potential export sales are high enough to justify largely replacing the foreign intermediaries with the company's own foreign sales and service branches. Financial commitment increases with increasing business, as does exchange rate and political risk. If the company is aiming to achieve globalisation, it is at this stage that it begins to acquire the local knowledge and experience that it will need. However, the management orientation is still **ethnocentric**.

(c)   **Overseas production**. Export sales are now so high that shipping and other exporting-related costs represent an opportunity for savings by establishing overseas production. At the same time, overseas production can exploit cheap labour and other resources. The company's management orientation is still largely **ethnocentric**. Some functions, such as R&D and marketing are centralised and there is centralised control of manufacturing operations with regular reports to headquarters. Worldwide synergies and economies of scale are sought and decisions on adapting to local conditions are made at headquarters. Products are still largely standardised.

(d)   **Insiderisation**. The company clones itself in its overseas markets, completing the corporate functionality in each location, rather than restricting itself to marketing. The aim is to develop a full marketing capability and offer products suited to local requirements. The management is shifting to a **polycentric** orientation and thinks of itself as a **multinational**. This approach reduces exchange rate and political risk but requires financial commitment. Economies of scale will be lost and there may be inefficiencies of co-ordination.

(e)   **The global company**. The global company differs from the multinational in that it has a **geocentric** management orientation. It takes a world view while recognising local differences and similarities. It minimises its local adaptation of products and the rest of the marketing mix to those things that actually add customer value and it makes use of the best of its global facilities and people to promote overall excellence. It is likely to centralise functions such as R&D, finance and HR, though not necessarily all in the same place. At the same time, its operations will be controlled locally. The primary skill of the global company is to integrate learning, skills, competences and technologies in order to achieve global efficiencies combined with local responsiveness. It manages the value chain so that each part is centred in an optimal location. It is subject to a number of problems.

- Differing cultural values may undermine the global corporate identity
- Senior executives with the right mix of attitudes and skills are likely to be scarce
- It is subject to a wide range of environmental risks, particularly political ones

Ohmae suggests there are five reasons why companies are moving towards the global stage. He calls these the **five Cs**:

(a)   **Customer**. Market convergence is driven by widespread customer demand for products with similar characteristics.

(b)   **Company**. The search for economies of scale drives expansion towards the global scale.

(c)   **Competition**. The very existence of global competitors motivates companies to expand for reasons of prestige and competitiveness. They may also be amenable to cost-reducing strategic alliances.

(d)   **Currency**. Exchange rate risk can be managed most easily when a company has major cash flows in the countries in which it operates.

(e)   **Country**. Multiple locations enable a company to exploit both absolute and comparative advantage. They also enable it to promote itself as locally oriented in each country, thus enhancing its image with the local government and markets.

There are other factors encouraging the globalisation of world trade.

(a)   **Financial factors** such as developing nation debt; often lenders require the initiation of economic reforms as a condition of the loan. This can lead to a reduction in local protectionism and a consequent increase in trade.

(b)   **Country/continent** connections, such as that between the UK and the Commonwealth which foster trade and tourism.

(c) **Legal and regulatory factors** such as industrial standards and protection of intellectual property, which encourage the development and spread of standardised technology and design.

(d) **Markets** trading in international commodities; commodities are not physically exchanged, only the rights to ownership. A buyer can, thanks to efficient systems of trading and modern communications, buy a commodity in its country of origin for delivery to a specific destination at some future time.

(e) **The internet**: major companies are developing online systems of internal co-ordination and procurement.

(f) **Government policy** in many countries seeks to control the balance of payments by discouraging imports. Government policy towards importers will also reflect their quite proper desire to expand their economies and hence, employment and improve the local standard of living. Local manufacture may thus be the only way to access some markets.

3.4 Designs for global businesses

FAST FORWARD

Bartlett and Ghoshal discern four types of organisations, depending on the strength or weakness of pressure to globalise and the need for local adaptation:

- Global environment: (geocentric) global product divisions
- International environment; (ethnocentric) international division
- Transnational environment; (polycentric) integrated systems and structures
- Multinational environment; (polycentric) national or regional divisions

Bartlett and Ghoshal find that the pressures driving globalisation exist independently of the need for local responsiveness; and that both vary from industry to industry. The relationship between these pressures influences both the management orientation and the structure of the company that operates internationally.

(a) The **global company**, if active in more than one industry, is likely to be organised into product divisions with global scope. Efficiency is likely to be a key strategic competency.

(b) Companies operating in industries that require **little local differentiation** and at the same time are not subject to pressure for globalisation will tend to be structured with an international or export division.

(c) The **multinational environment** drives a polycentric orientation, with largely autonomous local operating companies. Responsiveness to local demand is likely to be a key strategic competency.

(d) The **transnational environment** is particularly difficult to respond to. Global scale is desirable but local conditions require differentiated approaches. The structural response may be the **global heterarchy**. Each regional or national unit achieves global scale and influence within the overall organisation by exploiting its specialised competences on behalf of the whole company. Some headquarters functions, such as R&D may be diffused across the organisation. The role of the global strategic apex is to promote a corporate culture and shared values that will promote co-operation and co-ordination. *JS&W* call this type of company a **transnational**: we will discuss it in more detail later in this Study Text.

	Low requirement for local adaptation and responsiveness	High requirement for local adaptation and responsiveness
High pressure to globalise	**Global environment** Geocentric orientation Global product divisions (Chemicals, construction)	**Transnational environment** Polycentric orientation Integrated systems and structures (Pharmaceuticals, motor vehicles)
Low pressure to globalise	**International environment** Ethnocentric orientation International division (Paper, textiles)	**Multinational environment** Polycentric orientation National or regional divisions (Fast food, tobacco)

3.5 Market selection

In making a decision as to which market(s) to enter, the firm must start by establishing its objectives. Here are some examples.

(a)   What proportion of total sales will be overseas?

(b)   What are the longer term objectives?

(c)   Will it enter one, a few, or many markets? In most cases, it is better to start by selling in countries with which there is some familiarity and then expand into other countries gradually as experience is gained. Reasons to enter fewer countries at first include the following.

   (i)   Market entry and market control costs are high
   (ii)   Product and market communications modification costs are high
   (iii) There is a large market and potential growth in the initial countries chosen
   (iv) Dominant competitors can establish high barriers to entry

(d)   What types of country should it enter (in terms of environmental factors, economic development, language used, cultural similarities and so on)? Three major criteria should be as follows.

   (i)   Market attractiveness
   (ii)   Competitive advantage
   (iii) Risk

The matrix below can be used to bring together these three major criteria and assist managers in their decisions.

Evaluating which markets to enter

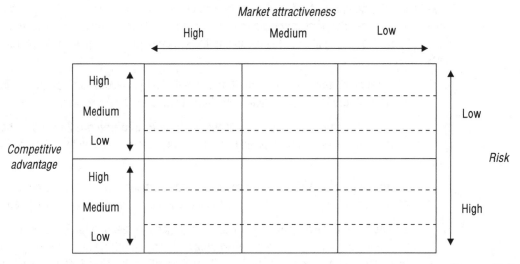

Source: Kotler

(a)   **Market attractiveness**. This concerns such indicators as GNP/head and forecast demand, and market accessibility.

(b)   **Competitive advantage**. This is principally dependent on prior experience in similar markets, language and cultural understanding.

(c)   **Risk**. This involves an analysis of political stability, the possibility of government intervention and similar external influences.

The best markets to enter are those located at the top left of the diagram. The worst are those in the bottom right corner. Obtaining the information needed to reach this decision requires detailed and often costly international marketing research and analysis. Making these decisions is not easy, and a fairly elaborate screening process will be instituted.

In international business, there are several categories of risk.

(a)   **Political risk** relates to factors as diverse as wars, nationalisation, arguments between governments etc.

(b) **Business risk.** This arises from the possibility that the business idea itself might be flawed. As with political risk, it is not unique to international marketing, but firms might be exposed to more sources of risk arising from failures to understand the market.

(c) **Currency risk.** This arises out of the volatility of foreign exchange rates. Given that there is a possibility for speculation and that capital flows are free, such risks are increasing.

(d) **Profit repatriation risk.** Government actions may make it hard to repatriate profits.

3.6 Modes of entry to foreign markets

FAST FORWARD

Modes of entry to foreign markets vary widely and include:

- Direct and indirect exporting
- Wholly owned overseas production
- Contract manufacture
- Joint ventures

The most suitable mode of entry depends on

- Marketing objectives
- Mode availability
- HR requirements
- Risks
- Firm size
- Mode quality
- Market research feedback
- Control needs

If an organisation has decided to enter an overseas market, the way it does so is of crucial strategic importance. Broadly, three ways of entering foreign markets can be identified: **indirect exports**, **direct exports** and **overseas manufacture**.

3.7 Choice of mode

The most suitable mode of entry varies:

(a) **Among firms in the same industry** (eg a new exporter as opposed to a long-established exporter)

(b) **According to the market** (eg some countries limit imports to protect domestic manufacturers whereas others promote free trade)

(c) **Over time** (eg as some countries become more, or less, hostile to direct inward investment by foreign companies)

A large number of considerations apply.

Consideration	Comment
The firm's marketing objectives	These relate to volume, time scale and coverage of market segments. Thus setting up an overseas production facility would be inappropriate if sales are expected to be low in volume.
The firm's size	A small firm is less likely than a large one to possess sufficient resources to set up and run a production facility overseas.
Mode availability	Some countries only allow a restricted level of imports, but will welcome a firm if it builds manufacturing facilities which provide jobs and limit the outflow of foreign exchange.
Mode quality	All modes may be possible in theory, but some are of questionable quality or practicality. The lack of suitably qualified distributors or agents would preclude the export, direct or indirect, of high technology goods needing installation, maintenance and servicing by personnel with specialist technical skills.
Human resources requirements	When a firm is unable to recruit suitable staff, either at home or overseas, indirect exporting or the use of agents based overseas may be the only realistic option.
Market feedback information	In some cases, a firm can receive feedback information about the market and its marketing effort from its sales staff or distribution channels. In these circumstances, direct export or joint ventures may be preferred to indirect export.

Consideration	Comment
Learning curve requirements	Firms which intend a heavy future involvement in an overseas market might need to gain the experience that close involvement in an overseas market can bring. This argues against the use of indirect exporting as the mode of entry.
Risks	Firms might prefer the indirect export mode as assets are safer from expropriation.
Control needs	Production overseas by a wholly owned subsidiary gives a firm absolute control while indirect exporting offers only limited control over the marketing mix to the exporter.

3.8 Exporting

Goods are made at home but sold abroad. It is the easiest, cheapest and most commonly used route into a new foreign market.

3.8.1 Advantages of exporting

(a) Exporters can **concentrate production** in a single location, giving **economies of scale** and **consistency of product quality**.

(b) Firms lacking experience can try international marketing on a **small scale**.

(c) Firms can **test** their international marketing plans and strategies before risking investment in overseas operations.

(d) Exporting **minimises operating costs**, administrative overheads and personnel requirements.

3.8.2 Indirect exports

Indirect exporting is where a firm's goods are sold abroad by other organisations who can offer greater market knowledge.

(a) **Export houses** are firms which facilitate exporting on behalf of the producer. Usually the producer has little control over the market and the marketing effort.

(b) **Specialist export management firms** perform the same functions as an in-house export department but are normally remunerated by way of commission.

(c) **UK buying offices of foreign stores and governments**.

(d) **Complementary exporting** ('piggy back exporting') occurs when one producing organisation (the carrier) uses its own established international marketing channels to market (either as distributor, or agent or merchant) the products of another producer (the rider) as well as its own.

3.8.3 Direct exports

Direct exporting occurs where the producing organisation itself performs the export tasks rather than using an intermediary. Sales are made directly to customers overseas who may be the wholesalers, retailers or final users.

(a) **Sales to final user**. Typical customers include industrial users, governments or mail order customers.

(b) Strictly speaking an **overseas export agent** or distributor is an overseas firm hired to effect a sales contract between the principal (ie the exporter) and a customer. Agents do not take title to goods; they earn a commission (or profit).

(c) **Company branch offices abroad**. A firm can establish its own office in a foreign market for the purpose of marketing and distribution as this gives greater control.

A firm can manufacture its products overseas, either by itself or by using an overseas manufacturer.

3.9 Overseas production

Benefits of overseas manufacture

- A **better understanding of customers** in the overseas market.
- **Economies of scale** in large markets.
- **Production costs are lower** in some countries than at home.
- **Lower storage and transportation costs**.
- **Overcomes the effects of tariff and non-tariff barriers**.
- Manufacture in the overseas market **may help win orders from the public sector**.

3.9.1 Contract manufacture

Licensing is a quite common arrangement as it avoids the cost and problems of setting up overseas.

In the case of **contract manufacture** a firm (the contractor) makes a contract with another firm (the contractee) abroad whereby the contractee manufactures or assembles a product on behalf of the contractor. Contract manufacture is suited to **countries** where the **small size of the market** discourages investment in plant and to **firms** whose main **strengths are in marketing** rather than production.

Advantages of contract manufacture

- No need to invest in plant overseas
- Lower risks associated with currency fluctuations
- Risk of asset expropriation is minimised
- Control of marketing is retained by the contractor
- Lower transport costs and, sometimes, lower production costs

Disadvantages of contract manufacture

- Suitable overseas producers cannot always be easily identified
- The need to train the contractee producer's personnel
- The contractee producer may eventually become a competitor
- Quality control problems in manufacturing may arise

3.9.2 Joint ventures

Some governments discourage or even prohibit foreign firms setting up independent operations, so joint ventures are the only option. That said, a joint venture with an indigenous firm provides local knowledge, quickly.

3.9.3 Wholly owned overseas production

Production capacity can be built from scratch, or, alternatively, an existing firm can be acquired.

(a) **Acquisition** has all the benefits and drawbacks of acquiring a domestic company.
(b) **Creating new capacity** can be beneficial if there are no likely candidates for takeover, or if acquisition is prohibited by the government.

Advantages

(a) The firm does **not have to share its profits** with partners of any kind.
(b) The firm does **not have to share or delegate decision-making**.
(c) There are **none of the communication problems** that arise in joint ventures.
(d) The firm is able to operate completely **integrated** international systems.
(e) The firm gains a more **varied experience** from overseas production.

Disadvantages

(a) The **investment** needed prevents some firms from setting up operations overseas.
(b) Suitable **managers** may be **difficult to recruit** at home or abroad.

(c) Some overseas **governments discourage**, and sometimes prohibit, **100% ownership** of an enterprise by a foreign company.

(d) This mode of entry **forgoes the benefits of an overseas partner's market knowledge**, distribution system and other local expertise.

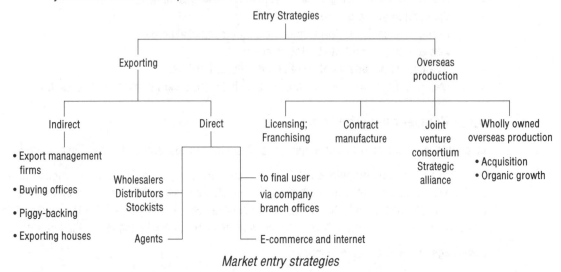

Market entry strategies

	Exporting	**Overseas production**
Advantages	Concentrates production; small start possible; minimises overheads	Lower distribution costs; overcomes trade barriers; possibly lower production costs
Key issues	Exchange rates, protectionism	Political risk; partnership; managing overseas facilities; more risky
Involvement	Usually less involved, but an exporter might depend on the **overseas** market	Usually more involved, but overseas subsidiaries might act independently: varying levels of control and risk

4 The corporate parent and value creation

There are three value-creating roles for the corporate parent:

- **Envisioning corporate intent**, communicating the vision to stakeholders and SBU managers, and acting in accordance with it
- **Intervention** to improve performance
- Provision of **services**, **resources** and **expertise**

Portfolio managers create value by applying financial discipline. They keep their own costs low.

Synergy managers pursue economies of scope through the shared use of competences and resources.

Parental developers add value by deploying their own competences to improve their SBUs' performance.

Earlier in this chapter, we mentioned Porter's views on conglomerate diversification and its potential to destroy value.

We have said that the defining feature of the corporate parent is that it has no direct contact with buyers and competitors. How then, does it create value?

4.1 Value creation

JS&W propose **three main value-creating roles** for the corporate parent:

(a) **Envisioning** is the process of creating a clear vision of **corporate intent**. This is important for three reasons.

(i)   The **corporate parent** itself needs a clear view of its own role if it is to avoid wasteful activity.

(ii)   **External stakeholders** in general, and existing and potential **investors** in particular, need a clear understanding of corporate intent if they are to understand what the organisation does and to make appropriate decisions about their relationships with it.

(iii) The **managers** responsible for the performance of individual SBUs need to know how their work fits in to the corporate scheme so that they know what is expected of them. Their motivation also depends to some extent on having a reasonable belief that the corporate parent knows what it is doing.

(b)   **Intervention** to improve performance or develop business strategy takes a number of forms:

(i)   **Monitoring and control** of performance against plans, targets and intentions
(ii)   Action to develop SBUs' **strategic capability**
(iii) **Coaching** and **training**
(iv)   Promoting **collaboration** between SBUs and the creation of **synergies**

(c)   The corporate parent may provide **services**, **resources** and **expertise** to its SBUs.

(i)   Financial assistance
(ii)   Resource sharing
(iii) Managerial assistance
(iv)   Central services, such as HRM, purchasing and treasury
(v)   Knowledge creation and management
(vi)   Access to external networks

It might be argued that external market forces and mechanisms such as takeover-enforced management change are capable of dealing with these issues without incurring the overhead cost associated with the existence of a corporate parent. JS&W suggest that the corporate parent is likely to produce better results, since it has both access to inside information and the co-operation of the SBU managers.

4.2 Value destruction

The existence of the corporate parent imposes **costs** related to its size; therefore **it must create value at least equal to these costs** if it is to be worth having. This may be challenging. In addition, the activities of the corporate parent may be economically disadvantageous.

(a)   The corporate hierarchy provides an arena for **managers' political ambition**. There is power to be achieved, but at a distance from the commercial realities of life in the SBUs. This is attractive to many.

(b)   The **size and complexity** of a very large corporation can hinder or obscure the development of a clear and useful **corporate vision**.

(c)   Corporate processes and hierarchy can **slow decision-making**, **stunt enterprise** and **absorb the energies** of SBU managers. This has the effect of blunting market responsiveness and harming overall efficiency.

4.3 Strategic rationale   12/10

JS&W identify three approaches to value creation that the corporate parent might adopt. They call these approaches **strategic rationales**.

4.3.1 Portfolio managers

The **portfolio manager** provides a service to investors by applying financial disciplines. It seeks out **undervalued companies** as purchase targets, acquires them, and improves their value and performance. Improvement may be achieved by asset stripping (the sale of attractive but inessential non-current assets), by disposing of under-performing elements or by installing new management. Portfolio managers **keep their own costs low** and provide **few central services**. Their SBUs are largely autonomous and their

managers are judged by financial results. Typically, this type of corporate parent presides over a **widely diversified conglomerate**; our earlier remarks about diversification and strategic success apply here.

4.3.2 Synergy managers

The **synergy manager**, reasonably enough, pursues economies of scope; that is, the benefits of synergy. We have already discussed potential sources of synergy: here we may simply remark that the synergy manager aims to achieve high efficiency in the **shared use of resources and competences**. To do this, it must overcome some difficulties:

(a)   The **costs** involved in sharing
(b)   The impact of **self-interest** among SBU managers
(c)   **Incompatibility of systems and culture** among SBUs
(d)   Variation in **local conditions**

Synergy managers must be **determined** if they are to achieve their goals. The central staff must integrate and control the efforts of the SBUs, which means they must be familiar with all of their operations and may reduce managerial motivation within the SBUs. The corporate parent must also be realistic about its ability to leverage the resources and competences it believes to offer synergistic benefits: it is easy to become subject to the **illusion of synergy**.

4.3.3 Parental developers

The **parental developer** adds value to its SBUs by deploying its own specific competences to aid them in their operations and development. To do this requires certain qualities in the corporate parent.

(a)   It must have **actual, demonstrable competences** to deploy, otherwise its efforts will be mere interference and a distraction to the SBUs.

(b)   Since it is unlikely that it can be equally good at everything, it must be prepared to divest itself of capabilities that can be **provided externally at lower cost**.

(c)   It must have sufficient understanding of its SBUs to discern genuine **opportunities for intervention**.

The parental developer may encounter a problem in the form of a high-performing SBU that offers no opportunities for the deployment of its competences. Logically, it would dispose of this business, since its relationship with it can only be one of adding cost, but the likelihood of any corporate parent actually doing this seems low. Alternatively, it could attempt to change its role in respect of such a SBU and become a portfolio manager or synergy manager. The danger of doing this is the potential for loss of focus and confusion as to just what it should be doing.

Exam focus point

> In the December 2010 exam, 10 marks were available for explaining the three strategic rationales and for assessing their relevance to the company in the scenario. Despite these being relatively theoretical marks, the examining team commented on the poor standard of answers given by candidates, with many scoring three or less of the ten possible marks. This appeared to be due to a lack of knowledge in this area of the syllabus.

 Case Study   **Corporate headquarters**

'The corporate head office should be fit for purpose, and justify itself in terms of added value,' says Michael Goold, founding director of the Ashridge strategic management centre in London. A dictatorial and over-mighty headquarters is unlikely to provide the support that the rest of the organisation needs.

In the late 1980s and early 1990s, there was a joke about the so-called 'inverse atrium rule' of head offices: the grander the corporate setting, the more trouble that organisation was likely to be in. Empire builders have long aimed to intimidate both competitors and colleagues with imposing HQs. It is an ancient human instinct , embodied by Shelley's Ozymandias, 'king of kings', whose resonant challenge to all-comers was: 'Look on my works, ye mighty, and despair!'

In an article in the *Strategic Management Journal*, Mr Goold, with Harvard's David Collis and Ashridge's David Young, describes four main roles that an effective head office has to perform.

First, there is unavoidable governance and compliance activity. While more people are needed for this than in the past, owing to today's more onerous regulational environment, Mr Goold warns against over-engineering. 'There is a danger that you end up double-checking everything, that there is too much monitoring going on, slowing down the work,' he says. 'This aspect of head office should be as lean and mean as possible.'

A second function of HQ is the 'value-added parenting' of other corporate activity, offering support to the executives from the centre. The acid test here is that the cost of this parenting should be less than the value it is generating in the rest of the business.

A third element of head office's work are shared services – HR, call centres, facilities management – many of which have been outsourced in recent years, or handed back to business units. And the fourth role is that of the 'core resource unit' – an example would be the research and development team in a pharmaceutical business.

While cutting out waste and duplication is obviously a good idea, it does not follow that headquarters should always be shrinking. As Mr Goold *et al* argue: 'Simply reducing the size of the headquarters is no guarantee of improved performance. Indeed, companies with larger headquarters typically outperform those with smaller headquarters.' On the other hand, globalisation may require leadership to be 'distributed' around the world. 'Core resource units' do not have to sit in the same building as compliance teams.

Stephan Stern, *Financial Times,* 10 April 2007

5 The corporate portfolio

A parent may deploy four policies towards its SBUs:

- Build
- Hold
- Harvest
- Divest

The SBU portfolio must be managed against three criteria:

- Balance
- Attractiveness
- Strategic fit

Matrix-based models are used to manage **portfolios:** the Ashridge model is the only one to address strategic fit and assumes the **parental developer** approach is used.

A corporate parent of any type will have to make decisions about acquiring, nurturing and disposing of subsidiaries.

Four **major strategies** can be pursued with respect to products, market segments and, indeed, SBUs:

(a) **Build**. A build strategy forgoes short-term earnings and profits in order to increase market share.

(b) **Hold**. A hold strategy seeks to maintain the current position.

(c) **Harvest**. A harvesting strategy seeks short-term earning and profits at the expense of long-term development.

(d) **Divest**. Divestment reduces negative cash flow and releases resources for use elsewhere.

A number of strategic tools have been developed to assist the decision process. These tools help the corporate parent to manage its portfolio of SBUs against three criteria:

(a) **Balance** in relation to markets and corporate needs

(b) **Attractiveness** in terms of profitability and growth

(c) **Strategic fit**, in terms of potential synergy and parenting capability

The balance and attractiveness criteria are addressed by a range of matrix-based tools; strategic fit is the subject of a single model, the Ashridge portfolio display.

5.1 The Boston classification   12/12, 12/10

FAST FORWARD

> The **Boston classification** classifies business units in terms of their **capacity for growth within the market** and the market's capacity for growth as a whole.

The **Boston Consulting Group** (BCG) developed a matrix based on empirical research that assesses businesses in terms of potential cash generation and cash expenditure requirements. SBUs are categorised in terms of **market growth rate** and **relative market share**.

Key term

> **Market share:** One entity's sale of a product or service in a specified market expressed as a percentage of total sales by all entities offering that product or service.'

(a) Assessing rate of **market growth** as high or low depends on the conditions in the market. No single percentage rate can be set, since new markets may grow explosively while mature ones grow hardly at all. High market growth rate can indicate good opportunities for profitable operations. However, intense competition in a high growth market can erode profit, while a slowly growing market with high barriers to entry can be very profitable.

(b) **Relative market share** is assessed as a ratio: it is market share compared with the market share of the **largest competitor**. Thus, a relative market share greater than unity indicates that the SBU is the market leader. BGG settled on market share as a way of **estimating costs** and thus **profit potential**, because both costs and market share are connected with **production experience**: as experience in satisfying a particular market demand for value increases, market share can be expected to increase also, and costs to fall. The connection between lower costs and higher market share was independently confirmed by PIMS studies.

Relative market share

		High	Low
Market growth	High	Stars	Question marks
	Low	Cash cows	Dogs

Boston Consulting Group matrix

The portfolio should be balanced, with cash cows providing finance for stars and question marks; and a minimum of dogs.

(a) In the short term, **stars** require capital expenditure in excess of the cash they generate, in order to maintain their position in their competitive growth market, but promise high returns in the future. Strategy: **build**.

(b) In due course, stars will become **cash cows**. Cash cows need very little capital expenditure, since mature markets are likely to be quite stable, and they generate high levels of cash income. Cash cows can be used to finance the stars. Strategy: **hold** or **harvest** if weak.

(c) **Question marks** must be assessed as to whether they justify considerable capital expenditure in the hope of increasing their market share, or should they be allowed to die quietly as they are squeezed out of the expanding market by rival products? Strategy: **build** or **harvest**.

(d) **Dogs** may be ex-cash cows that have now fallen on hard times. Although they will show only a modest net cash outflow, or even a modest net cash inflow, they are cash traps which tie up funds and provide a poor return on investment. However, they may have a useful role, either to complete a product range or to keep competitors out. There are also many smaller niche businesses in markets that are difficult to consolidate that would count as dogs but which are quite successful. Strategy: **divest** or **hold**.

The BCG matrix must be used with care.

(a)   It may be difficult to define 'high' and 'low' on both axes of the matrix.

(b)   The matrix has been used to assess **products** rather than **SBUs**, but *JS&W* say this should not be done; nor should it be applied to broad markets that include many market segments. They do, however, recommend it for assessing a **portfolio of international operations**, though with three caveats.

    (i)   The permitted forms of activity and ownership vary from country to country.
    (ii)   Political risk is not considered.
    (iii)   Shared resources are not considered.

(c)   The matrix is built around cash flows but **innovative capacity** may be the critical resource.

Exam focus point

You should now think back to our discussion of the product life cycle in this Study Text. We noted there that JS&W do not recommend the use of the BCG matrix for product portfolio purposes and recommended that you should initially think in terms of the product life cycle when answering questions that call for the analysis of product portfolios.

In December 2014, the Section A question focused on a group of companies operating in the transport industry. Candidates were required to evaluate the performance and contribution of the three operating companies. The use of the BCG matrix was highly appropriate in assessing the group's portfolio.

5.2 The public sector portfolio matrix

FAST FORWARD

The **public sector portfolio matrix** classifies activities in terms of their popularity and the resources available for them.

Montanari and Bracker proposed a matrix for the analysis of services provided by public sector bodies. This might be applied at the level of local or national government, or an executive agency with a portfolio of services. The axes are an assessment of service efficiency and public attractiveness: naturally, political support for a service or organisation depends to a great extent on the degree to which the public need and appreciate it.

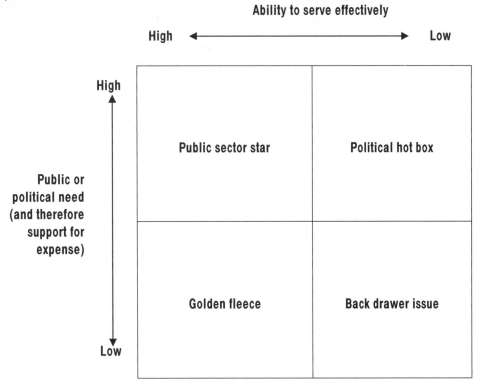

The public sector portfolio matrix

(a) A **public sector star** is something that the system is doing well and should not change. They are essential to the viability of the system.

(b) **Political hot boxes** are services that the public want, or which are mandated, but for which there are not adequate resources or competences.

(c) **Golden fleeces** are services that are done well but for which there is low demand. They may therefore be perceived to be undesirable uses for limited resources. They are potential targets for cost cutting.

(d) **Back drawer issues** are unappreciated and have low priority for funding. They are obvious candidates for cuts, but if managers perceive them as essential, they should attempt to increase support for them and move them into the **political hot box** category.

5.3 The Ashridge portfolio display

The **Ashridge model** assesses the benefit SBUs can derive from a corporate parent playing the parental developer role. **Heartland businesses** both have CSFs that fit the parent's resources and competences *and* provide opportunities for good use of them. **Alien businesses** have neither quality. **Ballast businesses** are well-understood by the parent but need little assistance. **Value trap businesses** need help but of a kind that the parent cannot provide.

As mentioned earlier, the Ashridge portfolio display is concerned with **strategic fit**, that is, the role of the corporate parent and the suitability of the range of SBUs it manages. The concept is based on the **parental developer** approach to the role of the corporate parent discussed earlier in this chapter. The principles embodied in the model can be approached from two directions.

(a) Corporate parents should build portfolios of businesses that they can develop effectively.
(b) Corporate parents should seek to build parenting skills that are relevant to their portfolios.

The coherence of the corporation overall may be assessed by reference to two variables.

(a) '**Feel**': The degree of fit between the parent's skills, resources and other characteristics and the SBUs' CSFs

(b) '**Benefit**': the degree of fit between the opportunities the SBUs present for parenting and the parent's skills resources and other characteristics

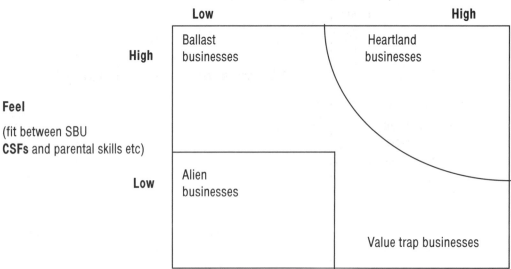

The Ashridge portfolio display

(a)   **Heartland businesses** can benefit from the attention of the parent without risk of harm from unsuitable developments.

(b)   **Ballast businesses** are well-understood by the parent, but need little assistance. They would do just as well if they were independent businesses. They should bear as little central cost as possible.

(c)   **Value trap businesses** provide good opportunities for parenting, but these opportunities do not relate to the SBU's CSFs. They should only be retained if they can be moved into the heartland; this will require the parent to acquire new skills and resources.

(d)   **Alien businesses** have no place in the portfolio. They need the attention of a skilled parent, but the actual parent does not have the skills and resources required to help them.

This analysis reverses the usual approach to portfolio management: it does not ask what the value of the SBUs is to the centre, but what value the centre can add to the SBUs. This raises two questions.

(a)   Is the **cost burden** of the parent **commensurate with the value it adds**? For example, if the corporate parent's role is limited to, say, relations with the financial markets, it should be small and economically run.

(b)   If a corporate parent has a justifiably interventionist role, **how many SBUs can it parent effectively**?

The trend in business recent years has been decentralisation of decision-making and a move towards **facilitiation** by the parent, rather than active intervention. A similar trend towards privatisation and deregulation has been apparent in the public sector.

Exam focus point

A Section B question in the December 2008 exam asked candidates to consider a potential acquisition by a corporate parent. The Ashridge Portfolio would have provided a useful framework for comparing the parent's skills with the 'parenting' required by the potential acquisition.

5.4 Better off tests

Michael Porter suggests that one of the key issues behind acquisitions should be in realising synergies between the existing company and the new acquisition.

To this end, he suggests that potential acquisitions should be assessed against three tests:

- **Better off test** – Will the company being acquired be better off after the acquisition? Will it gain competitive advantage from being in the group? Will the group be better off as a result of acquiring the company?

- **Attractiveness test** – Is the target industry structurally attractive? (Porter originally developed his tests in relation to diversification, and so was looking at companies making acquisitions in unrelated industries. However, the point about 'attractiveness' could be applied more generally to look at target companies, or countries.)

- **Cost of entry** – The cost of the acquisition (or the cost of entering a new market) must not capitalise all future profits from that acquisition (or market). In other words, will the future cash flows from the acquisition be greater than the amounts paid to acquire it?

Porter also identified another key point in relation to successful acquisitions, which could be called the **parenting test**. Has the company making the acquisition got the necessary skills as a corporate parent to get the best value out of the company being acquired? For example, have they got any experience of previous acquisitions?

6 Business unit strategy: generic strategies

> **Business unit strategy** involves a choice between being the lowest cost producer (**cost leadership**), making the product different from competitors' products in some way (**differentiation**) or specialising on a segment of the market (**focus**, by addressing that segment via a strategy of cost leadership or differentiation). **Porter** believes that a firm *must* choose one of these or be **stuck-in-the-middle**.

Competitive advantage is anything which gives one organisation an edge over its rivals. *Porter* argues that a firm should adopt a competitive strategy intended to achieve competitive advantage for the firm.

Competitive strategy means 'taking offensive or defensive actions to create a dependable position in an industry, to cope successfully with ... competitive forces and thereby yield a superior return on investment for the firm. Firms have discovered many different approaches to this end, and the best strategy for a given firm is ultimately a unique construction reflecting its particular circumstances'. (*Porter*)

6.1 The choice of competitive strategy

Porter believes there are three **generic strategies** for competitive advantage.

Key terms

> **Cost leadership** means being the lowest cost producer in the industry as a whole.
>
> **Differentiation** is the exploitation of a product or service which the *industry as a whole* believes to be unique.
>
> **Focus** involves a restriction of activities to only part of the market (a segment).
>
> *   Providing goods and/or services at lower cost (**cost-focus**)
> *   Providing a differentiated product or service (**differentiation-focus**)

Cost leadership and differentiation are industry-wide strategies. **Focus involves segmentation** but also the pursuit, **within the chosen segment only**, of a strategy of cost leadership or differentiation.

Exam focus point

> Porter's generic strategy model is one of a handful of truly vital theories that you **absolutely must master** for your exam. Study this section with great care and understand the implications of each strategy for the companies that might adopt them. Understanding this area of theory will not only equip you to make sensible suggestions in your answers to many questions, it will also enable you to appreciate important background detail in a wide range of question scenarios.

6.1.1 Cost leadership

A cost leadership strategy seeks to achieve the position of lowest-cost producer in the **industry as a whole**. By producing at the lowest cost, the manufacturer can compete on price with every other producer in the industry, and earn the higher unit profits, if the manufacturer so chooses.

How to achieve overall cost leadership

(a)   Set up production facilities to obtain **economies of scale**.

(b)   Use the **latest technology** to reduce costs and/or enhance productivity (or use cheap labour if available).

(c)   In high technology industries, and in industries depending on labour skills for product design and production methods, exploit the **learning curve effect**. By producing more items than any other competitor, a firm can benefit more from the learning curve, and achieve lower average costs.

(d)   Concentrate on **improving productivity**.

(e)   **Minimise overhead costs**.

(f)   **Get favourable access to sources of supply**.

Classic examples of companies pursuing cost leadership are Black and Decker and South West Airlines. Large out-of-town stores specialising in one particular category of product are able to secure cost leadership by economies of scale over other retailers. Such shops have been called **category killers**; an example is PC World.

6.1.2 Differentiation

A differentiation strategy assumes that competitive advantage can be gained through **particular characteristics** of a firm's products. Products may be divided into three categories.

(a)   **Breakthrough products** offer a radical performance advantage over competition, perhaps at a drastically lower price (eg float glass, developed by Pilkington).

(b)   **Improved products** are not radically different from their competition but are obviously superior in terms of better performance at a competitive price (eg microchips).

(c)   **Competitive products** derive their appeal from a particular compromise of cost and performance. For example, cars are not all sold at rock-bottom prices, nor do they all provide immaculate comfort and performance. They compete with each other by trying to offer a more attractive compromise than rival models.

How to differentiate

(a)   **Build up a brand image** (eg Pepsi's blue cans are supposed to offer different 'psychic benefits' to Coke's red ones).

(b)   **Give the product special features** to make it stand out (eg Russell Hobbs' Millennium kettle incorporated a new kind of element, which boils water faster).

(c)   **Exploit other activities of the value chain** (for example, quality of after-sales service or speed of delivery).

Note: We looked at the value chain earlier in this Study Text. If you cannot remember the activities described in the value chain, you should refer back to it to refresh your memory.

Generic strategies and the five forces

Competitive force	Advantages		Disadvantages	
	Cost leadership	**Differentiation**	**Cost leadership**	**Differentiation**
New entrants	Economies of scale raise entry barriers	Brand loyalty and perceived uniqueness are entry barriers		
Substitutes	Firm is not so vulnerable as its less cost-effective competitors to the threat of substitutes	Customer loyalty is a weapon against substitutes		
Customers	Customers cannot drive down prices further than the next most efficient competitor	Customers have no comparable alternative Brand loyalty should lower price sensitivity		Customers may no longer need the differentiating factor Sooner or later customers become price sensitive
Suppliers	Flexibility to deal with cost increases	Higher margins can offset vulnerability to supplier price rises	Increase in input costs can reduce price advantages	

Competitive force	Advantages		Disadvantages	
	Cost leadership	**Differentiation**	**Cost leadership**	**Differentiation**
Industry rivalry	Firm remains profitable when rivals go under through excessive price competition	Unique features reduce direct competition	Technological change will require capital investment, or make production cheaper for competitors Competitors learn via imitation Cost concerns ignore product design or marketing issues	Imitation narrows differentiation

6.1.3 Focus (or niche) strategy

In a focus strategy, a firm concentrates its attention on one or more particular segments or niches of the market, and does not try to serve the entire market with a single product.

 Case Study   **Internet dating**

Internet dating has grown hugely in popularity over the past decade and more recently, very specialised online dating services have begun to appear.

Uniformdating.com is one such specialised dating service which was launched to provide a dating platform specifically for individuals working in the uniformed services, including the police officers, firemen and women, soldiers, RAF personnel, pilots, doctors and nurses.

Uniformed personnel typically face a number of restrictions as part of their working lives, including working difficult shift patterns, working away or being on tour. These unique circumstances can place a significant strain on these people and the relationships they attempt to maintain. Uniformdating.com claims to understand these difficult circumstances and provide the solution via its matching services to help its members find their ideal match and form lasting relationships.

The site is not, however, restricted to those working in uniform and they welcome and encourage new members who are not necessarily from these professions, but who are looking to meet someone from the uniformed or emergency services. This allows the company not only to serve the main niche of uniformed personnel, but also to tap into the niche market of 'dating a man/woman in a uniform'.

Since its launch the site has grown hugely and, as of April 2012, claims to have "hundreds of thousands of uniformed members". It has successfully carved out this niche in the UK, USA, Canada and Australia.

Other, perhaps less well known, examples of online dating services targeting niche markets include Farmers Only and Geek2Geek. Farmers Only is a US and Canadian dating site aimed at 'down to earth folks only' serving single farmers, ranchers, cowboys, cowgirls and animal lovers. Geek2Geek, also US based, describes itself as 'the safe, friendly, and easy to use site where geeks and their admirers can find each other'. Its advertising explains that, 'traditional dating sites just don't work well for them' .

(a) A **cost focus strategy:** aim to be a cost leader for a particular segment. This type of strategy is often found in the printing, clothes manufacture and car repair industries.

(b) A **differentiation focus strategy:** pursue differentiation for a chosen segment. Luxury goods suppliers are the prime exponents of such a strategy.

Ben and Jerry's ice cream is a good example of a product offering based on differentiation focus.

Porter suggests that a focus strategy can achieve competitive advantage when '**broad-scope**' businesses fall into one of two errors.

(a)   **Underperformance** occurs when a product does not fully meet the needs of a segment and offers the opportunity for a **differentiation focus** player.

(b)   **Overperformance** gives a segment more than it really wants and provides an opportunity for a **cost focus** player.

Advantages

(a)   A niche is more secure and a firm can insulate itself from competition.

(b)   The firm does not spread itself too thinly.

(c)   Both cost leadership and differentiation require **superior performance** – life is easier in a niche, where there may be little or no competition.

Drawbacks of a focus strategy

(a)   The firm sacrifices economies of scale which would be gained by serving a wider market.

(b)   Competitors can move into the segment, with increased resources (eg the Japanese moved into the US luxury car market, to compete with Mercedes and BMW).

(c)   The segment's needs may eventually become less distinct from the main market.

6.2 Which strategy?

Although there is a risk with any of the generic strategies, Porter argues that a firm *must* pursue one of them. A **stuck-in-the-middle** strategy is almost certain to make only low profits. 'This firm lacks the market share, capital investment and resolve to play the low-cost game, the industry-wide differentiation necessary to obviate the need for a low-cost position, or the focus to create differentiation or a low-cost position in a more limited sphere.'

It is also important that both cost leadership and differentiation require superior performance. Therefore, most businesses should pursue some form of focus strategy as it is easier to dominate a niche than a complete market.

Case Study   Tesco: Stuck in the middle?

A report in the *Economist* (2013) highlighted the problems facing UK retail giant Tesco. According to the *Economist*, in December 2013 Tesco reported that 'same-store sales in Britain had dropped 1.5% in the third quarter', with the company's European and Asian operations falling by 4% and 5.1% respectively.

Spending power among British shoppers had failed to reach the heights that it achieved in 2007 and was predicted to be 10% lower in 2013 than six years earlier. However, discount retailers such as Aldi and Lidl experienced a steady increase in year-on-year sales, with the latter reporting an increase of 14% in 2013. Unlike Tesco, retailers such as Lidl have succeeded in offering a 'no-frills' shopping experience, with most produce being wheeled out from the warehouse on pallets straight onto the shop floor. Discounters had worked hard to shed the 'poor man's' stigma that had become synonymous with their brand, with many increasing advertising spending and improving the quality of the goods sold.

Tesco's problems had been further compounded as upmarket rival Waitrose reported an increase in sales of 9% in 2013. In late 2013, Tesco withdrew its supermarket operations in the US after its 'Fresh & Easy' venture failed to deliver the anticipated returns. In a bid to attract more customers in the UK, the then Tesco CEO Philip Clarke focused efforts on enhancing the retailer's online offering and investing in new convenience stores. Critics of Phillip Clarke's strategic vision argued that customers had 'fallen out of love with Tesco'. In his article 'Tesco, what went wrong', Kamal Ahmed (October 2014) highlighted that under Clarke's tenure, the retailer had 'bought posh coffee shops, restaurants and digital businesses, as it expanded the services it thought customers would be interested in'.

In July 2014, Tesco announced that Philip Clarke would be leaving the company later in the year. In September 2014, Dave Lewis took over as Tesco CEO.

By late 2014, Tesco's fortunes had worsened further, due to the growing popularity of the discount retailers. Zoe Wood of the Guardian reported that Tesco was continuing to 'lose shoppers in the face of a

fierce price war being waged by rivals and fast growing discount chains Aldi and Lidl'. The retailers like-for-like sales (which exclude gains from new shopfloor space – tumbled 5.5% in the final three months of the period. Tesco's profits in the UK more than halved to £499m. This was largely caused by falling sales and lower profit margins, resulting from a round of price cuts launched in the face of a mounting supermarket price war.

Commenting on the company's performance Dave Lewis said: 'I think we've got to be a little bit disappointed. Relative to the market, we've not been as competitive as I would have liked us to be. I think at Tesco we lose our way when we don't let the customer guide us.'

Wood notes Tesco's substantial problems overseas, 'with underlying sales falling in 8 out of 10 of Tesco's international markets'.

Sources:

'Stuck in the middle', (December 2013) published by *The Economist*, www.economist.com

'Tesco, what went wrong?', (October 2014) by Kamal Ahmed, published by the *BBC* www.bbc.co.uk

'Black day for Tesco as profits fall by 92%', (October 2014) by Zoe Wood, published by The Guardian; www.theguardian.com

Question	Hermes Telecommunications plc

The managing director of Hermes Telecommunications plc is interested in corporate strategy. Hermes has invested a great deal of money in establishing a network which competes with that of Telecom UK, a recently privatised utility. Initially Hermes concentrated its efforts on business customers in the South East of England, especially the City of London, where it offered a lower cost service to that supplied by Telecom UK. Recently, Hermes has approached the residential market (ie domestic telephone users) offering a lower cost service on long-distance calls. Technological developments have resulted in the possibility of a cheap mobile telecommunication network, using microwave radio links. The franchise for this service has been awarded to Gerbil phone, which is installing transmitters in town centres and at rail stations.

What issues of competitive strategy have been raised in the above scenario, particularly in relation to Hermes Telecommunications plc?

Answer

(a)   Arguably, Hermes initially pursued a cost-focus strategy, by targeting the business segment.

(b)   It seems to be moving into a cost leadership strategy over the whole market although its competitive offer, in terms of lower costs for local calls, is incomplete.

(c)   The barriers to entry to the market have been lowered by the new technology. Gerbil phone might pick up a significant amount of business.

6.3 Conceptual difficulties with generic strategy

In practice, it is rarely simple to draw hard and fast distinctions between the generic strategies as there are conceptual problems underlying them.

(a)   **Cost leadership**

(i)   **Internal focus.** Cost refers to internal measures, rather than the market demand. It can be used to gain market share: but it is the **market share which is important,** not cost leadership as such.

(ii) **Only one firm.** If cost leadership applies across the whole industry, only one firm will pursue this strategy successfully. However, the position is not clear-cut.

- More than one firm might **aspire** to cost leadership, especially in dynamic markets where new technologies are frequently introduced.

- The boundary between cost leadership and cost focus might be blurred.

- Firms competing market-wide might have different competences or advantages that confer cost leadership in different segments.

(iii) **Higher margins can be used for differentiation.** Having low costs does *not* mean you have to charge lower prices or compete on price. A cost leader can choose to 'invest higher margins in R&D or marketing'. Being a cost leader arguably gives producers more freedom to choose *other* competitive strategies.

(b) **Differentiation**. Porter assumes that a differentiated product will always be sold at a **higher price**.

(i) However, a **differentiated product** may be sold at the same price as competing products in order to **increase market share**.

(ii) **Choice of competitor.** Differentiation from whom? Who are the competitors? Do they serve other market segments? Do they compete on the same basis?

(iii) **Source of differentiation.** This can include **all** aspects of the firm's offer, not only the product. Restaurants aim to create an atmosphere or 'ambience', as well as serving food of good quality.

Focus probably has fewer conceptual difficulties, as it ties in very neatly with ideas of market segmentation. In practice, most companies pursue this strategy to some extent, by designing products/services to meet the needs of particular target markets.

'Stuck-in-the-middle' is therefore what many companies actually pursue quite successfully. Any number of strategies can be pursued, with different approaches to **price** and the **perceived added value** (ie the differentiation factor) in the eyes of the customer.

6.4 The strategy clock

FAST FORWARD The strategy clock develops Porter's theory, analysing strategies in terms of **price** and **perceived value added**.

Porter's basic concept of generic strategies has been the subject of further discussion. JS&W, quoting Bowman, describe the strategic options using the **strategy clock.**

The eight strategies shown on the clock represent different approaches to creating value for the customer and each customer will buy from the provider whose offering most closely matches their own view of the proper relationship between price and perceived benefits.

Each position on the clock has its own **critical success factor**, since each strategy is defined in market terms. Positions 1 and 2 will attract customers who are price conscious above all, with position 2 giving a little more emphasis to serviceability. These are typical approaches in commodity markets. By contrast, strategies 4 and 5 are relevant to consumers who require a customised product.

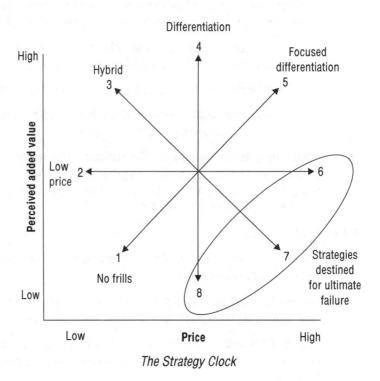

The Strategy Clock

6.4.1 Price-based strategies

Strategies 1 and 2 are price-based strategies.

(a)   A **no frills** strategy is appropriate under several conditions. It can be used for commodity-like products and the most price-conscious customers. It is also suitable where customers' switching costs are low and where there is little opportunity for competition on product features. This strategy may be used for market entry, to gain experience and build volume. This was done by Japanese car manufacturers in the 1960s, and is now being seen in the airline industry, with companies such as EasyJet and Ryanair successfully adopting a no-frills approach.

The no-frills airlines sell tickets at low prices but with limited customer services, and with a focus on keeping costs low at all times. They fly to less-congested, secondary airports, outside peak times, to reduce landing fees; they have fast turnaround times to maximise aircraft usage, and they make ticket sales over the internet to avoid travel agents' commissions. They have no reserved seats to encourage customers to turn up early to prevent delays, and do not offer complimentary food and drink like premium carriers, but instead generate ancillary revenue through in-flight sales.

(b)   A **low price** strategy offers better value than competitors. This can lead to price wars and thence, to reduced margins and lack of reinvestment for all players, and Porter's generic strategy of **cost leadership** is appropriate to a firm adopting this strategy.

6.4.2 Differentiation strategies

Strategies 3, 4 and 5 are all differentiation strategies. Each one represents a different trade-off between market share (with its cost advantages) and margin (with its direct impact on profit). Differentiation can be created in three ways:

*   Product features
*   Marketing, including powerful brand promotion
*   Core competences

The **hybrid** strategy seeks both differentiation and a lower price than competitors. The cost base must be low enough to permit reduced prices and reinvestment to maintain differentiation. This strategy may be more advantageous than differentiation alone under certain circumstances:

*   If it leads to growth in market share
*   If differentiation rests on core competences and costs can be reduced elsewhere

- If a low price approach is suited to a particular market segment
- Where it is used as a market entry strategy

The basic **differentiation** strategy comes in two variants, depending on whether a price premium is charged or a competitive price is accepted in order to build market share. The pursuit of a differentiation strategy requires detailed and accurate **market intelligence**. The **strategic customers** and their preferences must be clearly identified, as must the competitors and their likely responses. The chosen basis for differentiation should be inherently difficult to imitate, and will probably need to be developed over time.

A strategy of **focussed differentiation** seeks a high price premium in return for a high degree of differentiation. This implies concentration on a well-defined and probably quite restricted market segment. **Centres of excellence** in the public sector pursue a similar strategy.

(a) Focus is a common start-up strategy: expansion may prompt or require a gradual move to a less focussed differentiation.

(b) It is difficult to pursue focus with only part of an organisation: the less focussed part, even if it is to some extent differentiated, can damage the brand values of the focussed part.

(c) In the public sector, stakeholders expecting universal provision will object to focus on particular segments.

(d) Focus is aimed at a specific segment: if the non-focussed product is improved enough to become acceptable to this segment, the advantage of focus will be eroded. Alternatively, competitors may make even more focussed offerings to sub-segments, again eroding the focuser's original advantage

 Case Study   Watches

Leading global watch brands are positioned to appeal to particular buyer groups. Swiss brand Omega is over 150 years old, its watches are largely targeted at business professionals and watch collectors. Omega is the producer of quality precision watches and prides itself on its long time association with the Olympic Games, having been nominated as the official time keeper on 21 occasions. Fellow Swiss brand, TAG Heuer is classed as a luxury watch brand, targeted again at business professionals but also sports fans due to its partnership with the McClaren F1 team. Fossil watches, by contrast, was established in the US in the 1980s; its watches are targeted more as fashion items and are sold at considerably lower prices.

Exam focus point

The December 2007 exam included a question which asked why it would be inappropriate for a company pursuing a differentiation strategy to move to a no-frills position. Make sure you are aware of the unique characteristics of each type of strategy so that you can identify where they might be suitable (or unsuitable).

One of the requirements in the December 2014 exam asked for a discussion of how a road haulage company could pursue a hybrid strategy of offering low prices while attempting to differentiate, in order to achieve a competitive advantage. The use of Bowman' strategy clock was highly appropriate as it considers perceived added value and price.

6.4.3 Failure strategies

Combinations 6, 7 and 8 are likely to result in failure.

6.5 The TOWS matrix

We have already introduced the TOWS matrix and Weihrich's classification of strategies based upon it, in the chapter on strategic capability in Section A of this Study Text.

However, it will be useful to review it here, because each of the general classes of strategy it suggests could be useful to consider alongside the strategy clock, particularly when considering cash flows and the availability of resources. The TOWS matrix is also a relevant tool when developing product-market strategies, which we look at later in this chapter.

External factors (opportunities: threats)

Internal factors (strengths: weaknesses)	**SO** Use strengths to maximise opportunities (maxi-maxi strategy)	**ST** Use strengths to minimise threats (maxi-mini strategy)
	WO Minimise weaknesses by taking advantage of opportunities (mini-maxi strategy)	**WT** Minimise weaknesses and avoid threats (mini-mini strategy)

TOWS matrix

SO This is a strong position. A company might look to use this strength to expand globally or develop new products, building on its existing reputation.

ST This is a less strong position than 'SO' but an 'ST' company still has strengths it can draw on. Consider this example: A clothing manufacturing company with an established reputation for good quality products is now facing competition from cheap overseas competitors. The clothing company should adopt a differentiation strategy to use its reputation and brand to try to reduce the competitive threat. However, this strategy may not be successful if the cheap, imported clothes are also good quality, in which case the established company will need to consider moving its manufacturing plant abroad to a low cost location, and compete using a low price strategy.

WO A company has identified opportunities in the external environment, but internal organisational weaknesses (for example, inadequate manufacturing capacity, or poor distribution or marketing networks) prevent it from taking advantage of them. In this case, the company either needs to re-engineer its processes, or collaborate with a company which has the resources it needs. If the 'WO' company has sufficient funds, it may consider acquiring a company with the resources it needs (although it is unlikely that a 'WO' company will have sufficient funds to be able to do this).

WT A company faced with internal weaknesses and external threats may be in a precarious position and be forced into defensive strategies, for example, restructuring, or downsizing. Alternatively, it may look for a merger with another company, or, in the worst case scenario, it will have to go into liquidation.

An organisation in such a defensive position can only ever use strategy to protect itself. It cannot create success because it has neither the internal strengths nor the external opportunities needed to do so.

Successful companies, even if they temporarily use SO, WO and WT strategies, will attempt to get into a situation where they can work from strengths to take advantage of opportunities (SO strategy). They will strive to overcome weakness and make them strengths; and if they face threats, they will cope with them so that they can focus on opportunities.

7 Sustaining competitive advantage

FAST FORWARD

Different policies are required to sustain differentiation or price-based strategies. Lock-in is achieved when a product becomes the industry standard.

When we discussed competition in Chapter 3, we said that the business environment might be sufficiently stable to permit a build-up of **sustainable competitive advantage**. Alternatively, there might be **hypercompetition** and a need for rapid innovation and response to competitive moves. In Chapter 4, we went on to consider the **strategic capabilities** needed under these varying conditions. We will now consider the ways in which businesses can **form strategies** to respond to these two different conditions.

7.1 Sustaining price-based strategies

(a) **Low margins** can be sustained, either by increased volumes or by cross-subsidisation from another business unit.

(b) A **cost leader** can operate at a price advantage, but to be sustainable, cost leaders must constantly and aggressively drive down all of their costs.

(c) A cost leader or a company with extensive financial resources can win a **price war**.

(d) A **no-frills strategy** can succeed in the long term if it is aimed at a segment that particularly appreciates low price.

7.2 Sustaining differentiation

Sustaining differentiation is difficult. To begin with, it is more than just being *different*: the difference must be **valued by customers**. Secondly, a difference that a competitor can easily imitate gives no sustainable advantage.

(a) **Attempts at imitation can be obstructed** by, for example, securing preferred access to customers or suppliers through bidding or licensing procedures.

(b) Some resources are **inherently immobile**. This can be the result of **intangibility**, as in the case of brands; high customer switching costs, as with proprietary technology; or **co-specialisation**, which occurs when organisations' value chains are intimately linked.

(c) **Cost advantage** can be used to sustain differentiation, rather than price advantage by investing in innovation, brand management or quality improvement.

7.3 Lock-in

Lock-in is achieved in a market when a company's product becomes the **industry standard**. Direct competitors are reduced to minor niches and **compatibility** with the industry standard becomes a prerequisite for complementary products. Microsoft has achieved this position in the market for PC operating systems and is only challenged by Linux because the latter product is free to use. Sony regularly attempts to establish industry standards in order to achieve market dominance, with varying degrees of success. The original Walkman became the industry standard, but the Betamax video recording standard lost to VHS. The concept of lock-in is equally applicable to companies following strategies of cost leadership or differentiation.

Factors affecting lock-in

(a) **Perception of dominance**: potential competitors and suppliers of complementary products will only conform to an attempt to set standards if they perceive the standard-setter as dominant in the market, usually in terms of market share.

(b) **First mover advantage**: a standard is more likely to be set early in the lifecycle of a new product than when it is mature.

(c) **Self-reinforcement**: once dominance is achieved, conforming with the standard becomes necessary for survival.

(d) **Fierce defence**: a firm that achieves lock-in will defend its position vigorously. Visa threatened to impose coercive settlement fees on its top 100 card issuers if they attempted to move their operations to MasterCard.

Lock-in is also known as the **delta model**, which is the term used by Hax and Wilde, who described it in their book of the same name.

7.4 Strategy and hypercompetition

FAST FORWARD

> **Hypercompetition** makes it impossible to create lasting advantage with a steady policy: a series of short-term moves is required. These include repositioning on the strategy clock, counter attack, imitation and attacks on barriers to entry.

We discussed **hypercompetition** in Chapter 3. There we said that it was a condition of constant competitive change created by frequent, boldly aggressive competitive moves. This makes it **impossible to create lasting competitive advantage**. Under these conditions, continuing success depends on the dynamic capabilities discussed in Chapter 4 and on the effective exploitation of a series of short-term moves. Here are some examples.

7.4.1 Repositioning on the strategy clock

Repositioning may be possible. For example, a firm using a no frills strategy may move towards higher quality combined with a low price; that is from position 1 on the clock to position 2. Similarly, a differentiator may attempt to create a new market segment or niche and move towards a more focussed kind of differentiation.

7.4.2 Counterattacking against market-based moves

Market-based strategies that work under less competitive conditions are often successfully counterattacked.

(a)　**First mover advantage can be undermined** by leapfrogging into the lead with an improved product or making a flank attack on a new segment.

(b)　**Product/market moves can be imitated**, thus preventing the competitor from achieving advantage.

7.4.3 Attacking barriers to entry

(a)　**Rapid technological advance** shortens lifecycles and can allow competitors to outflank an initially **robust** strategic capability.

(b)　Attempts to dominate particular market segments or geographic markets may be overcome in several ways.

　　(i)　**Economies of scale** in a market can be countered by utilising the effects of similar economies achieved from a dominant position in another one. An example would be entering a foreign market with an undifferentiated product already established in the home market. **Cross subsidy** can also be used, perhaps to enable initial price competition.

　　(ii)　Dominance of the market's current pattern of **distribution** can be overcome by developing a different approach, such as selling by mail order, rather than through retail outlets.

(c)　Small competitors can **avoid direct confrontation** with resource-heavy dominant players by concentrating on niches, building trading alliances and by merging with other small companies.

7.4.4 Principles of hypercompetitive strategy

(a)　**Pre-empt imitation and remain unpredictable** by competing in new ways. This may involve destroying current advantages in order to develop new ones.

(b)　To attack **competitors' weaknesses** is to provoke them to overcome them.

(c)　A **series of small moves** disguises the strategy and provides a succession of temporary advantages.

(d)　**Misleading signals** of strategic intent can be used to confuse.

7.5 Collaboration as a strategy

FAST FORWARD

Collaboration may be a valid strategic option, reducing costs and building or overcoming barriers to entry.

Organisations do not only compete. **Collaboration** between buyers and sellers and between potential competitors can reduce costs below those of operating independently.

(a) Buyers and sellers may collaborate to ensure high quality, share the cost of research or reduce inventory levels, for example. Where high quality is of great importance, becoming an **accredited supplier** can be difficult, but will **enhance selling power**.

(b) Collaboration between members of a fragmented market **increases buying power**, as when small retailers co-operate to buy in large quantities.

(c) Collaboration between suppliers in an industry over such matters as marketing and research and development can help to **build barriers** to entry and against substitutes.

(d) On the other hand, collaboration may be the best way to obtain entry to some foreign markets; **aspiring entrants** can obtain local knowledge and access to the local infrastructure. Indeed, some governments require entrants to take a local partner.

(e) Suppliers may collaborate with consumers for a variety of reasons: examples include self-assembly of furniture and self-assessment of tax liability. Such **co-production** can help to hold down **costs** and increase a sense of **ownership**.

(f) **Knowledge sharing** may be required in the public sector, as a form of best practice. Also, collaboration may be required to improve standards, secure best value from spending or solve problems that cut across agency boundaries.

8 Using the value chain in competitive strategy

FAST FORWARD

The **value chain** can be used to design a competitive strategy, by deploying the various activities strategically.

The value chain model can be used to analyse a business's operations in order to establish where it achieves **competitive advantage through the creation of value**. It can also show where there is potential for **improved value addition** (especially in relationship to competitors) and where activities are being performed that do not add value; the aim here should be to eliminate such activities, or at least to reconfigure them so that they do contribute some value. However, using the value chain in this way, as with using any strategic management tool, requires careful thought and sound judgement. This may well involve the use of other strategic concepts, such as differentiation, competences and critical success factors, focussing the strategist's attention on areas where they might be applied.

8.1 Other uses of the value chain

As well as using the value chain to establish where it creates value for the customer, an organisation can also use the model in other strategically valuable ways:

- Identification of critical success factors
- Identification of activities suitable for out sourcing
- Identification of areas where value activities are not mutually supporting
- Identification of opportunities to use information strategically

9 Product-market strategy: direction of growth

FAST FORWARD

Product-market strategies involve determining which products should be sold in which markets, by market penetration, market development, product development and diversification. Diversification is assumed to be risky, especially diversification that is entirely unrelated to current products and markets. Alliances of various kinds are a possible approach to diversification. Withdrawal may be a valid option.

Key term

Product-market mix is a short hand term for the **products and services** a firm sells (or a service which a public sector organisation provides) and the **markets** it sells them to.

9.1 The importance of market share

Like some of the portfolio matrix tools we looked at in the last chapter, the PIMS framework regards **competitive strength** and **market attractiveness** as important determinants of profitability. However, perhaps the single most significant factor to emerge from the PIMS data is the link between profitability and **relative market share**. You will recall that relative market share was one of the axes of the **BCG matrix**.

There is a definite, observable correlation between market share and return on investment. This is probably the result of lower costs resulting from **economies of scale**. Economies of scale due to increasing market share are particularly evident in **purchasing** and the **utilisation of non-current assets**.

9.2 Product-market mix

Ansoff drew up a **growth vector matrix**, describing how a combination of a firm's activities in current and new markets, with existing and new products can lead to **growth**. Ansoff's original model was a four cell matrix based on product and market, shown as the heart of the diagram below. Lynch has produced an enhanced model that he calls the **market options matrix.** This adds the external options shown in the diagram. Withdrawal, demerger and privatisation are discussed at the end of this section.

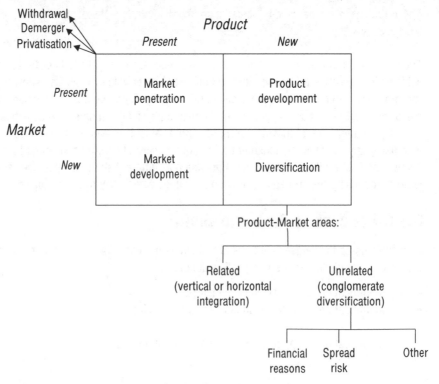

Lynch – Market options matrix

Note the resemblance between the basic Ansoff Matrix and the new product strategy matrix presented in Chapter 4 earlier in this Study Text.

9.2.1 Current products and current markets: market penetration

Market penetration. The firm seeks to do four things.

(a) **Maintain or to increase its share** of current markets with current products, eg through competitive pricing, advertising, sales promotion

(b) Secure dominance of growth markets

(c) Restructure a mature market by driving out competitors

(d) Increase usage by existing customers (eg airmiles, loyalty cards)

This is a relatively **low risk** strategy since it requires no capital investment. As such, it is attractive to the unadventurous type of company.

9.2.2 Consolidation

To consolidate is to seek to **maintain current market share**. This may be an appropriate strategy when the firm is already the market leader; if availability of funds is limited; or when an owner-manager is approaching retirement or wishes to avoid the loss of personal control that is a likely consequence of growth. Also, if it seems that profitability does **not** correlate with market share, consolidation may be a sensible option.

(a) Consolidation does not mean neglect. It is unlikely that competitors will halt their efforts, so the firm must continue to enhance its market offer in order to maintain its relative position.

(b) PIMS data indicates that **high product quality** is important if a consolidation strategy is to succeed. It can compensate to some extent for both a low market share and a low level of marketing expenditure.

9.2.3 Present products and new markets: market development

Market development is the process by which the firm seeks new markets for its current products. There are many possible approaches. Here are some examples:

(a) **New geographical areas** and export markets (eg a radio station building a new transmitter to reach a new audience).

(b) **Different package sizes** for food and other domestic items so that both those who buy in bulk and those who buy in small quantities are catered for.

(c) **New distribution channels** to attract new customers (eg organic food sold in supermarkets not just specialist shops).

(d) **Differential pricing policies** to attract different types of customer and create **new market segments**. For example, travel companies have developed a market for cheap long-stay winter breaks in warmer countries for retired couples.

This approach to strategy is also low in risk since it also requires little capital investment.

9.2.4 New products and present markets: product development

Product development is the launch of new products to existing markets. This has several advantages:

(a) The company can exploit its existing marketing arrangements such as promotional methods and distribution channels at low cost.

(b) The company should already have good knowledge of its customers and their wants and habits.

(c) Competitors will be forced to respond.

(d) The cost of entry to the market will go up.

This strategy is **riskier** than both market penetration and market development since it is likely to require **major investment** in the new product development process and, for physical products, in suitable production facilities.

9.2.5 New products: new markets (diversification)

Diversification occurs when a company decides to make **new products for new markets**. It should have a clear idea about what it expects to gain from diversification.

(a) **Growth.** New products and new markets should be selected which offer prospects for growth which the existing product-market mix does not.

(b) **Investing surplus** funds not required for other expansion needs, bearing in mind that the funds could be returned to shareholders. Diversification is a high risk strategy, having many of the characteristics of a new business start-up. It is likely to require the deployment of **new competences**.

We discuss divisionalisation and the role of the corporate headquarters further later in this Study Text.

9.3 Diversification and synergy

Synergy combined results produce a better rate of return than would be achieved by the same resources used independently. Synergy is used to justify diversification.

9.3.1 Obtaining synergy

Synergy is probably difficult to achieve in practice when one company takes over another. All too often, the expectations of synergy that help to justify a business combination fail to materialise. Synergy is probably more discussed in takeover bids than actually implemented.

Question	Diversification

A large organisation in road transport operates nationwide in general haulage. This field has become very competitive and with the recent down-turn in trade, has become only marginally profitable. It has been suggested that the strategic structure of the company should be widened to include other aspects of physical distribution so that the maximum synergy would be obtained from that type of diversification.

Suggest two activities which might fit into the suggested new strategic structure, explaining each one briefly. Explain how each of these activities could be incorporated into the existing structure. State the advantages and disadvantages of such diversification.

Answer

The first step in a suggested solution is to think of how a company operating nationwide in general road haulage might diversify, with some synergistic benefits. Perhaps you thought of the following.

(a) To move from **nationwide to international haulage**, the company might be able to use its existing contacts with customers to develop an international trade. Existing administration and depot facilities in the UK could be used. Drivers should be available who are willing to work abroad, and the scope for making reasonable profits should exist. However, international road haulage might involve the company in the purchase of new vehicles (eg road haulage in Europe often involves the carriage of containerised products on large purpose-built vehicles). Since international haulage takes longer, vehicles will be tied up in jobs for several days, and a substantial investment might be required to develop the business. In addition, in the event of breakdowns, a network of overseas garage service arrangements will have to be created. It might take some time before business builds up sufficiently to become profitable.

(b) Moving from general haulage to **speciality types of haulage**, perhaps haulage of large items of plant and machinery, or computer equipment. The same broad considerations apply to speciality types of haulage. Existing depot facilities could be used and existing customer contacts might be developed. However, expertise in specialist work will have to be 'brought in' as well as developed within the company and special vehicles might need to be bought. Business might take some time to build up and if the initial investment is high, there could be substantial early losses.

9.4 Other strategies

Withdrawal may be an appropriate strategy under certain circumstances.

(a)   Products may simply disappear when they reach the end of their life cycles.

(b)   Underperforming products may be weeded out.

(c)   Sale of subsidiary businesses for reasons of corporate strategy, such as finance, change of objectives, lack of strategic fit.

(d)   Sale of assets to raise funds and release other resources.

Exit barriers make this difficult.

(a)   Cost barriers include redundancy costs and the difficulty of selling assets.

(b)   Managers might fail to grasp the idea of decision-relevant costs ('we've spent all this money, so we must go on').

(c)   Political barriers include government attitudes. Defence is an example.

(d)   Marketing considerations may delay withdrawal. A product might be a loss-leader for others, or might contribute to the company's reputation for its breadth of coverage.

(e)   Psychology. Managers hate to admit failure, and there might be a desire to avoid embarrassment.

(f)   People might wrongly assume that carrying on is a low risk strategy.

Divestment and **demerger** have become more common as companies seek to reverse the diversification strategies they once pursued. There are several reasons for this:

(a)   To **rationalise** a business as a result of a strategic appraisal, perhaps as a result of portfolio analysis. Another reason might be to concentrate on core competences and synergies.

(b)   To sell off **subsidiary companies** at a profit, perhaps as an exit route after managing a turnaround.

(c)   To allow market valuation to reflect growth and income prospects. Where a low growth, steady income operation exists alongside a potentially high growth new venture, the joint P/E is likely to be too high for the cash cow and too low for the star. The danger is that a predator will take over the whole operation and split the business in two, allowing each part to settle at its own level.

(d)   Satisfy investors: diversified conglomerates are unfashionable. Modern investment thinking is that investors prefer to provide their own portfolio diversification.

(e)   To **raise funds** to invest elsewhere or to reduce debt.

 Case Study   Philips

Philips, the Dutch manufacturer of consumer electronics, divested some non-core businesses in order to concentrate on core businesses as a strategy for improving profitability. It sold its production of white goods (large kitchen appliances) to an American firm, Whirlpool. There was overcapacity in the market. Philips was suffering from declining profitability and did not have the resources to invest in all its product ranges.

 Case Study   The Royal Bank of Scotland sells Citizens Bank

The following example illustrates the importance of considering the wider business environment and the impact it has on organisational investment and divestment decisions. In May 2014, the Royal Bank of Scotland (RBS) announced plans to sell its US subsidiary, Citizens Bank. RBS purchased Citizens Bank in 1988 and 'turned it into one of the biggest regional banks in the US'. At the height of the global recession in 2008, the UK government moved to support RBS as part of a bank bail out programme, since which RBS has 'been under pressure to sell its foreign holdings'.

RBS's decision to divest its Citizen Bank operations have in part been driven by claims of breaching regulations for misselling mortgages in the US. Citizens Bank has approximately five million customers and assets of $122.2bn, operating nearly 1,400 branches. The share sale is expected to raise £2.75bn. As

the BBC reported, CEO of RBS, Ross McEwan said, 'The divestment of Citizens is a key component of our plan to continue to strengthen RBS's capital position. The achievement of our plan will allow us to focus fully on the needs of our customers'.

Source:

'RBS US subsidiary Citizens in public share sale' (May 2012) published on the *BBC*

www.bbc.co.uk

Demerger can realise underlying asset values in terms of share valuation. ICI's demerger of its attractive pharmaceuticals business led to the shares in the two demerged companies trading at a higher combined valuation than those of the original single form.

Privatisation has been pursued by governments all over the world to raise funds and transform culture and performance.

10 Method of growth   12/13

FAST FORWARD

The **method of growth** can vary.

- Companies can grow organically, building up their own products and developing their own market
- They may choose to acquire these ready-made by buying other companies. Acquisitions are risky because of the incompatibility of different companies
- Many firms grow by other means, such as joint ventures, franchising and alliances

Exam focus point

The compulsory question in the December 2013 exam paper required students to explain and evaluate three methods of pursuing growth (internal growth, acquisition and strategic alliance) in relation to the organisation described in the case study scenario.

10.1 Organic growth

Organic growth (sometimes referred to as **internal development**) is the primary method of growth for many organisations, for a number of reasons. Organic growth is achieved through the development of internal resources.

10.1.1 Reasons for pursuing organic growth

(a)   **Learning.** The process of developing a new product gives the firm the best understanding of the market and the product.

(b)   **Innovation.** It might be the only sensible way to pursue genuine technological innovations, and exploit them. (Compact disk technology was developed by Philips and Sony, who earn royalties from other manufacturers licensed to use it.)

(c)   There is **no suitable target for acquisition.**

(d)   Organic growth can be **planned more meticulously** and offers little disruption.

(e)   It is often **more convenient** for managers, as organic growth can be financed easily from the company's current cash flows, without having to raise extra money.

(f)   The **same style of management and corporate culture** can be maintained.

(g)   **Hidden or unforeseen losses are less likely** with organic growth than with acquisitions.

(h)   **Economies of scale** can be achieved from more **efficient use of central head office** functions such as finance, purchasing, personnel and management services.

10.1.2 Problems with organic growth

(a) **Time** – sometimes it takes a long time to descend a **learning curve**.

(b) **Barriers to entry** (eg distribution networks) are harder to overcome: for example, a brand image may be built up from scratch.

(c) The firm will have to **acquire the resources independently.**

(d) Organic growth may be **too slow for the dynamics of the market**.

Organic growth is probably ideal for market penetration, and suitable for product or market development, but it might be a problem with extensive diversification projects.

10.2 Acquisitions and mergers

Exam focus point

An article titled 'Takeovers, mergers and managing business units' (2010) written by Ken Garrett is available in the technical articles section for P3 on the ACCA website. It would be worth taking the time to study this article.

10.2.1 The purpose of acquisitions

(a) **Marketing advantages**

 (i) Buy in a new product range
 (ii) Buy a market presence (especially true if acquiring a company overseas)
 (iii) Unify sales departments or to rationalise distribution and advertising
 (iv) Eliminate competition or to protect an existing market

(b) **Production advantages**

 (i) Gain a higher utilisation of production facilities
 (ii) Buy in technology, intellectual property and skills
 (iii) Obtain greater production capacity
 (iv) Safeguard future supplies of raw materials
 (v) Improve purchasing by buying in bulk

(c) **Finance and management**

 (i) Buy a high quality management team, which exists in the acquired company
 (ii) Obtain cash resources where the acquired company is very liquid
 (iii) Gain undervalued assets or surplus assets that can be sold off
 (iv) Obtain tax advantages (eg purchase of a tax loss company)

(d) **Risk-spreading**

(e) **Independence**. A company threatened by a take-over might take over another company, just to make itself bigger and so a more expensive target for the predator company.

(f) **Overcome barriers to entry**

Many acquisitions **do** have a logic, and the **acquired company can be improved** with the extra resources and better management. Furthermore, much of the criticisms of **takeovers** has been directed more against the notion of **conglomerate diversification** as a strategy, rather than takeover as a **method of growth**.

Case Study   Disney – Lucasfilm

In 2012, the American entertainment company Disney announced it was acquiring Lucasfilm, the production company behind the Star Wars films. The deal cost Disney $4.05bn (£2.5bn) and consisted of cash and share based payments. Following the announcement of the acquisition, Disney's CEO, Robert Iger, confirmed plans to develop a new Star Wars film ready for release in 2015, owing to substantial demand from fans for the franchise to continue.

Early signs for the new venture look positive with Lucasfilm's founde,r George Lucas continuing to serve in the capacity as a creative consultant. Josh Dickey, film editor at Variety magazine, commented that the acquisition represents a 'great fit' between both companies, adding that 'they're (Disney) so good at branding and brands. They're so good at working with existing intellectual property and making it resonate with fans and marketing it very well.' This is not Disney's first large scale acquisition, having previously purchased Pixar and Marvel; both of which have led to a number of highly successful films.

Source: 'Disney buys Star Wars maker Lucasfilm from George Lucas', 31 October 2012, *BBC*

10.2.2 Problems with acquisitions and mergers

(a) **Cost**. They might be too expensive, especially if resisted by the directors of the target company. Proposed acquisitions might be referred to the government under the terms of anti-monopoly legislation.

(b) **Customers** of the target company might resent a sudden takeover and consider going to other suppliers for their goods.

(c) **Incompatibility**. In general, the problems of assimilating new products, customers, suppliers, markets, employees and different systems of operating might create 'indigestion' and management overload in the acquiring company. A proposed merger between two UK financial institutions was called off because of incompatible information systems.

(d) **Asymmetric information**. John Kay suggests that the acquisitions market for companies is rarely efficient.

    (i) The existing management 'always knows more about what is for sale than the potential purchaser. ... Successful bidders are often only the people who were willing to pay too much – that is the reason why their bid succeeds'.

    (ii) 'At the same time, good buys may be ignored, because there is no potential purchaser confident that he really is making a good buy.'

(e) **Driven by the personal goals** of the acquiring company's managers, as a form of sport, perhaps.

(f) **Corporate financiers and banks** have a stake in the acquisitions process as they can charge fees for advice.

(g) **Poor success record of acquisitions.** Takeovers benefit the shareholders of the acquired company often more than the acquirer. According to the Economist Intelligence Unit, there is a consensus that fewer than half all acquisitions are successful.

(h) **Firms rarely take into account non-financial factors**. A survey by London Business School examining 40 acquisitions (in the UK and US) revealed some major flaws.

    (i) All acquirers conducted financial audits, but only 37% conducted anything approaching a management audit: despite detailed audits of equipment, property, finances etc, few bothered with people.

    (ii) Some major problems of implementation relate to **human resources and personnel issues** such as morale, performance assessment and culture. Especially in service industries and 'knowledge-based' or creative businesses, many of the firm's assets are effectively the staff. If key managers or personnel leave, the business will suffer.

10.3 Joint ventures

Short of mergers and takeovers, there are other ways by which companies can co-operate.

(a) **Consortia:** organisations co-operate on specific business areas such as purchasing or research.

(b) **Joint ventures:** Two firms (or more) join forces for manufacturing, financial and marketing purposes and each has a share in both the equity and the management of the business.

(i) **Share costs**. As the capital outlay is shared, joint ventures are especially attractive to smaller or risk-averse firms, or where very expensive new technologies are being researched and developed (such as in the civil aerospace or petrochemical industries).

(ii) **Cut risk**. A joint venture can reduce the risk of government intervention if a local firm is involved (eg Club Méditerranée pays much attention to this factor).

(iii) Participating enterprises **benefit from all sources of profit**.

(iv) **Close control** over marketing and other operations.

(v) Overseas joint ventures provide **local knowledge, quickly**.

(vi) **Synergies**. One firm's production expertise can be supplemented by the other's marketing and distribution facility.

(c) A **licensing agreement** is a commercial contract whereby the licenser gives something of value to the licensee in exchange for certain performances and payments.

(i) The licenser may provide rights to produce a patented product or to use a patented process or trademark as well as advice and assistance on marketing and technical issues.

(ii) The licenser receives a **royalty**.

(d) **Subcontracting** is also a type of alliance. Co-operative arrangements also feature in supply chain management, JIT and quality programmes.

10.3.1 Disadvantages of joint ventures

(a) **Conflicts of interest** between the different parties.

(b) **Disagreements** may arise over profit shares, amounts invested, the management of the joint venture, and the marketing strategy.

(c) One partner may wish to **withdraw** from the arrangement.

(d) There may be a temptation to neglect **core competences**. Acquisition of competences from partners may be possible, but alliances are unlikely to create new ones.

 Case Study   Starbucks' Indian joint venture

In January 2012, Starbucks announced plans to bring its coffee shops to India via an $80m joint venture with Tata Global beverages, one of the world's largest coffee plantation companies. As part of the agreement, Tata was to provide coffee beans for use in the new outlets. Although formally established as Tata Starbucks Ltd, it was agreed that all coffee shops would operate under the Starbucks livery. The first Starbucks outlet opened in Mumbai in late 2012. In January 2013, it was reported by *The Hindu* newspaper that Tata Starbucks had opened two new outlets at Indira Gandhi International airport. Since this time, the venture has gone from strength to strength. By June 2014, the Starbucks website reported that it had 45 outlets in operation in India.

Source: The Hindu (http://www.thehindu.com) & Starbucks (http://www.starbucks.co.uk)

10.4 Franchising   12/12, 6/09

Exam focus point

A Section B question in the December 2012 Paper offered 10 marks for highlighting the advantages and disadvantages of franchising for the organisation featured in the scenario.

Franchising is a method of expanding the business on less capital than would otherwise be possible, because **franchisees** not only pay a capital lump sum to the franchiser to enter the franchise but they also bear some of the running costs of the new outlets. For suitable businesses, it is an **alternative business strategy to raising extra capital** for growth. Probably the most well-known franchisers are McDonalds, but other franchisers include Budget Rent-a-car, Dyno-rod, Express Dairy, Holiday Inn, Kall-Kwik Printing, Kentucky Fried Chicken, Sketchley Cleaners and Body Shop.

The franchiser and franchisee each provide different inputs to the business.

(a) The **franchiser**

    (i) Name, and any goodwill associated with it

    (ii) Systems and business methods, business strategy and managerial know-how

    (iii) Support services, such as advertising, training, research and development, and help with site decoration

(b) The **franchisee**

    (i) Capital, personal involvement and local market knowledge

    (ii) Payment to the franchiser for rights and for support services

    (iii) Responsibility for the day-to-day running, and the ultimate profitability of the franchise

10.4.1 Advantages of franchising

(a) **Reduces capital requirements**. Firms often franchise because they cannot readily raise the capital required to set up company-owned stores. John Y. Brown, the former president of Kentucky Fried Chicken, maintained that it would have cost KFC $450 million to establish its first 2,700 stores if it had run them as company-owned stores, and this was a sum that was not available to the corporation in the early stages of its life.

(b) **Reduces managerial resources required**. A firm may be able to raise the capital required for growth, but it may lack the managerial resources required to set up a network of company-owned stores. Recruiting and training managers and staff accounts for a significant percentage of the cost of growth of a firm.

Under a franchise agreement, the franchisees supply the staff required for the day-to-day running of the operation.

(c) **Improves return on promotional expenditure through speed of growth**. A retail firm's brand and brand image are crucial to the success of its stores. Companies often develop their brand through extensive advertising and promotion, but this only translates into sales if they have a number of stores that customers can visit after seeing their advertisements.

To reap the benefits of its national or regional advertising efforts, the company needs to attain the minimum efficient scale, in terms of number of stores, as quickly as possible.

Because franchising provides quicker access to capital and managerial resources, a firm can expand more quickly through franchising than through opening new company-owned stores. Faster expansion through franchising, in turn, should allow companies to achieve a favourable return on their promotional campaigns.

(d) **Benefits of specialisation**. Because the franchisee and the franchiser both contribute different resources to the franchise, franchising provides an effective way of reducing costs: each party concentrates on their core areas, and increases their efficiency in those areas.

In general, franchisers are more cost-efficient than franchisees in performing functions that decrease in cost with a substantial level of output. By contrast, franchisees are more efficient in performing functions which are more efficient at a smaller scale. For example, in the fast-food business, product development and national promotion are more efficiently handled on a large scale (by the franchiser), whereas the production of food itself is handled better on a relatively smaller scale (by the franchisee).

(e) **Low head office costs**. The franchiser only needs a small number of head office staff because there is a considerable delegation of operational responsibility to the franchisees. For example, in the fast-food business, the franchisees provide the staff who work in the restaurants, and so the franchisees incur the HR and payroll costs associated with that.

(f) **Reduced supervision costs**. Company-owned retail stores are run by employee managers who may often perform poorly if they are not supervised. A company, therefore, has to supervise its store managers, and this will result in central overhead costs. However, under a franchise arrangement, because franchisees have invested capital in their own stores, and because their

earnings come from the profits of those stores, they are motivated to work hard to maximise the success of the stores. Consequently, the franchiser will have much lower supervision costs.

(g)   **Risk Management**. When opening new stores, a corporation does not know with certainty the business potential and the chances of success of different locations. Under a franchising arrangement, the franchiser can judge the profitability potential of different sites without incurring a significant business risk. If a particular store fails, the franchisee bears the brunt of the failure.

However, franchising also helps franchisees reduce their risks. Franchised stores typically open more quickly, and become profitable more quickly, than independent company-owned stores. The franchisee benefits from the franchiser's managerial experience and from the established brand name. In effect, when a franchisee enters a lease agreement with the franchiser, it is leasing managerial know-how and brand recognition, as well as the physical store it is operating.

10.4.2 Disadvantages of franchising

(a)   **Profits are shared**. The franchisee receives the revenue from the customer at the point of sale and then pays the franchiser a share of the profits.

(b)   The **search for competent candidates** is both costly and time consuming where the franchiser requires many outlets (eg McDonald's in the UK).

(c)   **Control** over franchisees. (McDonald's franchisees in New York recently refused to co-operate in a marketing campaign).

(d)   **Risk to reputation**. A franchisee can damage the public perception of a brand by providing inferior goods or services.

(e)   **Potential for conflict**. There may be disagreement over the respective rights and obligations of the franchiser and franchisee, for example, over the level of support to be provided or the fees payable. These terms need to be clearly set out in a contract when the franchise is granted to reduce the chances of conflict arising. Conflict may also occur if either side is acting in bad faith, for example, if the franchisee is providing inferior goods or services which risk damaging the franchiser's brand.

10.5 Alliances   12/12

Exam focus point

A Section B question in the December 2012 Paper offered 7 marks for an evaluation of the different forms of strategic alliance which might be appropriate to the organisation featured.

Some firms enter long-term **strategic alliances** with others for a variety of reasons.

(a)   They **share development costs** of a particular technology.

(b)   The **regulatory environment prohibits take-overs** (eg most major airlines are in strategic alliances because in most countries – including the US – there are limits to the level of control an 'outsider' can have over an airline).

(c)   **Complementary markets or technology**.

(d)   **Learning.** Alliances can also be a 'learning' exercise in which each partner tries to learn as much as possible from the other.

(e)   **Technology**. New technology offers many uncertainties and many opportunities. Such alliances provide funds for expensive research projects, spreading risk.

(f)   **The alliance itself can generate innovations**.

(g)   The alliance can involve **'testing' the firm's core competence** in different conditions, which can suggest ways to improve it.

(h)   Regulation may prevent take over.

Strategic alliances only go so far, as there may be disputes over control of strategic assets.

10.5.1 Choosing alliance partners

Hooley et al suggest the following factors should be considered in choosing alliance partners.

Drivers	What benefits are offered by collaboration?
Partners	Which partners should be chosen?
Facilitators	Does the external environment favour a partnership?
Components	Activities and processes in the network
Effectiveness	Does the previous history of alliances generate good results? Is the alliance just a temporary blip? For example, in the airline industry, there are many strategic alliances, but these arise in part because there are legal barriers to cross-border ownership.
Market-orientation	Alliance partners are harder to control and may not have the same commitment to the end-user.

Alliances have some limitations

(a) **Core competence**. Each organisation should be able to focus on its core competence. Alliances do not enable it to create new competences.

(b) **Strategic priorities.** If a key aspect of strategic delivery is handed over to a partner, the firm loses flexibility. A core competence may not be enough to provide a comprehensive customer benefit.

The problems with strategic alliances are explored in the following case study.

Case Study   **Peugeot and General Motors**

In February 2012 General Motors (GM) and PSA Peugeot Citroen announced a global alliance that the two companies said would save them $2bn annually within about five years. The original agreement between the carmakers said they would share vehicle platforms, components and modules, and create a global purchasing joint venture (with a purchasing power of $125bn a year) to buy commodities and parts.

Speaking at the time the alliance was announced, GM's chief executive described the deal as 'a broad-scale global strategic alliance that will improve each company's competitiveness and will contribute to long-term profitability in Europe particularly, but around the world as well'.

The tie-up aimed to give GM and PSA, which had joint sales of about 12m, global industry leadership in production of 'B' compact and 'D' upper-middle segment cars.

The two companies said the alliance was not a merger, and said that it would not change any existing plans to rationalise their operations in Europe, where both PSA and GM's Opel unit had been losing money.

GM and PSA said the cost synergies would be split evenly between the two carmakers, while continuing to compete and sell cars under their own brands.

PSA's chief executive said that the alliance grew out of 'a growing realisation of very concrete synergies that exist between our companies.'

GM and PSA's alliance initially focused on small and midsize cars, multi-purpose vehicles and small sport utility vehicles, or crossovers. At the time, the two companies said they would even consider developing a new common platform for low-carbon vehicles.

However, in late 2013, Bloomberg reported that GM had moved to sell its 7% holding in PSA amid the struggling French carmaker's efforts to seek financial help from a Chinese partner.

Since the alliance was formed, 'the partnership had struggled to meet its original goals, with PSA saying that savings from the cooperation were estimated to be 40 percent less than originally planned'. Bloomberg reported that 'the scaled back alliance and persistent losses had propelled PSA to pursue deeper cooperation with Dongfeng Motor Corp to boost sales in China and other growth regions as the European market declined for a sixth straight year'.

Georges Dieng, a Paris based analyst talking to Reuters news in October 2013, commented that, 'Peugeot thought it had found a long-term partner, but the alliance seems to be disintegrating'. Reuters reported that apart from joint purchasing, 'just two mini vans have survived from about forty projects initially floated. The dropped plan to replace the Peugeot 208, Citroen C3 and Opel Corsa with a common small car was "absolutely key" to the partnership,' added analyst Kristina Church.

'The loosening of ties signals GM's renewed commitment to manage its own European turnaround independently following in domestic rival Ford's footsteps'.

Alliances between rival carmakers have a patchy track record. Daimler demerged from Chrysler in 2007 after an acrimonious partnership that lasted nine years, and Volkswagen and Suzuki went to arbitration after an alliance they concluded in 2009 hit the rocks in 2011.

Adapted from three online articles:

1) 'GM and Peugeot confirm alliance' by John Reed (February 2012) published on the *Financial Times* website; www.ft.com

2) 'Peugeot Plunges After GM Sells Entire 7% Holding' by Chris Reiter and David Ruth (December 2013) published on the *Bloomberg* website; www.bloomberg.com

3) 'New blow to Peugeot as GM alliance scaled back' by Laurence Frost (October 2013) published on the *Reuters* website; www.reuters.com

10.5.2 IS based alliances

The cost of major IS based methods of working, combined with their inherent communications capability have made alliances based on IS a natural development. There are four common types.

(a) **Single industry partnerships**: for example, UK insurance brokers can use a common system called IVANS to research the products offered by all of the major insurance companies.

(b) **Multi-industry joint marketing partnerships**: some industries are so closely linked with others that it makes sense to establish IS linking their offerings. A well-known example is holiday bookings, where a flight reservation over the internet is likely to lead to a seamless offer of hotel reservations and car hire.

(c) **Supply chain partnerships:** greater and closer co-operation along the supply chain has led to the need for better and faster information flows. Electronic data interchange between customers and suppliers is one aspect of this improvement, perhaps seen most clearly in the car industry, where the big-name manufacturers effectively control the flow of inputs from their suppliers.

(d) **IT supplier** partnerships: a slightly different kind of partnership is not uncommon in the IT industry itself, where physical products have their own major software content. The development of these products requires close co-operation between the hardware and software companies concerned.

11 Strategy and market position

FAST FORWARD

Strategies may be based upon market position, as leader, challenger, follower or nicher.

So far in this chapter, we have considered the broader aspects of strategy as they affect the overall stance of the organisation. In this section, we will examine some of the options that apply most appropriately to the strategic management of individual products or brands. An appreciation of scale is important when considering strategy. The strategies we discuss below may be regarded as detailed strategy for a major global organisation. On the other hand, they may constitute the essence of corporate strategy for a smaller company.

Most of the material in this section is based on *Strategic Marketing Management* by Wilson, Gilligan and Pearson.

11.1 Strategies for market leaders

PIMS research has revealed the advantages of being the market leader. A company in this position may try to do three things.

(a) **Expand the total market** by seeking increased usage levels; and new uses and users. These aims correspond to market penetration and market development.

(b) **Protect the current market share**. The most common way of doing this is by means of continuous product innovation.

(c) **Expand market share**. This may be pursued by enhancing the attractiveness of the product offering in almost any way, including increased promotion, aggressive pricing and improved distribution.

Military analogies have been used to describe defensive strategies for market leaders. These were described earlier in this Study Text.

11.2 Strategies for market challengers

The market challenger seeks to **build market share** in the hope of eventually overtaking the existing leader. However, this does not necessarily mean attacking the market leader head-on. This is a risky strategy in any case, because of the leader's resources in cash, promotion and innovation. Instead, the challenger may attack smaller regional firms or companies of similar size to itself that are vulnerable through lack of resources or poor management.

Military analogies have also been used to describe the challenger's attacking options. These were described earlier in this Study Text.

11.3 Strategies for market followers

The market follower accepts the status quo and thus avoids the cost and risk associated with innovation in product, price or distribution strategy. Such a **me-too** strategy is based on the leader's approach. This can be both profitable and stable. However, to be consistently successful, such a strategy must not simply imitate. The follower should compete in the most appropriate segments, maintain its customer base and ensure that its turnover grows in line with the general expansion of the market. It should be aware that it may constitute an attractive target for market challengers. The follower must therefore control its costs and exploit appropriate opportunities.

11.4 Strategies for market nichers

Avoiding competition by **niching** is a profitable strategy for small firms generally and for larger organisations where competition is intense. The key to niching is **specialisation**, but there are other considerations:

(a) The chosen market must have some growth potential while being uninteresting to major competitors.

(b) The firm must be able to serve its customers sufficiently well to build up sufficient goodwill to fend off any attacks.

(c) It must be possible to build up sufficient size to be profitable and purchase efficiently.

Serving a single niche can be risky: a sudden change in the market can lead to rapid decline. **Multiple niching** can overcome this problem.

12 Success criteria

Exam focus point

The Section A question in the December 2011 exam required students to provide an independent assessment of the strategy proposed by the organisation described in the case study. The use of the SAF model outlined in the next section provided a framework which could be applied to the scenario. The post-exam report noted that using the model helped candidates to produce a well structured answer.

FAST FORWARD

Strategies are evaluated according to their **suitability** to the firm's strategic situation, their **feasibility** in terms of resources and competences and their **acceptability** to key stakeholders groups (eg shareholders).

Organisations must select strategies to pursue in a rational way. JS&W suggest three **success criteria** to guide strategy choice:

- **Suitability**
- **Feasibility**
- **Acceptability**

12.1 Suitability

Suitability relates to the **strategic logic** of the strategy. The strategy should fit the organisation's current strategic position and should satisfy a range of requirements:

- **Exploit** strengths: that is, **unique** resources and **core competences**
- **Rectify** an organisation's **weaknesses**, or deal with problems identified in it
- **Neutralise** or deflect environmental **threats**
- Help the firm to **seize opportunities**
- **Satisfy the goals** of organisation
- **Fill the gap** identified by gap analysis
- Generate/maintain **competitive advantage**
- Involve an acceptable level of **risk**
- Suit the **politics** and corporate **culture**

A number of techniques can be used to assess suitability. These are discussed below.

12.1.1 Life cycle analysis

FAST FORWARD

The A D Little lifecycle/portfolio matrix assesses suitability in terms of **industry maturity** and **competitive position**.

The **product life cycle** concept may be used to assess potential strategies.

The **industry life cycle** may be combined with an appraisal of the company's strength in its markets using a **life cycle/portfolio matrix**. This was originally designed by consultants Arthur D Little.

	Embryonic	Growth	Mature	Ageing
Dominant	Fast grow Start up	Fast grow Attain cost leadership Renew Defend position	Defend position Attain cost leadership Renew Fast grow	Defend position Focus Renew Grow with industry
Strong	Start up Differentiate Fast grow	Fast grow Catch up Attain cost leadership Differentiate	Attain cost leadership Renew, Focus Differentiate Grow with industry	Find niche Hold niche Hang in Grow with industry Harvest
Favourable	Start up Differentiate Focus Fast grow	Differentiate, focus Catch up Grow with industry	Harvest, hang in Find niche, hold niche Renew, turnaround Differentiate, Focus Grow with industry	Retrench Turnaround
Tenable	Start up Grow with industry Focus	Harvest, catch up Hold niche, hang in Find niche Turnaround Focus Grow with industry	Harvest Turnaround Find niche Retrench	Divest Retrench
Weak	Find niche Catch up Grow with industry	Turnaround Retrench	Withdraw Divest	Withdraw

COMPETITIVE POSITION

The position of the company on the **industry maturity** axis of this matrix depends on the assessment of eight factors including market growth rate, growth potential and number of competitors. Each stage has its own strategic implications. For instance, an ageing market will be subject to falling demand, so heavy marketing expenditure is unlikely to be justified.

Competitive position

(a)   A **dominant** position allows the company to exert influence over the behaviour of competitors. It is rare in the private sector.

(b)   A **strong** position gives considerable freedom of choice over strategy.

(c)   A **favourable** position arises in a fragmented market, often when the company has strengths to exploit.

(d)   A **tenable** position is vulnerable to competition and profitability may depend on specialisation.

(e)   A **weak** position arises from inability to compete effectively. Firms of any size can find themselves in this condition.

12.1.2 Business profile analysis

In **business profile analysis,** the expected effects of a strategy on the corporation are forecast. A business profile is then created by scoring the forecast state against the favourable parameters established by the empirical findings of PIMS research. There are eleven of these parameters; they relate to market position, financial strength, quality and operational efficiency. The forecast profile may be compared with the current profile in order to assess the proposed strategy for suitability.

12.1.3 Strategy screening

It is not enough merely to assess strategies for suitability. Eventually, choices must be made. Such choices may be assisted by **strategy screening** methods, which include **ranking, decision trees** and **scenario planning**. Ranking and decision trees are dealt with later in this Study Text. Scenarios have already been described. Potential strategies may be screened by assessing their suitability against each potential scenario. This leads not so much to a choice as to the establishment of a series of **contingency plans**.

12.1.4 Consistency

Strategies must be internally consistent: generic strategy, market options choice and method of development must all work together satisfactorily. For example, a strategy of cost leadership would not be supported by a decision to acquire a chain of luxury distributors.

12.1.5 The TOWS matrix

The TOWS matrix was discussed earlier in this Study Text. We noted that Weirich categorised strategies into four groups that linked strengths, weaknesses, opportunities and threats in a logical fashion. There is an **inherent suitability** about strategies that fall into these groups, since they are founded on the fundamentals of the organisation's strategic position.

JS&W (and your syllabus) discern a logical link between the Ansoff Matrix and the TOWS matrix, since detailed strategic options based on the former may be validated and even generated by considering the latter. Thus, for example, a specific market development opportunity might exploit an under-used strength: this is an SO strategy.

12.2 Feasibility

Feasibility asks whether the strategy can be implemented and, in particular, if the organisation has adequate **strategic capability**. The Ms model we looked at earlier in this Study Text can provide a framework to use here.

Machinery	Has the organisation got the machinery required to deliver this strategy? Can any new machinery be obtained?
Make-up	Is the organisational structure appropriate to the strategy?
Management	Does the management team have the skills required to deliver the strategy?
Markets	Does the organisation have strong enough products or a strong enough brand for the strategy to work?
Materials	Does the organisation have access to the materials required to deliver the strategy?
Men and women	Will the strategy require extra staff? Will the strategy require staff to acquire new skills? If so, how long will this take?
Methods	Can the strategy be implemented, given the organisation's current production methods (either in-house or outsourced)?
Money	Can the organisation raise any finances that may be required? Will it be able to keep up with repayments if loan funding is required?

In addition, the organisation also needs to assess whether it has the ability to deal with the likely **responses that competitors** will make, and enough **time** to implement the strategy.

Strategies which do not make use of the existing competences and which therefore call for new competences to be acquired, might not be feasible, since gaining competences takes time and can be costly.

Two important financial approaches to assessing the feasibility of particular strategies are **funds flow** analysis and **breakeven** analysis. The principles of both should be familiar to you from your earlier studies in financial and management accounting.

Resource deployment analysis makes a wider assessment of feasibility in terms of **resources** and **competences**. The resources and competences required for each potential strategy are assessed and compared with those of the firm. A two stage approach may be followed.

(a) Does the firm have the necessary resources and competences to achieve the **threshold** requirements for each strategy?

(b) Does the firm have the core competences and **unique resources** to maintain **competitive advantage**?

When assessing feasibility in this way, it is important to remember that it may be possible to acquire new competences and resources or to stretch existing ones. Such innovation is likely to be difficult to imitate.

12.3 Acceptability

The acceptability of a strategy depends on expected performance outcomes and the extent to which these are acceptable to stakeholders.

(a) **Financial considerations**. Strategies will be evaluated by considering how far they contribute to meeting the dominant objective of increasing shareholder wealth.

We will look at financial management decisions in more detail later in this Study Text, but there are a number of the financial indicators which should be considered to assess the acceptability of a strategy.

(i)	Return on investment	(v)	Cash flow
(ii)	Profits	(vi)	Price/Earnings
(iii)	Growth	(vii)	Market capitalisation
(iv)	EPS	(viii)	Cost-benefit analysis

Profitability analysis techniques include **forecast ROCE**, **payback period** and **NPV**, all of which you should be familiar with. These methods should not be overemphasised.

(i) They are developed for assessing **projects** where cash flows are predictable. This is unlikely to be easy with wider **strategies**.

(ii) There may be **intangible** costs and benefits associated with a strategy, such as an enhanced product range or image or a loss of market share. **Cost-benefit analysis** is probably more appropriate for dealing with such development. See below.

Shareholder value analysis has the potential to provide a more realistic assessment of overall strategy than traditional financial measures such as NPV and forecast ROCE. This is because its emphasis on value management and understanding the organisation's system of value drivers requires managers to take an integrated view of current and potential future strategies and their overall effects.

(b) **Customers** may object to a strategy if it means reducing service, but on the other hand, they may have no choice.

(c) **Banks** are interested in the implications for cash resources, debt levels and so on.

(d) **Government**. A strategy involving a takeover may be prohibited under competition legislation.

(e) **The public**. The environmental impact may cause key stakeholders to protest. For example, out of town superstores are now frowned upon by national and local government in the UK.

(f) **Risk**. Different shareholders have different attitudes to risk. A strategy which changes the risk/return profile, for whatever reason, may not be acceptable. Financial ratio projections and sensitivity analysis may be useful in the assessment of risk.

Cost-benefit analysis may be an appropriate approach to acceptability where intangible effects are important, which is particularly the case in the public sector. This type of analysis attempts to put a monetary value on intangibles such as safety and amenity so that the impact of a strategy on all parties may be assessed.

12.4 Strategy selection

12.4.1 Planning and enforced choice

The techniques dealt within this chapter are appropriate to the use of the rational model and may be useful when less formal approaches are taken. They also have a role when strategic developments are **imposed from outside** the organisation. This may come about, for instance, as a result of a major change in the environment, as when the oil shocks of the 1970s stimulated off-shore production, or because of the influence of a dominant stakeholder.

Formal evaluation of imposed strategy

(a)   The first role of formal evaluation is to assess the degree of **risk** inherent in the imposed strategy. This may indicate that a medium-term programme to reduce risk is required; this could be incorporated into the overall plan.

(b)   Secondly, techniques such as **scenario planning** can be used to establish contingency plans in case the imposed strategy leads to unacceptably low performance.

12.5 Real options

The analysis and use of **financial options** as business tools is not examinable in paper P3. However, the option concept is very useful in the context of selecting strategies. The selection of a particular course of strategic action may offer **options for future strategy**. The availability of such an option should be considered when evaluating strategies.

A possible course of action may open up further possibilities: one important case is the possibility of making further, follow-on investments. This is equivalent to a call option in financial strategy. For example, if a manufacturing business decides to open a retail outlet, it acquires the option to stock complementary products from other manufacturers. If the NPV of the basic outlet strategy is assessed as negative, this negative sum represents the price of the option to expand the range at a future date.

Using this type of conceptual approach allows more subtle evaluation of possible strategies to be undertaken and permits more sophisticated choices to be made between alternatives. In particular, the option to abandon a chosen strategy at low cost will make that strategy more attractive than one with a high cost of abandonment. This choice might rise where there are two possible approaches to manufacturing a new product.

(a)   Purchase of high efficiency, highly specialised machinery
(b)   Purchase of lower efficiency, general purpose machinery

Option (a) may offer lower costs if the venture succeeds, but the ability to use option (b)'s machinery for another purpose reduces its cost of abandonment, should the venture fail.

- Many large businesses consist of a corporate parent and a number of SBUs. The defining characteristic of the corporate parent is that it has no direct contact with the buyers or competitors, its role being to manage the overall scope of the organisation in terms of diversity of products, markets and international operations.

- Diversity of products and markets may be advantageous for three reasons.

  - **Economics of scope** may arise in several forms of **synergy**.
  - **Corporate management skills** may be extendible.
  - **Cross-subsidy** may enhance **market power**.

  Related diversification, whether horizontal or vertical usually works better than conglomerate, or unrelated, diversification.

- Despite wide-ranging measures to liberalise trade and the resulting major growth in world trade, there has been little globalisation of services. Language differences and restrictions on population movement hamper the growth of international markets for labour, even when it is highly skilled.

- Perlmutter identifies four orientations in the management of international business.

  - **Ethnocentrism** is a home country orientation
  - **Polycentrism** adapts totally to local environments
  - **Geocentrism** adapts only to add value. It 'thinks globally, acts locally'.
  - **Regiocentrism** recognises regional differences

- Ohmae describes five stages in the evolution of a global business.

  - **Exporting** is an extension of home sales, using foreign intermediaries. It is low risk and **ethnocentric**.

  - **Overseas branches** arise when turnover is large enough. It requires greater investment and is still **ethnocentric**.

  - **Overseas production** exploits cheap labour and reduces exporting costs. The orientation is still **ethnocentric** and the business is still largely run from its HQ.

  - **Insiderisation** is a shift to **polycentrism**, with full functional organisations being set up overseas. This reduces exchange rate and political risk but economies of scale may be lost and there may be problems of co-ordination. The company is a **multinational**.

  - **The global company** takes a world view while recognising total differences: it has a **geocentric** orientation. It integrates learning, skills and competences to achieve global efficiencies while retaining local responsiveness.

- Ohmae offers five reasons for globalisation.

  - **Customer:** market convergence
  - **Company:** economies of scale
  - **Competition:** keeping up
  - **Currency:** exchange rate risk
  - **Country:** absolute and comparative advantage; local orientation

- Bartlett and Ghoshal discern four types of organisations, depending on the strength or weakness of pressure to globalise and need for local adaptation.

  - Global environment; (geocentric); global product divisions
  - International environment; (ethnocentric); international division
  - Transnational environment; (polycentric); integrated systems and structures
  - Multinational environment; (polycentric); national or regional divisions

- Modes of entry to foreign markets vary widely and include

  - Direct and indirect exporting
  - Wholly owned overseas production
  - Contract manufacture
  - Joint ventures

  The most suitable mode of entry depends on

  - Marketing objectives
  - Mode availability
  - HR requirements
  - Risks
  - Firm size
  - Mode quality
  - Market research feedback
  - Control needs

- There are three value-creating roles for the corporate parent.

  - **Envisioning corporate intent**, communicating the vision to stakeholders and SBU managers, and acting in accordance with it.

  - **Intervention** to improve performance.

  - Provision of **services, resources** and **expertise**

  Portfolio managers create value by applying financial discipline. They keep their own costs low.
  Synergy managers peruse economies of scope through the shared use of competences and resources.
  Parental developers add value by deploying their own competences to improve their SBUs' performance.

- A parent may deploy four policies towards its SBUs

  - Build
  - Hold
  - Harvest
  - Divest

  The SBU portfolio must be managed against three criteria

  - Balance
  - Attractiveness
  - Strategic fit

  Matrix-based models are used to manage **portfolios**: the **Ashridge model** is the only one to address strategic fit and assumes the **parental developer** approach is used.

- The **Boston classification** classifies business units in terms of their **capacity for growth within the market** and the market's capacity for growth as a whole.

- The **public sector portfolio matrix** classifies activities in terms of their popularity and the resources available for them.

- The **Ashridge model** assesses the benefit SBUs can derive from the corporate parent playing the parental developer role. **Heartland businesses** both have CSFs that fit the present's resources and competences *and* provide opportunities for good use of them. **Alien businesses** have neither quality. **Ballast businesses** are well-understood by the parent but need little assistance. **Value trap businesses** need help but of kinds the parent cannot provide.

- **Business unit strategy** involves a choice between being the lowest cost producer (**cost leadership**) making the product different from competitors' products in some way (**differentiation**) or specialising on a segment of the market (**focus**, by addressing that segment via a strategy of cost leadership or differentiation). **Porter** believes that a firm *must* choose one of these or be **stuck-in-the-middle**.

- The strategy clock develops Porter's theory, analysing strategies in terms of **price** and **perceived value added**.

- Different policies are required to sustain differentiation or price-based strategies. Lock-in is achieved when a product becomes the industry standard.

- **Hypercompetition** makes it impossible to create lasting advantage with a steady policy: a series of short-term moves is required. These include repositioning on the strategy clock, counter attack, imitation and attacks on barriers to entry.

- **Collaboration** may be a valid strategic option, reducing costs and building or overcoming barriers to entry.

- The **value chain** can be used to design a competitive strategy, by deploying the various activities strategically.

- **Product-market** strategies involve determining which products should be sold in which markets, by market penetration, market development, product development and diversification. Diversification is assumed to be risky, especially diversification that is entirely unrelated to current products and markets. Alliances of various kinds are a possible approach to diversification. Withdrawal may be a valid option.

- The **method of growth** can vary.

  - Companies can grow organically, building up their own products and developing their own market.

  - They may choose to acquire these ready-made by buying other companies. Acquisitions are risky because of the incompatibility of different companies.

  - Many firms grow by other means, such as joint ventures, franchising and alliances.

- Strategies may be based upon market position, as leader, challenger, follower or nicher.

- Strategies are evaluated according to their **suitability** to the firm's strategic situation, their **feasibility** in terms of resources and competences and their **acceptability** to key stakeholders groups (eg shareholders).

- The A D Little lifecycle/portfolio matrix assesses suitability in terms of **industry maturity** and **competitive position**.

Quick Quiz

1   What is related diversification?

2   What are JS&W's three strategic rationales for corporate parents?

3   What are the axes of the BCG matrix?

4   What are the axes of the Ashridge portfolio display?

5   What are Porter's three generic strategies?

6   What are the axes against which the strategy clock is constructed?

7   What is lock-in?

8   What are the four product-market options which are illustrated in Ansoff's matrix?

9   List three advantages of franchising.

10 What criteria are used to assess strategies?

Answers to Quick Quiz

1   Development beyond current products and markets but within the capabilities or value network of the organisation.

2   Portfolio manager, synergy manager, parental developer.

3   Market growth rate and relative market share.

4   Fit between SBU opportunities and parental skills and resources (benefit) and fit between CSFs and parental skills and resources (feel).

5   Cost leadership, differentiation, focus.

6   Price and perceived value added.

7   The product becomes the industry standard.

8   • Market penetration (present product, present market)
    • Market development (present product, new market)
    • Product development (new product, present market)
    • Diversification (new product, new market)

9   Possible answers:
    • Reduces capital requirements
    • Reduces managerial resources required
    • Speed of growth is faster than organic growth
    • Benefits of specialisation between franchiser and franchisee
    • Low head office costs
    • Reduces supervision costs
    • Reduces risk associated with opening new outlets

10 Suitability in terms of strategic logic; feasibility in terms of resources required; and acceptability to shareholders.

Now try the questions below from the Practice Question Bank

Number	Level	Marks	Time
Q3	Exam	8	15 mins
Q7	Preparation	n/a	36 mins

Organising and enabling success

Organising for success

Introduction

The static pyramidal hierarchy has formed the basis of ideas about organisational structure for many years. This structural form has the advantage of being easily understood and of providing clear lines of responsibility and communication. However, the challenges of the modern business environment have led not only to new structural designs, but also to a complete re-evaluation of basic assumptions about organisation structure.

Study guide

		Intellectual level
C1	**Organising and enabling success**	
(a)	Advise on how the organisation can be structured to deliver a selected strategy	3
(b)	Explore generic processes that take place within the structure, with particular emphasis on the planning process	3
(c)	Discuss how internal relationships can be organised to deliver a selected strategy	2
(d)	Discuss how organisational structure and external relationships (boundary-less organisations; hollow modular and virtual) and strategic alliances (joint ventures, networks, franchising, licensing) and the supporting concepts of outsourcing, offshoring and shared services, can be used to deliver a selected strategy.	2
(f)	Explore (through Mintzberg's organisational configurations) the design of structure, processes and relationships	3

Exam guide

Questions on structure were fairly uncommon under the old syllabus. However, JS&W's fresh approach, emphasising **processes** and **relationships** casts a new light on this rather specialised topic and brings it into the mainstream of strategic thinking. You cannot afford to neglect this chapter. We can expect questions that demand input on structure, ranging from passing comment all the way up to detailed proposals for change and development.

The structure of the organisation will be important in the context of scenario-based questions, and ensuring harmony between structure, process and relationships will be important throughout.

Models

Mintzberg's organisational configurations (Section 5 of this chapter) are explicitly referenced in the Study Guide and so could be specifically required in a question.

1 Challenges and concepts

FAST FORWARD

Globalisation, other aspects of rapid environmental change and, above all, the need to **exploit knowledge** make the **structures**, **processes** and **relationships** that make up configurations vital for strategic success.

JS&W identify three major groups of challenges for twenty first century organisation structures.

(a) **Flexibility of organisational design**. The rapid pace of **environmental change** and increased levels of **environmental uncertainty** demand flexibility of organisational design.

(b) **Effective systems**. The creation and exploitation of **knowledge** requires effective systems to link the people who have knowledge with the applications that need it.

(c) **Globalisation**. Globalisation creates new types and a new scale of **technological complexity** in communication and information systems; at the same time, **diversity of culture**, practices and approaches to personal relationships bring their own new problems of organisational form.

Of these three sets of issues, the need to capture, organise and exploit knowledge is probably the most pressing for most organisations. An important element of response to this need is therefore an emphasis on the importance of facilitating effective **processes** and **relationships** when designing **structures**. JS&W use the term **configuration** to encompass these three elements.

1.1 Organisational configuration

Key term

An organisation's **configuration** consists of the structures, processes, and relationships through which it operates. *JS&W*

(a) **Structure** has its conventional meaning of organisation structure.

(b) **Processes** drive and support people: they define how strategies are made and controlled; and how the organisation's people interact and implement strategy.

(c) **Relationships** are the connections between people within the organisation and between those inside it and those on the outside.

Effective processes and relationships can have varying degrees of formality and informality and it is important that formal relationships and processes are aligned with the relevant informal ones.

It is very important to be aware that structures, processes and relationships are **highly interdependent**: they have to work together intimately and consistently if the organisation is to be successful.

2 Types of structure

An organisation's formal structure reveals much about it.

(a) It shows who is **responsible** for what.

(b) It shows who **communicates** with whom, both in procedural practice and, to great extent, in less formal ways.

(c) The upper levels of the structure reveal the **skills the organisation values** and, by extension, the **role of knowledge and skill** within it.

Self contained organisations

Historically, organisational structures have tended to be **'self contained'** as they are distinct from external groups such as customers, competitors and suppliers.

JS&W review seven basic 'self contained' structural types:

- Functional
- Multi-divisional
- Holding company
- Matrix
- Transnational
- Team
- Project

Exam focus point

Students need to be aware of the clear distinction between self contained and boundary-less organisational structures. We shall explore the boundary-less organisation later in this chapter.

2.1 The functional structure

FAST FORWARD

In a functional structure, people are organised according to the type of work that they do.

In a functional organisation structure, departments are defined by their **functions,** that is, the work that they do. It is a traditional, common sense approach and many organisations are structured like this. Primary functions in a manufacturing company might be production, sales, finance, and general administration. Sub departments of marketing might be selling, advertising, distribution and warehousing.

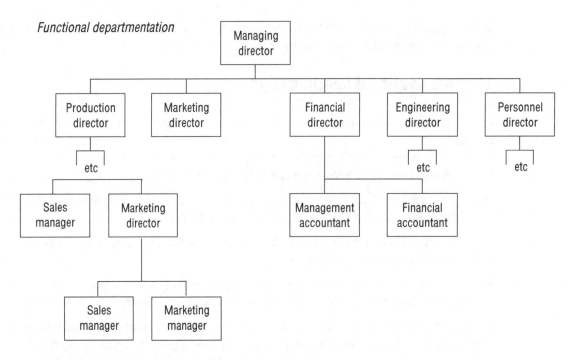

Functional departmentation

2.1.1 Advantages of functional departmentation

- It is based on work specialism and is therefore logical
- The firm can benefit from economies of scale
- It offers a career structure

2.1.2 Disadvantages

- It does not reflect the actual business processes by which **value is created**
- It is hard to identify where profits and losses are made on individual products
- People do not have an understanding of how the *whole* business works
- There are problems of co-ordinating the work of different specialisms

2.2 The multi-divisional and holding company structures

FAST FORWARD

The **multi-divisional structure** divides the organisation into semi-autonomous divisions that may be differentiated by territory, product, or market. The holding company structure is an extreme form in which the divisions are separate legal entities.

(a) Divisionalisation is the division of a business into **autonomous regions** or product businesses, each with its own revenues, expenditures and profits.

(b) Communication between divisions and head office is restricted, formal and related to performance standards. Influence is maintained by headquarters' power to hire and fire the managers who are supposed to run each division.

(c) Divisionalisation is a function of organisation size, in numbers and in product-market activities.

Mintzberg believes there are inherent problems in divisionalisation.

(a) A division is partly **insulated** by the holding company from shareholders and capital markets, which ultimately reward performance.

(b) The economic advantages it offers over independent organisations 'reflect fundamental inefficiencies in capital markets'. (In other words, different product-market divisions might function better as independent companies.)

(c) The divisions are **more bureaucratic** than they would be as independent corporations, owing to the performance measures imposed by the strategic apex.

(d) Headquarters management have a tendency to **usurp divisional profits** by management charges, cross-subsidies, head office bureaucracies and unfair transfer pricing systems.

(e) In some businesses, it is impossible to identify completely independent products or markets for which divisions would be appropriate.

(f) Divisionalisation is only possible at a fairly senior management level, because there is a limit to how much independence in the division of work can be arranged.

(g) It is a halfway house, relying on personal control over performance by senior managers and enforcing cross-subsidisation.

(h) Many of the problems of divisionalisation are those of **conglomerate diversification**. Each business might be better run independently than with the others. The different businesses might offer different returns for different risks which shareholders might prefer to judge independently.

The multi-divisional structure might be implemented in one of **two forms**.

(a) **Simple divisionalisation**

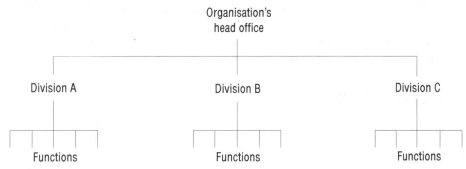

This enables concentration on particular product-market areas, overcoming problems of functional specialisation at a large scale. Problems arise with the power of the head office, and control of the resources. Responsibility is devolved, and some central functions might be duplicated.

(b) The **holding company** (group) structure is a radical form of divisionalisation. **Subsidiaries are separate legal entities**. The holding company can be a firm with a permanent investment or one that buys and sells businesses or interests in businesses: the subsidiaries may have other shareholders.

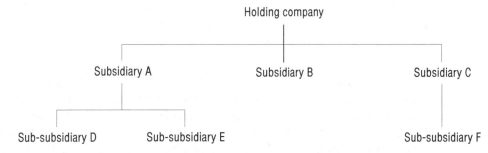

Divisionalisation has some advantages, despite the problems identified above.

(a) It focuses the attention of subordinate management on business performance and results.

(b) **Management by objectives** is the natural control default.

(c) It gives more authority to junior managers, and therefore provides them with work that grooms them for more senior positions in the future.

(d) It provides an organisation structure which reduces the number of levels of management. The top executives in each division should be able to report direct to the chief executive of the holding company.

Exam focus point

FAST FORWARD

Matrix structures attempt to ensure co-ordination across functional lines by the embodiment of dual authority in the organisation structure.

Matrix structure provides for the formalisation of management control between different functions, whilst at the same time maintaining functional departmentation. It can be a mixture of a functional, product and territorial organisation.

A golden rule of classical management theory is **unity of command**: an individual should have one boss. (Thus, staff management can only act in an advisory capacity, leaving authority in the province of line management alone.) Matrix and project organisation may possibly be thought of as a reaction against the classical form of bureaucracy by establishing a structure of **dual command,** either temporary (in the form of projects) or permanent (in the case of matrix structure).

2.4 Matrix organisation

Case Study

Matrix management

Matrix management first developed in the 1950s in the USA in the aerospace industry. Lockheed, the aircraft manufacturers, were organised in a functional hierarchy. Customers were unable to find a manager in Lockheed to whom they could take their problems and queries about their particular orders, and Lockheed found it necessary to employ 'project expediters' as customer liaison officials. From this developed 'project co-ordinators', responsible for co-ordinating line managers into solving a customer's problems. Up to this point, these new officials had no functional responsibilities.

Owing to increasingly heavy customer demands, Lockheed eventually created 'programme managers', with authority for project budgets and programme design and scheduling. These managers therefore had functional authority and responsibilities, thus a matrix management organisation was created.

The matrix organisation imposes the multi-disciplinary approach on a permanent basis. For example, it is possible to have a product management structure superimposed on top of a functional departmental structure in a matrix; product or brand managers may be responsible for the sales budget, production budget, pricing, marketing, distribution, quality and costs of their product or product line, but may have to co-ordinate with the R&D, production, finance, distribution, and sales departments in order to bring the product on to the market and achieve sales targets.

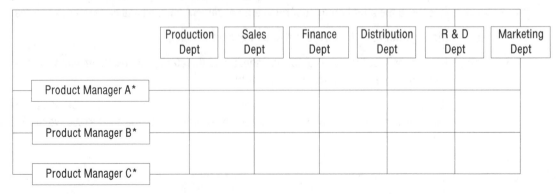

* The product managers may each have their own marketing team; in which case the marketing department itself would be small or non-existent.

The authority of product managers may vary from organisation to organisation.

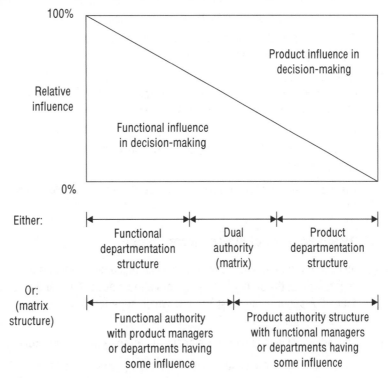

Once again, the division of authority between product managers and functional managers must be carefully defined.

Matrix management thus **challenges classical ideas** about organisation by rejecting the idea of one person, one boss.

A subordinate cannot easily take orders from two or more bosses, and so an arrangement has to be established, perhaps on the following lines.

(a) A subordinate takes orders from one boss (the functional manager) and the second boss (the project manager) has to ask the first boss to give certain instructions to the subordinate.

(b) A subordinate takes orders from one boss about some specified matters and orders from the other boss about different specified matters. The authority of each boss would have to be carefully defined. Even so, good co-operation between the bosses would still be necessary.

2.4.1 Advantages of a matrix structure

(a) It offers greater **flexibility**. This applies both to **people,** as employees adapt more quickly to a new challenge or new task, and develop an attitude which is geared to accepting change; and to **task and structure**, as the matrix may be short-term (as with project teams) or readily amended (eg a new product manager can be introduced by superimposing his tasks on those of the existing functional managers). Flexibility should facilitate efficient operations in the face of change.

(b) It should improve **communication** within the organisation.

(c) Dual authority gives the organisation **multiple orientations** so that functional specialists do not get wrapped up in their own concerns.

(d) It provides a **structure for allocating responsibility to managers for end-results**. A product manager is responsible for product profitability, and a project leader is responsible for ensuring that the task is completed.

(e) It provides for **inter-disciplinary co-operation** and a mixing of skills and expertise.

A matrix organisation is most suitable in the following situations.

(a)   There are a fairly large number of different functions, each of great importance.

(b)   There could be communications problems between functional management in different functions (eg marketing, production, R&D, personnel, finance).

(c)   Work is supposed to flow smoothly between these functions, but the communications problems might stop or hinder the work flow.

(d)   There is a need to carry out uncertain, interdependent tasks. Work can be structured so as to be **task centred**, with task managers appointed to look after each task, and provide the communications (and co-operation) between different functions.

(e)   There is a need to achieve common functional tasks so as to achieve savings in the use of resources – ie product divisions would be too wasteful, because they would duplicate costly functional tasks.

(f)   There are many geographic areas with distinct needs, but the firm wishes to exploit economies of scale.

2.4.2 Disadvantages of matrix organisation

(a)   Dual authority threatens a **conflict** between managers. Where matrix structure exists, it is important that the authority of superiors should not overlap and areas of authority must be clearly defined. A subordinate must know to which superior they are responsible for each aspect of their duties.

(b)   One individual with two or more bosses is more likely to suffer **role stress** at work.

(c)   It is sometimes more **costly** – eg product managers are additional jobs which would not be required in a simple structure of functional departmentation.

(d)   It may be **difficult for the management to accept** a matrix structure. It is possible that a manager may feel threatened that another manager will usurp his or her authority.

(e)   It requires consensus and agreement which may slow down decision-making.

2.5 The transnational structure

FAST FORWARD

The transnational structure attempts to reconcile global scope and scale with local responsiveness.

Earlier in this Study Text, we discussed designs for global business. We now return to that topic.

In international strategy, it has been difficult to combine **responsiveness to local conditions** with the degree of co-ordination necessary to achieve major **economies of scale**. The essence of the extreme case of the problem is an enforced choice between a low-cost product originally specified for a single market (typically the USA), which is potentially uninteresting or even actively shunned in other markets, and a range of low volume, and therefore high-cost, products, each specified for and produced in a single national market. These two cases are known as the **global** and the **multi-domestic** approaches to organisation and they have their own characteristic organisational structures. The global approach leads to **global divisions**, each responsible for the worldwide production and marketing of a related group of standardised products. The multi-domestic approach leads to the setting up or acquisition of local subsidiaries, each with a great deal of autonomy in design, production and marketing.

The **transnational structure** attempts to combine the best features of these contrasting approaches in order to create **competences of global relevance**, **responsiveness to local conditions** and **innovation and learning** on an organisation-wide scale. Bartlett and Ghoshal describe it as a **matrix** with two important general features.

(a)   It responds specifically to the challenges of globalisation.
(b)   It tends to have a high proportion of fixed responsibilities in the horizontal lines of management.

The transnational has three specific operational characteristics:

(a) National units are **independent operating entities**, but also provide capabilities, such as R&D, that are utilised by the rest of the organisation.

(b) Such shared capabilities allow national units to achieve global, or at least regional, **economies of scale**.

(c) The global corporate parent adds value by establishing the **basic role of each national unit** and then supporting the **systems, relationships and culture** that enable them to work together as an effective network.

If it is to work, the transnational structure must have very clearly defined managerial roles, relationships and boundaries.

(a) **Managers of global products or businesses** have responsibilities for strategies, innovation, resources and transactions that transcend both national and functional boundaries.

(b) **Country managers** must feed back local requirements and build unique local competences.

(c) **Functional managers** nurture innovation and spread best practice.

(d) **Managers at the corporate parent** lead, facilitate and integrate all other managerial activity. They must also be talent spotters within the organisation.

2.5.1 Disadvantages of the transnational structure

The transnational structure makes great demands on its managers, both in their immediate responsibilities and in the complexity of their relationships within the organisation. The complexity of the organisation can lead to the difficulties of control and the complications introduced by internal political activity.

2.6 The team-based structure

FAST FORWARD

Both team and project based structures extend the matrix approach by using cross-functional teams. The difference is that projects naturally come to an end and so project teams disperse.

A team-based structure extends the matrix structure's use of both vertical functional links and horizontal, activity-based ones by utilising **cross-functional teams**. Business processes are often used as the basis of organisation, with each team being responsible for the processes relating to an aspect of the business. Thus, a purchasing team might contain procurement specialists, design and production engineers and marketing specialists in order to ensure that outsourced sub-assemblies are properly specified, and contribute to brand values and are promptly delivered at the right price.

2.7 The project-based structure

The project-based structure is similar to the team-based structure except that projects, by definition, have a **finite life** and so, therefore, do the project teams dealing with them. This approach is very flexible and is easy to use as an adjunct to more traditional organisational forms. Management of projects is a well-established discipline with its own techniques. It requires clear project definition, if control is to be effective; and a comprehensive project review, if longer-term learning is to take place. We deal with project management in more detail later in this Study Text.

2.8 Choosing a structure

An organisation structure must provide a means of exercising appropriate **control**; it must also respond to the three challenges identified earlier: **rapid change**, **knowledge management** and **globalisation**.

JS&W summarise the seven basic types in a table. They emphasis that no single model of organisation is suitable for all purposes: managers must make choices as to which challenges they regard as most pressing.

	Control	Change	Knowledge	Globalisation
Functional	* * *	*	* *	*
Multi-divisional	* *	* *	*	* *
Holding	*	* * *	*	* *
Matrix	*	* * *	* * *	* * *
Transnational	* *	* * *	* * *	* * *
Team	*	* *	* * *	*
Project	* *	* * *	* *	* *

Goold and Campbell propose nine tests that may be used to assess proposed structures. The first four relate to the organisation's **objectives** and the **restraints** under which it operates.

(a) **Market advantage**: where processes must be closely co-ordinated in order to achieve market advantage, they should be in the same structural element.

(b) **Parenting advantage**: the structure should support the parenting role played by the corporate centre. For example, a portfolio manager would need only a small, low cost corporate centre.

(c) **People test**: the structure must be suited to the skills and experience of the people that have to function within it. For example, skilled professionals used to a team-working approach might be frustrated by a move to a functional hierarchy.

(d) **Feasibility test**: this test sweeps up all other constraints, such as those imposed by law, stakeholder opinion and resource availability.

The tests forming the second group are matters of **design principle**.

(a) **Specialised cultures**: specialists should be able to collaborate closely.

(b) **Difficult links**: it is highly likely that some inter-departmental links will be subject to friction and strain. A good example would be the link between sales and production when there are frequent problems over quality and delivery. A sound structure will embody measures to strengthen communication and co-operation in such cases.

(c) **Redundant hierarchy**: the structure should be as flat as is reasonably attainable.

(d) **Accountability**: effective control requires clear lines of accountability.

(e) **Flexibility**: the structure must allow for requirements to change in the future, so that unexpected opportunities can be seized, for example.

3 Processes

FAST FORWARD

Control processes determine how organisations function. They may be analysed according to whether they deal with inputs or outputs and whether they involve direct management action or more indirect effects. **Balanced scorecards** are direct output-based processes.

Processes are an important part of how organisations work. JS&W analyse them into four categories according to whether they deal with inputs or outputs and whether they operate by direct contact or through more indirect means. You should note that all of the processes discussed here are **control** processes.

3.1 Types of control process

	Input	Output
Direct	Supervision Planning processes	Performance targets Balanced scorecard
Indirect	Self-control Cultural processes	Internal markets

BPP
LEARNING MEDIA

3.2 Input controls

3.2.1 Supervision

Direct supervision can be used for strategic control in addition to its traditional lower-level role. It is often used for overall control in small organisations and in larger ones displaying little complexity. This technique requires that the managers thoroughly understand all aspects of the business. Direct personal control is also used in a crisis when firm and rapid action is vital.

3.2.2 Planning processes

'Planning processes' is the phrase JS&W use to mean **budgetary control**. They also regard schemes for the standardisation of work processes, such as ISO 9000:2000 certification, and IT-based enterprise resource planning systems as falling into this category. Simple and stable environments are best for this kind of approach. If different business units are faced by markedly different strategic imperatives, standardised planning systems are less applicable.

3.2.3 Self-control

Control can be exercised indirectly by promoting a high degree of **employee motivation**. When combined with autonomy, this can lead to both the exploitation of knowledge and effective co-ordination of activities by individuals interacting with one another. The role of management is then not to supervise but to provide appropriate channels for interaction, and for knowledge creation and information use.

Leadership is of fundamental importance to this technique, and depends particularly on providing role models, supporting autonomous processes and providing resources.

3.2.4 Cultural processes

Cultural control processes are **indirect** and **internalised by employees** as they absorb the prevailing culture and its norms of behaviour and performance. Culturally conditioned behaviour can provide effective responses to environments that are both dynamic and complex; it can be just as effective in a bureaucracy as in an informal, innovative, project-based organisation, for example. Training and development systems are an important aspect of the cultural control system.

Cultural processes also form important **links between organisations**, especially those that are highly dependent on the talent and knowledge of the people working in them; such people need an element of discussion, debate and cross-fertilisation in order for them to work effectively.

There is also a negative aspect to cultural processes, in that they can create **rigidities** of thought and behaviour, fossilising what was successful once, but may come to form an obstacle to progress.

3.3 Output controls

3.3.1 Performance targets

Performance can be judged against pre-set targets or **key performance indicators** (KPIs). This system is objective and permits the establishment of a hierarchy of supporting objectives that cascades down through the managerial structure. Managers are then free to organise their work and staff as they think best, so long as they achieve the targets set for them.

The extensive autonomy of method permitted by this system makes it useful in **large organisations** where the centre cannot possibly control everything in detail. It is also useful in **regulated markets**, such as privatised utilities. These tend to retain strong monopolistic tendencies that are kept in check by external regulators' setting of targets for key indicators such as service levels.

In the **public sector**, control of inputs has been traditional, but there has been a move towards targets for outputs in order to improve services.

A problem with performance targets is that it can be difficult to identify appropriate KPIs. High-level financial KPIs, such as Return on Investment (ROI), are well-established and present no difficulty.

However, even where data is easily expressed in quantitative form, non-financial targets that are actually useful can be difficult to define. The problem is even greater with aspects of performance that are **largely qualitative**, such as customer satisfaction. As a result, attention tends to be directed towards the easily measured financial aspects of performance.

One of the essential PER Performance Objectives focuses on how you have contributed to improving departmental performance, either at your own workplace or at an external organisation. The ACCA recognise that one approach to improving performance is through the establishment and close monitoring of performance measures.

3.3.2 The balanced scorecard

The **balanced scorecard** approach emphasises the need for a broad range of KPIs and builds a rational structure that reflects longer term prospects as well as immediate performance.

The balanced scorecard seeks to translate mission and strategy into objectives and measures, and focuses on **four different perspectives**, as follows.

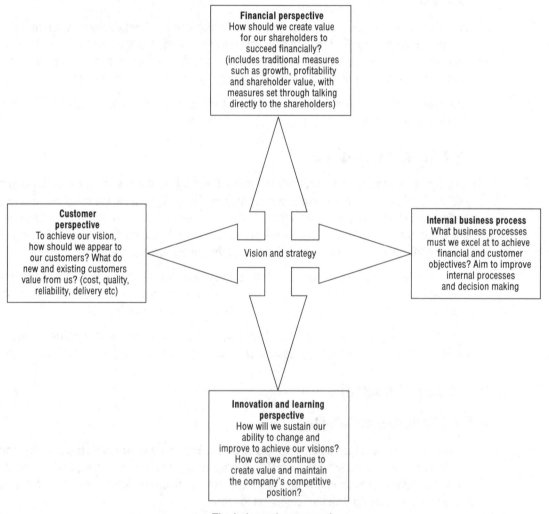

The balanced scorecard

Performance targets are set once the key areas for improvement have been identified, and the balanced scorecard is the **main monthly report**.

The scorecard is **balanced** in the sense that managers are required to think in terms of all four perspectives, to **prevent improvements being made in one area at the expense of another**.

Kaplan and Norton, who first described the balanced scorecard, recognise that the four perspectives they suggest may not be perfect for all organisations: it may be necessary, for example, to add further perspectives related to the environment or to employment.

3.3.3 Problems

As with all techniques, problems can arise during application.

Problem	Explanation
Conflicting measures	Some measures in the scorecard, such as research funding and cost reduction, may naturally conflict. It is often difficult to determine the balance which will achieve the best results.
Selecting measures	Not only do appropriate measures have to be devised but the number of measures used must be agreed. Care must be taken that the impact of the results is not lost in a sea of information. The innovation and learning perspective is, perhaps, the most difficult to measure directly, since much development of human capital will not feed directly into such crude measures as rate of new product launches or even training hours undertaken. It will, rather, improve economy and effectiveness and support the achievement of customer perspective measures.
Expertise	Measurement is only useful if it initiates appropriate action. Non-financial managers may have difficulty with the usual profit measures. With more measures to consider, this problem will be compounded.
Interpretation	Even a financially-trained manager may have difficulty in putting the figures into an overall perspective.

The scorecard should be used **flexibly**. The process of deciding **what to measure** forces a business to clarify its strategy. For example, a manufacturing company may find that 50% – 60% of costs are represented by bought-in components, so measurements relating to suppliers could usefully be added to the scorecard. These could include payment terms, lead times, or quality considerations.

3.3.4 Linkages

Disappointing results might result from a **failure to view all the measures as a whole**. For example, increasing productivity means that fewer employees are needed for a given level of output. Excess capacity can be created by quality improvements. However, these improvements have to be exploited (eg by increasing sales). The **financial element** of the balanced scorecard reminds executives that improved quality, response time, productivity or new products benefit the company only when they are translated into improved financial results, or if they enable the firm to obtain a sustainable competitive advantage.

The vertical vector

Kaplan and Norton's original perspectives may be viewed as hierarchical in nature, with a **vertical vector** running through the measures adopted.

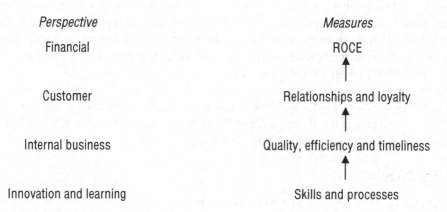

Perspective	Measures
Financial	ROCE
Customer	Relationships and loyalty
Internal business	Quality, efficiency and timeliness
Innovation and learning	Skills and processes

3.3.5 Market processes

Organisations are used to market relationships with entities, such as suppliers, outside the boundaries of their own systems. Attempts have been made to bring the responsiveness, self-regulating discipline and efficiency of the market **inside those boundaries**. Examples include autonomous **central service** units such as IT consultancy and the use of **transfer pricing** between divisions. Market solutions are particularly useful in complex or dynamic environments. They have also been used to promote innovation and responsiveness to local needs in the UK National Health Service as a replacement for centralised control.

3.3.6 Problems with market control processes

- Excessive management time spent bargaining
- Tendency for the creation of new bureaucracy to monitor effects
- Dysfunctional competition and legalistic contracting
- Destruction of cultures of collaboration

4 Relationships

Organisational relationships may be analysed into two categories: internal and external. Internal relationships concerning responsibility and authority for decision-making are particularly important.

4.1 Internal relationships

There are two important issues in internal relationships.

- The degree of centralisation
- The way the centre relates to the business units

4.1.1 Centralisation

FAST FORWARD

Centralisation offers control and standardisation; **decentralisation** utilises talent and local knowledge.

Key terms

Centralisation means a greater degree of central control.

Decentralisation means a greater degree of delegated authority to regions or sub-units.

4.1.2 Advantages of centralisation

Advantage	Comment
Control	Senior management can exercise greater control over the activities of the organisation and co-ordinate their subordinates or sub-units more easily.
Standardisation	Procedures can be standardised throughout the organisation.
Corporate view	Senior managers can make decisions from the point of view of the organisation as a whole, whereas subordinates would tend to make decisions from the point of view of their own department or section.
Balance of power	Centralised control enables an organisation to maintain a balance between different functions or departments.
Experience counts	Senior managers ought to be more experienced and skilful in making decisions.
Lower overheads	When authority is delegated, there is often a duplication of management effort (and a corresponding increase in staff numbers) at lower levels of hierarchy.
Leadership	In times of crisis, the organisation may need strong leadership by a central group of senior managers.

4.1.3 Advantages of decentralisation

Advantage	Comment
Workload	It reduces the stress and burdens of senior management.
Job	It provides subordinates with greater job satisfaction by giving them more say in making decisions which affect their work.
Local knowledge	Subordinates may have a better knowledge than senior management of 'local' conditions affecting their area of work.
Flexibility and speed	Delegation should allow greater flexibility and a quicker response to changing conditions. If problems do not have to be referred up a scalar chain of command to senior managers for a decision, decision-making will be quicker.
Training	Management at middle and junior levels are groomed for eventual senior management positions.
Control	By establishing appropriate sub-units or profit centres to which authority is delegated, the system of control within the organisation might be improved.

4.2 Contingency approach

Centralisation suits some functions more than others.

- The **research and development function** might be centralised into a single unit, as a resource for each division.
- Sales departments might be decentralised on a territorial basis.

4.2.1 Strategic management relationships

 **FAST FORWARD**

Goold and Campbell identified three major approaches to running divisionalised conglomerates: **strategic planning**, **strategic control** and **financial control**.

A vital feature of the relationship between the corporate centre and its business units is how responsibility for strategic decisions is divided between them.

There are **three generally accepted possible roles for the centre**:

- Determination of overall strategy and the allocation of resources
- Controlling divisional performance
- Provision of central services

All three of these roles have been subject to debate.

Centralised determination of strategy has been challenged as inappropriate in a diversified conglomerate. Similarly, **resource allocation**, it has been suggested, is the proper role of **capital markets**; and the rigour of the vetting carried out by central staffs has been questioned.

Controlling divisional performance is subject to all the arguments for and against decentralisation already discussed. The ability of the centre to prevent **strategic drift** has been questioned, though the radical market alternative can only work in drastic ways, such as takeover.

Centralised provision of certain **services**, such as legal and HR departments, is promoted as enhancing efficiency through the attainment of economies of scope. However, it is also suggested that many of these services can be contracted for locally at no greater cost and with the advantage of precluding any tendency to empire-building at the centre.

4.2.2 Research

Goold and Campbell researched the role of the centre in 16 British-based conglomerates. They concentrated on the first two roles summarised above, which they referred to as **planning influence** and **control influence**. The variation in these roles allowed the identification of eight distinct **strategic management styles**.

Planning influence was exercised in a variety of ways, but a fairly smooth spectrum of styles was observable, ranging from minimal, where the centre is little more than a holding company, to highly centralised, where the managers in the business units have responsibility only for operational decisions.

Control influence was exercised by the agreement of **objectives**, the monitoring of **results** and the deployment of **pressures and incentives**. This gave rise to three distinct categories of control influence: **flexible strategic**, **tight strategic** and **tight financial**.

Of the eight strategic management styles they defined, Goold and Campbell found that three of them were particularly common; each was associated with one of the three **control influence** categories mentioned above and with a different degree of **planning influence**.

<table>
<tr><td>Exam focus point</td><td>You should note that this analysis of strategic management styles is completely separate from JS&W's description of the three corporate rationales, discussed earlier in this Study Text.</td></tr>
</table>

4.3 Strategic management styles

4.3.1 Strategic planning

The strategic planning style is associated with the flexible strategic type of control influence and a fairly high degree of central planning influence. The **centre establishes extensive planning processes** through which it works with business unit managers to make substantial contributions to strategic thinking, often with a unifying overall corporate strategy. Performance targets are set in broad terms, with an **emphasis on longer-term strategic objectives**. Such organisations build linked international businesses in core areas. Business units tend to follow bold strategies and often achieve above industry average **growth** and **profitability**.

4.3.2 Strategic control

The strategic control style involves a **fairly low degree of planning influence** but uses **tight strategic control**. The centre prefers to leave the planning initiative to the business unit managers, though it will review their plans for acceptability. **Firm targets are set** for a range of performance indicators and performance is judged against them. The centre concentrates on rationalising the portfolio. Such companies achieve **good profits** but are **less successful at achieving growth**.

4.3.3 Financial control

The centre exercises influence almost entirely through the budget process. It takes little interest in business unit strategy and controls through profit targets. Careers are at stake if budgets are missed. Strategies are **cautious** and rarely global. Business unit managers tend to sacrifice market share to achieve high profits. As a result, these companies produce **excellent profits**, but **growth comes mainly from acquisitions**.

Question
Head office

XYZ has over 500 profit centres (ranging from baggage handling equipment to stockings) and revenues of £7bn. Head office staff amount to 47. Each profit centre must provide the following.

(a)   The **annual profit plan**. This is agreed in detail every year, after close negotiation. It is regarded as a commitment to a preordained level of performance.

(b)   **A monthly management report**, which is extremely detailed (17 pages). Working capital is outlined in detail. Provisions (the easiest way to manipulate accounts) are highlighted.

Is XYZ a strategic planner, a strategic controller or a financial controller?

Answer

XYC is a financial controller.

4.4 External relationships

FAST FORWARD

> External relationships are increasingly co-operative, rather than adversarial. Various forms of partnership, alliance or consortium may lead to the development of a **network organisation**.

Traditionally, external commercial relationships have been, to a greater or lesser extent, **adversarial**, in that each organisation has attempted to obtain for itself as much as possible of the value created overall in the value network. While this is still characteristic of most external relationships, many new ones have been created that focus more on **co-operation** than rivalry. These new structures are known as boundary-less organisations.

4.4.1 Boundary-less organisation structure

FAST FORWARD

> The **boundary-less organisation structure** involves the organisation collaborating with outside parties to make it more flexible during times of change. Hollow and modular organisation structures are underpinned by the use of **outsourcing. Hollow organisations** are created by outsourcing non-value adding activities to third parties. **Modular organisations** outsource a particular part of a production process, which is subsequently assembled in-house to create a completed product.

Boundary-less organisations are those which have structured their operations to allow for collaboration with external parties. Building relationships with suppliers, competitors and customers should increase the organisations flexibility to respond to change. There are various forms of boundary-less organisation, these include **hollow, modular**, **virtual and network** organisation structures. Each is discussed in more detail in this section.

Other boundary-less structures such as **strategic alliances (joint ventures, franchising** and **licensing)** were discussed earlier in the Study Text.

4.4.2 Hollow organisation structure

The hollow structure shares some similarities with the network organisation (see later). Outsourcing is central to the creation of the hollow organisational structure, as non-core processes such as human relations, payroll and logistics are outsourced to specialist providers.

Outsourcing non-core processes enables an organisation to concentrate on its core value adding activities, being those areas that provide the organisation with a competitive advantage. Value adding activities often relate to R&D, marketing and manufacturing. The outsourcing of certain functions effectively makes the organisation a 'hollowed out' entity, allowing it reduce its workforce and cut costs. The remaining staff are then free to manage the relationships created with the third party outsourcer.

Steps involved in creating a hollow organisation structure

Steps	Comment
1	Identify those non-value adding activities which do not underpin the entity's competitive performance. As we shall see later in the Study Text, the use of Harmon's process-strategy matrix is a useful tool for organisations to use in identifying those non-value adding activities. Once all relevant activities have been assessed, the most appropriate strategy to manage them can be implemented. Strategies may focus on improving existing processes, automating or outsourcing them. This we shall discuss in greater detail later in the text.
2	Explore the market for suitable outsource providers to take over certain business activities to allow these to be performed more efficiently.
3	Establish a working relationship with each outsource provider to ensure that the entity's operations are not hindered by the arrangement.
4	Bring the outsourcers own objectives in line with those of the entity through the use of incentives. For example if outsourcers can reduce costs and pass savings on then this may result in a longer term agreement being established between the parties.

 Case Study

Nike and Outsourcing

Sportswear company, Nike has suffered over the years from a bad press due to management's decision in the early 1990s to outsource non-core manufacturing operations to parts of the world with lower labour costs. Nike has been accused of allowing subcontractors to get away with paying workers less than the recognised minimum wage in some developing countries. There have also been accusations that some outsource parties have employed children to work in manufacturing plants, often in poor working conditions.

In part, Nike has been able to overcome some previous hostility by using the money saved through its outsourcing operations to undertake aggressive marketing campaigns to rebuild the company's tattered image.

Nike has also been able to get its outsource manufacturers to work with the company to improve the conditions for their workers. As part of Nike's ongoing re-branding exercise, the company became the first in the industry to publish a list of the factories it has agreements with.

Max Nisen highlights that, 'instead of denying every allegation, Nike has mostly managed to put the most difficult chapter in its history behind it and other companies who outsource could stand to learn a few things from Nike's turnaround'.

Adapted from an article:

'How Nike solved it's sweatshop problem' by Max Nisen (May 2013) published on the *Business Insider* website; www.businessinsider.com

4.4.3 Modular organisation structure

A modular organisation shares some of the same features as the hollow organisation structure. A modular organisation structure involves an organisation outsourcing some parts of its production to specialist providers. The core company will then assemble the outsourced components in-house to produce a final product. This type of structure is commonly used in hi-tech industries, such as aircraft manufacture. One argument in favour of outsourcing component production to third parties is that it should lower production costs and improve the efficiency of the organisation's internal operations. The components manufactured by the outsource parties tend to be of stand alone manufacture (product modules) to allow for easier assembly. For example, an outsource partner will provide the engines which the aircraft manufacturer can then bolt onto the finished plane.

4.4.4 Outsourcing, offshoring and shared servicing

FAST FORWARD

Outsourcing and offshoring involve external providers taking on activities previously carried out in-house. **Offshoring** involves using external providers in different countries. **Shared servicing** is an alternative approach where shared service centres consolidate the transaction-processing activities within a company. Cost savings are often highlighted as being the main motivator for all three types of arrangement.

4.4.5 Outsourcing

The concept of the boundary-less organisation has become increasingly possible due to the emergence of outsourcing. **Outsourcing** involves an organisation contracting out certain internal business functions to a third party. Organisations very often outsource those functions which are considered to be non-critical. As previously mentioned, Harmon's process-strategy matrix, which we shall discuss in more detail in a later chapter, recommends outsourcing those business processes which are of a high to low level of complexity with a low level of strategic importance.

At its simplest, outsourcing may involve hiring in a cleaning company to maintain the upkeep of the organisation's premises. This would remove the need for the organisation to retain its existing in-house cleaners. Commonly, the decision to outsource is based on anticipated cost savings and the freeing up of management time. The role of outsourcing is explored in more detail later in the Study Text.

4.4.6 Offshoring

Offshoring is a form of outsourcing that involves an external entity based in a different country providing an organisation with a particular product or process which had previously been provided in-house. Offshoring became particularly popular in the late 1990s when a number of well-known UK financial institutions (banks and insurance companies) decided to set up customer call centre operations in countries such as India. This shift saw the new call centres run by external third parties which provided the required staff and facilities.

Advantages and disadvantages of offshoring

Advantages of offshoring	Disadvantages of offshoring
Cost savings are often cited as the main motivation behind the decision to offshore.	**Quality**. Allowing third party providers to act as the interface between the organisation and its customers (eg through operating a call centre) increases the scope for quality issues to arise.
Focus on core activities. Managing non-core functions is often regarded as a distraction which can be alleviated by offshoring.	**Public perceptions**. Organisations may receive bad press if consumers in the home market perceive moves to offshore operations as leading to domestic jobs losses.
Capability. Offshoring can help organisations which lack expertise in delivering a particular process.	**Loss of control**. Offshoring increases the scope for third parties not to meet agreed service levels. This highlights the need for service level agreements. The danger here is that more management time is spent managing the relationship with the offshore partner.

Advantages of offshoring	Disadvantages of offshoring
Skills. Some countries lend themselves to offshoring due to local conditions. For example in India there is a growing number of English speaking people, often highly educated, which may help to attract large organisations.	
Flexibility. Offshoring may increase the flexibility of an organisation's operations as agreements with third parties to supply a service can be established for the short and long term.	

Case Study

RSA and offshoring

In October 2013, RSA (formerly Royal & Sun Alliance) which owns the More Than insurance brand, announced that it was creating 350 jobs in the UK. The move saw the company close its offshore Indian call centres.

John Elliott, RSA's personal lines customer service director said, 'The Indian teams are brilliant at following process transactions. But for a company trying to go from good to great service, we need consistency and excellence. The missing ingredient has been culture, and that's something we haven't been able to recreate in India. There are parts of the market that don't feel reassured dealing with somebody overseas, wherever it is'.

Adapted from an article:

'RSA brings back 350 call centre jobs back to the UK', by Steve Hawkes (October 2013), published on the *Telegraph* website; www.telegraph.co.uk

4.4.7 Shared servicing

An alternative to outsourcing is shared servicing, where shared service centres consolidate the transaction-processing activities of many operations within a company. Shared service centres aim to achieve significant cost reductions whilst improving service levels through the use of standardised technology and processes. Many large organisations have moved to centralise their IT support functions. It is common now for one IT helpdesk to serve the entire organisation, as opposed to individual divisions or departments having their own designated IT support.

Advantages to using this approach include:

(a) Reduced headcount due to economies of scale, resulting from bringing operations to a single location.

(b) Associated reduction in premises and other overhead costs.

(c) Knowledge sharing should lead to an improvement in quality of the service provided.

(d) Allows standard approaches to be adopted across the organisation, leading to more consistent management of business data.

4.4.8 Alliances

The very great cost advantages available from economies of scale are a major driver of expansion. Indeed, the minimum efficient scale for capital intensive industries such as motor vehicle manufacture is so high that operations on at least a continental scale are necessary to achieve it. Such a degree of expansion requires huge amounts of capital; various forms of **complex organisation** result from the pressure to pool resources. These include **partnerships**, **alliances**, **consortia** and the unintegrated structures resulting from **takeovers** and **mergers**.

The various forms of partnership structure were discussed in Chapter 6 in the context of strategic options. Structures such as franchises and joint ventures inevitably depend on the **management of relationships**, though the legal form can vary from loose co-operation on more or less market terms, to joint ownership.

The legal form of these complex organisations is of less importance than the degree of co-operation actually achieved, and will anyway vary between the jurisdictions involved. Co-operation may be possible in any of the activities in the value chain. If co-operation is to convey mutual benefit, it must place both parties in a stronger position to achieve one or more of their strategic objectives, without at the same time undermining their ability to achieve others. A good example is **airline code sharing**.

Code sharing is a commercial agreement that allows an airline to put its two-letter identification code on the flights of another airline as they appear in computerised reservations systems. The airlines can then sell tickets for journeys that involve two or more flights without operating all the flights themselves. For example, US Airways and the German airline, Deutsche BA, operate code share flights from the US to destinations in Germany. Customers fly on a US Airways aircraft between the US and Munich; and on Deutsche BA aircraft, from Munich to Berlin, Cologne/Bonn, Dusseldorf and Hamburg, still using the US Airways ticket designator. Airlines that share codes typically co-ordinate schedules to minimise connection times and provide additional customer services, such as one-stop check-in and baggage checked through to the final destination.

The main problem of such structural relationships is the integration of knowledge to create a successful product. This becomes more difficult as the number of partners increases.

4.4.9 Network organisations

The idea of a **network structure** is applied both within and between organisations. Within the organisation, the term is used to mean something that resembles both the **organic** organisation discussed later in this chapter and the structure of informal relationships that exists in most organisations alongside the formal structure. Such a loose, fluid approach is often used to achieve innovative response to changing circumstances.

The network approach is also visible in the growing field of **outsourcing** as a strategic method. Complex relationships can be developed between firms, who may both buy from and sell to each other, as well as the simpler, more traditional practice of buying in services such as cleaning.

Writers such as Ghoshal and Bartlett point to the likelihood of network organisations becoming the corporations of the future, replacing formal organisation structures with innovations such as **virtual teams**. Virtual teams are interconnected groups of people who may not be in the same office (or even the same organisation) but who:

- Share information and tasks
- Make joint decisions
- Fulfil the collaborative function of a team

Organisations are now able to structure their activities very differently:

(a)   **Staffing.** Certain areas of organisational activity can be undertaken by freelance or contract workers. Charles Handy's shamrock organisation (see below) is gaining ground as a workable model for a leaner and more flexible workforce, within a controlled framework. The question is: how can this control be achieved?

(b)   **Leasing of facilities** such as machinery, IT and accommodation (not just capital assets) is becoming more common

(c)   **Production** itself might be outsourced, even to offshore countries where labour is cheaper. (This, and the preceding point, of course beg the question: which assets and activities do companies retain, and which ones do they 'buy-in'?)

Interdependence of organisations is emphasised by the sharing of functions and services. Databases and communication create genuine interactive sharing of, and access to, common data.

JS&W give four examples of network organisation structures:

(a)   **Teleworking**, which combines independent work with connection to corporate resources.

(b) **Federations of experts** who combine voluntarily. This is common in the entertainment industry.

(c) **One stop shops** for professional services in which a package of services is made available by a co-ordinating entity. The point of access to such a conglomerate might be a website.

(d) **Service networks** such as the various chains of franchised hotel that co-operate to provide centralised booking facilities.

Network structures are also discerned between competitors, where **co-operation on non-core competence matters** can lead to several benefits:

- Cost reduction
- Increased market penetration
- Experience curve effects

Typical areas for co-operation between **competitors** include R&D and distribution chains. The spread of the Toyota system of manufacturing, with its emphasis on JIT, quality and the elimination of waste, has led to a high degree of integration between the operations of industrial **customers** and their **suppliers**.

4.4.10 The shamrock organisation

FAST FORWARD

> The **shamrock organisation**, or flexible firm, has a core of permanent managers and specialist staff supplied by a contingent workforce of contractors and part-time and temporary workers. This form is popular during recessions.

Largely driven by pressure to reduce personnel costs and to adapt to new market imperatives, there has been an increase in the use of part-time and temporary contracts of employment. These allow rapid downsizing in times of recession or slow growth and can save on the costs of benefits such as pensions, holiday pay and health insurance. The growth in the proportion of the workforce employed on such less-favourable contracts has attracted political attention but continues. It has produced the phenomenon of the **flexible firm** or, as Handy calls it, the **shamrock organisation**.

Key term

> Handy defines the **shamrock organisation** as a 'core of essential executives and workers supported by outside contractors and part-time help'. This structure permits the buying-in of services as needed, with consequent reductions in overhead costs. It is also known as the **flexible firm**.

The first leaf of the shamrock is the **professional core**. It consists of professionals, technicians and managers whose skills define the organisation's core competence. This core group defines what the company does and what business it is in. They are essential to the continuity and growth of the organisation. Their pay is tied to organisational performance and their relations will be more like those among the partners in a professional firm than those among superiors and subordinates in today's large corporation.

The next leaf is made up of **self-employed professionals or technicians** or smaller specialised organisations who are hired on contract, on a project-by-project basis. They are paid in fees for results, rather than in salary for time. They frequently **telecommute**. No benefits are paid by the core organisation, and the worker carries the risk of insecurity.

The third leaf comprises the **contingent work force**, whose employment derives from the external demand for the organisation's products. There is no career track for these people and they perform routine jobs. They are usually temporary and part-time workers who will experience short periods of employment and long periods of unemployment. They are paid by the hour or day or week for the time they work.

A fourth leaf of the shamrock may exist, consisting of **consumers** who do the work of the organisation. Examples are shoppers who bag their own groceries and purchasers of assemble-it-yourself furniture.

This type of organisation provides three kinds of flexibility.

(a) **Personnel costs** can respond to market conditions of supply and demand for different types of labour and to the employer's financial position.

(b) Overall **personnel numbers** can be changed as required.

(c) The **skills** available can be modified fairly rapidly and multi-skilling can be encouraged.

There are other implications for employment patterns.

(a)   All staff will have to be prepared to widen their availability, possibly moving from site to site as required.

(b)   Staff must accept varying patterns of working hours, perhaps working on **annual hours** contracts which require extended shifts in busy times balanced with shorter ones in slack times.

(c)   Contracts of employment will be far less prescriptive of duties and responsibilities.

4.4.11 The virtual organisation

A **virtual organisation** is a geographically distributed network with little formal structure, probably held together by IT applications, partnerships and collaboration.

The idea of a **virtual organisation** or **cybernetic corporation** has attracted considerable attention as the usefulness of IT for communication and control has been exploited. The essence of the virtual organisation is the electronic linking of spatially dispersed components.

While there is some disagreement among academics as to a precise definition of the virtual organisation, a consensus exists with regard to **geographical dispersion** and the centrality of **information technology** to the production process. Many also agree that the virtual organisation has a temporary character. Other characteristics are a **flexible structure** and a **collaborative culture**.

However, an organisation is not a virtual organisation merely because it uses IT extensively and has multiple locations. Many academics would exclude organisations that use communications extensively, but not in a way **critical to completing the production process**.

Key term

A **virtual organisation** is a temporary or permanent collection of geographically dispersed individuals, groups, organisational units (which may or may not belong to the same organisation), or entire organisations that depend on electronic linking in order to complete the production process.

JS&W use the term rather less rigorously, to mean any network organisation that is 'held together not through formal structure and physical proximity of people, but by partnership, collaboration and networking'.

4.4.12 Collaborative organisational structures

Collaboration with customers

Exam focus point

Students need to be able to discuss how organisations interact and collaborate with their customers. An understanding of **user contribution systems** and **crowdsourcing** are key terms that you need to learn.

Understanding what customers want from companies is a major issue. The use of customer feedback surveys are not new. However, advances in internet technologies have led to the development of **user contribution systems**. Such systems allow for closer interaction between individuals and companies. **Crowdsourcing** involves obtaining information from a large group of people often external to the organisation for the purpose of helping to generate ideas and suggestions which can be implemented to improve organisational performance.

Organisations have collaborated with their customers for many years through the use of feedback questionnaires and customer satisfaction surveys. In recent times, many large organisations have created **user contribution systems** as a means of extracting and collating customer contributions.

New technologies such as Web 2.0 have enabled the widespread use of user contribution systems. People are now able to freely interact with each other and organisations by passing on information or expressing their opinions on a company's latest products and services via websites and online forums. Interaction between the individual and the company may be of a behavioural nature, as an individuals purchasing behaviour can be tracked.

Buchanan and Huczynski (in their text, *Organisational Behaviour*) highlight six motivations for individuals to interact with organisations through user contribution systems when no financial incentive exists:

Reasons	Comment
By-product of purchase	Individual users of a website provide data to an organisation when making a purchase. Such data is gathered as a by-product of the underlying interaction, ie the purchase. When making a purchase on eBay, this information is collected to show how many transactions an individual has participated in to date.
Practical solutions	Websites such as Delicious.com allow users to store and share web bookmarks. This enables other users to access a list of useful websites.
Social rewards	Users of social networking site Facebook are able to interact with friends and family by joining an online community.
Reputation	Some users choose to interact in order to enhance their own reputation. For example, being rated as a top rated seller on eBay.
Self-expression	Contribution systems provide individuals with the scope to express their opinions and give feedback. For example, shoppers on Amazon are able to leave recommendations on purchases.
Altruism	Some individuals interact in order to help others or bring certain issues to the attention of a greater range of people.

User contribution systems provide organisations with the opportunity to better understand customers and their needs. Organisations can use this information to their advantage by producing enhanced products and services, which may lead to reduced costs and help to attract further customers. This customer acquisition can be achieved through the use of tailored marketing messages, offering discounts on certain purchases and providing purchase recommendations.

4.4.13 Crowdsourcing

Crowdsourcing involves obtaining information from a large group of people. News agencies often ask individuals to phone in when they are aware of breaking news stories or even traffic jams on the road. Such information can then be used to inform and help other users.

In a commercial context, large companies are able to use internet technologies to ask online users for creative ideas on a particular matter or to provide information which the organisation can then use to solve particular problems.

 Case Study   IBM Innovation Jam

Computer giant IBM undertakes regular collaborative exercises to allow employees and external contributors to share their thoughts to help the company address significant challenges. This exercise is known as an online 'jam' session.

'An IBM jam is a guided online discussion with thousands of trusted collaborators from which we extract insights, discoveries and decisions. Since 2001, IBM has used jams to involve its more than 400,000 employees around the world in far-reaching exploration and problem-solving. ValueJam in 2003 gave IBM's workforce the opportunity to redefine the core IBM values for the first time in nearly 100 years. During IBM's 2006 innovation jam, IBM brought together more than 150,000 people from 104 countries and 67 companies. As a result, ten new IBM businesses were launched with seed investment totalling $100 million'.

Source: The details of IBM's Innovation Jam can be found on the *IBM* website; www.collaborationjam.com

Crowdsourcing and user contribution systems

Crowdsourcing can be considered to be distinct from user contribution systems as an organisation decides which contributions it will use. As illustrated above, IBM use the 'jam' sessions as a sounding board for ideas and suggestions, with only those deemed most appropriate taken forward for development.

Drawbacks of crowdsourcing

Lack of credibility: The use of free information does have its drawbacks – the use of community generated contributions are likely to lack the credibility which would have been obtained, had input been received from paid professionals with expertise in a particular field. Crowdsourcing may not be appropriate when higher risk issues are debated.

Collaborators do not have to collaborate: This is an important issue for companies which use the suggestions of others. Collaborators engage of their own free will, meaning that they have no obligation to continue providing contributions in the future.

5 Stereotypical configurations   6/13, 12/10

In Section 1, we pointed out that it is very important to be aware that structures, processes and relationships are **highly interdependent**: they have to work together intimately and consistently if the organisation is to be successful. This means, among other things, that the basic assumptions and characteristics of the three components must be more or less compatible, since they have to integrate so closely. Thus, it might be difficult to combine a strict **financial control** style of leadership at the corporate parent with a **transnational** structural approach, or to use **cultural control** throughout the **shamrock organisation**, simply because of the use of temporary workers.

As a result of this need for compatibility, the number of successful overall configurations is small. Mintzberg identifies only **six ideal types**. Of these, five fit neatly into a taxonomy based on their five main structural components; the sixth, less so.

FAST FORWARD

> Henry Mintzberg's theory of organisational configuration is a way of expressing the main features by which both formal structure and power relationships are expressed in organisations. He suggests that there are five ideal types of organisation, each of which configures five standard components in a significantly different way. Each component of the organisation has its own **dynamic**, which **leads to a distinct type of organisation**. The sixth type is the missionary organisation.

Exam focus point

In June 2013 the compulsory question required students to discuss how an understanding of organisational configurations would have helped a newly appointed CEO at a hospital introduce a strategic planning system. The examining team noted that students appeared to lack an understanding of organisational configurations. This is an important area that students should not avoid when preparing to sit paper P3.

The five components

(a) The **strategic apex** wishes to retain control over decision-making. It achieves this when the co-ordinating mechanism is **direct supervision**. The force this most relates to is the **force for direction** (in other words, the need for people to be told what to do).

(b) The **technostructure's** reason for existence is the design of **procedures** and **standards**. For example, the preparation of accounts is highly regulated. This acts as a **force for efficiency**.

(c)   The members of the **operating core** seek to minimise the control of administrators over what they do. They prefer to work autonomously, achieving what other co-ordination is necessary by **mutual adjustment**. As professionals, they rely on outside training (such as medical training) to standardise skills. This corresponds to the **force for proficiency**.

(d)   The managers of the **middle line** seek to increase their **autonomy** from the strategic apex, and to increase their control over the operating core, so that they can concentrate on their own segment of the market or with their own products. This corresponds to the **force for concentration** (on individual product areas).

(e)   **Support staff** only gain influence when their expertise is vital. **Mutual adjustment** is the co-ordinating mechanism. This corresponds to the **force for learning**.

The **forces for co-operation and competition** largely describe how these elements relate to each other.

5.1 The simple structure (or entrepreneurial) structure

The **strategic apex** wishes to retain control over decision-making, and so exercises what Mintzberg describes as a **pull to centralise**. Mintzberg believes that this leads to a **simple structure**.

(a)   **The simple structure is characteristic of small, young organisations**.

(b)   In small firms, a single entrepreneur or management team will dominate (as in the power culture). If it grows, the organisation might need more managerial skills than the apex can provide. Strategies might be made on the basis of the manager's hunches.

(c)   Centralisation is advantageous as it reflects management's full knowledge of the operating core and its processes. However, senior managers might intervene too much.

(d)   It is risky as it depends on the expertise of one person. Such an organisation might be prone to **succession crises**. Who takes over if the boss dies? This problem is often encountered in family businesses.

(e)   This structure can handle an environment that is relatively simple but fast moving, where standardisation cannot be used to co-ordinate activities.

(f)   **Co-ordination is achieved by direct supervision**, with few formal devices. It is thus flexible.

(g)   This structure has its own particular characteristics: wide span of control; no middle line and hence, minimal hierarchy; and no technostructure, implying little formalisation or standardisation of behaviour.

5.2 The machine bureaucracy

The **technostructure** exerts a pull for standardisation of work processes. It creates a **machine bureaucracy**.

(a)   This is the classic bureaucracy, working on a sophisticated and well-tuned set of **rules and procedures**. Machine bureaucracies are associated with routine technical systems and repetitive tasks. The bureaucracy can function if people leave, as jobs are designed precisely.

(b)   **The technostructure is the key part**. Power rests with analysts who standardise other people's work. The key management philosophy is **scientific management**.

(c)   The work of the operating core is highly standardised. Direct supervision by the strategic apex is limited as **standardisation of work processes ensures co-ordination**.

(d)   There is a strong emphasis on the **division of labour**, and in particular **on control**. Uncertainty has to be eliminated. The elaborate middle line monitors and directs the operating core. Outsourcing would be embraced reluctantly so the firm employs its own legal and PR specialists. (For example, many big firms have a central legal department.)

(e)   Formal communication is most important. Authority is hierarchical.

(f)   Conflict is rife between different departments, between line and staff, and between operating core and management.

(g)   The environment must be simple and stable.

(h)   The machine bureaucracy is the most efficient structure for integrating sets of simple and repetitive tasks.

(i)   Machine bureaucracies cannot adapt rapidly. They are designed for specialised purposes. They are driven by performance, not problem solving.

5.3 The professional bureaucracy

The **operating core** has a pull for standardisation, not of work processes but of **individual skills**. A machine bureaucracy would lay down exactly how financial transactions should be posted, whether people understood them or not. A **professional bureaucracy** would employ accountants who should know what is involved. The operating core seeks to minimise the influence of administrators (mainly the middle line and technostructure) over work. Examples are hospitals and accountancy firms.

(a)   It hires trained specialists who are all imbued with the skills and values of the profession. A school is an example. Teachers' work in the classroom is not directly supervised but all teachers are trained.

(b)   **Co-ordination is achieved by standardisation of skills**, which originate outside its structure. (Teacher training occurs at independent colleges.)

(c)   **Power is often based on expertise**, not formal position in the organisation hierarchy.

(d)   Work processes are **too complex** to be standardised by a technostructure.

(e)   The **operating core** is the key part. There is an elaborate support staff to service it. A technostructure might exist for budgeting, but not for designing work processes.

(f)   Work is decentralised. **Professionals control their own work**, and seek collective control over the administrative decisions which affect them.

(g)   There might be **two** organisation hierarchies: one, relatively informal, for the operating core doing the work; another, more formal for the support staff. An example is a barristers' chambers. Barristers are co-ordinated by their head clerk, but they retain collective authority over the clerk. The clerk, on the other hand, will exercise direct control over secretarial services.

(h)   Professional administrators also manage much of the organisation's boundary.

(i)   It can be democratic.

(j)   The professional bureaucracy cannot always cope with any variations of standards, as control is exercised through training.

Question	Bureaucracy

How would a machine bureaucracy and a professional bureaucracy ensure that accounting transactions are correctly posted?

Answer

The machine bureaucracy would devise very precise procedures and rule-books telling untrained clerks exactly what to do in any situation.

The professional bureaucracy would employ trained and perhaps qualified accounts staff, whose professional training would give them the expertise to make the right decision.

5.4 The divisional (or diversified) form

The middle line seeks as much autonomy for itself as possible. It exerts a **pull to balkanise** (ie to split into small self-managed units). The result is the **divisional form**, by which autonomy is given to managers

lower down the line. The prime co-ordinating mechanism is **standardisation of outputs**: these are usually performance measures such as profit, which are set by the strategic apex.

(a) Divisionalisation is the division of a business into **autonomous regions** or product businesses, each with its own revenues, expenditures and profits.

(b) Because each division is monitored by its objective performance towards a single integrated set of goals determined by the strategic apex, **each division is configured as a machine bureaucracy**.

(c) Communication between divisions and head office is restricted, formal and related to performance standards. Influence is maintained by headquarters' power to hire and fire the managers who are supposed to run each division.

(d) Divisionalisation is a function of organisation size, in numbers and in product-market activities.

5.5 The adhocracy

The **support staff** exert a pull of their own, towards **collaboration**. The **adhocracy** does not rely on standardisation to co-ordinate its activities, yet it is much more complex than the simple structure which also does not use standardisation.

(a) The adhocracy is **complex and disorderly**. There is little formalisation of behaviour. Specialists are deployed in market-based project teams which group together and disperse as and when a project arises and ends. Co-ordination is informal, by mutual adjustment.

(b) The adhocracy relies on the expertise of its members, **but not through standardised skills**. Instead, the **mix** of skills is important. For example, a film is made by a director, actors, camera people, set designers and so on.

(c) A matrix structure might exist, but there are a large number of management roles such as project managers. Managers do not plan or supervise, but co-ordinate.

(d) Decision-making power depends on the type of decision and the situation in which it is made, rather than level in hierarchy. 'No-one ... monopolises the power to innovate'.

(e) Strategy is hard to determine in the adhocracy. It depends partly on the projects that come along (like a film studio). The strategic apex does not **formulate** strategies, but is engaged in battles over **strategic choices** (eg which films shall we make?) and liaisons with the outside parties.

(f) The adhocracy is positioned in a dynamic and complex environment.

(g) The adhocracy is driven to bureaucratise itself as it ages. The organisation will eventually **specialise in what it does best**, driving it to more stable environmental conditions and predictable work processes, leading perhaps to a professional bureaucracy.

The adhocracy is concerned with **innovation**.

(a) The **operating adhocracy** seeks to **innovate** to serve its clients, whereas the professional bureaucracy seeks perfection. (Mintzberg uses an analogy of a theatre company. An adhocratic theatre company produces new plays. A professional bureaucratic one would seek to produce ever more perfect renditions of Shakespeare.) The operating core is retained.

(b) The **administrative adhocracy** innovates to serve its **own convenience**. Note that the operating core is split off, frequently subcontracted or automated, or even forms a separate organisation. The support staff are important, a central pool of expert talent from which project teams are drawn.

Adhocracies sometimes exist because the complexity of their technical systems require a trained support staff to operate them.

(a) The adhocracy is an ambiguous environment for work. This elicits complex human responses, as many people dislike ambiguity.

(b) The adhocracy is not suitable for **standardised** work; it is better at dealing with unique projects.

(c) It has a high cost of communication, and workloads are unbalanced.

A question in the December 2010 exam asked candidates to explain how an understanding of organisation configuration could have helped predict the failure of the implementation of a proposed structure in the organisation discussed in the scenario. This question specifically referenced Henry Mintzberg's configuration stereotypes to help student's identify what they were being asked to do. The examining team noted that very few candidates answered this question well, with perhaps less than one in ten being familiar with the work of Mintzberg. They also mentioned that students without this knowledge failed to use a logical approach of focusing on the key words 'structure' 'control' and 'processes' to see that the proposed structure would clash with the existing culture. Had they done this, they could have converted a marginal fail into a marginal pass.

This demonstrates the importance of ensuring you are familiar with all areas of the syllabus before attempting the P3 exam. However, this also shows the importance of stopping, thinking and applying your own logic and wider knowledge to the scenario to produce a sensible answer when faced with an inability to recall theoretical knowledge in the exam.

5.6 Concluding thoughts

The usefulness of Mintzberg's theory of structural configuration is that it covers many issues, over and above formal organisation structure.

- The type of work the organisation does (customised or standardised)
- The complexity it has to deal with (simple or complex)
- The environment (stable or dynamic)

We can summarise some of these in the table below.

	Co-ordination mechanism	Key part	Environment	Possible characteristics
Simple	Direct supervision	Strategic apex	Simple/dynamic (even hostile)	Small, young, centralised, personality-driven. Crisis of leadership
Machine bureaucracy	Standardised work processes	Techno-structure	Simple/stable	Old, large, rule-bound, specialised
Professional bureaucracy	Standardised skills	Operating core	Complex/stable	Decentralised, emphasis on training
Divisional form	Standardised outputs	Middle line	Varies; each division is shielded to a degree	Old, large, divisions are quasi-autonomous, decentralised, bureaucratic
Adhocracy	Mutual adjustment	Support staff	Complex/dynamic	High automated, 'organic'

5.6.1 The missionary organisation

Mintzberg mentions one other co-ordinating factor: **mission**. A **missionary organisation** is one welded together by ideology or culture. There is job rotation, standardisation of values (norms) and little external control (eg like a religious sect). This relates to ideology, the **force for co-operation**. This kind of configuration features simple systems and network relationships in team structures. It works well in a simple and static environment

Which organisation configurations are suggested in the following cases?

(a)   Creation Co provides public relations services to clients. It is run by five partners, with a staff of copy editors, designers, party-throwers and people with contacts in the press. Clients contact one of the partners who assembles a team to solve the client's problem, though the partner does not direct the solution.

(b)   The St Imelda Hospital is involved in providing physiotherapy to accident victims. It recruits trained physiotherapists, each of whom is allocated a patient. The hospital does not determine exactly what sort of treatments should be used.

Answer

(a)   Adhocracy
(b)   Professional bureaucracy

6 Configuration and strategy

FAST FORWARD

Chandler concluded that structure is determined by strategy. JS&W suggest that practical combinations of structures, processes and relationships are few and those that succeed tend to be robust and difficult to change because their dynamic interactions tend to produce **reinforcing cycles of behaviour**. Strategy and structure thus tend to support and preserve one another.

There has been debate as to which of strategy and structure is the **independent variable** and which the **dependent**. Chandler concluded that structure was determined by strategy, but it has been suggested that once a large organisation has settled into a particular structural form, the hierarchical, communication and cultural practices associated with that form will predispose it towards a particular strategic stance. JS&W expand on this suggestion with their description of **reinforcing cycles** and **configuration dilemmas**.

6.1 Reinforcing cycles

The very fact that there are only six ideal types of organisational configuration indicates that the three strands, structure, processes and relationships, are constrained in the ways in which they can combine effectively in practice. They do not offer a menu of independent choices; only certain combinations work. JS&W say 'configurations found in practice tend to be very **cohesive**, **robust** and **difficult to change**' (original emphasis).

This tendency is explained by the **dynamic interaction** between the various elements of configuration, environment and strategy. This interaction leads to **reinforcing cycles** of behaviour that tend to preserve the *status quo*. Thus, for example, a **machine bureaucracy** will seek out stable environmental conditions in which to compete with a standardised, cost effective product; this will make good use of its standardised processes and tight management and reinforce its defensive culture – which will predispose it to seek out stable environmental conditions.

This interdependence can strengthen the organisation, but the danger is that it can lead to strategic drift if one of the elements involved is changed. The circle of reinforcement is broken and the organisation may decline until a new reinforcing cycle is developed.

This tendency for things to get worse before they get better is illustrated by the **change and performance J curve**. Change tends to lead to a fall in performance that continues until a set of reinforcing factors is assembled; only then can performance improve past its original level.

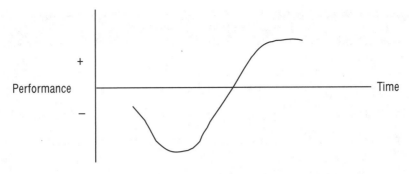

The change and performance J curve

There is an important lesson here for the **management of change**, which is that attention must be paid simultaneously to all three of structure, process and relationships if the change is to be carried through successfully.

6.2 Configuration dilemmas

Even within the six stereotypical configurations, there will be **problems of optimisation**, since many of the features that might be adopted have both advantages and disadvantages. Some of these problems can be resolved into simple choices, but most require a balance to be struck between opposed extreme positions.

A **hierarchical structure** may be necessary for direction and control, but is less good than a **network approach** for fostering learning and innovation. Similarly, **vertical lines of accountability** may push subordinates to greater efforts, but this may be at the expense of **horizontal relationships**.

Empowerment can promote the use of initiative, but is difficult to combine with overall control and may lead to chaotic activity. Similar considerations apply to centralisation, as discussed earlier in this chapter.

Dilemmas such as these may be managed in three ways:

(a)   The organisation may be **divided** and different approaches used in each part. For example, the accounting and HRM departments may function best if organised in a standardised, bureaucratic way, while the adhocracy may provide a more effective model for such activities as marketing and R&D. This has been called the **dual core** approach.

(b)   A **combination** of features may be possible, if difficult to achieve. JS&W give the examples of ABB and Unilever, which are said to be 'networked multi-divisionals'.

(c)   Frequent **reorganisation** may be used to prevent any particular approach from becoming dominant in the longer term.

Chapter Roundup

- Globalisation, other aspects of rapid environmental change and, above all, the need to **exploit knowledge** make the **structures**, **processes** and **relationships** that make up configurations vital for strategic success.

- In a functional structure, people are organised according to the type of work that they do.

- The **multi-divisional structure** divides the organisation into semi-autonomous divisions that may be differentiated by territory, product, or market. The holding company structure is an extreme form in which the divisions are separate legal entities.

- **Matrix structures** attempt to ensure co-ordination across functional lines by the embodiment of dual authority in the organisation structure.

- The **transnational structure** attempts to reconcile global scope and scale with local responsiveness.

- Both team and project based structures extend the matrix approach by using cross-functional teams. The difference is that projects naturally come to an end and project teams disperse.

- **Control processes** determine how organisations function. They may be analysed according to whether they deal with inputs or outputs and whether they involve direct management action or more indirect effects. **Balanced scorecards** are direct output-based processes.

- **Centralisation** offers control and standardisation; **decentralisation** utilises talent and local knowledge.

- Goold and Campbell identified three major approaches to running divisionalised conglomerates: **strategic planning**, **strategic control** and **financial control**.

- External relationships are increasingly co-operative, rather than adversarial. Various forms of partnership, alliance, consortium may lead to the development of a **network organisation**.

- The **boundary-less organisation structure** involves the organisation collaborating with outside parties to make it more flexible during times of change. Hollow and modular organisation structures are underpinned by the use of **outsourcing**. **Hollow organisations** are created by outsourcing non-value adding activities to third parties. **Modular organisations** outsource a particular part of a production process, which is subsequently assembled in-house to create a completed product.

- Outsourcing and offshoring involve external providers taking on activities previously carried out in-house. **Offshoring** involves using external providers in different countries. **Shared servicing** is an alternative approach where shared service centres consolidate the transaction-processing activities within a company. Cost savings are often highlighted as being the main motivator for all three types of arrangement.

- The **shamrock organisation**, or flexible firm, has a core of permanent managers and specialist staff supplied by a contingent workforce of contractors and part-time and temporary workers. This form is popular during recessions.

- A **virtual organisation** is a geographically distributed network with little formal structure, probably held together by IT applications, partnerships and collaboration.

- Understanding what customers want from companies is a major issue. The use of customer feedback surveys are not new. However, advances in internet technologies have led to the development of **user contribution systems**. Such systems allow for closer interaction between individuals and companies. **Crowdsourcing** involves obtaining information from a large group of people, often external to the organisation for the purpose of helping to generate ideas and suggestions which can be implemented to improve organisational performance.

Chapter roundup (cont'd)

- Henry Mintzberg's theory of organisational configuration is a way of expressing the main features by which both formal structure and power relationships are expressed in organisations. He suggests that there are five ideal types of organisation, each of which configures five standard components in a significantly different way. Each component of the organisation has its own **dynamic**, which **leads to a distinct type of organisation**. The sixth type is the missionary organisation.

- Chandler concluded that structure is determined by strategy. JS&W suggest that practical combinations of structures, processes and relationships are few and those that succeed tend to be robust and difficult to change because their dynamic interactions tend to produce **reinforcing cycles of behaviour**. Strategy and structure thus tend to support and preserve one another.

Quick Quiz

1   What are the three components of an organisation's configuration?

2   What specific features does a transnational have?

3   What are the perspectives of the standard balanced scorecard and how do they fit together?

4   What are the three strategic management styles identified by Goold and Campbell?

5   What are the five organisational components described by Mintzberg?

Answers to Quick Quiz

1   Structures, processes and relationships

2   Independent national operating companies that also provide expertise used globally; as a result global, or at least regional, scale economies; a global parent that establishes the basic roles of the national units and supports the systems, relationships and culture that enable them to work together.

3   The **innovation** perspective's measures of skills and processes should support the **internal business** perspective's measures of quality, efficiency and timeliness, which support the **customer** perspective's measures of relationships and loyalty, which support the overall **financial** perspective measure, ROCE.

4   Strategic planning, strategic control, financial control.

5   Strategic apex, middle line, operating core, technostructure, support services.

Now try the question below from the Practice Question Bank

Number	Level	Marks	Time
Q8	Preparation	n/a	36 mins

Managing strategic change

Topic list	Syllabus reference
1 Diagnosis: situation analysis for change	C2(a),(b),(c)
2 Styles of change management	C2 (d)
3 Change management roles	C2
4 Change management levers	C2
5 Pitfalls of change management	C2

Introduction

It will be unusual for an organisation's strategy to remain unchanged for any appreciable period of time and the same is true of the methods and processes used for implementing it. The influence of environmental developments is such that strategies will inevitably change and evolve; the only question is how rapid the change will be.

The management of change is thus an integral and important part of strategic management and is the subject of this chapter. Following JS&W, we will start by considering the **diagnosis of change requirements**. The work to be done here consists of establishing the type of change required; exploring the organisational context and the cultural influences involved; and analysing the forces that support or hinder the change required.

We will then examine the impact of **management style** and the **roles played by** managers and other **agents of change**. There are a number of **levers of change** that managers can use and we consider these next. Finally, we consider the **common pitfalls** that have hampered change programmes in the past.

Study guide

		Intellectual level
C2	**Managing strategic change**	
(a)	Explore different types of strategic change and their implications	2
(b)	Determine and diagnose the organisational context of change using Balogun and Hope Hailey's contextual features model and the cultural web	3
(c)	Establish potential blockages and levers of change	2
(d)	Advise on the style of leadership appropriate to manage strategic change	2

Exam guide

It is very important to be aware that strategic change may be implicit in a scenario rather than being the explicit subject of a question requirement. You must be able to recognise the factors that drive change and constrain the ways in which it may be effected.

Models and theories

The Study Guide for this chapter refers explicitly to two models:

- Balogun and Hope Hailey's contextual features model
- The cultural web

These models could be specifically required in a question.

We have already looked at the cultural web in Chapter 5 so it is not repeated here. However, it is important that you appreciate the way culture influences the context of change.

1 Diagnosis: situation analysis for change

There are three main change management considerations.

- The type of change required, whether adaptation, evolution, reconstruction or revolution
- The wider context of change, including the time available; capability to implement change; capacity and readiness; and power
- Forces facilitating and blocking change

A wide range of stimuli may lead an organisation's managers to recognise the need for strategic change. Consideration of the broader contexts of the **environment** and the organisation's **strategic capability** may show that large scale developments are necessary; the need to put strategy into action may call for more detailed but no less far-reaching adjustment of processes, relationships, technologies and so on. In any event, the management of change starts with an understanding of **three main considerations**:

(a) The **type** of change required
(b) The **wider context** of the change
(c) **Forces facilitating** and **blocking** change

1.1 Types of change

JS&W, quoting Balogun and Hope Hailey, analyse change on two axes: these are its **scope** and its **nature**.

The **scope** of change is its extent: the measure of scope is whether or not the methods and assumptions of the existing **paradigm** must be replaced.

The **nature** of change may be incremental and built on existing methods and approaches, or it may require a 'big bang' approach if rapid response is required, as in times of crisis.

Scope of change

		Realignment	Transformation
Nature of change	**Incremental**	Adaptation	Evolution
	'Big bang'	Reconstruction	Revolution

Types of change

(a) **Adaptation** is the most common type of change. It does not require the development of a new paradigm and proceeds step by step.

(b) **Reconstruction** can also be undertaken within an existing paradigm but requires rapid and extensive action. It is a common response to a long-term decline in performance.

(c) **Evolution** is an incremental process that leads to a new paradigm. It may arise from careful analysis and planning or may be the result of **learning processes**. Its transformational nature may not be obvious while it is taking place.

(d) **Revolution** is rapid and wide ranging response to extreme pressures for change. A long period of **strategic drift** may lead to a crisis that can only be dealt with in this way. Revolution will be very obvious and is likely to affect most aspects of both what the organisation does and how it does them.

1.2 The context of change (Contextual features model) 6/14,12/12, 12/10

Exam focus point

The compulsory question in the December 2010 exam required candidates to identify and analyse the contextual factors of a strategic change. The scenario focused on the purchase by a parent company of a smaller, struggling entity. The parent company had different business interests in the fishing industry and was in the process of finalising its takeover of a seafood restaurant chain. There were 13 marks available for applying and justifying an appropriate model (such as the contextual features model) to use in the scenario.

The compulsory question in the June 2014 exam required candidates to evaluate the effect of contextual features on the introduction of strategic change at a company involved in the printer cartridge market. This requirement was worth 14 marks. The Balogun and Hope Hailey model was specifically provided in the scenario in the form of a diagram. As a result, candidates were not required to recall the model, but were expected to apply their knowledge to the scenario. The examining team highlighted that a number of candidates seemed unfamiliar with the contextual features model. 'They were forced to guess what each of the contextual factors is and many answers made little reference to the scenario. Many candidates did not focus their answers on strategic change and consequently candidates did not score too well on this part of the question'.

The context of change is provided by the organisational setting; this has many aspects and can therefore be very complex. However, this complexity can be approached in a manageable way by considering it under eight general headings proposed by Balogun and Hope Hailey. One of the eight headings is **scope**: this has already been discussed. The rest are discussed below.

The headings represent a wide range of influences and the specific considerations affecting the impact of each may vary from organisation to organisation. For example, the first on the list, **time available**, may be largely determined by stakeholder sentiment in one organisation; and by anticipated political change, in another, with different aspects of the market situation influencing both.

1.2.1 Aspects of context

(a) The **time available** may vary dramatically, but can often be quite limited when responding to competitive or regulatory pressure.

(b) The **preservation** of some organisational characteristics and resources may be required.

(c) **Diversity** of general experience, opinion and practice is likely to ease the change process: homogeneity in these factors is unlikely to do so.

(d) The **capability** to manage and implement change is obviously important. To a great extent, this depends on past experience of change projects, both among managers and among lower-level staff.

(e) **Capacity** to undertake change depends on the availability of resources, particularly finance, and IS/IT, and management time and skill. We have looked at IS/IT earlier in this Study Text, but it is important to note that unrealisable or out-dated systems could become a blockage in the change process.

(f) The degree of workforce **readiness** for change will affect its success. Readiness may be contrasted with **resistance** to change, which can exist at varying levels of intensity and may be widespread or confined to pockets.

(g) The **power** to effect change may not be sufficient to overcome determined resistance among important stakeholder groups. This can apply even at the strategic apex, where, for example, major shareholders, trustees or government ministers may constrain managers' freedom of action.

Exam focus point

The June 2008 exam featured a question on strategic change, and the examining team noted it was the least popular of the optional questions. The examining team also noted that, despite the question being clearly built around Balogun and Hope Hailey's matrix of the nature and scope of change and the contextual features model, many candidates' answers suggested they were unfamiliar with this area of the syllabus.

The models in questions are explicitly referenced in the Study Guide, so make sure you learn them well enough to be able to answer a question based on them.

1.2.2 Questions

An examination of context leads to four questions.

(a) Is the organisation able to **achieve** the change required?
(b) Does the context affect the **means** by which change should be achieved?
(c) Should the context itself be **restructured** as a preliminary to strategic change?
(d) Will constraints present in the context make it necessary to proceed in **stages**?

1.3 Culture and change

If you think about the elements of context outlined above, you will quickly realise that they are all affected to some extent by **cultural considerations**. For example, even the adequacy or otherwise of the time available may be affected by culturally-influenced attitudes to speed of action, caution and risk.

The **cultural web** (which we have looked at earlier in this Study Text) may be used as a tool to establish specific implications of the desired overall strategic change by facilitating comparison between the current position and the desired future outcome. For example, consideration of **power structures** may make it clear that there should be a move away from some aspects of uncontrolled **devolution of power** and towards a **clearer definition of responsibility**. Similarly, it might be decided that dress is a powerful **symbol** and that a corporate livery should be provided for customer-facing staff.

1.4 Forcefield analysis

Forcefield analysis consists of the identification of the factors that promote and hinder change. Promoting forces should be exploited and the effect of hindering forces reduced.

It is traditional to represent these forces by **arrows** whose individual dimensions correspond to their perceived strengths. Promoting and hindering forces are then shown pointing from opposite sides to a vertical linear datum line. This representation is useful for purposes such as brainstorming and staff briefings, but two lists in order of magnitude are just as useful for purposes of analysis. The example below concerns a public sector organisation that is introducing performance review.

We have already encountered the idea of force fields when we were considering project management. Be aware that change management and project management are intimately linked: any project is quite likely to result in change, while change is often implemented through projects.

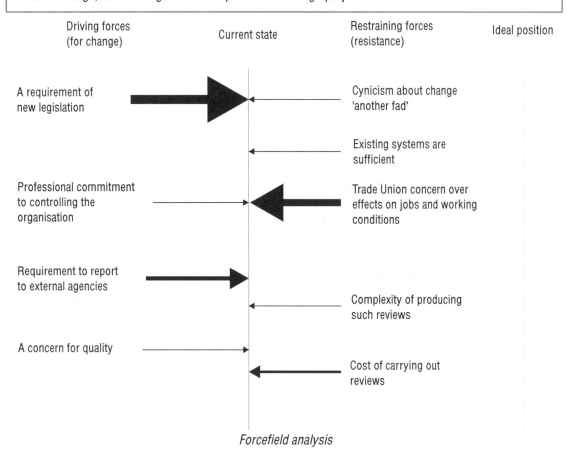

| Driving forces (for change) | Current state | Restraining forces (resistance) | Ideal position |

Forcefield analysis

Senior (drawing on the advice of Carnall and Huczyuski and Buchanan) suggests a practical route to applying the force field analysis idea.

(a) Define the problem in terms of the current situation and the desired future state.

(b) List the forces supporting and opposing the desired change and assess both the strength and the importance of each one.

(c) Draw the force field diagram.

(d) Decide how to strengthen or weaken the more important forces as appropriate and agree with those concerned. Weakening might be achieved by persuasion, participation, coercion or bargaining, while strengthening might be achieved by a marketing or education campaign, including the use of personal advocacy.

(e) Identify the resources needed.

(f) Make an action plan including event timing, milestones and responsibilities.

JS&W state that, typically, elements of the **cultural web** emerge as important forces promoting or hindering change. The web can thus be used alongside forcefield analysis as a diagnostic tool.

2 Styles of change management

There are five change management styles.

- Education and communication
- Collaboration/participation
- Intervention
- Direction
- Coercion/edict

Progression down the list of styles corresponds to progression through the four types of change noted above.

2.1 Five management styles

We have looked at leadership earlier in this Study Text and one of the aspects of a leader's role will be to implement strategic change. However, it is important that the style in which the change is managed is appropriate to the context.

JS&W identify five styles of change management:

- Education and communication
- Collaboration/participation
- Intervention
- Direction
- Coercion/edict

2.1.1 Education and communication

Education and communication is an approach based on persuasion: the reasons for change and the means by which it will be achieved are explained in detail to those affected by it. It is appropriate when change is **incremental**. This style is time-consuming, but can be useful if there has been misinformation in the past. However, it is a top-down approach and depends on a **willingness** to accept management's plans as appropriate. This may not, in fact, be present.

2.1.2 Collaboration/participation

Collaboration, or **participation**, brings those affected by strategic change into the change management process, drawing them into issue identification, prioritisation and the creation of new routines to implement newly established strategy, for example. It may improve decision quality by bringing wider experience and knowledge to bear. However, it may be time-consuming and it will be **subject to the influence of the existing culture and paradigm**, which may limit its potential effectiveness. This approach is both ethical, in basic deontological terms, and advantageous in practice, since it can nurture a positive attitude, thus building both **readiness** and **capability** for change. It is suited to incremental change.

2.1.3 Intervention

Intervention is undertaken by a **change agent** (see below) who delegates some aspects of the change process to teams or individuals, while providing guidance and retaining overall control. Delegated aspects can include both design and implementation activities. Final responsibility for achieving the necessary change remains with the change agent, but this kind of participation can build **commitment** and a **sense of ownership**. This style is appropriate for incremental change.

2.1.4 Direction

Direction is a top-down style in which **managerial authority** is used to establish and implement a change programme based on a clear future strategy. It is thus suited to **transformational change**. It has the potential advantages of speed and clarity, but may lead to **resistance**. Its success depends in part on the adequacy of the proposed strategy: if this is inappropriate, the best managed of change programmes will not result in wider strategic success.

2.1.5 Coercion

Coercion is an **extreme form of direction**, being based on the use of power to impose change. It is likely to provoke opposition but may be the best approach in times of confusion or crisis.

2.2 Using styles

There may be advantages to making use of more than one of the change management styles outlined above.

2.2.1 Context

Specific aspects of the organisational context already discussed will influence the use that can be made of the five styles. Clear and appropriate **direction** can be a strong motivating force and may enhance **readiness** to change, while **collaboration/participation** and **intervention** may help to build **capability** to change.

2.2.2 Scope and nature

Using Balogun and Hope Hailey's matrix of the scope and nature of change (shown in Section 1.1), we might suggest that progression down the list of styles may correspond reasonably well with progression from top left to bottom right of the matrix. In **adaptation**, where time is not critical and the extent of the change required is small, styles from the collaborative-communicative end of the spectrum may be appropriate. **Revolution**, on the other hand will require a great element of **direction** and even of **coercion**. The intermediate cases are likely to require a combination of **participation** and **direction**, with the emphasis on the former in **evolution** and on the latter in **reconstruction**.

2.2.3 Power structures

In many cases, it will be appropriate to **echo an organisation's normal power structure** when managing change. Direction or intervention is likely to be more suitable in a firmly hierarchical organisation than these would be in a network or learning organisation, except in time of crisis, for example.

2.2.4 Personality type

Management style is a tool. Good managers will be capable of using a **style appropriate to the conditions** they have to work in. However, many managers' personality types will incline them to the style with which they are most comfortable. This effect is likely to interact with the effect of power structure mentioned above.

2.2.5 Combining styles

It will often be appropriate to use a combination of styles in a change programme, taking different approaches with different stakeholders. Providers of capital are likely to respond better to **education and communication** than to **direction**, for example, while something approaching **coercion** may be necessary in some internal areas simply because of the pressure of time.

3 Change management roles

FAST FORWARD

A **change agent** is an individual or group that helps to bring about strategic change in an organisation.

Strategic leaders act as change agents in one of five styles:

- Strategy
- Human assets
- Expertise
- Control
- Change

Middle managers implement and control top-down change; translate overall change strategy for local contexts; and advise strategic managers.

Outsiders may be brought in at the strategic apex in order to re-make the paradigm. New middle managers can enhance change capability; consultants can fill planning and facilitating roles.

Key term

A **change agent** is an individual or group that helps to bring about strategic change in an organisation.
JS&W (amended)

Change agency is an activity that might be concentrated in one person, but which is just as likely to be spread among the members of a group, such as a project team or management staff generally. Outsiders, such as consultants, may share in change agency.

JS&W examine change agency by considering the roles played by three distinct groups.

- Strategic leaders
- Middle management
- Outsiders

3.1 Strategic leadership

Key term

> Leadership is the process of influencing an organisation (or group within an organisation) in its efforts towards achieving an aim or goal.   *JS&W*

JS&W, quoting Farkas and Wetlaufer, identify five approaches to strategic leadership.

- Strategy
- Human assets
- Expertise
- Control
- Change

3.1.1 The strategy approach

The leader taking the strategy approach focuses on strategic analysis and the formulation of strategy. Other managers take responsibility for routine operations and for the management of change.

3.1.2 The human assets approach

The development of the organisation's people is the main activity of leaders who take the human assets approach: other managers take responsibility for strategic management. Such leaders are concerned to recruit the right people and to develop an appropriate culture. Their approach to change management is to recruit people to whom the responsibility can be devolved.

3.1.3 The expertise approach

The expertise approach focuses on some form of technical expertise as a source of competitive advantage and concentrates on building expertise through systems and procedures. This focus also forms the basis of change management. Other managers also concentrate on their areas of expertise.

3.1.4 The control approach

The control approach is also known as the 'box' approach. The strategic leader following this approach concentrates on setting procedures and control measures and monitoring performance so as to achieve uniform, predictable performance. Other managers are expected to use this approach and change management is based on careful control.

3.1.5 The change approach

The leader using the change approach focuses on continual change and expends much effort on communication and motivation. Other managers are expected to act largely as change agents.

3.1.6 Charismatic and transactional leadership

We discussed leadership in general terms earlier in this Study Text. The five approaches outlined above may be fitted into a general model of leadership that recognises two general types: charismatic and transactional.

(a)   Transactional leaders focus on systems and controls and generally seek improvement rather than change. This approach is also called instrumental leadership.

(b) **Charismatic leaders** energise people and build a vision of the future. Change management is a natural part of what they do. This approach is also known as **transformational** leadership and we referred to it in this way in our earlier discussion.

Using this analysis, we may say that the **control** approach is a form of **transactional leadership**, while the other four approaches fall into the **charismatic** category.

3.2 Middle management

Strategic leaders pursuing change may see their middle managers as implementers, at best, and possibly, as potential blockers. Their commitment to change is important and they have significant roles to play in change management.

(a) **Implementation** and **control** where change is introduced in a top-down way

(b) **Translation** of the overall change strategy into forms suited to specific local contexts: this may require r**einterpretation** and **adjustment** of strategic factors such as relationships with suppliers and customers.

(c) Provision of **advice** to higher management on requirements for change and potential obstacles

3.3 Outsiders

Outsiders may contribute to the change process in a range of roles.

(a) A new **chief executive** may be appointed to bring a fresh point of view and break down the constraints of the existing paradigm. A **hybrid** chief executive is one who has appropriate experience of the industry, or even of the organisation, but is not part of the existing culture.

(b) New **managers** in other positions can enhance the capability to change and increase **diversity** of opinion and practice. However, their success is likely to depend on the visible backing of the chief executive.

(c) **Consultants** may be employed to fill a number of planning and facilitating roles. Like newly appointed managers, they bring a fresh approach and are not constrained by the existing paradigm. This enables them to challenge things that are taken for granted. Also, their appointment signals the importance of the change process.

(d) Other external **stakeholders** are capable of influencing change and may have a part to play.

4 Change management levers

FAST FORWARD

A **turnaround strategy** is required when a business is in terminal decline. Such a strategy uses its own change management techniques. More widely applicable change management levers are often related to aspects of the cultural web.

- Challenging the paradigm
- Changing routines
- Use of symbolic processes
- Political activity and use of power structures
- Communication and monitoring
- Tactics, including careful timing, care over job losses and exploration of quick successes

Many of the levers that can be used to implement change are related to aspects of the **cultural web**. We will consider these in this section, but first we will consider the special case of **turnaround**.

4.1 Turnaround

When a business is in terminal decline and faces closure or takeover, there is a need for rapid and extensive change in order to achieve cost reduction and revenue generation. This is a **turnaround strategy**. JS&W identify **seven elements of such a strategy**.

4.1.1 Crisis stabilisation

The emphasis is on reducing costs and increasing revenues. An emphasis on reducing direct costs and improving productivity is more likely to be effective than efforts to reduce overheads.

(a)   **Measures to increase revenue**

    (i)   Tailor marketing mix to key market segments
    (ii)   Review pricing policies to maximise revenue
    (iii)   Focus activities on target market segments
    (iv)   Exploit revenue opportunities if related to target segments
    (v)   Invest in growth areas

(b)   **Measures to reduce costs**

    (i)   Cut costs of labour and senior management
    (ii)   Improve productivity
    (iii)   Ensure clear marketing focus on target market segments
    (iv)   Financial controls
    (v)   Strict cash management controls
    (vi)   Reduce inventory
    (vii)   Cut unprofitable products and services

Severe cost cutting is a common response to crisis but it is unlikely to be enough by itself. The **wider causes of decline** must be addressed.

4.1.2 Management changes

It is likely that new managers will be required, especially at the strategic apex. There are four reasons for this.

(a)   The old management allowed the situation to deteriorate and **may be held responsible by key stakeholders**.

(b)   **Experience of turnaround management** may be required.

(c)   Managers brought in from outside will not be **prisoners of the old paradigm**.

(d)   A **directive approach** to change management will probably be required.

4.1.3 Communication with stakeholders

The support of key stakeholder groups – groups with both a high level of power and a high degree of interest in an organisation – such as the workforce and providers of finance – is likely to be very important in a turnaround; it is equally likely that stakeholders did not receive full information during the period of deterioration. A **stakeholder analysis** (discussed earlier in this Study Text) should be carried out so that the various stakeholder groups can be informed and managed appropriately.

4.1.4 Attention to target markets

A **clear focus on appropriate target market segments** is essential; indeed, a lack of such focus is a common cause of decline. The organisation must become customer-oriented and ensure that it has good flows of marketing information.

4.1.5 Concentration of effort

Resources should be concentrated on the best opportunities to create value. It will almost certainly be appropriate to **review products and the market segments** currently served, and to eliminate any distractions and poor performers. A similar review of internal activities would also be likely to show up several candidates for **outsourcing**.

4.1.6 Financial restructuring

Some form of **financial restructuring** is likely to be required. In the worst case, this may involve trading out of insolvency. Even where the business is more or less solvent, capital restructuring may be required, both to provide cash for investment and to reduce cash outflows in the shorter term.

4.1.7 Prioritisation

The eventual success of a turnaround strategy depends in part on management's ability to **prioritise necessary activities**, such as those noted above.

4.2 Challenging the paradigm

The entrenched assumptions and habits of mind that JS&W refer to as **the paradigm** constitutes an important obstacle to strategic change. The paradigm must, therefore, be **challenged** if change is to be achieved. There are several approaches to this process of challenge; JS&W give four examples.

(a)   Newcomers to the organisation are likely to trust **objective evidence** that new conditions require new approaches. Unfortunately, evidence is rarely overwhelming, or even complete, and there is a natural tendency to reinterpret, discount or even deny it. Persistence is required when objective evidence is relied on.

(b)   A **careful analysis** of just what is taken for granted, possibly through **workshop sessions**, may enhance an objective assessment of new ideas. The aim is to lead those involved to challenge their own assumptions.

(c)   **Scenario construction** can be used to bring managers to a better understanding of changing conditions by presenting a range of possible futures and their implications for the organisation.

(d)   It may be appropriate to take firm action to **bring senior managers close to the daily reality** of what the organisation does, perhaps by extended visits to places and processes with direct customer contact.

4.3 Changing routines

Routines are the **habitual behaviours** that members of the organisation display, both internally and externally. They are *not* procedures or processes but the **wider ways of doing things** that are typical of the organisation. They are closely linked to the paradigm. The problem of routines is that they can subvert change efforts. For example, it is unlikely that simply explaining required new processes and procedures will lead to their effective adoption: existing routines will mould the way they are put into operation.

When a **top-down change programme** requires the introduction of new methods, the detail of implementation can be driven by the careful identification of **critical success factors** and the **competences** they demand.

When change is to be introduced in a **less directed** way, change agents may focus on routines, **extending** existing ways of doing things toward what is required and then '**bending** the rules of the game' when sufficient stakeholder support has been created.

4.4 Symbolic processes

Symbols were mentioned earlier in this Study Text during our discussion of culture and the cultural web. Their importance in the context of change is that they can often be used as levers of change. However, it is important to understand that the significance of a given symbol may vary from person to person; this makes their use as a tool of management difficult.

(a)   New **rituals** can be introduced and old ones abolished in order to communicate and implement change. For example, the replacement of a strictly hierarchical approach to management with a culture of coaching and empowerment can be signalled and reinforced by the introduction of social occasions such as office parties that will allow staff to meet relatively informally.

(b)   Formal **systems and processes** can have symbolic aspects, typically when they signal status and power relationships, but also when they direct attention to new concerns, such as customer service.

(c)   Changes to **physical aspects** of the workplace can have strong symbolic effect, as, for instance, when open-plan offices or hot-desking are introduced.

(d)   The **behaviour** of leaders and change agents has very powerful symbolic effect and must reflect intended change if the intention is not to be undermined: staff will respond far better to example than to edict.

(e)   **Language** can have symbolic significance beyond the bald meaning of the words used. Well-chosen words can inspire and motivate change; similarly, the use of badly chosen words can undermine their inherent meaning.

(f)   **Stories** have an important symbolic role, but are not easy to exploit since much corporate communication is automatically dismissed as mere marketing puff.

4.5 Power and politics

Politics is about the exercise of **power** and the use of **influence**. Managers and other important individual stakeholders establish and exploit **power structures** and **networks of influence** that are intertwined with both formal hierarchies and the informal aspects of the organisation's life. The implementation of strategy is inevitably influenced by the operation of these structures and networks. Change management is also, therefore, subject to political influence and change managers should take due account of political processes.

JS&W suggest three objectives of **political activity** that may be sought by change managers.

- Building the **power base**
- Overcoming **resistance**
- Achieving **compliance**

Four **political mechanisms** may be used to exert influence in these areas.

- Manipulation of **resources**
- Relationships with **powerful groups and individuals** (elites)
- Exploitation of **subsystems**
- **Symbolic activity**

4.5.1 Resources

The ability to control the allocation of resources (or even merely to influence their allocation) is recognised as a distinct and important **form of power** within the organisation. It can be used, both to **enable specific developments** in the change programme and, more subtly, to **build support and influence** that will assist with the processes of overcoming resistance and ensuring compliance.

4.5.2 Elites

Association with **respected and influential stakeholders** can enhance the personal status and thus the power base of the change agent. Similarly, association with a **high status change agent** can assist more junior managers to overcome resistance to change.

Sometimes it is necessary to **eliminate centres of resistance** by removing people from the organisation in order to ensure compliance with change requirements.

4.5.3 Subsystems

A power base can be established by building up **networks and alliances** among those sympathetic to change. It may then be possible to outmanoeuvre and marginalise the resistance. Equally, however, it may not; also, such manoeuvring by change agents may provoke stronger resistance. It will be useful to analyse power and influence using the stakeholder mapping model explained earlier in this Study Text.

4.5.4 Symbols

Change managers may utilise existing symbols and symbolic activities or challenge them as seems appropriate.

4.6 Communication and monitoring

It is obvious that change management must include effective communication and explanation of the **need for change**, what the plan is intended to **achieve** and what it involves. Good communication is a very important factor in overcoming resistance to change, particularly in the matter of building trust. Strategic complexity may make this difficult, but a clear vision must be provided.

A wide range of **communication media** is available and it is important that **appropriate selections** are made. Media that provide richness, immediacy and interactivity are appropriate when complex and important material is to be communicated, while more routine matters can be dealt with in less complex ways. It is important for change agents to be aware that what seems simple and routine to them may have significantly greater importance for ordinary members of the organisation.

The **intervention style** of change management inherently provides extensive means of communication in the form of the individuals and teams involved. These people form an important route through which information can flow into the organisation.

Communication efforts should include clear and plentiful opportunities and routes for **feedback**, so that omissions, poorly constructed messages, misunderstandings and anxiety can be dealt with.

Care must be taken with **emotional aspects** of communication so that appropriate media, language and symbols are used.

Monitoring of behaviour to ensure that required changes are not subverted is essential.

4.7 Tactics

The change process can be forwarded by the use of specific tactics of change management.

4.7.1 Timing

The time at which actions are taken can be selected for tactical effectiveness.

(a)   A **crisis** can be used to justify extensive change, so monitoring a mounting crisis and delaying action until it is ripe may enhance acceptance.

(b)   **Windows of opportunity** may occur, as, for example, when a takeover occurs.

(c)   **Messages** about timing must be coherent so that, for example, rapid action is not undermined by the retention of procedures that enforce long time frames.

(d)   Fear and anxiety about change as such may be reduced if unpleasant consequences can be **decoupled in time** from the main change programme: an example would be a programme of redundancy that does not commence until other change objectives such as the outcomes of product and market reviews have been implemented.

4.7.2 Job losses

The threat of job losses associated with change is likely to be bad for morale and provoke resistance. Redundancy programmes must be managed with care.

(a)   A single, rapid and extensive round of cuts is preferable to a long drawn out programme of smaller reductions: the former can be stressful but the latter creates **long-term uncertainty and anxiety**.

(b)   Where **delayering** is required, it may be possible to concentrate the job losses among managers identified as being opposed to change: these are likely to be more senior figures.

(c)   Those who lose their jobs should be dealt with as sympathetically and **compassionately** as possible; the provision of services such as outplacement, counselling and retraining may help.

4.7.3 Quick success

Momentum for change can be created by putting simple but highly visible improvements into successful operation. Even where the overall position is difficult and requires a complex solution, such **quick wins** are often available: it is common for them to emerge in the form of suggestions from the lower echelons of the organisation.

Even where there are no obvious easy options, it may be possible to create some by **concentrating the available resources** on specific problems, rather than spreading them thinly.

5 Pitfalls of change management

FAST FORWARD

> Change programmes may be subverted and lead to unintended consequences. This has four implications for change management.
>
> - Monitoring and control are vital
> - The existing culture must be understood
> - The organisation's people should be involved in the change process
> - The extent of the challenge must be recognised

JS&W quote Harris and Ogbonna, who identify **eight unintended outcomes** of change programmes.

(a) **Ritualisation of change**. When change programmes extend into the longer-term, there is a danger that organisation members will come to view the initiatives as mere ritual with little real significance.

(b) **Hijacked process of change**. Change initiatives can be hijacked for unintended purposes: for example, improved technology provided to improve performance may be used simply to cut staffing levels, defeating the overall objective.

(c) **Erosion**. The successful introduction of new initiatives may suffer erosion from the effects of other events and processes, as, for example, when high staff turnover hampers staff development.

(d) **Reinvention**. Recalcitrant staff may reinvent the nature and implications of the change programme in a way that accommodates previous undesirable practices. This is a failure of monitoring and control.

(e) **Ivory tower change**. When change is imposed from the top-down, its proponents may be seen as inhabiting an ivory tower, out of touch with operational reality and lacking in credibility as a result.

(f) **Lack of attention to symbols**. Change managers who pay insufficient attention to symbols can both fail to make the change relevant to day to day reality and succeed in sending the wrong messages.

(g) **Uncontrolled efforts**. If practical adjustments, to systems, for example, do not fit well with the overall intent of the change programme, staff are likely to become confused and demotivated.

(h) **Behavioural compliance**. Apparent behavioural compliance may disguise lack of commitment. People may appear to comply with the changes, without actually 'buying into' them.

These problems underline the complexity of the change management task. JS&W identify four specific implications for change management.

(a) **Monitoring** and **control** are vital aspects of change management, as is the flexibility to adjust programmes as they unfold.

(b) It is essential to understand the **existing culture** and its effects, since they are highly likely to hinder planned change.

(c) It will generally be advantageous to **involve the organisation's people** in the change process.

(d) Change represents a **major challenge** and may be more difficult to implement than it seems at first.

Chapter Roundup

- There are three main change management considerations.

    - The type of change required, whether adaptation, evolution, reconstruction or revolution

    - The wider context of change, including the time available; capability to implement change; capacity and readiness; and power

    - Forces facilitating and blocking change

- There are five change management styles.

    - Education and communication
    - Collaboration/participation
    - Intervention
    - Direction
    - Coercion/edict

    Progression down the list of styles corresponds to progression through the four types of change noted above.

- A **change agent** is an individual or group that helps to bring about strategic change in an organisation.

    Strategic leaders act as change agents in one of five styles

    - Strategy
    - Human assets
    - Expertise
    - Control
    - Change

    Middle managers implement and control top-down change; translate overall change strategy for local contexts; and advise strategic managers.

    Outsiders may be brought in at the strategic apex in order to re-make the paradigm. New middle managers can enhance change capability; consultants can fill planning and facilitating roles.

- A **turnaround strategy** is required when a business is in terminal decline. Such a strategy uses its own change management techniques. More widely applicable change management levers are often related to aspects of the cultural web.

    - Challenging the paradigm
    - Changing routines
    - Use of symbolic processes
    - Political activity and use of power structures
    - Communication and monitoring
    - Tactics, including careful timing, care over job losses and exploration of quick successes

- Change programmes may be subverted and lead to unintended consequences. This has four implications for change management.

    - Monitoring and control are vital
    - The existing culture must be understood
    - The organisation's people should be involved in the change process
    - The extent of the challenge must be recognised

Quick Quiz

1. What is meant by the scope of change?

2. Which styles of management are required to effect revolution?

3. What is a change agent?

4. What is the difference between charismatic leadership and transactional leadership?

5. What are the objectives of political activity that may be sought by change managers?

6. How can change managers create opportunities for early success?

Answers to Quick quiz

1   The scope of change is the degree of change required – whether it can be transformational or whether a more fundamental realignment is required.

2   Direction and, probably, coercion

3   A change agent is an individual or group that helps to bring about strategic change in an organisation

4   Transactional leaders focus on systems and controls, while charismatic leaders seek to energise people and build a vision of the future.

5   Building a powerbase; overcoming resistance; achieving compliance

6   By concentrating resources on potentially solvable problems rather than spreading them thinly.

Now try the question below from the Practice Question Bank

Number	Level	Marks	Time
Q9	Examination	12	22 mins

8: Managing strategic change | Part C Organising and enabling success

Business process change

Business
process change

Topic list	Syllabus reference
1 The background to process change	D1 (a), (b), (c) D2(b), D3(a)
2 Harmon's process-strategy matrix	D2(c)
3 A process redesign methodology	D2(a), (f)
4 Process commoditisation and outsourcing	D2(d), (e)

Introduction

This chapter is the first in which we consider the 'middle layer' of the relational diagram of the syllabus.

Strategies are, to some extent at least, delivered by means of processes. We have already seen how processes fit with structures and relationships in configurations and we have examined control processes in some detail. In this chapter, and the next, we go on to examine processes in the wider sense, the contribution they make to organisations and strategy and, overall, how processes may be improved and made more effective.

Furthermore, it is worth noting here that improvements to processes may also be an important source of potential emergent strategies – an area we look at in the final chapter of this Study Text.

Study guide

		Intellectual level
D1	**Business change**	
(a)	Explain that business change projects are initiated to address strategic alignment	2
(b)	Apply the stages of the business change lifecycle (alignment, definition, design, implementation, realisation)	3
(c)	Assess the value of the four view (POPIT – people, organisation, processes and information technology) model to the successful implementation of business change	3
D2	**The role of process and process change initiatives**	
(a)	Advise on how an organisation can reconsider the design of its processes to deliver a selected strategy	3
(b)	Appraise business process change initiatives previously adopted by organisations	3
(c)	Establish an appropriate scope and focus for business process change using Harmon's process-strategy matrix	3
(d)	Explore the commoditisation of business processes	3
(e)	Advice on the implications of business process outsourcing	3
(f)	Recommend a business process redesign methodology for an organisation	2
D3	**Improving the processes of the organisation**	
(a)	Evaluate the effectiveness of current organisational processes	3

Exam guide

The syllabus places considerable emphasis on processes. This is a very practical topic and it is easy to see that the examining team will have plenty of scope for practical questions based on it. An obvious route would be to ask you to use the process-strategy matrix to select processes for improvement and the process redesign methodology discussed in Section 3 to show how to proceed.

It is also important to think how business processes and business process re-engineering link to other areas of the P3 syllabus. The diagram below illustrates some of the key linkages.

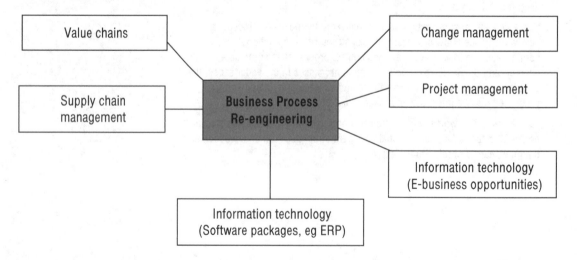

BPP
LEARNING MEDIA

Models

Harmon's **process – strategy matrix**, **the business change lifecycle** and **POPIT (four view model)** are each explicitly referenced in the Study Guide and so could be specifically required in a question.

However, do not overlook the other sections of this chapter. This chapter contains a lot of very examinable material around business process change and redesign, and outsourcing.

1 The background to process change

Business processes of all kinds have been subject to efforts towards their improvement for many years. The industrial revolution brought new techniques for manufacturing and also for administration. Josiah Wedgwood is best known for innovation in pottery and ceramic goods but he also made rapid strides in the development of cost accountancy, including the establishment of standard costs, for example. Other important figures in the history of management innovation include the experts known to us as the Scientific Management School and figures such as Henry Ford, Alfred Sloan and Peter Drucker. The search for better ways of doing things has been going on for a long time. In this section (which is largely based on Chapter 1 of *Business Process Change* by Paul Harmon) we will revise some of the important steps along the way.

Exam focus point

An article titled 'Business process change' (2008) written by Adrian Thomas is available in the technical articles section for P3 on the ACCA website. The article outlines the importance of business processes in delivering strategy and explores how organisations can analyse existing processes with a view to improving organisational performance. It would be worth taking the time to study this article.

1.1 Organisations as systems

FAST FORWARD

General system theory would see the organisation as an **open system**, interacting with its environment.

1.2 Systems theory

Key term

Curtis defines a **system** as a collection of interrelated parts which, taken together, forms a whole such that:

(a)   The collection has some purpose
(b)   A change in any of the parts leads to or results from a change in some other part or parts.

An organisation is a type of system.

1.3 Open and closed systems

General systems theory makes a distinction between open, closed and semi-closed systems.

(a)   **A closed system is isolated from its environment and independent of it**, so that no environmental influences affect the behaviour of the system, nor does the system exert any influence on its environment.

(b)   **An open system is connected to, and interacts with, its environment**. It takes in influences from its environment and also influences this environment by its behaviour. An open system is a stable system which is nevertheless continually changing or evolving

(c)   **Few systems are entirely closed**. Many are **semi-closed**, in that their relationship with the environment is in some degree restricted. An example of a semi-closed system might be a pocket calculator. Its inputs are restricted to energy from its batteries and numerical information entered into it in a particular way (by the operator depressing a sequence of keys). The calculator is restricted in what it will do.

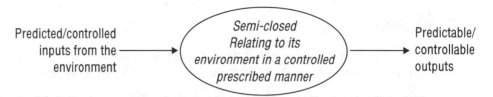

Predicted/controlled inputs from the environment → **Semi-closed** *Relating to its environment in a controlled prescribed manner* → Predictable/controllable outputs

Social organisations, such as businesses and government departments, are by definition open systems.

Organisations have a variety of interchanges with the environment, obtaining inputs from it, and generating outputs to it.

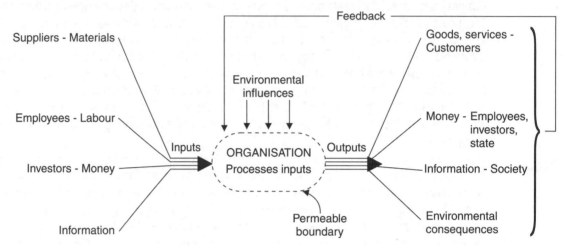

This general background is clearly linked to Porter's **value chain** model, which shows how the functioning of the **internal sub-systems** of the organisation contribute to its overall capability to add value. The ways in which the system and its sub-systems function constitute the organisation's **processes and relationships**.

The value chain was discussed in detail earlier in this Study Text, but if you cannot remember, it you would be well advised to review it now. The groundwork for the current emphasis on understanding business processes was laid by Michael Porter in his value chain model.

1.4 The business change lifecycle

FAST FORWARD **The business change lifecycle** provides a framework for assessing the key stages involved in undertaking a business change project.

Exam focus point

The examining team has indicated that the lifecycle model should enable students to gain a greater understanding of the business change concept. The lifecycle could be used to frame answers to future examination questions.

Business change is an important issue for most organisations. To reflect this fact, the business change lifecycle model has been included in the P3 syllabus. The lifecycle provides a broad umbrella framework from which different process change methodologies can operate. These will be explored later in the Study Text. The business change lifecycle model has been included to complement existing areas in the syllabus such as project management and organisational change. The model provides a step by step framework for considering a proposed business change project.

As with any project methodology, the business change lifecycle framework has a beginning, middle and end. Each aspect of the framework is considered in turn throughout the next section.

Business change lifecycle

Source: Adapted from 'Business analysis', 2nd edition, Paul, Yeates & Cadle

1.4.1 Alignment

The external environment

A common theme in modern business concerns the need to constantly assess the external environment. As the environment changes, management need to consider the potential impact external developments may have on the ability of the organisation to achieve its objectives.

From time to time, businesses may be required to align (or re-align) their goals with the environment. External regulation, or developments by competitors, will often require organisations to undertake some form of business change in order to respond effectively. In recent years, there have been a number of high profile cases involving companies which have failed to react to external pressures and have gone out of business as a result.

When business change is required, organisations need to determine the most appropriate approach to achieve it. Proposed action is often implemented through a business change project.

Case Study
Morrisons: Part One

This case study highlights the need for organisations to continually monitor the external environment.

UK supermarket sector

Competition in the UK supermarket sector is fierce. According to Tesco, the market leader, the 'UK grocery market was worth £163.2 billion in 2012 and is forecast to rise to £196.2 billion by 2017. Price wars and innovation in retailing among the big four supermarkets (Tesco, Sainsbury's, Asda and Morrisons) are common.

In 1996, Tesco launched its dot.com business in response to increasing customer demand for online shopping. When first established. Tesco.com operated from one office with a 'handful of computers', and deliveries were made from a single store. Since this time, revenue has grown from £25m to £1.5bn.

Both Asda and Sainsbury's have followed suit in recent years, unveiling their own online shopping websites.

Morrisons

Morrisons, the fourth largest supermarket chain for a number of years, avoided establishing its own online presence. *The Guardian* highlighted that former Morrisons CEO, Sir Ken Morrison, who stepped down in 2008, was keen to shun 'new fangled fancies', in favour of 'keeping it simple: shops the same size selling the same stuff so that costs were low and profit margins high'.

Falling behind

In recent years, Morrisons has fallen behind its main competitors. In 2013, Morrisons announced worse than expected like-for-like sales, the *Yorkshire Post* reporting a decline of 5.6% compared to the previous year, with profit forecasts reported at the lower end of market predictions.

In response to these external pressures, Morrison's CEO, Dalton Philips, announced plans for the company to offer its own online service. The move aims to provide customers with greater guarantees over the freshness of foods purchased online. Customers will be able to purchase fresh bread from the bakery and specify the thickness of the cuts of meat purchased from the supermarket's online butchery.

Adapted from four online sources:

1) 'Tesco UK' published on the Tesco website: www.tescoplc.com

2) 'What is Tesco.com?' published on the Tesco website; http://dotcom.tesco-careers.com

3) 'Morrisons banks Ocado tie-up to click with shoppers' by Sarah Butler (October 2013) published on *The Guardian* website; www.guardian.com

4) 'Morrisons delivery vans hit the road as grocer goes live with online service' (January 2014) published on the *Yorkshire Post* website; www.yorkshirepost.co.uk

Bottom-up change

It should, however, be noted that not all proposals for business change come directly from the external environment. Operational staff in an organisation may also push for changes to existing business processes in order to deliver short-term improvements. However, short-term change initiatives implemented in a haphazard fashion can prove detrimental to the organisation's overall performance. Proposed business change projects should be considered in relation to the organisation's overall long-term strategy and objectives.

1.4.2 Definition

Forming the business case

Once the need for change has been established, the practicalities of defining the improvement begin. This will lead to the establishment of a formal project team designated to explore and evaluate the available options to achieve the desired change. This evaluation will often involve a 'gap analysis' where the project team assess the organisation's current position and processes. 'Gaps' between the current position and targeted end state are then revealed. The gap analysis should help to provide the project team with an idea of the work required to implement a successful change.

Gap analysis

The 'gaps' identified will help to determine the type of business change required. For example, a process change upgrading a company's existing website is likely to result in a relatively basic change, whereas changes of a more complex nature will require a fundamental rethinking of existing processes. This is known as business process re-engineering (BPR), and we will look at BPR in more detail later in this chapter.

Gap analysis gives particular consideration to the organisation's core resources, including its people and IT infrastructure. The project team may conduct face-to-face interviews with users of existing processes, and may even observe staff while they work to better understand the improvements needed.

Need for a holistic view

Taking a holistic view of any proposed business change is particularly important in helping the project team gain an understanding of how different activities and resources interact. Most business change programmes will affect more than one area of the business.

For example, the decision to introduce a new corporate website is likely to require a focus on both the human and technical elements. Understanding how these elements interrelate helps to raise questions that the project team will need to consider. These could include:

- Are those affected by the change likely to need training to use the website effectively?

- Will customers want to use it?

- Will it affect what our customers purchase from us?

- Will the introduction of a new website require improvements to the existing site or a complete upgrade of the existing IT infrastructure?

- Will the change be supported by the use of in-house technical support or be provided by a third party?

 Case Study   **Morrisons: Part Two**

On 10 January 2014, Morrisons launched its own online grocery store. Initially serving customers based in the Midlands, deliveries were rolled out to other regions throughout 2014.

Supporting infrastructure

Morrisons made the decision to roll out its online offering by establishing an alliance with Ocado. In May 2013, it was reported that Morrisons had agreed to pay £170m to buy Ocado's distribution centre in Dordon. The purchase agreement gave the company the right to use Ocado's delivery technology for the next 25 years. Interestingly, Ocado will provide the staff and vehicles as part of the arrangement while operating under the Morrison's brand name.

Morrison's chief executive, Dalton Philips, announced that the deal with Ocado moved Morrisons from a 'standing start, straight into the fast lane of online retailing'.

Customers

Morrison's online offering let customers access its site through Facebook and allowed users to import their favourite purchases from other shops. On the day of the website's launch, Morrisons reported a 'strong interest in its dot.com offering with many thousands registering their interest'.

The decision to roll out its online shop through the use of a third party was due in part to years of under investment in the company's IT infrastructure which had left the company trailing behind its main rivals.

<u>Adapted from two articles</u>:

1) 'Morrisons signs deal with Ocado to launch online service' by Graham Ruddick (May 2013) published on *The Telegraph* website; www.telegraph.co.uk

2) 'Morrisons begins online food deliveries' (January 2014) published on the Morrisons website; www.morrisons-corporate.com

Contents of the business case

Proposals for change are drawn together to produce a business case. This sets out supporting recommendations to help management decide the most appropriate change project to undertake. The business case will include the associated costs of the change options identified.

Benefits of change

The project team will set out the improvement objectives that the desired change will achieve. For example, a new call management system at a call centre should lead to improved call response times, which will lower the number of customer complaints and boost sales.

Most organisations will appoint a benefit owner to assess whether the project delivers the anticipated benefits. The benefit owner may be an individual or group of people closely connected to the change process to help the project team ensure that the business plan is delivered. The role of the benefit owner is explored in more detail later in the Study Text.

1.4.3 Design

The **POPIT model (four view model)** focuses the project team's attention on four inter-related areas when undertaking a business process change. Some analysts argue that project teams focus too much on the process and technological aspects of business change and ignore the impact change has on people and the organisation.

The POPIT (four view model)

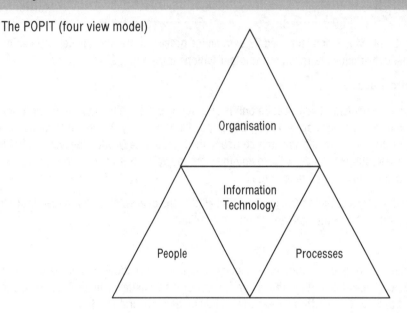

Source: Adapted from Business Analysis (2nd edition), Paul, Yeates & Cadle

1.4.4 POPIT model

Once a change project has been selected, the work of detailing how the new process will actually work begins. A useful framework to consider at this stage is the POPIT model, sometimes referred to as the four view model. POPIT provides the project team with four key areas that need consideration when enhancing a business process.

Exam focus point

> The examining team has indicated that candidates should be prepared to use the POPIT model as a framework for answering a question in the exam. For example, a case study could illustrate a scenario where elements of the model have been neglected, and candidates could then be asked to assess the impact of this on the implementation of a change project.

Usefulness of POPIT

In recent years, concern has started to grow among business analysts that too many business change projects have failed to adequately consider the four perspectives of the POPIT model. All too often, attention is heavily focused on the technological and process aspects of change without fully understanding how a change will affect people and the organisation as a whole. The application of the POPIT model forces project teams to take a far more holistic view of business change, identifying those issues may hinder the project's success.

The table below sets out the four views of the POPIT model and the consideration each is likely to require.

POPIT heading	Areas for consideration
Organisational context	**Management support** The project team should assess the level of management support for business change. As illustrated above in the case study, historically Sir Ken Morrison was not an advocate of introducing online shopping systems at Morrisons. This stance led to a delay in its introduction. **Cross-functional working** In order for processes to work effectively, it is critical that departments co-operate beyond functional boundaries. Therefore, the project team need to consider how departments interact with one another. Departments should be configured to 'add value' during process change. Functional departments such as the accounts and human resources teams do not operate in isolation. **Jobs and responsibilities** Consideration will need to be given to the job roles and responsibilities of existing employees. Business change projects should ensure that all staff affected have clear, well-defined job roles and associated responsibilities. If people know what is expected of them and they are provided with the resources to carry out their responsibilities, this should lead to optimal performance once a change is implemented.
Processes	**IT support** The level of IT support within an organisation should be assessed. Organisations with poor IT support in place are likely to need to address such weaknesses as part of process improvement. **Manual processes & system workarounds** Existing processes which require physical documents and paperwork to be passed around the organisation should be identified as part of the design stage of process change, as there may be scope to eliminate these.
People	**Skills** Ensuring that staff have the right level of skill to carry out a given process is critical. A significant proportion of the process design stage may be designated to enhancing staff skill levels through the use of training. Involving staff at the process design stage may help to ensure a smoother implementation phase, as any problems with the proposed changes can be identified and corrected prior to any further development. **Staff motivation** Most business change will only be successful if consideration is given to staff morale. Reward systems which influence staff motivation may need to be aligned with the organisation's goals.

POPIT heading	Areas for consideration
Information Technology	**Information systems** Business processes need to be configured so that they help facilitate the flow of critical information. The board of directors will want internal and external information which they can use to make decisions about the strategic direction of the business. Middle management will require information about key aspects of performance which affect the ability of their department to achieve the overarching strategy. For example, a breakdown of production down time. Operational level staff will need information about operational performance which affects the organisation on a day-to-day basis. For example, daily sales data.

1.4.5 Implementation

Force field analysis

The implementation stage of business change is likely to be the most challenging. This is due to the influence of certain stakeholder groups. Failure to gain the support and acceptance of staff may undermine any changes.

As highlighted earlier in the Study Text, the use of a force field analysis can prove particularly useful in identifying those forces driving and restraining change. By understanding the motives of those resisting change, an organisation should be better placed to weaken such opposition.

Communication

The use of a communication plan which highlights the benefits of the change is likely to prove central to overcoming resistance. Communication needs to be of a professional nature to help build confidence and create staff 'buy in' to the new processes.

 Case Study   NHS National Programme for IT – Part One

In 2002, the UK government unveiled an ambitious IT project to overhaul the National Health Service's (NHS) IT infrastructure. Daniel Martin, writing in the *Daily Mail*, reported that the 'National Programme for IT' project was intended to modernise existing processes by developing 'a national email system with the ability to transfer X-rays and prescriptions electronically. It included an "electronic care record", a process intended to allow hospitals and surgeries to share patient's medical information'.

In 2011, the government announced its intention to scrap the project, having spent £12.7bn on it to date. The decision followed findings issued by the Major Projects Authority (MPA) which found that the IT scheme was 'not fit to provide services to the NHS'. The MPA report concluded 'there can be no confidence that the programme has delivered or can be delivered as originally conceived'.

Alistair Maughan, writing in *Computer Weekly*, states that 'it is a hallmark of successful ICT and outsourcing projects that there should be good consultation with all stakeholders involved, particularly end-users'. The National Programme for IT had been dogged by the concerns of key stakeholders about the project's aims. Local NHS trusts were deeply suspicious over the loss of control over existing systems. Doctors raised concerns over the accessibility of the system, and the British Medical Association expressed unease over the increased risk to patient privacy amid concerns of losing patient data.

As Maughan suggests, 'few projects can succeed over the outright opposition of the proposed users'.

Adapted from two articles:

1) '£12bn NHS computer system is scrapped' by Daniel Martin (September 2011) on the *Daily Mail* website; www.dailymail.co.uk

2) 'Six reasons why the NHS National Programme for IT failed', by Alistair Maughan on the *Computer Weekly* website; www.computerweekly.com

Rewards

Management may attempt to incentivise staff to embrace new processes by offering one-off payments or flexible working conditions during the implementation stage. Longer-term incentives such as the re-designing existing performance appraisal schemes and introducing performance-related pay, may also help to embed a new process.

Training

This may take the form of group or one-to-one sessions where training on how to use a new process is provided. In cases of IT enabled change, it is common for staff to be provided with technical support from an IT help desk.

Systems

As a significant number of modern business change projects involve the use of IT, the project team should ensure that the technology undergoes sufficient systems testing. A lack of testing and insufficient attention to the need for data migration are common problems with IT-related process change.

Data migration is concerned with transferring existing data from one system to another. It is a common feature of most IT system upgrade projects.

 Case Study NHS National Programme for IT – Part Two

The Major Projects Authority, which reviewed the failings of the 'National Programme for IT', highlighted that 'the project had not been delivered in line with the original intent, as targets on dates, functionality, usage and levels of benefit had been delayed and reduced'.

Maughan highlights the need to avoid the so called 'Mastermind factor', which can creep in during the implementation of projects that are not going well. In essence, this involves an 'I've started, so I'll finish' approach whereby project managers do not step back and review whether the project is on course to achieve its intended objectives.

Adapted from two articles:

1) '£12bn NHS computer system is scrapped' by Daniel Martin (September 2011) published on the *Daily Mail* website; www.dailymail.co.uk

2) 'Six reasons why the NHS National Programme for IT failed', by Alistair Maughan published on the *Computer Weekly* website; www.computerweekly.com

1.4.6 Realisation of the benefits of change

The final stage in the lifecycle is designated to assessing whether the intended benefits of undertaking a change process have been realised.

Benefit owner

The benefit owner assigned during the definition stage will play a significant role during this phase. Benefits can be assessed by benchmarking performance to the original business case while asking: 'Did we achieve what we wanted to achieve?'

The adoption of key performance indicators and a balanced scorecard approach may help management assess whether a particular area of business performance has been enhanced as a result of implementing the change project.

Financial and non-financial benefits

A business change project may result in financial and non-financial benefits. As illustrated earlier, Morrisons' decision to offer online shopping was motivated by the scope to increase its financial performance through boosting sales, but also by increasing its brand awareness among customers (non-financial performance).

Often when assessing the financial benefits derived from a business change project, management will use a range of techniques including ROI, pay back period calculations and NPV workings. You should be familiar with these techniques from your earlier studies.

Holistic approach

Organisations need to review the benefits realised to ensure that process change does not result in undesired side effects. A number of well-known UK retailers, including Tesco and Boots, have introduced self-service checkouts as a means of reducing customer waiting times in store. However, their introduction has also resulted in increased instances of theft. This emphasises the need for a holistic approach to benefits realisation, as the negative aspects of change may be as important as the positive features derived.

A good benefits realisation review should identify which intended benefits have not materialised, as well as those which have. Identifying the benefits which have not materialised early on may allow for corrective action to be taken and to enable the full benefit to be realised. In some cases, unanticipated benefits may emerge which did not form part of the original business plan.

As illustrated by the earlier case study about the National Programme for IT, it is important to ensure that project output does not deviate from the original business plan. A review of the project work undertaken should be conducted at each stage of the change lifecycle to help ensure that the intended end benefits will be achieved.

1.5 Business process re-engineering

FAST FORWARD

Business process re-engineering is a useful approach based on challenging basic assumptions about business methods and even the objectives they are designed to achieve. IT can be very useful here, but simply to automate a process is not the same as re-engineering it.

Business process re-engineering involves fundamental changes in the way an organisation functions. For example, processes which were developed in a paper-intensive processing environment may not be suitable for an environment which is underpinned by IT.

Why focus on processes?

Many businesses recognise that value is delivered **through processes,** but still define themselves in terms of their functional roles. To properly harness the resources within a business, a clear agreement of the management and implementation of processes is needed. **Without this focus** on processes:

(a)   It is **unclear how value is achieved** or can continue to be achieved.

(b)   The **effects of change** on the operation of the business are **hard to predict**.

(c)   There is no basis to achieve **consistent** business improvement.

(d)   **Knowledge is lost** as people move around or out of the business.

(e)   Cross-functional interaction is not encouraged.

(f)   It is difficult to align the strategy of an organisation with the people, systems resources through which that strategy will be accomplished.

The main writing on the subject is Hammer and Champy's *Reengineering the Corporation* (1993), from which the following is taken.

Key term

> **Business process re-engineering** is the fundamental rethinking and radical redesign of business processes to achieve dramatic improvements in critical contemporary measures of performance, such as cost, quality, service and speed.

The key words here are **'fundamental'**, **'radical'**, **'dramatic'** and **'process'**.

(a) **Fundamental** and **radical** indicate that BPR assumes nothing: it starts by asking basic questions such as, 'Why do we do what we do?', without making any assumptions or looking back to what has always been done in the past.

(b) **'Dramatic'** means that BPR should achieve 'quantum leaps in performance', not just marginal, incremental improvements.

(c) **'Process'** is explained in the following paragraphs.

BPR is not automation or rationalisation. **Automation** is the use of computerised working methods to speed up the performance of existing tasks. **Rationalisation** is the streamlining of operating procedures to eliminate obvious inefficiencies. Rationalisation usually involves automation.

1.5.1 Principles of BPR

Hammer presents **seven principles** for BPR:

(a) Processes should be designed to achieve a desired **customer-focused outcome,** rather than focusing on existing **tasks**. The whole process should be **market-driven**.

(b) Personnel who use the **output** from a process should **perform** the process. For example, a company could set up a database of approved suppliers; this would allow personnel who actually require supplies to order them themselves, perhaps using online technology, thereby eliminating the need for a separate purchasing function.

(c) Information processing should be **included** in the work that **produces** the information. This eliminates the differentiation between information gathering and information processing.

(d) **Geographically-dispersed** resources should be treated as if they are **centralised.** This allows the benefits of centralisation to be obtained, for example, economies of scale through central negotiation of supply contracts, without losing the benefits of decentralisation, such as flexibility and responsiveness.

(e) Parallel activities should be **linked,** rather than **integrated.** This would involve, for example, co-ordination between teams working on different aspects of a single process.

(f) Workpeople should be **self-managing**, exercising greater autonomy over their work. The traditional distinction between workers and managers can be abolished: decision aids such as expert systems can be provided where they are required.

(g) Information should be captured **once** at **source.** Electronic distribution of information makes this possible.

1.5.2 Is there a BPR methodology?

Davenport and Short prescribe a **five-step approach** to BPR:

Step 1 Develop the **business vision and process objectives**. BPR is driven by a business vision which implies specific business objectives such as cost reduction, time reduction, output quality improvement, Total Quality Management and empowerment.

Step 2 **Identify the processes** to be redesigned. Most firms use the 'high impact' approach, which focuses on the most important processes or those that conflict most with the business

vision. Lesser number of firms use the exhaustive approach that attempts to identify all the processes within an organisation and then prioritise them in order of redesign urgency.

Step 3 Understand and **measure the existing processes** – to ensure previous mistakes are not repeated and to provide a baseline for future improvements.

Step 4 **Identify change levers**. Awareness of IT capabilities could prove useful when designing processes.

Step 5 Design and **build a prototype** of the new process. The actual design should not be viewed as the end of the BPR process – it should be viewed as a prototype, with successive alterations. The use of a prototype enables the involvement of customers.

1.6 IT and BPR

IT is not the solution in itself, it is an **enabler**. BPR uses IT to allow an organisation to do things that it is not doing already. For example, teleconferencing reduces the cost of travelling to meetings – a re-engineering approach takes the view that teleconferencing allows more frequent meetings.

As *Hammer* and *Champy* put it, 'It is this disruptive power of technology, its ability to break the rules that limit how we conduct our work, which makes it critical to companies looking for competitive advantage.'

1.6.1 Problems with BPR

There are concerns that BPR has become misunderstood. According to an independent study of 100 European companies, BPR has become allied in managers' minds with narrow targets such as **reductions in staff numbers** and other **cost-cutting** measures.

In addition to this perception about headcount, several other criticisms have been levelled at the way the idea has been implemented:

(a) Any successful BPR programme is likely to result in significant **changes** that will affect staff widely.

(b) BPR as practised is a kind of **scientific management**: a rational approach to improving efficiency. It neglects the direct link to **effectiveness** originally envisaged and may, by reducing the number of managers in an organisation, reduce innovation and creativity at the same time. Hamel and Prahalad call this process **hollowing out**.

(c) While BPR practice generally seeks to empower workers, it assumes they will work within structures and systems imposed by others. This places strict limits on the scope for releasing their potential with such modern ideas as **teamworking** and **coaching**.

(d) Established systems often have valuable but unrecognised features, particularly in the area of **control**. When a process is re-engineered from scratch, particularly when done with a view to cutting costs, such desirable features as segregation of duties and management supervision may be lost.

1.7 Workflow systems

FAST FORWARD
Workflow systems and **enterprise resource planning** automate existing manual processes. The software engineering approach improves on this and can substitute software for some human interventions.

The first software-based **workflow systems** appeared in the early 1990s. They were essentially systems for the automation of document flows and were based on electronic copies of scanned original documents. The early systems had no potential for improvements to major organisation processes.

Subsequently, **enterprise resource planning** (ERP) systems were developed to provide a menu of communication and control links between **software application packages**. ERP worked best in well-understood applications such as accounting and inventory management. We discuss the adoption of software packages later in this Study Text, but it is important to recognise the linkage between software and business processes.

Like the original workflow systems, ERP systems are essentially a form of **automation of existing processes** and therefore **qualitatively different from BPR**, as discussed above.

1.8 Software engineering

The application of software to business processes has continued, with efforts being made to extend its potential scope to include aspects that would normally require human intervention, such as decision-making. The **software engineering** approach emphasises system efficiency and consistency; there is also a focus on refining business analysts' inputs into software development.

1.9 The Rummler-Brache methodology

The Rummler-Brache methodology sees processes as cross-functional wholes and considers them from three structural levels and three design perspectives.

In 1990, *Rummler and Brache* published *Improving Performance: how to Manage the White Space on the Organisation Chart*. As its title suggests, this book was about designing and managing business processes as **cross-functional wholes**. The authors suggested that organisational process change must be considered at three different structural levels and *at the same time* from three separate perspectives: there are thus **nine areas of concern**, all of which must be addressed satisfactorily if a programme of process change is to be successful.

Structural levels

(a) The organisation as a whole
(b) The process
(c) The job or performance level

Perspectives

(a) Goals and measures of achievement
(b) Design and implementation of processes
(c) Management

Effective organisations will have strong links both up and down the structural levels and across the perspectives. For example, process goals and measures must not only relate accurately to both overall organisational and detailed job goals and measures; they must also form part of a well-designed and implemented process that is managed to operate efficiently.

1.10 Quality improvement methods

There has been a series of quality improvement initiatives including **Total Quality, Six Sigma and ISO 9000 certification**.

There were a number of attempts to introduce a systematic approach to improving quality of output in the 1990s. **Statistical process control**, **total quality management** and all the implications of the **Toyota system of manufacturing** fall under this general heading, as do **Six Sigma**, which used a statistical approach to measurement, and **ISO 9000:2000**. The implementation of ISO 9000:2000 has developed from the simple documentation and management of procedures to a more change-oriented system. At the same time, there has been significant cross-fertilisation between these various initiatives.

1.11 The internet

The influence of the internet has moved beyond unwieldy and expensive **EDI**, enabling extensive and cheap communication.

Electronic data interchange was the main networking technique for integrating large-scale corporate IT systems in the early 1990s. It was rather unwieldy and expensive to operate and so was only used by larger companies and their more important suppliers. The growth of the internet and of its **World Wide Web** aspect in particular means that similar capabilities are now available at much reduced cost. Despite the setback caused by the bursting of the **dotcom bubble**, the internet has had a major effect on business processes. Larger organisations use it to manage and circulate information, as well as making extensive use of it for retailing, while many small businesses trade exclusively over the Web.

We will return to look at the internet and e-business more comprehensively later in this Study Text.

1.12 The effect of business consolidations

FAST FORWARD

Business considerations and the dispersal of manufacturing bring new demands for software integration and operations control and co-ordination.

Extensive redesign of processes often takes place as a result of **mergers and acquisitions**. There has been significant growth in this kind of process development as a result of accelerating globalisation. The acquisition of **foreign subsidiaries**, in particular, usually leads to extensive work to integrate systems or to redesign and replace them where they are incompatible.

At the same time, large scale manufacturing operations have become much more dispersed as work is transferred to low-wage economies in order to control costs. Controlling and co-ordinating such dispersed and complex operations have required the development of new, standardised systems.

1.13 The current position

FAST FORWARD

Improvement projects should be tied to **specific performance goals**. Change management must be to a high standard. IT specialists must take a strategic view if they are to make appropriate input.

Harmon makes several comments about the current state of the art business process change.

First, he emphasises the need to tie improvement projects to **specific corporate goals**: if this is not done, the project will lose focus, develop a life of its own and solve unimportant problems as a result.

Second, he remarks on the difficulty of installing new processes when the operational staff and managers do not support the changes involved. Considerable effort must be expended on **change management**, including obtaining 'buy-in' and **aligning incentives** with the new processes.

The **role of IT specialists** is a third concern. Harmon feels that they have a special contribution to make because of the ubiquity of IT systems within the organisation: IT specialists are increasingly required to take a strategic view of the corporation as a whole so that they can support the line managers who have responsibility for operating and improving business processes. At the same time it is necessary for those line managers to understand the difficulties and concerns of the IT specialists.

1.13.1 Terminology

FAST FORWARD

Harmon suggests three terms:

- **Process improvement** is a tactical, incremental technique.
- **Process re-engineering** is a strategic level rethinking of core processes.
- **Process redesign** is for intermediate scale processes that need significant change.

Harmon suggests a specific terminology for process change efforts that emphasises the scale of what is contemplated.

(a)   **Process improvement** is a **tactical level**, **incremental** technique that is appropriate for developing smaller, stable existing processes.

(b) **Process reengineering** is used at the **strategic level** when major environmental threats or opportunities mandate fundamental re-thinking of large scale, core processes that are critical to the operation of the value chain.

(c) **Process redesign** is an intermediate scale of operation appropriate for **middle sized processes** that require **extensive improvement or change**.

2 Harmon's process-strategy matrix   6/13, 12/11, 12/09

FAST FORWARD

The process strategy matrix analyses processes in terms of their **complexity** on one axis and their **strategic importance** (the value they add) on the other.

It is clear from the overall account given above, that there are a number of options available when the need for process change is established. Harmon describes a tool intended to aid consideration of these options by categorising the organisation's identified processes into four groups. This is the **process-strategy matrix**, which is yet another two axis matrix.

The degree of **process complexity and dynamics** is plotted on the vertical axis; the horizontal axis shows the degree of **strategic importance of the process**. Process 'dynamics' means the extent to which the process is subject to adjustment in response to external stimuli. The effect of this analysis is to create four classes of processes, each of which is amenable to a particular improvement strategy.

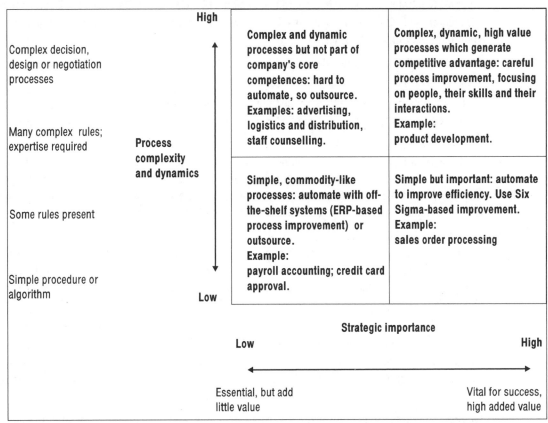

The process-strategy matrix

Exam focus point

The June 2013 exam included a question in which students were asked to use Harmon's process-strategy matrix to analyse the characteristics of three process areas featured in the scenario. Students were required to suggest how each process (payroll, legal advice and a website upgrade) should be sourced and implemented. Harmon's Matrix provided an excellent framework for this question; encouraging students to look at the complexity of the different processes and their strategic importance as being critical factors in the sourcing discussion.

Case Study

Make-It

Analysing a process scenario

Make-It is a manufacturing company that has the following main processes:

Inventory management. Make-It holds a standardised set of materials for 85% of the items it makes. The remaining 15% of items are specific to bespoke customer orders, and are made specifically for those jobs.

Manufacturing. The manufacturing process is computer controlled, with few manual interventions. The only major exception to this rule is that Make-It has a 'hand-made' range of products where the finishing is done by hand.

Logistics. All finished goods are shipped to customers based on their individual order dates, leading to a range of complicated route plans. Make-It's managers feel that they are spending too much time and effort on this area.

Support functions. These include payroll, invoicing, HR, and marketing. These are all areas that are quite straightforward for Make-It's business, but are currently labour intensive (eg the payroll inputs each month are very time-consuming).

New product design. Product design is becoming increasingly important due to the increasing demand for innovative bespoke products.

The management at Make-It have carried out a process review, to decide whether any of the processes should be redesigned. They have applied Harmon's process-strategy matrix to decide how important and complex each process is.

Inventory management. This is generally quite a simple process, but it is a very important one for a manufacturing business. Therefore it should be automated as far as possible to maximise efficiency. However, the 15% of inventory relating to the bespoke products may require more manual intervention, and co-ordination with the product design, logistics and manufacturing processes.

Manufacturing. This process has very high strategic importance. The computer controlled production is likely to be relatively simple, and so little change is likely to be required for this automated process. However, the preparation of the hand made range is likely to be both strategically important and potentially complex. Therefore, Make-It's management should focus considerable effort on analysing and redesigning this process.

Logistics. Logistics and product delivery is of lower strategic importance than manufacturing because it is not part of the product itself. However, it still plays an important part of the marketing mix in relation to 'place'. All the same, 'logistics' is not a core competence of Make-It's business, and so they should consider outsourcing this process, buying in the expertise they need. However, there may be concerns over losing control over this element of their supply chain.

Support functions. These processes are relatively simple, and have low strategic importance. Therefore, Make-It should consider either outsourcing them or automating them. For example, the payroll function could be outsourced to a payroll bureau, while invoicing could be automated using off-the-shelf accounting software.

New product design. This is likely to be both an important and complex process. It will be important that Make-It not only makes innovative use of technology, but also recruits the best designers possible given the increasing demand for bespoke products. New product design (particularly with respect to the bespoke products) is a key source of competitive advantage and so needs to be continuously reviewed and improved.

3 A process redesign methodology

FAST FORWARD

Harmon proposes a methodology for process redesign. This methodology has much in common with the **business change lifecycle** and **project management techniques** dealt with later in this Study Text. It has five phases: planning, analysis, redesign, development and transition.

Exam focus point

It is very easy to envisage that the examining team might set a question that requires you to describe how a specific process redesign project might proceed. If you cannot recall exactly how Harmon's methodology proceeds, you could base your answer on the business change lifecycle model. Failing this, do not be afraid to use your knowledge of the general principles of project management.

Harmon proposes a **business process redesign** methodology. It is clear from its nature that it is best fitted to the category of work described in Section 1.13.1 (c) above. That is to say, it seems appropriate for 'middle sized processes that require extensive improvement or change'.

The methodology is over-complex for **process improvement** (an 'incremental technique ... for developing smaller, stable existing processes'): indeed, *Harmon* covers process improvement in an earlier part of his book. Nevertheless, passing reference to major strategic change suggests that he does envisage its use at the other end of the scale, for **process reengineering** ('fundamental re-thinking of large scale, core processes').

3.1 Advantages of having a methodology

(a) A plan provides **discipline** for the overall process and helps to prevent it from losing focus.

(b) Successful implementation depends on **acceptance by staff and managers** who will have to operate the new process: the methodology emphasise the need for obtaining support at all appropriate stages.

3.2 The methodology in outline

The methodology has five phases.

Phase 1 **Planning**
Goals are set, project scope is defined, project team members and other roles are identified and the overall schedule is developed.

Phase 2 **Analysis**
Current workflow is documented, problems identified and a general approach to a redesign plan is established.

Phase 3 **Redesign**
Possible solutions are considered and the best chosen; objectives for the next phase are defined.

Phase 4 **Development**
All functional implications are followed through, aspects are improved, including management and information systems.

Phase 5 **Transition**
The redesigned process is implemented; modifications are undertaken as required.

3.3 Initiating a redesign

Major process redesign can be very expensive in terms of managers' and specialists' time and it is, therefore, likely that redesign projects will only be undertaken when called for by managers at the **strategic apex**. Harmon calls these managers the **executive committee**. He also suggests that there may be a **process architecture committee** responsible for the organisation's responses to perceived threats and opportunities; this committee takes specific responsibility for the effectiveness of business processes

overall. Under this structure, the executive committee would set overall goals and strategies, delegating decisions about process development to the process architecture committee.

Harmon recommends that the organisation be **structured around its systems and processes,** rather than functionally. Where this is done, a process that is selected for redesign will have a process manager in charge of it; this manager becomes the **project sponsor** for the redesign project. More traditionally structured organisations will have to appoint a project sponsor. The project sponsor does not undertake detailed redesign work: this role is concerned with overall decision-making and championing the redesign at the highest levels.

A **process redesign steering committee** is required. This body has high level representation of all the departments involved in the process. It has two main functions. The first is to be responsible for approving the work of the redesign team. The second is to ensure that managers and staff affected by the redesign support the changes to be made and will implement them.

A **project facilitator** must be appointed to act as project manager. This important role may be allocated to a consultant, since skill at facilitating project redesign is required, rather than familiarity with the specific business processes under consideration. In any case, it is important that the facilitator remains neutral and is not committed to any functional or departmental group.

3.4 Planning

The facilitator and the redesign team need a **project charter** or overall plan to define the scope of their work; this should include an account of how the process they design supports the organisation's overall strategy and goals and how it relates to other processes and stakeholders.

Ideally, this plan will have been defined at a higher echelon of management, such as the executive committee or the process architecture committee. If this has not been done, it will be for the project sponsor, facilitator and the steering committee, once appointed, to develop this plan themselves. The facilitator will then take charge of the outline plan and refine it after appropriate consultation.

The planning phase ends with the agreement of a **detailed project plan**, including **time and cost budgets**, at the executive committee level. To reach this stage, the project sponsor, facilitator and steering group must produce extensive documentation. This will state the project's assumptions, goals, constraints, scope and success measures. It will outline the changes that are required and how they fit in with the rest of the organisation. It is particularly important that resource and systems constraints are considered in detail.

At the same time, the members of the **process redesign team** must be identified.

3.5 Analysing the existing process

This phase may not be present in all projects.

(a)   Some organisations may already have full analysis documentation.
(b)   There may not be an existing process.
(c)   It may be decided to omit this phase if radical change is envisaged.

Where this phase is undertaken, it results in the **full documentation** of the processes and sub-processes concerned. This involves the use of process flow diagrams and organisation charts. Goals, activities, inputs and outputs are identified, named and described in detail. Known problems with the system are noted, as are descriptions of past attempts to improve them. It is also necessary to consider **how the process is managed**, what personal managerial responsibilities are involved and whether improvements to the management system are required. In particular, **performance measures and incentives** should be examined.

When the analysis is complete, the **project goals and assumptions** should be re-examined and revised as necessary. A coherent and robust redesign plan may then be created and presented to higher management. Approval by those who must later implement and manage the new design is essential and support from these senior managers is an indispensable output from this stage.

3.6 Designing the new process

Design of the new process itself is only part of this phase: there are other important aspects.

(a) Design of **supporting management roles and responsibilities** is required, as are the supporting performance measures.

(b) Rationalisation of **reporting responsibilities** may be possible and desirable. A new organisation structure may result.

(c) Where very complex processes are concerned, it may be appropriate to **run simulations and prepare cost estimates** on two or more possible new designs. This is likely to require the use of software tools.

(d) The new design must be **fully documented**.

The final essential output from this phase is, once again, approval from senior management. To achieve this, it will be necessary to explain the new process in detail.

3.7 Development

This phase of the process follows the design through into all of its **functional and resource implications**. New IS resources of hardware and software are specified and designed; job descriptions are created and staff training provided; other necessary resources are acquired. The **project sponsor** has the role of co-ordinating the provision of the resources needed.

At this stage, the implications of organising by processes, rather than by functions, become apparent. The new process is more likely to be effective if it, and the staff and resources committed to it, are managed by a process manager rather than by a group of separate functional managers. This is, therefore, the time at which a change to a **process structure** is best made; this would be a major project in its own right.

The development phase ends when all the new arrangements have been tested and found satisfactory and the new process is ready for installation.

3.8 Transition

The success of the transition phase depends on successful **change management**: it can be harmed or even prevented by opposition or passive resistance. There must be support from the top and close liaison with the managers who have to make the new process work. This may lead to revisions to the process. Eventually, this phase merges into routine monitoring of the process for efficiency and potential further improvements.

4 Process commoditisation and outsourcing 6/11, 6/10

FAST FORWARD

Outsourcing enables organisations to benefit from their suppliers' scale economies.

The establishment of standards for processes will make them easier to outsource. Some processes may thus be commoditised.

Exam focus point

An article titled 'Outsourcing' written by Ken Garrett is available in the technical articles section for P3 on the ACCA website. It would be worth taking the time to study this article.

As we discussed in Chapter 7, outsourcing and offshoring offer modern organisations many benefits, including a reduction in the workload of management and the freeing up of time to allow staff to concentrate on the organisation's core competences.

Generally speaking, outsourcing is appropriate for peripheral activities: to attempt to outsource core competences could lead to the collapse of the whole organisation. However, it can be difficult to identify with clarity just what an organisation's core competences are and it is not too difficult to imagine an organisation whose core competence was, in fact, outsourcing. Certainly, the motor manufacturing industry seems to be moving in this direction.

A further advantage of outsourcing is that external suppliers may capture **economies of scale** and experience effects that mean that costs may be reduced by using their services, rather than in-house provision.

 **Case Study**   The London Fire Brigade

In March 2012, the London Fire Brigade (LFB) – the largest fire service in the UK – made the controversial decision to outsource its 999 control centre to outsourcing giant, Capita.

The deal will see Capita run the call centre on behalf of the brigade and also supply the new 999 control system. Existing staff, including 999 control officers and back office employees, will be transferred to Capita and it is expected that the new systems will go live later in 2012.

According to the LFB, this will save £5m over the 10 year life of the contract and will allow the service to focus on its core business of putting out fires and saving lives.

Other fire brigades in the UK, also under pressure to make savings, are said to be monitoring the LFB initiative to consider whether a similar approach could be taken in their areas.

However, critics have argued that the moves to 'privatise' the handling of the fire service's 999 calls will put lives at risk based on a concern that private companies winning such contracts would not be held accountable for mistakes.

Adapted from an article:

'London fire brigade to outsource 999 control centre' (March 2012) published on

The Guardian website; www.theguardian.com

Getting the best out of outsourcing depends on **successful relationship management,** rather than through the use of formal control systems.

Successful outsourcing depends on three things.

(a)   The ability to **specify with precision** what is to be supplied: this involves both educating suppliers about the strategic significance of their role and motivating them to high standards of performance.

(b)   The ability to **measure** what is actually supplied and thus establish the degree of conformance with specification

(c)   The ability to **make adjustments elsewhere** if specification is not achieved.

FAST FORWARD

There are also **practical considerations** relating to outsourcing.

- It can save on costs by making use of a suppliers' economies of scale
- It can increase effectiveness where the supplier deploys higher levels of expertise
- It can lead to loss of control, particularly over quality
- It means giving up an area of threshold competence that may be difficult to reacquire

 Case Study   Outsourcing requires the right in-house skills

UK public sector cuts in response to the ongoing tough financial climate has led to inevitable job cuts and a commitment to increasing the proportion of outsourced services the government buys from small and medium-sized businesses.

However, research carried out by totaljobs.com has indicated that a lack of vital exepertise is already damaging the sector's ability to manage contracts. More than 100 senior managers from local and central government were involved in the research and over one third of those consulted admitted a lack of skills was the key reason for cancelling outsourcing contracts in 2011.

The research highlights the importance for commissioners of outsourced services need to understand the value as well as the cost. It suggests this is addressed via the establishment of a centralised panel to help spread best practice in looking beyond top-line costs and higlighting the benefits that might accrue from delivering services in different ways.

As the report highlights, blurring the distinction between the public and private sectors requires a new approach to exchanging knowledge and developing skills. The shifting careers landscape provides a once-in-a-generation opportunity to demolish the barriers between public and private sector working cultures to achieve better outcomes for all. The public sector is crying out for new ideas with two-fifths of public sector decision-makers keen to improve their own in-house consultancy skills.

Much can be learned from the working practices of both the public and private sector, but real value can only be achieved by uniting the best elements of each. A one-size-fits-all approach is no longer the answer. More focus is needed on locality, and working to meet regional needs. Establishing an advisory group to bring such ideas together is the best path to securing a strongly performing public service outsourcing for the future.

<u>Adapted from an article</u>:

'Outsourcing requires the right in-house skills' by Mike Booker (March 2012) published on

The Guardian website; www.theguardian.com

Outsourcing of non-core activities is widely acknowledged as having the potential to achieve important cost savings. However, process outsourcing is still uncommon for a number of reasons, one of which is the difficulty of assessing the cost-effectiveness of what is purchased. Cost should be fairly clear, but the quality of what is purchased is extremely difficult to assess in advance.

- Companies perceive their processes are not comparable with the competences of outside suppliers
- Companies perceive that processes are not standard (like products are), and so they think it is difficult to assess whether a process will be improved by outsourcing it

In short, companies have no idea how an outside business might perform their processes, so they keep the processes in-house.

A key problem has been a lack of **process standards**. However, Davenport suggests that this situation is changing following the introduction of the Capability Maturity Model (CMM) as a process standard for software development.

The success of the CMM in improving software development processes appears to have prompted other business domains to adopt a similar model (the CMMI model). Consequently, there is a move towards process standardisation which will allow companies to determine whether a business capability can be improved by outsourcing it. These standards will also make it easier to compare service providers and evaluate the costs versus benefits of outsourcing.

The establishment of standards for a wide range of processes will have important consequences, since **processes themselves will become commodities**.

- The level of outsourcing will increase
- Prices of outsourced processes will fall, as the market matures and the number of providers increases
- The quality of process performance will improve, because companies will only focus on processes that are truly core to their organisation
- The flow of jobs offshore will accelerate
- The basis of competition will change, because, as processes become standardised, they will no longer act as a basis of competitive advantage

Process standardisation may also mean it is possible for companies to combine certain processes with competition. If the processes no longer offer competitive advantages, the companies can set up shared-

service centres, thereby benefitting from economies of scale. So process standards could actually lead to more collaboration among competitors.

4.1 Advantages and disadvantages of outsourcing

Although we have suggested (above) that process standardisation will increase the level of business process outsourcing, ultimately organisations will only choose to outsource if they are convinced of the advantages of doing so.

Advantages

(1) Can save on costs by making use of a specialist providers' **economies of scale**

(2) Can **increase effectiveness** where the supplier deploys higher levels of expertise (eg in software development)

(3) Allows the organisation to focus on its own **core activities**/competencies

(4) Can deliver benefits and change more quickly than business process reorganisation in-house

(5) Service level agreements mean that the company knows the level of service they can expect

(6) **Cost control**. The creation of a 'customer/contractor' relationship introduces a focus on cost control which is sometimes lost when functions are performed internally

Disadvantages

(1) There may be problems finding a single supplier who can manage complex processes in full. If more than one supplier has to be used for a single process then the economies of scale are likely to be reduced

(2) Firms may be **unwilling to outsource whole processes** due to the significance of those processes or the confidentiality of certain aspects of them. (This could be a particular problem if the contractor company is also working for competitors.) Again, if processes are fragmented in this way, the economies of scale may be reduced

(3) Outsourcing can lead to **loss of control,** particularly in relation to **quality issues**. This occurs when agreed service levels are not met. The firm which is outsourcing activities now has to develop competences in relationship management (with the outsourced suppliers) in place of its competences in the processes it has outsourced

(4) Firms may be tied to **inflexible, long term contracts**

(5) If there are specialist skills involved in the work, it may be difficult to switch to a new supplier if there are problems, or at the end of a contract period. This gives the external contractor significant bargaining power

(5) Firms may be unwilling to give up an area of threshold competence that may be difficult to reacquire. If they lose the competence, they will become dependent on suppliers; again, giving the supplier significant bargaining power

The outsourcing decision needs to be treated with care. The advantages it delivers will largely be seen in the short term, but the disadvantages could affect an organisation in the longer term. Therefore, both the short-term and longer-term implications need to be considered before an organisation chooses to outsource.

<table>
<tr><td>Exam focus
point</td><td>When evaluating whether or not a process should be outsourced, take care to apply your answer directly to the scenario, rather than simply churning out the list of pros and cons above. The June 2010 exam included a 12 mark requirement in a Section B question asking for the benefits to the organisation in question of outsourcing IT. Many candidates failed to use the information in the scenario, falling back on lists such as the above and therefore missed many of the marks available.</td></tr>
</table>

Chapter Roundup

- General systems theory would see the organisation as an **open system**, interacting with its environment.

- **The business change lifecycle** provides a framework for assessing the key stages involved in undertaking a business change project.

- The **POPIT model (four view model)** focuses the project teams attention on four interrelated areas when undertaking a business process change. Some analysts argue that project teams focus too much on the process and technological aspects of business change and ignore the impact that change has on people and the organisation.

- **Business process re-engineering** is a useful approach based on challenging basic assumptions about business methods and even the objectives they are designed to achieve. IT can be very useful here, but simply to automate a process is not the same as re-engineering it.

- **Workflow systems** and **enterprise resource planning** automate existing manual processes. The software engineering approach improves on this and can substitute software for some human interventions.

- **The Rummler-Brache methodology** sees processes as cross-functional wholes and considers them from three structural levels and three design perspectives.

- There has been a series of quality improvement initiatives including **Total Quality, Six Sigma and ISO 9000 certification**.

- The influence of the internet has moved beyond unwieldy and expensive **EDI**, enabling extensive and cheap communication.

- Business considerations and the dispersal of manufacturing bring new demands for the software integration and operations control and co-ordination.

- Improvement projects should be tied to **specific performance goals**. Change management must be to a high standard. IT specialists must take a strategic view if they are to make appropriate input.

- Harmon suggests three terms:

  - **Process improvement** is a tactical, incremental technique.
  - **Process re-engineering** is a strategic level rethinking of core processes.
  - **Process redesign** is for intermediate scale processes that need significant change.

- The process strategy matrix analyses processes in terms of their **complexity** on one axis and their **strategic importance** (or the value they add) on the other.

- Harmon proposes a methodology for process redesign. This methodology has much in common with the **project management techniques** dealt with later in this Study Text. It has five phases: planning, analysis, redesign, development and transition.

- **Outsourcing** enables organisations to benefit from their suppliers' scale economies.

  The establishment of standards for processes will make them easier to outsource. Some processes may thus be commoditised.

- There are also **practical considerations** relating to outsourcing.

  - It can save on costs by making use of a suppliers' economies of scale.
  - It can increase effectiveness where the supplier deploys higher levels of expertise.
  - It can lead to loss of control, particularly over quality.
  - It means giving up an area of threshold competence that may be difficult to reacquire.

1   Define BPR in one sentence.

2   What are the structural levels specified in the Rummler-Brache methodology?

3   What are the perspectives specified in the Rummler-Brache methodology?

4   Arrange Harmon's three specified approaches to process change in ascending order of scale.

5   What are the axes of the process-strategy matrix?

6   What is the process-strategy matrix's prescription for dealing with processes that are complex and dynamic but add little value?

7   What are the phases of Harmon's process redesign methodology?

8   List three benefits of outsourcing.

1   BPR is the fundamental rethinking and radical redesign of business processes to achieve dramatic improvements in performance

2   The organisation as a whole; the process; the job or performance level

3   Goals and measures; design and implementation; management

4   Process improvement, process redesign, process re-engineering

5   Process complexity and dynamics; and strategic significance

6   Such processes are difficult to automate: they should be outsourced

7   Planning, analysis, redesign, development, transition

8   Possible answers:

    –   Reduce costs by making use of specialist providers' economies of scale
    –   Increase effectiveness where outsourced supplier has specialist expertise
    –   Focus on core competencies
    –   Can deliver benefits and changes more quickly
    –   Certainty over service levels
    –   Improved control over costs

Now try the question below from the Practice Question Bank

Number	Level	Marks	Time
Q10	Preparation	n/a	15 mins

10

Improving processes

Topic list	Syllabus reference
1 Managing and measuring processes	D3(a)
2 Process redesign patterns	D3(b)-(e)
3 Standard software packages	D4(b), (d)
4 Establishing software requirements	D4(a)
5 Choosing research techniques	D4(a)
6 Assessing software packages	D4(c)
7 Selecting software packages	D4(c)

Introduction

Having established a framework for the consideration of process change, we may now proceed further into the practical detail of how to go about it. We start with some further, simple ideas and then proceed to the main subject of this chapter, the selection of software packages.

Study guide

		Intellectual level
D3	**Improving the processes of the organisation**	
(a)	Evaluate the effectiveness of current organisational processes	3
(b)	Describe a range of process redesign patterns	2
(c)	Establish possible redesign options for improving current processes of an organisation	2
(d)	Assess the feasibility of possible redesign options	3
(e)	Assess the relationship between process redesign and strategy	3
D4	**Software solutions**	
(a)	Establish information system requirements required by business users	2
(b)	Assess the advantages and disadvantages of using a generic software solution to fulfil those requirements	2
(c)	Establish a process for evaluating, selecting and implementing a generic software solution	2
(d)	Explore the relationship between generic software solutions and business process redesign	2

Exam guide

The examining team is known to be interested in software approaches to process change, so we confidently await regular demonstrations of this interest in the form of questions that address the material in this chapter.

Models and frameworks

The Study Guide for this chapter does not explicitly reference any models, although Harmon's work on process redesign patterns links very closely to D3(b). Nonetheless, no specific models will be explicitly required in a question on process improvement.

1 Managing and measuring processes

FAST FORWARD

> Organisations should be structured around processes rather than functions. This means that the hierarchy of management objectives and performance measures will be similarly structured. Process improvement becomes part of every manager's task.

As we noted earlier, Harmon recommends a management structure based on processes rather than functions, since it is the efficiency of the organisation's processes that determine its success. In practical terms, this can lead to a **matrix structure**.

This approach implies that the **hierarchy of objectives** should also be structured on process lines, as should the organisation's **measures of performance** (we mentioned this approach early in Chapter 1). Objectives and performance measures flow down in a co-ordinated way from mission to major processes, to sub-processes, to activities and to individual tasks. The roles of managers at all levels are thus built around process performance: they plan, set targets, provide training, measure performance and take control action in terms of the **processes for which they are responsible**. This approach fits well with the balanced scorecard approach.

Harmon says:

> "If an organisation establishes process measures that extend from the process to the activity, and if managers continuously check these measures and take actions when there are deviations, then process improvement becomes part of every manager's job. In effect, **measures determine how the activity should be performed**." (Emphasis added by BPP).

This has a vital implication for process improvement: any changes made at a lower level **must be followed through** into the detail of management responsibility at **higher levels**. The immediate supervisor has to deal with a different way of doing things and achieve different outcomes. The supervisor's manager needs to know about these changes in the supervisor's role and so on, up the hierarchy.

2 Process redesign patterns   6/11

In the previous chapter, we considered a proposed general approach to the project management of the activities involved with the redesign of a process. In this section, we will look more closely at the techniques that are available for use in the redesign activity itself. Harmon calls these techniques **redesign patterns**.

Key term

> A **process redesign pattern** is a general approach to redesigning processes for their improvement.

FAST FORWARD

Harmon describes four **basic redesign patterns**.

(a)   **Re-engineering** starts with a clean sheet of paper.
(b)   **Simplification** eliminates redundant process elements.
(c)   **Value-added analysis** eliminates activities that do not add value.
(d)   **Gaps and disconnects** target problems at departmental boundaries.

The feasibility of any proposed redesign must be considered.

2.1 Re-engineering

We introduced BPR in the previous chapter, using these words: '**business process re-engineering** is the fundamental rethinking and radical redesign of business processes to achieve dramatic improvements in critical contemporary measures of performance, such as cost, quality, service and speed.'

The BPR approach is used when large-scale change is to be introduced. The aim is to achieve major efficiency improvements. This pattern is hardly **redesign** at all, since its philosophy is to question all assumptions and start from scratch. Re-engineering can achieve **very large-scale improvements**, but it is inevitably **highly disruptive** and has a **high risk of dramatic failure**.

2.2 Simplification

Simplification is a far less radical pattern of redesign. It proceeds on the assumption that most established business processes are likely to have developed **elements of duplication or redundancy**. This assumption is probably most valid in relation to large-scale processes that cut across departmental or functional boundaries and it is, therefore, in such instances that simplification is most likely to be fruitful approach. The effort involved is usually moderate.

The simplification approach commences with **identification and modelling** of all the systems, activities and sub-processes involved in the business process under investigation. Each element is then subject to challenge: it may not actually be necessary; it may provide information that is available elsewhere; it may be a bottleneck; it may repeat something done in another place. Whenever possible, activities are removed from the process so that duplication and unnecessary complexity are gradually eliminated. This pattern is likely to produce **improvements**, though their **scale can vary widely**, from the relatively minor to the impressive.

Judgement and flexibility are needed to use this approach, since apparently similar activities may incorporate subtle differences that are important in one departmental context but not in another. An element of redesign may be required in addition to simple cuts: for example, it may be possible to achieve a net saving by designing a single process to replace two existing ones.

2.3 Value-added analysis

The aim of value-added analysis is to eliminate processes that do not add value. Value-added analysis approaches processes from the point of view of the customer. Here, 'customer' means whoever receives the output of the process, so internal customers are included.

Value-adding activities satisfy three conditions.

- The customer is willing to pay for the output
- The process changes the output in some way
- The process is performed correctly at the first attempt

Four categories of activity are defined as **non-value-adding**.

- Preparation and set-up activities
- Control and inspection activities
- Movement of a product
- Activities that result from delay or failure of any kind

There is a third category: **value-enabling activities**. These are essential preliminaries to value-adding activities. If you think about this for a moment, you will see that, just as with the simplification approach, judgement is required here: an obvious instance lies in the area of preparation and set-up. We have defined such activities as non-value-adding, but, surely, they are essential preliminaries? An example might help here.

 Case Study   Toyota

When Toyota restarted production cars in the late 1940s, the prevailing western technology for producing body panels was based on extremely careful set-up of presses and very long production runs. Set-up had to be painstaking in order to avoid sub-standard output, some of which might not be discovered until it had been incorporated into a part-finished car. The problem was the alignment of the press dies. These weighed many tonnes and so took a team of specialists up to a day to reposition. In these circumstances, very long production runs were required to make the whole process economic. This implied the use of a large number of presses in order to provide the hundreds of different panels required and often led to excessive inventory holdings.

Toyota was not able to use this system: it had only a few presses and could only sell a few thousand cars each year. Taiichi Ohno, the chief production engineer, therefore developed a system using simple adjustment mechanisms and roller mountings for the dies. This made it possible for ordinary production workers to change dies in a tiny fraction of the time previously thought necessary. An unexpected bonus of this approach was that, since the output panels were needed for immediate assembly, any misalignment or other fault was discovered immediately and wastage was thus reduced.

How does this example help us? It is clear that Ohno's system of changing dies is an essential, minimal, value-enabling preliminary to the value activity of pressing body panels; the traditional way is extremely expensive and, with its natural consequences of over-stocking and high wastage, adds little if any value.

Bearing in mind that the overall intention is to eliminate non-value-adding activities, we may thus suggest that where preparation and set up are concerned, we should aim to ensure that they qualify as value-enabling activities by making them as simple and cost effective as possible.

The Toyota example illustrates another aspect of the importance of processes and process redesign. This is the link between processes and strategy. The standard process was created in the context of the strategy of the US motor industry of the time: this involved vast volumes and was to some extent a seller's market, so healthy margins would easily absorb the waste inherent in the method. Toyota could not pursue this strategy: it was forced to minimise costs and maximise its utilisation of its resources. The redesign of the pressing process helped it to do so.

Like the simplification approach, value-added analysis commences with **identification and modelling** of all the systems, activities and sub-processes involved in the business process under investigation. Each element is then **categorised** according to the criteria discussed above. Harmon suggests that, typically, only 20% of the activities making up a process are identifiable as value-adding, with most of the remainder falling into the value-enabling category. When all of the clearly value-adding and value-enabling activities have been identified, the remainder may be examined in detail. The Toyota body press example above indicates how careful consideration can lead to the development of new methods that eliminate much non-value-adding work in preliminary activities.

(a)   It may be possible to minimise control and inspection activities by processes of **empowerment**.

(b)   Physical movement of products can be minimised by careful **workplace layout**, which is an aspect of production engineering. **Workflow systems** eliminate transit time for documents by scanning all documents to produce electronic copies which are transferred at the click of a mouse.

(c)   Activities that result from delay or failure require careful investigation to establish **patterns or modes of failure** that may be subject to correction. Again, empowerment may offer some potential for making improvements. This is especially true in the whole area of customer complaints, where a rapid satisfactory resolution is a powerful tool for improving customer loyalty.

This improvement pattern is capable of producing results on a scale similar to that achieved by the simplification approach; that is to say, varying between extensive and fairly small.

2.4 Gaps and disconnects

In the previous chapter, we discussed Rummler and Brache and their book, *Improving Performance: how to Manage the White Space on the Organisation Chart*. In this book, the authors suggest that a major problem with many processes is likely to be failures of communication between business departments and functions. These failures can produce continuing **gaps and disconnects,** both in the processes themselves and in the management of those processes.

This approach commences in the usual way, with **identification and modelling** of the selected process, but its focus is on occasions when information or materials pass from one department or function to another, since this is where gaps and disconnects are to be found.

Rummler identifies over thirty potential areas in which gaps and disconnects are likely to occur. These are fairly evenly divided between the three levels we mentioned when discussing the book in the previous chapter.

(a)   The organisation as a whole
(b)   The process
(c)   The job or performance level

It is only at the second and third of these levels that problems relating to actual **workflow** and **activities** appear. At the organisational level, they are entirely concerned with the **design of processes** and the **monitoring** and **control** of **process outcomes**. These are clearly **management activities**.

2.5 Feasibility

The purpose of considering feasibility is not so much to find out if a proposed project can achieve its objective as to establish whether or not it can do so in a **cost-effective** manner. Given sufficient resources, most proposals that lie outside the realms of fantasy can be implemented, but **not all are worth undertaking**. The feasibility study is the mechanism by which the organisation filters out proposals that would cost too much, cause too much disruption, make excessive demands on human and other resources or have side effects whose undesirability outweighs their advantages. The assessment of feasibility can be broken down into a number of areas.

2.5.1 Technical feasibility

The assessment of technical feasibility will depend on the nature of the technology involved.

(a)   Does all the necessary technology exist or is significant **innovation** required?

(b)   Is the technology mature enough to use or is further **development** likely to be required?

(c)   How **specialised** is the required technology and is **the expertise** to make use of it available?

Technical feasibility also includes **technical matters that do not relate to technology**; that is to say, matters of technical expertise, such as marketing, financial strategy and human resource management. We might wish to know, for example, whether it were feasible to communicate effectively with a particular identified market segment.

2.5.2 Social feasibility

Any change is likely to have effects upon people, both those in the organisation concerned and those outside it. The social feasibility of a project depends on the nature and extent of those effects. There are obvious human resource management implications to most projects, in the area of forming, leading and motivating the project team. The progress and outcome of a process improvement project may also have important consequences for employees outside the team, such as increased demand for certain categories of staff, redundancies, training requirements and changed work patterns.

2.5.3 Environmental concerns

Consideration of a project in environmental terms is usually not so much about feasibility as about **acceptability**. Several different stakeholder groups are likely to have environmental concerns and their opinions and reactions may affect both the progress of a project itself and the desired characteristics of its deliverables.

2.5.4 Financial feasibility

It is appropriate to submit proposed changes to **cost-benefit analysis**, though this can be very difficult when the benefits are largely in intangible form. Part of the difficulty lies in identifying the benefits and part in assigning monetary values to them. Dealing with intangible or qualitative benefits is likely to be particularly important in the public and voluntary sectors, where objectives such as improved road safety or education are common. We will return to this later in the Study Text.

2.6 Illustration of process redesign patterns   6/10, 6/09

**Exam focus
point**

In the P3 exam, it is unlikely that you will be asked simply to describe Harmon's four basic process redesign patterns. It is much more likely to be a scenario describing the current processes and asking you to suggest potential improvements, as was the case in the June 2011 paper in which candidates were required to identify a range of re-design options that an examining body could consider for improving its question handling process. Candidates were also required to evaluate the benefits of each of their suggested options.

Note that process redesign is also linked to issues of project management, and possibly IT, which also feature in the middle layer of the relational model of syllabus capabilities for P3.

As in so much of this paper, it is being able to apply your knowledge which is crucial. The case study that follows illustrates the application of the process redesign patterns.

 Case Study

Process diagram

In the previous chapter, we looked at a fictitious manufacturing company (Make-It) to illustrate the application of Harmon's process-strategy matrix. Imagine that one of the items Make-It makes is a wooden chair, with a cushioned seat.

The production of the chair involves a number of processes. It starts with requisitioning materials from inventory, and then preparing them. After that the chair is assembled, and then finished (which includes being polished).

We can show the construction process as a process diagram:

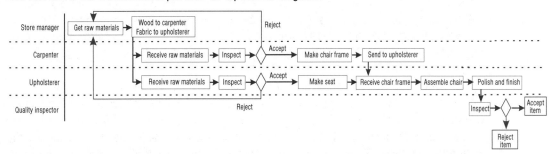

Once the diagram is complete, we can see who is responsible for what areas of the process, and whether there are any aspects of it which can be improved. For example:

- Are there any elements of duplication or redundancy?
- Are there any gaps or disconnects?
- Are there any activities which do not add value?

In this case, we have assumed that the carpentry work involved in carving the wood is a specialised job, so the carpenter should not also be assembling the chair. Therefore, there is no duplication as a result of having both a carpenter and an upholsterer involved in the process.

However, there is potential redundancy in the raw material inspection. If the storeroom manager inspected the materials before giving them to the carpenter and the upholsterer, then they could concentrate on their core activities of using the materials to make a chair.

There are also some potential issues in the order of the construction process. If the upholsterer makes the seat cushion before receiving the chair frame from the carpenter, there is a risk that the size may not be right. (There is no indication that all the chairs are made to the same size, or that the carpenter tells the upholsterer the exact dimensions of the chair being made). Therefore, there is potentially a disconnection between the two processes, and we suggest this could be resolved by the upholsterer waiting until the carpenter has finished the chair frame before making the seat cushion.

You might also question whether the final quality inspection adds value, but we have assumed it does. The customer will only want to pay for the chair if it is well-built, and the quality inspection ensures this.

The diagram can now be redrawn to show the proposed changes:

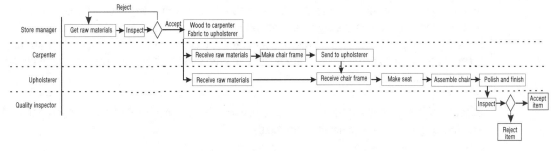

However, note that before implementing these changes, management should discuss them with all the people involved to make sure there are not any reasons which would mean the changes are not suitable or feasible.

Exam focus point

> Business process diagrams provide a useful way of summarising the activities in a business process, and in this way can also identify potential areas of improvement in the process.
>
> You will not be asked to draw a business process diagram in your exam, but you may be asked to interpret one.

3 Standard software packages

> ERP systems are based on limited, standardised modules. This means that the organisation must adapt to the standard system, rather than designing its own most appropriate and efficient process. However, the alternative, adapting a standard package to local requirements, destroys the advantages of purchasing the standard package and introduces further complications. Nevertheless, packages have their own disadvantages.

The use of computers to automate business processes began over half a century ago in the UK. J Lyons & Co had made many improvements in its administrative techniques and set about developing its own computer in association with Cambridge University. The result was the **LEO 1 computer**: LEO stands for Lyons Electronic Office. LEO 1 ran its first payroll in December 1953. The LEO system was the archetypal **tailored**, or **bespoke**, IS; not only was the software created specifically for the company's purposes, the hardware was too.

In the forty years that followed, computers were widely utilised for a wide range of business procedures, including the well-known manufacturing and resource control systems, **MRP** and **MRPII**. The result of this process was the widespread acquisition of standardised software packages by large companies from the 1990s onward. These packages were originally standalone applications for such business functions as accounting and HRM but their vendors developed their products into packages that could deal with major parts of a business's system infrastructure in an integrated way. By extension from the MRP acronym, these integrated systems became known as **enterprise resource planning** (ERP) systems.

3.1 ERP – general characteristics

In general, standard ERP packages are robust systems that incorporate wide experience of business procedures and their automation. They are, however, based on **standardised modules** and are not necessarily optimised for any given commercial application. Claims by vendors that their products can give a competitive edge are questionable: competitors can easily buy the same product. The best that can be said is that an ERP system should provide an effective way of doing things.

The standardised, one size fits all nature of ERP software also means that attempting to improve business processes by installing it **reverses the normal method**. As Harmon says, with ERP 'you begin with a solution'. Rather than analysing what happens currently and then developing an improved system, ERP forces the organisation to adjust itself to the requirements of the software.

Exam focus point

> Be prepared to contrast Harmon's reservations about standard packages with Davenport's view that process standards will have a positive effect on how business is conducted. There is a debate between those who think that packages represent best practice (eg Davenport) and those (like Harmon) who see them as merely average practice. There is merit in both views but specific problems and context may lead to one conclusion or the other.

Because of this generic nature, many clients insist on having their ERP software tailored to fit their own existing systems. This is generally a **mistake**.

- The cost advantage of buying off the shelf is destroyed
- Introduction is delayed
- Reliability is reduced
- New versions of the same software will be useless until they too have been modified

A **middle course** between utilising a standard package and developing a bespoke application is to **purchase the source code** for a package and **modify it in-house** as required. This destroys the advantages of purchasing a standard package and adds its own disadvantages.

- Internal developers are initially unfamiliar with the programs and data structures
- Pre-existing errors in the source code will not be fixed by the vendor
- Upgrades issued by the vendor cannot be relied on to work properly
- The underlying design may not in fact have the necessary development potential

Generally, it is cheaper and more effective to redesign the organisation's processes to fit a standard package than to do the opposite.

3.2 Advantages of software packages over in-house development

(a) **Cost savings** should be available because the vendor can spread the cost of systems development over a large number of installations.

(b) **Time savings** should be very significant, since developing a new application can be extremely time consuming.

(c) **Quality** should be guaranteed both by the vendor and, except for launch customers, by earlier installation by other customers.

(d) **Documentation and training** should be immediately available and of high quality, since these are important selling points.

(e) **Maintenance support** should be good and would normally include help desk service and routine software amendments to correct faults as they become apparent.

(f) Comprehensive **package evaluation** should be possible. This might include use for a trial period and visits to existing installations.

3.3 Disadvantages of software packages

(a) **Property rights** over the software usually reside with the supplier. This has three important potential consequences for the user.

   (i) The supplier controls future development of the software.

   (ii) The supplier controls the support available and may discontinue it, forcing the customer to purchase an upgrade.

   (iii) The supplier may sell the product rights to another supplier, perhaps to the prejudice of the customer.

(b) The **financial stability** and survival of the supplier is not guaranteed.

(c) **Competitive advantage** cannot be obtained from standard software packages available to all.

(d) **Inadequate performance** is quite likely: the customer may have to accept restricted functionality or pay for tailored amendments, with the accompanying disadvantages already discussed. Further problems may be caused by unwanted standard features: these may cause difficulties in training and implementation.

(e) **Legal redress** for lack of functionality will almost certainly not be available.

(f) **Changing requirements** can erode a package's functionality. Potential purchasers evaluate a package against their current requirements. These may change as time passes or may not have been properly specified in the first place. In either case, the package fails to provide full satisfaction.

Exam focus point

A question in the June 2011 exam asked candidates to explain the advantages of using a software package and the implications of using a software package for the organisation's redesign process. The examining team stressed that too many students provided answers which were too long and simply provided general disadvantages of using off-the-shelf software packages, rather than bespoke solutions. As a result, few marks were awarded on this part of the question.

4 Establishing software requirements

FAST FORWARD

The first phase of any IS project is likely to be the collection of information. There are seven techniques:

- Interviews
- Questionnaires
- Written questions
- Observation

- Protocol analysis
- Workshops
- Prototyping

Each technique has its advantages and disadvantages, so it will be normal to use a combination of them.

When an organisation contemplates the acquisition or development of a new IS, whether a component or a complete system, the first stage of the project is the **collection of information** so that system requirements may be firmly established. This must be done carefully and with an insistence on the verification of data: personal impressions and opinions are of little value. Also, it may be necessary to revisit work that has already been done in order to extend or confirm the data.

It is important that analysts have adequate face-to-face communication skills, since much of their work will involve close contact with the staff whose work they investigate. Staff may be suspicious, taciturn or otherwise uncooperative and analysts may have to work hard to gain their confidence. An important aspect of this process is initial research undertaken in order to become familiar with the basics of the business systems in use.

Skidmore and Eva describe seven techniques for fact gathering.

4.1 Interviews

Interviews allow analysts and stakeholders to meet and are thus particularly appropriate during the early stages of investigation. Interviews are used to collect information and promote understanding of a range of topics.

- The business background and technical context and constraints
- Current procedures and data flows
- Known problems with the existing system
- Requirements for the new system

Interviews must be **carefully planned and conducted** if they are to produce satisfactory results.

(a) It is important not to **rush to conclusions** at this early stage. Solutions based on incomplete information are unlikely to be appropriate.

(b) Projects to introduce new systems can be **unsettling for staff** since they often lead to job losses and other unwelcome changes. Interviewers must be careful to avoid any element of interrogation or criticism and should be appreciative of interviewees' assistance.

(c) Interviewers should make **comprehensive notes** during interviews and write them up promptly.

(d) It is usual to start at the top with the project sponsor and work down the hierarchy through managers to the staff that actually operate the existing system. This allows for the establishment of **an overview that is gradually supplemented with more detailed information**.

(e) Interviews should take place in the interviewee's workplace. This enhances **interviewee confidence**, ensures that current **documents** are available and allows for the initial observation of **working conditions and practices**.

(f) Interview preparation should include the establishment of clear **objectives** and the preparation of an agenda and questions. The agenda should be sent to the interviewee in sufficient time to allow for suitable preparation.

(g) Interviews must be controlled if they are to be effective. A rambling conversation is unlikely to produce the required information. A possible sequence is **context-detail-problems-requirements**.

(h) During the **context** phase, interviewees describe their current roles and tasks.

 (i) Further **detail** of procedures, documents and records is then elicited.

 (ii) **Problems** and how they arise may then be discussed.

 (iii) Finally, a wish list of **requirements** for the new system can be considered.

(i) **Question technique** is an important aspect of control and there is a range of question types that may be used.

 (i) **Closed questions** use words such as 'when', 'who' and 'how many' and require short, simple, positive answers. They are used to obtain basic facts and as a means of controlling the interviewee who likes to answer at length.

 (ii) **Open questions** invite discursive answers and use words such as 'tell me about'. These questions allow the interviewer to obtain detailed information about procedures and problems. They are also useful for encouraging interviewees who are reluctant to speak.

 (iii) **Anecdotal questions** are a kind of open question: the interviewer invites the respondent to provide illustrations or examples of the way in which events have occurred in the past.

 (iv) **Probing questions** are used to obtain more details about an earlier answer. These questions promote a fuller consideration of a topic.

 (v) **Verification questions** are a kind of probing question: they ask for specific confirmation of the interviewer's impression on a topic and use such phrases as, 'Would it be correct to say that …'.

 (vi) **Sequencing questions** are used to establish the correct order of events in a procedure.

4.2 Questionnaires

Questionnaires do not permit the use of question types other than closed, nor do they permit the interpretation of body language. However, they can be useful for gathering data from a large number of geographically scattered respondents and, with careful design, may be used to assess attitudes and aspirations. Also, they are not affected by distortions and errors introduced by the interviewer. **Question design** is obviously of great importance.

(a) The questionnaire should be as short as possible and the questions should be both **concise and precise**.

(b) Each question should ask for a single, separate response and not combine two queries.

(c) **Leading questions**, which are those that suggest a particular response, must not be used.

(d) Questions must use words and expressions that the respondents will **understand immediately**, including local jargon and technical terms, where applicable.

(e) The **method of response**, such as box ticking or number circling, must be made clear.

Once drafted, questionnaires should be **tried out** on a sample of respondents to ensure that it works. This trial should include an analysis of responses.

4.3 Written questions

Written questions may be used when a person is not available for interview, or as a supplement to an earlier interview. They differ from questionnaires in that they can be **tailored to specific purposes** and allow for **open questions**.

4.4 Observation

Observation of working processes is an important tool for collecting information and works well as a complement to interviewing. It can be carried out **informally**, such as when visiting the workplace for other purposes, or **formally**, in which case the prior agreement of managers and staff is required.

Observation may be used to establish the detail of document flows, by following an example through all the processes it is subject to, and for understanding how processes and people interact by observing a workplace as a whole.

4.5 Protocol analysis

Protocol analysis starts with a person **performing a task and describing what is happening**. It combines the interaction of the interview techniques with the generation of data that cannot be explained in words alone. It also ensures that nothing is taken for granted by the person providing the information, since the demonstration includes all aspects of what has to be done.

4.6 Document analysis

Document analysis is very important, since all formal transactions are likely to be recorded on a document of some kind. The analyst should obtain copies of all types of documents in use. The documents themselves must be assessed for **usability and relevance** to current procedure and analysed to establish the size and format of the **data fields** they contain. The **use** of the documents must also be established. This will include such matters as volumes and frequencies of use, the purpose of each, where the data comes from, who is responsible for completing it, where, how and for how long it is filed and so on.

4.7 Workshops

Workshops are particularly useful when there are **too many stakeholders** to interview individually; when **project scope is unclear**, as may be the case with new systems; and when there is disagreement about **system requirements**. A workshop run by a skilled facilitator can resolve this kind of problem and lead to acceptable consensus. Workshops also allow for creative interaction and can achieve more than other methods.

A series of workshops may be required, probably starting with senior stakeholders in order to decide high-level objectives and requirements. This stage may be followed by workshops for users to deal with more detailed matters.

Ideally, workshops will take place off-site in order to avoid disruption.

4.8 Prototyping

Prototyping is carried out using software to present a mock-up of how the eventual system will look and work. Users can then comment. This is very useful when the proposed system specification is very complex or when it lacks detail or precision. Another approach is to demonstrate an existing package that offers some of the required functionality, though it must be made clear that this is not being proposed as a solution.

4.9 Investigations when computers are already in use

The techniques discussed above may need some modification or change of emphasis when computers are already in use.

(a) Interviews and questionnaires will largely concern the functionality of the existing system.
(b) Observation is likely to be screen and keyboard based and will require attention to seating for observer and operator.
(c) Document analysis will relate to screen layouts in use. Storage will probably be in database form and investigation will require interviews with technical staff.

5 Choosing research techniques

The research techniques discussed above have distinct characteristics that make each of them more or less suitable as circumstances vary. Skidmore and Eva provide an assessment based on six specific problems that may occur.

(a) Staff may be **averse to change** and find it difficult to contribute ideas about future requirements and possible developments. Skidmore and Eva call this **present orientation**.

(b) Staff may be **vague** in their responses.

(c) There may be an element of '**taken for granted**' in staff's approach to existing systems: this results in failure to specify all aspects of the current situation.

(d) Much knowledge is **tacit** and is difficult to elicit in words.

(e) When a largely or completely **new system** is proposed, staff may have little concept of what it might achieve, except in the broadest terms.

(f) The analyst may be **inexperienced** in the work context under investigation and misunderstand or misinterpret raw information.

Using these criteria, we may analyse the techniques discussed as good (G), very good (VG), or not good (NG) as shown in the table below.

	Change aversion	Vagueness	Taken for granted	Tacit knowledge	New system	Inexperience
Interview	G	G	G	NG	G	G
Observation	NG	G	VG	G	NG	VG
Protocol analysis	NG	NG	VG	VG	G	VG
Document analysis	G	NG	G	G	NG	VG
Workshop	VG	NG	VG	NG	VG	G
Prototype	VG	NG	VG	G	VG	G

6 Assessing software packages   6/12, 6/09

FAST FORWARD

Software packages may be assessed against ten high-level requirement categories, each of which is made up of more detailed specific requirements. Not all high-level categories will receive the same weighting.

Imperatives are non-negotiable, absolute requirements and must be established very early on in the project.

Skidmore and Eva suggest that software packages may be assessed against ten high-level categories of requirement.

- Functional requirements
- Non-functional requirements
- Technical requirements
- Design requirements
- Supplier stability requirements
- Supplier citizenship requirements
- Initial implementation requirements
- Operability requirements
- Cost constraints
- Time constraints

These high-level categories will not all be equally significant and it is an important early task to allocate **relative weights** to them, according to their individual importance to the customer. These weightings will be used later in a quantitative assessment of candidate packages. A convenient way to represent this is with a score out of a total of 100. A general indication of likely weighting for each high level requirement is given in the discussion below.

Each high-level requirement is essentially a **category of more detailed requirements**, each of which must be specified very carefully and given its own weighting: these weightings will also be used in the detailed evaluation of packages.

A further early consideration is the establishment of **imperatives**. Imperatives are **non-negotiable, absolute requirements** that candidate packages **must** satisfy. The role of imperatives is to reject unsuitable packages from further consideration, so they must be carefully considered and not established unless definitely applicable. Imperatives are likely to arise in **technical**, **supplier** and **cost** requirements.

6.1 Functional requirements

Functional requirements are the things the new software must do to **support business or operational functions**. These requirements are established using the investigative techniques already discussed. They will normally be given a very high relative weight. Both **current** and **anticipated future** requirements must be considered. Typical weighting overall: 30

6.2 Non-functional requirements

Non-functional requirements are so called simply to distinguish them from functional requirements; they are **not** non-essential and **must** be supported by the package. Their point of distinction is that they do not relate directly to business functionality. Examples are legal compliance, archiving and audit requirements. Non-functional requirements are also established using the investigative techniques already discussed. Typical weighting overall: 10

6.3 Technical requirements

Technical requirements relate to the details of IT and might include preferences such as the hardware platform to be used, the operating system to be supported and the software development language to be used. Some technical requirements might well be **imperatives**. Typical weighting overall: 10

6.4 Design requirements

Flexibility is an important feature for a package, since current requirements may develop into rather different ones in the future. There are three main factors that determine flexibility:

(a) **Architecture** is the internal structure of the system and how its parts interact. Problems of compatibility can limit future development, but the Open Applications Group of suppliers work to open architecture standards that allow their products to be linked to one another without difficulty.

(b) The **internal design** of such elements of package software as files and databases has a significant affect on flexibility: modular design is desirable, as is simplicity of code.

(c) A high degree of **configurability** will allow a package to be tailored to user requirements without expensive code modifications. Ideally, a package should be configurable without programmer intervention.

Typical weighting for design requirements overall: 5

6.5 Supplier stability requirements

Purchasers will need support throughout the future, so they will be concerned that their chosen supplier is financially stable and unlikely to go out of business. They will also wish to purchase from a well-established supplier with a good reputation in the industry. A wide range of factors and considerations will influence a decision here:

(a) **Size and location** may be important: a small local supplier, or at least one with a local office, may provide a more personal service; a much larger one may have more experience and be more stable.

(b) Aspects of **financial stability**, such as profitability, turnover and length of successful trading history, may be **imperatives**. Similar considerations may apply to the supplier's **legal status**, **ownership** and **structure**.

(c)   A good **reputation in the industry** for expertise, service and fair dealing will be desirable.

(d)   **Accreditation** as a provider of certain hardware and software products may be required, as may wider industry accreditations.

(e)   **Quality assurance** will be an important consideration and possibly an **imperative**: it may be appropriate to inspect the provider's procedures and certification.

(f)   The use of **automated software tools** may be an indicator of the supplier's technical maturity.

(g)   Vendors must have proper **insurance cover**.

(h)   **Dispute resolution** should be the subject of a robust and equitable procedure.

(i)   There may be **outstanding issues** such as pre-existing litigation, takeover possibilities and directors' involvement in insolvency proceedings to take into account.

Typical weighting for supplier stability requirements overall: 15

6.6 Supplier citizenship requirements

The topics dealt with under the heading of citizenship might also be called matters of **social responsibility**. Purchasers might wish to take account of policy and practice on a range of issues.

* Diversity
* Health and safety
* Trade unions
* Charities and donations
* Sustainability and the environment

Typical weighting for supplier citizenship requirements overall: 2

6.7 Initial implementation requirements

It is vital that the installation stage of a new package is carried out successfully. This requires skill and involves several important processes.

Typical weighting for initial implementation requirements overall: 10

6.7.1 Data migration and file creation

The **creation of new files** and possibly the **conversion of old ones** will be required. Many commercial applications are based on extensive files of, for example, customer data. Before a new application can start processing, the basic file structures must therefore be created. Where it is intended that pre-existing data should be available for processing, the existing files must be loaded, possibly after being converted to a new, compatible format.

Data migration involves the conversion of existing data, whether manual or computerised, into data for use by the new system.

If data is to be moved from one system into the file structures and field headings of another, an evaluation of the structures in the new system will be needed to ensure that the allocation for field headings is consistent with those in the existing system.

When converting existing data there is a risk of error so conversion programs will have to be written and tested.

Manual input. It may not be possible to migrate all the existing data to the new system so some may have to be manually entered into the new system. Where data is entered manually, extensive checking is needed because there is a high risk of error. For example, where figures are manually keyed in, there is an increased risk of transposition errors which would reduce the quality of the input data.

File conversion is a complex and time consuming process and assistance from the contractor may be an **imperative**.

6.7.2 Software installation

Installation might be required of the supplier; this might include initial loading, testing and troubleshooting. Both the software package and any hardware required should be installed by the package supplier in order to avoid disputes over responsibility for problems.

6.7.3 System implementation

Implementation is the introduction of the new system into service. It may be achieved by simply changing from the old to the new at a given point in time, such as the start of work on a particular day (**direct changeover**), or there may be a period of **parallel running**. The first method is a high risk strategy and likely to require technical support, possibly from vendor staff on site. Parallel running requires extra staff, which the vendor may be able to supply. However, parallel running permits cross-checking of the respective outputs as both the new and old systems process current data. An upper time limit for parallel running should be set though, because although parallel running is a low risk approach compared to a direct changeover, it is costly to operate because it uses double resources.

Nonetheless, parallel running highlights the importance of **testing the solution**. Once the new system has been introduced, there needs to be a period of testing to ensure that the data in the new system is accurate and the system is running as intended.

As an alternative to either direct changeover or parallel running, an organisation may opt for a phased approach.

Pilot operation. The new system is installed on a branch by branch, or location by location, basis. This approach is particularly well-suited to large or geographically dispersed projects, and allows the system to be tested in a single location before being rolled out to all the others.

Restricted data running. Under this approach, a single part of the system file is run on the new system initially, and then once it has been tested and found to be working as intended, other parts of the system are converted. Again, the benefit of this approach is that it limits the impact any errors could have on the overall data quality.

Note that a phrased approach can still either be direct or parallel run at each stage of its roll-out.

6.7.4 User Training

Training in the new system will be required: its nature, content, cost and location must all be considered. Four key considerations are:

- Who needs to be trained?
- Will training be provided on the job or through structured courses?
- Will training be provided internally or by external experts?
- Will all staff be trained at the same time or will training be phased over time?

6.8 Operability requirements

Implementation requirements continue beyond the initial phase and into the productive life of the system.

(a) **Documentation** should be clear, complete, easy to use, helpful and kept up to date.

(b) Continuing **support** will be required and considerations will include such matters as helpline availability, response times and policy on support for superseded versions of software.

(c) **Upgrade policy** includes such matters as cost, frequency, documentation and method of distribution.

(d) **Legal protection** is required to cover the possibility of the supplier's business being wound up. The source code should be lodged **in escrow**.

Typical weighting for operability requirements overall: 2

6.9 Time and cost constraints

Overall requirements relating to time and, particularly, cost will almost certainly be **imperatives**. However, it may also be appropriate to consider time and cost **trade-offs** against other issues in the overall requirement.

Typical weighting for cost constraints: 20; for time constraints: 2

7 Selecting software packages   6/14, 6/12

Skidmore and Eva suggest that once the evaluation requirements have been set, the process of selecting a package may be thought of as falling into five phases:

- Obtaining tenders
- First pass selection
- Second pass selection
- Implementation
- The long-term relationship

Exam focus point

Question 3 in June 2014 focused on a construction company which had purchased a new CRM software package. The company had poorly executed the evaluation, selection and implementation of the software solution. The first requirement for 15 marks asked candidates to suggest a process for evaluating, selecting and implementing software packages and to explain how this process would have prevented the problems experienced by the company.

The examining team noted that 'very few candidates focused on a process that encompassed evaluation, selection and implementation. Too many answers identified a problem in the scenario and then suggested how this might have been avoided. Such an approach did gain credit, but it tended to lead to long disjointed answers, with much repetition and no overall coherent process'.

7.1 Identifying potential suppliers

The selection procedure is built around a detailed **invitation to tender** (ITT), but before this can be issued, potential suppliers must be identified. One way to do this is to **advertise the general system requirement** in the trade press and ask for responses from suppliers. This very open approach may be legally required, particularly in the public sector, but it may attract an unmanageably large number of responses, many of which may be of little value. Some less appropriate suppliers may be weeded out by making a small charge for the issue of the ITT.

A more structured approach is to **research the market** using trade directories, internet searches and personal business awareness.

In either case, the aim should be to identify a reasonable number of potential suppliers for further consideration. Some allowance must be made for wastage in the early stages – so, if, say, eight to twelve formal tenders are required, it may be necessary to identify fifteen to twenty candidates.

7.2 The invitation to tender

When a suitable number of potential suppliers has been identified, ITTs may be issued to them. The ITT is a fairly complex document and will include a number of sections. These are described below.

(a) **Administrative information**

    (i)   Where, how, to whom and by when the tender should be submitted
    (ii)   Procedure for dealing with queries
    (iii) Rules about tendering
    (iv) Confidentiality arrangements

(b)   Information about the **client organisation**

(c)   **The project**

      (i)   **Objectives**

      (ii)   **Scope**

      (iii)   Project **imperatives** as described earlier

      (iv)   **Project owner**

      (v)   Access to **client resources**, such as staff and existing systems

(d)   The **response format** may be specified, especially if it is intended to make comparisons using standardised numerical scores

(e)   **Package requirements** will be stated in terms of the ten requirement categories discussed in Section 6 above

(f)   Client **project management** procedures

(g)   An exposition of the **evaluation procedures** that will be used to assess the tenders

The ITT is likely to be accompanied by a request for detailed information about the tendering organisation, including such items as legal, financial, employment and trading status and policies.

7.3 First pass selection

The object of the first pass selection is to produce a short list of, say, three candidate tenders that can be subjected to further evaluation. The first pass is based largely on information provided in the tenders that is relevant to the ten requirement categories. This must be assessed against each component of those ten categories. The quantitative analysis is extensive and a spreadsheet is commonly used to carry out the weighting arithmetic and to record the various scores.

7.3.1 Functional and non-functional requirements

Functional and non-functional requirements are considered separately but using the same quantitative method. The ITT asks suppliers to rate their products against the various functional and non-functional requirements. The rating is carried out by estimating the effort required to modify the package to fit the various components of each high-level requirement. Skidmore and Eva suggest a five point scale.

Score	
4	No modification required
3	Up to one day's work required
2	Two to five days' work required
1	Six to ten days' work required
0	More than ten days' work required

The suppliers' scores are multiplied by the requirement ratings and the results summed up to provide a total assessment for each of the two high-level requirements.

7.3.2 Technical and design requirements

It will be possible to assess conformity with many **technical** and **design** requirements as a **simple positive or negative**, scoring 4 or 0 respectively; other aspects may require a degree of judgement. Assessment will be based on the tenders or on supplementary information obtained from suppliers. Scores are evaluated as above.

7.3.3 Supplier and implementation requirements

There are four high-level requirements in this group: supplier **stability** and **citizenship**; and **initial implementation** and **operability**. It will be possible to assess many items from the tenders; others will

require subjective assessment in a facilitated workshop attended by suitable members of staff. Scores are evaluated in the usual way.

7.3.4 Cost

If all the tenders satisfy the **cost imperative**, they may be graded relative to the cheapest. Cost (and time) trade-offs may also be assessed.

7.4 Second pass selection

There are **two elements** to the second pass selection.

First, the quantitative assessment outlined above is used to create a **shortlist** of candidate packages that may be then examined further.

This further examination is based on an objective reassessment of those elements of the first pass that were based on the suppliers' claims. It is carried out by running each package through a series of **specific test scenarios**; a **user panel** then awards scores for each function. The demonstration can be provided by the suppliers performing against a script or by client staff using demonstration packages. The second method tends to be more convenient.

The **second element** of the second pass selection concerns **reference sites** and **financial investigation**.

(a) Reference sites are places where the packages are already installed and in operation. Suppliers should provide information about these sites in their tenders. Reference sites should be visited and assessed in detail.

(b) Financial investigation should be undertaken in order to check the information provided by the suppliers.

Either of these aspects of assessment may lead to significant adjustment to earlier scores and even reveal that one or more imperatives have not been satisfied.

7.5 Implementation

Because packages, by their very nature, may be expected to be fully functional and because of the work done during the assessment, it should not be necessary to include much **testing** in the initial implementation. Testing is likely to be restricted to volume running, checking interfaces with other systems and final usability checking.

Similarly, **standard package documentation** is unlikely to require much adjustment, though there may be some work required to integrate it with existing process documentation.

Training in the use of the package should be provided by the vendor, though the user will be responsible for training in the organisation's wider processes that relate to the package.

File creation and **conversion** are likely to be more involved, as already discussed. These are specialised jobs and vendor assistance is likely to be necessary. Vendors may quote a low price for this service as an inducement to buy.

7.6 Managing the long-term relationship   12/12

Buying a package tends to make the user organisation dependent on the supplier, bringing an inevitable element of risk. Risk can be managed via risk avoidance and risk mitigation.

Key terms

> **Risk avoidance** involves choosing not to do something that may bring about risk. For example, deciding not to embark on a new way of working, or buying a particular software package, due to the level of inherent risk that it would introduce.
>
> **Risk mitigation** involves taking steps to either reduce the level of risk, or reduce the impact, should the risk occur.

> **Risk mitigation – risk reduction**. Reducing the risk by changing the way that a particular activity is carried out. For example, IT risk can be minimised by adopting a best practice apporach when aquiring or operating IT systems.
>
> **Risk mitigation – impact reduction.** Some risks cannot be eliminated or reduced to an acceptable level. In these cases, they should be mitigated by assessing the likely impact of the risk and taking steps to reduce this impact. For example, an organisation may issue procedures for quarentining and diabling a systems virus before it spreads throughout the system.

When buying a software package, the user can mitigate the risk in several ways.

(a)   Maintain a good relationship, avoiding conflict
(b)   Make supplier evaluation a continuing process to obtain early warning of potential problems
(c)   Have a contingency plan to migrate to another supplier
(d)   Maintain an escrow agreement

7.6.1 Escrow agreements

An escrow agreement involves placing the source code of a computer programme into secure storage with a third party agent. The source code is released to the organisation that has purchased the software licence (the licensee) if the developer is no longer able to continue to operate and maintain the software, for example due to bankruptcy. In effect, an escrow agreement can form an important part of the risk mitigation strategies in relation to information technology contracts and software licenses.

Escrow agreements are best suited to bespoke or business critical software which cannot be easily replicated or replaced, and the source code and associated intellectual property rights cannot be purchased as part of the overall software purchase.

An escrow agreement provides the licensee with a contingency plan, meaning that they can continue to operate the software, should anything happen to the developers. An escrow agreement is also beneficial to the developers as it allows them to avoid passing on 'trade secrets' to the users of the software, therefore preventing it being replicated.

However, before entering into an escrow agreement, the licensee must ensure that the escrow provider is capable of transferring the software and all customer data to its backup system. Access to the source code may not translate to access to a fully operational system. For example, the materials placed in escrow should include not only the source code itself, but also any supporting documentation and any associated software development tools. In other words, the escrow package needs to contain sufficient material to enable the licensee to have everything it needs to maintain and operate the software upon release of the software package.

Chapter Roundup

- Organisations should be structured around processes rather than functions. This means that the hierarchy of management objectives and performance measures will be similarly structured. Process improvement becomes part of every manager's task.

- Harmon describes four **basic redesign patterns**:

  (a) **Re-engineering** starts with a clean sheet of paper.
  (b) **Simplification** eliminates redundant process elements.
  (c) **Value-added analysis** eliminates activities that do not add value.
  (d) **Gaps and disconnects** target problems at departmental boundaries.

  The feasibility of any proposed redesign must be considered.

- ERP systems are based on limited, standardised modules. This means that the organisation must adapt to the standard system, rather than designing its own most appropriate and efficient process. However, the alternative, adapting a standard package to local requirements, destroys the advantages of purchasing the standard package and introduces further complications. Nevertheless, packages have their own disadvantages.

- The first phase of any IS project is likely to be the collection of information. There are seven techniques.

  - Interviews
  - Questionnaires
  - Written questions
  - Observation
  - Protocol analysis
  - Workshops
  - Prototyping

  Each technique has its advantages and disadvantages, so it will be normal to use a combination of them.

- Software packages may be assessed against ten high-level requirement categories, each of which is made up of more detailed specific requirements. Not all high-level categories will receive the same weighting.

  Imperatives are non-negotiable, absolute requirements and must be established very early on in the project.

- Skidmore and Eva suggest that once the evaluation requirements have been set, the process of selecting a package may be thought of as falling into five phases.

  - Obtaining tenders
  - First pass selection
  - Second pass selection
  - Implementation
  - The long-term relationship

1   What are the three conditions that value adding activities satisfy?

2   What are the four basic redesign patterns Harmon describes?

3   List three disadvantages of using bought software packages rather than developing in-house software

4   What are the seven techniques for information gathering to establish software requirements?

5   In the context of assessing software packages, what are imperatives?

Answers to Quick Quiz

1   The customer is willing to pay for the output; the process changes the output in some way; the process is performed correctly at the first attempt

2   Re-engineering; simplification; value-added analysis; gaps and disconnects

3   Possible answers:

 –   Property rights over the software reside with the supplier, so the supplier controls any future developments and the support available to maintain the software

 –   The financial stability and survival of the supplier is not guaranteed

 –   Competitive advantage cannot be obtained by an organisation if standard software packages are also available to, and used by, its competitors

 –   Inadequate performance due to restricted functionality or a lack of tutoring

 –   Changing user requirements can erode a package's functionality

4   Interviews; questionnaires; written questions; observations; protocol analysis; workshops; prototyping

5   Imperatives are non-negotiable, absolute requirements that software packages must satisfy. Any packages which do not satisfy these requirements will be rejected from further consideration

Now try the question below from the Practice Question Bank

Number	Level	Marks	Time
Q11	Examination	25	45 mins

Information technology

11

E-business

Topic list	Syllabus reference
1 Principles of e-business	E2(a), (b)
2 Organisations and their customers	E2(c), (d)
3 Hardware and software infrastructure and controls	E1(a)-(d)
4 Big Data	C1 (e)
5 IT and strategy	E2 (c), (d)
6 Supply chain management	E3(a)–(d)
7 E-procurement	E3(e), (f)

Introduction

Your syllabus includes an extensive section on information technology and e-business. This is a relatively new, rapidly expanding and fundamentally important aspect of strategic implementation. Indeed, in many organisations, it may be regarded as a fundamental aspect of strategy and certainly of the business model. In this chapter and the next, we will consider this vital new area of business.

Study guide

		Intellectual level
C1	**Organising and enabling success**	
(e)	Discuss how big data can be used to inform and implement business strategy	2
E1	**Principles of information technology**	
(a)	Advise on the basic hardware and software infrastructure required to support business information systems	2
(b)	Identify and analyse the general information technology controls and application controls required for effective accounting information systems	2
(c)	Analyse the adequacy of general information technology controls and application controls for relevant application systems	3
(d)	Evaluate controls over the safeguarding of information technology assets to ensure the organisational ability to meet business objectives	3
E2	**Principles of e-business**	
(a)	Discuss the meaning and scope of e-business	2
(b)	Advise on the reasons for the adoption of e-business and recognise barriers to its adoption	3
(c)	Evaluate how e-business changes the relationships between organisations and their customers	3
(d)	Discuss and evaluate the main business and marketplace models for delivering e-business	3
E3	**E-business application: upstream supply chain management**	
(a)	Analyse the main elements of both the push and pull models of the supply chain	2
(b)	Discuss the relationship of the supply chain to the value chain and the value network	2
(c)	Assess the potential application of information technology to support and restructure the supply chain	3
(d)	Advise on how external relationships with suppliers and distributors can be structured to deliver a restructured supply chain	3
(e)	Discuss the methods, benefits and risks of e-procurement	2
(f)	Assess different options and models for implementing e-procurement	2

Exam guide

We would expect aspects of e-business to be relevant to many questions, both in Section A of your exam and in Section B. Think back to the relational diagram of the main syllabus capabilities: information technology is in the middle tier, and so you should be asking yourself how it affects business strategy (the top tier). At one level, you need to consider how the proper co-ordination and alignment of IT systems is essential to support strategic implementation; but at another level, you also need to consider how IT can shape that strategy itself – through e-business and e-commerce.

We would expect that from time to time, there might be complete questions linked directly to e-business and e-marketing.

Models and frameworks

The Study Guide refers, in general terms, to business and marketplace models for delivering e-business, and to push and pull models of the supply chain. Therefore, a good general understanding of these models could be required in a question.

1 Principles of e-business   12/10

1.1 E-business – meaning and scope

Electronic business, or e-business, is the automation of business processes of all types through electronic means. This may be restricted to email or may extend to a fully-featured website or an e-marketplace. E-business that includes a financial transaction is known as e-commerce. E-business is radically different from ordinary business and brings six categories of benefit.

- Costs are reduced.
- Capability is increased.
- Communications are improved.
- Control is enhanced.
- Customer service is improved.
- Competitive advantage may be achieved, depending on competitors' reactions.

Adoption of e-business methods may be hindered by a range of obstacles, including lack of skills; lack of internet use and awareness among businesses and the wider population; and fears about privacy, effectiveness, cost, security and so on.

Key term

E-business has been defined by IBM as 'the transformation of key business processes through the use of internet technologies'.

E-business processes include not only online marketing and sales, but supply-chain and channel management; manufacturing and inventory control; financial operations; and employee workflow procedures across an entire organisation. Essentially, e-business technologies empower customers, employees, suppliers, distributors, vendors and partners by giving them powerful tools for information management and communications.

There are **different levels of e-business**; some businesses do not need a website but deal all day with other businesses and customers online via email and an e-marketplace. Other businesses have a website that helps them sell their products all around the world. It is up to each business to determine what level of e-business is right for it.

E-business is often confused with **e-commerce**.

(a)   Any transaction with an electronic process using internet technologies is **e-business**.

(b)   If there is a **financial transaction** involved with the electronic process using internet technologies, it is **e-commerce**. For example, buying a book on Amazon.com is both e-commerce and e-business. Creating a map with directions from your office to the post office on Yahoo.com is e-business (no e-commerce is involved).

E-commerce has many aspects.

(a)   Electronic ordering of goods and services that are delivered using traditional channels such as post or couriers (indirect electronic commerce)

(b)   Online ordering, payment and delivery of intangible goods and services such as software, electronic magazines, entertainment services and information services (direct electronic commerce)

(c)   Electronic fund transfers (EFT)

(d)   Electronic share trading

(e)   Commercial auctions

(f)   Direct consumer marketing and after-sales service

There are several features of e-business and the internet that make it radically different from what has gone before.

(a)   It **challenges traditional business models** because, for example, it enables suppliers to interact directly with their customers, instead of using intermediaries such as retail shops, travel agents, insurance brokers, and conventional banks.

(b)   Although the internet is global in its operation, its benefits are not confined to large (or global) organisations. **Small companies** can move instantly into a global market place, either on their own initiative or as part of a **consumer portal**.

(c)   It offers a **new economics of information** because, with the internet, much information is free of charge to the user. Those with internet access can view many of the world's major newspapers and periodicals without charge.

(d)   It supplies an almost incredible **level of speed** of communication, giving virtually instant access to organisations, plus the capacity to complete purchasing transactions within seconds.

(e)   It has created **new and cheaper networks of communication** – between organisations and their customers (either individually or collectively), between customers themselves (through mutual support groups), and between organisations and their suppliers.

(f)   It stimulates the appearance of **new intermediaries** and the disappearance of some existing ones. Businesses are finding that they can cut out the middle man, with electronic banking, insurance, publishing and printing as primary examples.

(g)   It has led to **new business partnerships** through which small enterprises can gain access to customers on a scale which would have been viewed as impossible a few years ago.

(h)   Work is becoming **independent of location**. Clerical, administrative and knowledge work can be done at any location. This can reduce establishment and travelling costs, especially if people work at home, but the loss of personal interaction can affect **motivation** and **job satisfaction**.

(i)   The **nature of work** is changing, since increased quantities of available data and more powerful methods of accessing and analysing it mean that greater attention can be paid to **customising product offerings to more precisely defined target segments**.

1.2 Adopting e-business

Driven by competitive pressures, companies are employing e-business for a variety of purposes.

(a)   **Increase revenues** through optimal customer and partner management.

(b)   **Reduce costs** through automated sales, administration and service activities.

(c)   Enable greater **channel efficiency** and effectiveness: efficiency benefits arise from improved communication using email and other internet technologies and effectiveness benefits obtain from the ability to gather information.

(d)   Gain **visibility.**

(e)   **Control and automate** customer and partner-facing operations.

The e-business **adoption pyramid** illustrates the order in which e-business facilities tend to be adopted.

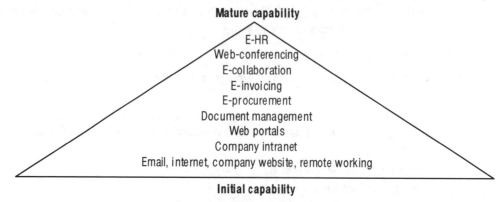

The e-business adoption pyramid

Most businesses start with the key e-business facilities of email, internet and company websites and in addition, many also have remote working facilities. These facilities seem to constitute the key communication tools essential for businesses in the present technological environment.

Benefits of e-business

(a) **Cost reduction** – in procurement and reduced headcount needed to handle consumer and business enquiries. Cost of sales and promotion may be reduced and lower prices passed on to customers.

(b) **Capability** – may be able to increase penetration in new countries and may help reduce the amount of goods stored.

(c) **Communication** – to customers can be improved with updates of product or service information.

(d) **Control** – the website can be used to monitor interest in product or service from customers.

(e) **Customer service** – many basic enquiries about products can be dealt with on the website. Opening times (for stores or offices) and special offers can be promoted. This may reduce the number of phone enquiries. Business customers can use the e-commerce system to track delivery and manage inventory better through reducing time for ordering.

(f) **Competitive advantage** – will be dependent on the use of e-commerce by competitors.

1.3 Barriers to e-business and e-commerce adoption

Barriers (also referred to as obstacles, impediments or hindrances) to e-business adoption work differently according to perception, country, economic issues, technology, culture, law and ethics, and organisational type.

The barriers to e-business appear greater to organisations with just a few employees. They use **three arguments**:

- E-business is not relevant to them.
- Staff do not have the required skills and knowledge.
- Their customers do not use e-business.

1.3.1 Other barriers

(a) **Country** – successful e-business depends on a critical mass of internet users, which has not been reached in many countries. Also, the combination of connection and usage charges tends to inhibit the uptake of the internet in many countries and, by extension, reduces e-commerce activity. Obviously, as more people go online and charges become competitive, the value of the whole network and the opportunities for e-business will increase tremendously and this initial barrier will be overcome.

(b) **Economic issues** – much of the consumer world still pays cash, rather than taking credit. The lack of ability or interest in credit transactions is an enormous barrier to e-commerce. Also, the issue of transaction security over the internet is of concern to many consumers.

(c) **Culture** – different languages and cultural platforms compound the complexity of doing e-business overseas. Cultural features such as risk aversion, attitudes to privacy and lifestyle differences may affect internet usage. The use of Hofstede's cultural dimensions can help e-businesses to understand their customers better. For example, cultures rating high on **uncertainty avoidance** and low on **individualism** are likely to be difficult markets for introducing consumer e-business.

(d) **Organisational type** – surveys of sectors such as retail, tourism and manufacturing have identified a number of major concerns including: privacy, trust, uncertainty of financial returns and lack of reliable measurement, fraud, lack of support and system maintenance. For small and medium-sized enterprises, there is a wide range of barriers:

(i) Cost of implementation
(ii) Need for immediate return on investment
(iii) Complexity of technologies like electronic data interchange (EDI) which could require new skills
(iv) Lack of organisational readiness, with many small and medium-sized enterprises having limited existing IT resources
(v) Lack of perceived benefits
(vi) Lack of assertiveness by the owner/manager
(vii) Security, including confidentiality and fraud

2 Organisations and their customers

FAST FORWARD

> Both businesses and customers can originate e-commerce activity; thus there are four main categories: B2B, B2C, C2B and C2C. **Channel structures** are the means by which products and services are delivered to customers. **Disintermediation** removes intermediaries from supply channels while **reintermediation** establishes new ones. **Countermediation** is the creation of a new intermediary by an established company to compete via a business with established intermediaries.

2.1 Varieties of e-commerce

Exam focus point

An article titled 'E-commerce' (2005) written by Jim Stone is available in the technical articles section for P3 on the ACCA website. It would be worth taking the time to study this article.

E-commerce can be divided into four main categories:

- B2B (Business-to-Business)
- B2C (Business-to-Consumer)
- C2B (Consumer-to-Business)
- C2C (Consumer-to-Consumer)

B2B (Business-to-Business) – involves companies doing business with each other, as when manufacturers sell to distributors and wholesalers sell to retailers. Pricing is based on quantity of order and is often negotiable.

Case Study   **Alibaba**

Alibaba, which operates predominantly in China, is the world's largest e-commerce company. According to the company's website, its mission is to 'make it easy to do business anywhere'. Alibaba was set up in 1999 by a Chinese English teacher (Jack Ma), with the aim of helping small Chinese businesses trade globally. As Linda Yueh, the BBC's chief business correspondent explains, Alibaba is effectively a 'combination of eBay and Amazon. It is an online company with multiple revenue streams that are more conventional than a social network site. Alibaba.com is a B2B, or business-to-business, website. It links up businesses around the world looking for suppliers. For instance, they link wholesalers to distributors around the world, from the UK to China to the US'. Businesses can trade almost anything from olive oil to computer components.

Adapted from two online sources:

1) 'Company overview' published on the *Alibaba* website: www.alibabagroup.com/en/about/overview

2) 'Alibaba: The next Facebook?' by Linda Yueh (June 2013) published on the *bbc* website; www.bbc.co.uk

B2C (Business-to-Consumer) – involves businesses selling to the general public, typically through catalogues with **shopping cart software**.

C2B (Consumer-to-Business) – a consumer posts their project with a set budget online and within hours, companies review the consumer's requirements and bid on the project. The consumer reviews the bids and selects the company that will complete the project.

C2C (Consumer-to-Consumer) – an excellent example of this is found at eBay, where consumers sell their goods and services to other consumers. Another technology that has emerged to support C2C activities is that of the payment intermediary PayPal. Instead of purchasing items directly from an unknown, untrusted seller, the buyer can instead send the money to PayPal, who forward it to the vendor's account.

The transaction alternatives between businesses and consumers are shown in the matrix below:

Delivery by

		Business	Consumer
Exchange initiated by	Business	B2B Business models eg BPP.com	B2C Business models eg Amazon.com
	Consumer	C2B Business models eg Priceline.com	C2C Business models eg eBay.com

Varieties of e-commerce

Companies using internal networks to offer their employees products and services online (but not necessarily via the internet) are engaging in **B2E** (Business-to-Employee) e-commerce.

Other forms of e-commerce that involve transactions with the government include:

- **G2G** (Government-to-Government)
- **G2E** (Government-to-Employee)
- **G2B** (Government-to-Business)
- **B2G** (Business-to-Government)
- **G2C** (Government-to-Citizen)
- **C2G** (Citizen-to-Government)

B2M (Business to Machine) is another emerging area within e-commerce. The general idea is that companies can link to **remote machines** via the internet. For example, with this technology, owners of vending machines know exactly how much inventory is in each machine and their accounting system produces a restocking report advising the delivery driver accordingly. In this manner, companies can monitor their machines remotely to determine if they need repairing or restocking. This information is then used to schedule efficient delivery before the inventory runs out.

2.2 Market place channel structures

Channel structures are the means by which a manufacturer or selling organisation delivers products and services to its customers. The simplest channel structure is **direct**: the business deals directly with the customer without the assistance of any **intermediaries**. The more complex the channel structure, the more intermediaries (wholesalers and/or retailers) are used in the supply chain. Intermediaries offer a wide range of services and facilities: they include agents, traders, brokers, dealers, wholesalers/distributors and providers of specialised information.

The main changes to channel structures facilitated through the internet include **disintermediation** (direct selling), **reintermediation** (new intermediaries) and **countermediation** (the creation of a new intermediary by an established company).

2.2.1 Disintermediation

Disintermediation is the removal of intermediaries in a supply chain that formerly linked a company to its customers. Instead of going through traditional distribution channels, with intermediaries such as a distributor, wholesaler, broker or agent, companies may now deal with every customer directly via the internet. Dell computers have taken this option and removed any intermediaries from their downstream supply chain (between them and their customers).

2.2.2 Examples

You can already bypass publishers to get a book printed at tiny cost through self-publishing sites such as Lulu.com. Gambling is being changed by online sites arranging bets directly between individuals, not through bookmakers, with Betfair being a market leader in this respect. In the UK, voice communication is being revolutionised by enabling people to use free internet telephony systems such as Skype, rather than BT. Even benevolent intermediaries such as libraries may be under threat if all reference books are scanned by Google and made available to everyone.

Disintermediation may be initiated by **consumers** because they are aware of **supply prices** direct from the manufacturer or wholesaler. Alternatively, it may be instigated by the author or creator of a work, such as Stephen King selling his books directly to the public. There are also third party aggregators or buyer's clubs that link consumers with producers to obtain lower prices.

Reverse auction sites that allow consumers to specify an item they wish to purchase, allowing producers and others to bid on the item.

Traditional value chain in publishing

| Author | → | Publisher | → | Wholesaler | → | Retailer | → | Customer |

E-market value chain – Amazon

| Author | → | Publisher | → | Wholesaler | → | Retailer | → | Customer |

(with Retailer branching above from Wholesaler to Customer)

E-market value chain – the print on-demand paradigm

| Author | → | Publisher | → | Wholesaler | → | Retailer | → | Customer |

(with Author linking directly to Customer)

2.2.3 Reintermediation

Reintermediation is the establishment of new intermediary roles for traditional intermediaries that were disintermediated. In some cases, a new element of a supply chain simply replaces a single displaced element, such as Amazon.com replacing retailers. In other cases, a reintermediating entity replaces multiple supply chain elements. These new intermediaries do one of two things.

(a) Provide customers with **new, important value-added services** not provided in the new direct customer-supplier relationship. An example is Kelkoo, which is a shopping/price comparison search engine.

(b) Provide customers with **more efficient means** of transacting business.

The ever-increasing number of 'hubs', 'portals', 'aggregators', 'clearing houses' and 'exchanges' shows that entirely new ways of doing business are being created. Those organisations (or individuals) clever enough to recognise the opportunities provided by the web are reinventing themselves as 'cybermediaries' or 'infomediaries' – intermediaries offering value-added services to consumers and vendors over the internet.

2.2.4 New types of intermediary

Search engines and directories. Search engines such as Google provide search facilities based on data generated by software engines that search the web. Directories such as Yahoo provide a general index of a large variety of different sites.

Search agents (Search bots) gather material from other sites. For example, Shopbot searches across online shops.

Portals provide a gateway to the web and may also offer **signposting**, selected **links** and other services to attract users. Internet Service Provider's (ISP) home pages such as www.aol.com are an example of portals, and the large ISPs offer a wide range of added value services. Variations on the portal as a gateway are: a horizontal portal or user customised gateway (eg my Yahoo); a vertical portal or special interest portal, eg CNET – a portal for users interested in developments in IT; and an enterprise information portal, which is an organisation's home page for employees, including corporate info and selected links.

'E-tailers' or consumer shopping sites such as Amazon. While starting out as simply a bookshop on the web, it has added a variety of products and types of services. By contrast, Tesco is an offline retailer which is offering web-based order and delivery services.

Malls are sites that group together different online stores as tenants. An example is the Scottish Shopping Mall (www.scottish-retailer.com). Malls provide cyber-infrastructure, but do not own inventory or sell products directly.

Auction sites such as eBay support online auctions.

Publisher websites are traffic generators that offer content of interest to consumers.

Virtual resellers are intermediaries that exist to sell to consumers. They are able to obtain products directly from manufacturers, who may hesitate to go directly to consumers for fear of **alienating retailers** upon which they still largely depend.

Website evaluators direct consumers to a producer's site via a new type of site that offers some form of evaluation, which may help to reduce some of the risk.

Forums, **fan clubs**, and **user groups** can play a large role in facilitating customer-producer feedback and supporting market research.

Financial intermediaries. Any form of e-commerce will require some means of making or authorising payments from buyer to seller.

2.2.5 Countermediation

Countermediation is the creation of a new intermediary by an established company in order to compete via e-business with established intermediaries. Examples include B&Q setting up diy.com to help people who want to do their own DIY, and Opodo.com which has been set up by a collaboration of nine European airlines. Tescodiets.com, which the established food retailer Tesco bought from eDiets, is another example of a countermediation strategy. Countermediation also refers to possible partnerships with another independent intermediary, eg mortgage broker Charcol and Orange, which was Freeserve.

2.2.6 Examples

Airlines. The impact of the internet is seen clearly in the transportation industry. Airlines now have a more effective way of bypassing intermediaries (ie travel agents) because they can give their customers immediate access to flight reservation systems. EasyJet was the first airline to have over half of its bookings made online.

Travel agents. The internet has also produced a new set of online travel agents who have lower costs because of their ability to operate without a high street branch network. Their low-cost structure makes them a particularly good choice for selling low margin, cheap tickets for flights, package holidays, cruises and so forth.

In 2004, British Airways stopped paying commission to travel agents for flight bookings, intending to move to an entirely internet-based system for bookings. In 2005, the European industry saw significant consolidation when Sabre Holdings, the US owner of Travelocity, bought Lastminute.com.

Tesco has operated on the internet since 1994 and is the UK's largest internet grocery business. In 2000, it formally launched its Tesco.com site. In addition to its online grocery business, Tesco has also established Tesco Direct as its online marketplace for electrical appliances, home furnishings and other non-grocery products.

Financial services. The impact of the internet is especially profound in the field of financial services. New intermediaries enable prospective customers to compare the interest rates and prices charged by different organisations for pensions, mortgages and other financial products. This means that the delivering companies are **losing control of the marketing** of their services, and there is a **downward pressure on prices**, especially for services which can legitimately be seen as mere commodities (eg house and contents insurance).

2.3 Business models for e-commerce

FAST FORWARD

Rappa describes nine business models. E-commerce business models may also be categorised by characteristics such as value proposition, revenue model and market opportunity.

Rappa classified nine generic business models:

1	**Brokerage model**	Those that bring buyers and sellers together and facilitate transactions (often fee based)
2	**Advertising model**	Supported by advertising revenue, a website will provide content and services together with advertising (eg banner ads)
3	**Infomediary model**	Collecting data about consumers and their purchasing habits and selling this information to other businesses
4	**Merchant model**	Selling of goods and services on the traditional retail model
5	**Manufacturer model**	Direct selling by the creator of a product or service to consumers, cutting out intermediaries
6	**Affiliate model**	Offering financial incentives to affiliated partner sites
7	**Community model**	Where users themselves invest in a site, eg by the contribution of content, money or time. This can be combined with other models, eg advertising or subscription
8	**Subscription model**	Where consumers (users) pay for access to the site, usually for high added-value content, eg financial information, newspapers, journals
9	**Utility model**	A model based on metered usage or pay-as-you-go

Other ways of categorising an e-commerce business model

(a)   **Value proposition** defines how a company's product or service fulfils the need of customers.

(b)   **Revenue model** describes how the firm will earn revenue, produce profits, and produce a superior return on invested capital. The five primary revenue models are advertising, subscription, transaction fee, sales and the affiliate revenue model.

(c)   **Market opportunity** refers to the company's intended **market space** and the overall potential financial opportunities available to the firm in that market space.

(d)   **Competitive environment** refers to the other companies operating in the same market space selling similar products.

(e)   **Competitive advantage** is achieved by the firm when it can produce a superior product and/or bring the product to market at a lower price than most, or all, of its competitors.

(f)   **Market strategy** is the plan that details exactly how the organisation intends to enter a new market and attract new customers.

(g)   **Organisational development** describes how the company will organise the work to be accomplished.

(h)   **Management team**: employees of the company responsible for making the business model work.

3 Hardware and software infrastructure and controls

System architecture is the arrangement of software, machinery and tasks in an information system needed to achieve a specific functionality.

The **internet** enables computers across the world to communicate via telecommunications links.

The **World Wide Web** is a navigation system within the internet. It is based on a technology called **hypertext** which allows documents stored on host computers on the internet to be linked to one another.

An **intranet** is used to disseminate and exchange information 'in-house' within an organisation.

An **extranet** is used to communicate with selected people outside the organisation.

In general, all of the machines on the internet can be categorised into two types: servers and clients. The machines that provide services to other machines are servers; and the machines that are used to connect to those services are clients.

Each machine on the internet is assigned a unique address called an IP address.

There are several levels to the interaction between a client and a server, from the physical pieces of wire making the connection, through the transfer and checking of data, security problems of access and logging on, to the final presentation to and interaction with the user. The International Standards Organisation (ISO) has defined seven levels in a standard called Open Systems Interconnection (ISO).

A **protocol stack** is a group of protocols that all work together to allow software or hardware to perform a function. The TCP/IP protocol stack is a good example. It uses four layers that map to the OSI model.

Alternatives to PC-based internet access include interactive digital television and wireless or mobile access.

Tutorial note

Section 3 of this chapter covers some fairly technical material about hardware and software. You will not be examined specifically on this, so you do not need a detailed knowledge of it. However, you need to be aware of the underlying ideas to appreciate that an organisation must have a suitable IT infrastructure to support its strategy.

Also, remember that information systems and information technology can play an important role in allowing organisations to achieve their strategic objectives overall.

PER Performance Objective 6 recognises this, and indicates that candidates should be able to demonstrate how software packages used in the workplace help to support their own work objectives. As ACCA highlight, this may include 'using technology to gather and present information, calculate and interpret data and to communicate with others'.

Technology plays a central role in virtually every finance team, and professional accountants need to recognise the importance of technology for handling information and supporting business.

3.1 E-commerce infrastructure

Many technologies must be integrated for supporting e-business:

- PC
- Modem
- Routers
- Servers
- Email
- Internet and web protocols
- Web connectivity software
- Database management software
- Shopping cart software
- Shipment tracking software

System architecture is the arrangement of software, machinery and tasks in an information system needed to achieve a specific **functionality**.

The table below shows how the different components of the e-business infrastructure relate to each other. They can be shown as different layers with defined interfaces between each layer.

E-business architecture	Infrastructure	Players
E-business services – application layer	E-commerce software systems Customer Relationship Management system Performance enhancement Supply chain management, data mining and content management systems	Microsoft, IBM, Ariba, BroadVision Peoplesoft, Siebel Akamai
Systems software layer	Web browser, operating systems, server software and standards, networking software and database management systems Encryption software	Microsoft, Sun, Linux Oracle, Sybase, IBM, Microsoft. Verisign, Checkpoint
Transport or network layer	Web servers. Physical network – routers and transport standards (TCP/IP)	IBM, Dell, Sun Cisco, Lucent
Storage/physical layer	Permanent magnetic storage on web servers. Optical back-up. Temporary storage in RAM	
Content and data layer	Web content for internet, intranet and extranet sites. Customers' data. Transactions data. Payment systems Streaming media solutions Hosting services	PayPal, Microsoft, Real Networks, Apple IBM, WebIntellects

The **application layer** uses business rules to determine pricing based on various discount strategies for different types of customers.

The **data layer** retrieves basic price and product description information from a company-wide database.

3.2 The internet

The **internet** enables computers across the world to communicate via telecommunications links. Information can be exchanged through email or through accessing and entering data via a **website**: a collection of screens providing information in text and graphic form, any of which can be viewed by clicking the appropriate link (shown as a button, word or icon) on the screen.

The **World Wide Web** is a navigation system within the internet. It is based on a technology called **hypertext** which allows documents stored on host computers on the internet to be linked to one another. When you view a document that contains **hypertext links**, you can view any of the connected documents or pages simply by clicking on a link. The web is the most powerful, flexible and fastest growing information and navigation service on the internet. In order to 'surf' or navigate the web, users need a **web browser** that interprets and displays hypertext documents and locates documents pointed to by links. Internet Explorer is the browser from Microsoft: alternatives include Mozilla Firefox and Enigma.

Access to the internet will become easier and easier. Most new PCs now come pre-loaded with the necessary software, and cheaper internet devices are beginning to reach the market: Microsoft and America Online (AOL), among others, have been exploring inexpensive 'set-top' TV/internet connections. Developments in telecom networks are already rendering modems unnecessary. Personal digital assistants (PDAs) wireless internet-compatible cellular phones and wireless laptop connections (such as Apple's 'air port') allow users to surf the web and send and receive email from almost any location, without cords or cables.

While we tend to use the terms internet and World Wide Web interchangeably, the internet describes the entire system of networked computers and the World Wide Web describes the method used to access information contained on computers connected to the internet. The availability of a common internet infrastructure – of computers, networks and protocols – and the development of an easy to use **graphical user interface** (GUI) have been the catalysts for the growth of e-commerce. It has created an open community that is easy to join and easy to use.

Most large communications companies have their own dedicated **communication backbones** connecting various regions. In each region, the company has a Point of Presence (POP). The POP is a place for local users to access the company's network, often through a local phone number or dedicated line. There is no overall controlling network. Instead, there are several high-level networks connecting to each other through Network Access Points or NAPs.

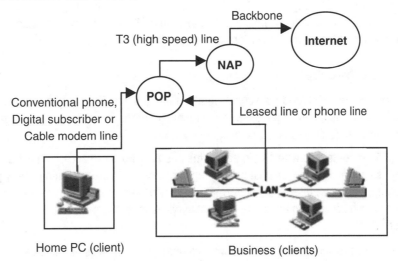

Physical and network infrastructure components of the internet.

3.3 Intranets and extranets

'Inter' means 'between': 'intra' means 'within'; ''extra' means 'outside'. This may be a useful reminder of some of the inter-related terminology in this area.

(a)   The **internet** is used to disseminate and exchange information among the public at large.

(b)   An **intranet** is used to disseminate and exchange information 'in-house' within an organisation. Only employees are able to access this information.

(c)   An **extranet** is used to communicate with selected people outside the organisation.

3.3.1 Intranets

An **intranet** is an internal network used to share information. Intranets utilise internet technology and protocols. The **firewall** surrounding an intranet fends off unauthorised access.

The idea behind an intranet is that companies set up their own mini version of the internet. Each employee has a browser, used to access a server computer that holds corporate information on a wide variety of topics, and in some cases, also offers access to the internet.

Potential applications include company newspapers, induction material, online procedure and policy manuals, employee web pages where individuals post details of their activities and progress, and internal databases of the corporate information store.

Intranets are used for many purposes:

(a)   **Performance data:** linked to sales, inventory, job progress and other database and reporting systems, enabling employees to process and analyse data to fulfil their work objectives.

(b)   **Employment information:** online policy and procedures manuals (health and safety, disciplinary and grievance), training and induction material, internal contacts for help and information.

(c) **Employee support/information:** advice on first aid, healthy working at computer terminals, training courses offered and resources held in the corporate library and so on.

(d) **Notice boards** for the posting of messages to and from employees: notice of meetings, events, trade union activities.

(e) **Departmental home pages:** information and news about each department's personnel and activities to aid identification and cross-functional understanding.

(f) **Bulletins or newsletters:** details of product launches and marketing campaigns, staff moves, changes in company policy, links to relevant databases or departmental home pages.

(g) **Email** facilities for the exchange of messages between employees in different locations.

(h) **Upward communication:** suggestion schemes, feedback, questionnaires.

A **firewall** is a security device that effectively isolates the sensitive parts of an organisation's system from those areas available to external users. It examines all requests and messages entering and exiting the intranet and blocks any not conforming to specified criteria.

3.3.2 Extranets

Extranets are web based but serve a combination of users. Whereas an intranet resides behind a **firewall** and is accessible only to people who are members of the same company or organisation, an **extranet** provides various levels of accessibility to **outsiders**.

Only those outsiders with a valid **username** and **password** can access an extranet: varying levels of access rights enable control over what people can view. Extranets are becoming a very popular means for business partners to exchange information. They can share data or systems to provide smoother transaction processing and more efficient services for customers. An extranet may be used for a variety of purposes:

(a) To provide a pooled service which a number of business partners can access and exchange **news** which is of use to partner companies and clients

(b) To share **training** or **development resources**

(c) To publicise loyalty schemes, sponsorships, exhibition attendance information and other **promotional tools**

(d) To exchange potentially large volumes of **transaction data** efficiently

(e) To provide **online presentations** to business partners and prospects

The basic components of an extranet are an internet connection which goes via a **router**, an HTTP server, a firewall and the essential data and files. All the infrastructure and applications can sit inside the firewall or outside in a secure area called a demilitarised zone (DMZ). An organisation could connect its browser based purchase order system to the product catalogue database on a supplier's intranet (see diagram below).

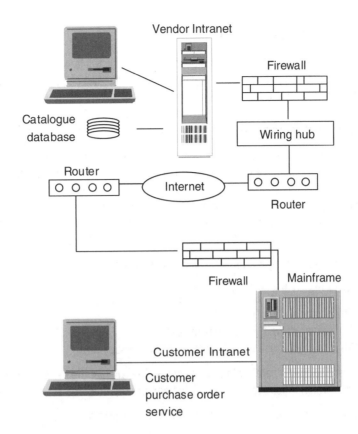

3.4 Electronic mail

The term **electronic mail** is used to describe various systems for sending data or messages electronically via a telephone or data network and a central server computer. Email has replaced letters, memos, faxes, documents and even telephone calls, combining many of the possibilities of each medium with new advantages of speed, cost and convenience. Messages are written and read in a special program such as Microsoft Outlook (for an individual) or part of a groupware package such as Microsoft Exchange or Novell, if used in a large company. This software has convenient features such as: message copying (to multiple recipients); integration with an address book (database of contacts); automatic alert messages sent when the target recipient is unable to access his or her email immediately, with alternative contact details; stationery and template features, allowing corporate identity to be applied; facilities for mail organisation and filing.

Some websites, eg Hotmail and Yahoo provide free email facilities and only require a web browser.

3.5 Client/server architecture

In general, all of the machines on the internet can be categorised into two types: servers and clients. The machines that provide services to other machines are **servers;** and the machines that are used to connect to those services are **clients.** It is possible and common for a machine to be both a server and a client, but for our purposes here, you can think of most machines as one or the other.

A server machine may provide one or more services on the internet. For example, a server machine might have software running on it that allows it to act as a web server, an email server and a file transfer protocol (FTP) server. Clients that come to a server machine do so with a specific intent, so clients direct their requests to a specific software application running on the overall server machine. For example, if you are running a web browser on your machine, it will most likely want to talk to the web server application on the server machine; your Telnet application will want to talk to the Telnet server and your email application will talk to the email server.

3.5.1 Internet protocol (IP)

To keep all of these machines straight, each machine on the internet is assigned a unique address called an IP address. A server has a static IP address that does not change very often. A home machine that is dialling up through a modem often has an IP address that is assigned by the ISP when the machine dials in. That IP address is unique for that session – it may be different the next time the machine dials in. This way, an ISP only needs one IP address for each modem it supports, rather than one for each customer.

As far as the internet's machines are concerned, an IP address is all you need to talk to a server but because most people have trouble remembering the strings of numbers that make up an IP addresses, and because IP addresses sometimes need to change, all servers on the internet also have human-readable names, called domain names. For example, www.amazon.com is a permanent, human-readable name. It is easier for most of us to remember than it is to remember 72.21.203.1; you can type the URL http://72.21.203.1 and arrive at the machine that contains the web server for Amazon's home page.

When you type a URL into a browser, the following steps occur.

The browser breaks the URL into three parts:

* The protocol ('http')
* The server name ('www.amazon.com')
* The file name (where applicable, eg gp/homepage.html)

The browser communicates with a name server to translate the server name, 'www.amazon.com', into an IP address, which it uses to connect to that server machine.

The browser then forms a connection to the web server at that IP address on port 80.

Following the HTTP protocol, the browser sends a GET request to the server, asking for the file, http://www.amazon.com/gp/homepage.html'.

The server sends the HTML text for the web page to the browser.

The browser reads the HTML tags and formats the page onto your screen.

3.5.2 Open Systems Interconnection (OSI) standard

There are several levels to the interaction between a client and a server, from the physical pieces of wire making the connection, through the transfer and checking of data, security problems of access and logging on, to the final presentation to, and interaction with, the user. Each level has its own standards, and many standards encompass several levels. In an attempt to bring some order to this, the International Standards Organisation (ISO) has defined seven levels in a standard called Open Systems Interconnection (OSI). At each layer, certain things happen to the data that prepare it for the next layer. The seven layers are:

Application	Layer 7 actually interacts with the operating system or application whenever the user chooses to transfer files, read messages or perform other network-related activities
Presentation	Layer 6 takes the data provided by the Application layer and converts it into a standard format that the other layers can understand
Session	Layer 5 establishes, maintains and ends communication with the receiving device
Transport	This layer maintains flow control of data and provides for error checking and recovery of data between the devices. Flow control means that the Transport layer looks to see if data is coming from more than one application and integrates each application's data into a single stream for the physical network
Network	Layer 3 deals with the routing from one point in a network to another. It determines the way that the data will be sent to the recipient device. Logical protocols, routing and addressing are handled here
Data-link	Layer 2 defines the rules for sending and receiving information between two specific nodes on a network
Physical	This is the level of the actual hardware. It defines the physical characteristics of the network such as connections, voltage levels and timing

3.5.3 Protocol stacks

A **protocol stack** is a group of protocols that all work together to allow software or hardware to perform a function. The TCP/IP protocol stack is a good example. It uses four layers that map to the OSI model as follows:

Network Interface	Combines the Physical and Data layers and routes the data between devices on the same network. It also manages the exchange of data between the network and other devices.
Internet	Corresponds to the Network layer. The Internet Protocol (IP) uses the IP address, consisting of a Network Identifier and a Host Identifier, to determine the address of the device it is communicating with.
Transport	Corresponding to the OSI Transport layer, this is the part of the protocol stack where the Transport Control Protocol (TCP) can be found. TCP ensures that connection is maintained and that data is transferred correctly
Application	Combines the Session, Presentation and Application layers of the OSI model. Protocols for specific functions such as email (Simple Mail Transfer Protocol, SMTP) and file transfer (File Transfer Protocol, FTP) reside at this level.

As you can see, it is not necessary to develop a separate layer for each and every function outlined in the OSI Reference Model. But developers are able to ensure that a certain level of compatibility is maintained by following the general guidelines provided by the model.

3.6 Alternative internet access technologies

Alternatives to PC-based internet access include interactive digital television and wireless or mobile access.

3.6.1 Interactive digital television (iDTV)

iDTV is displayed using a digital signal delivered by a range of media including cable, satellite and terrestrial (by aerial). Consumer interactions are provided by a remote control which enables users to select different viewing options through signals sent to a set top box. From a marketing perspective, a key aspect is how the return path to the provider operates. This is required to provide interactions which involve exchange of information such as a consumer completing an online offer form in response to an interactive TV ad or a purchase transaction. For satellite or terrestrial viewers, the return path is provided by the phone line and requires a dial-up and local-call charge in the same manner as the internet. This currently acts as a barrier in comparison with cable which is an always-on, two-way connection.

3.6.2 Mobile or wireless commerce (m-commerce)

When wireless devices are used for e-commerce applications, this is referred to as mobile commerce or m-commerce.

As well as offering voice calls, mobile phones are used for email and short message service (SMS) (otherwise known as 'texting') that lets users receive and send short text messages to other mobile phones.

Mobile phone characteristics

- They can be accessed from anywhere
- Their users can be reached when they are not in their normal location
- It is not necessary to have access to a power supply or a fixed line connection
- They provide security, since each user can be identified by their unique identification code

In 1999, the first of a new generation of mobile phones, known as **Wireless Application Protocol** (WAP) phones was introduced that offered the opportunity to access information on websites specially tailored for display on the small screens of mobile phones. WAP pages are accessed using wireless techniques from a **WAP gateway** that is connected to a traditional web server where the WAP pages are hosted.

BPP LEARNING MEDIA

In 2001, new services became available on **General Packet Radio Service** (GPRS). This is approximately five times faster than GSM (Global System for Mobile Communications) and is an always-on service charged according to usage. Display is still largely text-based and based on the WAP protocol.

In 2003, the third generation (3G) of mobile phone technology became available based on **Universal Mobile Telephone System** (UMTS). UMTS is a realisation of a new generation of broadband multimedia mobile telecommunications technology with high speed data transfer enabling video calling. 3G technologies enabled network operators to offer users a wider range of more advanced services while achieving greater network capacity through improved spectral efficiency. Following the success of 3G, in 2012 4G was launched in the UK. 4G allows users to access multimedia content online faster, with download speeds comparable to a user's home broadband.

Many facilities available from a desktop PC are offered on a handheld unit. This later led to the development of smartphones and iPads, which are handheld computers integrated with mobile technology. These allow yet more advanced applications to be installed and run and they operate in much the same way as a regular computer, allowing the user instant access to facilities such as the internet, email, and mobile banking. Unlike their predecessors, the user views information on a smartphone or iPad in the same way as they would using a PC, rather than viewing cut down 'mobile' versions.

3.6.3 Wi-Fi internet access

Wireless Fidelity (Wi-Fi) is a technology that facilitates the mobile use of laptop computers and personal handheld devices away from the home or office. Wi-Fi networks are created through an array of local **hotspots** throughout metropolitan areas.

Hotspots can now be found in most major airports, hotels, bookstores, coffee houses, shopping centres, and even car dealerships.

Municipal Wi-Fi is a newer application that is gaining popularity quickly. Numerous cities across the country are partnering with ISPs such as EarthLink to build wireless networks that blanket every inch of their city.

This new technology removes the need to be near a localised hotspot and provides wireless access to all residents and businesses within the city limits, including open spaces such as parks and highways.

3.7 Information technology controls

FAST FORWARD

For an organisation's IT assets to operate effectively, it is critical that adequate control measures are in place. To help prevent theft, fraud and human error, four types of control are needed to protect IT assets.

These are:

- **Physical access controls**
- **Logical access controls**
- **Operational controls**
- **Data input controls**

Organisations may have in place a range of IT controls. These can be classified in one of four ways:

- Physical access controls
- Logical access controls
- Operational controls
- Data input controls

3.7.1 Controls over physical access

Controls over physical access are predominantly directed toward preventing unauthorised individuals gaining access to an organisation's IT and IS assets. Controls will also be aimed at stopping damage to the IT infrastructure which may occur as a result of natural hazards, eg having fire proof doors to the room where network servers are housed.

Simple controls

Relatively straightforward measures to prevent unauthorised physical access may include ensuring that doors leading to an organisation's IT systems remain locked when not in use. The practicality of such a control may be undermined if the door remains in regular use.

Locks can be combined with:

(i)   A keypad system, requiring a code to be entered
(ii)   A card entry system requiring a card to be 'swiped'

Other controls may focus on the use of personnel. Ensuring that receptionists and security guards are on duty outside of working hours may help control human access. This can be supplemented by the use of intruder alarms.

Advanced physical access controls

The best form of access control would be one which recognised individuals immediately, without the need for personnel or cards. However, biometric machines which can identify a person's fingerprints or scan the pattern of a retina are expensive, so are used only in highly sensitive industries, like defence.

 Case Study   BBC

In 2013, BiometricsUpdate.com reported that the British Broadcasting Corporation (BBC) was investigating the introduction of biometric security measures as part of a security overhaul. BBC's Head of Capital Development stated, 'Access ID is currently used – not biometrics yet, but we are looking at it. We think it will be more acceptable now, as it is used in schools and colleges.'

The BBC often have freelance workers and non employees working on the premises, and one of the issues the Head of Capital Development highlighted was how to manage a public thoroughfare which might go through a news room.

Adapted from the article:

'BBC mulls biometric access control' by Adam Vrankuli (April 2013) published on the *Biometrics Update* website; biometricsupdate.com

3.7.2 Controls over logical access

Logical access controls are aimed at ensuring that only authorised users of IT systems are provided with access to those systems. Such measures are directed towards identifying and confirming the authenticity of the user. A common mechanism in protecting computerised data is through the use of **passwords**.

Passwords can be applied to data files, program files and to parts of a program.

(a)   One password may be required to read a file, but another to write a new data to it.

(b)   The terminal user can be restricted to the use of certain files and programs (eg in a banking system, junior grades of staff are only allowed to access certain routine programs).

If the password entered matches a password issued to an authorised user, or is valid for that particular terminal, the system permits access. Otherwise, the system does not allow access, and the terminal may lock. Attempted unauthorised access should be recorded.

Keeping track of failed attempts can alert managers to repeated efforts to break into the system. In these cases, the culprits might be caught, particularly if there is an apparent pattern to their efforts.

Many of the world's leading banks now require customers visiting a branch or attempting to access online services to obtain a key code from an authentication device. This is often in addition to the use of a password prior to the system permitting user access.

3.7.3 Operational controls

Operational controls are aimed at ensuring that an organisation's day-to-day activities run effectively. Most organisations establish operational controls aimed at influencing an individual's behaviour.

Segregation of duties

Strong internal company policies often stop situations arising which lead to one individual having too much power over a particular function. This is often achieved through ensuring a segregation of duties. Ensuring a segregation of duties between staff involved in the processing of sensitive information is key in preventing instances of fraud. For example, the person dealing with processing the monthly payroll should not have responsibility for adding new employees to the payroll or authorising the monthly payment of salaries from the organisation's bank. There have been numerous cases of fraudsters adding fictitious employees to the payroll to claim additional pay.

Exam focus point

Although the syllabus focus here is on operational controls within an IT environment, many of these controls will not be constrained only to an IT context, eg segregation of duties isn't only an IT related control, as you will recall from your F8 studies.

Audit trail

In the context of IT systems and controls, an audit trail is a record showing who has accessed a computer system and what operations that individual has performed. Audit trails are useful, both for maintaining security and for recovering lost transactions. Accounting systems include an audit trail component that is able to be output as a report.

The original concept of an audit trail is to enable a manager or auditor to follow transactions stage by stage through a system to ensure that they have been processed correctly. The intention is to identify errors and detect fraud.

Modern integrated computer systems have cut out much of the time-consuming stage-by-stage working of older systems, but there should still be some means of identifying individual records; and input and output documents associated with the processing of any individual transaction.

In addition, there are separate audit trail software products that enable network administrators to monitor the use of network resources. An audit trail should be provided so that every transaction on a file contains a unique reference (eg a sales system transaction record should hold a reference to the customer order, delivery note and invoice).

3.7.4 Controls over data input

Input controls should ensure the accuracy, completeness and validity of data input into a computer system. Such controls are integrated into the software used.

Controls are likely to focus on:

- **Data verification**: This involves ensuring data entered matches source documents

- **Data validation**: Involves ensuring that data entered is not incomplete, unreasonable or duplicated, eg a system should flag and reject invoice numbers which have been duplicated when input

    Various checks can be used, depending on the data type.

    (i)   **Check digits**. A digit calculated by the program and added to the code being checked to validate it. For example, it is common to set up individual supplier accounts using accounting software. The program will assign the respective supplier a code and will only accept postings to valid codes.

    (ii)   **Control totals**. For example, a batch total totalling the entries in the batch.

    (iii) **Range checks**. Used to check the value entered against a sensible range, eg the parameters for an organisation's nominal ledger coding may require that statement of financial position

codes must be between 5000 and 9999; for example, account code 6200 may relate to inventory.

(iv) **Limit checks**. Similar to a range check, but usually based on an upper limit. For example must be less than $999,999.99. The aim is that the software should identify unreasonable input values. In the case of a small company posting, a sales invoice for $1.3m to the accounts software should be rejected.

(v) **Compatibility checks**. Ensure that two entries to the system are compatible. The value of a sales invoice posting should be compatible to the sales tax posting.

(vi) **Format check**. Only accepts postings to the system which are in the correct format; otherwise be rejected. For example, dates must be posted in a particular format, 21/11/14.

Controls over data input are aimed at ensuring the quality of the system's output, eg if the data input into a system is incorrect, then the quality of the output will be compromised, and will reduce its usefulness to managers for the purposes of control and decision-making. The focus of such mechanisms is to ensure that only valid data is accepted by the system. Data validation is likely to centre upon ensuring that data entered into a system has been posted to the correct account codes, that only acceptable values are allowed and that input data is in a suitable format.

3.8 Manual accounting process and computerised processes

FAST FORWARD

To ensure that computerised accounting systems are working effectively, it is critical that the input data is treated correctly. This requires the consideration of two key issues, firstly establishing the rules to ensure that all data input is processed in the same way; and secondly, to ensure that there is a way of assessing whether the controls are working. Controls can be reviewed through the use of 'test data'.

Exam focus point

The examining team has highlighted that those students attempting paper P3 need to understand the control implications that arise when using a computerised accounting system. An appreciation of the rules which govern how accounting entries are treated when posted to the software is essential. A question may ask you to suggest ways in which internal system controls can be improved.

Today, most organisations operate computerised accounting processes, replacing manual accounting systems.

In many ways, the use of computerised accounting systems has helped to reduce the scope for human error in the processing of data. As illustrated earlier in this section, accounting software correctly installed and set up should ensure that all data input follows a standardised set of rules to ensure that entries of the same type are treated in the same manner. For example, a good system should ensure that entries posted to the program are sent to the correct accounts, making it impossible to post a one-sided entry, ie only posting the debits and failing to post the credits.

3.8.1 Chart of accounts

Establishing the rules a system will follow is of paramount importance if it is to work effectively. When the software is first installed, a **chart of accounts** should be set up to define how each accounting transaction will be treated. The aim is to ensure that assets, liabilities, revenue and expenditure are segregated. The chart of accounts will list the different account names which will feed through to the financial statements. As mentioned in the previous section, each account name will be assigned a numeric code. When entries are posted to the system, the value will be posted to the respective code – for example, the rent and rates code. When the chart of accounts is set up it is important that consideration is given to the business's information and reporting requirements from the accounting system.

3.8.2 Controlling the chart of accounts

Once established, ensuring that there are adequate controls over the chart of accounts is critical. The organisation needs to have in place control mechanisms to ensure that new account codes are not added

or deleted by users without the approved level of authority to make such amendments. Management should conduct regular reviews of the chart (on an annual basis) to ensure that it still covers the organisation's needs.

3.8.3 Verifying the rules are working

To ensure that the accounting software posting rules are working effectively, management should conduct system tests. You should be familiar with the use of test data as a test of control from your earlier auditing studies.

Test data involves entering data (eg a sample of transactions) into an entity's computer system and comparing the results obtained with pre-determined results. Test transactions are selected from previously processed transactions or are created to test specific processing characteristics of a computer system. Test data can be used to check that controls which prevent the processing of invalid data are working in a number of ways, including:

- Entering data with non-existent customer codes
- Submitting unrealistic amounts into the system
- Posting transactions which break customer credit limits

In each case, provided the controls are working correctly such data will not be accepted.

3.9 Continuity planning and disaster recovery

Continuity planning is an umbrella term used to explain the plans and processes an organisation will follow in the event of its business operations being disrupted. **Disaster recovery** is devoted to ensuring the continuation of an organisation's IT systems in the event of some form of disaster.

Exam focus point

When a disaster occurs, safeguarding the organisation's IT assets is likely to be of critical importance for most modern businesses. The ability of the entity to respond quickly is central to ensuring the continuity of operations. It is possible that an exam question may focus on an evaluation of an entity's disaster recovery process.

3.9.1 Continuity planning

What is continuity planning?

Continuity planning focuses on ensuring the survival of an organisation and its operations in the short term. Many internal and external threats to an organisation's operations exist, which could severely affect the organisation's ability to achieve its objectives if they materialise. Events such as natural disasters and computer network failures are likely to be highly detrimental to an organisation's operations.

Continuity planning involves the creation and validation of a practised logistical plan. This plan sets out procedures to recover and restore partially or completely interrupted critical functions within a set amount of time after a disaster has occurred.

A completed business continuity planning cycle results in a formal printed manual. For a small organisation, this manual could consist of a printed document stored safely away from the organisation's main location, containing the contact details for crisis management staff, general staff, customers, suppliers, the location of offsite data back-up storage media and other vital materials. Organisations need to ensure that the underlying continuity plan is realistic and easy to follow in a crisis.

3.9.2 Disaster recovery

Disaster recovery is part of continuity planning. It is focused on the continuation of an organisation's IT infrastructure. Disaster recovery is predominantly concerned with the processes and procedures that an organisation uses to allow its IT systems to continue in operation in the event of a disaster occurring. In the event of critical functions being interrupted, a company's disaster recovery processes are directed at restoring operations within an acceptable time frame.

Why it matters

Disaster recovery is a highly important issue for most organisations, given the extensive use of computers in modern business. For those organisations which primarily trade online, having a disaster recovery plan can make the difference between survival and failure.

A disaster can occur where the system for some reason breaks down, leading to potential losses of equipment, data or funds. Disasters can be caused by events including:

- Natural disaster; fire and floods

- Man-made disasters; sabotage of IT systems by intruders or malicious attacks on an organisation's website

In the event of a computer system breakdown, a good disaster recovery plan should provide for:

(a)   Standby procedures so that some operations can be performed while normal services are disrupted
(b)   Recovery procedures once the cause of the breakdown has been discovered or corrected
(c)   Personnel management policies to ensure that (a) and (b) are implemented properly

Contents of a disaster recovery plan

The contents of a disaster recovery plan will include the following:

Section	Comment
Definition of responsibilities	It is important that somebody (a manager or co-ordinator) is designated to take control in a crisis. This person can then delegate specific tasks or responsibilities to other designated personnel.
Priorities	Limited resources may be available for processing. Some tasks are more important than others. These must be established in advance. Similarly, the recovery programme may indicate that certain areas must be tackled first.
Back-up and standby arrangements	These may be with other installations, with a company that provides such services (eg maybe the hardware vendor), or reverting to manual procedures.
Communication with staff	The problems of a disaster can be compounded by poor communication between members of staff.
Public relations	If the disaster has a public impact, the recovery team may come under pressure from the public or from the media.
Risk assessment	Some way must be found of assessing the requirements of the problem, if it is contained, with the continued operation of the organisation as a whole.

The disaster recovery plan is dependent on effective back-up procedures for data and software, and arrangements for replacement – and even alternative premises.

The plan must cover all activities, from the initial response to a disaster, through to damage limitation and full recovery. Responsibilities must be clearly spelt out for all tasks.

Ideally, the plan should be tested. A simulation, ideally under normal business conditions, will demonstrate whether hardware and software operate effectively and staff can operate under alternative arrangements.

Hardware duplication

Hardware duplication may be required to permit a system to function in case of breakdown. The provision of back-up computers tends to be quite costly, particularly when these systems have no other function. Many organisations will use several similar computer systems and find that a significant level of protection against system faults can be provided by shifting operations to one of the systems still functioning.

Where an organisation has only a single system to rely on, recourse to a back-up facility is unavailable. In these instances one response would be to negotiate a maintenance contract which provides for back-up facilities.

Case Study

Hurricane Katrina

In 2005, Hurricane Katrina battered the Gulf Coast of the US, causing $200bn worth of damage. The disaster severely damaged the regions communications infrastructure, knocking down 1,000 wireless towers. Essential utilities, including hospitals and TV broadcasters, were forced to shut.

SunGard, a company specialising in disaster recovery services, kept its Gulf Coast customers operating during the initial aftermath of the hurricane. The company relocated the majority its clients to its own SunGard 'hotsites'. A 'hotsite' provides users with backed-up data and computer power away from the client's premises. As a result of the hotsites, SunGard's clients were able to keep their systems online in the aftermath of Hurricane Katrina.

SunGard also provided mobile 'hotsites' where computer servers and equipment were dispatched on large 18 wheel lorries for clients to operate from.

Adapted from an article:

'How Disaster Recovery Plans work', by Dave Ross, published on the *How Stuff Works* website; HowStuffWorks.com

4 Big data

FAST FORWARD

Big data is the term used to describe the growth of structured and unstructured data. Some experts argue that big data may be as important to business as the internet.

Laney suggests that big data can be defined by considering the three V's:

- Volume
- Velocity
- Variety

Big data analytics refers to the analysis and identification of insights in vast quantities of data. Historically, organisations have been restricted as to the amount of data that they can process due to the storage limitations of existing computer systems.

McKinsey's 2011 report, 'Big data: The next frontier for innovation, competition and productivity' suggests five ways in which big data can create value for organisations:

- Creating transparency
- Performance improvement
- Market segmentation and customisation
- Decision making
- New products and services

Critics, however, argue that big data is simply the latest buzzword which has become an obsession of business leaders and the media alike. Critics claim that big data analytics tend to be too focused on the discovery of correlations between data sets, with little interest given to the causation of such relationships.

In this section, we shall explore the role of big data in helping companies design and implement their strategies. (The syllabus refers specifically to the role of big data in informing and implementing strategy.) However, due to its heavy dependence on IT systems and links with e-business, it is explored here in Chapter 11. Throughout this section, we look at the way organisations collect and use data to support and inform the process of strategic development.

Organisations today have more transactional data than they have ever had before – about their customers, suppliers and about their operations.

More generally, the growth of the internet, multimedia, wireless networks, smartphones, social media, sensors and other digital technology are all helping to fuel a data revolution. In the so-called 'Internet of Things,' sensors embedded in physical objects such as mobile phones, motor vehicles, smart energy meters, RFID tags, tracking devices and traffic flow monitors all create and communicate data which is shared across wired and wireless networks that function in a similar way to the internet. The timing and location of cash withdrawals from ATM machines could also be a potential source of data.

Consumers using social media, smartphones, laptops and tablets to browse the internet, to search for items, to make purchases and to share information with other users also all create trails of data. Similarly, internet search indexes (such as Google Trends) can be sources of data for big data analytics.

4.1 What is big data?

'Big data is a popular term used to describe the exponential growth and availability of data, both structured and unstructured. Big data may be as important to business and society as the internet has become.'

(SAS, *big data – What it is and why it matters*. [Online] SAS. www.sas.com)

As we shall explore, in a commercial setting, big data is being used to identify trends that may exist in vast quantities of data in the pursuit of value creation.

4.1.1 Three Vs of big data

Laney suggests that big data can be defined by considering the three Vs: volume, velocity and variety.

Volume – The vast volume of data generated is a key feature of big data. The main benefit of big data analytics comes from the ability to process very large amounts of information. The bigger the data, the more potential insights it can give in terms of identifying trends and patterns, and in terms of getting a deeper understanding of customer requirements. For example, as more customers use the internet, smart phones and social media in their everyday lives, these can now also be sources of data for organisations alongside any data they may capture internally – for example, from customer loyalty cards or the transactions recorded in EPOS tills.

However, the 'volume' aspect of big data also presents the most obvious challenges to conventional IT structures, due to volume of storage space required for the data.

Velocity – refers to the speed at which 'real time' data is being streamed into the organisation, and with which it is processed within the organisation. Online retailers are able to compile records of each click and interaction a customer makes while visiting a website, rather than simply recording the final sale at the end of a customer transaction. Moreover, retailers who are able to utilise information about customer clicks and interactions quickly – for example, by recommending additional purchases – can use this speed to generate **competitive advantage**.

It is important to recognise that the competitive advantage an organisation can gain from 'velocity' relates to the speed with which data is processed and the velocity of a system's outputs, as well as the speed with which data initially flows into it.

Variety (or variability) – A common theme in relation to big data is the diversity of source data, with a lot of the data being unstructured (ie not in a database). For example, keywords from consversations people have on Facebook or Twitter, and content they share through media files (tagged photographs, or online video postings) could be sources of unstructured data.

This variety presents a challenge to organisations as they need to find ways of capturing, storing and processing the data. If data is too big, moves too fast, or doesn't fit with the structures of an organisation's existing information systems, then in order to gain value from it, an organisation needs to find an alternative way to process that data.

In this respect, big data analytics is likely to be crucial to making use of the potential value of big data.

4.1.2 Big data analytics

Big data analytics refers to the ability to analyse and reveal insights in data which had previously been too difficult or costly to analyse, due to the volume and variability of the data involved.

The aim of big data analytics is to extract insights from unstructured data or from large volumes of data.

Being able to extract insights from the data available is crucial for organisations to benefit from the availability of big data – for example, to help them understand the complexity of the environment in which they are operating, and to respond swiftly to the opportunities and threats presented by it; or to develop new insights and understanding into what customers need or want.

Case Study	The rise of big data analytics

In March 2014, the BBC's Matthew Wall reported on the growing emphasis that big business is now placing on the role of big data.

It's not big, it's just bigger

Laurie Miles, Head of Analytics for big data specialist SAS, explains that 'the term big data has been around for decades, and we've been doing analytics all this time. It's not big, it's just bigger'. Miles highlights that, for many years, organisations held traditional structured data, which could be neatly stored and organised in databases. However, over the last 20 years, the rise of the internet has lead to a 'proliferation of so-called unstructured data, generated by all our digital interactions, from email to online shopping, text messages to tweets, Facebook updates to YouTube videos'. This has resulted in increasingly large and complex data sets, which have become harder to analyse. It is predicted that 90% of all the data in existence today has been created in the past few years.

The big challenge

The challenge for big business has been to capture and analyse these vast quantities of data, which may be of use in a commercial context. Miles notes 'data is only as good as the intelligence we can glean from it, and that entails effective data analytics and a whole lot of computing power to cope with the exponential increase in volume'.

Wall reports that a significant number of large entities have already turned to big data analytics with the aim of gaining a competitive advantage over their rivals. Proponents of big data analytics argue that the insights gained may lead to improvements throughout the entire organisation.

'Practically, anyone who makes, grows and sells anything can use big data analytics to make their manufacturing and production processes more efficient and their marketing more targeted and cost-effective.'

The article draws an important distinction between the role of big data analytics compared to historic data analysis. Big data is not just about understanding historic business intelligence, but instead combines several 'real time' data sets, which make it increasingly useful to big businesses.

The big questions

It should be noted that the rise of big data has had its implications. Organisations looking to exploit the opportunities presented have encountered a significant shortage of individuals with the required skills in the job market to analyse the data. As Duncan Ross, Director of Science at Teradata, highlights: 'big data needs new skills, but the business and academic worlds are playing catch up. The job of the data scientist didn't exist five years or 10 years ago'.

Questions have also been raised over who ultimately owns the data that organisations hold and who is responsible for keeping such data safe from hackers. Does it belong to the individual or customer, the company, the service provider hosting the data or the national jurisdiction where the data is held? Such questions are unlikely to go away in the short term, as Miles highlights, it is a 'legal minefield'.

Adapted from: Wall, M (March 2014) *Big data: Are you ready for blast-off?* [Online] BBC www.bbc.co.uk

4.2 The strategic importance of big data

Historically, only the largest corporations have had sufficient resources to be able to process big data. Now, however, it is becoming possible for all organisations to access and process the volumes of big data potentially available to them, due to cost-effective approaches such as cloud-based architectures and open source software.

In a June 2011 report, 'Big data: The next frontier for innovation, competition and productivity' issued by the McKinsey Global Institute, it was suggested that, 'big data has now reached every sector in the global economy. Like other essential factors of production such as [physical] assets and human capital, much of modern economic activity simply couldn't take place without it'.

This suggests that the ability to capture and analyse big data, and the information gained by doing so, have become **important strategic resources for organisations**. Making effective use of big data could confer **competitive advantage** on an organisation. Alternatively, in time, competitors who fail to develop their capabilities to use big data and information as strategic resources could be left behind by those who do.

While these might initially seem to be quite bold claims, big data can certainly create value for organisations through its ability to drive innovation and by helping organisations gain greater and faster insight into their customers.

Similarly, analysing data from as many sources as possible when making decisions, can also increase the amount of useful information available to managers when they are making decisions.

Exam focus point

It is particularly important that you understand how big data can help to keep management informed of developments which may affect the ability of the organisation to meet its objectives. This is likely to be essential for most organisations during the implementation of its strategy.

4.3 The value of big data

McKinsey's big data report suggests there are five broad ways in which big data can create value for organisations.

4.3.1 Creating transparency

Making data more easily accessible to relevant stakeholders, in a timely manner, can create value in its own right – for example, by revealing insights from data which had previously been too costly or complex to process. This transparency could relate to data within an organisation as well as external data – through better integration and analysis of data produced by different parts of an organisation. Furthermore, improved transparency in data should help organisations during the process of strategic implementation and the achievement of corporate objectives.

For example, consider a manufacturing company which is operating in a highly competitive market where innovation and speed in product development are considered critical to success. The company has a corporate objective 'to deliver products the customer demands at the time they are required', and as a result, the company is pursuing a strategy of ongoing product development. The integration of data from across the company's various departments (research and development, engineering and manufacturing units) should enable concurrent engineering and may help to significantly reduce time to market, as well as improving quality.

However, in many cases, the increased transparency resulting from big data is likely to relate to external data. For example, analysing shopper's transactions, alongside social and geographical data, can reveal peer influence among customers – ie the extent to which shopper's choices are shaped by their friends and neighbours, as well as by the marketing efforts of the company itself.

4.3.2 Performance improvement

The increasing amount of transactional data they store in digital form provides organisations with an increasing amount of accurate and detailed performance data – in real or almost real time. By analysing

the variability in performance – and the causes of that variability – organisations then manage performance to higher levels.

For example, improving profitability is often a key financial objective for most commercial organisations. The use of big data analytics can help organisations monitor strategies aimed at improving profitability by allowing management to identify why certain product lines sell more slowly than expected. Operational managers can either take action to improve sales of those lines, or else divert resources into more popular product lines.

The following case study provides an interesting insight into how retailer Tesco has been able to reduce costs and improve the efficiency of its in-store refrigerators through the use of real time performance data.

| Case Study | Big data in action |

In May 2013, Tesco, the market-leading supermarket chain, unveiled plans to save €20m a year by exploiting the use of big data analytics to help ensure that its in-store refrigerators operate at the right temperature. A report by *Computerweekly.com* highlighted the findings of a joint project between Tesco Ireland and IBM aimed at 'optimising the performance of its in-store refrigerators'. The project used highly sophisticated computer systems to analyse Tesco's refrigeration data.

As Goodwin highlights, 'without realising it, many Tesco stores in Ireland were running their refrigerators at a lower temperature than necessary'. John Walsh, Tesco's Energy and Carbon Manager in Ireland, noted that, 'ideally, we keep our refrigerators at between -21°C and -23°C, but in reality we found we were keeping them colder. That came as a surprise to us'.

Tesco was able to capture this data from in-store sensors that monitor the performance of individual refrigeration units. The sensors then process 'the data in real time, and display the results on a Google map that shows the performance of refrigerators in more than 120 Irish stores', says Goodwin. As the article highlights, Tesco has achieved maintenance cost savings, as engineers are now able to investigate potential faults remotely, 'diagnose the problem and turn up with the right part. Previously, engineers would turn up to the store, diagnose the problem and have to return to the depot to collect the equipment they needed'.

Adapted from: Goodwin, B (May 2013) 'Tesco uses Big Data to cut cooling costs by up to €20m' [Online] *Computerweekly.com*. www.computerweekly.com

4.3.3 Market segmentation and customisation

The volume and variety within big data enables organisations to create highly specific segments within its markets and to tailor its products and services precisely to meet the needs of customers in those segments.

The idea of market segmentation is already a key concept within strategic marketing, (the concept of e-marketing is covered in greater detail in Chapter 12). However, big data could facilitate the real-time micro-segmentation of customers for targeted promotions and advertising.

McKinsey also highlights that big data could also be valuable in segmenting public sector markets. Traditionally, public sector markets have not segmented citizens (service users) in the same way that private sector companies have segmented customers and potential customers. However, big data could enable public sector organisations to pursue strategies which build upon the effective tailoring of products and services.

4.3.4 Decision making

The sophisticated analytics tools which are used to uncover previously hidden patterns and trends in data could also be used to improve decision making. For example, trends identified in in-store and online sales for a retailer – in real time – could be used to determine inventory and pricing strategies. In some cases, decisions will be made by managers in store (based on analytics from the datasets) but in other cases, the

decisions themselves could even become automated. So, for example, a retailer could use algorithms to optimise decisions about inventory levels and pricing in response to current and predicted sales data.

4.3.5 New products and services

Companies can use data about social trends and consumer behaviours to create new products and services to meet customer's needs, or to enhance existing products and services so that they meet customers' needs more exactly. For example, the emergence of real-time location data, from traffic light sensors and satellite navigation systems, could enable insurance companies to refine the pricing of their insurance policies according to where, and how, people drive their cars.

More generally, big data could also provide new business opportunities in its own right. For example, Facebook's advertising business incorporates analysis of a user's actions as well as their friends' actions. Equally, Amazon could be seen as an example of a company which has built its business strategy using data and analytics; for example, through the way it makes recommendations for customers linked to the purchases made by other customers with similar interests.

4.4 Data and customers

So far in this section, we have looked at the way organisations can use big data to understand more about what their customers want. However, Web 2.0 technologies (which we discuss in a later chapter) mean that data is increasingly available to customers as well as organisations.

For example, online customer reviews are now commonplace, and smartphone applications now enable customers to evaluate and compare product prices in real time. This increased availability of data creates a new market transparency which can give customers a greater insight into what they are buying and who they are buying from.

In this respect, the data helps customers to base purchasing decisions not only on price, but also on a company's social reputation – for example, in terms of customer's feedback in relation to the quality of service they have received.

Case Study   **Big data: Helping to shape strategy**

The following case study outlines how companies are now using data about their customers to analyse their competitors in order to shape their own competitive strategy.

In 2013, Donna Ferguson, writing in *The Guardian* newspaper, illustrated how a number of major supermarket chains have taken to using big data as a means to better understand their rivals.

The use of in-store loyalty cards as a means of capturing data about customers and their shopping habits to enable the effective targeting of shoppers with promotions, is not a new occurrence. Tesco's Clubcard and Sainsbury's Nectar card schemes have been in existence for many years.

Today, retailers have started to exploit data about their shoppers by tracking purchases made by individual debit and credit cards. As Guy-Montague-Jones of *The Grocer* highlights, retailers are able to 'build up a demographic profile of you, and collect data about how loyal you are, what you buy and how much you spend'.

Retailers that operate online shops are now able to use data about a shoppers' previous purchasing behaviour to target individuals with particular products when they log on. Analysis of shopping patterns are now even being used to help store managers decide what items to stock. Ferguson notes that 'Sainsbury's discovered that a cereal brand called Grape-Nuts was worth stocking – despite weak sales – because the shoppers who bought it were extremely loyal to Sainsbury's, and were often big spenders'.

Furthermore, following extensive data analysis, Sainsbury's purchased the remaining 50% of Sainsbury's bank, which it did not own, as those individuals who used the bank's services were found to 'become more loyal and spend more in-store'.

Competitor analysis

Establishing new stores

The supermarket chain Waitrose has taken to using shoppers' Visa card data obtained in-store to analyse which competing stores customers are using when not frequenting a Waitrose outlet. This data has been used to help the company decide where to locate new stores. The article highlights that the data analytics firm Beyond Analytics was hired by Waitrose to integrate 'Visa transaction data with Waitrose's own data to figure out what proportion of potential customers were buying groceries from other supermarkets, and the general locations of these competitors'.

Trends in shopping patterns

Rival supermarket Morrisons has historically shunned loyalty card schemes. However, it recently confirmed that it will 'buy in' demographic data about its shoppers to extrapolate trends in shopping patterns to help it target offers at customers. Clearly, if Morrisons' rivals are aware of the data that the company is buying in, then they will be able to target existing customers with their own promotional offers in a bid to undermine competing moves.

Selling data

Ferguson notes that big brands have become increasingly prepared to pay 'a lot of money' to purchase data about shopping patterns from the major supermarkets. 'A brand of say, coffee will approach Sainsbury's, Morrisons or Tesco and ask to buy access to customers purchasing rival brands, so it can put an offer to these customers.'

Adapted from: Ferguson, D (June 2013) 'How supermarkets get your data – and what they do with it.'
[Online] *The Guardian*. www.theguardian.com

4.5 Criticisms of big data

An article in *The Financial Times* entitled 'Big data: are we making a big mistake', raised a number of criticisms over the ability of big data to deliver the anticipated benefits.

Critics argue:

(a) Big data is simply a buzzword, a vague term that has turned into an obsession in large organisations and the media. Very few examples exist where analysing vast amounts of data have resulted in significant new discoveries.

(b) There is a focus on finding correlations between data sets and less of an emphasis on causation. Critics suggest that it is easier to identify correlations between two variables than to determine what is actually causing the correlation.

(c) A failure to understand the factors giving rise to a correlation mean that analysts have no idea what factors may cause the correlation to break down.

 Case Study

Google Flu Trends

Google Flu Trends was presented as a means of tracking and predicting the spread of influenza across the US.

The programme used algorithms which identified correlations between the symptoms people searched for online and flu symptoms. However, after providing a swift and accurate account of flu outbreaks for several winters, in the 2012-3 season, Flu Trends overstated the spread of flu-like illnesses across the US by almost a factor of two.

The cause of this problem was that ultimately Google did not know what linked the search terms with the spread of flu, and Google's algorithms weren't designed to identify what caused what. They were simply finding statistical patterns in the data; and as such, focused on correlation rather than causation.

One explanation of the Flu Trends failure in 2012-3 is that there were a number of news stories in December about the dangers of flu, and those provoked internet searches by people who were healthy.

(d)   Analysing a data set, regardless of its size is not necessarily representative of the entire data population as a whole. *The Financial Times* suggests that, if an organisation wishing to understand the public mood solely used the social networking site Twitter to analyse all of the tweets made, this would not represent the views of all members of society. Research indicates that Twitter users tend to be young, urban individuals.

(e)   The costs and upheaval involved in enhancing data architectures and IT applications in order to store and analyse big data sets may prove prohibitive for smaller organisations. Furthermore, in order to gain a meaningful insight from big data, it is important that organisational capabilities are fully considered. Entities which lack the right mix of people with appropriate skills and capabilities to analyse and interpret captured data are unlikely to realise the full potential offered by the hidden relationships contained in big data.

5 IT and strategy

FAST FORWARD

The internet has the capacity to transform many businesses via the introduction of new technology and skills and, eventually, the repositioning of the offering to fit the new market conditions.

A **strategy for e-commerce** should be considered at the highest level of management and it is particularly necessary that it should conform to the standard criteria for strategic choice: suitability, acceptability and feasibility.

Suitability. For most companies, e-commerce will be a supplement to more traditional operations, with the website forming a supplementary medium for communication and sales.

Acceptability. The e-commerce strategy must be acceptable to important stakeholders. Distributors are particularly important here.

Feasibility. Feasibility is a matter of **resources**. The fundamental resource is cash, but the availability of the skilled labour needed to establish and administer a website will be crucial to the e-commerce strategy.

5.1 Strategy for e-commerce

The internet has the capacity to transform many businesses via the introduction of new technology and skills and, eventually, the repositioning of the offering to fit the new market conditions. Commentators highlight so-called **megatrends** which, coupled with the internet, are changing the face of organisations.

(a)   New **distribution channels**, revolutionising sales and brand management

(b)   The continued **shift of power** towards the consumer

(c)   **Growing competition** locally, nationally, internationally and globally

(d)   An acceleration in the **pace of business**

(e)   The **transformation of companies** into extended enterprises involving virtual teams of business, customer and supplier working in collaborative partnerships

(f)   A re-evaluation of how companies, their partners and competitors **add value,** not only to themselves, but in the wider environmental and social setting

(g)   Recognition of **knowledge** as a strategic asset

Most experts agree that a successful strategy for e-commerce cannot simply be bolted on to existing processes, systems, delivery routes and business models. Instead, management groups have, in effect, to start again, by asking themselves **fundamental questions**.

- What do customers want to buy from us?
- What business should we be in?

- What kind of partners might we need?
- What categories of customer do we want to attract and retain?

In turn, organisations can visualise the necessary changes at **three interconnected levels**.

Level 1 – The simple **introduction of new technology** to connect electronically with employees, customers and suppliers (eg through an intranet, extranet or website).

Level 2 – **Re-organisation** of the workforce, processes, systems and strategy in order to make best use of the new technology.

Level 3 – **Repositioning** of the organisation to fit it into the emerging e-economy.

So far, very few companies have gone beyond levels 1 and 2. Instead, pure internet businesses such as Amazon and AOL have emerged from these new rules: unburdened by physical assets, their competitive advantage lies in **knowledge management** and **customer relationships**.

5.2 Building an e-commerce strategy

A **strategy for e-commerce**, while not necessarily constituting the organisation's overall strategy, is likely to have wide implications and to involve and affect more than one function or department within the organisation. It should, therefore, be considered at the highest level of management and it is particularly necessary that it should conform to the **standard criteria for strategic choice**: suitability, acceptability and feasibility. It should work well with any existing operations; be acceptable (to distributors in particular) and not make impractical demands for cash and skilled labour.

5.2.1 Suitability

There are a few large organisations, such as Amazon, whose overall strategy is based on e-commerce. However, for most companies, e-commerce will be a **supplement to more traditional operations**, with the website forming a supplementary medium for communication and sales. It is important that the e-commerce strategy supports the overall strategy generally. One way of approaching this would be to consider the **extended marketing mix** and the need for **balance**, **consistency** and **mutual support** between the elements. A very simple example would consider the question of whether to confine the website to an essentially communications role, or to incorporate a fully featured online shopping facility. A specialist chain store dealing in, say, camping and outdoor equipment would expect to expand its market if it developed online shopping. On the other hand, a manufacturer of specialist luxury goods, such as the most expensive fountain pens, would probably have a policy of distributing through carefully selected retailers. It is unlikely that online shopping would appeal to the target market segment: they would probably enjoy the shopping experience and would want to try the products before they bought them.

5.2.2 Acceptability

The e-commerce strategy must be **acceptable to important stakeholders**. Distributors are particularly important here. Pursuing our luxury goods example, we would expect that retailers chosen for their attractive premises, skilled and attentive staff and air of luxury would be unhappy to find their position usurped by a website.

5.2.3 Feasibility

Feasibility is a matter of **resources**. The fundamental resource is cash, but the availability of the **skilled labour** needed to establish and administer a website will be crucial to the e-commerce strategy. It may be appropriate to employ **specialist consultants** for these purposes.

Under this heading, we might identify the following points for consideration:

(a) The first thing to do is to try to establish precise **objectives** for the new strategy element. It may not be possible to do this conclusively and consideration of objectives may have to proceed alongside the processes outlined below, all passing through several iterations.

(b)   An estimate and analysis of **costs** and **benefits** should be undertaken. This should cover all the possible options, such as what services are to be offered, whether a full catalogue is to be put online, whether internet selling is envisaged, whether a search function is required, and so on.

(c)   A detailed **budget** should be prepared, probably using estimates from the cost and benefit analysis. Where internet selling is to be offered, **pricing policy** must be established: there is a theory that customers expect goods and services to be discounted when sold online, since they are aware that administrative costs are likely to be lower than in more traditional forms of distribution.

5.3 Strategy process models for e-business

FAST FORWARD

IT has the capacity to transform businesses. Corporate and e-business strategies thus become complementary, each supporting and influencing the other.

The traditional landscape of the business environment has changed from being a market*place* to one that is more of a market*space* – an information and communication-based electronic exchange environment. The impact of this is evident in the following changes:

(a)   The **content of transaction is different:** information about a product often replaces the product itself.

(b)   The **context of transaction is different:** an electronic screen replaces the face-to-face transaction.

(c)   The **enabling infrastructure of transactions is different:** computers and communications infrastructure may replace typical physical resources especially if the offering lends itself to a digital format.

The significant issue faced by managers today is one of **transformation**: 'How do I transform the bricks and mortar company of yesterday to the click and mortar company of today in order to be competitive in the inevitable digital economy of tomorrow?'

Until the emergence of e-business, IS had largely played a **facilitative** (and relatively peripheral) role in business, focusing on improving operational efficiencies, cost structures, and effectiveness. Now, however, it would be fair to claim that e-business would not be possible if it were not for the information systems that facilitate it. The role of IS has become central to e-business.

E-business strategy is defined as the approach by which the application of internal and external electronic communications can support and influence corporate strategy. There is a **two-way relationship** between corporate and e-business strategies, with e-business strategy not only supporting corporate strategy, but influencing or impacting it.

Differences between traditional business strategy and e-business strategy

	Traditional business strategy	E-business strategy
Planning horizons	Predictability and long-term execution plans	Adaptability and responsiveness within a short time period
Process models	Prescriptive strategy: the three elements (analysis, development and implementation) are linked together sequentially	Emergent strategy: the distinction between the three elements may be less clear and they are interrelated
Planning cycles	One time development effort	Iterative strategic development because the pace of change is rapid
Power base	Positional power and strength in the market place	Success based on manipulation of critical information
Core focus	Production and factory goods orientation	Customer orientation

According to Kalakota and Robinson, **continuous planning with feedback** has evolved as the strategy of choice for the fluid and volatile e-environment. This method of continuous planning with feedback is structured around four steps.

Step 1 **Knowledge building and capability evaluation**: identify and acquire a comprehensive understanding/vision of customer needs. Develop a clear understanding of what capabilities are needed in order to address the identified customer needs. Communicate this understanding of customer needs to all employees of the organisation.

Step 2 **Develop a comprehensive e-business design**: this entails developing the competence to address customer needs. If the customer wants self-service, then the business design must provide and facilitate it.

Step 3 **E-business blueprint**: the vital link between the e-business design, the business goals, and the technology foundation. If a self-service business model is to be implemented, then the e-business blueprint helps determine the required application framework. It maps the projects and performance milestones that must be achieved.

Step 4 **Application development and deployment**: translate the key milestones and projects into integrated applications. There should be two feedback loops:

(a) At the micro level, employees know how their individual job performance impacts corporate objectives.

(b) At the macro level, feedback on the overall corporate objectives is provided. This facilitates an understanding about what is working and what is not, so that refinements/remedial actions may be undertaken.

5.4 Stage models

FAST FORWARD Several stage models have been proposed for assessing maturity of capability. Such models can also be used as guides to future development.

Rayport and Jaworski suggest a four-stage model of the evolution of internet-based B2B e-commerce, believing that, in general, an organisation goes through these stages in utilising the internet for its business-to-business activities:

1	**Emission – Broadcast**	The company begins by creating an **informational website** for its clients
2	**Interaction**	Using the internet for **interaction with customers** such as emails, customer survey and feedbacks
3	**Transaction**	The use of the internet to take, manage and support **transactions with customers** such as online ordering systems
4	**Collaboration**	The use of the internet to provide **inter-organisational activities**, that can be accessed and utilised by the company and its trading partners

The model of Rao et al suggests the following stages of e-commerce development and their characteristics:

Stage 1	Stage 2	Stage 3	Stage 4
Presence	**Portals**	**Transaction integration**	**Company integration**
Content	Profiles	B2B/B2C	B2B
Window to the web	Two-way communications	Communities	Full integration
No integration	Email	E-marketplaces	E-business
Email	Order placing	Auctions	Uses e-commerce systems to manage CRM and supply chain
	Cookies	3rd party emarketplaces	
	No online financial transactions	Low-level collaboration	Value chain integration
		Online financial transactions	High-level collaboration

Stages of growth models give a better understanding of the factors influencing the strategy that an organisation is considering and so management are able to do a more successful job of planning. The management principles will differ from one stage to another, and different technologies, and perhaps different areas of the organisation, are in differing stages at any one time. Therefore, these models also make explicit the need for a portfolio of strategies to cater for these differences.

The stages approach is useful for several purposes:

(a) A small or medium sized enterprise may use it for comparison with its major competitors; it may indicate gaps and lead to strategic actions.

(b) It can provide a roadmap to assist companies to determine whether or not it is sensible to progress to a subsequent stage.

(c) It can explain past, current and future involvement in e-business.

(d) It can be used for guidance and direction as to where to proceed further, as well as where an organisation might focus its goals and resources.

(e) It can help an organisation reduce the complexity of its e-business initiatives by breaking them into smaller, more flexible and manageable portions. By doing so, an organisation is able to focus more on the task at hand, constantly evaluating and assessing the progression of its e-business initiatives.

(f) It can assist in identifying phases of development required and provide milestones that can be understood by management.

(g) It may help control costs and allow for alteration during the development process.

Exam focus point

Make sure you understand how e-business affects an organisation's relationships with its customers, and therefore the implications it can have for restructuring the organisation's downstream supply chain. We are going to look at supply chain management in the next part of this chapter.

6 Supply chain management

FAST FORWARD

A **supply chain** encompasses all activities and information flows necessary for the transformation of goods from the origin of the raw material to when the product is finally consumed or discarded.

A supply chain always includes push and pull elements. The pull based element is particularly relevant on IS for feedback and control, since it aims to eliminate buffer inventory by increasing responsiveness.

Exam focus point

An article titled 'The strategic use of IT' (October 2010) written by Ken Garrett was published in *Student Accountant*, and is available on the ACCA website. It would be worth taking the time to study this article.

In Chapter 4, we mentioned an article titled 'Value chains, value networks and supply chain management,' also written by Ken Garrett. This is available in the Technical Articles section for P3 on the ACCA website. The article focuses on the role of the value chain in creating value for customers and considers different types of supply chain models. You are strongly advised to read this article.

6.1 Supply chain basics

Key supply chain activities include production planning, purchasing, materials management, distribution, customer service, and sales forecasting. These processes are critical to the success of any operation whether they are manufacturers, wholesalers, or service providers.

Electronic commerce and the internet are fundamentally changing the nature of supply chains, and redefining how consumers learn about, select, purchase, and use products and services. The result has been the emergence of new business-to-business supply chains that are consumer-focused rather than product-focused. They also provide customised products and services.

6.2 Push and pull models of the supply chain

6.2.1 Traditional supply chain – push model

In a supply chain based on the **push model**, an organisation produces goods according to schedules based on historical sales patterns.

A push-based supply chain is slow to respond to changes in demand, which can result in overstocking, bottlenecks and delays, unacceptable service levels and product obsolescence. Where there are several links in the distribution chain, the system's inability to respond to variations in consumption leads to the establishment of buffer inventory at each stage of distribution. Poor co-ordination can lead to large fluctuations in the levels buffer inventory, even where actual consumption patterns vary only marginally. This kind of uncoordinated amplification of minor feedback signals is called the 'bull whip effect'.

Features of a push system

- Forecasts of sales drive production and replenishment
- Long-term forecasts
- Inventory pushed to next channel level, often with the aid of trade promotions
- Inability to meet changing demand patterns
- Potential product obsolescence
- Excessive inventory and low service levels
- Bull whip effect

6.2.2 The pull model

Driven by e-commerce capabilities to empower clients, many companies are moving to a customer-driven **pull model**, where production and distribution are **demand driven**. The consumer requests the product and 'pulls' it through the delivery channel. There is an emphasis on the supply chain **delivering value to customers** who are actively involved in product and service specifications.

This new business model is less product-centric and more directly focused on the individual consumer. To succeed in the business environment, companies have recognised that there is an ongoing **shift in the balance of power** in the commerce model, from suppliers to customers.

Features of a pull system

- Demand drives production and replenishment
- Centralisation of demand information and of replenishment decision-making
- Reduced product obsolescence
- Expanded ability to meet changing demand patterns
- Lower inventories and higher service levels
- Reduced bull whip effect

In the pull model, customers use electronic connections to pull whatever they need out of the system. The push model involves a linear flow that keeps many members of the supply chain relatively isolated from end users. With the new customer-driven pull model, it is no longer a linear process. The new supply chain has each participant scrambling to establish direct electronic connections to the end customer. The result is that electronic supply-chain connectivity gives end customers the opportunity to become better informed through the ability to research and give direction to suppliers. Ultimately, customers have a direct voice in the functioning of the supply chain.

E-commerce creates a much more efficient supply chain that benefits both customers and manufacturers. Companies can better serve customer needs, carry less inventory and send products to market more quickly.

6.2.3 IS implications

Push-based systems rely less on sophisticated IS support, since high inventory levels are used to cope with variations in customer demand. Pull-based systems, like Just-in-Time (JIT), need accurate and quick

information on actual demand to move inventory and schedule production in the chain: therefore, they require integrated internal systems and linkages throughout the supply chain.

A supply chain is almost always a **combination of both push and pull**, where the interface between the push-based stages and the pull-based stages is known as the push-pull boundary. An example of this would be Dell's **build-to-order** supply chain. Inventory levels of individual components are determined by forecasting general demand, but final assembly is in response to a specific customer request. The push-pull boundary would then be at the beginning of the assembly line. At this point on the supply chain timeline, it is typically coordinated through a **buffer inventory**.

6.3 Relationship with the value chain and the value network

FAST FORWARD

IS may be used to improve the working of the links between activities in the value chain and between value chains in the value network. One important consequence of this is that improved communication with customers results, making it easier for them to purchase.

Knowledge brought forward from earlier studies

The **value chain** concept has already been described in detail earlier in this Study Text. Here is the diagram to refresh your memory.

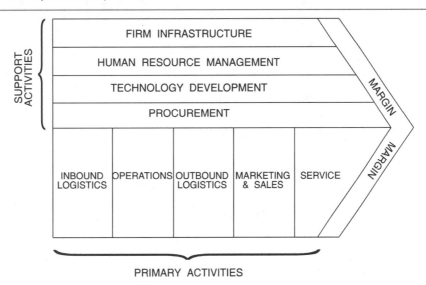

6.3.1 Using the value chain with IS

Management can use this model to assess the degree of **effectiveness** and **efficiency of resource use**.

(a) **Efficiency** is the measure of how well the resources are being used and measures could include profitability, capacity use and yield gained from that capacity.

(b) **Effectiveness** is the assessment of how well the resources are allocated to the most competitively significant activities within the value chain.

An analysis of resource utilisation

(a) **Identify the value activities**. This stage should include an assignment of costs and added value and an identification of the **critical activities**. These are the various value activities which underpin the production and delivery of products or services, including the supply and distribution chains.

(b) **Identify the cost or value drivers**. The factors that sustain the competitive position are called **cost drivers** or **value drivers**. For example, e-commerce allows transportation companies of all sizes to exchange cargo documents electronically over the internet. It enables shippers, freight forwarders and trucking firms to streamline document handling without the monetary and time investment required by the traditional document delivery systems. By using e-commerce, companies can reduce costs, improve data accuracy, streamline business processes, accelerate business cycles, and enhance customer service.

(c) **Identify the linkages.** An organisation's value activities and the linkages between them are sources of **competitive advantage**. There may be important links between the primary activities. For example, good communications between sales, operations and purchasing can help cut inventory; the purchase of more expensive or more reliable machinery and equipment may lead to cost savings and quality improvements in the manufacturing process. Competitors can often imitate the separate activities of an organisation but it is more difficult to copy the linkages within and between value chains.

6.3.2 Value network

Knowledge brought forward from earlier studies

A **value network** can be defined as the links between an organisation and its strategic and non-strategic partners that form its external value chain. Activities that add value do not stop at the organisation's boundaries.

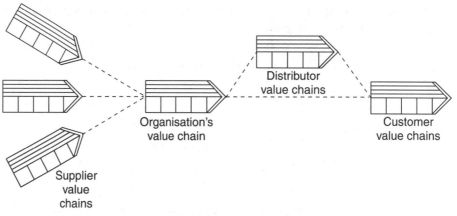

Value network

The impact of e-business on the value network

E-business is a vital element in the value network. It will help companies deliver better services to their customers, accelerate the growth of the e-commerce initiatives that are critical to their business, and lower their operating costs.

Using the internet for e-business will allow customers to access price information, place delivery orders and track shipments. The internet makes it easier for customers to do business with companies. For example, anything that simplifies the process of arranging transportation services will help build companies' business and enhance shareholder value. The only tools needed to take advantage of this solution are a personal computer and an internet browser. By making more information available about the commercial side of companies, businesses will make their website a place where customers will not only get detailed information about the services the company offers, but also where they can actually conduct business with the company. Ultimately, websites can provide a universal, self-service system for customers. E-commerce functions are taking companies a substantial step forward by providing customers with a faster and easier way to do business with them.

6.4 Impact of IT on the value chain $\qquad$ 6/12

A Section B question in the June 2012 exam required candidates to evaluate how technology could be used to support the supply chain operations of the organisation featured in the scenario.

Value chain analysis can be used to assess the impact of IS/IT and identify processes within the value chain where it can be used to add value.

(a) **Inbound logistics** covers receiving, storing and handling raw material inputs. The use of IT includes inventory control and systems such as Material Requirements Planning (MRP), Enterprise Resource Planning (ERP) and JIT.

(b) **Operations** are concerned with the transformation of the raw material inputs into finished goods or services. IT can be used to automate and improve tasks; examples include robots, process control, and machine tool control, Computer Aided Manufacturing (CAM), Computer Integrated Manufacturing (CIM) and Enterprise Resource Planning (ERP).

(c) **Outbound logistics** is concerned with the storing, distributing and delivering the finished goods to the customers. IT makes it possible to follow the progress of goods from pickup to delivery.

(d) **Marketing and sales** are responsible for communication with the customers. Supermarkets use EPOS system information on inventory to aid speedy ordering and replenishment.

(e) **Service** covers all of the activities that occur after the point of sale, eg installation, repair and maintenance. Customer databases allow organisations to sell after-sales services.

Alongside all of these primary activities are the secondary, or support, activities of procurement, technology, human resource management and corporate infrastructure.

(a) At the inbound logistics stage of **procurement**, IT can automate purchasing decisions and can be used as a link to a supplier with EDI.

(b) **Technology development** includes Computer Aided Design (CAD) aiding operations to produce engineer's drawings and component design.

(c) **Human resource** applications include the maintenance of a skills database and staff planning.

Having identified areas that could be more efficient or effective from the value chain analysis, the IS/IT strategy can be used to try and determine how those activities, and in particular, the competitively significant activities, can be improved.

(a) Can **linkages** between the different activities be improved by the use of IT? For example, information from support activities may be made available to primary activities on a more timely basis.

(b) Can IS/IT improve the **information flow** through the primary activities? For example, linking sales and marketing with operations or outbound logistics using a central database to provide sales and marketing with online details of products being produced.

(c) Can more effective **links** be formed with external entities? For example, can inbound logistics be improved by using EDI?

(d) Can IS/IT be used to **decrease the cost** of any activity? For example, is there room for more automation or transformation of activities, or even re-engineering using currently available IT tools and techniques?

6.5 Taking advantage of IT

Porter and Millar advocate five steps that senior executives may follow to take advantage of opportunities that the information revolution has created.

Porter and Millar advocate five steps that senior executives may follow to take advantage of opportunities that the information revolution has created.

Step 1   **Assess information intensity**. A high level of information content in either products or processes indicates that IT can play a strategic role.

Step 2   **Determine the role of IT in industry structure**. IT may have the potential to radically change the way in which the industry operates, including changing the basis of competition and moving its boundaries.

Step 3   **Identify and rank the ways in which IT might create competitive advantage**. Possible value chain-based applications include opportunities for reducing cost or enhancing differentiation and establishing new links between activities. There may also be opportunities to enter new market segments and to introduce new products.

Step 4   **Investigate how IT might spawn new businesses.** These might be based on the exploitation of new categories of information and the sale of information-processing capacity.

Step 5   **Develop a plan to exploit IT**. Effectively, this is the creation of a comprehensive strategy and has implications for most parts of the organisation.

For any organisation, it is possible to assess the **information content** (the information intensity), of the value chain activities and linkages. Porter and Millar's **information intensity matrix** considers the role of IT and suggests how it can be exploited for competitive advantage. The matrix evaluates the information intensity of the value chain (how product value is transformed through activities and linkages in the value chain) against that of the product (what the buyer needs to know to obtain the product and to use it to obtain the desired result). When assessing the degree of information in the product, oil, for example, has a low information content while banking has a high information content.

The degree of information in the value chain also varies. It is low in the case of a cement manufacturer who makes a simple product in bulk, but high in the case of a complex, sophisticated process such as oil refining.

Information content of the product

	Low	High
High	Oil refining	Banking, Airlines
Low	Cement	Fashion

(Left axis: **Information intensity of the value chain**)

Information intensity matrix

If the information content of the **product** is high, IT can be used to **enhance product delivery** as, for example, with internet sites for newspapers. When the information in the **value chain** is high, it implies that sophisticated information systems are required to **manage the linkages** optimally.

The segment where the information content of both the product and the value chain are **high** includes banking and financial services. For example, ATMs, credit cards, debit cards and customer databases have all been integrated to give a much more personalised service as well as lowering service costs. There are banks in the UK such as First Direct that have no branches and retail online, through ATMs and 24 hour telephone phone links.

The segment where the information content of both the product and the value chain are **low** contains traditional process-manufactured, widely available commodity products with several potential producers, such as bricks and cement. The fact that information content is low does not mean that there is no scope for exploiting IT to achieve a business advantage. Firms in this segment might be low-cost producers who are looking for linkages in the value chain to contribute to overall cost leadership. For example, there could be a niche market for specialist bricks in garden design, where expertise is in short supply. Information about their use could provide added value. The production process offers little scope for IT but, since the process is presumably well known and closely controlled, information could be used to provide a more efficient operation. For example, airline pilots are encouraged to use autopilot to fly planes because consumption of fuel increases by as much as 30% during a manually controlled flight.

6.6 Restructuring the supply chain

Supply chain management options can be portrayed as a continuum, from **vertical integration** to **virtual integration**.

Vertical disintegration means that various diseconomies of scale or scope have broken a production process into separate companies, each performing a limited subset of activities required to create a finished product.

A **virtually integrated company** is one in which **core** business functions, as well as non-core functions, take place in external organisations. Virtually integrated companies are so tightly organised that it is often difficult to determine where one legal entity ends and another starts.

Supply chain management options can be portrayed as a continuum, from **vertical integration** to **virtual integration**.

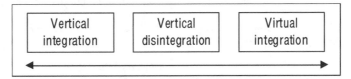

6.6.1 Vertical integration

Vertical integration is a style of ownership and control with companies united through a hierarchy and sharing a common owner. It has been extensively discussed elsewhere in this Study Text.

6.6.2 Vertical disintegration

Vertical disintegration is a specific organisational form of production. As opposed to integration, in which production occurs within a single organisation, vertical disintegration means that various diseconomies of scale or scope have broken a production process into separate companies, each performing a limited subset of activities required to create a finished product.

One major reason for vertical disintegration is to **share risk**. Also, in some cases, smaller firms can be more responsive to changes in market conditions. Vertical disintegration is thus more likely when operating in volatile markets. Stability and standardised products more typically engender integration, as it provides the benefits of scale economies.

6.6.3 Example

Filmed entertainment was once highly vertically integrated into a handful of large studios that handled everything from production to theatrical presentation. After the Second World War, the industry was broken into small fragments, becoming highly vertically disintegrated, with specialised firms that only performed certain tasks such as editing, special effects, trailers and so on.

6.6.4 Virtual integration

A **virtually integrated company** is one in which **core** business functions, as well as non-core functions, take place in external organisations. Virtually integrated companies are so tightly organised that it is often difficult to determine where one legal entity ends and another starts. As a result, they operate as a single organisation with shared goals, processes and (sometimes) corporate cultures.

6.6.5 Example

An example of this restructuring is what has happened in the car industry. Henry Ford's original vision included controlling as many aspects of the end vehicle production as possible; from the production of raw materials in steel mills and rubber plantations, through all of the design, manufacturing, assembly and distribution activities. He managed a truly vertically integrated supply chain. Today the vision for most

automotive vehicle manufacturers is to become virtual companies, owning only the brand and the customer. The design, system development, product sourcing, logistics, and even final assembly can all be outsourced to supply chain partners. Increasingly, the goal is to replace physical assets with information in such a way that every member of this extended supply chain benefits. This forces the move from an environment of **hard wired integration**, where relationships are at arms-length and adversarial, even across functional boundaries within the organisation, to an environment based on **negotiated sourcing**, where non-core activities are outsourced and collaborative partnerships are the norm.

6.6.6 Two kinds of integration

In most industries today, it is not enough simply to optimise internal structures and infrastructures based on business strategy. The most successful manufacturers seem to be those that have carefully linked their internal processes to external suppliers and customers in **unique supply chains**. Upstream and downstream integration with suppliers and customers has emerged as an important element of manufacturing strategy. Typically, the goal is to create and coordinate manufacturing processes seamlessly across the supply chain in a manner that most competitors cannot very easily match.

At the tactical level, the literature suggests that there are **two interrelated forms of integration** that manufacturers regularly employ.

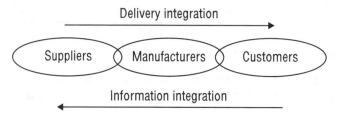

1   Co-ordinating and integrating the **forward physical flow** of deliveries between suppliers, manufacturers and customers, using just-in-time, mass customisation in the supply chain or by exploiting third party logistics
2   Backward co-ordination of information technologies and the flow of data for customers to suppliers

Information technologies allow multiple organisations to co-ordinate their activities in an effort to truly manage a supply chain. Integration using IT includes electronic data interchange (EDI) as well as sharing data for traditional planning and control systems.

According to Hayes and Wheelwright, if this need to develop shared operational activities is accepted, then the strategic issues become **direction**, **degree** and **balance**.

(a)   In which **direction** should integration progress, towards customers and/or towards suppliers?

(b)   To what **degree** of integration should such activity be developed? How far should the company take downstream or upstream integration?

(c)   To what extent does each stage of the supply chain focus on supporting the total supply chain?

The fundamental concerns of direction and degree are the boundaries of the firm and whether the organisation should broaden or narrow the span of its operations, whereas balance deals with the resulting vertically-linked activities, in terms of how dependent the suppliers and customers are on the firm, relative to how dependent the firm is on its suppliers and customers.

The challenges for manufacturing firms are shifting from **internal efficiency** to **supply chain efficiency**. The outward-shifting focus to the supply chain calls for information technology support systems that can handle information exchange between supply chain partners. The information can be integrated through ordinary means of communications such as telephone, fax and email; it can also be integrated through dedicated supply chain planning software.

E-business is revolutionising the way supply chains are configured and managed and, in response, many supply chains are becoming more virtual. They are developing into looser affiliations of companies, organised as a supply network, where direct ownership is changing dramatically.

In all sectors, e-business is increasing the pressure for supply chain responsiveness in three ways.

(a) **Increased competition**. Easier market entry enables new entrants to steal significant market share at the expense of unresponsive existing suppliers.

(b) **Increased volumes and speed of data**. There is a requirement to gather, process and act on massively increasing volumes of data in a rapid and intelligent manner.

(c) **More demanding customer requirements**. These include reduced cost, shorter lead times and reliability of supply.

Additionally, what is not well recognised is the increased capability of customers to bypass their traditional supplier and **cut out the middle man**. This threat is equally applicable right along the supply chain, with the consumer bypassing the retailer, and businesses bypassing tiers of their suppliers. To remain in the chain, companies do not just have to demonstrate the value they add, but also demonstrate their ability to manage their own suppliers.

7 E-procurement 6/11

7.1 The methods, benefits and risks of e-procurement

FAST FORWARD

E-procurement is the purchase of supplies and services through the internet and other information and networking systems, such as Electronic Data Interchange (EDI).

It is typically operated through a secure website, possibly using a paperless system based on a purchasing card. It brings time and efficiency improvements but it also brings threats to control and security. Implementation may proceed according to a variety of models, but initially it is easiest to introduce IS to only part of the improvement cycle.

An important part of many B2B sites, e-procurement is also referred to by other terms, such as **supplier exchange**.

Traditionally, e-procurement has been seen as a simple process from creation of need to placing an electronic purchase order with a supplier and the possible payment by an electronic bank payment system such as BACS. Today the transactional process is considered to be only part of the e-procurement function. It includes purchasing, transportation, goods receipt and warehousing before the goods are used. A properly implemented system can connect companies and their business processes directly with suppliers while managing all interactions between them. This includes management of correspondence, bids, questions and answers, previous pricing, and multiple emails sent to multiple participants.

It focuses on the complete purchasing mix, or the **five rights of purchasing**, which are that goods and services must be delivered:

- At the right **time**
- In the right **quantity**
- In the right **quality**

- At the right **price**
- From the right **vendor**

7.1.1 Methods

Typically, e-procurement websites allow authorised and registered users to log in using a password. The supplying organisation will set up its website so that it recognises the purchaser, once logged in, and presents a list of items that the purchaser regularly buys. This saves searching for the items required and also avoids the need to key in name, address and delivery details. Depending on the approach, buyers or sellers may specify prices or invite bids. Transactions can be initiated and completed. Once the purchases are made, the organisation will periodically be billed by the supplier. Ongoing purchases may qualify customers for volume discounts or special offers.

A very limited form of electronic procurement is the **purchasing card**, which is a paperless purchase and payment system aimed at the end-user who can now order and pay for goods directly with a small number of suppliers. Buyers identify themselves with their card number when placing an order; the supplier checks the purchase card number and, if correct, authorises it with the bank. The bank pays the supplier in 2 to 5 days, and the supplier ships the goods.

7.1.2 Benefits of e-procurement

Cost reduction	Might include process efficiencies, reduction in the actual cost of goods and services, and reduced purchasing agent overheads.
Reduced inventory levels	Knowing product numbers, bid prices and contact points can help businesses close a deal while other suppliers are struggling to gather their relevant data.
Control	The ability to control parts inventories more effectively.
Wider choice of supplier	In theory, resources can be sourced from suppliers anywhere in the world, perhaps at much lower prices than could be obtained if the organisation only considered local suppliers.
Improved manufacturing cycles	Moving to e-sourcing speeds up the sourcing process dramatically, but the increased efficiency and speed can also put the rest of a supply chain in chaos if it is not prepared to step up its performance to meet the increased speed in the purchasing link of the chain.
Intangible benefits	Staff are able to concentrate on their prime function and there is financial transparency and accountability.
Benefits to suppliers	Reduction in ordering and processing costs, reduced paperwork, improved cash flow and reduced cost of credit control.

7.1.3 Risks of e-procurement

(a) **Control.** If anyone can order goods from anywhere, there is a major risk that unauthorised purchases will be made. There is also an increased likelihood that purchases will be made from suppliers who cannot deliver the required quality (or cannot deliver at all).

(b) **Organisational risk.** In moving to an e-procurement tool, an adopting company will make a substantial investment in the software, but for any number of reasons, the implementation may never take flight. Users may not adapt to it well. Suppliers may reject the technology or new process. Technical issues may stall the implementation. Also, managing the internal processes around the changeover is challenging.

(c) **Data security.** Putting a company's spending online means dealing with the security issues that come with any internet-related deployment. This brings up questions like: Who has access to our data? Where is it stored? How is it protected? What happens if we change providers? Do we get our data back? Do they sell spending data to our competitors?

(d) **Management loses spending control.** There is a perceived risk that moving to e-procurement will put spending decisions in the wrong hands internally and management will lose decision-making control over who spends how much on what.

(e) **Supply chain problems.** Moving to e-sourcing speeds up the sourcing process dramatically but the increased efficiency and speed can also destabilise the rest of a supply chain if it is not able to step up its performance to meet the increased speed in the purchasing link of the chain.

Exam focus point

Nine marks were available as part of an optional question in the June 2011 P3 exam. The question required students to explain the principles of e-procurement and evaluate its potential application at the company in question. This was, on the whole, answered very well by candidates with many scoring full marks.

7.2 Options and models for implementing e-procurement

Model	How it works	Examples
Public Web	Individual buyers find individual suppliers on the web and make a purchase. There is no structural relation between buyer and supplier.	Webshops like www.amazon.com
Exchange	Suppliers and buyers trade through a third party open marketplace. They have no structural relationship even though they may regularly deal with each other.	www.autobuytel.com
Supplier centric	An individual supplier gives access to buying organisations for a pre-negotiated product range. Buyer and supplier have a contractual relationship.	www.dell.com www.cisco.com
Buyer centric	Individual companies have contracts with a number of different suppliers. The catalogue and ordering system are maintained within the buying organisation. The system is fully integrated into corporate financial control and reporting systems.	Many software suppliers
B2B Marketplace	An independent third party has agreements with a number of buying and supplying organisations. Buyers and suppliers deal with each other through a marketplace. Both are bound by agreements with the marketplace.	www.productview.com

In terms of the options available to organisations, historically, it has been easier to implement systems that only cover part of the procurement cycle.

For example, buyers may choose a minimal involvement such as an inventory control system or a web based catalogue or they may integrate the entry of the order through a database workflow system. Some networked accounting systems allow staff in the buying department to enter an order, which can then be used by accounting staff to make payment when the invoice arrives.

Enterprise Resource Planning (ERP) systems integrate all the facilities. Such integrated business software systems power a corporate information structure, thus helping companies to control their inventory, purchasing, manufacturing, finance and personnel operations. They allow an organisation to automate and integrate most of its business processes, share common data and practices across the whole enterprise and produce and access information in a real-time environment. ERP may also incorporate transactions with an organisation's suppliers. They help large national and multinational companies in particular to manage geographically dispersed and complex operations. For example, an organisation's UK sales office may be responsible for marketing, selling and servicing a product assembled in the US using parts manufactured in France and Hong Kong. ERP enables the organisation to understand and manage the demand placed on the plant in France.

Chapter Roundup

- **Electronic business**, or e-business, is the automation of business processes of all types through electronic means. This may be restricted to email or may extend to a fully-featured website or an e-marketplace.

  E-business that includes a financial transaction is known as **e-commerce**. E-business is radically different from ordinary business and brings six categories of benefit.

  - Costs are reduced.
  - Capability is increased.
  - Communications are improved.
  - Control is enhanced.
  - Customer service is improved.
  - Competitive advantage may be achieved, depending on competitors' reactions.

  Adoption of e-business methods may be hindered by a range of obstacles including lack of skills; lack of internet use and awareness among businesses and the wider population; and feats about privacy, effectiveness, cost, security and so on.

- Both businesses and customers can originate e-commerce activity; thus there are four main categories: B2B, B2C, C2B and C2C. **Channel structures** are the means by which products and services are delivered to customers. **Disintermediation** removes intermediaries from supply channels while **reintermediation** establishes new ones. **Countermediation** is the creation of a new intermediary by an established company to compete via a business with established intermediaries.

- Rappa describes nine business models. E-commerce business models may also be categorised by characteristics such as value proposition, revenue model and market opportunity.

- **System architecture** is the arrangement of software, machinery and tasks in an information system needed to achieve a specific functionality.

  The **internet** enables computers across the world to communicate via telecommunications links.

  The **World Wide Web** is a navigation system within the internet. It is based on a technology called **hypertext** which allows documents stored on host computers on the internet to be linked to one another.

  An **intranet** is used to disseminate and exchange information 'in-house' within an organisation.

  An **extranet** is used to communicate with selected people outside the organisation.

  In general, all of the machines on the internet can be categorised into two types: servers and clients. The machines that provide services to other machines are servers. And the machines that are used to connect to those services are clients.

  Each machine on the internet is assigned a unique address called an IP address.

  There are several levels to the interaction between a client and a server, from the physical pieces of wire making the connection, through the transfer and checking of data, security problems of access and logging on, to the final presentation to and interaction with the user. The International Standards Organisation (ISO) has defined seven levels in a standard called Open Systems Interconnection.

  A **protocol stack** is a group of protocols that all work together to allow software or hardware to perform a function. The TCP/IP protocol stack is a good example. It uses four layers that map to the OSI model.

  Alternatives to PC-based internet access include interactive digital television and wireless or mobile access.

- For an organisation's IT assets to operate effectively, it is critical that adequate control measures are in place. To help prevent theft, fraud and human error four types of control are needed to protect IT assets. These are:

  - **Physical access controls**
  - **Logical access controls**
  - **Operational controls**
  - **Data input controls**

To ensure that computerised accounting systems are working effectively, it is critical that the input data is treated correctly. This requires the consideration of two key issues: firstly, establishing the rules to ensure that all data input is processed in the same way; and secondly, to ensure that there is a way of assessing whether the controls are working. Controls can be reviewed through the use of test data.

Continuity planning is an umbrella term used to explain the plans and processes an organisation will follow in the event of its business operations being disrupted. **Disaster recovery** is devoted to ensuring the continuation of an organisation's IT systems in the event of some form of disaster.

- Big data is the term used to describe the growth of structured and unstructured data. Some experts argue that big data may be as important to business as the internet.

  Laney suggests that big data can be defined by considering the three V's:

  - Volume
  - Velocity
  - Variety

  Big data analytics refers to the analysis and identification of insights in vast quantities of data. Historically, organisations have been restricted as to the amount of data that they can process due to the storage limitations of existing computer systems.

  McKinsey's 2011 report, 'Big data: The next frontier for innovation, competition and productivity,' suggests five ways in which big data can create value for organisations:

  - Creating transparency
  - Performance improvement
  - Market segmentation and customisation
  - Decision making
  - New products and services

  Critics however argue that big data is simply the latest buzzword which has become an obsession of business leaders and the media alike. Critics claim that big data analytics tend to be too focused on the discovery of correlations between data sets with little interest given to the causation of such relationships.

- The internet has the capacity to transform many businesses via the introduction of new technology and skills and, eventually, the re-positioning of the offering to fit the new market conditions.

  A **strategy for e-commerce** should be considered at the highest level of management and it is particularly necessary that it should conform to the standard criteria for strategic choice: suitability, acceptability and feasibility.

- **Suitability.** For most companies, e-commerce will be a supplement to more traditional operations, with the website forming a supplementary medium for communication and sales.

  Acceptability. The e-commerce strategy must be acceptable to important stakeholders. Distributors are particularly important here.

  Feasibility. Feasibility is a matter of **resources**. The fundamental resource is cash, but the availability of the skilled labour needed to establish and administer a website will be crucial to the e-commerce strategy.

- IT has the capacity to transform businesses. Corporate and e-business strategies thus become complementary, each supporting and influencing the other.

- Several stage models have been proposed for assessing maturity of capability. Such models can also be used as guides to future development.

- A **supply chain** encompasses all activities and information flows necessary for the transformation of goods from the origin of the raw material to when the product is finally consumed or discarded.

  A supply chain always includes push and pull elements. The pull based element is particularly relevant on IS for feedback and control, since it aims to eliminate buffer inventory by increasing responsiveness.

BPP
LEARNING MEDIA

- IS may be used to improve the working of the links between activities in the value chain and between value chains in the value network. One important consequence of this is that improved communication with customers results, making it easier for them to purchase.

- Porter and Millar advocate five steps that senior executives may follow to take advantage of opportunities that the information revolution has created.

- Supply chain management options can be portrayed as a continuum from **vertical integration** to **virtual integration**.

  Vertical disintegration means that various diseconomies of scale or scope have broken a production process into separate companies, each performing a limited subset of activities required to create a finished product.

  A **virtually integrated company** is one in which **core** business functions, as well as non-core functions, take place in external organisations. Virtually integrated companies are so tightly organised that it is often difficult to determine where one legal entity ends and another starts.

- **E-procurement** is the purchase of supplies and services through the internet and other information and networking systems, such as Electronic Data Interchange (EDI).

  It is typically operated through a secure website, possibly using a paperless system based on a purchasing card. It brings time and efficiency improvements but it also brings threats to control and security. Implementation may proceed according to a variety of models, but initially it is easiest to introduce IS to only part of the improvement cycle.

1   What distinguishes e-commerce from e-business?

2   What is disintermediation?

3   How does the infomediary model of e-business work?

4   What is system architecture?

5   Is the bull whip effect associated with the push model or the pull model of the supply chain?

6   What are the axes of Porter and Millar's information intensity matrix?

7   What are the models available for implementing e-procurement?

Answers to Quick Quiz

1   E-business involves transactions over the internet. If an e-business transaction is of a financial nature, it is e-commerce

2   The removal of intermediaries from a supply chain

3   The infomediary collects data about consumers and their purchasing habits and sells it to other businesses

4   The arrangement of software, machinery and tasks in an information system needed to achieve a specific functionality

5   The push model

6   Information content of the product and information intensity of the value chain

7   Public web, exchange, supplier centric, buyer centric, B2B market place

Now try the question below from the Practice Question Bank

Number	Level	Marks	Time
Q12	Examination	25	45 mins

E-marketing

Introduction

This second chapter on e-business is largely concerned with marketing aspects and the way that various aspects of internet technology can be used to build and maintain marketing relationships.

Study guide

		Intellectual level
E4	**E-business application: downstream supply chain management**	
(a)	Define the scope and media of e-marketing	2
(b)	Highlight how the media of e-marketing can be used when developing an effective e-marketing plan	2
(c)	Explore the characteristics of the media of e-marketing using the '6I's of Interactivity, Intelligence, Individualisation, Integration, Industry structure and Independence of location	2
(d)	Evaluate the effect of the media of e-marketing on the traditional marketing mix of product, promotion, price, place, people, processes and physical evidence	3
(e)	Describe a process for establishing a pricing strategy for products and services that recognises both economic and non-economic factors.	2
(f)	Assess the importance of online branding in e-marketing and compare it with traditional branding	3
E5	**E-business application: customer relationship management**	
(a)	Define the meaning and scope of customer relationship management	2
(b)	Explore different methods of acquiring customers through exploiting electronic media	2
(c)	Evaluate different buyer behaviour amongst online customers	3
(d)	Recommend techniques for retaining customers using electronic media	3
(e)	Recommend how electronic media may be used to increase the activity and value of established, retained customers	3
(f)	Discuss the scope of a representative software package solution designed to support customer relationship management	3

Exam guide

This is very practical material relating to strategic implementations or, as JS&W put it, **strategy into action**. As such, it could well be examined in a dedicated question requiring in-depth knowledge, probably in Section B. However, e-business application is also likely to be relevant to many questions in Section A of your exam.

Models and frameworks

The '6I' characteristics of e-marketing are explicitly referenced in the Study Guide, along with the '7Ps' of the extended marketing mix, so these could be specifically referred to in an exam question.

1 E-marketing

E-marketing is the application of IS and internet techniques to the achievement of marketing objectives. Most marketing activities can be enhanced by the use of such techniques, including branding, customer service and sales.

1.1 E-marketing – scope and media

Key term

> **E-marketing** is described by Chaffey in *E-business and E-commerce Management* as 'the application of the internet and related digital technologies to achieve marketing objectives'.

Marketing objectives include identifying, anticipating and satisfying customer requirements profitably.

- **Identifying** – using the internet to find out customers' needs and wants

- **Anticipating** – the demand for digital services

- **Satisfying** – achieving customer satisfaction raises issues over whether the site is easy to use, whether it performs adequately and how are the physical products dispatched

Essentially, e-marketing means using digital technologies to help sell goods or services. The basics of marketing remain the same – creating a strategy to deliver the right messages to the right people. What has changed is the number of options available. These include pay per click advertising, banner ads, email marketing and affiliate marketing, interactive advertising, search engine marketing (including search engine optimisation) and blog marketing.

Though businesses will continue to make use of traditional marketing methods, such as advertising, direct mail and PR, e-marketing adds a whole new element to the marketing mix and is a valuable complement. It gives businesses of any size access to the mass market at an affordable price and, unlike TV or print advertising, it allows truly personalised marketing.

1.1.1 Key marketing functions the internet can perform

(a) **Creating company and product awareness** – communicating essential information about the company and its brands. Such information may have a financial orientation to help attract potential investors, or it may focus on the unique features and benefits of its product lines.

(b) **Branding** – is a marketing communications activity. The intent is to have the public perceive a brand in a positive manner. With the amount of advertising being devoted to the internet increasing each year, the frequency of visits to a site will also increase. Consequently, a website will play a more prominent role in building brand image. Online communications should therefore be similar in appearance and style to communications in the traditional media so as to present a consistent brand image.

(c) **Offering incentives** – many sites offer discounts for purchasing online. Electronic coupons, bonus offers, and contests are now quite common. Such offers are intended to stimulate immediate purchase before a visitor leaves a website and encourage repeat visits.

(d) **Lead generation** – the internet is an interactive medium. Visitors to a site leave useful information behind when they fill in boxes requesting more information (eg, name, address, telephone number, and email address). A site may also ask for demographic information that can be added to the company's database. This information is retained for future mailings about similar offers, or they can be turned over to a sales force for follow-up if it is a business-to-business marketing situation.

(e) **Customer service** – in any form of marketing, customer service is important. Satisfied customers hold positive attitudes about a company and are apt to return to buy more goods. Right now, customer service is perceived as a weak link in internet marketing. Customers are concerned about who they should call for technical assistance or what process to follow should goods need to be returned. Some customer service tactics commonly used include frequently asked questions

(FAQs) and return email systems. It is apparent that organisations will have to spend more time and money developing effective customer service systems.

(f) **Email databases** – organisations retain visitor information in a database. Emailing useful and relevant information to prospects and customers helps build stronger relationships. An organisation must be careful that it does not distribute spam on the internet. Spam refers to the delivery of unsolicited or unwanted email.

(g) **Online transaction** – organisations are capable of selling online if the website is user friendly. Sites that are difficult to navigate create frustration in visitors. Presently, the business-to-business market is booming with business transactions. Organisations in the supply chain are linking together to achieve efficiencies in the buying-selling process.

1.1.2 Specific benefits of e-marketing

(a) **Global reach** – a website can reach anyone in the world who has internet access. This allows organisations to find new markets and compete globally for only a small investment.

(b) **Lower cost** – a properly planned and effectively targeted e-marketing campaign can reach the right customers at a much lower cost than traditional marketing methods.

(c) **The ability to track and measure results** – marketing by email or banner advertising makes it easier to establish how effective your campaign has been. You can obtain detailed information about customers' responses to your advertising.

(d) **24-hour marketing** – with a website your customers can find out about your products even if your office is closed.

(e) **Personalisation** – if the customer database is linked to the website, then whenever someone visits the site, they can be greeted with targeted offers. The more they buy from the organisation, the more the organisation can refine the customer profile and market effectively to them.

(f) **One-to-one marketing** – e-marketing helps to reach people who want to know about the products and services instantly. For example, many people take their mobile phones or tablet computers with them wherever they go. Combine this with the personalised aspect of e-marketing, and you can create very powerful, targeted campaigns.

(g) **More interesting campaigns** – e-marketing helps to create interactive campaigns using music, graphics and videos. For example, sending customers a game or a quiz – whatever will interest them.

(h) **Better conversion rate** – customers are only ever a few clicks away from completing a purchase. Unlike other media which require people to get up and make a phone call, post a letter or go to a shop, e-marketing is seamless.

Together, all of these aspects of e-marketing have the potential to add up to more sales.

As a component of e-commerce, it can include information management; public relations; customer service and sales.

1.2 Developing an effective e-marketing plan

It is important to recognise that planning for e-marketing does not mean starting from scratch. Any online e-communication must be **consistent with the overall marketing goals** and **current marketing efforts** of the organisation.

The key strategic decisions for e-marketing are common with strategic decisions for traditional marketing. They involve selecting target customer groups and specifying how to deliver value to these groups. Segmentation, targeting, differentiation and positioning all contribute to effective digital marketing.

The **SOSTAC ® planning framework** developed by Paul Smith provides a structured and effective approach to marketing strategy. It can be used by managers in the private, public and non-profit sectors.

S = Situation Analysis	Where are we now? What is the external environment in which we are operating? What are our own strengths and weaknesses?
O = Objectives	Where do we want to get to? What is our goal?
S = Strategies	How do we get there? What do we need to do to be successful?
T = Tactics	What are the individual steps we need to take to achieve our objective?
A = Actions	What are the things we need to do? What is our 'to-do' list? Who will do what?
C = Control	What will we measure to know we are succeeding? How will we know when we have arrived?

The planning framework is expanded in the diagram below to show the techniques/actions that make up each stage:

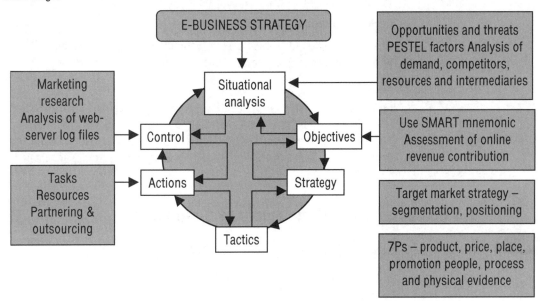

Framework for e-marketing planning

In developing an effective e-marketing plan, the media of e-marketing used at certain stages will include the following.

Competitor analysis	Scanning competitor internet sites
	Competitor benchmarking to compare e-commerce services within a market
	Competitive intelligence systems give a structured approach to monitoring and disseminating information on competitor activities
Intermediary analysis	Identify and compare intermediaries for a marketplace
	Search portals and look for new approaches for traffic building
	Research whether competitors are using disintermediation or reintermediation

Internal marketing audit	Focus on e-market measurement:

Channel promotion	Channel behaviour	Channel satisfaction	Channel outcomes	Channel profitability
Acquisition costs Referrers	Who? How?	Opinions? Attitudes? Brand impact?	Leads? Sales?	ROI? Profitability?

Internal marketing audit (cont.)	Applying web analytics tools to measure the contribution of leads, sales and brand involvement currently delivered by online communications such as search engine marketing, online advertising and email marketing in conjunction with the website
	Create online CRM capabilities to understand customers' characteristics, needs and behaviours and to deliver targeted, personalised value
Objective setting	Online revenue contribution
Strategy	Identify target market by assessing size, segments, needs and competitive action
	Online value proposition (OVP)
Tactics	Use internet to vary the extended product
	Look at new channel structures
	Research people replacements: auto responders, email notification, call-back facility, FAQs, on-site search engines and virtual assistants
	Branding
	Managing the continuous online marketing communications such as search engine marketing, partnerships, sponsorships and affiliate arrangements and campaign-based e-marketing communications such as online advertising, email marketing and microsites to encourage usage of the online service and to support customer acquisition and retention campaigns

1.3 Characteristics of the media of e-marketing   12/13, 6/11

FAST FORWARD

The employment of e-marketing may be analysed and planned using the six Is.

- Independence of location
- Industry structure
- Integration
- Interactivity
- Individualisation
- Intelligence

The six Is of marketing developed at Cranfield by McDonald and Wilson in 1999, summarise the ways in which the internet can add customer value and hence improve the organisation's marketing effectiveness.

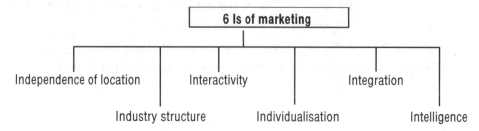

By considering and questioning each of these aspects of new media marketing, managers can develop plans to accommodate the characteristics of new media.

Independence of location	Do you exploit any opportunities to deliver information-based products and services electronically? Electronic media gives the possibility of communicating globally – giving opportunities of selling into markets that may not have been previously accessible.
Industry structure	Industry restructuring includes the following: Redesigning business processes Redrawing the market map in form of new market segments or increasing the marketing boundaries Adopting IT enabled services (ITeS)
Integration	Do you have detailed knowledge of individual customers, influencers or consumers? Do you share this knowledge across all customer-facing parts of the business? Advertising products/services on the web is easy. It is more difficult, but absolutely crucial to gather vital customer information, obtain customer feedback, use existing knowledge about the customer and exploit the web's interactive nature to add value through product configuration, online pricing and so on.
Interactivity	Do you use interactive media to allow your customers to communicate with you? Do you listen to what they say and respond appropriately in a continuing dialogue? Traditional media are mainly 'push' media – the marketing message is broadcast from company to customer – with limited interaction. On the internet, it is usually a customer who seeks information on a website – it is a 'pull' mechanism. The growing use of carefully targeted direct mail as a means of communicating with individual customers has led some to call this 'the age of addressability'
Individualisation	Do you use your customer knowledge to tailor products and services to the needs of particular individuals or segments? Do you tailor all your communications to the characteristics of the recipients? Communications can be tailored to the individual, unlike traditional media where the same message is broadcast to everyone. As we saw in the previous chapter, the increasing use of big data has enabled companies like Amazon to tailor their marketing message and purchase recommendations to customers based on purchases made by other customers with similar interests.
Intelligence	Do you inform your marketing strategy with intelligence gleaned from your operational systems at the customer interface eg, through analysis of customer needs, segmentation, prioritising segments according to customer lifetime value etc? The internet can be used as a low cost method of collecting marketing information about customer perceptions of products and services. The website also records information every time a user clicks on a link. Log file analysers will identify the type of promotions or products customers are responding to and how patterns vary over time.

Example

The best-known example of electronic commerce – book-selling, exemplifies how the internet can be used for an interactive dialogue with a known customer.

Websites such as Amazon.com exploit the web's interactive nature to allow the customer to search for books on particular topics, track the status of an order placed earlier, and ask for recommendations of books similar to their favourites, read reviews placed by other customers, and so on. The website builds knowledge of the customer which allows it, for example, to notify them by email if a new book appears on a topic of particular interest.

The June 2008 exam included a Section B question which asked candidates to identify how electronic media could provide a training college with different marketing opportunities to traditional media (such as advertising and direct mail). The '6 I' framework was a particularly effective tool to use when answering this question, because the marketing implications of each 'I' for the college could be compared and contrasted between traditional and electronic media.

The June 2011 exam offered 16 marks for evaluating how the principles of **interactivity**, **intelligence**, **individualisation and independence of location** might be applied in marketing the products and services of a used car dealership. Remember when answering questions such as this, to apply your answer specifically to the scenario given and not simply churn out generic lists. For example, the majority of students who sat this particular paper failed to recognise that 'expanding globally' due to independence of location might not be appropriate for a used car dealership!

1.4 E-marketing and the 7Ps   12/10

FAST FORWARD

More specific concepts for the development of e-marketing may be based on the 7Ps.

- The augmented **product** can be extended through website information and interactivity.
- **Pricing** can be made transparent; dynamic pricing may be used.
- The global reach of the internet has great implications for **place**, with the creation of new marketplaces and channel structures.
- **Promotion** can be previously targeted via customer databases.
- **People** can be replaced by software to a varying extent.
- **Processes** may be automated.
- **Physical evidence** consists of the customer's experience of using the organisation's e-marketing tools in general and of its website in particular

Marketing on the internet brings many new opportunities not readily available or affordable using conventional marketing methods.

The marketing mix is the combination of marketing activities that an organisation engages in, so as to best meet the needs of its targeted market. Because of changes in the market and the behaviour of the customers, future marketing should focus more on delivering value to the customer and become better at placing the customer – and not the product – in the centre. In some texts, the 4 Ps have been renamed the 4 Cs.

- Product becomes **customer value**
- Place becomes **customer convenience**
- Promotion becomes **customer communication**
- Price becomes **customer cost**

Another change proposed because marketing has expanded into service delivery, means that the original 4Ps of the marketing mix have been joined by three more Ps (Dibb & Simkin, 1994) (see diagram below):

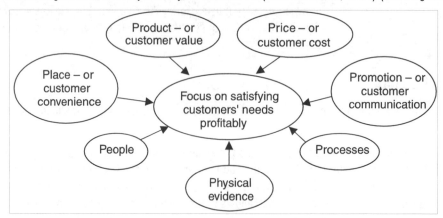

In this section, we can show how e-commerce provides the opportunities for the marketer to vary the seven elements of the marketing mix.

1.4.1 Product (or customer value)

This is the element of the marketing mix that involves researching customers' needs and developing appropriate products. Philip Kotler, in *Principles of Marketing,* devised a very interesting concept of benefit building with a product. He suggested that a product should be viewed in three levels.

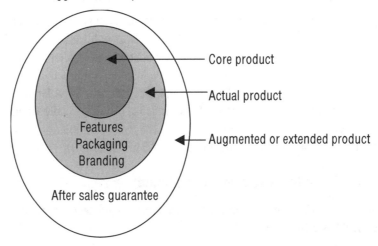

Core product – what is the core benefit the product offers? Customers who purchase a camera are buying more than just a camera – they are purchasing memories.

Actual product – all cameras capture memories. The strategy at this level involves organisations **branding**, **adding features** and benefits to ensure that their product offers a differential advantage from their competitors.

Augmented or **extended product**: What additional non-tangible benefits can you offer? Competition at this level is based around after sales service, warranties, delivery and so on.

What does buying products online offer over one-to-one sales?

(a) The ability to deliver interactivity and more detailed information through the internet is the key to enhancing the augmented or extended product offering online.

(b) The buyer knows immediately about product features – the facts, not a sales person's interpretations.

(c) The buying process is customised for returning visitors, making repeat purchases easier. Organisations can also offer immediately ancillary products along with the main purchase. EasyJet, for example, can readily bundle its flights, hotels and car hire through suitable design of its website.

(d) The product can also be customised to consumers needs eg www.nike.com offers customised trainers to users online. Users can design and see their trainers online before they order.

1.4.2 Price (or customer cost)

The internet has made pricing very competitive. Many costs, such as store rental and staff costs, have disappeared for completely online stores, placing price pressures on traditional retailers.

(a) The internet increases customer knowledge through **increased price transparency,** since it becomes much quicker to shop around and compare quoted prices by visiting supplier websites. Even more significant is the use of price comparison sites by consumers. Sites such as Kelkoo.com give a single location that empowers the consumer to quickly find out the best price from a variety of suppliers for a range of products, from books and CDs to white goods. Such easy access to information helps to maintain prices within the online world.

(b) **Dynamic pricing** gives the ability to test prices or to offer differential pricing for different segments or in response to variations in demand. For some product areas such as ticketing, it may be possible to dynamically alter prices in line with demand. Tickets.com adjusts concert ticket prices according to demand and has been able to achieve 45% more revenue per event as a result.

(c) Different types of pricing may be possible on the internet, particularly for digital, downloadable products. Software and music has traditionally been sold for a continuous right to use. The internet offers new options, such as payment per use; rental at a fixed cost per month or a lease arrangement. Bundling options may also be more possible.

(d) The growth of online auctions also helps consumers to dictate price. The online auction company eBay has grown in popularity with thousands of buyers and seller bidding daily.

(e) E-pricing can also easily reward loyal customers. Technology allows repeat visitors to be tracked, easily allowing loyalty incentives to be targeted towards them.

(f) Payment is also easy; PayPal or online credit cards allow for easy payments. However, the downside to this is internet fraud, which is growing rapidly around the world.

Price is a crucial part of the marketing mix. The concept of price and the process of establishing a pricing strategy are considered in-depth in Section 1.5 of this chapter.

1.4.3 Place (or customer convenience)

Allen and Fjermestad argue that the internet has the greatest implications for **place** in the marketing mix, since it has a global reach.

E-Business Models

Types of marketplaces	Set up by	Main aim
Controlled by sellers	Single vendor seeking many buyers	To retain value and power in any transaction
Controlled by buyers	One or more buyers	To shift value and power in marketplace onto the buyer's side Buyer intermediaries can also be there to act as agents
Neutral marketplaces	Third party intermediaries to match many buyers to many sellers	To match buyers to sellers at an auction Commission based

Choosing a marketplace depends on four factors:

- Are there transactions or benefits to be realised?
- Is the electronic market for the product developing quickly?
- Does the company have substantial market share or buying power?
- Would a neutral intermediary be beneficial?

Types of e-commerce marketplace

- B2C and B2B (eg, Dell and Alibaba)
- C2C (eBay)
- Auctions, (eBay, QXL)
- Consumer reviews (Bizrate)
- Games (There.com)
- C2B
- Customer bids (Priceline)

New channel structures – strategies need to be developed for the following forms.

(a) **Disintermediation** – is there an option for selling direct? When assessing this option, there will be a number of barriers and facilitators to this change. A significant threat arising from the introduction of an internet channel is that while disintermediation gives a company the opportunity to sell direct and increase profitability on products, it can also threaten distribution arrangements with existing partners.

(b) **Reintermediation** – new intermediaries created through re-intermediation, for example Lastminute.com or Travelocity, should be evaluated for suitability for partnering with affiliate arrangements. These intermediaries receive a commission on each sale resulting from a referral from their site. Reintermediation is particularly common in the travel industry, where online reintermediaries are replacing traditional travel agents.

(c) **Countermediation** – should the organisation partner with another independent intermediary, or set up its own independent intermediary? For example, a group of European airlines have joined forces to form Opodo, which is intended to counter independent companies such as Lastminute.com or eBookers offering discount fares.

Navigation – there are three aspects of navigation that are key to achieving competitive advantage online.

(a) **Reach** – this is the potential audience of the e-commerce site. Reach can be increased by moving from a single site to representation with a large number of different intermediaries.

(b) **Richness** – this is the depth or detail of information which is both collected about the customer and provided to the customer. This is related to the product element of the mix.

(c) **Affiliation** – this refers to whose interest the selling organisation represents – consumers or suppliers. This particularly applies to retailers. It suggests that customers will favour retailers who provide them with the richest information on comparing competitive products.

Localisation – providing a local site, usually a language specific version, is referred to as localisation. A site may need to support customers from a range of countries; they may have different product needs, language differences and cultural differences.

1.4.4 Promotion (or customer communication)

Marketing communications are used to inform customers and other stakeholders about an organisation and its products.

(a) There are new ways of applying each of the elements of the **communications mix** (advertising, sales promotions, PR and direct marketing), using new media such as the web and email. Most organisations today have some form of webpage used in most, if not all, advertisements. Placing banner advertisements on other web pages is a common form of e-promotion. Website public relations (WPR) is another approach to promoting online. Newsworthy stories based on product or service launches can be placed on the company's webpage, or WPR articles sent to review sites for consumers to read.

(b) The internet can be used at different stages of the **buying process**. For instance, the main role of the web is often in providing further information rather than completing the sale. Think of a car purchase. Many consumers will now review models online, but most still buy in the real world.

(c) Promotional tools may be used to assist in different stages of **customer relationship management** from customer acquisition to retention. In a website context, this includes gaining initial visitors to the site and gaining repeat visits using, for example, direct email reminders of site proposition and new offers.

(d) The internet can be integrated into **campaigns**. For example, we are currently seeing many direct response print and TV ad campaigns where the web is used to manage entry into a prize draw and to profile the entrant for future communications.

These general technological trends impact across the promotional mix.

Promotion activity	Impact/opportunity	Examples of supporting technology
Advertising	Reach more customers worldwide Target audiences more specifically Increase response via interactivity	Websites and ads Specialist TV channels Direct Response TV, SMS text messaging
Sales promotion	Target segment/individual interests and preferences Facilitate/motivate response Online discounts (lower admin costs)	Customer databases, EPOS data Online entry/coupons Online transaction
Direct marketing	Personalised, one-to-one messages Permission-based database/contacts to enhance response rate Speed and interactivity of response Direct response/transaction	Database Email, website, SMS requests for info Email + website links E-commerce sites
PR and publicity	Speed of information dissemination and response to crisis/issues	Email media releases and online information
Marketing/sales support	Publicising sponsorships Publicising exhibition attendance Up-to-date information for sales force & call centre staff	Website Website/email clients Access to product/inventory and customer database
Internal marketing	Staff access to information relevant to their jobs Co-ordination/identification of dispersed offices and off-site staff	Intranet newsletters, bulletins, policy info Email, tele- and video-conferencing
Network marketing	Supplier/client access to information relevant to business relationship	Extranet: access to selected information

1.4.5 People

The **people** element of the marketing mix is the way an organisation's staff interact with customers and other stakeholders during sales and pre and post sales. Smith and Chaffey (2001) suggest that online, part of the consideration for the people element of the mix is the consideration of the tactics by which people can be replaced or automated.

(a)   **Auto responders** automatically generate a response when a company emails an organisation, or submits an online form.

(b)   **Email notification** may be automatically generated by a company's systems to update customers on the progress of their orders. Such notifications might show, for example, three stages: order received; item now in stock; order dispatched.

(c)   **Call-back facility** requires that customers fill in their phone number on a form and specify a convenient time to be contacted. Dialling from a representative in the call centre occurs automatically at the appointed time and the company pays.

(d)   **Frequently Asked Questions (FAQ)** can pre-empt enquires. The art lies in compiling and categorising the questions so customers can easily find both the question and a helpful answer.

(e)   **On-site search engines** help customers find what they are looking for quickly. Site maps are a related feature.

(f)   **Virtual assistants** come in varying degrees of sophistication and usually help to guide the customer through a maze of choices.

1.4.6 Process

The **process** element of the marketing mix is the internal methods and procedures companies use to achieve all marketing functions such as new product development, promotion, sales and customer service. The restructuring of the organisation and channel structures described for product, price, place and promotion all require new **processes**.

Exam focus point

Note the link here to process redesign: changes in the business structures usually need to be supported by changes in business process.

1.4.7 Physical evidence

The physical evidence element of the marketing mix is the tangible expression of a product and how it is purchased and used. In an online context, physical evidence is customers' experience of the company through the website and associated support. It includes issues such as ease of use, navigation, availability and performance. Responsiveness to email enquiries is a key aspect of performance. The process must be right to enable an acceptable response within the notified service standards such as 24 hours.

1.4.8 Example

A university can put its reading list on a website and students wishing to purchase any given book can click directly through to an online bookseller such as Amazon.com. The university gets a commission; the online bookseller gets increased business; the student gets a discount. Everyone benefits except the traditional bookshop.

Benefits of e-marketing
It promotes **transparent pricing** – because potential customers can readily compare prices not only from suppliers within any given country, but also from suppliers across the world.
It facilitates **personalised attention** – even if such attention is actually administered through impersonal, yet highly sophisticated IT systems and customer database manipulation.
It provides sophisticated **market segmentation** opportunities. Approaching such segments may be one of the few ways in which e-commerce entrepreneurs can create **competitive advantage**.
The website can either be a **separate** or a **complementary** channel.
A new phenomenon is emerging called **dynamic pricing**. Companies can rapidly change their prices to reflect the current state of demand and supply.

These new trends are creating **pressure** for companies. The main threat facing companies is that **prices will be driven down by consumers' ability to shop around**.

1.5 Price and pricing strategies   6/14, 12/11

FAST FORWARD

One of the most complex decisions involved in the marketing mix is deciding on the **price** of the product or service. There are eight steps in the process of establishing prices:

- Select a pricing objective
- Assess target market's evaluation of price and its ability to buy
- Determine the nature and price elasticity of demand
- Analyse demand, cost and profit relationships
- Evaluate competitor's prices
- Determine the basis for pricing
- Select a primary strategy
- Determine the final price

Key term	**Price** is the value placed on what is exchanged.

| Exam focus point | An article titled 'Business strategy and pricing' (February 2011) written by Ken Garrett was published in *Student Accountant*, and is available on the ACCA website. It would be worth taking the time to study this article.

Question 2 in June 2014 required candidates to suggest a pricing strategy for an IT training company. The question required candidates to consider both financial and non-financial matters in determining an appropriate price for courses. The scenario set out an initial price of $750 per delegate attending a training course. Financial details had been provided for a similar company for the purpose of calculating expected values for use in analysing the suggested price. The examining team noted that the question was not well answered, 'financial analysis was often limited, with little use of expected values. The non-financial analysis was often poorly structured and was not well integrated with the financial analysis'.

The 16 marks available were given an equal weighting between the financial and non-financial considerations. It is important that you devote sufficient time to both elements when answering questions. Better candidates recognised this and therefore scored higher marks. |
| --- | --- |

One of the most complex decisions involved in the marketing mix is deciding on the **price** of the product or service. Buyers have only limited resources and have to make decisions about what they will and will not buy. In order to do this, they consider the usefulness of the product, or the benefits they expect to derive from it, and compare this to the cost to determine if the exchange will be worthwhile. This is what makes price so important.

Price directly affects how well an organisation performs competitively, and is also closely linked to the perceptions of value for money held by the customers.

If the price is too high, the exchange may not be perceived as worthwhile, and customers may not buy the product.

If the price is too low, then one of two things could happen:

(1)   The product sells well, however, the revenue per item is lower than it could be if the price were higher, less revenue is earned which, in turn, means less profit than may be possible with a higher price.

(2)   The consumer perceives the price to be too low and interprets this as meaning quality has been compromised. The customer does not buy the product at all.

Getting this balance right (and not setting a price either too high or too low) can be difficult and the organisation will have to take many factors into account when setting the price for their products and services. An **eight stage process** can be used:

(1)   Select a pricing objective
(2)   Assess target market's evaluation of price and its ability to buy
(3)   Determine the nature and price elasticity of demand
(4)   Analyse demand, cost and profit relationships
(5)   Evaluate competitors' prices
(6)   Determine the basis for pricing
(7)   Select a pricing strategy
(8)   Determine the final price

We will consider each of these eight steps to illustrate the price setting process.

Exam focus point	The December 2011 exam included a Section B question which offered 15 marks for identifying and discussing the factors that need to be taken into consideration when pricing an e-learning product. This question was an unpopular choice and a general lack of knowledge in this area was evident in many of those who did attempt it.

1.5.1 Pricing objectives

The first stage of setting a price is to select a **pricing objective**. This pricing objective must be consistent with the:

- **Overall objectives of the organisation**
- **Marketing objectives**

Inconsistency can impact on the ability of the organisation to achieve its overall goals, can lead to internal conflicts and confusion, and can cause poor decisions to be made further down the line.

Pricing objectives form the basis of decisions made at later stages of the price setting process. Therefore, these objectives should be explicitly stated and should include the time within which the objectives should be achieved.

Organisations should have one or more pricing objectives for each product. Different pricing objectives can be chosen for the same product aimed at different market segments.

Pricing objectives typically change over time.

1.5.2 Assessing the target market's evaluation of price and its ability to buy

The second stage involves understanding the amount that an individual will pay for something. This depends on a number of factors.

(a) **Type of product** – people will be more sensitive to changes in the price of food than they are to changes in the price of new cars. This may be for two reasons. Firstly, food is a necessity, whereas a car is a luxury. Secondly, this may be due to the percentage of income spent on such goods.

(b) **Target market** – business travellers are less concerned about train prices than those travelling for leisure purposes.

(c) **Purchase situation** – people are willing to pay more for soft drinks and popcorn at a cinema than they would in a supermarket.

The key to this stage is to understand the buying power of the customers, and also how important one product is to them over another. Value for money perceptions of the customer are important here.

1.5.3 Determining demand

The next stage is to determine the demand for the product by considering its relationship with price. For most products, the quantity demanded falls as the price increases, as illustrated by the classic demand curve shown as D1 below.

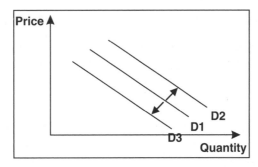

This relationship will hold true so long as all other factors remain constant. However, the other factors in the marketing mix also affect demand. If one of those other factors changes, this may cause the demand curve to shift, as illustrated by D2 and D3 in the diagram above. The direction of the shift will depend on what the other factor is and its impact on demand.

The steepness of the demand curve will be determined by the **price elasticity of demand**. The more sensitive demand is to changes in price, the more **elastic** demand is said to be. For example, demand for basic food items and utilities might be relatively **inelastic**. This means that changes in the price only have a slight effect on the demand for these products and the demand curve will be **steep**. They are essential

items that will still be demanded, even when prices rise. The change in demand is less than proportional to the change in price. Demand for more luxury products, such as exotic holidays on the other hand, is more **elastic**. This means that if the price increases, the fall in demand will be greater than proportional to the increase in demand and therefore total revenue for the product will fall. This demand curve will be much **flatter**.

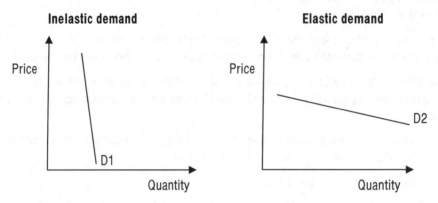

However, not all products conform to this model. Some products, such as designer clothing, sell better the higher the price. This is because the price is associated by the customer with high quality and exclusivity. A fall in price would cause the item to be within the price range of more people, and as such no longer 'exclusive', and so demand would fall. The demand curve for products such as this is shown below.

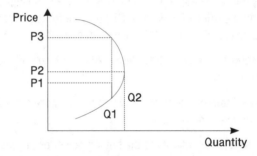

1.5.4 Analysis of demand, cost and profit relationships

The next step involves developing an understanding of demand, cost and profit relationships. There are two approaches for doing this

- **Marginal analysis**
- **Break-even analysis**

Marginal analysis

Marginal analysis is concerned with how a change in production (or sales volume) by one unit affects an organisation's costs and revenues. Marginal cost is the extra cost incurred when one more unit is produced.

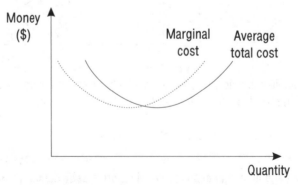

The marginal cost curve is typically U-shaped. This is because marginal costs decrease as output increases due to economies of scale. However, at some point diseconomies of scale (eg more supervision and larger workforce) appear and marginal costs begin to rise.

Marginal revenue is the change in total revenue that occurs when one more unit is sold.

Due to the downward sloping demand curve faced by most organisations, the only way additional units can be sold is through the lowering of prices. Therefore, each additional product sold provides less revenue than the previous one. When marginal revenue falls to zero, the sale of more units actually harms the profits.

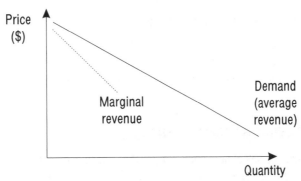

Profit is maximised where **marginal cost equals marginal revenue**. Up to this point, the additional revenue generated per unit is more than the additional cost. After this point, the additional cost exceeds the additional revenue.

Unfortunately, in reality the cost (supply) and revenue (demand) change regularly and rapidly. However, it is still beneficial to organisations to have an understanding of the relationship between the marginal cost and marginal revenues when setting prices of existing products.

Marginal analysis offers little help in the pricing of new products as costs and revenues will not yet be established.

Break-even analysis

The **break-even point** is the point at which the costs of producing a product equal the revenue made from selling it. It is important to know how many units are required to break-even when determining the price.

$$\text{Break-even point} = \frac{\text{fixed costs}}{\text{price} - \text{variable costs}}$$

To use break-even analysis effectively, the break-even point for a range of different prices should be established. This allows the effects on total revenue, total cost and the break-even point for each price under consideration to be assessed. Although it may not indicate the correct price to charge, it will identify any price alternatives that should definitely be avoided.

The diagram below illustrates the relationship between the costs, revenues, profits and losses involved in determining the break-even point.

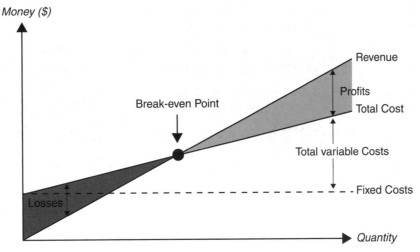

The problem with break-even analysis is that it focuses on recovering costs and breaking even, rather than on how to achieve a pricing objective, eg a return on investment or percentage of market share.

1.5.5 Evaluation of competitors' prices

The price set will be influenced by the prices of competitors. Evaluating these is step five of the price setting process.

Setting a price is much easier when the amount charged by the competition is known. However, this is not always an easy task, particularly in producer and reseller markets. Even if the organisation has access to the price lists, these may not reflect the true prices where these are established through negotiation.

Competitor prices are important to organisations as they can help them to ensure that their own prices are in line. Some organisations may choose to make their own price slightly higher to indicate 'quality' to the customer. Others may choose to use price as a competitive tool by selecting prices that undercut the competition.

1.5.6 Determine a basis for pricing

Stage six involves selecting a basis for pricing. Prices can be determined on the basis of cost, demand, competition, or marketing.

Price basis	Features	Limitations	Suitable uses
Cost-based pricing	A monetary amount or percentage is added to the product cost. It involves calculating desired profit margins and is a simple method to implement. There are two main types of cost-based pricing: cost plus, and mark-up. **Cost-plus pricing**: Seller's costs are determined and then an amount or percentage is added to these costs to determine price. In industries where this approach is common and sellers have similar costs, price competition may be relatively low. **Mark-up pricing**: Price is determined by adding a pre-determined percentage of the cost (the mark-up) to the cost of the product. The same percentage is often used for the prices of items within a single product category and similar mark-ups may be used across an industry at the retail level.	Does not relate to a specific pricing approach, nor does it ensure the attainment of pricing objectives Some costs are difficult to determine. Seller may increase costs to gain larger profits.	Appropriate when production costs are hard to predict, or production takes a long time, eg custom-made equipment or commercial construction projects. Popular in periods of rapid inflation as raw materials used may fluctuate in price.
Demand-based pricing	The price is high when demand is high, and low when demand is weak. Compared to cost-based pricing, this method allows higher profits to be achieved.	The effectiveness of the pricing depends on the ability of the price setter to estimate demand accurately.	Leisure amenities, eg peak time and off peak gym memberships.

Price basis	Features	Limitations	Suitable uses
Competition-based pricing	Prices are set in relation to competitors. The price may be above, in line with, or below those of competitors depending on the strategy of the organisation. This method should help attain a pricing objective to increase sales or market share. It can also be combined with cost approaches to arrive at price levels necessary to attain a profit.	True amounts charged by competitors can be difficult to determine.	Useful where products are almost homogeneous and price is the key variable of the marketing strategy eg domestic supply of gas or electricity.
Marketing-oriented pricing	This kind of pricing takes account of a wide range of factors: • Marketing strategy • Competition • Costs • Product line pricing • Value to the customer • Negotiating margins • Price-quality relationships • Political factors • Explicability • Effect of distributors/retailers The price set must reflect the product's marketing strategy, ie target market profile, brand positioning and sales targets. The price must also be in line with the rest of the marketing mix (the other 6 of the 7Ps).	This is the most complex approach to pricing. It is a detailed and time consuming process.	This approach takes account of many different factors that influence price. It is appropriate where sufficient time and resources are available to carry out the necessary analysis.

1.5.7 Selection of pricing strategy

A **pricing strategy** is an approach designed to influence and determine pricing decisions. It helps to solve the practical problems of establishing prices.

There are five main types of pricing strategies

- **Differential pricing**
- **New product pricing**
- **Product-line pricing**
- **Psychological pricing**
- **Professional pricing**
- **Promotional pricing**

Differential pricing

This involves charging different prices to different customers for the same quality and quantity of product. There are four ways this can be done.

Negotiated pricing	The final price is established through bargaining between the seller and buyer. This is common for products such as houses and cars as well as for second-hand items.
Secondary market pricing	One price is set for the primary market and another (usually lower) price is set for another market. This might be used by a restaurant that offers cheap deals for eating earlier in the evening.
Periodic discounting	Temporarily reducing prices on a systematic basis, for example many retailers hold January and summer sales. The disadvantage of these is that, due to their predictable pattern, customers learn to expect the reductions and wait to make their purchases then.
Random discounting	Temporary reductions are made as above but on an unsystematic basis. This means the customer cannot predict when the sales are likely to be and so will purchase in line with their own requirements rather than waiting for the reductions to be made.

New product pricing

When a new product is launched, a base price will have to be set for it. This can be done in two key ways.

Price skimming	The price is set at the highest possible price that customers who most desire the product will pay. This provides the most flexible base price as demand is not very price sensitive at the introductory stage of a new product. For example, when flat screen TVs were first introduced they were extremely expensive compared to regular TVs. Now that they have become the norm, their price has fallen dramatically. By setting the price at the highest level possible, a lot of profit can be made from sales of only a few units to customers who desperately want to be the first to own a new product. This high profit helps organisations recover the high research and development costs they will have faced in the run up to its launch and will probably have limited production capacity, so will need to earn a higher revenue per unit.
Penetration pricing	A price is set below the prices of competing brands in order to penetrate a market and produce a larger unit sales volume. This approach is less flexible than price skimming as it is harder to raise than to lower a price. Often a penetration price may be used for a product after first skimming the market with a higher price. Penetration pricing is most useful where it is believed that competitors could easily enter the market.

Product-line pricing

Product-line pricing means establishing and adjusting prices of multiple products within a product line. There are four main ways of doing this.

Captive pricing	The basic product is priced low, but related products are priced high. For example, a printer may be sold at a low price, but the ink cartridges may be very expensive.
Premium pricing	The highest quality, or most versatile, products are given the highest price and the rest of the products in the range are priced to appeal to price-sensitive customers or those that desire specific features.
Bait pricing	One item in the product line is priced very low with the aim of selling a higher-priced item in the line. It may advertise its cheaply priced most basic model in the hope the customer will actually purchase a more expensive version.
Price lining	A limited number of prices are set for lines of merchandise, eg various styles and brands of clothing that all sell for $40, and another higher quality line that all sell for $65. If price lining is used, the demand curve looks like a series of steps.

Psychological pricing

Psychological pricing encourages customers to base their decisions on emotional, rather than rational, responses. There are seven key techniques for doing this.

Reference pricing	This involves pricing a product at a moderate level and then positioning it next to a more expensive model or brand.
Bundle pricing	Packaging two or more complementary products and selling them for a single price, which is usually lower than they would cost if both items were purchased separately. Examples could be shampoo and conditioner, or hand wash and hand cream. This kind of pricing is also common in travel services, banking and car sales.
Multiple-unit pricing	Two or more identical products are packaged together and sold for a single price, usually at a lower price than it would cost to purchase a single unit. Examples are tins of baked beans and bars of soap.
Everyday low prices (EDLP)	A consistent low price (rather than regular discounting) is set for a product that is sufficiently below the prices of competitors for customers to feel that they are receiving a good deal. The benefits of using EDLP are that the organisation incurs less promotional expenditure and has greater stability in sales. Procter and Gamble and Wal-Mart both use EDLP.
Odd/even pricing	Some customers prefer odd number pricing, ie would be more likely to buy a product costing $99.99 than a product of $100. Some customers are not fooled by the 'saving' and prefer to pay an even price $20, rather than $19.99. Fewer organisations adopt the even pricing approach.
Customary pricing	Prices are set based mostly on tradition, eg telephone calls from call boxes in the UK cost the same for years. This was dealt with by BT by altering the number of units but keeping the price the same, so although your money ran out quicker, you still perceived it to cost the same as it always had.
Prestige pricing	Prices are set artificially high to give the product a 'quality' image. Holidays, cars, electrical and beauty products are often priced in this way.

Professional pricing

Professional pricing is used by people who are very skilled or experienced in their particular field to price their services. Rather than setting their fees based on their time and involvement, they may set a standard fee, regardless of the problems involved in carrying out the work. Recruitment agency fees provide an example of how this could be used if the price was a set percentage of the salary negotiated for the selected candidate. Professionals have an ethical responsibility not to overcharge unknowing customers.

Promotional pricing

The pricing is related to a short-term promotion of a particular product. There are four ways that this can be done.

Price leaders	Products are sold below the usual mark up, usually for a price just below, or near, cost. Price leaders get people in the shop, and they then make other purchases on which greater profits are made. Supermarkets regularly use this tactic.
Misleading pricing	These are pricing policies which intentionally mislead customers. Many countries have legislation controlling the use of this.
Special event pricing	Advertised 'sales' or price cutting that is linked to a holiday, season or event to increase sales volume.
Comparison discounting	Setting a price at a specific level and comparing it to a higher price. This higher price could be the previous price of the product, the recommended retail price. This technique is regularly used. If overused, customers stop believing that the higher price is the normal price.

1.5.8 Determining the final price

The basis for pricing and pricing strategies should inform and structure the selection of a final price. In practice, rather than follow this systematic approach, many prices are set by trial and error or after only limited planning. This is not recommended as it often leads to unsuitable prices being set.

In the absence of government price controls, pricing is a flexible and convenient way of adjusting the marketing mix. Prices can usually be adjusted very quickly; the other components of the marketing mix do not have this flexibility or freedom.

Prices may have to be revised on an ad hoc basis in response to market developments. However, the organisation must not lose sight of the longer-term implications for the brand, or the fundamental relationship between demand, costs and profits.

1.6 Comparison of traditional and online branding

FAST FORWARD

IT and the internet have particular implications for branding.

- The domain name is a vital element of the brand
- Brand values are communicated within seconds via the experience of using the brand website
- Online brands may be created in four ways:
    - Migrate the traditional brand
    - Extend the traditional brand
    - Partner with an existing digital brand
    - Create a new digital brand

Key term

A **brand** is a name, symbol, term, mark or design that enables customers to identify and distinguish the products of one supplier from those offered by competitors.

A brand is a tool which is used by an organisation to differentiate itself from competitors. For example, what is the value of a pair of Nike trainers without the brand or the logo?

The value of brands in today's environment is phenomenal. Brands have the power of instant sales; they convey a message of confidence, quality and reliability to their target market, which is particularly important in e-commerce where there are often concerns over privacy and security.

Aspects of a well-formed brand in traditional delivery channels
Brand name awareness – achieved through marketing communications to promote the brand identity and the other qualities of the brand
Perceived quality – awareness counts for nothing if the consumer has had a bad experience of a product or associated customer service
Positive brand associations – include imagery, the situation in which a product is used, its personality and symbols
Brand loyalty – the commitment of a segment to a brand

These customer touch-points combine to build a good brand presence. However, screen-based delivery adds a new level of complexity to the problem. For the first time, customers are interacting in machine-mediated experiences, as opposed to human-mediated. How can a machine be made to express a company's positive brand attributes, like respect and reliability, the same way a person does?

There are essential elements common to both traditional media and new screen-based systems. A successful brand, online or off, represents an entire customer experience. In a bricks-and-mortar environment this includes such matters as: how the customer is welcomed into the store; how products are packaged and presented and how staff and customers interact.

These elements can be translated to the online shopping experience to include the e-tailer's home or welcome page website design and page navigation and online support.

1.6.1 Visual identity

An effective visual identity is important online, as is a memorable **domain name**. The one big difference in branding on the internet from branding in conventional marketing is introduced by domain names. For example, the domain name www.coca-cola.com is fast becoming the brand first seen by the consumer, rather than the distinctive red and white label on the can. Unfortunately, there are a limited number of names available, and each name has been given to the first applicant. The World Intellectual Property Organisation has now taken up this issue, at least in terms of the worst exploitative excesses. Even so, there may be many legitimate claimants for a .com name who operate in very different sectors, and the new extensions (such as .biz and .TV) do not totally resolve the problem. Every supplier still wants .com since this is where the customers look first.

Despite these similarities, online branding differs in important ways from traditional branding and must be approached differently. A company's entire character, identity, products, and services, can be communicated in seconds on the web and customers make judgments just as fast.

1.6.2 Online brand options

Migrate traditional brand online – this can make sense if the brand is well known and has a strong reputation eg, Marks & Spencer, Orange and Disney. However, there is a risk of jeopardising the brand's good name if the new venture is not successful.

Extend traditional brand – a variant. For example, Aspirin's land based brand positioning statement is 'Aspirin – provides instant pain relief'. Management felt it did not hold true for a meaningful web presence, because you can't get instant pain relief on the web. So it was changed to 'Aspirin – your self help brand' which offered visitors to their website what they described as 'meaningful health oriented intelligence and self help'.

Partner with existing digital brands – co-branding occurs when two businesses put their brand name on the same product as a joint initiative. This practice is quite common on the internet and has proved to be a good way to build brand recognition and make the product or service more resistant to copying by private label manufacturers. A successful example of co-branding is the Senseo coffeemaker, which carries both the Philips and the Douwe Egberts brands. Another is the Braun and Oral B plaque remover.

Create a new digital brand – because a good name is extremely important, some factors to consider when selecting a new brand name are that it should suggest something about the product, be short and memorable, be easy to spell, translate well into other languages and have an available domain name.

2 Customer relationship management   6/13, 6/10

FAST FORWARD

Customer Relationship Management (CRM) is the establishment, development, maintenance and optimisation of long-term mutually valuable relationships between consumers and organisations.

It has three phases: acquisition, retention and extension. An accurate and detailed online database fundamental to customer relationship management.

Exam focus point

A question requirement in the June 2013 exam asked students to evaluate how the organisation described in the case study scenario could use a CRM system to acquire and retain customers. The examining team was disappointed to report that many students did not appear to be familiar with the use of CRM.

2.1 Meaning and scope of customer relationship management

Key term

Customer Relationship Management (CRM) is the establishment, development, maintenance and optimisation of long-term mutually valuable relationships between consumers and organisations.

What CRM involves	Company benefits realised as a result
• Organisations must become 'customer centric' • Organisations must be prepared to adapt so that they take customer needs into account and then deliver them • Market research must be used to assess customer needs and satisfaction	• Improved customer retention • Improved cross selling • Improved profitability (per customer and in general)

Dave Chaffey outlines three phases of CRM in e-business and e-commerce management:

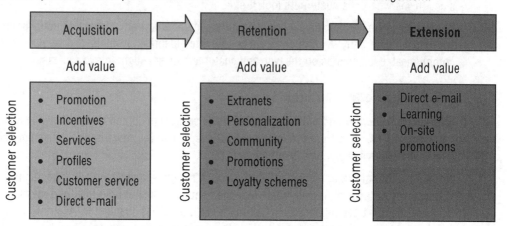

Chaffey's three phases of customer relationship management

Customer acquisition is the process of attracting customers for their first purchases.

Customer retention ensures that customers return and buy for a second time. The organisation keeps them as customers. This is most likely to be the purchase of a similar product or service, or the next level of product or service.

Customer extension introduces products and services to loyal customers that may not wholly relate to their original purchases. These are additional, supplementary purchases.

In recent times, emphasis has increased on building and maintaining good long-term relationships with customers. This is because such relationships are more profitable than constantly searching for new customers, owing to repeat purchasing and ease of service.

2.1.1 The nature of the customer

Not all customers are the same. Some appear for a single cash transaction and are never seen again. Others make frequent, regular purchases in large volumes, using credit facilities and building up a major relationship. Yet another type of customer purchases infrequently but in transactions of high value, as, for instance, in property markets. This variation will exist to a greater or lesser extent in all industries, though each will have a smaller typical range of behaviour. However, even within a single business, customers will vary significantly in the frequency and volume of their purchases, their reasons for buying, their sensitivity to price changes, their reaction to promotion and their overall attitude to the supplier and the product.

Segmentation of the customer base can have a major impact on profitability, perhaps by simply tailoring promotion to suit the most attractive group of customers.

The **stakeholder concept** suggests a wider concern than the traditional marketing approach of supplying goods and services which satisfy immediate needs. The supplier-customer relationship extends beyond the basic transaction. Today's highly competitive business environment means that customers are only retained if they are very satisfied with their purchasing experience. Any lesser degree of satisfaction is likely to result in the loss of the customer. Companies must be active in monitoring customer satisfaction because very few will actually complain. They will simply depart. Businesses which use intermediaries must be particularly active, since research shows that even when complaints are made, the principals hear about only a very small proportion of them.

Research indicates that **the single largest reason why customers abandon a supplier is poor performance by front-line staff**. Any scheme for customer retention must address the need for careful selection and training of these staff. It is also a vital factor in **relationship marketing**.

2.1.2 Intermediaries

Many businesses sell to intermediaries rather than to the end consumer. Some deal with both categories; they have to recognise that **the intermediary is just as much a customer as the eventual consumer**. We have discussed the impact of the **strategic customer** elsewhere in this Study Text. Intermediaries who do not take title to goods are equally worthy of consideration. Examples are manufacturers who maintain their own sales organisation but appoint agents in geographically remote areas and companies who combine autonomous operations with franchising. While it is reasonable to give the highest priority to the needs of the **ultimate consumer** and insist on some control over the activities of the intermediary, it must be recognised that intermediaries will only perform well **if their own needs are addressed**. For instance, a selling agent who has invested heavily in inventory after being given exclusive rights in an area should be consulted before further investment demands are made by the launch of a new product.

2.2 Relationship marketing

Relationship marketing is defined very simply by Grönroos as the management of a firm's market relationships.

Kotler says 'marketing can **make promises** but only the whole organisation can **deliver satisfaction**'. Adcock expands on this by remarking that relationship marketing can only exist when the marketing function fosters a customer-oriented **service culture** which supports the network of activities that deliver value to the customer.

Relationship marketing is thus as much about **attitudes** and **assumptions** as it is about techniques. The marketing function's task is to encourage habits of behaviour at all levels and in all departments that will enhance and strengthen the alliance. It must be remembered, however, that the effort involved in long-term relationship building is **more appropriate in some markets than in others**. Where customers are purchasing intermittently and switching costs are low, there is always a chance of business. This tends to be the pattern in commodity markets. Here, it is reasonable to take a **transactions approach** to marketing and treat each sale as unique. A **relationship marketing approach** is more appropriate where switching costs are high and a lost customer is thus probably lost for a long time. Switching costs are raised by such factors as the need for training on systems; the need for a large common installed base and high capital cost and the incorporation of purchased items into the customer's own designs.

2.2.1 Differences between transactional and relationship marketing

Transactional	Relationship
Importance of single sale	Importance of customer relation
Importance of product features	Importance of customer benefits
Short time scale	Longer time scale
Less emphasis on service	High customer service
Quality is concern of production	Quality is concern of all
Competitive commitment	High customer commitment
Persuasive communication	Regular communication

2.2.2 Implementing relationship marketing

The conceptual or philosophic nature of relationship marketing leads to a simple principle, that of **enhancing satisfaction by precision in meeting the needs of individual customers**. This depends on extensive two-way communication to establish and record the customer's characteristics and preferences

and build a long-term relationship. Adcock mentions three important practical methods which contribute to this end.

- Building a customer database
- Developing customer-oriented service systems
- Extra direct contacts with customers

Modern **computer database systems** enable the rapid acquisition and retrieval of the individual customer's details, needs and preferences. Using this technology, relationship marketing enables the sales person to greet the customer by name, know what they purchased last time, avoid taking their full delivery address, know what their credit status is and what they are likely to want. It enables new products to be developed that are precisely tailored to the customer's needs and new procedures to be established that enhance satisfaction. It is the successor to **mass marketing**, which attempted to be customer-led but which could only supply a one-size-fits-all product. The end result of a relationship marketing approach is a mutually satisfactory relationship that continues indefinitely.

2.2.3 Lifetime value

In determining which customers are worth the cost of long-term relationships, it is useful to consider their lifetime value. This depends on three things:

- Current profitability computed at the customer level
- The propensity of those customers to stay loyal
- Expected revenues and costs of servicing such customers over the lifetime of the relationship

Building relationships makes most sense for customers whose **lifetime value** to the company is the highest. Thus, building relationships should focus on customers who are currently the most profitable, likely to be the most profitable in the future, or likely to remain with the company for the foreseeable future and have acceptable levels of profitability.

Relationship marketing is grounded in the idea of establishing a **learning relationship** with customers. At the lower end, building a relationship can create cross-selling opportunities that may make the overall relationship profitable. For example, some retail banks have tried selling credit cards to less profitable customers. With valuable customers, customer relationship management may make them more loyal and willing to invest additional funds. In banking, these high-end relationships are often managed through private bankers, whose goals are not only to increase customer satisfaction and retention, but also to cross-sell and bring in investment.

2.2.4 Software

The goal of relationship management is to increase customer satisfaction and to minimise any problems. By engaging in 'smarter' relationships, a company can learn customers' preferences and develop trust. Every contact point with the customer can be seen as a chance to record information and learn preferences. Complaints and errors must be recorded, not just fixed and forgotten. Contact with customers in every medium, whether over the internet, through a call centre, or through personal contact, is recorded and centralised.

Many companies are beginning to achieve this goal by using customer relationship management (CRM) software. Data, once collected and centralised, can be used to customise service. In addition, the database can be analysed to detect patterns that can suggest better ways to serve customers in general. A key aspect of this dialogue is to learn and record preferences.

 Case Study

The Ritz

The Ritz Carlton Hotel makes a point of observing the choices that guests make and recording them. If a guest requests extra pillows, then extra pillows will be provided every time that person visits. At upmarket retailers, personal shoppers will record customers' preferences in sizes, styles, brands, colours and price ranges and notify them when new merchandise appears or help them choose accessories.

2.3 Different methods of acquiring customers through exploiting electronic media

FAST FORWARD

Electronic media may be used to acquire customers by using a wide range of techniques. These vary from analogues of traditional mass-communications methods such as advertising and newsletters, through specialised online forms such as search engine registration, to previously targeted means such as personalised emails and website messages to logged in return customers.

Techniques to achieve acquisition include traditional online mass media techniques and specialised online techniques.

(a)   **Search engine registration and directories** provide an index of content on registered sites that can be searched by keyword. Skilled website design can put a supplier high up among search results.

(b)   **Newsgroups and forums** providing expert opinion and useful help are a way for businesses to communicate with their peers and customers in an informal environment.

(c)   **Newsletters** allow an organisation to send news about the company, new products or services and any new information that has been posted on the website.

(d)   **Link building and partnership campaigns** can greatly benefit a business, significantly boosting its online presence. Reciprocal links are an exchange of links between two site owners. Types of link building include article and press release syndication, email campaigns and directory submission. Affiliate networks are based on paying commission on sales referred from other sites.

(e)   **Viral marketing** is about creating a buzz about products or services. Viral marketing relies on word of mouth or, in the online sense, getting people to share the online application with others. This can be achieved by providing webpages that can easily be sent to other people, for example. For businesses, viral marketing can emphasise the value of their goods or services, promote special offers and generate interest in the business or their products and services through word of mouth.

(f)   **Banner advertising** is similar to advertisements seen in newspapers and magazines. They are the graphical strips commonly seen across the top of website pages. Many companies use banner advertising in affiliate programs, emails and related websites. Depending on what medium is chosen to place the banner, the organisation could pay by impression, mile, click or action.

(g)   **Email** marketing represents the single largest shift in the way humans communicate since the invention of the telephone.

2.4 Differences in buyer behaviour

FAST FORWARD

The processes involved in making a purchase may be complex or relatively simple, depending on the nature of the need.

The greatest contrast lies between business and consumer purchases. Online purchaser behaviour is complicated by the special conditions of the online environment.

Segmentation of online consumer purchasers may be based on general online activity and the degree of confidence and competence displayed.

An important part of the marketing process is to understand why a customer or buyer makes a purchase. Without such an understanding, businesses find it hard to respond to the customer's needs and wants.

Research suggests that customers go through a five-stage decision-making process in any purchase. This is shown in the diagram below:

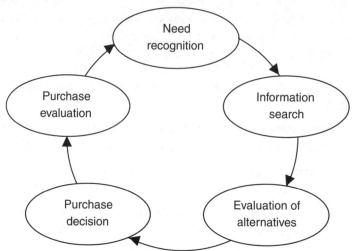

Five-stage decision-making process

The model implies that customers pass through all stages in every purchase. However, in more routine purchases, customers often skip or reverse some of the stages.

Step 1   The buying process starts with **need recognition**: for example, I am hungry, we need a new sofa, I have a headache, or responds to a **marketing stimulus**, as, for example, when passing a restaurant and being attracted by the smell.

Step 2   The customer then needs to decide how much information (if any) is required. If the need is strong and there is a product or service that meets the need close to hand, then a purchase decision is likely to be made there and then. If not, then the process of **information search** begins. A customer can obtain information from personal, commercial, public and experiential sources.

Step 3   In the **evaluation** stage, the customer must choose between the alternative brands, products and services. Where a purchase is 'highly involving' the customer is likely to carry out extensive evaluation.

Step 4   The purchase decision is made.

Step 5   The final stage is the post-purchase **evaluation of the decision**. It is common for customers to experience concerns after making a purchase decision. This arises from the phenomenon known as **cognitive dissonance**. This occurs when the customer receives different information from two trusted sources and experiences confusion and a lack of certainty. The customer, having bought a product, may feel that an alternative would have been preferable. In these circumstances, that customer will not repurchase immediately, but is likely to switch brands next time.

2.4.1 Types of buying behaviour

Types of buying behaviour – there are four typical types of buying behaviour based on the type of product that is to be purchased.

(a)   **Complex buying behaviour** occurs when the individual purchases a high value brand and seeks a lot of information before the purchase is made.

(b)   **Habitual buying behaviour** occurs when the individual buys a product out of habit, such as a newspaper.

(c) **Variety seeking buying behaviour** occurs when the individual likes to shop around and experiment with different products.

(d) **Dissonance reducing buying behaviour** occurs when buyers are highly involved with the purchase of the product, because the purchase is expensive or infrequent. There is little difference between existing brands. An example would be buying a diamond ring since there is perceived to be little difference between existing diamond brand manufacturers.

2.4.2 Business and consumer markets

The major differences in buyer behaviour are between the B2B and B2C markets.

Differences	B2B	B2C
Market structure	Fewer buyers but larger purchases Demand largely derived from consumer demand, eg car industry buys steel because consumers buy cars	Many buyers with smaller purchases
Nature of the buying unit	Buying unit differs – more rational approach, more people involved	Individuals or families
Type of purchase	Purchase products to meet specific business needs – want a customised product package Emphasise economic benefits	Purchase products to meet individual or family needs Purchase from intermediaries
Type of buying decision	Business purchases involve a more complex decision-making process with formal, lengthy purchasing policies.	Buy on impulse or with minimal processes
Communication differences	Existing customers can be contacted directly. Information is placed on the web to support customers and encourage loyalty Website content should be tailored to the needs of users, influencers and deciders	Promoting the website uses methods such as banner ads and search engines

2.4.3 Internet consumers

Segmentation using buyer behaviour – there have been many studies to identify the behaviour of different groups of internet user.

One study identified six different groups of active internet users and their motivations

- **Simplifiers** – easier than the real world
- **Surfers** – new experiences
- **Bargainers** – good deals
- **Connectors** – chatroom users
- **Routiners** – news, stock prices, finance
- **Sportsters** – sports news

Netpoll has established a different user typology:

(a) **Gameboy** – still at school and living at home. Accesses the internet mainly at home. Into playing online games. Thinks he is pretty net-savvy.

(b) **CyberLad** – accesses the internet at work and at home. Thinks he knows it all as far as the net is concerned.

(c) **Net Sophisticate** – straddles the border between cool and nerd. Could be a gee-whiz creative at agency or unemployed and living at home with mum.

(d) **CyberSec** – works as a PA to the boss of a small organisation. Super-competent, well turned out and also very much 'one of the girls'. Accesses the internet only at the office.

(e) **Hit 'n' Runner** – can be either be male or female. Successful professional or high-flying marketing exec. Accesses the internet at work and only for information. Very impatient if finding information is difficult or if the site is slow to download.

(f) **InfoJunky** – either male or female. Possibly a middle-rank civil servant or a partner at a small firm of solicitors. Is under the impression that the time spent online is a big benefit to the job. Given that he/she gets side-tracked, this is very debatable.

(g) **CyberMum** – married with kids and works in a 'caring' profession. Her husband thought it would be a good idea if they got online when he started spending one week in four at company HQ in Holland, so that they could exchange email messages. She would like to be able to shop online, if only she knew how it worked.

2.5 Retaining customers using electronic media

FAST FORWARD

> Retention of online customers may be based on careful use of customer databases and by offering wider benefits. Databases allow for personalised communications, promotions and offers. Wider benefits may be offered by access to extranets and online communities.

Much has been written about how to attract customers using search engines, indexes, portals and other advertising media, but far less has been written about how to persuade them to remember any site and return to it when they need another item or, in particular, to return to that site when they do not need anything but may be susceptible to impulse purchases. This factor has been called **stickiness**. Trying to attract 'sticky customers' (customers who will bring repeat business) is a crucial goal for many online businesses.

Customer retention marketing is a tactically-driven approach based on customer behaviour. It is the core activity going on behind the scenes in:

*   **Relationship marketing**
*   **Loyalty marketing**
*   **Database marketing**
*   **Permission marketing** – consumers giving their consent to receive marketing information improves the targeting and relevance of promotional messages, thus improving response and conversion rates

The basic philosophy is that active customers are happy (retained) customers; and they like to feel like winners. They like to feel they are in control and smart about choices they make, and they like to feel good about their behaviour.

Marketers take advantage of this by offering **promotions** of various kinds. These promotions range from discounts and sweepstakes to loyalty programs and higher concept approaches such as thank-you notes and birthday cards. **Retaining customers means keeping them active**, otherwise they will slip away and eventually no longer be customers.

Other techniques for retaining customers include personalisation, the use of extranets, online communities, online sales promotions and opt-in email marketing.

2.5.1 Personalisation

Database, document generation and web technologies have improved the ease and sophistication of targeting and personalisation of contact between organisations and customers. Here are some examples.

(a) Allowing users to customise web pages for their personal interests and tastes

(b)   Making individually-targeted product offers and recommendations based on browsing/buying behaviour

(c)   Sending personally addressed and targeted-content messages to customers

(d)   Encouraging users/customers to form **virtual communities** (for example, using chat rooms, discussion boards and newsgroups)

2.5.2 Extranets

For many companies, extranets are still only web-based systems that provide password-protected areas allowing users (customers, resellers) to fill out forms or perform simple online transactions. HTTP-based extranets allow companies to deliver information through a browser interface but offer very limited ability to interact with core business systems and applications.

On the customer side, extranets offer secure tunnels to remote databases, which let users access inventory data, examine special discounts, view delivery status, research products, place and fulfills orders, and collaborate via a secure internet connection. By opening customer access in this way, extranets offer businesses a significant customer retention opportunity – the customer is almost literally attached to the business.

2.5.3 Online communities

A community is a multi-way online environment where members encourage each other to contribute content and interact.

According to a top e-business technology consultant, the most important objective for a small business when establishing a business presence online is to create a community where people interested in the product or service can feel at home 'hanging out'.

Interactivity benefits

(a)   Within commercial sites, community members account for one-third of all users, but two thirds of all transactions.

(b)   Active posters make nine times as many visits to a website as passive users.

(c)   Active members are twice as loyal to a site as all other users.

Types of community are shown below:

Communities of purpose where members share a vocation or profession	**Communities of circumstance** where members share a personal situation

Communities of purpose where members share a common objective

Communities of interest where members share a hobby or interest	**Communities of geography** where members live in the same area

Some sites are inherently sticky because they serve a particular natural community, for example, a fan club or football team. These will generate their own news regularly and will be visited frequently by both dedicated and lukewarm adherents without special stimulus. Other sites are also going to attract regular visitors because of their nature, such as Amazon, eBay and Loot, whose primary purpose is well known and is of frequent use for certain people. Revenue there comes from direct sales or commission on transactions, or even from advertisers based on the number of visitors.

2.5.4 Opt-in email

Opt-in emails are promotional emails that have been requested by the individual receiving them. Unlike promotional emails that get sent out to large lists of recipients without regard to whether or not they want the information, opt-in emails are only sent to people who specifically request them.

Opt-in emails are targeted and often personalised and carry information about specific topics or promotions that users are interested in learning about. Typical opt-in emails contain newsletters, product information or special promotional offers. For example, if a user frequented a website that sold books and music online, that user could opt in to receive announcements when his or her favourite author or musician released new material. The promotional email may even present the recipient with a special promotional offer to purchase the product at a discount available only to those on the opt-in list.

2.6 Increasing the activity and value of established, retained customers

FAST FORWARD

Customer activity may be enhanced by the use of data mining and cookies.

CRM is concerned with the creation, development and enhancement of individualised customer relationships with carefully targeted customers and customer groups.

Paul Postma, in *The New Marketing Era,* highlights two major shifts in the way customer information is used in the new marketing era:

(a)   'In a traditional market approach, people have all sorts of ideas about the target group, or they think up some obvious target group for a certain product. Without a marketing database, people are able to approach this target group only as a generic whole, by choosing the correct advertising medium and tailoring the creative ideas to the prescribed target group. In the new approach…we no longer calculate the market from within the company, but instead communicate, listen and record. The **database** will teach us what the market has to say…'

(b)   'In the new marketing era, we are shifting from derivative and self-reported information to **behavioural analysis**… Information technology makes it possible to determine behaviour, even at an individual level, and even in mass markets. This information is by far the most trustworthy when forecasting future behaviour.'

2.6.1 Database marketing

Database marketing has been defined by Shaw and Stone as 'an interactive approach to marketing, which uses individually addressable marketing media and channels to extend help to a company's target audience, stimulate their demand and stay close to them by recording and keeping an electronic database memory of customer, prospect and all communication and commercial contacts, to help them improve all future contacts and ensure more realistic planning of all marketing'.

A database, in marketing terms, is a collection of data that can be organised to give marketing information. The customer database is one example.

Allen et al suggest the following projects which can be conducted using database marketing techniques.

Project	Method
Identify the best customers	Use RFM analysis (Recency of the latest purchase, Frequency of purchases, and Monetary value of all purchases) to determine which customers are most profitable to market to
Develop new customers	Collect lists of potential customers to incorporate into the database
Tailor messages based on customer usage	Target mail and email based on the types and frequency of purchases indicated by the customer's purchase profile
Recognise customers after purchase	Reinforce the purchase decision by appropriate follow-up

Cross-sell related and complementary products	Use the customer purchase database to identify opportunities to suggest additional products during the buying session
Personalise customer service	Online purchase data can prompt customer service representatives to show that the customer is recognised, their needs are known and their time (for example, in giving details) is valued
Eliminating conflicting or confusing communications	Present a coherent image over time to individual customers – however different the message to different customer groups. (For example, don't keep sending 'dear first-time customer' messages to long-standing customers!) Remember the Integrated Marketing Communications approach

New data management techniques have been developed to provide marketers with better and quicker access to data analysis.

2.6.2 Data mining

Data mining is a set of statistical techniques that are used to identify trends, patterns and relationships in data. Data mining is closely linked to Big Data, which we explored in Chapter 11.

Data mining techniques have been available for many years, but they have only recently grown popular, as more data is being created, data processing power (in the form of computers) is becoming more accessible and data mining software tools are becoming available. Most data mining models are one of two types:

(a)   **Predictive**: using known observations to predict future events (for example, predicting the probability that a recipient will opt out of an email list)

(b)   **Descriptive**: interrogating the database to identify patterns and relationships (for example, profiling the audience of a particular advertising campaign).

The logical extension of database marketing is referred to by Kotler as **customer specific marketing** and by Peppers and Rogers as **one-to-one marketing**. The company collects data on individual customers, their past web-browsing and purchase habits, demographic and even psychographic characteristics. It is then possible to customise or personalise the organisation-customer interface to suit individual customer profiles: whether on the telephone (using Computer Telephony Integration), by mail (using data merged from database files into word-processing programmes), by email (ditto) or by website (personalising and customising pages for known surfers).

2.6.3 Cookies

Cookies are a technology that allows a website to remember individual visitors' surfing and/or purchase history and preferences. This information is placed on the visitor's hard disk and when they revisit the site, it references the cookie and is able to show the visitor product selections and recommendations, and offer personalised welcomes and streamlined ordering (through remembering names, addresses, and credit card details).

2.7 Web 2.0 technologies   12/12

Technologies known collectively as **Web 2.0** have spread rapidly among consumers in recent years. As the popularity of **Web 2.0** has grown, companies have noted the way consumers have engaged with the technologies, and have realised this could have important business implications – particularly in relation to marketing and new product development strategies.

The phrase 'Web 2.0' has become synonymous with a new generation of web technologies and software, and, possibly more importantly, their impact on how web users interact with content, applications and each other.

2.7.1 User experience and participation

Web 2.0 allows internet users (and potential customers for businesses) to no longer simply be recipients of information, but to participate in the creation, sharing and evaluation of content. In other words, users can actively take part in 'many-to-many' communications. A crucial aspect of Web 2.0 is that it focuses on **user experience** and **participation**.

This is also important for businesses, because Web 2.0 allows firms of all sizes to engage with customers, staff and suppliers in new ways. In particular, it allows firms to have a more customer-focused approach to new product development – because customers can actually be involved in the design of the new products.

Web 2.0 has highlighted the significance of **dynamic social interactions** in the environment, rather than considering business and business transactions as a set of static business processes.

When looking at internal strategic capabilities (Chapter 4) we identified the **importance of knowledge** to businesses. Web 2.0 plays an important role in this 'knowledge economy' through supporting creativity, **collaboration**, **knowledge sharing**, and ultimately, innovation.

2.7.2 Features of Web 2.0

We will now look at some of the key aspects of Web 2.0.

Web-based communities

Probably the most popular aspect of Web 2.0 has been social networking sites, such as Facebook and MySpace, which now attract more than 100 million visitors a month.

Web-based communities are enhanced by:

- **Social networking** – Social Networks (such as Facebook, MySpace and Twitter) allow users to make contact with other users.

- **Blogs** – Blogs provide an easy way for users to publish their own content. Blogs are usually text based. Users can publish audio and visual content as podcasts, and the growth of sites such as YouTube illustrates how popular podcasts have become.

- **Wikis** – Wikis allow user groups to collaborate in editing content. Wikipedia, the collaborative online encyclopaedia, is the best known example of this.

- **Instant messaging** – This allows real time conversations between two or more participants using pop-up dialogue boxes (eg instant messaging is now available in Skype).

These web-based communities mean that web **users are now participants in the web experience,** rather than simply being observers.

2.7.3 Socialisation of knowledge sharing

Web 2.0 technologies encourage the socialisation of knowledge sharing through:

- **Tagging of information**: A tag is a keyword assigned by a user to describe a piece of information (such as a file, an image, or an internet bookmark). Tagging is a key feature of many Web 2.0 applications and is commonly used on file storing and file sharing sites. Once a file has been tagged, the tag allows it to be found again when a relevant search enquiry is made.

  Tagging also highlights an important point which businesses need to consider. The new technologies mean that the amount of information on the internet is rising constantly. However, information is no use if it can't be found. **Search Engine Optimisation** is therefore increasingly important for businesses – making sure the information on a business website is findable and relevant.

- **Mashups**: A mashup is a web publication that combines data from more than one source into a single webpage. For example, a restaurant review website, could take the location details of all the local restaurants in an area and map them onto a single Google map page.

- **Feedback** on sources of information

- **Promoting collective intelligence**: Collective intelligence refers to both structured and unstructured group collaboration. It describes the way people's opinions or behaviours can be aggregated so that others can learn from their collective decision making.

  The online auction site eBay uses collective intelligence to let potential buyers see how efficient and trustworthy vendors are. Equally, Amazon and a number of online sites include product reviews, allowing people who have purchased an item to comment on the item and rate its performance.

  Amazon also uses collective intelligence to make product recommendations based on purchasing patterns. When a user selects an item to buy, he or she is presented with a list of other items purchased by people who have already bought the current selection, which may encourage a user to make follow up purchases.

- **User generated content** (UGC): websites can now have sections of content **created by their readers**. One of the main ideas behind Web 2.0 technologies is that users can generate the content of sites themselves, and the technologies allow users to create, capture and share information across the web. The video streaming website, YouTube, is a popular example of this.

- **Consumer generated content** (CGC): websites can now contain shared **feedback from consumers**; for example, product reviews. This has important implications for businesses, because it means customers can communicate with other (potential) customers very easily. If a customer receives poor customer service, they can now tell everyone else about it, which could damage the business' reputation, and lead to a decline in sales.

  The most widely known example of CGC is the user reviews developed by Amazon noted above. Many customers look at other users' product reviews when assessing prospective purchases.

2.7.4 Applications of Web 2.0 for business

In recent years, we have seen the emergence of a number of new online companies. Many are probably also run by young entrepreneurs for whom technology will play a key role in their business strategy:

- The business can find partners, collaborators, customers and suppliers through social networks and blogs

- The business can use blogs, and social networks for publicity and to market itself, and it can encourage customers to leave feedback on its site (customer generated content)

- The business can manage the development, creation and delivery of its products through virtual workspaces and wikis that support collaboration, innovation and the management of workflow. The collaborative nature of Web 2.0 enables external third parties to participate in product development

- The business can get market intelligence through blogs and online reference sites. It can also get feedback on how customers perceive its own products or services

Staff - Importantly also, if the businesses want to attract and retain young, dynamic employees they will need to provide them with tools they are familiar with, and offer a work environment that fits with their lifestyle.

Marketing – Web 2.0 can have significant implications for marketing approaches. Teenagers and young adults can be an important demographic for many businesses, and sites such as Facebook and Twitter play an important part in their lives. In this way, running campaigns through popular social networking sites can offer businesses a way of engaging with these users, allowing them to reach a demographic which has traditionally been difficult to reach.

However, if companies do engage in social networking or publish blogs, they need to monitor how these are perceived by the online communities (see the case study later in this Chapter titled 'Social media risks'). **Brand management** remains very important – perhaps even more so because of the way users can publish negative feedback on poorly designed or presented content.

An article published on the *Forbes* website highlights the increasing use of social media marketing and information systems by businesses looking for a 'big return' on their investment in marketing activities.

The article highlights a number of good reasons for organisations to turn to social media marketing.

Brand recognition

Social media can be used as a means of brand-building. 'With consistent effort and great content, you can build a reputation for your brand around your company's values, benefits, and advantages.'

Community

Social media is particularly effective at creating a community. 'When your followers become part of your community, you gain instant access to them. That means you can find out what challenges they are facing and what they like and don't like about your offerings. You can engage in ongoing dialogue that can be more valuable than any kind of paid market research.'

Repeat Exposure

Forbes notes that social media provides organisations with the opportunity to 'remind followers over and over again about what companies have to offer, which can shorten the sales cycle dramatically'.

Influence

By building a social media following, this can create a 'snowball effect'. In essence, the greater the social media audience, the greater scope for attracting new 'customers, media interviews, joint venture partnerships, and all kinds of other opportunities'. *Forbes* highlights that effective social media marketing through sharing posts, videos and other content can lead to an increased 'hit' rate on a company's websites.

Big Wins

'While many businesses large and small are trying to justify the cost and time investment for managing social media marketing, an important benefit often gets overlooked: Big Wins. For example, if someone from LinkedIn connects your business with a significant government contract, then that would certainly qualify as a Big Win. If a major media outlet finds your business on Twitter and interviews the MD for a national article, then that is also a Big Win – one that you can't measure based on revenues directly generated.'

Source: Adapted from 'The hidden benefits of social media marketing', by Stephanie Chandler, December 2013, *Forbes* [online]

Developing ideas – Also, by allowing web users to provide feedback and share ideas, Web 2.0 is encouraging a model in which people outside an organisation can have an impact on that organisation's strategy.

In this way, the internet becomes, in effect, a research tool, where companies can find out about customers' opinions about products and services. Web 2.0 allows businesses to aggregate opinions from many different individuals to guide idea generation and strategic decision making.

Consequently, customer networks and social interaction have become much more important in marketing.

 Case Study

Social media risks

In September 2013, accounting firm Grant Thornton published a report titled 'Social media risks and rewards'. The report explored the increasing use of social media by large companies and the new types of risk that such communication brings. The growing importance of social media among big business is evident from the report's findings:

- More than half of (55%) of the executives who responded to the survey feel that social media will be an important component of corporate marketing efforts going forward.

- Two thirds (66%) of respondents expected their company's use of social media to increase slightly or significantly over the next 12 months.

The report identifies four main risks of using social media:

(1) Damage to brand reputation
(2) Disclosure of proprietary and/or confidential information
(3) Corporate identify theft
(4) Legal, regulatory and compliance violations

'Nearly three quarters (71%) of executives surveyed were concerned about the potential risks involved in the use of social media, but believe the risks can be mitigated or avoided'.

The report highlights some memorable examples of companies which have failed to manage their social media communications effectively, including blunders by Gap and Netflix.

Gap

In 2012, when Hurricane Sandy struck parts of America causing severe devastation, retailer Gap posted a tweet via Twitter which advised customers to 'stay safe, and perhaps shop at Gap.com'. Gap apologised shortly afterwards and removed the message.

Netflix

The US Securities and Exchange Commission (SEC) investigated Netflix in 2012 after the company's CEO, Reed Hastings, posted information on Facebook which boosted its share price.

Reed Hastings' comment raises an interesting issue about social media communications and associated risks. As social media starts to play an increasing role in how businesses communicate, careful consideration needs to be given to ensure that private messages expressing personal opinions are not perceived as official corporate communications.

Source: Adapted from 'Social media risks and rewards', by Thomas Thompson, Jan Hertzberg and Mark Sullivan (September 2013), Grant Thornton [online]

3 Software and CRM

FAST FORWARD

There are four main areas of CRM automation:

- **Sales** – lead management, order tracking, sales support
- **Service** – help desk, FAQs problem resolution
- **Marketing** – prospect database, campaign management
- **Reporting** – presentation of performance data

E-commerce systems must be integrated with back office systems such as inventory management and sales ledger.

Systems choice is subject to considerations previously dealt with, concerning design, integration, modality and customisation.

There are three aspects of CRM that can each be implemented in isolation from one another:

(a) **Operational CRM** provides support to front office business processes, including sales, marketing and service. Each interaction with a customer is generally added to a customer's contact history, and staff can retrieve information on customers from the database as necessary. Many call centres use some kind of CRM software to support their call centre agents.

(b) **Collaborative CRM** covers the direct interaction with customers. This can include a variety of channels, such as internet, email, automated phone/Interactive Voice Response (IVR).

(c)   **Analytical CRM** analyses customer data for a variety of purposes, eg risk assessment and fraud detection, in particular for credit card transactions.

Many businesses invest in a CRM system to improve their customer services. The CRM system brings information like customer data, sales patterns, marketing data and future trends together with the aim of identifying new sales opportunities, delivering improved customer service, or offering personalised services and deals.

In addition to improving sales and profitability, the CRM system is very effective in handling customer complaints and can have a tremendous effect on a company's reputation.

Whilst IT and software are not the entire story for CRM, they are vital to its success. CRM software collects data on consumers and their transactions. Huge databases store data on individuals and groups of individuals. Organisations will track individuals, and try to market products and services to them based upon similar buyer behaviour seen in other individuals.

The customer interacts with the company via email, telephone, web or face-to-face, through the company's back office, sales team, marketing division and so on. As the interaction progresses to a sale, service query or quote the information from that interaction is stored and fed through middleware into a **database**. This data can then be drawn upon by sales, service, marketing or business to add a greater functionality to those departments.

Major areas of CRM focus on service automated processes, personal information gathering and processing, and self-service. It attempts to integrate and automate the various customer serving processes within a company. It typically involves four general areas:

(a)   **Sales automation** including lead management, order tracking and sales support, plus integration with desktop applications to share contacts, send email and manage calendars.

(b)   **Service management** including basic helpdesk functionality, case management, escalation with basic workflow, problem ticket tracking and FAQs.

(c)   **Marketing automation** to manage a database of prospects. Further down the line, more sophisticated campaign management can be brought into play to track the origin and status of prospects and monitor marketing effectiveness.

(d)   **Management reporting**, including easy to understand graphical views of different slices of the data such as by territories or order status.

These areas should all be focused around building a single view of the customer. Integration should initially be sought between key modules.

Typical CRM objectives include reducing customer complaints, increasing communication with customers, increasing customer loyalty, and of course, increasing the variety or volume of products sold. Good sales people will know what their customers' requirements are, and when they are needed, but in a channel sales environment it is necessary to apply this level of knowledge company-wide to maximise opportunities for sale. Managers selecting CRM systems will be concerned with the following key technical issues:

- CRM applications
- Integration with back-office systems
- The choice of single-vendor solutions or a more fragmented choice

3.1 CRM applications

(a)   **Electronic marketing**: a high volume of all communication takes place via email. A basic application for any CRM system would be to send an email to any customer who had previously purchased certain items which would lead the organisation to believe that they may be interested in related items. CRM systems allow this list to be created in minutes and campaigns put into action instantly. A logical extension of this strategy is to send them a way of ordering as well as a promotional message, as research has shown that this can treble the effectiveness of the campaign.

(b) **Target mailing** will reduce costs and increase response rate. A simple example of this is to send this season's catalogue to customers who purchased from the last catalogue. To achieve this, the mailing lists need to be linked to sales history.

(c) **Sales analysis** is widely used by large sophisticated channel marketing businesses, but this strategy is basically simple and easy to implement using an integrated CRM system. For example, it should be easy to generate a list of customers who have not purchased for over a year. These could then be targeted by email, direct mail or telephone by asking them if they want to receive the next catalogue, and offering them some sort of discount to become a customer again. It is also possible to understand simple relationships; for example, anybody purchasing a computer printer must need to buy toner cartridges. A simple gap analysis allows a list to be formed of the details of anyone who has purchased a printer without toner cartridges, and thus provides a targeted list for a sales campaign. Again, a fully integrated CRM system will enable this.

(d) **Order building**: another role for the CRM system should be to provide the organisation's order taker or website with key data about each customer. Customers placing orders can then be reminded of their usual order requirements, any related products on offer and further product information. As well as increasing sales, this also helps to build the customer relationship.

Integrated CRM software is also known as **front office solutions**. This is because they deal directly with the customer, eg applications for sales, marketing and customer service.

Many call centres use CRM software to store all of their customers' details. When a customer calls, the system can be used to retrieve and display information relevant to the customer. By serving the customer quickly and efficiently, and also keeping all information on a customer in one place, a company aims to make cost savings, and also encourage new customers.

CRM solutions can also be used to allow customers to perform their own service via a variety of communication channels. For example, you might be able to check your bank balance via your WAP phone without ever having to talk to a person, saving money for the company, and saving you time.

A CRM solution is characterised by its functionality.

(a) **Scalability** is the ability to be used on a large scale and to be reliably expanded to whatever scale is necessary.

(b) **Multiple communication channels** provide the ability to interface with users via different devices such as phone, WAP, internet and so on.

(c) **Workflow** is enhanced by the ability to route work automatically through the system to different people based on a set of rules.

(d) **Databases** provide centralised storage (in a data warehouse) of all information relevant to customer interaction.

(e) **Customer privacy** is enhanced by, for example, data encryption and the destruction of records to ensure that they are not stolen or abused.

Integration with back-office systems

For CRM to be truly effective, the e-commerce platform must be seamlessly incorporated into the back office system (finance, payroll and HR applications). A simple example is that when product information in the back office system is altered (such as inventory levels), this should also update the website. When customers place orders on the web, they should be able review their order history whether placed on the website or over the telephone.

When contemplating a CRM system, management will have previously invested in systems for other business functions. These legacy systems will be at the application and database levels within the organisation and it will not be financially viable to abandon these applications so their integration is a vital part of the decision to implement a CRM system.

3.2 The choice of single-vendor solutions or a more fragmented choice

CRM software is available either as a complete purchase from a software vendor or outsourced from an application service provider, or ASP. ASPs host the CRM applications and sell subscription-based services. ASPs are more affordable than standalone software and require little maintenance on the organisation's part. However, ASPs are often static in what they offer and will not provide the level of customisation offered by purchased software.

CRM software is often sold in modules, so checking on modular availability can help trim costs. Before shopping, think about the organisation's goals. Is retaining existing customers important? Reducing time in the sales cycle? Or is it more valuable to expand into an online market? The data that is collected, analysed, and reported on should directly support these objectives. CRM systems typically offer so many tracking options that it is easy to get caught up in data overload, collecting every possible piece of information about each and every customer, potential customer, and transaction. But it is far wiser to save time, effort, and money by deciding in advance what information is most worthwhile to collect, how it will be measured and what will be done with it.

In an ideal world, the organisation would choose to have a single integrated database such that any employee would have total visibility about a customer and could access all visit, sales and support histories; the system would be bought from a single vendor for ease of implementation and support.

In reality, most organisations will have different applications for different communications channels, separate databases in different functional areas and multiple vendors. E-commerce systems are often separate from traditional systems. Such fragmentation makes implementation and maintenance of such systems a headache for managers and will often result in poor levels of customer service for the customer. The solution that many companies are looking to move to is close to the situation above.

However, the best option might be to adopt a CRM system phase by phase. The company needs to identify the areas where the return on investment would be highest and adopt CRM technology there.

Another good approach is to automate one of the key departments with an inexpensive CRM solution and if the project becomes successful, adopt a cross-company CRM solution.

For either of these options the present customer related information that is going to be integrated with the CRM system should be carefully analysed, consolidated, structured and cleaned up prior to adoption.

Chapter roundup

- E-marketing is the application of IS and internet techniques to the achievement of marketing objectives. Most marketing activities can be enhanced by the use of such techniques, including branding, customer service and sales.

- The employment of e-marketing may be analysed and planned using the six Is.

  - Independence of location
  - Industry structure
  - Integration
  - Interactivity
  - Individualisation
  - Intelligence

- More specific concepts for the development of e-marketing may be based on the 7Ps.

  - The augmented **product** can be extended through website information and interactivity
  - **Pricing** can be made transparent; dynamic pricing may be used
  - The global reach of the internet has great implications for **place**, with the creation of new marketplaces and channel structures
  - **Promotion** can be previously targeted via customer databases
  - **People** can be replaced by software to a varying extent
  - Processes may be automated
  - **Physical evidence** consists of the customer's experience of using the organisation's e-marketing tools in general and of its website in particular

- One of the most complex decisions involved in the marketing mix is deciding on the price of the product or service. There are eight steps in the process of establishing prices:

  - Select a pricing objective
  - Assess target market's evaluation of price and its ability to buy
  - Determine the nature and price elasticity of demand
  - Analyse demand, cost and profit relationships
  - Evaluate competitor's prices
  - Determine the basis for pricing
  - Select a primary strategy
  - Determine the final price

- IT and the internet have particular implications for branding.

  - The domain name is a vital element of the brand
  - Brand values are communicated within seconds *via* the experience of using the brand website
  - Online brands may be created in four ways

    - Migrate the traditional brand
    - Extend the traditional brand
    - Partner with an existing digital brand
    - Create a new digital brand

- **Customer Relationship Management** (CRM) is the establishment, development, maintenance and optimisation of long-term mutually valuable relationships between consumers and organisations.

  It has three phases: acquisition, retention and extension. An accurate and detailed online database is fundamental to customer relationship management.

- Electronic media may be used to acquire customers by using a wide range of techniques. These vary from analogues of traditional mass-communications methods such as advertising and newsletters, through specialised online forms such as search engine registration, to previously targeted means such as personalised emails and website messages to logged-in return customers.

- The processes involved in making a purchase may be complex or relatively simple, depending on the nature of the need.

  The greatest contrast lies between business and consumer purchases. Online purchaser behaviour is complicated by the special conditions of the online environment.

  Segmentation of online consumer purchasers may be based on general online activity and the degree of confidence and competence displayed.

- Retention of online customers may be based on careful use of customer databases and by offering wider benefits. Databases allow for personalised communications, promotions and offers. Wider benefits may be offered by access to extranets and online communities.

- Customer activity may be enhanced by the use of data mining and cookies.

- There are four main areas of CRM automation.

  - **Sales** – lead management, order tracking, sales support
  - **Service** – help desk, FAQs problem resolution
  - **Marketing** – prospect database, campaign management
  - **Reporting** – presentation of performance data

  E-commerce systems must be integrated with back office systems such as inventory management and sales ledger.

  Systems choice is subject to considerations previously dealt with, concerning design, integration, modality and customisation.

Quick Quiz

1. The SOSTAC planning framework can be used to develop a marketing strategy. What does SOSTAC stand for?

2. What are the six Is of marketing?

3. What are the four ways an online brand be created?

4. What are the three phases of CRM identified by Chaffey?

5. What are the five phases of making a purchase?

6. What is scalability?

Answers to Quick Quiz

1   Situation analysis; Objectives; Strategies; Tactics; Actions; Control.

2   Independence of location, industry structure, interactivity, individualisation, integration and intelligence

3   • Migrate the traditional brand
    • Extend the traditional brand
    • Partner with an existing digital brand
    • Create a new digital brand

4   Acquisition, retention, extension

5   Need recognition, information search, evaluation of alternatives, purchase decision, post purchase evaluation

6   An attribute of software that enables that software to be used reliably on a range of scales as necessary.

Now try the question below from the Practice Question Bank

Number	Level	Marks	Time
Q13	Examination	25	45 mins

Project management

Project management

Introduction

Project management is an important aspect of putting strategy into action. In the first place, many organisations' business consists largely of projects: civil engineering contractors and film studios are two obvious examples. Secondly, even where operations are more or less continuous, the need for continuing strategic innovation and improvement in the way things are done brings project management to the forefront of attention. Finally, even relatively low-level, one-off projects must be managed with a view to their potential strategic implications.

Project management is also very closely linked to business process change and information technology issues. For example, major changes in technology are usually implemented through projects and project management.

Study guide

		Intellectual level
F1	**The nature of projects**	
(a)	Determine the distinguishing features of projects and the constraints they operate in	2
(b)	Discuss the implications of the triple constraint of scope, cost and time	2
(c)	Discuss the relationship between organisational strategy and project management	2
(d)	Identify and plan to manage risks	2
(e)	Advise on the structures and information that have to be in place to successfully initiate a project	3
(f)	Explain the relevance of projects to process re-design, e-business systems development and quality initiatives	2
F2	**Building the business case**	
(a)	Describe the structure and contents of a business case document	2
(b)	Analyse, describe, assess and classify benefits of a project investment	3
(c)	Analyse, describe, assess and classify costs of a project investment	3
(d)	Evaluate the costs and benefits of a business case using standard techniques	3
(e)	Establish responsibility for the delivery of benefits	2
(f)	Explain the role of a benefits realisation plan	2
F3	**Managing and leading projects**	
(a)	Discuss the organisation and implications of project-based team structures	2
(b)	Establish the role and responsibilities of the project manager and the project sponsor	2
(c)	Identify and describe typical problems encountered by a project manager when leading a project	2
(d)	Advise on how these typical problems might be addressed and overcome	3
F4	**Planning, monitoring and controlling projects**	
(a)	Discuss the principles of a product breakdown structure	2
(b)	Assess the importance of developing a project plan and discuss the work required to produce this plan	3
(c)	Monitor the status of a project and identify project risks, issues, slippage and changes	2
(d)	Formulate response for dealing with project risks, issues, slippage and changes	2
(e)	Discuss the role of benefits management and project gateways in project monitoring	2
F5	**Concluding a project**	
(a)	Establish mechanisms for successfully concluding a project	2
(b)	Discuss the relative meaning and benefits of a post-implementation and a post-project review	2
(c)	Discuss the meaning and value of benefits realisation	2

(d)	Evaluate how project management software may support the planning and monitoring of a project	3
(e)	Apply 'lessons learned' to future business case validation and to capital allocation decisions	3

Exam guide

The examining team has indicated that the importance of project management will be recognised, both by Section B questions which deal with it explicitly, and also through issues in the Section A scenario. It is possible that topics that have been examined in the old syllabus Paper 2.1 *Information systems*, such as project initiation, project slippage, project completion and risk management, will re-emerge in your exam in a more complex and substantial form.

You should also remember that project management is also linked very closely to the business process change and IT issues dealt with by your syllabus. Its treatment here builds on the syllabus for Paper F1 *Accountant in Business*, Section E, which deals with leading and managing individuals and teams.

Models

The Study Guide for this chapter does not refer to any specific models of project management, and so no specific models will be explicitly required by a question.

However, note the way the Study Guide emphasises the **practical aspects of project management**, suggesting that these practical applications will be important in answering exam questions on project management.

1 The nature of project management

FAST FORWARD

A **project** is an undertaking that has a beginning and an end and is carried out to meet established goals within cost, schedule and quality objectives. It often has the following characteristics:

- A defined beginning and end
- Resources allocated specifically to it
- Intended to be done only once (although similar separate projects could be undertaken)
- Follows a plan towards a clear intended end-result
- Often cuts across organisational and functional lines

1.1 What is a project?

To understand project management, it is necessary to first define what a project is.

Key terms

A **project** is 'an undertaking that has a beginning and an end and is carried out to meet established goals within cost, schedule and quality objectives'. (Haynes, *Project Management*)

Resources are the money, facilities, supplies, services and people allocated to the project.

In general, the work which organisations undertake involves either **operations** or **projects**. Operations and projects are planned, controlled and executed. So how are projects distinguished from 'ordinary work'?

Projects	Operations
Have a defined beginning and end	Ongoing
Have resources allocated specifically to them, although often on a shared basis	Resources used 'full-time'
Are intended to be done only once	A mixture of many recurring tasks

Projects	Operations
Follow a plan towards a clear intended end-result	Goals and deadlines are more general
Often cut across organisational and functional lines	Usually follows the organisation or functional structure

An activity that meets the first four criteria above can be classified as a project, and therefore falls within the **scope of project management**. Whether an activity is classified as a project is important, as projects should be managed using **project management techniques**.

Common examples of projects include:

- Producing a new product, service or object
- Changing the structure of an organisation
- Developing or modifying a new information system
- Implementing a new business procedure or process

Exam focus point

Note the links back to previous sections of your syllabus here: business process change (Section D) and information technology (Section E).

The December 2007 exam included a question looking at changes to a downstream supply chain. Such changes need to be investigated and implemented through projects.

1.2 What is project management?

FAST FORWARD

Project management is the combination of systems, techniques, and people used to control and monitor activities undertaken within the project. It will be deemed successful if it is completed at the specified level of **quality**, **on time** and within **budget**. Achieving this can be very difficult: most projects present a range of significant challenges.

Key term

Project management: Integration of all aspects of a project, ensuring that the proper knowledge and resources are available when and where needed, and above all to ensure that the expected outcome is produced in a timely, cost-effective manner. The primary function of a project manager is to manage the trade-offs between performance, timeliness and cost.

The objective of project management is a successful project. A project will be deemed successful if it is completed at the **specified level of quality**, **on time** and **within budget**.

Constraint	Comment
Quality	The end result should conform to the project specification. In other words, the result should achieve what the project was supposed to do
Budget	The project should be completed without exceeding authorised expenditure
Timescale	The progress of the project must follow the planned process, so that the 'result' is ready for use at the agreed date. As time is money, proper time management can help contain costs

Quality, **cost** and **time** are regarded as the yardsticks against which project success is measured. It is common to add a fourth constraint, **scope**, and even to use it to **replace quality** as a fundamental constraint and target. The **scope** of a project defines all the work that is to be done and all the deliverables that constitute project success. Under this analysis, the quality constraint is restricted to a narrower meaning and the difference between scope and quality becomes the difference between doing a job and doing it well – or badly.

The process involved in project management can be summarised in the figure below. (We will look at these processes in more detail throughout this chapter.)

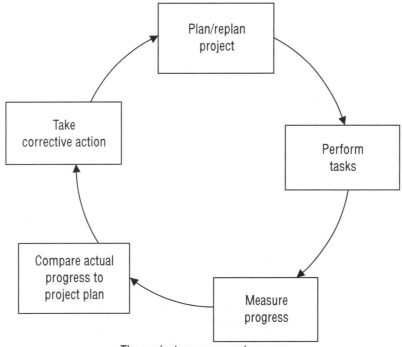

The project management process

1.2.1 Projects present some management challenges

Challenge	Comment
Teambuilding	The work is carried out by a team of people often from varied work and social backgrounds. The team must 'gel' quickly and be able to communicate effectively with each other
Expected problems	Expected problems should be avoided by careful design and planning prior to commencement of work
Unexpected problems	There should be mechanisms within the project to enable these problems to be resolved quickly and efficiently
Delayed benefit	There is normally no benefit until the work is finished. The lead-in time to this can cause a strain on the eventual recipient who is also faced with increasing expenditure for no immediate benefit
Specialists	Contributions made by specialists are of differing importance at each stage
Potential for conflict	Projects often involve several parties with different interests. This may lead to conflict

1.2.2 A note on terminology

Unfortunately, the terminology used in project management is not standardised, as we have already seen in the case of **scope** and **quality**. This is partly because large organisations develop their own methodologies and partly because there are at least two major, widely used methodologies that are taught as professional disciplines. These are **PRINCE2**, developed in the UK and used globally, and the **project management body of knowledge** (PMBOK) approach and terminology developed by the US Project Management Institute (PMI). Your syllabus does not mandate the use of any specific scheme of terminology, so we will use a selection of technical terms as they become appropriate in the discussion that follows. Where there are equivalents or near-equivalents, we will give them in brackets, together with their provenance, where appropriate, thus: '… project charter (PRINCE2: project initiation document)…'.

1.3 Projects and strategy

Adaptation to environmental change makes project management an important feature of strategic implementation. Also, strategic management thinking can be a useful input into project management. Strategic project management envisages strategy as a stream of projects intended to achieve organisational breakthroughs.

1.3.1 Linking projects with strategy

Grundy and Brown see three links between **strategic thinking** and **project management**.

(a) Many projects are undertaken as **consequences of the overall strategic planning process**. These projects may change the relationship between the organisation and its environment or they may be aimed at major organisational change.

(b) Some important projects arise on a bottom-up basis. The need for action may become apparent for operational rather than strategic reasons: such projects must be given careful consideration to ensure that their overall effect is **congruent with the current strategy**.

(c) Strategic thinking is also required at the level of the **individual project**, in order to avoid the limitations that may be imposed by a narrow view of what is to be done.

1.3.2 Project managing strategy

Project management in its widest sense is fundamental to much strategy. This is because very few organisations are able to do the same things in the same ways year after year. Continuing **environmental change** forces many organisations to include extensive processes of **adaptation** into their strategies. Business circumstances change and new conditions must be met with new responses or initiatives. Each possible new development effectively constitutes a project in the terms we have already discussed.

Grundy and Brown suggest three reasons for taking a project management view of strategic management.

(a) **Strategic planning**. Much strategy appears to develop in an incremental or fragmented way; detailed strategic thinking may be best pursued through the medium of a **strategic project** or group of projects. Project management is a way of making *ad hoc* strategy more deliberate and therefore better-considered.

(b) **Strategic implementation** is more complex than strategic analysis and choice; a project management approach, as outlined above, has an important role to play here, but must become capable of handling more complex, ambiguous and political issues if it is to play it effectively. When an apparent need for a project emerges, it should be screened to ensure that it supports the overall strategy.

(c) Even at the smaller, more traditional scale of project management, **wider strategic awareness is vital** if project managers are to deliver what the organisation actually needs.

Of course, not all new developments are recognised as worthy of project management. For example, the installation of a new, shared printer in an office would probably be regarded as a matter of routine, though it would no doubt have been authorised by a responsible budget holder and installed and networked by a suitable technician. There would probably have been a small amount of training associated with its use and maintenance and it might have been the subject of a health and safety risk assessment. All these processes taken together look like a project, if a very small one.

In contrast to the multitude of such small events, modern organisations are likely to undergo significant change far less often, but sufficiently frequently and with developments that have sufficiently long lives for project management to be an **important aspect of strategic implementation**. Project management and **change management** are thus intimately linked.

An atmosphere of change and continuing development will be particularly evident in relation to information systems and technology, organisation structure and organisation culture.

1.3.3 Project management as a core competence

FAST FORWARD

Kerzner suggests that where project management is a core competence, a continuous improvement approach should be taken to developing and consolidating the methodology.

Project management can be a **core strategic competence** for companies working in such industries as consulting and construction. Such companies must ensure that they maintain and improve their project management abilities if they are to continue to be commercially successful.

Kerzner describes a five level **project management maturity model** of continuous organisational improvement in the methodology of project management. Organisations should aspire to progress to the highest level, which is a state of **continuous improvement**. The five levels need not necessarily follow one another in a linear fashion: they may overlap, but the degree of overlap allowed is reflected in the risk associated with the overall process.

Level 1 **Common knowledge**
The importance of project management to the organisation is understood and training in the basic techniques and terminology is provided.

Level 2 **Common processes**
The processes employed successfully are standardised and developed so that they can be used more widely, both for future projects and in concert with other methodologies such as total quality management.

Level 3 **Singular methodology**
Project management is placed at the centre of a single corporate methodology, achieving wide synergy and improving process control in particular. A separate methodology may be retained for IS matters.

Level 4 **Benchmarking**
Competitive advantage is recognised as being based on process improvement and a continuing programme of benchmarking is undertaken.

Level 5 **Continuous improvement**
Benchmarking information is critically appraised for its potential contribution to the improvement of the singular methodology. Organisations such as this strive for project management excellence. Common characteristics at this level of project management maturity are the creation of lessons learned after each project and the application of lessons learned from previous projects into subsequent projects.

Models such as Kerzner's are a guide to progress; in particular they indicate corporate training needs and career development routes for project managers.

The need for continuous improvement is necessary because, despite best efforts, many projects fail. By analysing the reasons for the failures and identifying the lessons learned, the chances of future success can be improved. Taking the lessons learned forward into future projects helps avoid similar mistakes and to strengthen and improve both the project management and management processes.

1.3.4 Strategic project management

Grundy and Brown suggest that it is often appropriate for organisations to combine project management and strategic management into a process that they call **strategic project management**. This envisages strategy as a **stream of projects**.

Key term

> **Strategic project management** is the process of managing complex projects by combining business strategy and project management techniques in order to implement the business strategy and deliver organisational breakthroughs.
> *Grundy and Brown*

The link between strategy and project is most clearly seen in the concept of the **breakthrough project**.

> A **breakthrough project** is a project that will have a material impact on either the business's external competitive edge, its internal capabilities or its financial performance. *Grundy and Brown*

Breakthrough projects are a feature of the Japanese technique of *hoshin* or 'breakthrough management'. *Hoshin* requires that there should be not more than three concurrent breakthrough projects. This has distinct advantages.

- Resources are concentrated where they will do the most good
- Projects of marginal value are avoided
- Managerial attention remains focussed

The link from strategy to project management is a process influenced by both **internal** and **external change**. Vision gives rise to ideas for **strategic breakthroughs**. These lead to the establishment of **strategic programmes** and these, in turn generate **strategic projects**.

2 The project lifecycle   6/13

> The project life cycle concept describes the progression of many projects through four stages: definition, design, delivery and development.

Projects may be thought of as having a **lifecycle**. This concept is useful for understanding the processes involved in project management and control, since the resources required and the focus of management attention vary as projects move from one stage to the next.

2.1 A typical four stage project lifecycle

Maylor describes a typical four stage project lifecycle.

2.1.1 Project definition

Project definition is the first stage. Its essential element is the definition of the purpose and objectives of the project. This stage may include abstract processes of conceptualisation, more rigorous analysis of requirements and methods, feasibility studies and, perhaps most important, a definition of scope. The scope of a project in this sense is what is included and what is not, both in terms of what it is intended to achieve and the extent of its impact on other parts of the organisation, both during its execution and subsequently.

The project definition stage may also include the procedures required for **project selection**. We will discuss this further below, but for now we may simply point out that an organisation may be aware of a larger number of worthwhile projects than it has resources to undertake. Some rational process for deciding just which projects will proceed is therefore required.

2.1.2 Project design

The project design phase will include detailed planning for **activity**, **cost**, **quality** and **risk**. Final project authorisation may be delayed until this stage to ensure that the decision is taken in the light of more detailed information about planned costs and benefits.

2.1.3 Project delivery

The project delivery phase includes all the work required to deliver the planned project outcomes. Planning will continue, but the emphasis is on getting the work done. Sub-phases can be identified.

(a) The people and other resources needed initially are assembled at **start up**.
(b) Planned project activities are carried out during **execution**.
(c) **Completion** consists of success or, sometimes, abandonment.

(d)   The delivery phase comes to an end with **handover**. This is likely to include **project closure** procedures that ensure that all documentation, quality and accounting activities are complete and that the customer has accepted the delivery as satisfactory.

2.1.4 Project development

Handover brings the delivery phase to an end but the project continues through a further stage of management largely aimed at **improving the organisation's overall ability to manage projects**.

(a)   There should be an **immediate review** to provide rapid staff feedback and to identify short-term needs such as staff training or remedial action for procedure failures.

(b)   **Longer-term review** will examine the project outcomes after the passage of time to establish its overall degree of success. **Lifetime costs** are an important measure of success. There should also be longer-term review of all aspects of the project and its management, perhaps on a functional basis.

It is tempting to ignore the need for project review, especially since, done properly, it imposes significant costs in terms of management time and effort. It is, however, essential if the organisation is to improve the effectiveness of its project management in the future.

2.2 Project definition

Grundy and Brown summarise the process of project definition as the preparation of answers to a series of questions.

- What opportunities and threats does the project present?
- What are its objectives?
- What are its potential benefits, costs and risks?
- What is its overall implementation difficulty?
- Who are the key stakeholders?

A number of techniques that aid analytical thinking may be used when addressing these questions.

2.2.1 Defining the key issues – fishbone analysis

Fishbone analysis (root-cause, cause and effect or *Ishikawa* diagram analysis) is useful for establishing and analysing key issues. It can be used both on existing problems, opportunities and behavioural issues, and on those that may be anticipated, perhaps as a result of the construction of a scenario.

The essence of fishbone analysis is to break a perceived issue down into its smallest underlying causes and components, so that each may be tackled in a proper fashion. It is called fishbone analysis because the overall issue and its components are traditionally analysed and presented on a diagram such as the one that follows.

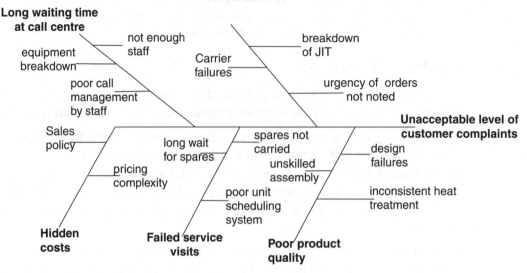

Fishbone analysis

The major issue or problem is shown at the right hand side of the page and the perceived causes and influences are shown, in no particular order, on the 'bones' radiating from the central spine. Each 'bone' can be further analysed if appropriate. It is common to use familiar models such as the Ms list of resources (men, money, machines and so on) to give structure to the investigation, though not necessarily to the diagram. The fish bone diagram itself is not, of course, essential to the process of analysis, but it forms a good medium for brainstorming a problem and for presenting the eventual results.

2.2.2 Determining performance drivers

Many strategic projects are aimed at or include improving some aspect of the performance of a department, activity or function: **performance driver analysis** is useful in such cases; essentially it is another brainstorming and presentation technique. It has a lot in common with the **force field analysis** we will encounter later in this Study Text, during our consideration of the management of change. The essential difference between the two is that force field analysis is concerned with factors affecting future change activity, while performance driver analysis is used to identify the factors that account for past (and current) performance.

The essence of the technique is to identify two groups of performance related influences: those that **enable good performance** and those that **hinder or prevent it**. The factors in these two groups are drawn as arrows against a baseline, the length of each arrow representing the perceived strength of the influence it represents.

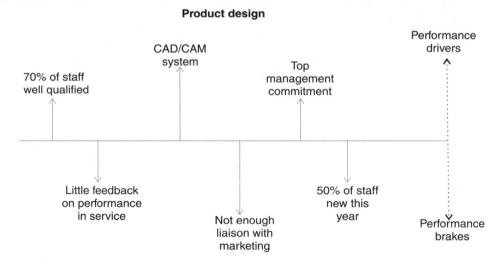

Performance driver analysis

2.2.3 Gap analysis

Gap analysis is widely used in business strategy to focus attention on the **anticipated gap** between **desired** future strategic performance and **likely** future performance if there is no intervention. It can be used in a similar way in project selection and definition as a route to establishing both what projects should be undertaken and what their scope should be.

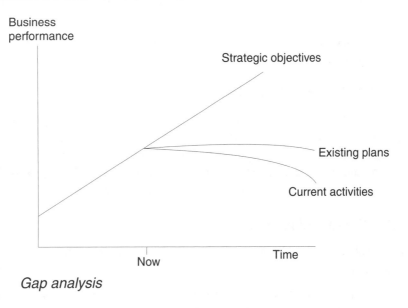

Gap analysis

2.2.4 From–to analysis

From–to analysis is appropriate for establishing the scope of strategic projects concerned with **organisational change** or **operational improvement**. The essence of the technique is to both define the **current state** ('from this') and the **desired state** ('to this') of relevant issues such as management style, control methods, power structures, communications practices, working methods, cost base and customer service. Deciding which issues are relevant is as important as deciding what should be done about them, so **fishbone analysis** might lead in to this technique. From-to analysis would supplement **gap analysis** by looking at the gap from a different perspective.

2.2.5 Stakeholder analysis

We have covered stakeholder analysis in general earlier in this Study Text, but we will look at project stakeholder analysis in more detail later in this chapter.

2.3 Initiating a project   6/12

FAST FORWARD

> Limits to resource availability mean that not all potential projects will be undertaken; rational methods are used to select projects.
>
> Project initiation tasks include the appointment of project manager and sponsor; stakeholder analysis and the definition of project scope. The business case explains why the project is needed, while the project charter gives authorisation for it to be undertaken.

2.3.1 Project selection

As already mentioned, it is likely that an organisation will be aware of a greater number of potentially advantageous projects than it has resources to undertake. It is therefore necessary to **select projects carefully** in order to make the best use of those limited resources. Project assessment and selection is analogous to strategic choice, not least because many projects are of strategic significance. The techniques used for making strategic choices are, therefore also applicable. The criteria of **suitability**, **acceptability** and **feasibility** are applicable to many project choice problems, perhaps reinforced by the use of more detailed assessment techniques such as those below.

(a) **Risk/return analysis** using DCF, expected values and estimates of attractiveness and difficulty of implementation

(b) **Weighted scoring** of project characteristics

(c) Assessment of **organisational priority**

(d) **Feasibility studies** addressing technical, environmental, social and financial feasibility; such studies are costly and time-consuming and are likely to be restricted to front-running project proposals

(e) **SWOT analysis**, assessing the strengths and weaknesses of individual projects against the opportunities and threats facing the organisation.

2.3.2 Project initiation tasks

When a project has been approved in general terms, it should be the subject of a number of management processes and tasks in order to start it up and move it into the execution phase. The exact nature of these processes may well vary from project to project and according to the particular project management methodology adopted. Schwalbe lists **pre-initiating tasks** and **initiating tasks**. The pre-initiating tasks follow on directly from the formal project selection process.

2.3.3 Pre-initiating tasks

Pre-initiating tasks are the responsibility of the senior managers who decide that the project should be undertaken.

(a) Determination of project goals and constraints. This involves setting the project scope, but also identifying time or cost constraints

(b) Identification of the **project sponsor**

(c) Selection of the **project manager**

2.3.4 Project constraints

We noted at the start of this chapter that a project will be deemed successful if it is completed on time, within budget, and to the specified scope.

However, it is important to note that in any project, there is a trade-off between project scope, time and cost.

There are several aspects to consider for each of these elements.

Project scope

Project scope varies according to either **quantity** or **quality**.

- How many tasks or activities are to be included in the project?
- What level of quality is required for each task?

Time

- There is likely to be an overall deadline for when the project has to be completed

- Within this overall deadline, there is likely to be an operational 'time budget' containing the number of staff hours which can be devoted to the project

Cost

- A project should have a cost budget, and the project manager should aim to ensure costs remain within this budget

- Costs should be commensurate to the benefits the project will deliver, and the business case (see below) should demonstrate that the project's benefits exceed its costs

- Budget constraints will mean the project has limited resources – for example, contractors, materials or equipment

The trade-off between scope, time and cost can best be viewed as a triangle. Each of the three elements is constrained in itself, but also acts as a constraint on the others. If there is a change to one aspect of the triangle, there is likely to be a knock-on effect on the remaining aspects. For example, if the project scope is extended to include an extra activity, this is likely to increase costs and mean the project takes longer to complete (unless the quality of the remaining activities is sacrificed to adjust for the additional activity).

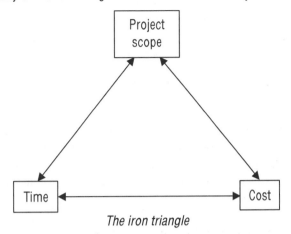

The iron triangle

Note. The roles and responsibilities of the project manager and project sponsor are discussed later in this chapter.

- **Senior management meeting** with project manager to review the process and expectations for managing the project
- Decision whether the project actually needs to be divided into two or more smaller projects

2.3.5 Initiating tasks

Initiating tasks are carried out by the **project manager**.

(a) Identification of **project stakeholders** and their characteristics
(b) Preparation of a **business case** for the project
(c) Drafting of a **project charter** (PRINCE2: project initiation document)
(d) Drafting an initial statement of **project scope**
(e) Holding a **project initiation meeting** (PMBOK: 'kick-off' meeting)

2.3.6 Risk management

Risk management is concerned with **identifying potential problems** and taking action to **eliminate or reduce the damage** that will result if the risks materialise. Failure to manage risks adequately could threaten the success of a whole project. For example, it could lead to missed deadlines, poor quality, or business disruption.

Risk management is the responsibility of the project manager, who should assess the likelihood and potential impact of each risk. Risk management resources should be concentrated in those areas where risk is high (**risk prioritisation**). There are two aspects of risk management:

(a) **Risk prevention**
(b) **Minimising the effect** of a risk event if it does occur

Risk assessment and management should be conducted at the start of the project, but should be revisited throughout the project to ensure that risks are understood and controlled. It is usually impossible to eliminate risk altogether so the project manager should recognise the existence of risks and prepare, in advance, plans for dealing with them if they occur.

As a project proceeds, the **nature of risk changes**. Old risks disappear and new ones appear. Consequently, risk management is a continuous process, so there needs to be an ongoing risk assessment procedure which regularly reviews and reassesses risks throughout a project.

In this respect, risk management is also part of controlling a project, and we will look at risk management in more detail as part of project control later in this chapter.

2.4 Stakeholder analysis

Project stakeholders are the individuals and organisations that are involved in, or may be affected by, project activities and outcomes.

We discussed the strategic importance of stakeholders earlier in this Study Text. Fairly obviously, where a project is of strategic significance, stakeholders will be considered at several points during the development of the strategy. The stakeholder concept can also be applied to the management of projects of less overall significance. This would form part of that strategic approach to project management advocated by Grundy and Brown.

It is important to understand who has an interest in a project, because part of the responsibility of the project manager is **communication** and the **management of expectations**. An initial assessment of stakeholders should be made early in the project's life, taking care not to ignore those who might not approve of the project, either as a whole, or because of some aspect such as its cost, its use of scarce talent or its side-effects. Each stakeholder's degree of interest in and support for (or opposition to) the project should be estimated.

2.5 Preparation of a business case

When the project selection process is complete and a project selected for action, there is likely to be a great deal of information available to justify the decision to proceed. However, it is unlikely that a full account of the project has been prepared. A **business case** is a reasoned account of **why** the project is needed, **what** it will achieve and **how** it will proceed.

The business case is a fundamental component of the PRINCE2 methodology, which is built on the assumption that a project is, in fact, **driven by its business case**. An important use of the business case in any project is to maintain **focus** and prevent **mission creep** by regular reference back to it. It is possible that final approval for a large project will depend upon the preparation of a satisfactory business case.

A business case is not, of course, something that is confined to commercial organisations: the principles are equally applicable to any organisation undertaking a project.

Building the business case is covered in detail later in this chapter.

2.6 The project charter

The **project charter** (or project initiation document) complements the business case: while the business case explains the **need** for work on the project to start, the charter gives **authorisation** for work to be done and resources used. The charter also has an important role in internal communication within the organisation, since it can be given wide distribution in order to keep staff informed of what is happening. The exact content of a charter will vary from organisation to organisation and from project to project, but some elements are likely to be present in all charters.

- Project title
- Project purpose and objectives
- Project start date and expected finish date

- Details of the project sponsor and project
- Authorisation by the main stakeholders

Other elements of information may be included.

- Outline schedule of work
- Budget information

- Outline of project scope and work sequence
- Further details of roles and responsibilities

2.7 Statement of project scope

As we have already indicated, the word **scope** is used in project management to mean both the outcomes that are required and the work that is to be done to achieve them. It is obviously of great importance that everyone involved in a project should have a common understanding of these matters. If this common understanding is not reached, sooner or later there will be acrimonious disputes. A careful specification of

project scope is therefore of great importance and the project management methodology in use may require that this be a separate document. Equally, it may be that the business case and the project charter between them provide a clear statement of agreed scope. Under the **PRINCE2** methodology, the **business case** performs the role of a statement of project scope.

It is likely that in larger projects, it will become necessary to **adjust the project scope**. This might occur, for example, if resources are unavoidably reduced or it becomes clear that a feasibility study was too optimistic or too pessimistic. When a change to project scope becomes apparent, it is important that it is **clearly stated** and that the revision is **approved by the interested stakeholders**.

2.8 Terminology again

If you have been paying attention, you will have noticed that there has been a certain amount of overlap in our account so far of the processes involved in getting a project off the ground. For example, there have been a couple of mentions of stakeholders and the whole problem of scope has been approached from several different directions. We make no apology for this – it is the result of the variety of project methodologies in use in the real world.

<table>
<tr><td>**Exam focus point**</td><td>Prepare your own summary of the activities and processes involved in project selection, definition, and initiation, mentioning each one just once. This will provide you with essential information for dealing with any question that involves the early stages of a project.</td></tr>
</table>

3 Building the business case   12/10

<table>
<tr><td>**FAST FORWARD**</td><td>The business case is a key document which is initially used to secure funding for a project, then revisited and revised during the life of the project to ensure the project remains on track and the identified benefits are realised.</td></tr>
</table>

<table>
<tr><td>**Key term**</td><td>A **business case** is a key document for a project. It is used to propose a course of action to senior management for their consideration.</td></tr>
</table>

<table>
<tr><td>**Exam focus point**</td><td>An article titled 'Project management – business cases and gateways' written by Ken Garrett is available in the technical articles section for P3 on the ACCA website. It would be worth taking the time to study this article.</td></tr>
</table>

The purpose of a business case is to:

- Secure funding for significant financial investment

- Provide information to decide whether or not to make the financial investment

- Enable the organisation to plan, manage and successfully complete the project so that the benefits which underpin the rationale for both the investment and the business changes are achieved

- Provide, where appropriate, arguments that define how the project will contribute to enhancing existing capabilities or create new ones

- Help ensure the effective coordination and management of the activities and resources involved

- Ensure the investment is understood from the viewpoints of both what benefits can be expected and how feasible it is to achieve those benefits, in comparison with alternative uses of funds and resources

The business case is not a one-off process; it will be continually developed and revised throughout the life of the project.

3.1 Structure of a business case

Business cases vary greatly in size depending on the preferences of the organisation in question. Whilst some prefer large documents, backed up with supporting evidence, documentation, calculations and analysis; others prefer short, summarised business cases.

Regardless of their size and format, they generally contain the same key elements.

- Introduction
- Management summary
- Description of the current situation
- Options considered
- Analysis of costs and benefits
- Investment appraisal
- Impact assessment
- Risk assessment
- Recommendations
- Appendices and supporting information

3.1.1 Introduction

The introduction defines the scope and objectives of the change and provides the necessary background information to illustrate why the business case is being put forward. It may also describe the methods used in developing the business case and thank key contributors to the study.

3.1.2 Management summary

This is the last piece of the business case to be prepared. It summarises the main points in only a few paragraphs. It should be carefully worded as it may be the only part of the business case which is actually read in detail by senior decision makers. It should cover:

- What the study was about
- What was discovered about the issues under consideration
- Details of the options considered and the main merits and drawbacks of each
- A clear statement of the recommendation being made and the decision required

3.1.3 Description of the current situation

This section details what is happening at the moment, and where the problems and opportunities lie. This section should be as short as possible as senior managers can become frustrated at reading large amounts of text, only to discover what they already knew! The exception is where the real problems are not in line with the current understanding of management, in which case more detailed explanation can be provided.

3.1.4 Options considered

This briefly details what options were considered and why they were rejected, followed by a full description of the recommended solution.

3.1.5 Analysis of costs and benefits   6/14

This section should provide the benefits first, followed by the costs. This is to help the reader appreciate the benefits before they are faced with the costs in achieving them. Preparation of the section involves a number of challenges.

- Working out where the costs will be incurred and what benefits may arise
- Remaining realistic about whether the benefits will actually be realised in practice

- Intangible elements, such as improved moral, can be difficult to value. In some organisations managers will not consider intangible benefits at all. This can make it difficult, or even impossible to make an effective business case. The best policy with intangible benefits is to state them but not value them, leaving the reader to come to their own conclusion about their worth

- Values are often based on assumptions which may or may not turn out to be accurate. Only assumptions that are common within the organisation should be made, and the values calculated based on these should always be under, rather than overstated

3.1.6 Investment appraisal

Once the costs and benefits have been assessed, they must be presented in a way that allows the reader to see whether, and when, the project will pay for itself.

3.1.7 Impact assessment

Any impacts the project may have on the organisation, in addition to the cost, should be described here. For example, changes may need to be made to the organisational structure, or specialist staff may need to be recruited.

All changes such as these should be clearly described, along with details of any costs these changes will incur.

3.1.8 Risk assessment

Strong business cases clearly identify the risks involved and illustrate the suitable countermeasures available. For every risk, the following should be stated.

- **Description** of the cause of the risk and its impact

- **Impact assessment** of the scale of the damage that would be suffered, should the risk event occur

- **Probability** of how likely that risk is to occur

- **Countermeasures** describing how the likelihood of the risk occurring can be reduced, how to lessen its impact if it occurs, and how the risk can be transferred (eg insurance)

- **Ownership** of the risk (the individual responsible for managing that risk should be defined)

3.1.9 Recommendations

This section should summarise the business case and clearly state the decisions that senior management are being asked to take.

3.1.10 Appendices and supporting information

Detailed information should be put into appendices to separate out the supporting detail from the main points included in the body of the case. Statistics, charts and the detailed cost/benefit calculations may also be put into the appendices.

3.2 Identifying the benefits

A business case should be based on the ability to measure each benefit and estimate expected improvements. Benefits can be classified as **observable**, **measureable**, **quantifiable** or **financial**.

Some projects are more successful than others at delivering benefits. To understand why this is, observation of methodologies used in projects was carried out and the **benefits management** approach was developed. This approach aims to avoid the loss of achievable benefits as well as to realise more extensive benefits than from previous investments. It is possible that this approach may also reduce costs, as those costs which deliver nothing of value can be eliminated.

Benefits management has much in common with change management and the business process change lifecycle model as it recognises that the way in which a major change is managed must be appropriate to the content of the change and the context of the organisation involved.

Benefits management is not a one-off process; it will be revised constantly throughout the life of the project. It is made up of five key stages as shown by the following diagram.

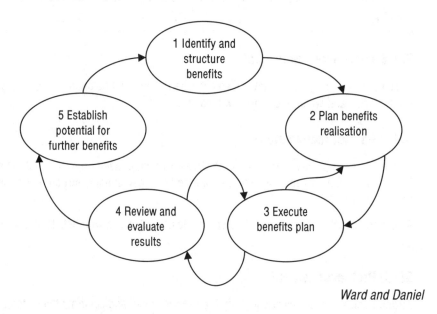

Ward and Daniel

The first stage of the diagram, **identifying and structuring benefits**, is important for inclusion in the business case. The point of the business case is to secure funding by demonstrating the benefits for the organisation that the project will bring.

The purpose of identifying and structuring benefits is to:

- Establish agreed objectives for the investment
- Identify all the potential benefits that may arise if the objectives of the investment are met (including where in the organisation it will occur)
- Understand how those benefits could be realised
- Determine ownership of the benefits
- Determine how the benefits can be measured to prove they have occurred
- Identify any issues that could delay the project or cause it to fail

- Produce an outline business case to decide whether to proceed with the project or stop investment at this stage

Notice that as part of this process, it is important to determine who **owns** the benefit and how it will be **measured**. If a perceived benefit cannot be measured, or no one owns it, then that benefit does not really exist.

3.2.1 Classifying and measuring benefits

A Section B question in the June 2012 exam required candidates to categorise and critically evaluate four proposed benefits given in the scenario. This required the application of the four types of benefit identified in the next section: observable, measurable, quantifiable and financial.

A business case should be based on the ability to **measure** each benefit and on specific evidence that enables the level or size of each expected improvement to be estimated. It should aim to express benefits in **financial** terms so that the overall expected return of the investment can be calculated. However, not all benefits can be quantified in this way.

However, **all** benefits can be measured in some way. Benefits can be classified as **observable, measurable, quantifiable** and **financial**.

Observable benefits are those which are measured by experience or judgement. 'Soft' benefits such as staff morale fall into this category.

Measurable benefits relate to an area of performance that could be (or already is being) measured, but it is not possible to quantify how much performance will increase as a result of the change.

Quantifiable benefits are those where the level of benefit that will result from the change can be reliably forecast based on the evidence in place.

Financial benefits are quantified benefits that have had a financial formula (such as cost or price) applied to them to produce a financial value for the benefits.

The examining team has stressed the importance of understanding the different ways that benefits can be classified.

An article titled 'Project management – business cases and gateways' (April 2011) written by Ken Garrett is available in the technical articles section for P3 on ACCA's website. It would be worth taking the time to study this article.

3.2.2 Observable benefits

The realisation of observable benefits can only be determined by judgement or experience. The benefit gained from the process is **observed**. However, if such benefits have been tracked over time, then it may become possible to measure, rather than just observe, their impact.

Observable benefits are unlikely to be sufficient to argue the business case. However, their impact should not be devalued or underestimated. They should be included in the business plan, even if there are plenty of other financial and quantifiable benefits to secure funding.

3.2.3 Measurable benefits

As their name suggests, measurable benefits relate to areas of the business where performance could be measured. The impact of the improvement, however, cannot yet be quantified. This will only be possible **after** the improvement has been put in place and the appropriate measurements taken. Performance is measured, both before and after the implementation, and the improvement can then be attributed to the investment. Process improvement benefits are often measurable benefits.

It is often necessary with such benefits to have more than one measure in order to determine if the benefit has been fully realised. These measures should be relevant to both the measure itself and the changes needed to realise it. This helps to ensure that the improvement can be directly attributable to the investment.

3.2.4 Quantifying benefits

A big challenge when defining benefits for inclusion in the business plan is to find a way of **quantifying** the benefits.

Quantifiable benefits differ from measurable benefits because it is possible to quantify the degree of improvement **before** the change is actually made.

Many investment cases are criticised for being unable to provide sufficient evidence to back up the assumptions made to quantify the benefits listed in their business case. If the quantification cannot be verified, then any financial figure placed on this benefit will be meaningless. This is therefore the most crucial stage in building a sound economic case for investment. There are five approaches to quantifying benefits.

1   **Evidence.** Relevant detailed evidence may be obtained from existing systems over an appropriate period of time. This method is particularly useful when the change requires **stopping** the carrying out of a certain process.

2   **Modelling and simulating** can be carried out using computer software to identify the level of performance that could be achieved if particular new processes are adopted, providing a basis for estimates for what could be achieved in the specific situation under review.

3   **Benchmarking**. Benefits can be quantified by evaluating the changes in relation to best practices in the industry, or in similar processes in different industries. This is a helpful technique for quantifying the effects of process improvement initiatives but less helpful when attempting to quantify the benefits of innovations.

4   **Reference sites** are examples of the change being made or of the technology being used in other organisations or industries. Unless it is a first-of-its-kind innovation, there should be a reference site available, often from the suppliers of the technology who will be keen to demonstrate its prior success. Once a relevant implementation has been identified, it will be necessary to determine:

   •   How the technology has been deployed

   •   What changes had to be made in order to obtain the required improvement in performance

   •   The starting point (in performance terms) of the reference organisation in order to determine how much of their achievement is relevant and feasible for the current organisation.

5   **Pilot implementations** can be used, both to test technology and to evaluate potential benefits from new systems and ways of working. This method is necessary where proof of the benefit is required. The process is tested on a small scale and the benefits are recorded, then extrapolated to provide the total expected benefit. Ideally, a comparable control group, working in the old way, will be monitored simultaneously to provide a baseline.

3.2.5 Financial benefits

A business case should aim to express as many of the benefits as possible in financial terms in order for the expected return of the investment to be calculated. However, over-reliance on financial benefits will limit the benefits included because, as we have seen, not all benefits can be reliably quantified and hence, no reliable financial value can be attached to it.

Quantifiable benefits can be converted to financial benefits by applying a financial formula (such as cost or price) to that benefit. However some quantified benefits, such as increased productivity, can be difficult to convert to a financial benefit, especially if the improved productivity arises from a saving in staff time. This is because the value placed on such benefits can be very subjective and varies greatly across organisations.

Financial benefits are only realisable through reductions in cost, avoidance of known future costs or costs associated with unacceptable risks, increases in revenue, or avoidance of revenue loss. Generally, reductions in costs are easier to identify, quantify and prove than increases in revenue. However, converting the benefit to a financial benefit will be relatively straightforward, assuming the benefits were appropriately quantified based on sound assumptions and evidence.

3.3 Identifying the costs

FAST FORWARD

Many costs will be incurred as part of a project, these will be both **capital** and **operational**. Care should be taken to ensure all costs are fully identified within the business case.

As we have seen with project benefits, predicting costs can also be difficult particularly as some (such as those associated with making business changes) may not be recorded. Types of costs that should be included as part of the project cost assessment include:

- **Purchase costs** such as hardware, software, consultancy and materials

- **Internal systems development costs** such as developing/purchasing software

- **Infrastructure costs**. These are costs that are incurred exclusively for the new system

- **Costs of carrying out the business changes** should be included to provide a complete financial view of the investment. This includes costs such as training, recruitment, redundancy, refitting buildings and so on

- **Ongoing costs**. These are the permanent costs involved in the new ways of working. They should be either explicitly stated as additional costs or netted off against the benefits

We can see from this that a project will include both **capital** and **operational** costs.

Key term

Capital expenditure acquires or produces an asset whose value continues to be used (or consumed) over several financial years.

Operating costs refer to any expenditure on things whose value is used up within the same financial year.

The majority of capital expenditure is likely to occur at the start of the project and prior to implementation. This could involve expenditure on items such as building new facilities, refits and refurbishment, new technology and systems and so on.

Operating expenditure can be non-recurrent, such as consultancy fees, or can be recurrent, such as staff salaries. Recurrent operating expenditure could continue long after the project has been completed and the finished solution implemented.

Recurrent operating costs are as relevant to the business case as the capital and non-recurrent operating costs incurred during the project itself. However, it is easy to overlook such costs as part of 'business as usual'. If such costs would not be incurred if the project did not go ahead, then those costs must be built into the business case if it is to be a true representation of the worth of the project.

3.4 Evaluation of the costs and benefits   6/11

Exam focus point

A requirement in the compulsory Section A of the Pilot Paper requires candidates to evaluate a cost-benefit technique that has been used in the scenario to justify investing in a project. Make sure you can identify which of the techniques have been used, as well as have a firm understanding of the limitations of the methods. You should also be familiar with the way benefits should be classified (ie observable, measurable etc as descibed above) to ensure the benefits included in such analyses are justified.

When investment decisions are made, an outlay of economic value (usually cash) is made in anticipation of future benefits. The outlay is usually large and is incurred at the start of the process. The benefits do not occur until later and then generally arrive in a number of smaller amounts over a period of time.

Investment decisions are important to businesses because they involve **large amounts of resource**, and once the investment has been undertaken, it can be **difficult and expensive to pull out** of it.

Given this, it is important that investment proposals are properly appraised before they are taken on. There are four key methods that are used for investment appraisal, they are:

- Accounting rate of return (ARR)
- Payback period (PP)
- Net present value (NPV)
- Internal rate of return (IRR)

All of these are valid methods which are used by many organisations.

3.4.1 Accounting rate of return

The accounting rate of return takes the average accounting operating profit that the investment will generate and expresses it as a percentage of the average investment made over the life of the project.

$$ARR = \frac{\text{Average annual operating profit}}{\text{Average investment to earn that profit}} \times 100$$

For a project to be acceptable, it must achieve a target ARR as a minimum. It is likely that this target would be based on the Return on Capital Employed (ROCE) perhaps of similar prior projects, or of the industry average.

If there are a number of competing projects that achieve the minimum ARR, the one that would be selected is the one with the highest ARR.

ARR has two main advantages:

- **Consistent** with the overall approach to measuring business performance (ROCE)
- Gives the result expressed as a **percentage**, managers generally feel comfortable with this

There are also several problems in using ARR:

(a) Ignores the **time** factor. For example, if two projects that require the same outlay give the same total return over five years, then ARR would rank them equally. However, it may be that in one the returns are concentrated in year 1 and in the other the returns are concentrated in year 5. A rational investor would prefer the one that gave the most returns quickly – however, ARR overlooks this.

(b) Is based on **profits not cash**. When measuring performance over the whole life of a project, cash is more important because it is used to acquire resources and for distribution to owners. Accounting profit is more appropriate for reporting achievement on a periodic basis, eg a year or half-year. Cash is more appropriate over the long term.

(c) ARR can create problems when considering competing investments of different **size**. This is because it deals with percentages. It would suggest that the best project to invest in would be the one with the biggest **percentage return**; however, it may be far better to select the project with the biggest **absolute return.**

Question

Arrow wants to buy a new item of equipment. Two models of equipment are available, one with a slightly higher capacity and greater reliability than the other. The expected costs and profits of each item are as follows.

	Equipment item X	Equipment item Y
Capital cost	$80,000	$150,000
Life	5 years	5 years
Profits before depreciation	$	$
Year 1	50,000	50,000
Year 2	50,000	50,000
Year 3	30,000	60,000
Year 4	20,000	60,000
Year 5	10,000	60,000
Disposal value	0	0

ARR is measured as the average annual profit after depreciation, divided by the average net book value of the asset.

Which item of equipment should be selected if the company's target ARR is 30%?

Answer

	Item X $	Item Y $
Total profit over life of equipment		
Before depreciation	160,000	280,000
After depreciation	80,000	130,000
Average annual profit after depreciation	16,000	26,000
Average investment = (capital cost + disposal value)/2	40,000	75,000
ARR	40%	34.7%

Both projects would earn a return in excess of 30%, but since **item X would earn a bigger ARR, it would be preferred to item Y**, even though the profits from Y would be higher by an average of $10,000 a year.

Exam focus point

A question in the June 2011 exam asked for a critical evaluation of comments made by the owner of an events company which organised folk music festivals. Students were required to evaluate the investment appraisal technique used (NPV) in selecting one of two IT projects. To perform well on this question, students needed to demonstrate an understanding of payback period calculations, discount rate and IRR.

3.4.2 Payback period

The **payback period** is the length of time it takes for an initial investment to be repaid out of the net cash inflows from the project.

This method overcomes the problem of time that is associated with the ARR method of project appraisal.

For a project to be acceptable, it would need to have a payback period shorter than a maximum payback period set by the organisation.

If there are several competing projects that meet the requirement above, then the one with the shortest payback period should be selected.

Payback period has the following advantages.

- Quick and easy to calculate
- Easily understood by managers
- The speed of cost recovery concept emphasises the importance of liquidity

Payback period also has the following problems:

- Ignores cash flows after the payback date, for example, two projects may take 5 years to repay the initial outflow; however, in years six and seven, one may generate significantly more than the other, yet they would be rated identically using this method
- Ignores many risks, eg the risk that demand will be lower than expected is not considered
- It is not linked to promoting increases in the wealth of the organisation and its owners; instead, it recommends projects that quickly pay for themselves

Question	Payback Period

An asset costing $120,000 is to be depreciated over ten years to a nil residual value. Profits after depreciation for the first five years are as follows.

Year	$
1	12,000
2	17,000
3	28,000
4	37,000
5	8,000

How long is the payback period to the nearest month?

Answer

Profits before depreciation should be used.

Year	Profit after depreciation	Depreciation	Profit before depreciation	Cumulative profit
	$'000	$'000	$'000	$'000
1	12	12	24	24
2	17	12	29	53
3	28	12	40	93
4	37	12	49	142
5	8	12	20	

$$\text{Payback period} = 3 \text{ years} + \left[\frac{(120 - 93)}{(142 - 93)} \times 12 \text{ months} \right]$$

= 3 years 7 months

3.4.3 Net present value

Net present value (NPV) is the sum of the discounted value of the net cash flows from the investment.

NPV is a good basis for investment decisions because it:

- Considers **all** the costs and benefits of each investment opportunity
- Makes a logical allowance for the **timing** of those costs and benefits

There are three key reasons why timing is an important consideration.

1   **Interest lost**. If the organisation has the funds in its control, then it could invest them and earn interest. The longer the funds are tied up in an investment, the longer the organisation does not have access to them and hence, the longer they will be unavailable to earn interest.

2   **Risk**. Investing in something that will bring about future benefits is risky – the benefits actually received may not be in line with what was expected. A degree of risk is accepted in all project investments. The greater the risk, the higher the rate of return is expected.

3   **Inflation**. Money loses purchasing power over time as a result of inflation; a dollar now is worth more than a dollar in a year's time.

NPV recognises the **time value of money** by working out the **present value** of future returns (ie if the cash flows from the investment were received today, how much would they be worth?).

The present value is worked out using the equation

$$PV \text{ of a cashflow} = \frac{\text{actual cashflow}}{(1+r)^n}$$

n = year of cashflow

r = the opportunity investing cost of capital expressed as a decimal (rather than a percentage)

The **NPV** is the sum of **all the cashflows** associated with a project, less the cost of the original investment.

Investments that return a positive NPV should be accepted. If several competing investments all have positive NPVs, then the one with the highest NPV should be selected.

NPV is a better method for investment appraisals than either the IRR (see below) or the PP. This is for a number of reasons.

- **Timing**. NPV takes account of the time value of money by discounting future cashflows to arrive at a present value of those cashflows. The net benefit after finance costs have been met is identified

- **Completeness**. This method considers all future cashflows, regardless of when they will occur. Although it treats them differently depending on when they are expected to occur, every cashflow is taken into account

- **Alignment** with business objectives. NPV is the only method of investment appraisal that produces an output that relates directly to the amount of wealth generated for shareholders

Question   NPV

Slogger has a cost of capital of 15% and is considering a capital investment project, where the estimated cash flows are as follows.

Year	Cash flow
	$
0 (ie now)	(100,000)
1	60,000
2	80,000
3	40,000
4	30,000

Required

Calculate the NPV of the project, and assess whether it should be undertaken.

Answer

Year	Cash flow $	Discount factor 15%	Present value $
0	(100,000)	1.000	(100,000)
1	60,000	1/(1.15)= 0.870	52,200
2	80,000	$1/1.15^2 = 0.756$	60,480
3	40,000	$1/1.15^3 = 0.658$	26,320
4	30,000	$1/1.15^4 = 0.572$	17,160
			NPV = 56,160

(*Note*. The **discount factor for any cash flow 'now' (time 0) is always 1**, whatever the cost of capital.)

The **PV of cash inflows exceeds the PV of cash outflows** by $56,160, which means that the project will earn a DCF yield in excess of 15%. It should therefore be **undertaken**.

3.4.4 Internal rate of return

The **internal rate of return (IRR)** is the discount rate that, when applied to its future cash flows, will produce an NPV of zero.

It is generally calculated using either trial and error, or a spreadsheet. A range of discount rates are calculated until the one that yields zero NPV is found.

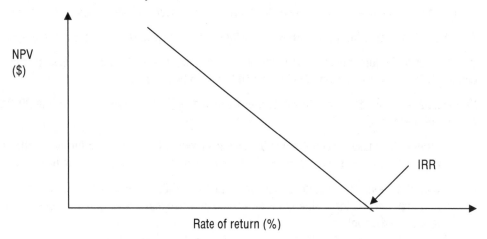

If the discount rate itself is zero, the NPV would be the sum of the net cash flows, ie no account would be taken of the time value of money. When the discount rate increases, there is a corresponding decrease in the NPV. The NPV is zero where it crosses the horizontal axis.

If we determine **a cost of capital where the NPV is slightly positive, and another cost of capital where it is slightly negative**, we can **estimate the IRR** by using the interpolation method. The **interpolation method assumes that the NPV rises in linear fashion between the two NPVs close to 0**. The real rate of return is therefore assumed to be on a straight line between the two points at which the NPV is calculated.

The **IRR interpolation formula** to apply is:

$$IRR = A + \left[\frac{P}{P-N} \times (B-A)\right]\%$$

where A is the (lower) rate of return

B is the (higher) rate of return

P is the NPV at A

N is the NPV at B

Note that N doesn't have to be negative, but if it is, then we effectively end up adding in the denominator.

Investments that have an IRR greater than the cost of capital should be accepted. If several competing investments all have IRRs greater than the cost of capital, then the one with the highest IRR should be selected.

| Question | Definite variables |

A company is trying to decide whether to buy a machine for $80,000 which will save costs of $20,000 per annum for five years and which will have a resale value of $10,000 at the end of year 5.

Required

If it is the company's policy to undertake projects only if they are expected to yield a DCF return of 10% or more, ascertain using the IRR method whether this project should be undertaken.

| Answer |

The first step is to calculate two net present values, both as close as possible to zero, using rates for the cost of capital which are whole numbers. One NPV should be positive and the other negative.

Choosing rates for the cost of capital which will give an NPV close to zero (that is, rates which are close to the actual rate of return) is a hit-and-miss exercise, and several attempts may be needed to find satisfactory rates. **As a rough guide**, try starting at a **return figure which is about two thirds or three quarters of the ARR**.

Annual depreciation would be $(80,000 – 10,000)/5 = $14,000.

The **ARR** would be (20,000 – depreciation of 14,000)/(½ of (80,000 + 10,000)) = 6,000/45,000 = 13.3%

Two thirds of this is 8.9% and so we can start by trying 9%.

Try 9%.	Year	Cash flow	PV factor	PV of cash flow
		$	9%	$
	0	(80,000)	1.000	(80,000)
	1–5	20,000	3.890	77,800
	5	10,000	0.650	6,500
				NPV = 4,300

This is **fairly close to zero**. It is also **positive**, which means that the **real rate of return** is **more than 9%**. We can use 9% as one of our two NPVs close to zero, although for greater accuracy, we should try 10% or even 11% to find an NPV even closer to zero if we can. As a guess, it might be worth trying 12% next, to see what the NPV is.

Try 12%.	Year	Cash flow	PV factor	PV of cash flow
		$	12%	$
	0	(80,000)	1.000	(80,000)
	1–5	20,000	3.605	72,100
	5	10,000	0.567	5,670
				NPV = (2,230)

This is **fairly close to zero** and **negative**. The **real rate of return** is therefore **greater than 9%** (positive NPV of $4,300) but **less than 12%** (negative NPV of $2,230).

Note. **If the first NPV is positive, choose a higher rate for the next calculation to get a negative NPV. If the first NPV is negative, choose a lower rate for the next calculation.**

So, IRR = $9 + \left[\dfrac{4,300}{4,300+2,230} \times (12-9) \right]\%$ = 10.98%, say 11%

If it is company policy to undertake investments which are expected to yield 10% or more, this project would be undertaken.

IRR has some features in common with NPV: all cash flows are taken into account, and the timing of the cashflows is handled logically. However, there are a number of problems associated with IRR:

- IRR does not relate directly to shareholder wealth

- IRR ignores the **scale of investment** so is not appropriate for comparing investments of different size

- IRR can also be unreliable where there are projects with unconventional cash flows, such as positive and negative cashflows in different years of the project's life. This can cause there to be several IRRs, or none at all, for a particular investment

IRR generally gives similar results to the NPV, but is viewed as an inferior approach due to the inherent problems listed here.

3.4.5 Investment appraisal in practice

In practice, most organisations use more than one method to appraise investment decisions.

NPV and IRR have become increasingly popular and are now the most widely used methods, particularly by larger organisations. Although NPV is superior to IRR, it is thought that the reason IRR is equally popular is the fact that it presents the results in terms of a percentage, rather than an absolute figure, which may be more acceptable to managers and easier to understand.

Despite the inherent problems with ARR and payback period, they are still widely used by many organisations. This is likely due to those methods being quick and easy to calculate and the easy to understand nature of their outputs.

Exam focus point

> Investment appraisal was specifically examined in an optional question of the June 2011 P3 exam. The question asked the candidates to critically evaluate a number of statements made in the scenario about investment appraisal. This was an unpopular question choice, suggesting that candidates are not confident in this area. Make sure you are familiar with the characteristics and limitations of each of the methods, and have a strong understanding of benefit classifications and their potential use in investment appraisal.

3.5 Responsibilities for delivering the benefits 6/14

FAST FORWARD

> A **benefit owner** should be assigned to each individual benefit. **Change owners** may also be required to ensure benefits are fully realised.

Once the costs and benefits of a project have been identified, an owner should be assigned to each individual benefit before it can be stated in the business case. The owner should be an individual who gains the advantage inherent in the stated benefit and therefore is willing to work with the project team to ensure the benefit is realised.

Key term

> A **benefit owner** is an individual or group who will gain advantage from a business benefit and who will work with the project team to ensure that benefit is realised.

The benefit owner will work with the project team, either personally or through the resources he or she has to ensure the benefit is realised. However, the benefit owners cannot be considered to be solely responsible for realising the benefit, since the changes necessary to deliver the benefit may need to be undertaken by others outside their sphere of control or influence. People who do this are known as **change owners**.

Sometimes it is appropriate to have more than one benefit owner due to the structure of the organisation. For example, if an organisation is based in two separate geographical locations, it may be appropriate to have one benefit manager in each of the sites.

However, there should not be a large group of benefit owners due to difficulties they may face in obtaining agreement within the group, and the risk that if they have to make decisions to influence the benefit's delivery, they are unlikely to have much influence on others in the organisation. Whilst these people should not be named as benefit owners, the views of these people affected by the project, especially in relation to what is in it for them and how they will be affected by the required changes, are vital to realising the benefits and should be expressly addressed.

The benefit owners will be responsible for establishing measures for benefits, and identifying how they will know when the benefit has been achieved (what evidence of achievement is required? How can the achievement of each change be assessed?)

In addition to identifying benefit owners, it is also necessary to identify **change owners**. These are named individuals of groups who will be responsible for making each of the identified changes happen successfully.

> A **change owner** is an individual or group who will ensure that an identified business or enabling change is successfully achieved.

The change owner should be the individual who is responsible for the area in which the identified change resides. The change owners may not be personally responsible for making the changes, but they are accountable for the changes being effected successfully. They must be committed to the project, dedicate sufficient personal time and knowledge to planning and managing the changes, and be influential enough to ensure the necessary resources are made available to carry out the changes.

A single change owner is best, if there are multiple change owners, change can be difficult to achieve as the responsibilities for resolving any problems that may arise may become unclear.

3.5.1 The nature of benefit and change ownership

Change owners should be senior or influential enough to ensure the change identified will be achieved successfully and when needed in the project plan. However, if a very senior person is the change owner, then they will not have day-to-day involvement in making the change happen and this will be delegated to others.

If difficulties are encountered in successfully achieving the change, then the change owner will use their resources or influence to ensure they are addressed and, if possible, overcome.

Benefit owners, although not necessarily responsible for changes, should have active (rather than passive) involvement in the project and should work closely with those who are managing the changes. They will have to address any issues that might cause uncertainty about achieving the benefits and they should use their knowledge and, where necessary, resources, to help resolve the problems. The benefit owner should also therefore be senior or influential enough to ensure that others understand and carry out their responsibilities in the project.

It is important to note that 'senior enough' does not mean that ownership of benefits or change has to be escalated to very senior levels. In smaller and mid-size projects, middle management levels are usually ideal for these roles. In large projects, however, where changes have to be coordinated across a number of business functions or processes, the involvement of more senior managers is often required.

In all cases, the important criteria for benefit and change owners is their interest and perceived commitment to the project. It should be a role that the appropriate individuals nominate themselves for. A lack of willingness to take on the responsibilities probably suggests a lack of interest or commitment to the project. Lack of interest by a number of the identified change or benefit owners, especially of the more critical changes or most significant benefits, should make an organisation question whether the investment is actually still worth pursuing.

FAST FORWARD

> A **benefits realisation** plan should be included as part of the business plan to demonstrate how the identified benefits will be measured, taken forward and achieved.

After the benefits have been quantified (or otherwise measured) and allocated to owners, the business case will need to identify how those benefits will be realised. This can be done by including a **benefits realisation plan** as part of the business case for the investment. The aim of this plan is to demonstrate how the identified benefits will be measured, taken forward and achieved. It will identify factors that will indicate when the change has been successful and the benefits are being realised, and will illustrate everything that has to happen in order for this to occur.

The benefits realisation plan will involve:

- Full descriptions of each benefit and change with responsibilities for delivery defined and agreed
- Measures, and where possible, expected values, for each benefit
- Measurements to establish the current baseline
- Agreed ownership of all the changes and actions in place to address issues that may affect the achievement of changes
- Evidence or criteria to be used to assess whether each change has been successfully carried out
- Complete and documented benefits dependency network identifying all the benefit and change relationships

The plans should also clearly define the drivers for change.

Key term

> **Drivers** are forces acting on an organisation which require it to make changes either to what it does or how it conducts its business activities.

Drivers for change can be either internal or external, but are specific to the context in which the organisation operates. They should be described in sufficient detail to ensure there is an understanding for the need for change and the implications of not taking action to respond to the drivers.

Drivers must be strategic to the future of the whole organisation, not just specific functions or departments. Localised priorities are often found to be in conflict with the overall best interests of the organisation. A business case will be greatly strengthened if it can demonstrate that it is linked to the priorities of the senior management of the organisation.

3.6.1 Investment objectives and business drivers

Organisational drivers will exist, whether or not the decision is taken to invest in the project. When the senior decision makers review the business case and benefits realisation plan, they will need to assess how the investment will achieve the necessary changes to address these drivers.

The benefits realisation plan should therefore establish an agreed set of **investment objectives**.

Rather than a long list of small and overlapping objectives, the plan should include only a few compelling and clearly stated investment objectives. The importance of the objectives is far more important than the number of them.

Each investment objective should explicitly address one or more of the drivers to ensure that the project will contribute to achieving the changes that are important to the future of the organisation.

Projects that do not address at least one of the business drivers should be rejected as it will be impossible to develop a credible business case for the project.

Organisations are affected by many drivers, and one single project will not be able to address them all. Each driver, by definition, is important to the future of the organisation so if a project addresses only one, it is not necessarily a low-priority project. This project could be the only way that a particular driver can be addressed, making it of high importance to the organisation.

3.6.2 A benefits dependency network

The benefits management process links the investment objectives and the resulting benefits to the business, organisational and IS/IT changes required for the benefits to be realised in a **benefits dependency network**.

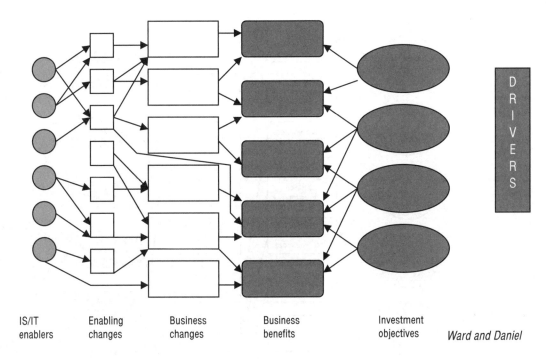

| IS/IT enablers | Enabling changes | Business changes | Business benefits | Investment objectives | *Ward and Daniel* |

Once the drivers, investment objectives and business benefits have been identified, it is necessary to identify the changes to the ways individuals and groups work that will be needed for the potential benefits to be realised. Each benefit should be considered in turn and the necessary changes should be identified and described on the benefits dependency network.

The changes that need to be made can be categorised as **business changes** or **enabling changes**.

Business changes are the new ways of working that will be permanently required, such as new roles and responsibilities, new or refined processes or new governance arrangements.

Enabling changes are one-off changes that may be required in order for the business changes to be brought about, or may be related to bringing in the new system. Examples might include training, process mapping and process design, decommissioning of legacy systems and definition of new roles and responsibilities.

Following on from the identification of the business changes and enabling changes, the information systems and technology required need to be considered. These are known as **IS/IT enablers**. The identification of the IS/IT enablers may lead to further changes, particularly enabling changes, to be required. If so, they need to be added to the relevant part of the network.

This process may also highlight that the organisation does not actually need to invest in any new IS or IT. It is often found that the changes could be undertaken, and many of the benefits realised with current systems.

Case Study   NHS

National Health Service

The National Health Service (NHS) in the UK carried out a project called 'Choose and Book' (www.chooseandbook.nhs.uk) which would allow patients to select a time and date for their appointment that is convenient for them. The previous system involved the patient's GP requesting an appointment (for instance, for an X-ray) from the local hospital who would then inform the patient of their appointment, resulting in wasted appointment slots when patients fail to attend. The new system allows the patient to choose their own time and date, reducing the number of wasted appointments,

The below shows a simplified benefits dependency network for this project.

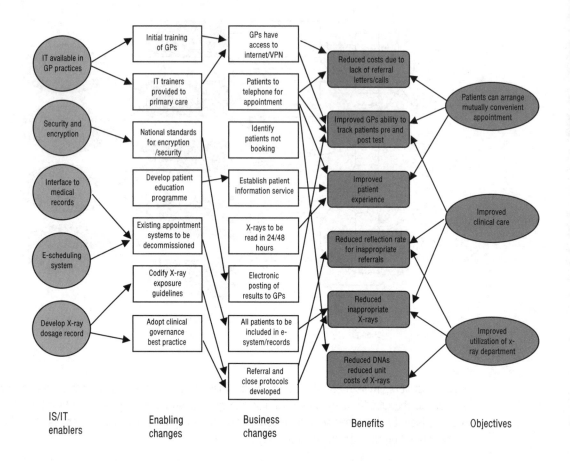

This network identifies several benefits, such as improved patient experience and reduced unit cost per X-ray. However, it also shows that if the system can be used to transmit test results back to GPs and update patient records, then additional benefits could also be expected. An example might be that patient treatment could be started sooner, as the doctor will be quicker informed of the patient's condition.

Working back towards the left, we can see the required changes to IT/IS in order to achieve these benefits. The diagram also highlights the dependency of some of the benefits on resources or capabilities outside the project, such as having an expert available to interpret the results of the X-ray,

Source: Ward and Daniel: *Benefits Management*

3.6.3 Executing the benefits plan

The next stage is to actually carry out the benefits plan. It will need to be revised, as issues and events that affect its viability arise. Interim targets and measures may need to be set to evaluate progress towards key milestones or the final implementation.

A business project manager is usually appointed to ensure that the project is delivered and the needs are met without unnecessary disruption or risk. The project manager should be the custodian of the benefits plan and ensure that each of the stakeholders carry out their respective responsibilities as defined in the plan.

The project manager will also have to decide what action to take in terms of reviewing the scope and specification of the project in light of any changes that have arisen. Any decision made should be based on the overall project objectives, not just the immediate problem, and all stakeholders should be involved in any decisions to change the plan. The plan may also be revised in light of any further benefits that have been identified during the implementation of the plan.

Of course, it is also possible that implementation will reveal that some benefits are no longer feasible or relevant. Again, the benefits plan will have to be modified accordingly, along with any associated business changes.

4 Strategic aspects of the project plan

Many large-scale projects, particularly those involving major change, are strategically significant, and project management can merge into strategic management. Force field analysis identifies enablers, constraints and showstoppers.

The unique nature of each project means that careful planning is an essential component of project management. Many project costs, time overruns and outright failures can be traced to failures of planning.

Project management as a discipline is commonly associated with fairly clearly defined issues such as preparing for a conference, organising an office move or installing a new IT system. Projects such as these can be of strategic importance, but even when they are, there is often an unspoken assumption that once the go-ahead is given, the job of project management is essentially one of detailed planning, organisation and control, with, perhaps, a little trouble-shooting thrown in. It is important to understand that this is unlikely to be the case with truly strategic projects: with projects such as the turnaround of an underperforming division or an initial move into a foreign market, **project management and strategic management are likely to merge into one another**. As a corollary, we can say that at the level of the strategic project, project planning is likely to make use of a strategic planning approach. A failure to think strategically is likely to lead to project failure.

4.1 Why do projects go wrong?

Project planning is fundamental to project success. **Realistic timescales** must be established, use of **shared resources** must be planned and, most fundamental of all, jobs must be done in a sensible **sequence**. However, even if all these aspects are satisfactory, there are other potential pitfalls that the project planner must avoid or work around. Here are some examples.

(a)   **Unproven technology**
      The use of **new technological developments** may be a feature of any project. The range of such developments extends from fairly routine and non-critical improvements, through major innovations capable of transforming working practices, costs and time scales, to revolutionary techniques that make feasible projects that were previously quite impracticable. As the practical potential of a technical change moves from minor to major, so too moves its potential to cause disruption if something goes wrong with it. A classic example is Rolls Royce's attempt to use carbon fibre in the design of the RB211 engine in the early 1970s. Not only did the project fail to meet its objectives, its failure led to the company's financial failure and subsequent takeover by government.

(b)   **Changing client specifications**
      It is not unusual for clients' notions of what they want to evolve during the lifetime of the project. However, if the work is to come in on time and on budget, they must be **aware** of what is **technically feasible**, **reasonable** in their **aspirations**, **prompt** with their **decisions** and, ultimately, **prepared to freeze the specification** so that it can be delivered.
      Note that the term 'client' includes *internal* specifiers.

(c)   **Politics**
      This problem area includes politics of all kinds, from those internal to an organisation managing its own projects, to the effect of national (and even international) politics on major undertakings.

Identification of a senior figure with a project; public interest and press hysteria; hidden agendas; national prestige; and political dogma can all have deleterious effects on project management. **Lack of senior management support** is an important political problem.

4.2 Force field analysis

Grundy and Brown suggest that force field analysis can be useful in project planning. This is an important example of the **close relationship between project management and strategic management** that appears in their analysis.

The emphasis of force field analysis is an assessment of the **degree of difficulty** that implementing a project is likely to encounter: the problems discussed above, and any of a wide range of other attitudes and conditions will affect the degree of difficulty encountered and this will be particularly the case with projects of a strategic nature. It is important that such matters are carefully considered as part of the planning process and force field analysis is one way of doing this.

The essence of force field analysis is the identification and assessment of the underlying forces tending to promote successful implementation or to hold it back. These forces may be referred to as **enablers** and **constraints**. The overall potential of each force must be estimated. As in the performance driver analysis already discussed, it is usual to show enablers and constraints as arrows against a baseline in a visual presentation.

A degree of objectivity can be brought into this analysis by seeking to **expose implicit assumptions** about these factors and the overall situation. This process can be moved forward by asking three questions.

- What is it about each force that allows it to be identified as an enabler or a constraint?
- How great is its potential influence on the change process?
- What other, less obvious factors does it depend on?

A further important part of the overall analysis is the identification of potential **showstoppers**. These are constraints that can make implementation so difficult as to cause overall project failure. These factors must be continuously monitored.

Management of constraints includes two important possibilities.

(a) It may be possible to turn one of the constraints around and turn it into a driver. Changing the mind of an unsympathetic stakeholder would be a good example.

(b) Careful examination of the context of the project may reveal **latent enablers** that could be called into play. For example, there may be sympathetic stakeholder groups whose driver potential has been ignored.

4.3 More on stakeholders

We suggested that a preliminary stakeholder analysis should form part of the project definition phase. It is appropriate to take this further at the planning stage. The project manager should be prepare to deal with varying degrees of support for the project. A **stakeholder grid** of the type discussed earlier in this Study Text should be prepared and an assessment made of overall stakeholder attitudes. This process should be repeated as required to reflect the changes that are likely to occur as the project progresses and stakeholders' attitudes develop.

5 Practical aspects of project planning

FAST FORWARD

Work breakdown structure is an analysis of the work involved in a project into a structure of phases, activities and tasks. **Dependencies** determine the order in which tasks must be carried out, while **interactions** between tasks affect them without imposing order.

5.1 Work breakdown structure

Work breakdown structure (WBS) is fundamental to traditional project planning and control. Its essence is the **analysis** of the work required to complete the project into **manageable components**.

A good way to approach WBS is to consider the **outputs** (or **deliverables**) the project is required to produce. This can then be analysed into physical and intangible components, which can in turn be further analysed down to whatever level of simplicity is required. Working backwards in this way helps to **avoid preconceived ideas** of the work the project will involve and the processes that must be undertaken. This approach, called **product breakdown**, is the basis of project planning under the PRINCE2 system.

The WBS can allow for several levels of analysis, starting with major project phases and gradually breaking them down into major activities, more detailed sub-activities and individual tasks that will last only a very short time. There is no standardised terminology for the various levels of disaggregation, though an **activity** is sometimes regarded as being composed of **tasks**.

The delivery phase of many projects will break down into significant stages or sub-phases. These are very useful for control purposes, as the completion of each stage is an obvious point for reviewing the whole plan before starting the next one.

5.1.1 Dependencies and interactions

A very important aspect of project planning is the determination of **dependencies** and **interactions**. At any level of WBS analysis, some tasks will be dependent on others; that is to say, **a dependent task cannot commence** until the task upon which it depends is completed. Careful analysis of dependencies is a major step towards a workable project plan, since it provides an **order in which things must be tackled**. Sometimes, of course, the dependencies are limited and it is possible to proceed with tasks in almost any order, but this is unusual. The more complex a project, the greater the need for analysis of dependencies.

Interactions are slightly different; they occur when tasks are linked but not dependent. This can arise for a variety of reasons: a good example is a requirement to share the use of a scarce resource.

The output from the WBS process is a list of tasks, probably arranged hierarchically to reflect the disaggregation of activities. This then becomes the input into the planning and control processes described below.

5.2 The project budget

FAST FORWARD The **project budget** plans the allocation of resources to the project and forms a basis for their control. Budgeting may be top-down or bottom-up.

Key term

> **Project budget.** The amount and distribution of resources allocated to a project.

Building a project budget should be an orderly process that attempts to establish a realistic estimate of the cost of the project. There are two main methods for establishing the project budget: **top-down** and **bottom-up**.

Top-down budgeting describes the situation where the budget is imposed **from above**. Project managers are allocated a budget for the project based on an estimate made by senior management. The figure may prove realistic, especially if similar projects have been undertaken recently. However, the technique is often used simply because it is quick, or because only a certain level of funding is available.

In **bottom-up budgeting** the project manager consults the project team, and others, to calculate a budget based on the tasks that make up the project. WBS is a useful tool in this process.

5.3 Gantt charts

FAST FORWARD

A **Gantt chart** shows the deployment of resources over time.

A **Gantt chart**, named after the engineer Henry Gantt who pioneered the procedure in the early 1900s, is a horizontal bar chart used to plan the **time scale** for a project and to estimate the **resources** required.

The Gantt chart displays the time relationships between tasks in a project. Two lines are usually used to show the time allocated for each task, and the actual time taken.

A simple Gantt chart, illustrating some of the activities involved in a network server installation project, follows.

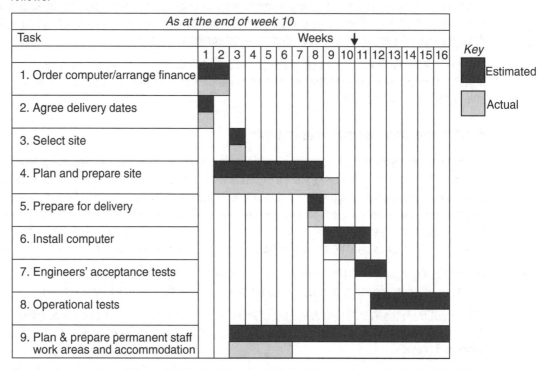

The chart shows that at the end of the tenth week, Activity 9 is running behind schedule. More resources may have to be allocated to this activity if the staff accommodation is to be ready in time for the changeover to the new system.

Activity 4 had not been completed on time, and this has resulted in some disruption to the computer installation (Activity 6), which may mean further delays in the commencement of Activities 7 and 8.

A Gantt chart does not show the interrelationship between the various activities in the project as clearly as a **network diagram** (covered later in this chapter). A combination of Gantt charts and network analysis will often be used for project planning and resource allocation.

5.4 Network analysis

FAST FORWARD

Network analysis illustrates interactions and dependencies. It is used to plan the sequence of tasks making up project scope and to determine the critical path. PERT uses probabilities to make estimates of likely completion and milestone dates.

Network analysis, also known as **Critical Path Analysis** (CPA), is a useful technique to help with planning and controlling large projects, such as construction projects, research and development projects, and the computerisation of systems.

CPA aims to ensure the progress of a project, so the project is completed in the **minimum amount of time**. It pinpoints the tasks **on the critical path**, which is the longest duration sequence of tasks in the project; a delay to any of these tasks would **delay the completion** of the project as a whole. The technique can also be used to assist in **allocating resources** such as labour and equipment.

5.4.1 Project evaluation and review technique (PERT)

Project evaluation and review technique (PERT) is a modified form of network analysis designed to account for **uncertainty**. For each activity in the project, **optimistic**, **most likely** and **pessimistic** estimates of times are made, on the basis of past experience, or even guess-work. These estimates are converted into a mean time and also a standard deviation.

Once the mean time and standard deviation of the time have been calculated for each activity, it should be possible to do the following.

(a)   Establish the duration of the critical path using **expected times**.
(b)   Calculate a **contingency time allowance**.

5.5 Resource histogram

A simple resource histogram showing programmer time required on a software development program follows:

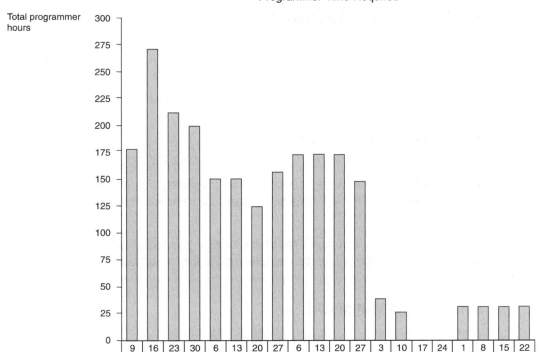

Programmer Time Required

Week ending

Some organisations add another bar (or a separate line) to the chart showing resource availability. The chart then shows any instances when the required resource hours exceed the available hours. Plans should then be made to either obtain further resource for these peak times, or to reschedule the work plan. Alternately, the chart may show times when the available resource is excessive, and should be redeployed elsewhere. An example follows:

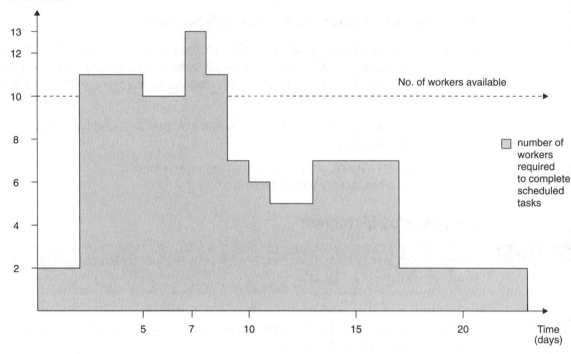

The number of workers required on the seventh day is 13. Can we re-schedule the non-critical activities to reduce the requirement to the available level of 10? We might be able to re-arrange activities so that we can make use of the workers available from day 9 onwards.

6 Project management   12/09

Key terms

The **project sponsor** provides and is accountable for the resources invested into the project and is responsible for the achievement of the project's business objectives.

The **project manager** takes responsibility for ensuring the desired result is achieved on time and within budget.

The **Project Board** (PMBOK: project steering committee) is the body to which the project manager is accountable for achieving the project objectives. It represents the interests of the project sponsor.

Project champion. Sometimes a project champion is appointed. This is a senior manager whose role is to represent the project to the rest of the organisation, communicating its vision and objectives and securing commitment to them.

Project owner. The project owner is the person for whom the project is being carried out and as such, they are interested in the end result being achieved and their needs being met.

6.1 Higher management

In all but the smallest organisations, it is likely that the project manager will be appointed by, and be responsible to, a higher level of management. Resources must be allocated to the project by a person or group with the power to do so and the project manager must be subject to supervision.

It is common to refer to the person or group providing the resources as the **project sponsor**, though the term **investment decision-maker** has also been used. The project sponsor may, in fact, be the strategic apex body of the organisation, or may be a person or committee at a lower level; the essential feature is that the project sponsor has the budgetary capability to authorise the project.

The project sponsor will not be involved in the management of the project and may not have the capacity to provide effective supervision for the project manager. Under these circumstances, the project sponsor may appoint a **project owner**, whose role will be to review project plans and progress at regular intervals and to arbitrate on any conflicts that may arise between project and line management. Of course, in smaller organisations, the roles of project sponsor and project owner may be combined.

xam focus oint

Some organisations use the terms project owner and project sponsor in a way exactly opposite to the usage we have outlined here! An example is the Scottish Executive construction works procurement guidance, which makes the project owner subordinate to the investment decision-maker and superior to the project sponsor. Be careful in your use of these terms and explain what you mean when you use them.

6.1.1 The project manager

FAST FORWARD

The person who takes ultimate responsibility for ensuring the desired result is achieved on time and within budget is the **project manager**. Duties of the project manager include: Planning, teambuilding, communication, co-ordinating project activities, monitoring and control, problem-resolution and quality control.

Some project managers have only one major responsibility: a specific project. However, anyone responsible for a project, large or small, is a project manager. As a result, many project managers, will have routine work responsibilities outside their project goals, which may lead to conflicting demands on their time.

The role a project manager performs is, in many ways, similar to those performed by other managers. There are, however, some important differences, as shown in the table below.

Project managers	Operations managers
Are often **generalists** with wide-ranging backgrounds and experience levels	Usually **specialists** in the areas managed
Oversee work in **many functional areas**	Relate closely to **technical tasks** in their area
Facilitate, rather than supervise team members	Have **direct technical supervision** responsibilities

6.2 The responsibilities of a project manager

The overall issue for all project managers is understanding how to balance the factors of scope, resources, time and risk.

However, a project manager also has responsibilities both to management and also to the project team.

6.2.1 Responsibilities to management

- Ensure resources are used efficiently – strike a balance between cost, time and results
- Keep management informed with timely and accurate communications
- Manage the project to the best of his or her ability
- Behave ethically, and adhere to the organisation's policies
- Maintain a customer orientation (whether the project is geared towards an internal or external customer) – customer satisfaction is a key indicator of project success

6.2.2 Responsibilities to the project and the project team

- Take action to keep the project on target for successful completion
- Ensure the project team has the resources required to perform tasks assigned
- Help new team members integrate into the team

- Provide any support required when members leave the team, either during the project or on completion

6.3 Duties of a project manager

The project manager's responsibilities give rise to a number of fairly standard duties and managerial activities

Duty	Comment
Outline planning	See above for project definition and initiation
Detailed planning	Work breakdown structure, budgeting, resource requirements, network analysis for scheduling
Obtain necessary resources	Resources may already exist within the organisation or may have to be bought in. Resource requirements unforeseen at the planning stage will have to be authorised separately by the project board or project sponsor
Team building	Build cohesion and team spirit in the project team
Communication	Keep all stakeholders suitably informed and ensure that members of the project team are properly briefed. Manage expectations
Co-ordinating project activities	Co-ordination will be required between the project team, external suppliers, the project owner and end-users
Monitoring and control	Monitor progress against the plan, and take corrective measures where needed
Problem-resolution	Even with the best planning, unforeseen problems may arise
Quality control	Understand and manage quality procedures; agree and manage any appropriate trade-off of functionality against achieving deadlines

It is also possible to view the **process of project management** as having **five stages**:

- Initiation
- Planning
- Leadership
- Controlling
- Completing

The first, second, fourth and fifth of these phases correspond closely to the phases of the **project life cycle**, which was discussed earlier in this chapter. The third phase, leadership, forms a major part of the subject matter of this section.

6.4 The skills required of a project manager

Project managers require the following **skills**: Leadership and team building, organisational ability, communication skills (written, spoken, presentations, meetings), some technical knowledge of the project area and interpersonal skills.

To perform these duties and meet these responsibilities, a project manager requires a wide range of skills.

Skill	Application to project management
Leadership and team building	A participative style of leadership is appropriate for much of most projects, but a more autocratic, decisive style may be required on occasion
	Be **positive** (but realistic) about all aspects of the project
	Understand where the project fits into the **big picture**
	Delegate tasks appropriately – and not take on too much personally
	Build team spirit through **co-operation** and recognition of achievement
	Do not be restrained by organisational structures – a high tolerance for ambiguity (lack of clear-cut authority) will help the project manager
Organisational	Ensure all project **documentation** is clear and distributed to all who require it
	Use project management **tools** to analyse and monitor project progress
Communication and negotiation	**Listen** to project team members
	Use **persuasion** to coerce reluctant team members or stakeholders to support the project
	Negotiate on funding, timescales, staffing and other resources, quality and disputes
	Ensure management is kept **informed** and is never surprised
Technical	By providing (or at least providing access to) the **technical expertise** and experience needed to manage the project
Personal qualities	Be **flexible**. Circumstances may develop that require a change in plan
	Show **persistence**. Even successful projects will encounter difficulties that require repeated efforts to overcome
	Be **creative**. If one method of completing a task proves impractical, a new approach may be required
	Patience is required, even in the face of tight deadlines. The 'quick-fix' may eventually cost more time than a more thorough, but initially more time-consuming, solution
Problem solving	Only the very simplest projects will be without problems. The project manager must bring a sensible approach to their solution and **delegate** as much responsibility as possible to team members so that they become used to **solving their own problems.** By the nature of a project there is always uncertainty and risk involved. The project manager needs to be able to react to these situations fast, and adopt an efficient problem solving attitude so as not to hold up the project at key moments
Change control and management	Major projects may be accompanied by the kind of far-reaching **change** that has wide-ranging effects on the organisation and its people. Here, however, we are concerned with **changes to the project itself**. Changes can arise from a variety of sources (not least the intended end-users) and have the potential to disrupt the progress of the project. They must be properly authorised, planned and resourced and records kept of their source, impact and authorisation if the project is not to become unmanageable. **Change control** is one of the components of the **PRINCE2** project management system

6.5 Leadership style

Exam focus point

An article titled 'Conflict management and the accountant as project manager' (2011) written by Dr Graham Morgan is available in the technical articles section for P3 on the ACCA website. It would be worth taking the time to study this article.

As in other forms of management, different project managers have different styles of leadership. There is no single best leadership style, as individuals react differently to different styles on different occasions. The key is adopting a style that suits both the leader and the team, and that is appropriate to the current situation.

The leadership style adopted will affect the way decisions relating to the project are made. Although an autocratic style may prove successful in some situations, such as very simple or repetitive projects, a more consultative style has the advantage of making team members feel more a part of the project. This should result in greater **commitment**.

Not all decisions will be made in the same way. For example, decisions that do not have direct consequences for other project personnel may be made with no (or limited) consultation. A **balance** needs to be found between ensuring decisions can be made efficiently, and ensuring adequate consultation.

The type of people that comprise the project team will influence the style adopted. For example, professionals generally dislike being closely supervised and dictated to. Some people however, prefer to follow clear, specific instructions and not have to think for themselves.

Project management techniques encourage **management by exception** by identifying, from the outset, those activities which might threaten successful completion of a project.

6.6 Organising for projects – the matrix structure

Many projects are organised as stand-alone enterprises, with their own dedicated staff. However, much project management is undertaken within a framework of routine operations, with staff being seconded to the project from their own departments or functions. This gives rise to a **matrix structure**. In general terms, a matrix structure provides for the formalisation of management control between different functions, whilst at the same time maintaining functional departmentation. This approach is widely used as a general approach to management in complex organisations. It is particularly suitable for structuring the management of projects. Many projects are **interdisciplinary**, and might require, for instance the contributions of an engineer, a scientist, a statistician and a production expert, who would be appointed to the team while retaining membership and status within their own functional department. A matrix approach enables such specialists to receive management and leadership inputs from both the project manager and their own functional manager.

6.7 The project team

FAST FORWARD

Project managers should have some understanding of the way that groups of people interact at work.

Teams enable people's talents and efforts to be combined and teamwork can have a motivating effect. Tuckman identified four stages in team development.

- Forming
- Storming
- Norming
- Performing

However, teams bring their own problems, including disharmony, risky shift, groupthink and political conflict. Handy suggests a contingency approach to team leadership. Belbin identified nine roles played by team members.

- Co-ordinator
- Plant
- Resource investigator
- Team worker
- Specialist
- Shaper
- Monitor-evaluator
- Implementer
- Finisher

Knowledge brought forward from earlier studies

A lot of the material covered in this section was introduced in the F1 syllabus. At P3 you may be required to **apply** your knowledge of teams and appropriate leadership styles in a scenario context. If you are not comfortable with this material, you should look back to the F1 material to refresh yourself with it.

Key term

A **group** is any collection of people who perceive themselves to be a group.

Unlike a random collection of individuals, a group shares a common sense of identity and belonging. They have certain attributes that a random crowd does not possess.

(a) A **sense of identity**. There is awareness of membership and acknowledged boundaries to the group which define it.

(b) **Loyalty to the group**, and acceptance within the group. This generally expresses itself as conformity or the acceptance of the norms of behaviour and attitudes that bind the group together and exclude others from it.

(c) **Purpose and leadership**. Most groups have an express purpose, whatever field they are in: most will, spontaneously or formally, choose individuals or sub-groups to lead them towards the fulfilment of those goals.

A **primary working group** is the immediate social environment of the individual worker. A **formal group** used for particular objectives in the work place is called a **team**. Project teams fall into this category by definition. Although many people enjoy working in teams, their popularity in the workplace arises because of their effectiveness in fulfilling the organisation's work.

6.7.1 Aspects of teams

Key term

A **team** is a 'small number of people with complementary skills who are committed to a common purpose, performance goals and approach for which they hold themselves mutually accountable'. (*Katzenbach and Smith*, 1994)

(a) **Work organisation.** Teams combine the skills of different individuals and avoid complex communication between different business functions.

(b) **Control.** Fear of letting down the team can be a powerful motivator, hence teams can be used to control the performance and behaviour of individuals. Teams can also be used to resolve **conflict**.

(c) **Knowledge generation**. Teams can generate ideas.

(d) **Decision-making.** Teams can be set up to investigate new developments and decisions can be evaluated from more than one viewpoint.

(e) **Communication.** Team work can enhance the flow of information.

(f) **Social needs.** People generally have a need for company and social interaction.

6.7.2 Multi-disciplinary teams

Many project teams will be deliberately structured as multi-disciplinary teams. Multi-disciplinary teams bring together individuals with different skills and specialisms, so that their skills, experience and knowledge can be pooled or exchanged. Team working of this kind encourages freer and faster communication between disciplines in the organisation.

(a) Team working increases workers' **awareness of their overall objectives** and targets.

(b) Team working **aids co-ordination**.

(c) Team working **helps to generate solutions to problems**, and suggestions for improvements, since a multi-disciplinary team has access to more 'pieces of the jigsaw'.

6.7.3 Development of the team

The **performance** and **effectiveness** of teams is influenced by a range of factors.

(a)   **Size** is important: larger groups can do more work, but individual productivity tends to fall. This is called the **Ringelmann effect**. This effect is held to be the product of **social loafing**, which arises when group members believe they will not receive a fair share of reward if they make a great effort, nor appropriate blame if they make an inadequate one.

(b)   **Cohesion** enhances output. Cohesion is reduced by membership turnover and if members have divided loyalties. Similarity of status enhances cohesion.

(c)   **Group roles**. Groups often develop roles that are played by individuals spontaneously. More formal roles are acknowledged by mechanisms such as election. Personal predisposition and talent are important in the emergence of such figures as leaders and nurturers in groups. We return to this concept later when we discuss the work of Belbin on team roles.

Four stages in team development were identified by Tuckman. Project managers should be aware of these stages and be prepared to manage and exploit them

Step 1   Forming

The team is just coming together, and may still be seen as a collection of individuals. Each member wishes to impress his or her personality on the group. The individuals will be trying to find out about each other, and about the aims and norms of the team. There will at this stage probably be a wariness about introducing new ideas. The objectives being pursued may as yet be unclear and a leader may not yet have emerged. This period is essential, but may be time wasting: the team as a unit will not be used to being autonomous, and will probably not be an efficient agent in the planning of its activities or the activities of others.

Step 2   Storming

This frequently involves more or less open conflict between team members. There may be changes agreed in the original objectives, procedures and norms established for the group. If the team is developing successfully, this may be a fruitful phase as **more realistic targets** are set and **trust** between the group members **increases**.

Step 3   Norming

A period of settling down: there will be agreements about work sharing, individual requirements and expectations of output. **Norms and procedures** may evolve which enable methodical working to be introduced and maintained.

Step 4   Performing

The team sets to work to execute its task. The difficulties of growth and development no longer hinder the group's objectives.

6.7.4 Characteristics of the ideal functioning team

(a)   Each individual gets the support of the team and a sense of identity and belonging that encourages loyalty and hard work on the group's behalf.

(b)   Skills, information and ideas are shared, so that the team's capabilities are greater than those of the individuals. **Synergy** is achieved through the pooling of skills.

(c)   New ideas can be tested, reactions taken into account and persuasive skills brought into play in group discussion for **decision making** and **problem solving**. The team provides a focus for **creativity** and **innovation**, especially in multi-disciplinary teams.

(d)   Each individual is encouraged to participate and contribute and thus becomes personally involved in and committed to the team's activities. Equally, control and discipline are enhanced by commitment to the team's expectations.

(e)   Goodwill, trust and respect can be built up between individuals, so that communication is encouraged and potential problems more easily overcome. This can contribute to **empowerment** when responsibility and authority are delegated to self-managing teams.

6.7.5 Problems with teams

Unfortunately, team working is rarely such an undiluted success. There are certain constraints involved in working with others.

(a) Awareness of **group norms** and the desire to be acceptable to the group may **restrict individual effort**.

(b) **Too much discord**. Where an individual is a member of more than one group, conflicting roles and relationships can cause difficulties in communicating effectively.

(c) **Personality problems** will arise if one member dislikes or distrusts another; is too dominant or so timid that the value of their ideas is lost; or is so negative in attitude that constructive communication is rendered impossible.

(d) **Rigid leadership** and procedures may stifle initiative and creativity in individuals. Team working requires that managers share power with the team. Some managers find this difficult to do. Also, a coaching style of management is most appropriate for teams and this must be learned.

(e) **Differences of opinion** and political conflicts of interest are always likely.

(f) **Too much harmony**. Teams work best when there is room for disagreement. They can become dangerously blinkered to what is going on around them, and may confidently forge ahead in a completely **wrong** direction. I L Janis describes this as **groupthink**. The cosy consensus of the group prevents consideration of alternatives, constructive criticism or conflict. Alternatively, efforts to paper over differences may lead to bland recommendations without meaning.

(g) **Corporate culture and reward systems**. Teams will fail if the company promotes and rewards the individual at the expense of the group. Similarly, when team rather than individual output is measured, it is easier for un-motivated individuals to get by with minimal effort.

(h) **Too many meetings**. Teams should not try to do everything together. Not only does this waste time in meetings, but team members are exposed to less diversity of thought. Decision-making by teams can be excessively time-consuming and may not offer any advantage over the normal process of decision-making by individual managers after consultation.

(i) **Powerlessness.** People will not bother to work in a team or on a task force if its recommendations are ignored.

(j) **Risky shift**. Group processes are such that individual characteristics can be reinforced and become exaggerated. A good example is the way that a group of risk-averse individuals may adopt a far less risk-averse approach to collective decision-making.

6.7.6 Creating an effective work team

The management problem is how to create effective, efficient work teams. Handy takes a contingency approach to the problem of team effectiveness.

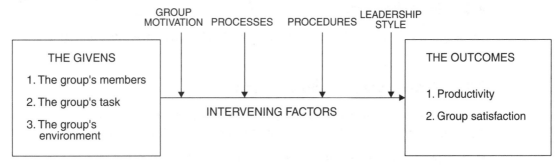

Management can operate on both **givens** and **intervening factors** to affect the **outcomes**.

6.8 The givens

6.8.1 The team

Belbin, in a study of business-game teams at Carnegie Institute of Technology in 1981, drew up a list of the most effective character-mix in a team. This involves eight necessary roles that should be played by team members.

Member	Role
Co-ordinator	Presides and co-ordinates: balanced, disciplined, good at working through others
Shaper	Highly strung, dominant, extrovert, passionate about the task itself, a spur to action
Plant	Introverted, but intellectually dominant and imaginative; source of ideas and proposals but with disadvantage of introversion
Monitor-evaluator	Analytically (rather than creatively) intelligent; dissects ideas, spots flaws; possibly aloof, tactless – but necessary
Resource-investigator	Popular, sociable, extrovert, relaxed; source of new contacts, but not an originator; needs to be made use of
Implementer	Practical organiser, turning ideas into tasks; scheduling, planning and so on; trustworthy and efficient, but not excited; not a leader, but an administrator
Team worker	Most concerned with team maintenance – supportive, understanding, diplomatic; popular but uncompetitive – contribution noticed only in absence
Finisher	Pushes the team to meet deadlines, attends to details; promotes urgency and follow-through; not always popular

The **specialist** joins the group to offer expert advice when needed. Notice that one team member may play two or more roles.

6.8.2 The task

The nature of the task must have some bearing on how a group should be managed.

(a)   If a job must be done urgently, it is often necessary to dictate how things should be done, rather than to encourage a participatory style of working.

(b)   Jobs which are routine, unimportant and undemanding will be insufficient to motivate either individuals or the group as a whole.

6.8.3 The environment

The team's environment relates to factors such as the physical surroundings at work and to inter-group relations.

6.8.4 Intervening factors and outcomes

Processes and procedures. Research indicates that a team that tackles its work systematically will be more effective than one that lives from hand to mouth, and muddles through.

Motivation and leadership style. High productivity outcomes may be achieved if work is so arranged that satisfaction of individuals' needs coincides with high output. Where teams are, for example, allowed to set their own improvement goals and methods and to measure their own progress towards those goals, it has been observed (by Peters and Waterman among others) that they regularly exceed their targets. The **style of leadership** adopted by the team leader can also affect its outcome. This depends on the circumstances.

Individuals may bring their own **hidden agendas** to groups for satisfaction. These are personal goals that may have nothing to do with the declared aims of the team, such as protection of a sub-group, impressing superiors and pursuit of inter-personal rivalry.

Project management has been examined fairly regularly and is a core part of the P3 syllabus. The December 2009 exam contained a Section B question which included a 12 mark requirement to identify the elements of good project management which has contributed to the success of the project described in the scenario. Make sure you are able to identify the application of elements of good project management in practice.

7 Controlling projects

FAST FORWARD

Progress reports should report progress towards key **milestones**. **Slippage** may be managed with a number of options, including incentives, working smarter, extra resources and rescheduling. Project changes must be carefully considered, communicated, documented and controlled. Risk management involves risk assessment and recording, and action to reduce, avoid, transfer or absorb risks.

7.1 Gateways

A key feature of many project management systems is the use of predefined gateways. These are important points to stop, report progress, review key issues and verify that the project should proceed.

Key term

A **gateway** is a project review point at which certain criteria must be met before the project can pass through the gateway and proceed to the next stage.

Gateways and benefits management should be incorporated into formal monitoring of projects in order to ensure that the project has remained on track, and any problems can be identified and rectified before they get out of hand. In order to ensure the benefits defined at the outset are realised, progress towards these should be reviewed and any further benefits identified. Any benefits that are no longer feasible or realistic should be recorded and the relevant steps taken to revise the benefits management plan.

The business case will also have to be revisited at these points. As we noted earlier, the business case is not a one-off event, it is a living document that develops along with the project. Projects must pass certain tests, particularly in relation to their business viability, in order to pass through these gateways and be allowed to proceed to the next stage.

Gateways are particularly helpful for identifying **scope creep**.

Key term

Scope creep relates to uncontrolled changes in the scope of a project.

If the project has been poorly defined, or is not controlled sufficiently, the scope of the project can steadily grow until it is dramatically different from that planned at the outset. This can cause significant delays in the project as well as causing it to exceed its intended budget.

Gateways have a number of other benefits. They are a useful **expectations management** tool, and they allow project sponsors and senior management to **review** their project investments as they proceed. If necessary this allows them to deflect resources to more successful projects.

7.2 Progress reports

Key term

A **progress report** shows the current status of the project, usually in relation to the planned status.

The frequency and contents of **progress reports** will vary depending on the length of, and the progress being made on, a project. The report is a control tool intended to show the discrepancies between where the project is, and where the plan says it should be. A common form of progress reports uses two columns – one for planned time and expenditure and one for actual. Any additional content will depend on the format adopted. Some organisations include only the raw facts in the report, and use these as a basis for discussion regarding reasons for variances and action to be taken, at a project review meeting. Other

organisations (particularly those involved in long, complex projects) produce more comprehensive progress reports, with more explanation and comment.

The report should monitor progress towards key milestones.

Key term

> A **milestone** is a significant event in the life of the project, usually completion of a major deliverable.

A progress report may include a **milestone slip chart** which compares planned and actual progress towards project milestones. Planned progress is shown on the X-axis and actual progress on the Y-axis. Where actual progress is slower than planned, progress slippage has occurred.

Milestone slip chart

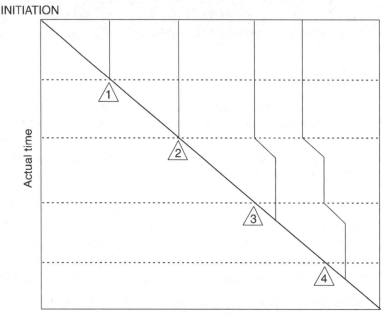

INITIATION

Actual time

Planned time

On the chart above, milestones are indicated by a triangle on the diagonal planned progress line. The vertical lines that meet milestones 1 and 2 are straight – showing that these milestones were achieved on time. At milestone 3 some slippage has occurred. The chart shows that no further slippage is expected as the progress line for milestone 4 is the same distance to the right as occurred at milestone 3. The progress report should also include an updated budget status – such a report could adopt the format shown in the following example.

7.3 Dealing with slippage

Exam focus point

> One of the question scenarios in the December 2008 exam described a software implementation project which was slipping behind schedule, and appeared unlikely to meet its target delivery data. The question asked candidates to evaluate a range of options available to the project manager to deal with the slippage.

When a project has slipped behind schedule, there are a range of options open to the project manager. Some of these options are summarised in the following table.

Action	Comment
Do nothing	After considering all options it may be decided that things should be allowed to continue as they are
Add resources	If capable staff are available and it is practicable to add more people to certain tasks it may be possible to recover some lost ground. Are extra funds available to hire more staff? Could some work be subcontracted?

Action	Comment
Work smarter	Consider whether the methods currently being used are the most suitable – for example, would prototyping be more effective at eliciting requirements?
Replan	If the assumptions that the original plan was based on have been proved invalid, a more realistic plan should be devised
Reschedule	A complete replan may not be necessary – it may be possible to recover some time by changing the phasing of certain deliverables
Introduce incentives	If the main problem is team performance, incentives such as bonus payments could be linked to work deadlines and quality. This is a positive incentive. In some cases, poor team performance may need to be addressed through more negative responses, for example, disciplinary action if staff are not working to the level required of them. Note: performance issues need not be limited to in-house staff. They could equally relate to contractors or suppliers, in which case the project manager will need to introduce incentives (positive or negative, as appropriate) to improve their performance
Briefings and motivation	If the project is long, it may be beneficial for the manager to hold update briefings with the team to renew their energy and enthusiasm and thereby increase productivity
Change the specification	If the original objectives of the project are unrealistic, given the time and money available, it may be necessary to negotiate a change in the specification
	This change could either be to reduce the **number of activities** included in the scope, or to reduce the level of **quality** required in each activity

There are also two specific courses of action a project manager should consider if a project starts to slip dramatically, but has a fixed deadline and so cannot be delayed. These are **fast-tracking** and **crashing**.

7.3.1 Fast-tracking

Fast-tracking involves taking activities that are normally done in sequence, and doing them in parallel instead (for example, starting construction alongside the design phase, instead of waiting for the design phase to be completed before beginning construction).

Note, however, that while fast-tracking can accelerate a project, it also involves the risk of increased costs and reworking later. For example, if the design is changed before it is finalised, yet some construction work has already been done, the change of design may result in having to re-do some of that construction work.

7.3.2 Crashing

Crashing involves assigning additional resources to the critical path. For example, if one person was working on a twelve day activity on the critical path, and it was essential to reduce the path length to eight days, a second person could be added to work on the activity.

Note that the second person may not be as efficient as the first or have all the right skills, and so he or she might need to work eight days just to reduce the path length by four (from twelve to eight).

Crashing usually leads to an increase in the cost of the project, but this may be considered an acceptable trade-off for getting the project back on schedule. However, an organisation should still aim to minimise the incremental cost incurred as a result of crashing.

7.4 Project change procedure

Some of the reactions to slippage discussed above would involve changes that would significantly affect the overall project. Other possible causes of changes to the original project plan include:

- The availability of new technology
- Changes in personnel
- A realisation that user requirements were misunderstood
- Changes in the business environment
- New legislation eg data protection

The earlier a change is made, the less expensive it should prove. However, changes will cost time and money and should not be undertaken lightly. When considering a change an investigation should be conducted to discover:

(a) The **consequences of not implementing** the proposed change.
(b) The **impact of the change** on time, cost and quality.
(c) The expected **costs and benefits** of the change.
(d) The **risks** associated with the change, and with the status-quo.

The process of ensuring that proper consideration is given to the impact of proposed changes is known as change control. Changes will need to be implemented into the project plan and communicated to all stakeholders.

7.5 Risk management

Projects and other undertakings carry an element of **risk**, for example, the risk of an inappropriate system being developed and implemented. Risk management is concerned with identifying such risks and putting in place policies to eliminate or reduce these risks. The identification of risks involves an overview of the project to establish what could go wrong, and the consequences. Risk management may be viewed as a six-stage process:

Stage 1   **Plan the risk management approach**
It is appropriate to determine the degree of **risk aversion** that will apply. The general rule is that as risk increases, so do potential returns. Minimising risk is expensive, so the degree of risk acceptable to the project sponsor and project board should be considered at an early stage.

Stage 2   **Identify and record risks**
Existing plans for time, costs and quality should be examined for risk potential. The critical path, cost estimates and quality assumptions should be examined with particular care. It will be useful for project staff to brainstorm and external advice may be sought: this could come from non-project staff within the organisation or from external sources.

Identified risks are recorded in a **risk register**. Schwalbe suggests the detail shown below should be recorded for each risk event in the risk register.

(a) An identification number
(b) A probability
(c) A name
(d) A description
(e) The root cause
(f) Possible indicators and symptoms: these are factors that tend to increase the chance that the risk event will occur
(g) Potential impact
(h) Potential responses
(i) An owner: this person monitors the risk event
(j) Current status: this will change as the project progresses; eventually the risk may become irrelevant

Stage 3 **Assess the risks**

There are two aspects to the assessment of risk.

(a)   The **probability** that the risk event will actually take place

(b)   The **consequences** of the risk event if it does occur

Several quantitative techniques may be useful in assessing risk, including expected values, sensitivity analysis, Monte Carlo simulation and programme evaluation and review technique (PERT). PERT requires the application of probabilities to the time planned for the activities identified in the critical path analysis.

The likelihood and consequences of risks may be plotted on a matrix. This approach allows unquantifiable risks to be considered alongside those to which a numerical value can be given.

Risk Assessment Matrix

	Low	Med	High
High	M	H	VH
Med	L	M	H
Low	VL	L	M

Potential impact

Threat likelihood

Stage 4 **Plan and record risk responses**

Developing a risk **contingency plan** that contains strategies for risks that fall into the VH segment should have priority, followed by risks falling into the two H segments. Following the principle of **management by exception**, the most efficient way of dealing with risks outside these quadrants may be to do nothing unless the risk presents itself. Extra time and finance should be held in reserve for dealing with likely contingencies.

Dealing with **risk** involves four strategies.

(a)   **Avoidance**: activities that could carry risk are not performed or are removed from a project. For example, an acquisition is rejected because of the potential legal liabilities attached to the potential acquisition target.

(b)   **Reduction** or **mitigation**: the potential for the risk cannot be removed, but mitigation can reduce the severity of any loss or the likelihood of the loss occurring, for example, by entering into an escrow agreement alongside the purchase of a bespoke software solution. (Refer back to Chapter 10 for further information on risk avoidance, reduction and mitigation).

(c)   **Transference**: the risk is passed on to someone else, perhaps by means of insurance, or possibly by building it into a supplier contract.

(d)   **Absorption**: the potential risk is accepted in the hope or expectation that the incidence and consequences can be coped with if necessary.

Stage 5   **Implement risk management strategies**

Stage 6   **Review the risk management approach and actions for adequacy**

Risk management is a continuous process. Procedures are necessary to regularly review and reassess the risks documented in the risk register.

As well as being an important part of your syllabus for this exam, project management is also likely to be an important part of your ongoing role as an accountant.

The ACCA Practical Experience Requirements require new members to demonstrate they can manage ongoing activities in their area of responsibility, and two components of this are:

* Monitor progress against agreed timetables and amend these timetables where necessary
* Identify potential risks associated with achieving stated objectives and how these will be managed.

7.6 Project completion   12/11

The project completion report shows the project outcomes, and any continuing issues. Post-project and post-implementation reviews should be carried out to examine the degree of success achieved, review methods and organisation and note lessons for future reference.

Exam focus point

A question in the December 2011 exam asked students to explain the purpose of a post-project review, post-implementation review and a benefits realisation review. The question then asked for an evaluation of the problems and lessons that should be learned from a project aimed at replacing a physical ordering system with an electronic system.

Key term

The **completion report** summarises the results of the project, and includes client sign-off.

On project completion, the project manager will produce a completion report. The main purpose of the completion report is to document (and gain client sign-off for) the end of the project.

The report should include a summary of the project outcome.

(a)   Project objectives and the outcomes achieved

(b)   The final project budget report showing expected and actual expenditure. If an external client is involved, this information may be sensitive – the report may exclude or amend the budget report

(c)   A brief outline of time taken compared with the original schedule

The completion report will also include provision for any continuing issues that will need to be addressed after completion. Such issues would be related to the project, but not part of the project. An example of such an issue would be a procedure for dealing with any bugs that become apparent after a new software program has been tested and approved.

Responsibilities and procedures relating to any such issues should be laid down in the report.

The manager may find it useful to distribute a **provisional report** and request feedback. This should ensure the version presented for client sign-off at the completion meeting is acceptable to all parties.

A more detailed review of the project follows a few months after completion, the post-completion audit.

7.6.1 Post-project and post-implementation reviews

Key term

> The **post-project review** is a formal review of the project that examines the lessons that may be learned and used for the benefit of future projects.

The review considers the success of the project by asking the following.

(a)   Was the project achieved on time and within budget?

(b)   Was the management of the project as successful as it might have been, or were there bottlenecks or problems? This review covers:

    (i)   Problems that might occur on future projects with similar characteristics.
    (ii)   The performance of the team individually and as a group.

In other words, any project is an **opportunity to learn how to manage future projects more effectively**.

The post-project review should involve input from the project team. A simple questionnaire could be developed for all team members to complete, and a reasonably informal meeting held to obtain feedback, on what went well (and why), and what didn't (and why).

 Case Study   **BBC and DMI**

In 2008, the BBC (British Broadcasting Corporation) launched the Digital Media Initiative (DMI) project. The project aimed to modernise the BBC's existing production operations, moving the corporation away from the use of video tape towards digital production.

In 2013, the project was abandoned after years of technical problems in getting the technology to work and delays in reporting on the project's progress. In an article published on the BBC website in February 2014, the corporation reported that the estimated project cost was £125.9m.

The Guardian newspaper, highlighting the findings of a National Audit Office inquiry, reported that the deteriorating fortunes of DMI were not adequately reported, either within management or, critically, to the BBC Trust. A 'code red' warning of the imminent project failure for example, from the BBC's own internal project management office from February 2012 wasn't reported to the trust until July that year.

The BBC Director General (the most senior executive officer at the organisation) at the time had believed that the technology was being used on programmes including the early evening 'One Show'.

A later report by the National Audit Office reported that 'the BBC had hoped to save £98m by introducing the new system. However, the final estimate of the benefits it brought to the BBC was zero. The report blamed the project's failure on confusion, a lack of planning and insufficient scrutiny'.

Commenting on the National Audit Office report, Margaret Hodge MP of the Public Accounts Committee (the body which oversees UK government spending) wrote, 'this report reads like a catalogue of how not to run a major programme. The BBC needs to learn from the mistakes it made and ensure that it never again spends such a huge amount of licence fee payer's money with almost nothing to show for it'.

The BBC responded, saying it had adopted new procedures for managing big projects in the light of the problems with the DMI project.

<u>Adapted from two online articles:</u>

1) 'Mark Thompson apologises over project failure at BBC', (February 2014) published on the *BBC* website; www.bbc.co.uk

2) 'BBC's Digital Media Initiative failed because of more than poor oversight', by Steve Hewlett (February 2014) published on *The Guardian* website; www.theguardian.com

This information should be formalised in a report. The post-project review report should contain:

(a) A **summary** should be provided, emphasising any areas where the structures and tools used to manage the project have been found to be unsatisfactory.

(b) A **cost-benefit review** should be included, comparing the forecast costs and benefits identified at the time of the feasibility study with actual costs and benefits.

(c) **Recommendations** should be made as to any steps which should be taken to improve the project management procedures used.

Lessons learned from this review should be fed back into **project management standards** to ensure future projects do not repeat the same mistakes.

At the end of the project, the finished solution will be implemented into the organisation. Sometime after this solution has been deployed a **post-implementation review** should be carried out. The timing of this will depend on the specific situation. However, typical periods range from six weeks to six months.

Key term	**Post-implementation reviews** are assessments of the completed working solution.

The post-implementation review focuses more specifically on the product that was produced by the project. It is carried out for three main reasons.

- To determine how well the project met its objectives, delivered the expected benefits and addressed the requirements that were originally defined

- To consider the working business solution to see if further improvements could be made to optimise the benefit delivered

- To identify lessons that can be learned and fed back into the **product production process**. This could involve improving processes such as research and development, and operational processes as well as making changes to who is involved in certain processes and the timings at which individual processes are carried out

In order to do this, work will centre around determining the current situation, identifying the benefits actually being delivered in comparison to those originally defined by the project, and identifying any further improvements that could be made and the learning points for the future.

Exam focus point	Make sure you understand the difference between a post-project review and a post-implementation review. The post-project review focuses on the project itself and the way it was carried out. The post-implementation review focuses on the actual product that is produced as a result of that project.
	This was examined in December 2011 where six marks were available for explaining the purpose of each of a post-project review, a post-implementation review, and a benefits realisation review. This straightforward test of theoretical knowledge was, in a number of cases, not well answered.
	A further twelve marks were then on offer for applying this knowledge to the scenario in order to identify the problems and lessons that should be learnt from a post-project review and a post-implementation review of the system implemented in the scenario.

Lessons learnt that relate to the way the project was managed should contribute to the smooth running of future projects.

A starting point for any new project should be a review of the documentation of any similar projects undertaken in the past.

7.6.2 Benefits realisation

It is obviously important that the benefits expected from the completion of a project are actually enjoyed. Has a project delivered what it was meant to? Has it been worthwhile?

Benefits realisation is concerned with the planning and management required to realise expected benefits. It also covers any required organisational transition processes.

The UK Office of Government Commerce has identified a **six stage procedure for benefits realisation**. This is most relevant to projects aimed at process improvement and changing the organisation's way of doing things.

Stage 1 **Establishing benefits measurement**
Measure the start state and record it in the benefits profile. The benefits profile defines each anticipated benefit and is used to track progress towards its realisation. Determine how benefit realisation will be measured. Benefits may be complex and spread across departments: designing usable and realistic measures may be difficult.

Stage 2 **Refining the benefits profile**
The benefits profile should be refined and controlled throughout the life of the project. Project managers should conduct regular benefits profile reviews in collaboration with key stakeholders.

Stage 3 **Monitoring benefits**
There should be regular monitoring of benefits realisation against the original business case and project programme. Adjustments may be required if it becomes clear the original plan is no longer realistic. It must be accepted that some projects will only be beneficial in enabling other projects to be successful.

Stage 4 **Transition management**
Projects are likely to bring change and this must be implemented in a proper way. Effective communications will be required, as will the deployment of good people skills.

Stage 5 **Support for benefit realisation**
Benefits realisation will mainly accrue after the end of the project. Where a project brings changes in methods and processes, there is likely to be a period for settling-down before benefits are fully realised. During this period, costs may rise and problems may occur. Careful management is required to overcome these short-term effects and to secure longer-term benefits. A philosophy of continuous improvement is required if further benefits are to be achieved.

Stage 6 **Measuring the benefits**
Benefits achieved should be established by comparison with the pre-improvement state recorded in the benefits profile.

8 Project management software

Project management software can be used to produce detailed project planning documentation, to update plans and to produce reports.

8.1 Project management software

We have now considered a number of aspects of project management, but we will end by looking at the ways project management software can support project planning and control.

Project management techniques are ideal candidates for computerisation. Project management software packages have been available for a number of years. Microsoft Project is a popular package, while SmartDraw software also contains Gantt charts, PERT charts and project schedules.

Software might be used for a number of purposes.

(a) **Planning**

Network diagrams (showing the critical path) and Gantt charts (showing resource use) can be produced automatically once the relevant data is entered. Packages also allow a sort of 'what if?' analysis for initial planning, trying out different levels of resources, changing deadlines and so on to find the best combination. In this way, software can be very useful for scheduling resource usage.

(b)   **Estimating**

As a project progresses, actual data will become known and can be entered into the package and collected for future reference. Since many projects involve basically similar tasks (interviewing users and so on), actual data from one project can be used to provide more accurate estimates for the next project. The software also facilitates and encourages the use of more sophisticated estimation techniques than managers might be prepared to use if working manually.

(c)   **Monitoring**

Actual data can also be entered and used to facilitate monitoring of progress and automatically updating the plan for the critical path and the use of resources as circumstances dictate. Monitoring project progress should help provide an early warning of any risks to the project.

(d)   **Reporting**

Software packages allow standard and tailored progress reports to be produced, printed out and circulated to participants and senior managers at any time, usually at the touch of a button. This helps with co-ordination of activities and project review.

8.2 What input data is required?

Most project management packages feature a process of identifying the main steps in a project, and breaking these down further into specific tasks.

A typical project management package requires four **inputs**.

(a)   The length of **time** required for each activity of the project
(b)   The **logical relationships** between each activity
(c)   The **resources** available
(d)   **When** the resources are available

8.3 Advantages of project management software packages

The **advantages** of using project management software are summarised below.

Advantage	Comment
Enables quick re-planning	Estimates can be **changed many times** and a new schedule produced almost instantly. Changes to the plan can be reflected immediately.
Document quality	Well-presented plans give a **professional** impression and are easier to understand.
Encourages constant progress tracking	The project manager is able to compare **actual** progress against **planned** progress and investigate problem areas promptly.
What if? analysis	Software enables the effect of various scenarios to be calculated quickly and easily. Many project managers conduct this type of analysis using **copies** of the plan in separate computer files – leaving the actual plan untouched.

Another advantage is that the software is able to analyse and present the project information in a number of ways.

8.4 Disadvantages of project management software packages

Some **disadvantages** of project management software are:

(a)   Some packages are difficult to use. Some people may achieve better results using simpler techniques (pen and paper!) but feel pressured into using project management software by company policy.

Often, project management software is unnecessary for small, stand-alone projects, where the scope of the project does not justify the time or costs involved in the software. However, project management software can be very useful for multiple, larger projects.

(b)   Some project managers become so interested in producing perfect plans that they spend too much time producing documents and not enough time managing the project. In particular, there is a danger they do not adjust the initial project plan to reflect actual progress through the project (for example, to reflect tasks that are completed late or are re-sequenced).

(c)   The project manager's level of interpersonal contact may suffer as he or she spends too much time looking at the software. (This problem is similar to the one some accountants suffer from when they spend too much time looking at spreadsheets, rather than talking to operational managers to understand what is really happening in the business.)

- A **project** is an undertaking that has a beginning and an end and is carried out to meet established goals within cost, schedule and quality objectives. It often has the following characteristics:

    - A defined beginning and end
    - Resources allocated specifically to it
    - Intended to be done only once (although similar separate projects could be undertaken)
    - Follows a plan towards a clear intended end-result
    - Often cuts across organisational and functional lines

- **Project management** is the combination of systems, techniques, and people used to control and monitor activities undertaken within the project. It will be deemed successful if it is completed at the specified level of **quality**, **on time** and within **budget**. Achieving this can be very difficult: most projects present a range of significant challenges.

- Adaptation to environmental change makes project management an important feature of strategic implementation. Also, strategic management thinking can be a useful input into project management. Strategic project management envisages strategy as a stream of projects intended to achieve organisational breakthroughs.

- Kerzner suggests that where project management is a core competence, a continuous improvement approach should be taken to developing and consolidating the methodology.

- The project life cycle concept describes the progression of many projects through four stages: definition, design, delivery and development.

- Limits to resource availability mean that not all potential projects will be undertaken; rational methods are used to select projects.

- Project initiation tasks include the appointment of project manager and sponsor; stakeholder analysis and the definition of project scope. The business case explains why the project is needed, while the project charter gives authorisation for it to be undertaken.

- The business case is a key document which is initially used to secure funding for a project, then revisited and revised during the life of the project to ensure the project remains on track and the identified benefits are realised.

- A business case should be based on the ability to measure each benefit and estimate expected improvements. Benefits can be classified as **observable**, **measurable**, **quantifiable** or **financial**.

- Many costs will be incurred as part of a project, these will be both **capital** and **operational**. Care should be taken to ensure all costs are identified within the business case.

- A **benefit owner** should be assigned to each individual benefit. **Change owners** may also be required to ensure benefits are fully realised.

- A **benefits realisation plan** should be included as part of the business plan to demonstrate how the identified benefits will be measured, taken forward and achieved.

- Many large-scale projects, particularly those involving major change, are strategically significant and project management can merge into strategic management. Force field analysis identifies enablers, constraints and showstoppers.

- Work breakdown structure is an analysis of the work involved in a project into a structure of phases, activities and tasks. **Dependencies** determine the order in which tasks must be carried out, while **interactions** between tasks affect them without imposing order.

- The **project budget** plans the allocation of resources to the project and forms a basis for their control. Budgeting may be top-down or bottom-up.

- A **Gantt chart** shows the deployment of resources over time.

- **Network analysis** illustrates interactions and dependencies. It is used to plan the sequence of tasks making up project scope and to determine the critical path. PERT uses probabilities to make estimates of likely completion and milestone dates.

- A resource **histogram** is a useful planning tool that shows the amount and timing of the requirement for a resource (or a range of resources).

- The person who takes ultimate responsibility for ensuring the desired result is achieved on time and within budget is the **project manager**. **Duties** of the project manager include: Planning, teambuilding, communication, co-ordinating project activities, monitoring and control, problem-resolution and quality control.

- **Project managers** require the following **skills**: Leadership and team building, organisational ability, communication skills (written, spoken, presentations, meetings), some technical knowledge of the project area and interpersonal skills.

- Project managers should have some understanding of the way that groups of people interact at work.

  Teams enable people's talents and efforts to be combined and teamwork can have a motivating effect, Tuckman identified four stages in team development.

– Forming	– Norming
– Storming	– Performing

  However, teams bring their own problems, including disharmony, riskshift, groupthink and political conflict. Handy suggests a contingency approach to team leadership. Belbin identified nine roles played by team members.

– Co-ordinator	– Shaper
– Plant	– Monitor-evaluator
– Resource investigator	– Implementer
– Team worker	– Finisher
– Specialist	

- Progress reports should report progress towards key **milestones**. **Slippage** may be managed with a number of options, including incentives, working smarter, extra resources and rescheduling. Project changes must be carefully considered, communicated, documented and controlled. Risk management involves risk assessment and recording; and action to reduce, avoid, transfer or absorb risks.

- The project completion report shows the project outcomes, and any continuing issues. There should be a post-completion audit process to examine the degree of success achieved, review methods and organisation and note lessons for future reference.

- **Project management software** can be used to produce detailed project planning documentation, to update plans and to produce reports.

Quick Quiz

1 What are the three main measures of project success?

2 What are the two main project management methodologies in the UK and the US?

3 What is a breakthrough project?

4 What are four phases of a typical project lifecycle?

5 What does a Gantt chart do?

6 Who provides the resources needed for a project?

7 What is a milestone?

8 Name two specific courses of action available to a project manager if a project starts to slip dramatically, but has a fixed deadline and so cannot be delayed.

9 What are the four risk management strategies?

10 What is the main benefit of carrying out a post-completion audit?

Answers to Quick Quiz

1   Quality, cost and time

2   PRINCE2 and PMBOK

3   One that will have a material effect on either the business's external competitive edge, its internal capabilities or its financial performance

4   Definition, design, delivery, development

5   It shows the deployment of resources over time

6   The project sponsor

7   A significant event in the life of the project, usually completion of a major deliverable

8   Fast-tracking; crashing

9   Avoidance, mitigation, transference, absorption

10   The opportunity make the management of future projects more effective

Now try the questions below from the Practice Question Bank

Number	Level	Marks	Time
Q14	Examination	20	36 mins

Finance

Finance

Introduction

The role of the finance function and that of the accountant in business is changing. This evolution is due to a growing expectation that finance professionals should not just communicate performance but play an active role in helping to shape strategy.

Finance may be regarded as the fundamental business resource, since it provides access to all other more specific resources, to the extent that they are available. The organisation's financial position will form a major part of the strategic position and will also constitute a strong influence on the process of strategic choice, for example, in assessing the acceptability and feasibility of different options. The consequences of strategic actions will also be financially evaluated. Finance is therefore relevant to all three of strategic position, strategic choice and strategic action and so has inherent strategic significance.

The majority of the material in this section of the Study Text should be familiar to you from your previous studies, so dealing with it should be a matter of revision and consolidation on knowledge.

Study guide

		Intellectual level
G1	**The link between strategy and finance**	
(a)	Explain the relationship between strategy and finance	3
	(i) Managing for value	
	(ii) Financial expectations of stakeholders	
	(iii) Funding strategies	
(b)	Discuss how the finance function has transformed to enabling an accountant to have a key role in the decision-making process from strategy formulation and implementation to its impact on business performance	2
G2	**Finance decisions to formulate and support business strategy**	
(a)	Determine the overall investment requirements of the business	2
(b)	Evaluate alternative sources of finance for these investments and their associated risks	3
(c)	Efficiently and effectively manage the current and non-current assets of the business from a finance and risk perspective	2
G3	**The role of cost and management accounting in strategic planning and decision making**	
(a)	Evaluate budgeting, standard costing and variance analysis in support of strategic planning and decision making	3
(b)	Evaluate strategic and operational decisions, taking into account risk and uncertainty (Including using decision trees)	3
(c)	Evaluate the following strategic options using marginal and relevant costing techniques. (i) Make or buy decisions (ii) Accepting or declining special contracts (iii) Closure or continuation decisions (iv) Effective use of scarce resources	3
(d)	Evaluate the role and limitations of cost accounting in strategy development and implementation, specifically relating to: (i) Direct and indirect costs in multi-product contexts (ii) Overhead apportionment in full costing (iii) Activity-based costing in planning and control	2
G4	**Financial implications of making strategic choices and of implementing strategic actions**	
(a)	Apply efficiency ratios to assess how efficiently an organisation uses its current resources.	2
(b)	Apply appropriate gearing ratios to assess the risks associated with financing and investment in the organisation.	2
(c)	Apply appropriate liquidity ratios to assess the organisation's short-term commitments to creditors and employees.	2
(d)	Apply appropriate profitability ratios to assess the viability of chosen strategies.	2
(e)	Apply appropriate investment ratios to assist investors and shareholders in evaluating organisational performance and strategy.	2

Exam guide

P3 is not a strategic financial management paper and we do not expect the examining team to present technically difficult questions on finance. Nonetheless, the evidence of the papers to date suggests you are likely to encounter numerical analysis of some kind in Question 1 and the examining team has indicated that there will continue to be opportunities for calculation. However, in P3 it is important that you link your financial skills and computations to business strategy, rather than simply performing calculations in their own right.

There is no certainty that the numerical analysis will be of a financial kind. It is possible that financial matters will appear in optional Section B questions (rather than the Section A case study), and in this case, the context could be the mutual impact of finance and strategy on one another (for example, benefits realisation from projects, or supplier evaluation in software selection), rather than simply doing computations.

1 The finance function

1.1 Transformation of the role of the accountant and the finance function

FAST FORWARD

> The role of the finance function and finance professional is changing. Today's finance professional is expected to take on a broader advisory and strategic role. This gradual evolution has given rise to the notion of the finance function acting as a **business partner**, where finance professionals share their finance expertise with operational teams. Furthermore, the '**hybrid accountant**', is now regarded as the modern model of an accountant in business, where they act as internal consultants and business analysts.

In this section, we explore how the traditional role of the finance function and that of the finance professional is continuing to evolve. In recent times there has been a noticeable shift in the role that finance plays in modern organisations, moving away from being a mechanism for simply reporting on performance, to taking on a broader advisory and strategic role.

1.1.1 The role of the traditional finance function

The specific activities and roles undertaken by the traditional finance function include:

(a)   Processing transactions, maintaining accounting records and delivering month-end reports efficiently and at low cost.

(b)   Communicating results to internal and external stakeholders.

(c)   Ensuring the effective operation of corporate governance and control. This has become increasingly important in the wake of various financial scandals and the requirements of legislation such the American Sarbanes-Oxley Act (which you should recall from your P1 studies).

1.1.2 The finance function as a business partner

The finance function has faced pressures to become more actively involved in business operations. Many finance functions have therefore re-focused their roles as business partners, adopting a more commercial, action-orientated approach. This means gaining broad knowledge of the business, participating as full members of operational teams and bringing financial expertise to the management process. They are expected to **integrate management accounting information** with **strategic management accounting data.**

Important areas where the finance functions role has developed have included:

- Providing more useful information on business units, projects, products and customers
- Collaborating in the formulation of corporate objectives, strategic plans and budgets
- Monitoring outcomes against plans and initiating responsive action to improve performance
- Supplying business cases for new investments
- Communicating and interpreting financial and non-financial information for a range of stakeholders
- Helping operational and strategic managers understand information on which decisions are based

- Designing information systems that provide greater support for management

1.1.3 The hybrid accountant

This evolution in the role of the finance function has had implications for finance professionals – leading to the creation of the term the '**hybrid accountant**', which is now regarded as the modern model of an accountant. Growing numbers of accountants spend the majority of their time as internal consultants or business analysts. They spend less time preparing standardised reports, but more time analysing and interpreting information. Moreover, many no longer work in an accounting department, but are based in the operating departments with which they work, meaning that they are increasingly involved with the operations of their business, and more actively involved in decision making.

 Case Study   **The complete finance professional**

The following extract was taken from a report, 'The complete finance professional 2013' published by ACCA. The report outlined findings from ACCA's global survey of CFO's on the skills and capabilities they see as being most relevant to their role. ACCA's research provides a useful insight into how the role of the finance professional is changing.

'Today's business environment is particularly challenging; public debt, currency instability, emerging market growth, commodity price rises, ongoing funding challenges and a broadening risk exposure present an uncertain climate.

Managing the multitude of risks faced, supporting strategic decision-making that drives sustainable long-term value, and simply controlling the organisation effectively are difficult but ever more important finance priorities for finance leaders.

For Chief Financial Officers and the finance functions they lead, the rules of the game have changed. The finance journey has seen the role of the function evolve from back office to centre stage in supporting organisations create and protect value. It has taken place against the backdrop of a global economy which is increasingly volatile and complex, more competitive, higher risk and rebalancing between west and east.

Many of the challenges and priorities that face the finance function are very evident in the aftermath of the financial and economic crisis in 2008-2009; in particular, the desire for sustainable wealth creation. The finance function has a critical role to play in helping deliver this ambition but it necessitates a subtly different type of finance leadership that is needed in global finance functions today.

A defining hallmark of finance leadership post-crisis has been the need for balance between the pursuit of growth and appropriate control of the organisation; in essence supporting the business to drive sustainable growth. Today's CFOs must bring a wealth of capabilities to the top finance job, and they must demonstrate a balanced finance understanding.

In practical terms, what do we mean by balanced finance leadership? Finance leaders have an important role to play in supporting the organisations strategy and partnering with the business effectively, but to do this sustainably the business first and foremost must be effectively controlled. Sustainable value creation requires effective risk management processes because poor risk management approaches are counter to creating longer term value; it requires strong financial management of the organisation because the inability to protect and maximise the funds the business creates is not consistent with long-term wealth creation; it requires CFOs to develop financial strategies that are beneficial in the longer term, knowing that most eyes will be on quarter-by-quarter results; it calls into play an adept understanding of the implications of poor investment decision-making in a complex investment landscape; it necessitates a clear understanding of past and possible future performance measurement; it mandates the need for strong governance of the organisation, and of course ensuring its regulatory responsibilities are met. This balanced finance stewardship is the building block of sustainable value creation in today's competitive business environment'.

Source: 'The complete finance professional 2013' report can be found on the ACCA website at www.accaglobal.com

1.2 Importance of decision making to organisations

A large part of the modern accountant's role is to work closely with the business to improve **strategic decision making** to enhance the business' ability to create value. This, however, does present some challenges for traditional accounting systems.

As ACCA's report highlights, the ever changing business environment requires finance professionals to support organisations in a far broader sense. In the context of developing business strategy, perhaps the most important of these job roles is the provision of information and analysis on which decisions are based. A key part of the modern accountant's role is to work closely with the business to improve decision making and to enhance the business' ability to create value.

This change in the focus of the modern accountant's role also reflects an increasing recognition that high quality decision-making is becoming critical to superior business performance and may form the basis of a competitive advantage.

1.2.1 The challenge for modern accountants

The challenge lies in providing more relevant information for decision making. Traditional accounting systems may not always provide this.

(a)   **Historical costs** are not necessarily the best guide to decision making. One of the criticisms of management accounting in a strategic context is that management accounting information is biased towards the **past rather than the future**.

(b)   **Strategic issues** are not easily detected by accounting systems. Much accounting information has been devised for internal consumption. However, it is important to balance this with external factors, especially as strategic management involves competitor and environmental considerations.

(c)   **Financial models** of some sophistication are needed to enable accountants to provide useful information.

In other words, to support strategic decisions, accounting itself needs to become more strategic. The rest of this section is devoted to exploring how accountants (and more specifically, management accountants) can add value to organisations acting as strategic management accountants.

1.3 What is strategic management accounting?

Strategic management accounting is a form of management accounting in which emphasis is placed on information about factors which are external to the organisation, as well as non-financial and internally generated information.

The role of the **strategic management accountant** covers **financial analysis, planning and control.**

Strategic management accounting is a form of management accounting in which emphasis is placed on information about factors which are external to the organisation, as well as non-financial and internally-generated information.

1.3.1 The role of the strategic management accountant

Ward suggests that the role of the strategic management accountant can be analysed as follows.

(a)   **Financial analysis** indicates the **current position** of a business and its financial performance in comparison with competitors, as well as breaking it down into product and customer profitability analyses. (The concept of customer profitability was discussed earlier in the Study Text in Chapter 3).

(b)   **Financial planning** quantifies the goals and objectives of the business, normally in a budget.

(c)   **Financial control**. Financial information is an essential part of the feedback mechanism comparing planned with actual performance.

However, although Ward focuses on the financial information which could be provided by a strategic management accountant, it is also important to remember the contribution of non-financial information to strategic management accounting; for example, in relation to a product or business unit's market share.

We also appreciate something of the context of strategic management accounting by reminding ourselves what strategy itself is:

'Strategy is the direction and scope of an organisation over the long term which achieves advantage in a changing environment, through its configuration of resources and competences with the aim of fulfilling stakeholder expectations.' *(Johnson, Scholes & Whittington)*

The references to the **environment** and to **stakeholders** are important here, because they highlight that strategy has an **external focus** as well as an internal one.

1.3.2 External orientation

The important fact which distinguishes strategic management accounting from other management accounting activities is its **external orientation** towards customers and competitors, suppliers and other stakeholders. For example, whereas a traditional management accountant would report on an organisation's own revenues, the strategic management accountant would report on market share or trends in market size and growth.

(a)   **Competitive advantage is relative**. Chapter 3 of the Study Text highlighted that understanding competitors and customers is likely to be of prime importance to most organisations.

For example, knowledge of competitors' costs, as well as a firm's own costs, could help inform strategic choices: a firm would be unwise to pursue a cost leadership strategy without first analysing its costs in relation to the cost structures of other firms in the industry.

(b)   **Customers** determine if a firm has competitive advantage.

1.3.3 Future orientation

Another criticism of traditional management accounts is that they are **backward-looking**. Decision making is a forward and outward looking process. Strategic management accountants will use **relevant costs** (covered later in this chapter) and revenues (ie **incremental** costs and revenues and **opportunity** costs) for decision making.

1.3.4 Goal congruence

Business strategy involves the activities of many different functions, including marketing, production and human resource management. The strategic management accounting system will require the **inputs of many areas of the business**.

(a)   Strategic management accounting translates the consequences of different strategies into a **common accounting language for comparison**.

(b)   It **relates business operations to financial performance** and, therefore, helps ensure that business activities are focused on shareholders' needs for profit.

(c)   It **helps to ensure goal congruence**, again by translating business activities into the common language of finance.

1.4 What information could strategic management accounting provide?

In general terms, strategic management accountants could expect to help an organisation through providing information which supports more effective strategic planning, better decision making, and improved control over an organisation's performance. However, bearing in mind the need for **goal congruence**, **external orientation** and **future orientation**, some more specific **examples** of how strategic management accounting information could be useful to an organisation during strategy formulation are provided below.

(a) **Competitor analysis**. Analysing competitors' costs and the activities competitors carry out. How do competitors' costs compare with ours? Are competitors vulnerable because of their cost structure or their product/service portfolio (or are we vulnerable because of our cost structure or our product/service portfolio)?

Analysing competitors' costs and performance also highlights the potential importance of **benchmarking**.

(b) **Financial effect of competitor response**. How might competitors respond to an initiative (eg to reduce prices; to introduce new products/services)? What might the impact of the competitor response be?

(c) **Product profitability**. A firm should want to know what profits or losses are being made by each of its products, and why.

(d) **Portfolio analysis**. What are the firm's key products or strategic business units – in terms of their contribution to revenue or profit? What strategies should be adopted for different products or business units (eg in relation to their relative market share and market growth; per BCG matrix)?

(e) **Customer profitability**. Some customers or groups of customers are worth more than others. Which customers are most important/profitable to us? Why are some groups of customers more profitable than others?

(f) **Pricing decisions**. How is customer demand for a product/service likely to vary at different prices? How will this affect profits and cash flows? How does the proposed price fit with the organisation's overall generic strategy? How does it compare to competitors' prices?

(g) **Product – market decisions**. What are the potential costs and benefits of launching new products and/or entering new markets? Should the organisation launch the products, or enter the markets? Alternatively, should the organisation discontinue a product or leave a market which does not seem to be performing well?

(h) **Capacity expansion**. Should the firm expand its capacity, and if so by how much?

(i) **Brand valuation**. What are the costs and benefits of investing in building brands?

(j) **Shareholder wealth**. Future profitability determines the value of a business.

1.5 Success factors for a strategic management accounting system (SMAS)

FAST FORWARD

A strategic management accounting system (SMAS) should:

- Aid strategic decisions
- Close the communication gap between accountants and managers
- Identify the type of decision
- Offer appropriate financial performance indicators
- Distinguish between economic and managerial performance
- Provide relevant information
- Separate committed from discretionary costs
- Distinguish discretionary from engineered costs
- Use standard costs strategically
- Allow for changes over time

Strategic management accounting has to bridge a gap between financial reporting, on the one hand; and the uncertainties of the future, on the other. We can now go on to identify the success factors of a strategic management accounting system. It should:

- Aid strategic decisions
- Close the communication gap between accountants and managers

- Identify the type of decision
- Offer appropriate financial performance indicators
- Distinguish between economic and managerial performance
- Provide relevant information
- Separate committed from discretionary costs
- Distinguish discretionary from engineered costs
- Use standard costs strategically
- Allow for changes over time

These are now discussed in more detail.

1.5.1 Aid strategic decisions

As part of a strategic management system, the SMAS will provide one-off information to support and evaluate particular strategic decisions and information for strategic management, in order to monitor strategies and the firm's overall competitive position. Changes in the external environment and competitor responses should be easily incorporated into the system.

1.5.2 Close the communication gap

The SMAS converts financial data into information for strategic decision-making. Financial data is off-putting to many people. Consequently, the originator of such information should make sure that it is tailored.

- Ask the recipient how he or she would like the **format** of the report
- Provide only the **relevant** supporting financial data
- Identify the **key assumptions** on which the information is prepared

1.5.3 Identify the types of decision

Ward states that, despite the one-off nature of many strategic decisions, it is possible to identify the following types of financial decision.

(a) **Changing the balance of resource allocation** between different business areas, for example, by increasing spending in one area.

(b) **Entering a new business area** (eg new product development, new markets). Some account will have to be taken of the timescale in which the strategy is expected to consume resources, as benefits may be some time in coming.

(c) **Exit decisions** which come in two forms.

    (i)   **Closing down** part of the business and selling off the assets

    (ii)   Selling the business as a **going concern**

To support such decisions, the SMAS should:

- Incorporate **future cash flows** rather than historic costs
- Include only those items which will be **changed** by the particular decision

1.5.4 Offer suitable financial performance indicators

Two general points can be made.

(a) **Financial data is not enough**. Customers drive a business, and competitors can ruin it, so performance measures which ignore key variables of customer satisfaction or competitor activity ignore critical strategic issues.

(b) **The financial information must suit the competitive strategies**. A report complaining about the expense of an advertising campaign ignores the fact that failing to advertise could lead to loss of market share.

1.5.5 Distinguish economic versus managerial performance

A business's **overall economic performance** results from both controllable and uncontrollable factors.

(a) **Risk**. Shareholders may be happy with the risk, if it is balanced by suitable return, but a manager may be unhappy if their career is at risk from pursuing a strategy, the success of which is outside their control.

(b) **Performance**. Judging a manager's contribution on the basis of the overall economic performance of the business may not reflect their contribution at all. Managers should therefore be judged on their contribution in areas over which they have control.

1.5.6 Provide relevant information

Relevant financial information should be provided, which presents strategic decisions from the organisation's viewpoint. Specific, tailored reports should support individual decisions and activities, perhaps with **profitability analyses** for each market segment.

1.5.7 Separate committed from discretionary costs

Ignore sunk costs. This has a number of ramifications for the making of business strategies.

- A cost may be **committed,** even though it has not actually been incurred
- **Discretionary costs** are those over which the decision-maker still has choice.

1.5.8 Distinguish between discretionary and engineered costs

Engineered costs are those which derive from a relatively predictable relationship between input materials and output units of production.

1.5.9 Use standard costs strategically

Standard costs (covered later in this chapter) consist of a physical usage element (eg volume of materials) and a price element. The split between the **price** and **usage** elements is indicative of:

- The extent to which the firm is **vulnerable** to suppliers raising prices
- The possible impact of **trade-offs** between, say, labour and materials

Trade-offs. If the relationships between the input material and output quantities are known, or variable, then standard costing can show the financial effects of different mixes.

(a) For example, if there is a trade-off between labour and raw materials, changes in the relative costs of these factors can indicate a suitable mix: more expensive labour would result in less of a valued raw material being used.

(b) If the price of a raw material escalates suddenly, the standard costing system can be amended with the new price, and a new mix analysis calculated which takes it into account.

Absorbing indirect/fixed overheads into products can lead to poor pricing decisions, in the short term. If a factory is working at 60% capacity utilisation, this could lead to higher indirect costs being absorbed per unit. This information, if wrongly interpreted, could be used to suggest a price rise, rather than a reduction to encourage more sales and hence, an increased utilisation of capacity.

2 Finance and strategy

In commercial organisations, managing for value is about creating shareholder value, while in the public sector; it is about obtaining value for money. Managers must understand the key cost and value drivers affecting their operations. Financial risk is determined exclusively by gearing, but there are several sources of business risk. Financial risk may be balanced against business risk, so that overall risk is managed.

In the first part of this chapter, we explored the evolution in the role of the finance function and that of the modern finance professional. In this section, we take a closer look at the main financial issues most organisations face.

JS&W suggest that organisations of all types must deal with three broad issues of finance.

- **Managing for value**
- **Funding**
- **Financial expectations of stakeholders**

2.1 Managing for value

For commercial organisations, managing for value is about **creating value** for shareholders, while in the public sector, it is about **obtaining best value** for the money spent.

2.1.1 Shareholder value

Shareholder value depends on long-term capacity to generate cash. This will enable the payment of dividends, which, in turn, will drive up the market value of the business, offering capital gain as an alternative form of value. Ability to generate cash is influenced by three main factors.

(a)   **Funds from operations**, which are determined by sales revenues and costs.

(b)   The net cost of financing the **capital base of non-current and current assets** required to support operations: an important aspect of this factor is the efficiency with which these assets are used.

(c)   **Capital structure** (gearing), which will determine the company's **cost of capital** (and its financial risk).

2.1.2 Best value in the public sector

Most public sector managers are concerned only with managing their budgeted cash spending. However, they should understand the significance of the factors outlined above as they apply to their responsibilities. A good example is the need for efficient exploitation of non-current assets.

2.1.3 Drivers of cost and value

Value creation does not occur and costs do not arise evenly across the organisation, so managers should have a firm grasp of the **key cost and value drivers** affecting their operations. Some of these may be outside the organisation, elsewhere in the value network, so the ability to influence suppliers and distributors may be crucial to success. This will depend on **relative bargaining power**, as discussed elsewhere in this Study Text.

Choice of **generic strategy** interacts with cost and value: strict control of cost is obviously fundamental to cost leadership, while differentiation will inevitably have cost implications associated with such matters as brand communications, product quality and customer service.

The structure of costs and value creation is likely to **change over time**, as, for example, illustrated by the cost and profit aspects of the **product life cycle**. The cash flow aspect of the **Boston matrix** analysis also illustrates this.

2.2 Funding strategies

There are likely to be several considerations relevant to funding decisions for commercial organisations. Among these are: the ownership structure; whether a company is quoted or privately held; and, perhaps most significantly, the attitude of the owners and senior managers to **risk**. One of the most important commercial funding decisions is **capital structure**, or **gearing**. Gearing up, with a high proportion of loan capital, enables holders of equity to benefit significantly when overall returns are in excess of the cost of debt, since the surplus accrues to them. The natural corollary to this is, however, that when times are hard and returns are depressed below the rate payable to lenders, it is the holders of equity that have to find the shortfall. This is **financial risk**.

The level of gearing and thus the degree of financial risk accepted, will be influenced by management's beliefs about the prospects for the company and the future movement of interest rates; these, in turn, depend to some extent on the future state of the economy generally.

Financial risk cannot be considered in isolation. There are several other important sources of risk, including political change and the dangers inherent in the physical environment. However, it is likely to be **business risk** that will require the most careful consideration. Business risk is the total of all the uncertainties that exist in any business venture and thus includes such aspects of uncertainty as sales success, public image, changes in the bargaining power of suppliers and so on.

2.2.1 Managing risk

JS&W point out that financial risk can, to some extent, be balanced against business risk in order to produce an acceptable level of risk overall. If business risk is perceived as being low, a higher level of financial risk may be acceptable and gearing increased. Similarly, if business risk increases, a proportionate response might be to aim to pay off an element of debt. The ability to **adjust the level of dividend paid** may be a useful adjunct to this concept.

JS&W illustrate the relationships involved here using the four cases of the Boston matrix, which parallel the life cycle model to some extent. We summarise their illustration in the table below.

	Launch (Question mark)	Growth (Star)	Maturity (Cash Cow)	Decline (Dog)
Business risk	Very high	High	Medium to low	Low
Financial risk	Keep very low	Keep low	May be increased	Can be high
Funding	Venture capital	Equity	Debt and equity	Secured Debt
Dividends	Nil	Nominal, if any	High	Total

2.2.2 Conglomerates

A large company is likely to seek a balanced portfolio of businesses at different stages of their lives. It is important that such conglomerates consider the **overall risk profile** of their operations. They should then adjust their funding strategy using the ideas illustrated above.

2.2.3 Funding and strategy

Funding arrangements can be a major influence on strategy.

(a)   A **highly geared company** is likely to avoid high levels of business risk.

(b)   The **form of ownership** may be changed in order to gain access to new sources of funds.

(c)   A strategy based on **acquisitions** may be driven by the need to reinvest surplus funds or to demonstrate a high level of growth to the market; wider strategic considerations may be neglected as a result.

2.3 Stakeholders' financial expectations

We discussed the general expectations of stakeholders earlier in this Study Text. These will inevitably make demands on available funds, some directly, as in employees' expectations for proper wages and salaries, and some more indirectly, as in various expectations of socially responsible action.

There will also be expectations of **solvency** and **liquidity** on the part of trading partners and providers of loan finance. Customers will expect **good value** in their purchases. This also applies to public sector organisations.

BPP LEARNING MEDIA

3 Financial management decisions

FAST FORWARD

In seeking to attain the financial objectives of the organisation or enterprise, a financial manager has to make decisions on three topics.

- Investment
- Financing
- Dividends

These three policy areas interact and decision makers must also manage the interactions.

3.1 Investment, financing and dividend decisions

Maximising the wealth of shareholders generally implies maximising profits consistent with long-term stability. Often short-term gains must be sacrificed in the interests of the company's long-term prospects. In the context of this overall objective of financial management, there are three main types of decisions facing financial managers: **investment** decisions, **financing** decisions and **dividend** decisions.

3.2 Investment decisions

The financial manager will need to **identify** investment opportunities, **evaluate** them and decide on the **optimum allocation of scarce funds** available between investments.

Investment decisions may be on the undertaking of new **projects** within the existing business, the **takeover** of, or **merger** with, another company or the **selling off** of a part of the business. Managers have to take decisions in the light of strategic considerations such as whether the business intends to **expand internally** (through investment in existing operations) or **externally** (through expansion).

3.3 Financing decisions

Financing decisions include those for both the long term (**capital structure**) and the short term (**working capital management**).

The financial manager will need to determine the **source, cost** and effect on **risk** of the possible sources of long-term finance. A balance between **profitability** and **liquidity** (ready availability of funds if required) must be taken into account when deciding on the optimal level of short-term finance.

3.4 Interaction of financing with investment and dividend decisions

When taking financial decisions, managers will have to fulfil the **requirements of the providers of finance**; otherwise finance may not be made available. This may be particularly difficult in the case of equity shareholders, since dividends are paid at the company's discretion; however, if equity shareholders do not receive the dividends they want, they will sell their shares, the share price will fall and the company will have more difficulty raising funds from share issues in future.

Although there may be risks in obtaining extra finance, the long-term risks to the business of **failing to invest** may be even greater and managers will have to balance these risks. Investment may have direct consequences for decisions involving the **management of finance**; extra working capital may be required if investments are made and sales expand as a consequence. Managers must be sensitive to this and ensure that a balance is maintained between receivables and inventory, and cash.

A further issue managers will need to consider is the **matching** of the **characteristics** of investment and finance. **Time** is a critical aspect; an investment which earns returns in the long-term should be matched with finance that requires repayment in the long-term.

Another aspect is the **financing of international investments**. A company which expects to receive a substantial amount of income in a foreign currency will be concerned that this currency may weaken. It can hedge against this possibility by borrowing in the foreign currency and using the foreign receipts to repay the loan. It may though be better to obtain finance on the international markets.

3.5 Dividend decisions

Dividend decisions may affect the view that shareholders have of the long-term prospects of the company, and thus the **market value of the shares**.

3.6 Interaction of dividend with investment and financing decisions

The amount of surplus cash paid out as **dividends** will have a direct impact on **finance** available for **investment**. Managers have a difficult decision here; how much do they pay out to shareholders each year to keep them happy, and what level of funds do they retain in the business to invest in projects that will yield long-term income? In addition, funds available from retained profits may be needed if debt finance is likely to be unavailable, or if taking on more debt would expose the company to undesirable risks.

4 Cash forecasts

FAST FORWARD

Cash forecasting should ensure that sufficient funds will be available when needed, to sustain the activities of an enterprise at an acceptable cost.

4.1 Cash budgets

Key term

A **cash budget** (or **forecast**) is a detailed budget of estimated cash inflows and outflows, incorporating both revenue and capital items.

Cash forecasts (or budgets) are used to plan the structure of an organisation's finances.

- How much cash is required?
- When it is required?
- How long it is required for?
- Whether it will be available from anticipated sources

A company must know **when** it might need to borrow and **for how long**, not just **what amount** of funding could be required.

4.2 Cash forecasts based on the statement of financial position (balance sheet)

A forecast based on the statement of financial position (balance sheet) is produced for **management accounting purposes** and so not for external publication or statutory financial reporting. **It is not an estimate of cash inflows and outflows**. A number of sequential forecasts can be produced, for example, a forecast of the statement of financial position at the end of each year for the next five years.

As an estimate of the company's statement of financial position at a future date, a statement of financial position forecast is used to identify either the **cash surplus** or the **funding shortfall** in the company's statement of financial position **at the forecast date**.

FAST FORWARD

As part of a business's risk analysis, different forecasts should be prepared with **changing financial** or **business variables**. The links between these variables and the figures in the forecasts may not be straightforward.

4.3 Sensitivity analysis

In a well-designed forecast a great number of **'what-if'** questions can be asked and answered quickly by carrying out **sensitivity analysis** and changing the relevant data or variables. In a cash flow forecast model, managers may wish to know the cash flow impact if sales growth per month is nil, $1/2$%, 1%, $1\frac{1}{2}$%, $2\frac{1}{2}$% or minus 1% and so on.

However, businesses will also want to estimate the magnitude of changes in sales and ultimately, profits, if economic or business variables change. This will be more problematic.

4.4 Changes in economic variables

Businesses need to be aware of likely changes in inflation, interest rates and so on. Governments and central banks issue regular updates and forecasts, and the financial press is also helpful.

However, businesses will also need to forecast:

(a) How the **predicted changes** will **affect demand**. The links may not be easy to forecast. Businesses should consider separately the effect of major increases on each type of product.

(b) How the **business** will **respond to changes in variables**. For example will the business automatically adjust prices upwards by the rate of inflation, or will it try to hold prices? What will its competitors do? If raw material prices increase, will the business try to change suppliers? What effect will this have on payment patterns?

4.5 Changes in business variables

Economic variables will clearly impact upon business variables such as **sales volumes** or **profit margins**. Businesses need to be aware of the other factors, such as changes in the competitive environment that could affect these variables and how this effect might work. The original forecast should itself have been based on **demand forecasts,** determined by market surveys and statistical models based on past changes in demand. However, if factors such as taste change, businesses need to recognise this might not just require marginal changes in forecasts, but a re-visiting of the base data, since the changes will ultimately render the previous surveys or models redundant.

5 Financing requirements

Cash deficits will be funded in different ways, depending on whether they are short- or long-term. Businesses should have procedures for investing **surpluses** with appropriate levels of risk and return.

5.1 Deficiencies

Any forecast **deficiency** of cash will have to be funded.

(a) **Borrowing**. If borrowing arrangements are not already secured, a source of funds will have to be found. If a company cannot fund its cash deficits, it could be wound up.

(b) The firm can make arrangements to **sell any short-term marketable financial investments** to raise cash.

(c) The firm can delay payments to suppliers, or pull in payments from customers. This is sometimes known as **leading and lagging**.

Because cash forecasts cannot be entirely accurate, companies should have **contingency funding**, available from a surplus cash balance and liquid investments, or from a bank facility. The approximate size of the contingency margin will vary from company to company, according to the cyclical nature of the business and the approach of its cash planners.

Forecasting gives management time to arrange its funding. If planned in advance, instead of a panic measure to avert a cash crisis, a company can more easily choose when to borrow, and will probably obtain a lower interest rate.

5.2 Cash surpluses

Many cash-generative businesses are less reliant on high quality cash forecasts. If a **cash surplus** is forecast, having an idea of both its size and how long it will exist could help decide how best to invest it.

In some cases, the amount of **interest** earned from surplus cash could be significant for the company's earnings. The company might then need a forecast of its interest earnings in order to indicate its prospective **earnings per share** to stock market analysts and institutional investors.

6 Obtaining equity funds

FAST FORWARD

Companies seeking extra equity finance can obtain it by **retaining cash** in the business for investment or by **issuing shares**.

6.1 Retained profits

For many businesses, the cash needed to finance investments will be available because the earnings the business has made have been retained within the business, rather than paid out as dividends. We emphasised earlier that this interaction of investment, financing and dividend policy is the most important issue facing many businesses.

6.1.1 Advantages of using retentions

(a)   Retentions are a **flexible source** of finance; companies are not tied to specific amounts or specific repayment patterns.

(b)   Using retentions does **not involve** a **change in the pattern** of **shareholdings**.

6.1.2 Disadvantages of using retentions

(a)   As mentioned above, shareholders may be **sensitive** to the **loss of dividends** that will result from retention for re-investment, rather than paying dividends.

(b)   Not so much a disadvantage as a misconception, that retaining profits is a cost-free method of obtaining funds. There is an **opportunity cost** in that if dividends were paid, the cash received could be invested by shareholders to earn a return.

6.2 Ordinary (equity) shares

Key terms

> **Equity** is the issued ordinary share capital plus reserves, statutory and otherwise, which represent the investment in a company by the ordinary shareholders.
>
> **Equity share capital** is a company's issued share capital, less capital which carries preferential rights. Ordinary share capital normally comprises ordinary shares.

Ordinary (equity) shares are those of the owners of a company.

The ordinary shares of UK companies have a nominal or face value, typically £1 or 50p. Outside the UK, it is not uncommon for a company's shares to have no nominal value.

The market value of a quoted company's shares bears **no relationship** to their **nominal value**, except that when ordinary shares are issued for cash, the issue price must be equal to or (more usually) *more than* the nominal value of the shares.

6.3 Reasons for share issues

A new issue of shares might be made in a variety of different circumstances.

(a)   The company might want to **raise more cash**, for example, for expansion of its operations.

(b) The company might want to issue new shares, partly to raise cash but more importantly, to obtain a **stock market listing**. When a UK company is floated, for example, on the main stock market, it is a requirement of the Stock Exchange that at least a minimum proportion of its shares should be made available to the general investing public if the shares are not already widely held.

(c) The company might issue new shares to the shareholders of another company, in order to **take it over**.

7 Bank loans

FAST FORWARD

Bank loans tend to be a **source** of **medium-term finance**, linked with the purchase of specific assets. Interest and repayments will be set in advance.

7.1 Loans and overdrafts

Banks often provide term loans as medium or long-term financing for customers. The customer borrows a fixed amount and pays it back with interest over a period or at the end of it. This contrasts with an overdraft facility, when a customer, through its current account, can borrow money on a short-term basis up to a certain amount. Overdrafts are repayable on demand.

7.2 Loan or overdraft

A customer might ask the bank for an overdraft facility when the bank would wish to suggest a loan instead; alternatively, a customer might ask for a loan when an overdraft would be more appropriate.

(a) In most cases, when a customer wants finance to help with day-to-day trading and cash flow needs, an **overdraft** would be the **appropriate method** of financing. The customer should not be short of cash all the time, and should expect to be in credit in some days, but in need of an overdraft on others.

(b) When a customer wants to borrow from a bank for only a **short period of time**, even for the purchase of a major asset such as an item of plant or machinery, an overdraft facility might be more suitable than a loan, because the customer will stop paying interest as soon as the account goes into credit.

(c) When a customer wants to borrow from a bank, but cannot see its way to repaying the bank except over the course of a few years, the **medium- or long-term nature** of the financing is best catered for by the provision of a loan rather than an overdraft facility.

7.2.1 Advantages of an overdraft over a loan

(a) The customer only pays interest when it is overdrawn.

(b) The bank has the flexibility to review the customer's overdraft facility periodically, and perhaps agree to additional facilities, or insist on a reduction in the facility.

(c) An overdraft can do the same job as a loan: a facility can simply be renewed every time it comes up for review.

(d) Being short-term debt, an overdraft will not affect the calculation of a company's gearing.

7.2.2 Advantages of a loan over overdraft

(a) Both the customer and the bank **know exactly** what the repayments of the loan will be and how much interest is payable, and when. This makes planning (budgeting) simpler.

(b) The customer does not have to worry about the bank deciding to reduce or **withdraw** an overdraft facility before being in a position to repay what is owed. Overdrafts are normally **repayable on demand**. There is an element of 'security' or 'peace of mind' in being able to arrange a loan for an agreed term.

(c) Loans normally carry a **facility letter** setting out the precise terms of the agreement.

7.3 Bank loan or other loan capital

A choice businesses often have is whether to seek funding through a bank loan or through other types of loan capital.

7.3.1 Advantages of bank loan over other forms of loan capital

(a) **Flexibility**. It may be possible to alter the terms of the bank loan as the finance requirements of the company change.

(b) **Confidentiality**. Although the bank will require information, the customer will not have to fulfil the publicity requirements that an issue of loan stock on the financial markets would need.

(c) **Speed**. It will be rather quicker to arrange a bank loan than fulfilling all the requirements of a public issue.

(d) **Costs**. A bank loan will mean that the issue costs of loan stock are avoided.

7.3.2 Disadvantages of bank loan over other forms of loan capital

(a) **Restrictions**. Restrictions such as collateral and possible restrictive covenants are required, as opposed to none for certain types of loan capital.

(b) **Financial information**. Detailed financial information such as budgets and management accounts may have to be submitted periodically to the bank, whereas other lenders will not require information in this detail.

7.4 Time scale of loan

For purchases of a non-current asset, the **term of the bank loan should not exceed** the **economic or useful life** of the asset purchased with the money from the loan. A business manager will often expect to use the revenues earned by the asset to repay the loan, and obviously, an asset can only do this as long as it is in operational use.

8 Loan capital

8.1 Loan stock

FAST FORWARD

> The term **bonds** is used to mean the various forms of long-term debt a company may issue, such as loan stock, which may be **redeemable** or **irredeemable**.

ey term

> **Loan capital** (or loan stock) is made up of debentures and other long-term loans to a business.

Loan capital or stock has a **nominal value**, which is the debt owed by the company, and interest is paid at a stated **coupon** on this amount. For example, if a company issues 10% loan stock, the coupon will be 10% of the nominal value of the stock, so that $100 of stock will receive $10 interest each year. The rate quoted is the gross rate, before tax.

ey term

> **Stock** is an amount of fully paid up capital, any part of which can be transferred.

Unlike shares, debt is often issued **at par**, ie with $100 payable per $100 nominal value. Where the coupon rate is fixed at the time of issue, it will be set according to prevailing market conditions given the credit rating of the company issuing the debt. Subsequent changes in market (and company) conditions will cause the market value of the bond to fluctuate, although the coupon will stay at the fixed percentage of the nominal value.

9 The budgetary process

FAST FORWARD

> A budget is a short-term plan expressed in financial terms. It converts strategic plans into specific targets. Budgets help organisations as they promote forward thinking, assist in the co-ordination of different aspects of the organisation, motivate managers and provide a basis for systems of control and authorisation.

Exam focus point

> A question in the December 2013 exam focused partly on the benefits of introducing a formal budgeting process to address inaccurate forecasting at the company featured in the case study scenario. The examining team noted that many students failed to explain the benefits of budgeting in relation to the scenario. It is important that you relate your answer back to the information provided; otherwise you are in danger of producing a general response which attracts few, if any, marks.

9.1 Budgets, long-term plans and corporate objectives

Budgets are an important planning tool for the organisation and are directly related to the mission and objectives of an organisation.

A budget is a business plan for the short term, usually one year. It is likely to be expressed in financial terms and its role is to convert the strategic plans into specific targets. It therefore fits into the strategic planning process as follows.

- The mission sets the overall direction
- The strategic objectives illustrate how the mission will be achieved
- The strategic plans show how the objectives will be pursued
- The budgets represent the short term plans and targets necessary to fulfil the strategic objectives

These budgets will then have to be **controlled** to ensure the planned events actually occur. This is as much a part of the budgeting process as actually setting the budget.

A budget is a **plan,** not a forecast. You plan to meet the targets in the budget; a forecast is a prediction of future position. Forecasts are helpful to budget setters and planners.

A **periodic budget** is a budget covering a period, eg a year.

A **continual**, or **rolling budget**, is continually updated.

Different budgets are prepared for each specific aspect of the business, and the contents of the individual budgets are summarised in **master budgets**. The contents of each of the individual budgets affect, and are influenced by, the contents of the others; they are linked together.

The sales budget is usually the first budget prepared, as the level of sales determines the overall level of activity for the period.

Planning (including budgeting) is the responsibility of managers, not accountants. Although management accountants help by providing relevant information to managers and contributing to decision making.

9.2 Benefits of budgets

There are five main benefits of budgets.

(1)   **Promotes forward thinking.** Potential problems are identified early, therefore giving mangers time enough to consider the best way to overcome that problem.

(2)   **Helps to co-ordinate the various aspects of the organisation.** The activities of the various departments and sections of an organisation must be linked so that the activities complement each other.

(3) **Motivates performance.** Having a defined target can motivate managers and staff in their performance. Managers should be able to relate their own role back to the organisational objectives, seeing as the budgets are based on these objectives.

(4) **Provides a basis for a system of control.** Budgets provide a yardstick for measuring performance by comparing actual against planned performance.

(5) **Provides a system of authorisation.** Allows managers to spend up to a certain limit. Activities are allocated a fixed amount of funds at the discretion of senior management, thereby providing the authority to spend.

These five uses may, however, conflict with each other. For example, a budget used as a system of authorisation may motivate a manager to spend to the limit, even though this is wasteful. This is particularly likely where the budget cannot be rolled over into the next period. In addition to this, budgets have some other limitations that could potentially arise.

(1) Employees may be **demotivated** if they believe the budget to be unattainable.
(2) **Slack** may be built in by managers to make the budget more achievable.
(3) Focuses on the **short-term results** rather than the underlying causes.
(4) Unrealistic budgets may cause managers to make decisions that are **detrimental** to the company.

9.3 Using budgets for control

Budgets are useful for exercising **control** over an organisation as they provide a yardstick against which performance can be assessed. This means finding out where and why things did not go to plan, then seeking ways to put them right for the future.

If the budget is found to be unachievable, it may need to be revised. Only realistic budgets can form the basis for control, and therefore they should be adaptable.

Budgets enable managers to manage by exception, that is, focus on areas where things are not going to plan (ie the exceptions). This is done by comparing the actual performance to the budgets to identify the **variances.** We will look at variances later in this chapter.

9.4 Making budgetary control effective

Successful budgetary control systems tend to share the same common features.

- **Senior management** take the system seriously. They pay attention to and base decisions on, the monthly variance report. This attitude cascades down through the organisation.

- **Accountability.** There are **clear responsibilities** stating which manager is responsible for each business area.

- **Targets** are **challenging but achievable**. Targets set too high, or too low, would have a demotivating effect.

- **Established data collection, analysis and reporting routines** which involve looking at actual versus budgeted results to calculate and report variances. This should be done automatically on a monthly basis.

- **Targeted reporting**. Managers receive specific, rather than general purpose, reports so that they do not have to wade through information to find the relevant sections.

- **Short reporting periods**, usually a month, so that things can't go too wrong before they are picked up.

- **Timely reporting.** Variance reports should be provided to managers as soon as possible after the end of the reporting period. This is so they can take action to prevent the same problems occurring in the next reporting period.

- **Provokes action.** Simply reporting variances does not cause change. Managers have to act on the report to create change.

9.5 Behavioural aspects of budgets

Budgets can be very effective in motivating managers. In particular, budgets have been found to:

- Improve performance

- Be most effective when they are demanding, yet achievable; though if they are unrealistically demanding, performance may deteriorate

- Are most effective when the managers have participated in the setting of their own targets

 Performance Objective 14 focuses on your involvement with budgets in the workplace. It is likely that having an understanding of budgets will be a key part of your future career as an accountant. The ACCA highlight that two key components of this will involve:

- Planning, monitoring and controlling the use of business and financial resources

- Analysing, evaluating and reporting on the financial performance and position of entities from internally available data and information

10 Standard costing and variance analysis

FAST FORWARD

Standards represent targets against which actual performance is measured and provide the basis for variance analysis. Variance analysis involves comparing actual and planned performance, identifying the differences and investigating the reasons for the variances.

We have just seen that budgets are short-term business plans that are expressed mainly in financial terms. They are often constructed of **standards**. A **standard** is a **carefully predetermined quantity target** which can be **achieved in certain conditions**. Budgets and standards are **similar** in the following ways.

(a) They both involve looking to the future and **forecasting** what is likely to happen, given a certain set of circumstances.

(b) They are both **used for control purposes**. A budget aids control by setting financial targets or limits for a forthcoming period. Actual achievements or expenditures are then compared with the budgets and action is taken to correct any variances where necessary. A standard also achieves control by comparison of actual results against a predetermined target.

As well as being similar, **budgets and standards are interrelated**. For example, a standard unit production cost can act as the basis for a production cost budget. The unit cost is multiplied by the budgeted activity level to arrive at the budgeted expenditure on production costs.

There are, however, **important differences between budgets and standards**.

Budgets	Standards
Gives planned total aggregate costs for a function or cost centre	Shows the unit resource usage for a single task, for example, the standard labour hours for a single unit of production
Can be prepared for all functions, even where output cannot be measured	Limited to situations where repetitive actions are performed and output can be measured
Expressed in money terms	Need not be expressed in money terms. For example, a standard rate of output does not need a financial value put on it

10.1 Standard quantities and costs

A **standard cost** is an estimated unit cost.

Standard costing involves the establishment of predetermined estimates of the costs of products or services, the collection of actual costs and the comparison of the actual costs with the predetermined estimates. The predetermined costs are known as standard costs and the difference between the standard and the actual cost is known as a **variance**. The process by which the total difference between standard and actual results is analysed is known as **variance analysis**.

Although standard costing can be used in a variety of costing situations such as batch and mass production, process manufacture, jobbing manufacture (where there is standardisation of parts) and service industries (if a realistic cost per unit can be established), the greatest benefit from its use can be gained if there is a degree of repetition in the production process so that average or expected usage of resources can be determined. It is therefore most suited to mass production and repetitive assembly work and less suited to organisations which produce to customer demand and requirements.

Standard costing has two principal uses.

(a) To **value inventories and cost production** for cost accounting purposes. It is an alternative method of valuation to methods like FIFO and LIFO which you will have covered in your earlier studies.

(b) To act as a **control device** by establishing standards (expected costs) and comparing actual costs with the expected costs, thus highlighting areas of the organisation which may be out of control.

Standards are budgeted physical quantities and financial values for one unit of input or output. They represent targets against which actual performance is measured and provide the basis for **variance analysis**. Standards can be set as **ideal** standards or **practical** standards.

(a) **Ideal standards** assume no inefficiency due to defects, downtime and so on, in order to encourage employees to strive for excellence. Ideal standards can be seen as long-term targets but they are not very useful for day-to-day control purposes. Ideal standards cannot be achieved, so if such standards are used for budgeting, an allowance will have to be included to make the budget realistic and attainable.

(b) **Practical standards** demand a high level of efficiency but do not assume perfect conditions. They are intended to be challenging but achievable. The realistic nature of these standards may improve motivation. These standards can be used for product costing, cost control, inventory valuation, estimating and as a basis for budgeting.

Information necessary for developing standards can be gathered by analysing the tasks and processes involved to develop suitable estimates. Another approach is to use past data such as costs, times and usage for the same or similar products and use this as a basis for the estimates.

One problem that may arise when standards are developed is that the manager responsible for meeting the standard is often involved in its development. This may mean that an element of slack is built into the standard in order to make it easier to achieve.

Standards are often used to measure routine processes. When the same process is carried out time and time again, a learning-curve effect tends to occur. This is because routine tasks are performed more quickly with experience. Although the speed of performing the task improves, standards often remain unchanged for many years. This effect must be taken into account, both when setting standards and when interpreting labour efficiency variances. For example, large adverse variances in the labour efficiency may be more likely if the process, or member of staff concerned, is new.

Standards are useful in providing data for income measurement and pricing decisions and there are a number of benefits for the control function of an organisation that can be achieved through the use of standards.

- Carefully planned standards are an aid to more accurate budgeting

- Standard costs provide a yardstick against which actual costs can be measured

- The setting of standards involves determining the best materials and methods which may lead to economies
- A target of efficiency is set for employees to reach and cost-consciousness is stimulated
- Variances can be calculated which enable the principle of 'management by exception' to be operated. Only the variances which exceed acceptable tolerance limits need to be investigated by management with a view to control action
- Standard costs and variance analysis can provide a way of motivation to managers to achieve better performance. However, care must be taken to distinguish between controllable and non-controllable costs in variance reporting

However, standards also have their limitations, particularly in modern manufacturing environments. The two main problems are that they do not provide a **useful basis** for exercising control (for instance ,where inappropriate action is taken to obtain favourable variances), and they **may not achieve their aim of motivating managers**. Indeed, standards set too highly can have a demotivating effect if they are not perceived to be achievable. Despite these problems, standards are still used widely.

10.2 Variance analysis

When actual performance is compared to standards and budgeted amounts, there will inevitably be **variances**. They may be favourable or adverse, depending on whether they result in an increase to, or a decrease from, the budgeted profit figure.

10.2.1 Sales variances

Sales volume variance is the difference between the original and flexed budget profit figures. This is an important variance because losing sales generally means losing profit as well. If it has the effect of making profit lower than budgeted, it is **adverse**; if it makes profit higher than budgeted, it is **favourable**.

Sales price variance is the difference between actual sales revenue and actual volume at the standard sales price. Higher sales prices (if all else remains constant) means an increase in profit.

10.2.2 Materials variances

Total direct materials variance is the difference between the actual and direct materials cost and the direct materials cost according to the flexed budget. If the actual material cost is higher than budget, it has an adverse effect on profit.

Direct materials usage variance is the difference between actual usage and budgeted usage for the actual volume of output, multiplied by the standard materials cost. If actual usage is higher than budgeted usage, then there will be an adverse effect on profit.

Direct materials price variance is the difference between actual materials cost and the actual usage multiplied by the standard materials cost. Again, if actual costs are higher than those budgeted, there will be an adverse effect on profit.

10.2.3 Labour variances

Total direct labour variance is the difference between the actual direct labour cost and the direct labour cost according to the flexed budget. If more is spent on labour than was budgeted, there will be an adverse effect on profit.

Direct labour efficiency variance is the difference between the actual labour time and budgeted time, for the actual volume of output, multiplied by the standard labour rate. It looks at the actual versus the budgeted number of hours used to produce the output. If actual time is greater than budgeted time, the effect on the profit will be adverse. The faster people work, the more profit can be made.

Direct labour rate variance is the difference between the actual labour cost and the actual labour time multiplied by the standard labour rate. This means it compares the actual cost of the hours worked against the anticipated cost based on a standard hour. Where actual costs exceed the standard, profit will be adversely affected.

10.2.4 Fixed overhead variances

Fixed overhead spending variance is the difference between the actual and budgeted spending on fixed overheads. Higher than budgeted overheads lead to less profit, so have an adverse effect.

10.2.5 Example: Flexible budgets and budgetary control

Penny manufactures a single product, the Darcy. Budgeted results and actual results for May are as follows.

	Budget	Actual	Variance
Production and sales of the Darcy (units)	7,500	8,200	
	$	$	$
Sales revenue	75,000	81,000	6,000 (F)
Direct materials	22,500	23,500	1,000 (A)
Direct labour	15,000	15,500	500 (A)
Production overhead	22,500	22,800	300 (A)
Administration overhead	10,000	11,000	1,000 (A)
	70,000	72,800	2,800 (A)
Profit	5,000	8,200	3,200 (F)

Note. (F) denotes a favourable variance and (A) an unfavourable or adverse variance.

In this example, the variances are meaningless for the purposes of control. All costs were higher than budgeted but the volume of output was also higher; it is to be expected that actual variable costs would be greater those included in the fixed budget. However, it is not possible to tell how much of the increase is due to **poor cost control** and how much is due to the **increase in activity**.

Similarly, it is not possible to tell how much of the increase in sales revenue is due to the increase in activity. Some of the difference may be due to a difference between budgeted and actual selling price but we are unable to tell from the analysis above.

For control purposes, we need to know the answers to questions such as the following:

● Were actual costs higher than they should have been to produce and sell 8,200 Darcys?
● Was actual revenue satisfactory from the sale of 8,200 Darcys?

Instead of comparing actual results with a fixed budget which is based on a different level of activity to that actually achieved, the correct approach to budgetary control is to compare actual results with a budget which has been **flexed** to the actual activity level achieved.

Suppose that we have the following estimates of the behaviour of Penny's costs:

(a)   Direct materials and direct labour are variable costs.

(b)   Production overhead is a semi-variable cost, the budgeted cost for an activity level of 10,000 units being $25,000.

(c)   Administration overhead is a fixed cost.

(d)   Selling prices are constant at all levels of sales.

Solution

The **budgetary control analysis** should therefore be as follows.

	Fixed budget	Flexible budget	Actual results	Variance
Production and sales (units)	7,500	8,200	8,200	
	$	$	$	$
Sales revenue	75,000	82,000 (W1)	81,000	1,000 (A)
Direct materials	22,500	24,600 (W2)	23,500	1,100 (F)
Direct labour	15,000	16,400 (W3)	15,500	900 (F)
Production overhead	22,500	23,200 (W4)	22,800	400 (F)
Administration overhead	10,000	10,000 (W5)	11,000	1,000 (A)
	70,000	74,200	72,800	1,400 (F)
Profit	5,000	7,800	8,200	400 (F)

Workings

1   Selling price per unit = $75,000 / 7,500 = $10 per unit

Flexible budget sales revenue = $10 × 8,200 = 482,000

2   Direct materials cost per unit = $22,500 / 7,500 = $3

Budget cost allowance = $3 × 8,200 = $24,600

3   Direct labour cost per unit = $15,000 / 7,500 = $2

Budget cost allowance = $2 × 8,200 = $16,400

4   Variable production overhead cost per unit = $(25,000 − 22,500)/(10,000 − 7,500)

= $2,500/2,500 = $1 per unit

∴ Fixed production overhead cost = $22,500 − (7,500 × $1) = $15,000

∴ Budget cost allowance = $15,000 + (8,200 × $1) = $23,200

5   Administration overhead is a fixed cost and hence budget cost allowance = $10,000

Comment

(a)   In selling 8,200 units, the expected profit should have been, not the fixed budget profit of $5,000, but the flexible budget profit of $7,800. Instead, actual profit was $8,200 ie $400 more than we should have expected.

One of the reasons for this improvement is that, given output and sales of 8,200 units, the cost of resources (material, labour etc) was $1,400 lower than expected.

These total cost variances can be analysed to reveal how much of the variance is due to lower resource prices and how much is due to efficient resource usage.

(b)   The sales revenue was, however, $1,000 less than expected because a lower price was charged than budgeted.

We know this because flexing the budget has eliminated the effect of changes in the volume sold, which is the only other factor that can affect sales revenue. You have probably already realised that this variance of $1,000 (A) is a **selling price variance**.

The lower selling price could have been caused by the increase in the volume sold (to sell the additional 700 units the selling price had to fall below $10 per unit). We do not know if this is the case but without flexing the budget we could not know that a different selling price to that budgeted had been charged. Our initial analysis above had appeared to indicate that sales revenue was ahead of budget.

The difference of $400 between the flexible budget profit of $7,800 at a production level of 8,200 units and the actual profit of $8,200 is due to the net effect of cost savings of $1,400 and lower than expected sales revenue (by $1,000).

The difference between the original budgeted profit of $5,000 and the actual profit of $8,200 is the total of the following.

(a) The savings in resource costs/lower than expected sales revenue (a net total of $400 as indicated by the difference between the flexible budget and the actual results).

(b) The effect of producing and selling 8,200 units instead of 7,500 units (a gain of $2,800 as indicated by the difference between the fixed budget and the flexible budget). This is the **sales volume contribution variance**.

A **full variance analysis statement** would be as follows.

	$	$
Fixed budget profit		5,000
Variances		
Sales volume	2,800 (F)	
Selling price	1,000 (A)	
Direct materials cost	1,100 (F)	
Direct labour cost	900 (F)	
Production overhead cost	400 (F)	
Administration overhead cost	1,000 (A)	
		3,200 (F)
Actual profit		8,200

If management believes that any of the variances are large enough to justify it, they will investigate the reasons for their occurrence to see whether any corrective action is necessary.

10.3 Reasons for variances

Variances may occur for a number of reasons. One possible reason is that the budget itself was not realistic. Unless they are achievable, budgets are not a useful method of control. However, there are many other reasons why variances may arise, as shown by the table below.

Variance	Possible reason for variance
Sales volume	Poor performance by sales staff
	Deterioration in market conditions between the time that the budget was set and the actual event
	Lack of goods or services to sell as a result of a production problem
Sales price	Poor performance by sales staff
	Deterioration in market conditions between the time that the budget was set and the actual event
Direct materials usage	Poor performance by production department staff, leading to high rates of scrap
	Substandard materials, leading to high rates of scrap
	Faulty machinery, causing high rates of scrap
Direct materials price	Poor performance by the buying department staff
	Using higher quality material than was planned
	Change in market conditions between the time the budget was set and the actual event

Variance	Possible reason for variance
Direct labour efficiency	Poor supervision
	A worker with a low skill grade taking longer to do the work than was envisaged for the correct skill grade
	Low-grade materials, leading to high levels of scrap and wasted labour time
	Problems with a customer for whom a service is being rendered
	Problems with machinery, leading to labour time wasted
	Dislocation of materials supply, leading to workers being unable to proceed with production
Direct labour rate	Poor performance by the human resources department
	Using a higher grade of worker than was planned
	Change in labour market conditions between the time of setting the budget and the actual event
Fixed overhead spending	Poor supervision of overheads
	General increase in costs of overheads not taken into account in the budget

Exam focus point

It is important that you are able to use flexed budgets and variance analysis in order to help you identify where problems lie in an organisation.

Also notice that adverse variances may not necessarily indicate problems. For example, consider a publishing company who has an adverse variance against their print budget (actual costs higher than budgeted costs). While this could indicate a problem in the printing processes, it could equally just be due to their being a greater demand for books, causing more books to be sold and therefore higher print costs to be incurred.

10.4 Investigating variances

Finding out why variances have occurred can be expensive. Reports and other information have to be scrutinised and discussions with individuals and groups may have to be carried out. Sometimes production may even have to be stopped.

Given the cost of investigating, and the number of small variances that will inevitably occur (hitting a target precisely is unlikely), organisations need a policy relating to which variances will be investigated and which will be accepted.

Knowing the reason for a variance is useful to help management bring things back under control and enables future targets to be met. In general, the following rules are useful.

- Significant **adverse** variances should be investigated as, if it continues to occur, it could become very costly

- Significant **favourable** variances should be investigated but with lower priority than for adverse variances. It may turn out that the target set was too low

- Insignificant variances should be kept under review. Although the individual variance may be insignificant, the cumulative effect (over time, or when considered along with related insignificant variances) may not be. In such cases, and investigation may be worthwhile

10.5 Limitations of control through variances and standards

Standards and variances are useful for decision making but they have limited application. For example, where spending is discretionary, such as for advertising or human resource development, there is no direct link between inputs and outputs. There are also potential problems when applying standard costing techniques.

(a) Standards can quickly become **out of date**. Regularly monitoring and updating standards can be costly and time consuming.

(b) Variances for which a manager is held accountable can be influenced by factors that are **out of the control** of that manager.

(c) **Lines of responsibility** between managers can be difficult to define.

(d) Once a standard has been met, there is **no incentive to improve**.

(e) May encourage undesirable behaviour, such as encouraging managers to build up excess inventories, leading to significant storage and financing costs. This could happen if managers exploit opportunities for bulk purchase discounts to attain a favourable direct materials price variance.

11 Probability, expected values and decision trees

FAST FORWARD

> Probability is a measure of likelihood, and expected values are weighted average values based on probabilities. These calculations and values are incorporated into decision trees to illustrate the possible choices and outcomes of decisions.

Decision trees can be very helpful tools for making strategic and operational decisions. Each branch of the tree represents the different outcomes that may occur. In order for the decision tree to be useful, each outcome should be assigned a probability and expected value. This is so that we can evaluate how likely each outcome is to occur, and what will be achieved, should that outcome actually occur. Let us first recap the basic concepts of probability and expected values before we go on to look at how these can assist decision making by incorporating them into decision trees.

11.1 Probability

Probability is a measure of **likelihood** and can be stated as a percentage, a ratio, or more usually, as a number from 0 to 1. It is a measure of the likelihood of an event happening in the long run, or over a large number of times.

$$\text{Probability of achieving the desired result} = \frac{\text{Number of ways of achieving desired result}}{\text{Total number of possible outcomes}}$$

Mutually exclusive outcomes are outcomes where the occurrence of one of the outcomes excludes the possibility of any of the others happening. For example, you can't roll one dice and score both 5 and 6 simultaneously.

The probability of mutually exclusive events occurring can be calculated by adding the probabilities together. For example, the probability of rolling a dice and scoring either a five or a six can be determined by adding together the probability of rolling 5 and the probability of rolling 6.

1/6 + 1/6 = 2/6

Independent events are events where the outcome of one event in no way affects the outcome of the other events. For example, simultaneously rolling a dice and tossing a coin. The probability of throwing a 5 and getting heads on the coin can be found by multiplying the probabilities of the two individual events.

1/6 × 1/2 = 1/12

The **general rule of addition** for two events, A and B, which are not mutually exclusive, is as follows.

Probability of (A or B) = P (AUB) = P(A) + P(B) − P(A and B)

For example, in a standard pack of 52 playing cards, what is the probability of selecting an ace or a spade?

Ace = 4/52
Spade = 13/52
Ace of spades = 1/52

Therefore, the probability of selecting an ace or a spade is:

4/52 + 13/52 − 1/52 = 16/52 = 4/13

Dependent or **conditional** events are events where the outcome of one event depends on the outcome of the others. The probability of two dependent events occurring is calculated by **multiplying** the individual probabilities together. **Contingency** tables can be useful for dealing with conditional probability.

For example, the probability of rolling a six, followed by another six is:

$1/6 \times 1/6 = 1/36$

Probability is used to help calculate **risk** in decision making. The higher the probability of an event occurring, the lower the associated risk will be.

Risk involves situations or events which may or may not occur, but whose probability of occurrence can be calculated statistically and the frequency predicted.

Uncertainty involves situations or events whose outcome cannot be predicted with statistical confidence.

11.2 Expected values

An **expected value** (or **EV**) is a weighted average value, based on probabilities. The expected value for a single event can offer a helpful guide for management decisions.

Although the outcome of a decision may not be certain, there is some likelihood that probabilities could be assigned to the various possible outcomes from an analysis of previous experience.

If the probability of an outcome of an event is p, then the expected number of times that this outcome will occur in n events (the expected value) is equal to n × p.

The concepts of probability and expected value are vital in **business decision making**. The expected values for single events can offer a helpful guide for management decisions.

- A project with a positive EV should be accepted
- A project with a negative EV should be rejected
- When choosing between options the alternative which has the **highest EV of profit** (or the **lowest EV of cost**) should be selected.

Where probabilities are assigned to different outcomes, we can evaluate the worth of a decision as the **expected value**, or weighted average, of these outcomes. The principle is that when there are a number of alternative decisions, each with a range of possible outcomes, the optimum decision will be the one which gives the highest expected value.

Expected values can be built into decision trees in order to aid decision making. The amount of expected profit is likely to be conditional on the result of various decisions. We will look at this in more detail below. First, let us briefly consider some limitations of using expected values as a basis for decisions.

11.2.1 Limitations of expected values

Evaluating decisions by using expected values has a number of limitations.

(a) The **probabilities** used when calculating expected values are likely to be estimates. They may therefore be **unreliable** or **inaccurate**.

(b) Expected values are **long-term averages** and may not be suitable for use in situations involving one-off decisions. They may therefore be useful as a **guide** to decision making.

(c) Expected values do not consider the **attitudes to risk** of the people involved in the decision-making process. They do not, therefore, take into account all of the factors involved in the decision.

(d) The time value of money may not be taken into account: $100 now is worth more than $100 in ten years' time.

Probabilities and expected values can be represented diagrammatically using **decisions trees** in order to aid decision making.

Exam focus point

An article titled 'Strategic planning in an age of turbulence' written by Ken Garrett is available in the technical articles for P3 on the ACCA website. The article explores issues faced by organisations operating in unpredictable environments. Consideration is given to the practical approaches management can use when making decisions. The usefulness of decision trees is covered in some depth. It would be worth taking the time to study this article.

11.3 Structure of decision trees   12/12

Exam focus point

A Section B question in the December 2012 exam required students to develop a decision tree from the information provided and discuss the implications and shortcomings of using decision trees in strategic decision making. The examining team commented that this question was not the most popular when it was attempted. However, a significant number of students appeared to be confident in constructing and interpreting decision trees.

Decision trees are diagrams which illustrate the choices and possible outcomes of a decision.

A **decision tree** is a pictorial method of showing a sequence of interrelated decisions and their expected outcomes. Decision trees can incorporate both the probabilities of, and values of, expected outcomes.

Decision trees provide a clear and logical approach to problem solving by:

- Showing all possible **choices** as **branches** on the tree
- Showing all possible **outcomes** as **subsidiary branches** on the tree

Decision trees begin with a decision point, usually represented by a square, and the various choices branch off from this, flowing from left to right.

If the outcome for any of those choices is certain, then the branch of the decision tree for that alternative is complete.

If the outcome of a particular choice is uncertain, then the various possible outcomes must be shown. This is done by inserting an **outcome point** on the branch. This is symbolised by a circle. Each possible outcome will then branch out from that outcome point. These are known as **subsidiary branches**.

The **probability** of each outcome occurring should be written on the branch of the tree that represents that outcome.

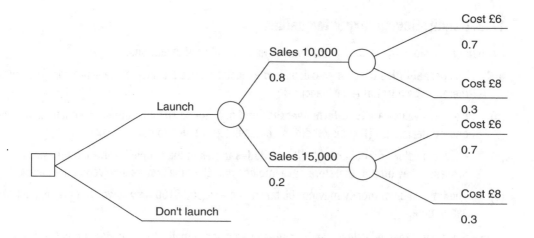

Sometimes, a **decision taken now** will lead to **other decisions** being taken in the future. When this situation arises, the decision tree can be drawn as a **two-stage tree**, as shown below.

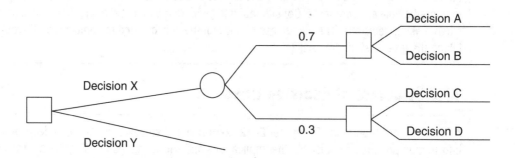

In this tree, a choice between A and B, or else a choice between C and D will be made, depending on the outcome which occurs after choosing X.

The decision tree should be in chronological order from left to right.

11.3.1 Evaluating decisions with a decision tree

The EV of each decision option can be evaluated, using the decision tree to help with keeping the logic properly organised. The basic rules are as follows.

(a)   We start on the **right hand side** of the tree and **work back** towards the left hand side and the current decision under consideration. This is sometimes known as the **rollback technique** or **rollback analysis**.

(b)   Working from **right to left**, we calculate the **EV of revenue, cost, contribution or profit** at each outcome point on the tree.

Consider the below decision tree which has been prepared for a new product that has been developed. The decision is whether the new product should be test marketed or abandoned. The outcomes are high, medium or low demand and are dependent on whether the result of the test marketing is positive or negative.

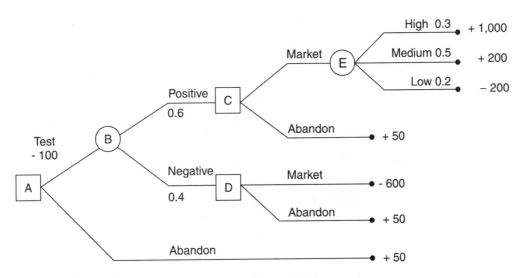

The right-hand-most outcome point is point E, and the EV is as follows.

	Profit X $'000	Probability p	px $'000
High	1,000	0.3	300
Medium	200	0.5	100
Low	(200)	0.2	(40)
		EV	360

This is the EV of the decision to market the product if the test shows a positive response. It may help you to write the EV on the decision tree itself, at the appropriate outcome point (point E).

(a) **At decision point C**, the **choice** is as follows.

   (i) Market, EV = + 360 (the EV at point E)
   (ii) Abandon, value = + 50

   The choice would be to market the product, and so the EV at decision point C is +360.

(b) **At decision point D**, the **choice** is as follows.

   (i) Market, value = – 600
   (ii) Abandon, value = +50

   The choice would be to abandon, and so the EV at decision point D is +50.

The second stage decisions have therefore been made. If the original decision is to test market, the company will market the product if the test shows positive customer response, and will abandon the product if the test results are negative.

The evaluation of the decision tree is completed as follows.

(a) **Calculate the EV at outcome point B.**

   0.6×360 (EV at C)
   + 0.4×50 (EV at D)
   = $216 + 20 = 236$.

(b) **Compare the options at point A**, which are as follows.

   (i) Test: EV = EV at B minus test marketing cost = 236 – 100 = 136
   (ii) Abandon: Value = 50

The choice would be to test market the product, because it has a **higher EV of profit**.

Evaluating decisions by using a decision tree has a number of limitations:

- The time value of money may not be taken into account
- Decision trees are not suitable for use in complex situations

- The outcome with the highest EV may have the greatest risks attached to it. Managers may be reluctant to take risks which may lead to losses
- The probabilities associated with different branches of the tree are likely to be estimates, and possibly unreliable or inaccurate

12 Evaluating strategic options using marginal and relevant costing techniques

FAST FORWARD

Relevant costs and marginal costing are useful when evaluating strategic options including accepting/rejecting special contracts, efficient use of scarce resources, make or buy decisions, and closing or continuation decisions.

12.1 Costs, output and breakeven

12.1.1 Fixed costs

Fixed costs are costs that do not change, no matter how many units of a product are produced. Staff costs are generally fixed costs. They will only change if there is a significant change in demand and the organisation decides to expand or scale back based on this and change its staffing requirement accordingly. 'Fixed' therefore usually relates to the short and medium term.

Fixed costs are affected by inflation and are almost always time-based, ie they vary with the length of time concerned.

12.1.2 Variable costs

Variable costs are costs that vary with the volume of activity; as production increases, so does the amount of variable cost incurred.

Some costs have an element of both fixed and variable costs. These are called **semi-fixed** or **semi-variable** costs. Telephones are a good example where a fixed line rental and a charge per minute are charged.

12.1.3 Breakeven analysis

The breakeven point occurs where total sales revenue equals total costs. The below chart shows the relationship between the different kinds of costs, revenue, profits and losses.

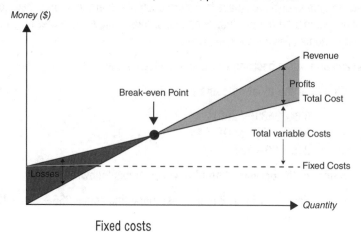

Break-even point: $\dfrac{\text{Fixed costs}}{\text{Sales revenue per unit} - \text{variable costs per unit}}$

The bottom part of this formula, sales revenue-variable costs, is known as the **contribution per unit.**

The **margin of safety** is the extent to which the planned volume of output or sales lies about the breakeven point.

BPP
LEARNING MEDIA

The relationship between contribution and fixed costs is known as **operational gearing**. An activity with high fixed costs compared with its variable costs is said to have high operational gearing. Increasing the level of gearing makes profits more sensitive to changes in the volume of activity.

12.1.4 Popularity and weaknesses of breakeven analysis

Breakeven analysis provides useful insights into the relationship between an organisation's fixed costs, variable costs and level of activity. It is a widely-used and popular planning tool.

There are, however, three main problems associated with breakeven analysis.

- **Non-linear relationships**. Breakeven assumes linear (straight line) relationships. This is unlikely in real life

- **Stepped fixed costs**. Most fixed costs are not fixed over **all** volumes of activity and are more likely to be stepped

- **Multi-product businesses**. Most businesses offer more than one product or service. It may be hard to identify which fixed costs belongs to which product, and the effect that the sale of one product may have on the sales of another

12.2 Marginal analysis

When an organisation is trying to decide between two or more possible courses of action, only **costs that vary with the decision** should be included in the decision analysis, ie it should only consider **relevant costs**.

When making these decisions, the key strategic objective should be the enhancement of shareholder wealth. As these decisions are short-term, the wealth will normally be increased by trying to generate as much net cash inflow as possible.

As fixed costs are ignored, **marginal cost** (the cost of producing one additional unit) usually equals the variable cost per unit. This will be true unless there is a step in the fixed costs, in which case that step, or increment, will be included as well as the variable costs.

Marginal analysis is useful in four key areas of decision making:

- Accepting/rejecting special contracts
- Determining the most efficient use of scarce resources
- Make-or-buy decisions
- Closing or continuation decisions

12.2.1 Accepting/rejecting special contracts

Marginal analysis can be used to decide whether or not a special contract should be accepted by determining the contribution (revenue less cost) that the price offered would yield. Positive contributions suggest the organisation would be better off accepting, rather than rejecting, the special contract.

However, there will also be other factors that are difficult, or impossible, to quantify which will also have to be considered before a final decision is made. For example, the contract itself may have a negative contribution, but it may lead to further more lucrative contracts, or help the organisation enter a new market.

12.2.2 Example: Picture This

Picture This Ltd makes photo frames. The fixed costs of operating the workshop for a month is $600. Each frame requires materials that cost $2.40. Each frame takes one hour to make, and the frame-makers

are paid $12 per hour. They are employed on a contract basis, so they are only paid if they work. The frames are sold wholesale for $16.80.

The frame-makers currently have some spare time available and an overseas retail chain has offered the business an order of 400 frames at a price of $15.60 each.

Without considering the wider issues, should the business accept the order?

Solution

The fixed costs are not relevant to this decision as they will be incurred regardless of whether or not the contract is accepted.

To determine whether the contract should be rejected or accepted, we must establish whether it would make a contribution

	$	
Additional revenue per unit	15.60	
Additional cost per unit	14.40	(12 + $2.40)
Additional contribution per unit	**1.20**	

For 400 extra units, the additional contribution will be (400 × $1.20) $480.

Since no additional fixed costs are incurred, the business will be $480 better off by accepting, rather than refusing, this contract.

12.2.3 Efficient use of scarce resources

Usually output is restricted by level of demand, rather than by the organisation's ability to produce. However, sometimes there is a limit to the amount that can be produced due to a scarce (limiting) factor, such as labour, space or machinery.

The most profitable combination of products will occur where the **contribution per unit of the scarce factor** is maximised.

12.2.4 Example: Scarce resources

A business makes three different products, as follows:

Product	A	B	C
Selling price per unit ($)	20	25	23
Variable cost per unit ($)	10	8	12
Weekly demand (units)	25	20	30
Machine time per unit (hours)	4	3	4

Fixed costs are not affected by the choice of product because all three products use the same machine. Machine time is limited to 148 hours a week.

Which combination of products should be manufactured if the business is to produce the highest profit?

Solution

	A	B	C
Selling price per unit ($)	25	20	23
Variable cost per unit ($)	(10)	(8)	(12)
Contribution per unit ($)	**15**	**12**	**11**
Machine time per unit	4 hours	3 hours	4 hours
Contribution per machine hour	$3.75	$4.00	$2.75
Order of priority	2nd	1st	3rd

Therefore produce:

20 units of product B using	60 hours
22 units of product A using	88 hours
	148 hours

This leaves unsatisfied the market demand for a further three units of product A and 30 units of product C.

12.2.5 Make or buy decisions

6/11

A common decision faced by businesses is whether to produce the product or service they sell themselves or whether to buy it from another business. Marginal costing can help with this by identifying the contribution of both options. As with accepting or rejecting contract decisions. However, there will be other factors that the organisation will have to take into account when making this decision. These other factors include loss of control of quality, potential unreliability of supply, and access to expertise and specialisation.

12.2.6 Example: Shark Ltd

Shark Ltd needs a component for one of its products. It can purchase the components from Ray Ltd, a subcontractor) for $20 each, or it can produce them internally for total variable costs of $15 per component. Shark Ltd has the spare capacity available.

Should the component be produced internally or subcontracted to Ray Ltd?

Solution

Shark Ltd should produce the component internally as this is $5 per unit cheaper than contracting out to Ray Ltd.

Question	Shark and Ray

How would the answer to the above differ if Shark Ltd had no spare capacity and could only produce the component internally by reducing its output of another of its products. Shark Ltd will lose contributions of $12 from the other product.

Answer

The relevant cost of internal production in this case would be

	$
Variable cost of production of the component	15
Opportunity cost of lost production of the other product	12
	27

In this case, Shark Ltd would subcontract the component to Ray Ltd as this would be $7 per unit cheaper than it would cost to produce the components internally.

12.2.7 Closing or continuation decisions

Many organisations produce separate financial statements for each department or section in order to attempt to assess the relative effectiveness of each one. By using these to look at the variable costs, the contribution for each can be determined. This means the organisation can determine the contribution to the overall organisation that the individual departments make. Departments that make a positive

contribution should not be closed even if individually it makes a loss. This is because the fixed costs would still be incurred and the organisation would be worse off without it.

12.2.8 Example: MogTown

MogTown Ltd is a retail shop with three departments, all located in the same premises. The three departments occupy similar sized areas of the premises. The results for the year that has just ended are as follows:

	Total $'000	Cat Food $'000	Cat Toys $'000	Cat Furniture $'000
Sales revenue	534	254	183	97
Costs	(482)	(213)	(163)	(106)
Profit/(loss)	52	41	20	(9)

This suggests that if the cat furniture department was closed, the company as a whole would be $9,000 more profitable per year.

However, when the fixed and variable costs are analysed, the contribution of each department can be determined. This gives the following results:

	Total $'000	Cat Food $'000	Cat Toys $'000	Cat Furniture $'000
	534	254	183	97
Variable costs	(344)	(167)	(117)	(60)
Contribution	190	87	66	37
Fixed costs (eg rent)	(138)	(46)	(46)	(46)
Profit/(loss)	52	41	20	(9)

This shows the cat furniture department actually makes a **positive contribution** of $37,000 and should not be closed. (Closing this department would make the company as a whole $37,000 **worse** off per year). The fixed costs would continue to be incurred, whether or not the department is closed.

13 Full costing

Full cost is the total amount sacrificed to achieve a particular objective. All running costs of a particular facility are part of the cost of output of that facility. Where there is more than one product, costs are split into direct and indirect costs. The direct costs are easily assigned to products. To determine the full cost a fair proportion of the indirect costs, or overheads, must also be allocated to each product.

Full cost is the total amount sacrificed to achieve a particular objective. It includes all amounts sacrificed, so all costs related to the production of the product or provision of the service would be included as part of the full cost.

Full costing works on the basis that all the costs of running a particular facility, eg a factory, are part of the cost of the output of that facility. For example, the rent is unlikely to change if we produce one more unit of the product. The cost per unit will therefore decrease as output increases and therefore is an important element of the cost of each unit of output.

Full costing is widely used in practice and can be a useful tool for assisting managers in decision making. It can be helpful in a number of ways, including:

Pricing and output decisions: full cost information allows managers to make decisions based on the price charged to the customer and the number of units required.

Exercising control: budgets are typically prepared on a full-cost basis and so actual performance based on full costs can be easily compared to the plans to identify, and take measures to address, any discrepancies between actual and planned performance.

Assessing relative efficiency: full costs can allow managers to compare their current processes with the cost of alternative methods of working, or the cost of operating in a different location. This can give managers an insight into the most efficient way of operating and so provide a basis for decisions related to the processes to be followed, or the location of a plant.

Assessing performance: Profit and income are important performance measures for an organisation and provide a basis for many decisions for managers. To measure profit, or income, the sales revenue needs to be compared to the associated expenses. One major expense will be the cost of making the product or service itself, ie the full cost.

13.1 Multi-product businesses

If a business has only one product or service, calculating the full cost is very straightforward. It involves simply adding together all the costs of production incurred during a period and dividing the total by the total number of units of output for the period.

However, most businesses produce more than one type of product or service and the units of output will therefore not be identical. Simply summing the costs and dividing by the number of units of output to get a cost per unit would not be reasonable in this situation.

Where the units of output are not identical, the first step is to separate the costs into **direct costs** and **indirect costs**.

Direct costs are costs that can be measured in respect of each particular unit of output, such as materials or labour. Collecting the direct costs can be easily done via a cost-recording system that is capable of capturing the cost of direct materials used on the job and the cost, based on the hourly rate and hours worked, of direct workers.

Indirect costs or **overheads** are all the other costs. They can't be directly measured in respect of each particular unit of output, eg rent, or utility bills.

Identifying the full cost per unit of output where the units of output differ is known as **job costing**.

To calculate the cost of a particular unit of output (job), we first identify the direct costs, and then charge each unit with a share of indirect costs, ie the overhead costs are **absorbed**. For this reason, full costing is also referred to as **absorption costing**.

Indirect costs, by definition, cannot be directly related to specific cost units. This raises the question of **how** such costs should be allocated to individual cost units or products.

13.2 Overhead apportionment

There is no 'correct' way to allocate overheads to particular jobs; by their very nature, overheads to do not directly relate to individual jobs. As long as the method used is acceptable to those who use the full-cost derived from it, then that method is suitable; the aim is simply to provide useful information to decision makers.

The best method for apportioning overheads, therefore, is the one which results in the provision of the most useful information. However, this can be difficult to assess.

The choice of an absorption basis is a matter of judgement and common sense. There are no strict rules or formulae involved. But the basis should realistically reflect the characteristics of a given cost centre, avoid undue abnormalities, and be 'fair'. The choice will be significant in determining the cost of individual products, but the total cost of production overheads is the budgeted overhead expenditure, no matter what basis of absorption is selected. It is the relative share of overhead costs borne by individual products and jobs which is affected by the basis of absorption.

The basis on which overheads are charged to jobs should remain consistent. If a different basis is used for different jobs, then either total overheads will not be fully charged to the jobs, or the jobs will be overcharged with overheads. Therefore, the objective of full costing – to charge all overheads to jobs done

- will not be achieved. If selling prices are based on full costs, this also may mean that the organisation does not charge high enough prices to cover all of its costs.

13.2.1 Dealing with overheads on a departmental basis

Although it is not possible to charge overheads to different jobs on different bases, it is possible to charge one segment of the total overheads on one basis and another segment on another basis. In practice, this is usually done by dividing a business into separate areas for costing purposes and charging overheads differently from one area to the next, according to the nature of work done there.

All but the smallest organisations are generally divided into departments for a number of reasons:

- It is more practical. Most businesses are too complex and large to be managed as a single unit

- Each department has its own area of expertise and is managed by a specialist

- Each department can have its own accounting records enabling the performance of that department to be assessed

Where costs are dealt with departmentally, each department is known as a **cost centre**. This is a function, activity, or physical area for which costs are separately identified.

The total overheads of the business must be divided between the departments, such that the sum of the departmental overheads is equal to the total overheads for the entire business.

The departments then charge all of their overheads to their specific jobs and so, between them, the departments will charge all of the overheads of the business to individual jobs.

13.2.2 Batch costing

An approach known as **batch costing** is used when the production of the good or service involves producing a batch of identical, or nearly identical, units of output, but where each batch is significantly different from the other batches. The cost for the batch is derived using a job-costing basis and this is divided by the number of units in the batch to determine the cost for each cost unit.

13.2.3 Predicting full costs in advance

Although full costs can only be calculated after the work has been done, they are often predicted in advance. This is often for the sake of pricing (eg car repair quote) where it is necessary to set the price before the customer will accept the job. This is often done even where no particular customer has been identified. Where the outcome is different to that originally predicted, corrections will have to be made to the full costs calculated.

13.3 Activity Based Costing

FAST FORWARD

Activity based costing (ABC) is an alternative to the traditional method of full costing. It involves the identification of the factors which cause the costs of an organisation's major activities. Support overheads are charged to products on the basis of their usage of the factor causing the overheads.

The traditional cost accumulation system of absorption costing was developed in a time when most organisations produced only a narrow range of products (so products underwent similar operations and consumed similar proportions of overheads). Also, overheads were only a very small fraction of total costs, because direct labour and direct material costs accounted for the largest proportion of the costs.

In addition, labour was at the heart of production with machinery only really used to support direct labour, so the market was relatively uncompetitive (due to limited transport links and technology), and the costs of information processing were high. The benefits of a more accurate system of overhead allocation would probably have been relatively small.

The world of industrial production has now fundamentally changed. Machines are at the heart of much production, a high proportion of costs are now made up of overheads (direct labour may now only account for as little as 5% of a product's cost), and organisations operate within a highly competitive international market. It therefore now appears difficult to justify the use of direct labour or direct material as the basis for absorbing overheads or to believe that errors made in attributing overheads will not be significant.

Traditional costing systems, which assume that all products consume all resources in proportion to their production volumes, tend to allocated too great a proportion of overheads to high volume products (which cause relatively little diversity and hence use fewer support services) and too small a proportion of overheads to low volume products (which cause greater diversity and use more support services). Activity based costing (ABC) attempts to overcome this problem.

> **Activity based costing (ABC)** involves the identification of the factors which cause the costs of an organisation's major activities. Support overheads are charged to products on the basis of their usage of the factor causing the overheads.

The major ideas behind activity based costing are as follows.

(a) **Activities cause costs**. Activities include ordering, materials handling, machining, assembly, production scheduling and despatching.

(b) **Producing products creates demand for the activities.**

(c) Costs are assigned to a product **on the basis of the product's consumption of the activities.**

The principal idea of ABC is to focus attention on **what causes costs to increase,** ie the **cost drivers**.

The **costs that vary with production volume**, such as power costs, should be traced to products using production **volume-related cost drivers**, such as direct labour hours or direct machine hours.

Overheads which do not vary with output but **with some other activity** should be traced to products using **transaction-based cost drivers**, such as number of production runs and number of orders received.

13.3.1 Cost Pools

ABC establishes separate cost pools for support activities such as despatching. As the costs of these activities are assigned directly to products through cost driver rates, reapportionment of service department costs is avoided.

Cost pools are similar to cost centres, except each cost pool is likely to relate to a particular **activity**, rather than being more general, as is the case with cost centres in traditional product costing.

13.3.2 ABC and service industries

ABC is perhaps even more relevant to the service industry than it is to manufacturing. This is because the lack of direct materials may mean an even greater proportion of costs are made up of overheads. Evidence suggests that ABC has been more widely adopted by service organisations rather than manufacturers.

13.3.3 ABC and decision making

Many of ABC's supporters claim that it can assist with decision making in a number of ways.

- Provides accurate and reliable cost information
- Establishes a long-run product cost
- Provides data which can be used to evaluate different ways of delivering business. It is therefore particularly suited to the following types of decision:
  - Pricing
  - Promoting or discontinuing products or parts of the business
  - Redesigning products and developing new products or new ways to do business

Note, however, that an ABC cost is **not a true cost** - it is **simply an average cost** because some costs, such as depreciation are still arbitrarily allocated to products. An ABC cost is therefore **not a relevant cost** for all decisions.

The traditional cost behaviour patterns of fixed cost and variable cost are felt by advocates of ABC to be **unsuitable** for longer-term decisions, when resources are not fixed, and changes in the volume or mix of business can be expected to have an impact on the cost of all resources used, not just short-term variable costs.

13.3.4 Criticisms of ABC

It has been suggested by critics that **activity based costing has some serious flaws**.

(a) Some measure of (arbitrary) cost apportionment may still be required at the cost pooling stage for items like rent, rates and building depreciation.

(b) Can a single cost driver explain the cost behaviour of all items in its associated pool?

(c) Unless costs are caused by an activity that is measurable in quantitative terms and which can be related to production output, cost drivers will not be usable. What drives the cost of the annual external audit, for example?

(d) ABC is sometimes introduced because it is fashionable, not because it will be used by management to provide meaningful product costs or extra information. If management is not going to use ABC information, an absorption costing system may be simpler to operate.

(e) The cost of implementing and maintaining an ABC system can exceed the benefits of improved accuracy.

(f) **Implementing** ABC is often problematic.

13.4 Criticisms of full (absorption) costing methods

Both the traditional and ABC methods of full costing have been criticised as they tend to use past (historic) costs, which could be considered to be irrelevant. This is because it is only possible to make decisions about the future, not about the past.

14 Ratio analysis   12/12, 6/12, 12/11, 6/10, 12/09, 6/09

Exam focus point

A Section B question in the December 2012 exam required candidates to evaluate whether the organisation featured in the scenario was able to fund its expansion using internally generated sources of finance. Candidates were expected to use the financial information provided in the scenario to support their answers by calculating a selection of appropriate ratios.

An article titled 'Performance appraisal' written by Bobbie Retallack is available in the technical articles section for P3 on the ACCA website. It would be worth taking the time to study this article.

FAST FORWARD

Ratios provide a means of systematically analysing financial statements. They can be grouped under the headings **profitability**, **liquidity**, **gearing** and **shareholders' investment**. It is important to calculate **relevant ratios** and to take into account the **limitations** of ratio analysis.

14.1 Uses of ratio analysis

Businesses carry out ratio analysis in order to **measure the progress of the enterprise** and of individual subsidiaries, so that managers know how well the company concerned is doing. The financial situation of a company will also obviously affect its share price. Is the company profitable? Is it growing? Does it have satisfactory liquidity? Is its gearing level acceptable? What is its dividend policy?

The key to obtaining meaningful information from ratio analysis is **comparison**: comparing ratios over time within the same business to establish whether the business is improving or declining, and comparing ratios between similar businesses to see whether the company you are analysing is better or worse than average within its own business sector.

A vital element in effective ratio analysis is understanding the **needs of the person** for whom the ratio analysis is being undertaken. **Investors,** for example, will be interested in the **risk and return** relating to their investment, so will be concerned with dividends, market prices, level of debt versus equity and so on. **Suppliers** and banks who have given loans are interested in receiving the payments due to them, so will want to know how liquid the business is. **Managers** are interested in ratios that indicate how well the business is being run, and also how the business is doing in relation to its **competitors**.

<exam focus
oint>

Try not to be too mechanical when working out ratios, and think constantly about what you are trying to achieve. You will only obtain credit in the exam for calculating ratios that are relevant.

The compulsory question in the December 2013 exam required students to consider whether a company specialising in the sale of small electrical machines and tools to trade and domestic customers should acquire a similar entity based overseas. The question provided students with key financial data relating to the acquisition target as well as data regarding the post-acquisition performance of two entities which the company had purchased previously.

The examining team commented that a significant number of students did not make enough use of this data, tending to use it superficially and failing to use the numbers to tell the story of each organisation's performance. Students were confident in calculating basic ratios, but failed to go further and expand on the practical considerations of acquiring an overseas target, eg the company lacked experience in operating in a foreign country.

It is therefore critical that you apply the financial data provided and make the numbers 'talk' as this provides you with evidence to support the practical points you raise.

14.2 Limitations of ratio analysis

Although ratio analysis can be a very useful technique, it is important to realise its limitations.

(a) **Availability of comparable information** - When making comparisons with other companies in the industry, industry averages may hide **wide variations** in figures. Figures for similar companies may provide a better guide, but then there are problems identifying which companies are similar, and obtaining enough detailed information about them.

(b) **Use of historical/out-of-date information** -Comparisons with the previous history of a business may be of limited use, if the business has recently undergone, or is about to undergo, **substantial changes**. In addition, ratios based on published accounts suffer from the disadvantage that these accounts are filed some months after the end of the accounting period. Comparisons over time may also be distorted by **inflation**, leading to assets being stated at values that do not reflect replacement costs, and revenue increasing for reasons other than more sales being made.

(c) **Ratios are not definitive** - Ideal levels vary industry by industry, and even they are not definitive. Companies may be able to exist without any difficulty with ratios that are rather worse than the industry average.

(d) **Need for careful interpretation** - For example, if comparing two businesses' liquidity ratios, one business may have higher levels. This might appear to be good, but further investigation might reveal that the higher ratios are a result of higher inventory and receivable levels which are a result of poor working capital management by the business with the better ratios.

(e) **Manipulation** - Any ratio including profit may be distorted by **choice of accounting policies**. For smaller companies, working capital ratios may be distorted, depending on whether a big customer pays, or a large supplier is paid, before or after the year-end.

(f) **Ratios lack standard form** - For example, when calculating **gearing,** some companies will include bank overdrafts; others exclude them.

Bear these limitations in mind when calculating and interpreting ratios, as the examiners' reports give many examples of misapplication of ratio analysis, and over-simplistic and misleading interpretations.

Financial data will frequently be provided in the exam, particularly in Question 1, but the examiner's reports indicate not enough use is made of it. Relatively easy marks are often available for calculating and interpreting ratios. However, make sure that you do *interpret* the data. You will not get many marks for simply extracting data that is immediately obvious from the scenario - for example, stating that net profit before tax has increased.

14.3 Broad categories of ratios

Ratios can be grouped into the following four categories:

- Profitability and return
- Debt and gearing
- Liquidity: control of cash and other working capital items
- Shareholders' investment ratios (or stock market ratios)

The **Du Pont** system of ratio analysis involves constructing a pyramid of interrelated ratios like that below.

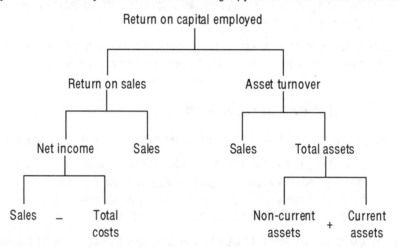

Such **ratio pyramids** help in providing for an overall management plan to achieve profitability, and allow the interrelationships between ratios to be checked.

Although you will have encountered most or all of the ratios that we are about to define before, make sure you know how to calculate them in the exam. One suggestion is to list all the ratios you need to know on a single sheet of paper and go through that sheet repeatedly, until you are confident you can calculate all the ratios.

14.4 Profitability and return: the return on capital employed (ROCE)

A company ought of course to be profitable, and obvious checks on **profitability** are:

- Whether the company has made a profit or a loss on its ordinary activities
- By how much this year's profit or loss is bigger or smaller than last year's profit or loss

It is impossible to assess profits or profit growth properly without relating them to the amount of funds (the capital) employed in making the profits. An important profitability ratio is therefore **return on capital employed (ROCE)**, which states the profit as a percentage of the amount of capital employed. **Profit** is usually taken as profit on ordinary activities before interest and taxation (PBIT), and **capital employed** is shareholders' capital plus long-term liabilities and debt capital. This is the same as total assets less current liabilities.

The underlying principle is that we must compare like with like, and so if capital means share capital and reserves plus long-term liabilities and debt capital, profit must mean the profit earned by all this capital together. This is PBIT, since interest is the return for loan capital.

$$\text{Thus ROCE} = \frac{\text{(PBIT)}}{\text{Capital employed}}$$

$$\text{Capital employed} = \begin{array}{l} \text{Shareholders' funds plus current liabilities plus} \\ \text{any long-term provisions for liabilities and charges.} \end{array}$$

14.4.1 Evaluating the ROCE

What does a company's ROCE tell us? What should we be looking for? There are three comparisons that can be made.

(a) The **change** in ROCE from one year to the next

(b) The **ROCE** being **earned** by other companies, if this information is available

(c) A comparison of the ROCE with **current market borrowing rates**

    (i) What would be the cost of extra borrowing to the company if it needed more loans, and is it earning an ROCE that suggests it could make high enough profits to make such borrowing worthwhile?

    (ii) Is the company making an ROCE which suggests that it is making profitable use of its current borrowing?

14.5 Analysing profitability and return in more detail: the secondary ratios

We may analyse the ROCE, to find out why it is high or low, or better or worse than last year. There are two factors that contribute towards a return on capital employed, both related to turnover.

14.5.1 Profit margin

A company might make a high or a low profit margin on its sales. For example, a company that makes a profit of 25c per $1 of sales is making a bigger return on its turnover than another company making a profit of only 10c per $1 of sales.

The profit margin can be calculated both in terms of gross profit margin and net profit margin. They do not necessary indicate the same thing.

14.5.2 Example: Profit margin

A company has the following summarised income statements for two consecutive years.

	Year 1	Year 2
	$	$
Turnover	70,000	100,000
Less cost of sales	42,000	55,000
Gross profit	28,000	45,000
Less expenses	21,000	35,000
Net profit	7,000	10,000

Although the net profit margin is the same for both years at 10%, the gross profit margin is not.

$$\text{Year 1} \ \frac{28,000}{70,000} = 40\% \qquad\qquad \text{Year 2} \ \frac{45,000}{100,000} = 45\%$$

Is this good or bad for the business?

Solution

An increased profit margin must be good because this indicates a wider gap between selling price and cost of sales. Given that the net profit ratio has stayed the same in the second year, however, expenses must be rising. In year 1, expenses were 30% of turnover, whereas in year 2 they were 35% of turnover. This indicates that administration, selling and distribution expenses or interest costs require tight control.

Percentage analysis of profit between year 1 and year 2

	Year 1	Year 2
	%	%
Cost of sales as a % of sales	60	55
Gross profit as a % of sales	40	45
	100	100
Expenses as a % of sales	30	35
Net profit as a % of sales	10	10
Gross profit as a % of sales	40	45

14.5.3 Asset turnover

Asset turnover is a measure of how well the assets of a business are being used to generate sales. For example, if two companies each have capital employed of $100,000, and company A makes sales of $400,000 a year, whereas company B makes sales of only $200,000 a year, company A is making a higher turnover from the same amount of assets. This will help company A to make a higher return on capital employed than company B.

Profit margin and asset turnover together explain the ROCE, and if the ROCE is the primary profitability ratio, these other two are the secondary ratios. The relationship between the three ratios is as follows.

Profit margin × Asset turnover = ROCE

$$\frac{PBIT}{Sales} \times \frac{Sales}{Capital\,employed} = \frac{PBIT}{Capital\,employed}$$

It is also worth commenting on the **change in turnover** from one year to the next. Strong sales growth will usually indicate volume growth as well as turnover increases due to price rises, and **volume growth** is one sign of a prosperous company.

14.6 Debt and gearing ratios

Debt ratios are concerned with how much the company **owes in relation to its size** and whether it is getting into heavier debt or improving its situation.

(a)   When a company is heavily in debt, and seems to be getting even more heavily into debt, banks and other would-be lenders are very soon likely to refuse further borrowing and the company might well find itself in trouble.

(b)   When a company is earning only a **modest profit** before interest and tax, and has a **heavy debt burden**, there will be very little profit left over for shareholders after the interest charges have been paid.

14.6.1 The debt ratio

The **debt ratio** is the **ratio** of a **company's total debts** to its **total assets**.

(a)   **Assets** consist of non-current assets at their balance sheet value, plus current assets.
(b)   **Debts** consist of all payables, whether current or non-current.

You can ignore long-term provisions and liabilities, such as deferred taxation.

There is no absolute rule on the **maximum safe debt ratio**, but as a very general guide, you might regard 50% as a safe limit to debt. In addition, if the debt ratio is over 50% and getting worse, the company's debt position will be worth looking at more carefully.

The following example shows the effect that gearing has on a business.

Example:

Suppose that two companies are identical in every respect, except for their gearing. Both have assets of $20,000 and both make the same operating profits (profit before interest and tax: PBIT). The only difference between the two companies is that Nonlever Co is all-equity financed and Lever Co is partly financed by debt capital, as follows:

	Nonlever Co	Lever Co
	$	$
Assets	20,000	20,000
10% Bonds	0	(10,000)
	20,000	10,000
Ordinary shares of $1	20,000	10,000

Because Lever has $10,000 of 10% bonds it must make a profit before interest of at least $1,000 in order to pay the interest charges. Nonlever, on the other hand, does not have any minimum PBIT requirement because it has no debt capital. A company, which is lower geared, is considered less **risky** than a higher geared company because of the greater likelihood that its PBIT will be high enough to cover interest charges and make a profit for equity shareholders.

14.6.2 Capital gearing

Capital gearing is concerned with the amount of debt in a company's **long-term** capital structure. **Gearing ratios** provide a long-term measure of liquidity.

$$\text{Gearing ratio} = \frac{\text{Prior charge capital (long-term debt)}}{\text{Prior charge capital} + \text{equity (shareholders' funds)}}$$

Prior charge capital is long-term loans and preferred shares (if any). It does not include loans repayable within one year and bank overdraft, unless overdraft finance is a permanent part of the business's capital.

14.6.3 Operating gearing

Operating gearing measures the proportion of fixed costs to total costs. High operating gearing means that a high proportion of cost is fixed. This has implications for business risk in that if turnover falls, there is little automatic relief in the reduction of variable costs. Operating gearing can be calculated as

$$\frac{\text{Contribution}}{\text{PBIT}}$$

14.6.4 Interest cover

The **interest cover** ratio shows whether a company is earning enough profits before interest and tax to pay its interest costs comfortably, or whether its interest costs are high in relation to the size of its profits, so that a fall in profit before interest and tax (PBIT) would then have a significant effect on profits available for ordinary shareholders.

$$\text{Interest cover} = \frac{\text{PBIT}}{\text{Interest charges}}$$

An interest cover of 2 times or less would be low, and it should really exceed 3 times before the company's interest costs can be considered to be within acceptable limits. Note that it is usual to exclude preference dividends from interest charges.

14.6.5 Cash flow ratio

The **cash flow ratio** is the ratio of a company's net annual cash inflow to its total debts:

$$\frac{\text{Net annual cash inflow}}{\text{Total debts}}$$

(a) **Net annual cash inflow** is the amount of cash which the company has coming into the business each year from its operations. This will be shown in a company's statement of cash flows for the year.

(b) **Total debts** are short-term and long-term payables, together with provisions for liabilities and charges.

Obviously, a company needs to earn enough cash from operations to be able to meet its foreseeable debts and future commitments, and the cash flow ratio, and changes in the cash flow ratio from one year to the next, provides a useful indicator of a company's cash position.

14.7 Liquidity ratios: cash and working capital

Profitability is, of course, an important aspect of a company's performance, and debt or gearing is another. Neither, however, addresses directly the key issue of liquidity. **A company needs liquid assets so that it can meet its debts when they fall due.**

Liquidity is the amount of cash a company can obtain quickly to settle its debts (and possibly to meet other unforeseen demands for cash payments too). **Liquid funds** consist of:

(a) **Cash.**

(b) **Short-term investments for which there is a ready market,** such as investments in shares of other companies. (Short-term investments are distinct from investments in shares in subsidiaries or associated companies.)

(c) **Fixed term deposits** with a bank or building society, for example, six month deposits with a bank.

(d) **Trade receivables.** These are not cash, but ought to be expected to pay what they owe within a reasonably short time.

(e) **Bills of exchange receivable.** Like ordinary trade receivables, these represent amounts of cash due to be received soon.

If an analysis of a company's published accounts is to give us some idea of the company's liquidity, profitability ratios are not going to be appropriate for doing this. Instead, we look at **liquidity ratios** and **working capital turnover ratios.**

Liquidity ratios

The **current ratio** is defined as:

$$\frac{\text{Current assets}}{\text{Current liabilities}}$$

In practice, a current ratio comfortably in excess of 1 should be expected, but what is comfortable varies between different types of businesses.

The **quick ratio**, or **acid test ratio**, is:

$$\frac{\text{Current assets less inventory}}{\text{Current liabilities}}$$

This ratio should ideally be at least 1 for companies with a slow inventory turnover. For companies with a fast inventory turnover, a quick ratio can be less than 1 without suggesting that the company is in cash flow difficulties.

An excessively large current/quick ratio may indicate a company that is **over-investing in working capital**, suggesting poor management of receivables or inventories by the company.

We can calculate **turnover periods** for inventory, receivables and payables (receivables and payables days). If we add together the inventory days and the receivables days, this should give us an indication of how soon inventory is convertible into cash. Both receivables days and inventory days therefore give us a further indication of the company's liquidity.

14.7.1 Example: Ratios

Calculate liquidity and working capital ratios from the accounts of a manufacturer of products for the construction industry, and comment on the ratios.

	20X8 $m	20X7 $m
Revenue	2,065.0	1,788.7
Cost of sales	1,478.6	1,304.0
Gross profit	586.4	484.7
Current assets		
Inventory	119.0	109.0
Receivables (note 1)	400.9	347.4
Short-term investments	4.2	18.8
Cash at bank and in hand	48.2	48.0
	572.3	523.2
Current liabilities		
Loans and overdrafts	49.1	35.3
Corporation taxes	62.0	46.7
Dividend	19.2	14.3
Payables (note 2)	370.7	324.0
	501.0	420.3
Net current assets	71.3	102.9

Notes

		20X8 $m	20X7 $m
1	Trade receivables	329.8	285.4
2	Trade payables	236.2	210.8

Solution

	20X8	20X7
Current ratio	$\dfrac{572.3}{501.0} = 1.14$	$\dfrac{523.2}{420.3} = 1.24$
Quick ratio	$\dfrac{453.3}{501.0} = 0.90$	$\dfrac{414.2}{420.3} = 0.99$
Receivables' payment period	$\dfrac{329.8}{2,065.0} \times 365 = 58$ days	$\dfrac{285.4}{1,788.7} \times 365 = 58$ days
Inventory turnover period	$\dfrac{119.0}{1,478.6} \times 365 = 29$ days	$\dfrac{109.0}{1,304.0} \times 365 = 31$ days
Payables' turnover period	$\dfrac{236.2}{1,478.6} \times 365 = 58$ days	$\dfrac{210.8}{1,304.0} \times 365 = 59$ days

As a manufacturing group serving the construction industry, the company would be expected to have a comparatively lengthy receivables' turnover period, because of the relatively poor cash flow in the construction industry. It is likely that the company compensates for this by ensuring that they do not pay for raw materials and other costs before they have sold their inventories of finished goods (hence the similarity of receivables' and payables' turnover periods).

The company's current ratio is quite low, but we do not know what the industry average is. It is possible that this position is comfortable for the construction industry.

The quick ratio is only a little lower than the current ratio. This suggests that inventory levels are strictly controlled, which is reinforced by the low inventory turnover period.

14.8 Stock market ratios

The final set of ratios to consider are those which help equity shareholders and other investors to assess the value and quality of an investment in the ordinary shares of a company.

We shall then consider their significance in the analysis of performance.

$$\text{Dividend yield} = \frac{\text{Dividend per share}}{\text{Market price per share}}$$

$$\text{Interest yield} = \frac{\text{Interest payable}}{\text{Market value of loan stock}}$$

$$\text{Earnings per shares} = \frac{\text{Profit after tax, extraordinary items and preference dividends}}{\text{Number of equity shares in issue and ranking for dividend}}$$

$$\text{Price/Earnings ratio} = \frac{\text{Market value per share}}{\text{Earnings per share}}$$

$$\text{Dividend cover} = \frac{\text{Earnings available for distribution to ordinary shareholders}}{\text{Actual dividend for ordinary shareholders}}$$

Investors are interested in:

- The value (market price) of the securities that they hold
- The return that the security has obtained in the past
- Expected future returns
- Whether their investment is reasonably secure

14.8.1 Dividend and interest yields

In practice, we usually find with quoted companies that the **dividend yield** on shares is less than the interest yield on debentures and loan stock (and also less than the yield paid on gilt-edged securities). The share price generally rises in most years, giving shareholders **capital gains**. In the long run, **shareholders** will want the **return on their shares**, in terms of **dividends received** plus **capital gains**, to exceed the return that investors get from fixed interest securities.

14.8.2 Earnings per share (EPS)

EPS is widely used as a measure of a company's performance and is of particular importance in comparing results over a period of several years. A company must be able to sustain its earnings in order to pay dividends and re-invest in the business so as to achieve future growth. Investors also look for **growth** in the EPS from one year to the next.

Example: Earnings per share

Walter Wall Carpets Co made profits before tax in 20X8 of $9,320,000. Tax amounted to $2,800,000.

The company's share capital is as follows.

	$
Ordinary share (10,000,000 shares of $1)	10,000,000
8% preference shares	2,000,000
	12,000,000

Required

Calculate the EPS for 20X8.

	$
Profits before tax	9,320,000
Less tax	(2,800,000)
Profits after tax	6,520,000
Less preference dividend (8% of $2,000,000)	(160,000)
Earnings	6,360,000
Number of ordinary shares	10,000,000

EPS   63.6c

EPS must be seen in the context of several other matters.

(a)   EPS is used for **comparing the results** of a company over time. Is EPS growing? What is the rate of growth? Is the rate of growth increasing or decreasing?

(b)   Is there likely to be a significant **dilution** of EPS in the future, perhaps due to the exercise of share options or warrants, or the conversion of convertible loan stock into equity?

(c)   EPS should not be **used blindly** to compare the earnings of one company with another. For example, if A plc has an EPS of 12c for its 10,000,000 10c shares and B plc has an EPS of 24c for its 50,000,000 25c shares, we must take account of the numbers of shares. When earnings are used to compare one company's shares with another, this is done using the P/E ratio or perhaps the earnings yield.

(d)   If EPS is to be a reliable basis for comparing results, it must be **calculated consistently**. The EPS of one company must be directly comparable with the EPS of others, and the EPS of a company in one year must be directly comparable with its published EPS figures for previous years. Changes in the share capital of a company during the course of a year cause problems of comparability.

Note that EPS is a figure based on **past data**, and it is easily manipulated by changes in accounting policies and by mergers or acquisitions.

14.8.3 Price/earnings ratio

The P/E ratio is, simply, a measure of the relationship between the **market value** of a company's shares and the **earnings** from those shares.

The value of the P/E ratio reflects the market's appraisal of the shares' future prospects. In other words, if one company has a higher P/E ratio than another, it is because investors either expect its earnings to **increase faster** than the other's or consider that it is a **less risky** company or in a more secure industry.

One approach to assessing what share prices ought to be, which is often used in practice, is a P/E ratio approach:

(a)   The relationship between the EPS and the share price is **measured** by the **P/E ratio**.

(b)   There is no reason to suppose, in normal circumstances, that the P/E ratio will vary much over time.

(c)   So if the EPS goes up or down, the share price should be expected to move up or down too, and the new share price will be the new EPS multiplied by the constant P/E ratio.

For example, if a company had an EPS last year of 30c and a share price of $3.60, its P/E ratio would have been 12. If the current year's EPS is 33c, we might expect that the P/E ratio would remain the same, 12, and so the share price ought to go up to 12 × 33c = $3.96.

Changes in the P/E ratios of companies over time will depend on several factors.

(a)   If **interest rates go up**, investors will be attracted away from shares and into debt capital. Share prices will fall, and so P/E ratios will fall.

(b)   If **prospects** for **company profits improve**, share prices will go up, and P/E ratios will rise. Share prices depend on expectations of future earnings, not historical earnings, and so a change in prospects, perhaps caused by a substantial rise in international trade, or an economic recession, will affect prices and P/E ratios.

(c)   **Investors' confidence** might be changed by a variety of circumstances, such as:

   (i)   The prospect of a change in government
   (ii)   The prospects for greater exchange rate stability between currencies

14.8.4 The dividend cover

The dividend cover is the number of times the actual dividend could be paid out of current profits and indicates:

(a)   The **proportion** of distributable profits for the year that is being **retained** by the company

(b)   The level of **risk** that the company will **not be able to maintain the same dividend** payments in future years, should earnings fall

A high dividend cover means that a high proportion of profits are being retained, which might indicate that the company is investing to achieve earnings growth in the future.

15 Comparison of accounting figures

Ratio analysis often forms the basis of comparisons of performance over time or with other organisations.

15.1 Results of the same company over successive accounting periods

Useful comparisons over **time** include:

- **Percentage growth** in **profit** (before and after tax) and percentage growth in turnover
- **Increases or decreases** in the **debt ratio** and the gearing ratio
- **Changes** in the **current ratio**, the inventory turnover period and the receivables' payment period
- **Increases** in the **EPS**, the dividend per share, and the market price

The principal advantage of making comparisons over time is that they give some indication of progress: are things getting better or worse? However, there are some weaknesses in such comparisons.

(a)   The effect of **inflation** should not be forgotten.

(b)   The progress a company has made needs to be set in the context of **what other companies have done**, and whether there have been any **special environmental or economic influences** on the company's performance.

15.1.1 Allowing for inflation

Ratio analysis is not usually affected by **price inflation**, except as follows.

(a)   **Return on capital employed** (ROCE) can be misleading if non-current assets, especially property, are valued at **historical cost net of depreciation** rather than at current value. As time goes by and if property prices go up, the non-current assets would be seriously undervalued if they were still recorded at their historical cost.

(b)   Some growth trends can be misleading, in particular, the **growth in sales turnover**, and the **growth in profits or earnings**.

15.2 Comparisons between different companies in the same industry

Making comparisons between the results of different companies in the same industry is a way of assessing which companies are outperforming others.

(a) Even if two companies are in the **same broad industry** (for example, retailing) they might not be direct competitors. Even so, they might still be expected to show **broadly similar performance** in terms of growth.

(b) If two companies are **direct competitors**, a comparison between them would be particularly interesting.

Comparisons between companies in the same industry can help investors to rank them in order of desirability as investments, and to judge relative share prices or future prospects. It is important, however, to make comparisons with caution: **a large company and a small company in the same industry might be expected to show different results**, not just in terms of size, but in terms of:

(a) **Percentage rates of growth** in sales and profits

(b) **Percentages of profits re-invested -** Dividend cover will be higher in a company that needs to retain profits to finance investment and growth.

(c) **Non-current assets** - Large companies are more likely to have freehold property in their statement of financial position than small companies.

15.3 Comparisons between companies in different industries

Useful information can also be obtained by comparing the financial and accounting ratios of companies in different industries. An investor ought to be aware of how companies in one industrial sector are performing in comparisons with companies in other sectors. For example, it is important to know:

(a) Whether sales growth and profit growth is higher in **some industries** than in others (For example, how does growth in the financial services industry compare with growth in heavy engineering, electronics or leisure?)

(b) How the **return on capital employed** and **return on shareholder capital compare** between different industries

(c) How the **P/E ratios and dividend** yields vary between industries

Chapter Roundup

- The role of the finance function and finance professional is changing. Today's finance professional is expected to take on a broader advisory and strategic role. This gradual evolution has given rise to the notion of the finance function acting as a **business partner**, where finance professionals share their finance expertise with operational teams. Furthermore, the **hybrid accountant** is now regarded as the modern model of an accountant in business, where they act as internal consultants and business analysts.

  A large part of the modern accountant's role is to work closely with the business to improve **strategic decision making** to enhance the business' ability to create value. This, however, does present some challenges for traditional accounting systems.

  Strategic management accounting is a form of management accounting in which emphasis is placed on information about factors which are external to the organisation, as well as non-financial and internally generated information.

  The role of the **strategic management accountant** covers **financial analysis, planning and control.**

  A strategic management accounting system (SMAS) should:

  - Aid strategic decisions
  - Close the communication gap between accountants and managers
  - Identify the type of decision
  - Offer appropriate financial performance indicators
  - Distinguish between economic and managerial performance
  - Provide relevant information
  - Separate committed from discretionary costs
  - Distinguish discretionary from engineered costs
  - Use standard costs strategically
  - Allow for changes over time

- In commercial organisations, managing for value is about creating shareholder value, while in the public sector, it is about obtaining value for money. Managers must understand the key cost and value drivers affecting their operations. Financial risk is determined exclusively by gearing, but there are several sources of business risk. Financial risk may be balanced against business risk, so that overall risk is managed.

- In seeking to attain the financial objectives of the organisation or enterprise, a financial manager has to make decisions on the following subjects.

  - Investment
  - Financing
  - Dividends

  These three policy areas interact and decision makers must also manage the interactions.

- **Cash forecasting** should ensure that sufficient funds will be available when needed, to sustain the activities of an enterprise at an acceptable cost.

- As part of a business's risk analysis, different forecasts should be prepared with **changing financial** or **business variables**. The links between these variables and the figures in the forecasts may not be straightforward.

- **Cash deficits** will be funded in different ways, depending on whether they are short- or long-term. Businesses should have procedures for investing **surpluses** with appropriate levels of risk and return.

- Companies seeking extra equity finance can obtain it by **retaining cash** in the business for investment or **issuing shares**.

- Bank loans tend to be a **source** of **medium-term finance**, linked with the purchase of specific assets. Interest and repayments will be set in advance.

Chapter Roundup (Cont'd)

- The term **bonds** describes various forms of long-term debt a company may issue, such as loan stock, which may be **redeemable** or **irredeemable**.

- A budget is a short-term plan expressed in financial terms. It converts strategic plans into specific targets. Budgets help organisations as they promote forward thinking, assist in the co-ordination of different aspects of the organisation, motivate managers and provide a basis for systems of control and authorisation.

- Standards represent targets against which actual performance is measured and provide the basis for variance analysis. Variance analysis involves comparing actual and planned performance, identifying the differences and investigating the reasons for the variances.

- Probability is a measure of likelihood, and expected values are weighted average values based on probabilities. These calculations and values are incorporated into decision trees to illustrate the possible choices and outcomes of decisions.

- Relevant costs and marginal costing are useful when evaluating strategic options including accepting/rejecting special contracts, efficient use of scarce resources, make or buy decisions, and closing or continuation decisions.

- Full cost is the total amount sacrificed to achieve a particular objective. All running costs of a particular facility are part of the cost of output of that facility. Where there is more than one product, costs are split into direct and indirect costs. The direct costs are easily assigned to products. To determine the full cost, a fair proportion of the indirect costs, or overheads, must also be allocated to each product.

- **Activity based costing (ABC)** is an alternative to the traditional method of full costing. It involves the identification of the factors which cause the costs of an organisation's major activities. Support overheads are charged to products on the basis of their usage of the factor causing the overhead.

- **Ratios** provide a means of systematically analysing financial statements. They can be grouped under the headings **profitability**, **liquidity**, **gearing** and **shareholders' investment**. It is important to calculate **relevant ratios** and to take into account the **limitations** of **ratio analysis**.

- **Ratio analysis** often forms the basis of comparisons with performance over time or with other companies.

Quick Quiz

1   What do JS&W consider to be the three main issues in strategic finance?

2   What is the name of the type of risk associated with gearing?

3   How might a company fund a forecast cash deficiency?

4   What are the advantages of using retained profits as a source of equity funds?

5   What is loan capital?

6   What is the formula for capital employed used in the ROCE calculation?

7   What is operating gearing?

8   Is inflation relevant to the calculation of ROCE?

Answers to Quick Quiz

1   Managing for value; funding; financial expectations of stakeholders

2   Financial risk

3   By borrowing; by selling marketable investments; and by managing cash flows to payables and from receivables

4   Retained profits are flexible in that there is no specific schedule of repayments. Also, there is no change in the pattern of shareholdings

5   Debentures and other long-term loans to a business

6   Shareholders' funds plus current liabilities plus any long-term provisions for liabilities and charges

7   The proportion of total costs that is made up of fixed costs

8   Yes: the use of historic cost net of depreciation would be misleading.

Now try the question below from the Practice Question Bank

Number	Level	Marks	Time
Q15	Examination	25	45 mins

People

Human resource management

15

Topic list	Syllabus reference
1 Strategic leadership	H1(a), (b)
2 Job design	H2(a), (c), (d)
3 HRM and knowledge work	H2(b)
4 Staff development	H3(a)–(d)

Introduction

This chapter looks at a number of human resource management topics. In Section 1, we look at the various aspects of leadership. We will then move on to look at how the people within the organisation contribute to its success. We will do this by exploring the range of approaches used to manage the workforce's efforts. These approaches are job design (Section 2), HRM and knowledge work (Section 3) and staff development (Section 4).

Study guide

		Intellectual level
	(Note that section H of the syllabus is underpinned directly by knowledge gained in F1, *Accountant in Business*. Students are expected to be familiar with the following Study Guide subject areas from that syllabus: A1, A2, B1-B3, D1, and D4-D6)	
H1	**Strategy and people: leadership**	
(a)	Explain the role of visionary leadership and identify the key leadership traits effective in the successful formulation and implementation of strategy and change management.	3
(b)	Apply and compare alternative classical and modern theories of leadership in the effective implementation of strategic objectives.	3
H2	**Strategy and people: job design**	
(a)	Assess the contribution of four different approaches to job design (scientific management, job enrichment, Japanese management and re-engineering)	3
(b)	Explain the human resource implications of knowledge work and post-industrial job design	2
(c)	Discuss the tensions and potential ethical issues related to job design	2
(d)	Advise on the relationship of job design to process re-design, project management and the harnessing of e-business opportunities	3
H3	**Strategy and people: staff development**	
(a)	Discuss the emergence and scope of human resource development, succession planning and their relationship to the strategy of the organisation	2
(b)	Advise and suggest different methods of establishing human resource development	3
(c)	Advise on the contribution of competency frameworks to human resource development	3
(d)	Discuss the meaning and contribution of workplace learning, the learning organisation, organisation learning and knowledge management	3

Exam guide

There is considerable practical detail in this chapter and it is easy to envisage a complete question covering these principles and how to embody them in a work situation.

You may also face a scenario where process redesign or information technology has an impact on job design. Be aware of the implications of different organisational structures for job design.

Models and theories

The Study Guide for this chapter indicates you need to be able to apply and compare alternative classical and modern theories of leadership in the effective implementation of strategic objectives. However, the guide does not explicitly reference any individual theories, so you will not be specifically required to use any single leadership theory to answer a question.

The Study Guide also refers explicitly to four approaches to job design – scientific management, job enrichment, Japanese management and re-engineering – so an assessment of any of these approaches could be specifically required in a question. However, remember that job design and staff development are also very practical (and examinable) topics, so make sure you cover the material in this chapter as a whole, rather than just focussing on the specific theories described in Section 1.

1 Strategic leadership 6/09

Knowledge brought forward from earlier studies

Paper F1, *Accountant in Business*, includes a section called 'Leading and managing individuals and teams'. This forms an important background to the material below.

xam focus oint

Note that whereas questions on leadership in F1 tested factual recall, questions in P3 will be context-based. For example, the scenario might indicate a leader behaving in a certain way and you will have to diagnose whether that behaviour is appropriate, using your knowledge of leadership styles but also analysing other areas of the business: the teams being led, organisational culture, the products and services being provided, organisational competencies and so on.

FAST FORWARD

The study of leadership has produced a wide range of theories; these may be analysed into four main groups.

- Trait theories
- Behavioural theories
- Contingency theories
- Transformational theories

1.1 Trait theories

Trait theories are based on the idea that some people are inherently suited to positions of leadership because they possess **appropriate personal qualities**. This approach can be seen as rooted in a class-based social structure, but extensive attempts were made to define specific leadership qualities. However, there was little agreement as to what those qualities actually were. This approach was overtaken in the mid-twentieth century by the belief that leaders were to be identified by what they did, rather than by who they were. Leadership came to be seen as a matter of **behaviour** and could therefore be taught.

Nevertheless, personal qualities and their development form a continuing strand in the progress of thought on leadership. Research has identified a number of traits that have been linked to leadership effectiveness with reasonable consistency, including emotional maturity and tolerance of stress. There is also evidence of a genetic basis for leadership ability differences.

1.2 Behavioural theories 6/13

Behavioural theories are often talking (broadly) about the same thing: a continuum of behaviours from:

(a) Wholly **task-focused**, directive leadership behaviours (representing high leader control) at one extreme, and

(b) Wholly **people-focused**, supportive/relational leadership behaviours (representing high subordinate discretion) at the other.

1.2.1 A continuum of leadership styles

Tannenbaum and Schmidt proposed a continuum of behaviours (and associated styles) based on the degree of authority used by a manager and the degree of freedom for the team.

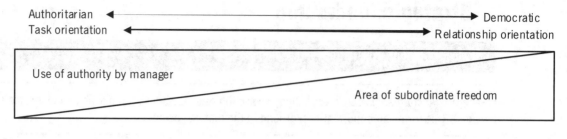

Authoritarian ◄──────────────────────────────► Democratic
Task orientation ◄──────────────────────────────► Relationship orientation

Use of authority by manager

Area of subordinate freedom

| Manager makes decision and announces it | Manager 'sells' decision | Manager presents ideas and invites questions | Manager presents intended decision, subject to amendment | Manager presents a problem, gets suggestions, and makes a decision | Manager defines limits and goals and asks the group to make the decision | Manager allows subordinates to act as they wish, within specified limits |

1.2.2 Blake and Mouton's Managerial Grid

Blake and Mouton carried out research (The Ohio State Leadership Studies) into managerial behaviour, and observed two basic dimensions of leadership: **concern for production** (or task performance) and **concern for people.**

Along each of these two dimensions, managers could be located at any point on a continuum, from very low to very high concern. Blake and Mouton observed that the two concerns did not seem to correlate, positively or negatively: a high concern in one dimension, for example, did not seem to imply a high or low concern in the other dimension. Individual managers could therefore reflect various permutations of task/people concern.

A questionnaire was designed to enable users to analyse and plot the positions of individual respondents on the grid. This was to be used as a means of analysing individuals' managerial styles and areas of weakness or 'unbalance', for the purposes of management development.

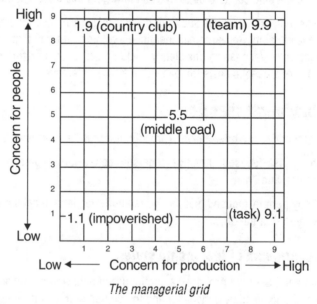

The managerial grid

The extreme cases shown on the grid are:

(a)   1.1 **impoverished:** the manager is lazy, showing little interest in either staff or work.

(b)   1.9 **country club:** the manager is attentive to staff needs and has developed satisfying relationships. However, there is little attention paid to achieving results.

(c)   9.1 **task oriented:** almost total concentration on achieving results. People's needs are virtually ignored.

(d)   5.5 **middle of the road** or the **dampened pendulum:** adequate performance through balancing (or switching between) the necessity to get out work with team morale.

(e)   9.9 **team:** high work accomplishment through 'leading' committed people who identify themselves with the organisational aims.

The grid thus offers a number of useful insights for the identification of management **training and development** needs. It shows, in an easily assimilated form, where the behaviour and assumptions of a manager may exhibit a lack of balance between the dimensions and/or a low degree of concern in either dimension or both. It may also be used in team member selection, so that a 1.9 team leader is balance by a 9.1 co-leader, for example.

However, the grid is a simplified model, and as such, has practical limitations.

(a)   It assumes that 9.9 is the desirable model for effective leadership. In some managerial contexts, this may not be so. Concern for people, for example, would not be necessary in a context of comprehensive automation: compliance is all that would be required.

(b)   It is open to oversimplification. Scores can appear polarised, with judgements attached about individual managers' suitability or performance. The grid is intended as a simplified 'snapshot' of a manager's preferred style, not a comprehensive description of his or her performance.

(c)   Organisational context and culture, technology and other 'givens' influence the manager's style of leadership, not just the two dimensions described by the grid.

(d)   Any managerial theory is only useful in so far as it is useable in practice by managers: if the grid is used only to inform managers that they 'must acquire greater concern for people', it may result in stress, uncertainty and inconsistent behaviour.

1.2.3 Theory X and Theory Y

Douglas McGregor *(The Human Side of Enterprise)* suggested that managers (in the US) tended to behave as though they subscribed to one of two sets of assumptions about people at work: Theory X and Theory Y.

(a)   **Theory X** suggests that most people dislike work and responsibility, and will avoid both if possible. Because of this, most people must be coerced, controlled, directed and/or threatened with punishment to get them to make an adequate effort. Managers who operate according to these assumptions will tend to supervise closely, apply detailed rules and controls, and use 'carrot and stick' motivators.

(b)   **Theory Y** suggests that physical and mental effort in work is as natural as play or rest. The ordinary person does not inherently dislike work: according to the conditions it may be a source of satisfaction or dissatisfaction. The potentialities of the average person are rarely fully used at work. People can be motivated to seek challenge and responsibility in their job, if their goals can be integrated with those of the organisation. A manager with this sort of attitude to his staff is likely to be a consultative, facilitating leader, using positive feedback, challenge and responsibility as motivators.

Both are intended to be extreme sets of assumptions – not actual types of people. However, they also tend to be self-fulfilling prophecies. Employees treated as if 'Theory X' were true will begin to behave accordingly. Employees treated as if 'Theory Y' were true – being challenged to take on more responsibility – will rise to the challenge and behave accordingly.

Theory X and Theory Y can be used to heighten managers' awareness of the assumptions underlying their motivational style.

1.3 Contingency theories

Contingency theory as applied to leadership suggests that no one style is likely to be entirely appropriate for all circumstances. For example, in an emergency, an autocratic approach is likely to be far more effective than an approach based on consultation and participative decision-making. The setting for the

exercise of leadership will vary from case to case. In particular, the nature of the group and its needs and desires are critical.

Contingency theories are based on the belief that there is no 'one best way' of leading, but that effective leaders adapt their behaviour to the specific and changing variables in the leadership context: the nature of the task, the personalities of team members, the organisation culture and so on.

1.3.1 Adair

Adair's action-centred, or situational model sees the leadership process in a context made up of three main variables, all of which are interrelated and must be examined in the light of the whole situation. These are **task needs**, the **individual needs** of group members, and the **needs of the group** as a whole. The total situation dictates the relative priority that must be given to each of the three sets of needs. Effective leadership is identifying and acting on that priority to create a balance between the needs. Adair's model is unusual in that it integrates both the **needs of the individual** and the **dynamics of the group**.

1.3.2 Fiedler

Fiedler found that people become leaders partly because of their own attributes and partly because of the nature of the **situation** they find themselves in. Leadership style depends on the personality of the leader, which is fixed. The extent to which the situation favours the leader depends on three things.

(a) **Position power**. This is the same thing as organisational authority.

(b) **Task structure**. Work is easier to organise and accountability easier to determine when the task is clear, well defined and unambiguous. The quality of performance is difficult to control when the task is vague and unstructured.

(c) **Leader-subordinate relations**. The leader's task is eased when subordinates have trust and confidence in him or her.

Fiedler found that a **task-oriented** approach was most productive when the situation was either **very favourable** to the leader or **very unfavourable**. In less extreme cases, a more **people-centred** approach was more effective.

1.3.3 Hersey and Blanchard

Hersey and Blanchard developed a model of leadership which appears to **map style theories on to the grid** suggested by Blake and Mouton. The leader should determine the **maturity** of followers. Maturity has three components.

(a) **Achievement motivation** (can the followers set high but realistic goals?)

(b) **Responsibility** (willingness and ability to assume it)

(c) **Education/experience**. Maturity in practice is divided into psychological maturity (eg attitude to work) and job maturity (eg problem solving ability)

Where maturity is high, the manager need exert little effort in support of either task or relationships and may **delegate** to a great extent.

Where maturity is low, on the other hand, an **autocratic** approach may be required, with great attention to the task but little need for attention to relationships.

Followers of moderate maturity will probably respond well to a high degree of concern for relationships combined with a moderate degree of attention to the task. **Participative** approaches are useful here.

1.4 Transformational theories

All of the models so far considered may be referred to collectively as **transactional theories** of leadership. This term is used to distinguish them from more recent approaches that have come to be known as **transformational theories** of leadership. Transformational theories generally accept that the world is a much less stable place than it was and that changes of all kinds are frequent and far-reaching. It is necessary for leaders of all kinds to accept this and to provide leadership that will help their organisations to respond in creative and effective ways.

There are a number of expectations of modern leaders:

- To **change** organisations and systems from within.
- To drive forward adventurous, **visionary strategies**. Leaders need to have a clear vision for the future, and what needs to be done to get there, so that they can inspire others to aim for that future as well.
- To motivate others. Visionary leaders motivate others to work harder by making work seem as natural as play, and by making their teams see the value and purpose in what they do.
- To provide **clarity of purpose** and direction.
- To be good communicators, both to communicate their vision and purpose, but also to listen to others' points of view and to gain their trust.

There are therefore three main themes within the transformational theories of leadership:

- Teams
- Vision
- Change

 Case Study   Bill Gates and Microsoft

Bill Gates founded the Microsoft Corporation in 1975, with his childhood friend Paul Allen. Gates correctly identified that as computer hardware became increasingly powerful, there would be a gap in the market for computer software.

Microsoft is now the global leader in software, services and solutions that enables people and businesses to maximise the value of computers in their lives.

However, one of the major factors behind the growth and success of the company has been Gates' readiness to restructure to keep it innovative and ready for each new phase in the fast changing world of computer technology.

In April 2002, Microsoft announced its fourth major reorganisation in five years, before, in 2005, Gates announced a further realignment of the company into three distinct newly formed divisions, each headed up by its own president.

One of these divisions will be responsible for 'entertainment and devices'. The other two are the Platforms Products and Services Division; and the Business Division.

The Microsoft Platforms and Services Division includes the three operating segments of Client; Server and Tools; and the Online Services Group.

From the fiscal year 2007, Microsoft changed to operate its business in five operating segments: (i) Online Client, (Subsequently re-named Windows and Windows Live Division) (ii) Server and Tools, (iii) Online Services Group, (iv) Business Division and (v) Entertainment and Devices Division.

The creation of the entertainment and devices division illustrates how Microsoft has diversified away from its original core competencies in developing computer language programmes and software into new areas such as console games via the Xbox system.

The divisional structure is designed to support Microsoft's drive for innovation and growth for the future, increasing the number of new products and services it delivers.

Over the years since it was founded, Gates' foresight, vision and leadership have been drivers for change, development and success in the Microsoft Corporation. On the one hand, Gates has continually strived to advance software technology with a view to making computing more accessible and fun for people; on the other, he has strived to make Microsoft an attractive and exciting place to work.

1.5 Leadership and strategy

Ultimately, the importance of leadership in strategy is that it cultivates **innovation** and **organisational change**. This is what **distinguishes leadership from management**.

Management provides the order and procedures to deal with the organisational requirements of business. Leadership, by contrast, champions change and shows how to cope with change. In this way, leaders **inspire** and **motivate** their followers in a way which managers do not.

Question	Leadership

Think of a business leader who you are familiar with, and identify the reasons which you think have contributed to their success. What leadership qualities and behaviours do they show?

2 Job design   6/10

FAST FORWARD

Job design is essentially about organising work and that has always been a major role of management. Four approaches are identified.

- **Scientific Management** is an engineering approach that seeks to apply a single, ideal solution to any given piece of work. It leads to work study, deskilling, efficiency and alienation.
- **Job enrichment** attempts to overcome the undesirable effects of the Scientific Management approach by making work more meaningful for the worker.
- The **Japanese model** emphasises enhanced worker responsibility in pursuit of higher quality and reduced waste.
- **Re-engineering** pursues major improvements in organisational systems while, at the same time, empowering workers to make the best use of their skills and abilities.
- Managers should be as **humane** as possible when undertaking **job design**.

Exam focus point

An article titled 'Strategy and People' (March 2011) written by Ken Garrett was published in *Student Accountant*, and is available on the ACCA website. It would be worth taking the time to study this article.

Key term

Job design is the process of combining tasks and responsibilities to form complete jobs and the relationship of jobs in the organisation.
Bratton

The importance of job design as a managerial responsibility has been apparent ever since there have been organised societies. Adam Smith described the economic advantages of job specialisation in *The Wealth of Nations*; in the later nineteenth century, **organising** a structure of tasks and jobs was identified by Fayol as one of the functions of management. A little later, Frederick Taylor founded his business and the approach still known as **Scientific Management** on the careful consideration and control of individual job content and technique.

Your syllabus requires us to consider four different approaches to job design:

- Scientific Management
- Job enrichment

- The Japanese model
- Re-engineering

2.1 Scientific Management

Frederick W Taylor argued that management should be based on 'well-recognised, clearly defined and fixed principles, instead of depending on more or less hazy ideas.' He was an engineer by training and mostly concerned with an **engineering efficiency** approach to production in order to increase productivity. His methods were later applied to many other types of work.

Taylor's early experience convinced him that workers had a natural tendency to do the minimum they could get away with: he described workers as 'marking time' or 'soldiering', rather than working productively. Since managers had very poor knowledge of how much output could reasonably be expected from a worker, the result was large scale under-achievement. It was always his principle that there was 'one best way' of doing a given job and the main thrust of much of his early work was therefore careful experimentation and measurement to find the **most effective methods**. This approach was the basis of what later became the widely used discipline of **work study**.

2.1.1 Principles of Scientific Management

Taylor described four ideas as the principles of his method.

(a) **The development of a true science of work**. 'All knowledge which had hitherto been kept in the heads of workmen should be gathered and recorded by **management**. Every single subject, large and small, becomes the question for scientific investigation, for reduction to law.'

(b) **The scientific selection and progressive development of workers:** workers should be carefully trained and given jobs to which they are best suited.

(c) **The bringing together of the science and the scientifically selected and trained men**. The application of techniques to decide what should be done and how, using workers who are both properly trained and willing to maximise output, should result in maximum productivity.

(d) **The constant and intimate co-operation between management and workers:** 'the relations between employers and men form without question the most important part of this art.'

2.1.2 Scientific Management in practice

Trade unionists, politicians of the left and those sympathetic to their ideas see Scientific Management as an extremely undesirable development, since it **minimised worker autonomy** and **maximised management control**. (This point of view can often be identified by the use of the term 'Taylorism' rather than Scientific Management.)

(a) **Work study techniques** established the 'one best way' to do any job. No discretion was allowed to the worker. Preparation and servicing tasks were allocated to unskilled workers. Subsequently, Henry Ford's approach to mass production broke each job down into its smallest and simplest component parts: these single elements became the newly-designed job. This process of **deskilling** makes such work unfulfilling and boring but very productive.

(b) **Planning the work and doing the work were separated.** First line management of work groups might involve several 'functional foremen,' each responsible for a different aspect of planning and controlling the work. Workers lost any control over what they did.

(c) **Workers received large pay increases** as the new methods greatly increased productivity and profits.

(d) All aspects of the **work environment** were tightly controlled in order to attain maximum productivity.

Despite the views of the detractors of Scientific Management, there is much that is relevant today in this approach and the pursuit of productivity through efficiency of method is still a major preoccupation for management at all levels. The whole field of process redesign, for example is essentially an application of the basic idea of improving performance in a designed way, as is much of the detail of modern quality management. However, we may identify two important and linked differences.

(a) The Scientific Management approach was for an external expert to prescribe the improvement: the modern approach is to involve the people concerned with the process.

(b) Taylor promoted the idea of 'one best way': modern approaches accept that more than one solution may be valid.

Also, there are genuine problems with Scientific Management in a modern setting.

(a) The **alienation** and **boredom** associated with the production-line approach lead to high levels of **labour turnover** and **absenteeism**.

(b)   While basic labour costs may fall, there is a penalty to pay in **increased costs of planning and supervision**.

(c)   Lack of **job satisfaction** can lead to lack of **commitment** and hence to **quality problems**.

2.2 Job enrichment

2.2.1 The human relations background

The development of the **human relations** school of thought can be traced back to experiments carried out in the early 1920s at Western Electric's Hawthorne plant in Chicago. The original experiments seemed to show that there was no clear relationship between improvements made to working conditions and productivity. Subsequent research extending over many years indicated the complex interplay of social, material and personal factors in determining much workplace behaviour and its influence on productivity. Awareness of **social and individual psychology** became a fundamental aspect of management technique, with an emphasis on measures such as employee **counselling** and the satisfaction of **social needs**. There was also an understanding that **financial reward alone** would be unlikely to motivate workers to high levels of output. However, the theory did not produce reliable results when applied in practical terms.

2.2.2 Motivation and job design

'**Neo-human relations**' was used by Rose as a label for the later work of psychologists such as Maslow, McGregor and Herzberg. These authors are best known in the wider field of management studies for their ideas about **motivation** and the potential of work and the work situation to provide higher psychological satisfactions. One important aspect of this consideration of work and motivation has been an emphasis on the **importance of job content** and a move towards **job enrichment**.

2.2.3 Job enrichment

Job rotation and **job enlargement** are simple approaches to the redesign of jobs.

(a)   **Job rotation**, or periodic movement around a group of different de-skilled tasks, can go some way towards reducing monotony and boredom, but offers little extra satisfaction.

(b)   **Job enlargement** reverses the process of de-skilling by combining a number of linked processes together in one job. This is in direct opposition to Ford's production line approach.

A more sophisticated approach is known as **job enrichment**: this may be distinguished from job enlargement in that the latter brings tasks together on a horizontal axis, while job enrichment involves an element of vertical amalgamation: an enriched job includes some elements of **responsibility for planning and control**.

Hackman and Oldham suggest that five core characteristics are required in enriched jobs if they are to produce positive outcomes:

(a)   The job requires the use of a **range of skills and talents**.

(b)   **Task identity** (sometimes called **closure**): the job includes all the tasks needed to complete an identifiable product or process.

(c)   **Task significance**: the job has an impact on other people's lives or work.

(d)   **Autonomy**: workers have a degree of discretion in scheduling and organising their work.

(e)   **Feedback**: workers are provided with information on the results of their performance.

These elements should lead to **three desirable psychological states**:

*   Experience of **meaningful work**
*   Experience of **responsibility for outcomes**
*   Knowledge of **actual results**

These, in turn, should produce **desirable outcomes**:

*   High productivity and quality
*   High job satisfaction and low absenteeism and labour turnover

However, this desirable progression, from job enrichment to desirable outcomes is subject to the effect of **moderators**.

- The level of knowledge and skill possessed by the employee
- The strength of the employee's need for growth in the job
- The influence of the work context over satisfaction

Thus, an ignorant, clumsy and unambitious person working in unsatisfactory conditions is unlikely to demonstrate the desired outcomes when his or her job is enriched.

xam focus
oint

If you consider the processes involved in job enrichment, you should discern potential links to process redesign and the changes inherent in adopting an e-business method. Each of these aspects of strategic implementation can provide extensive opportunities for job enrichment.

2.3 The Japanese model

Japanese industry has had enormous influence on western manufacturing practice. **Lean production** or 'the Toyota system' have been widely adopted and developed in an attempt to achieve Japanese levels of productivity and quality. Bratton suggests that three notable elements of the Japanese production model contribute to its influence on job design.

- Flexible manufacturing
- Minimisation of waste
- Quality methods

2.3.1 Flexible manufacturing

Flexibility of manufacturing means the ability to produce relatively small batches of a range of products without incurring excessive **set-up** costs. The principal features of the Japanese method of achieving this are multi-skilled workers and careful shop floor layout that makes a range of machinery and equipment available to each of them. **Machine cells** are a common feature of this approach. This approach stands in strong contrast to both the principles of Scientific Management and the assembly line layout; it inevitably brings a high degree of **job enrichment** through the **variety of work** and the **skills needed** to perform it.

2.3.2 Quality methods

Japanese manufacturers paid close attention to statistical quality control and Deming's other principles and methods very early in that country's post-1945 recovery. One of the results of this focus was the development of the **total quality** approach. This puts quality at the heart of the manufacturing process by abolishing inspection as an independent function and separate process within the organisation and making production workers responsible for the quality of their own output. This feature, together with participation in activities aimed at achieving **continuous improvement**, also produces job enrichment.

2.3.3 Minimisation of waste

Incorporating quality responsibility into production work is also an example of the Japanese approach to waste. Separate inspection processes (and the rework they lead to) add no value, therefore they are abolished. The **just-in-time** philosophy is a further example. Inventories of materials, components and work-in-progress must be financed with capital that could be better employed earning a return elsewhere. Inventories are therefore cut to an absolute minimum and capital released. To achieve this, the *kanban* system is used. A kanban is a signal calling for productive effort: a series of kanbans flows back from the final customer through all the various manufacturing and logistic stages of production. As a result, production is **pulled through** the factory by demand, **not pushed** by production schedule. This again places **enhanced responsibility** on individuals and work groups to respond appropriately. It is also a good illustration of one application of e-business methods – the use of electronic data interchange to link stages in the value network.

2.3.4 The problem of control

Bratton points out that the job enriching effects described above combine to make the company heavily **dependent on its workers**. In order to counterbalance this, Japanese companies have made use of a set of **social mechanisms that enhance the commitment** of their workers. The basic aim is the promotion of a **sense of community** that provides a socialisation into the norms of loyalty and motivation. Work groups tend to develop their means of disciplining members felt not to be conforming.

2.4 Re-engineering

Knowledge brought forward from earlier studies

We looked at business process change in more detail earlier in this Study Text, including a discussion of business process re-engineering (BPR) as it affects job design. You should refer to our earlier discussion and consider how BPR may be said to fit into the job design spectrum.

2.5 Ethics and job design

Knowledge brought forward from earlier studies

When we discussed ethics, we dealt with two important matters that are directly related to job design.

(a) One formulation of the **categorical imperative** is that people should not be treated simply as means to an end, but as an end in themselves.

(b) Natural law theory imposes a duty to respect the rights of others.

The managerial priorities of **control** and **cost reduction** can drive the process of job design towards infringement of these ethical principles.

(a) Jobs may be **deskilled** and organised in ways that prevent workers from deriving any satisfaction or fulfilment from them.

(b) Jobs may be automated or outsourced out of existence, thus bringing significant disruption and stress to workers' lives.

(c) Work groups may be broken up, limiting the potential of work to fulfil this is a difficult and complex problem. Managers should seek to balance their organisational responsibilities and the effect of their actions on their workers, seeking a humane course of action where possible.

2.6 An overview of job design

FAST FORWARD

Productivity through **work specialisation** leads to mechanisms of close managerial control. Together, these forces produce **job dissatisfaction** and **poor motivation**. All job design must attempt to reconcile these forces.

All job design must attempt to **reconcile two forces** that tend to work in opposition to one another.

(a) The need to **break work up** in order to exploit specialisation and the division of labour so as to maximise productivity

(b) The need to **integrate** and **control** the highly differentiated activities that result from (a)

From the point of view of the worker, specialisation can produce fragmented, unsatisfying work and poor social interaction, which, combined with its resultant control-based style of management, leads to low levels of **motivation and commitment**.

Scientific Management was based on extremes of specialisation and management control and ignored the potential psychological effects on the work force. Later developments have produced a different balance.

BPP
LEARNING MEDIA

2.7 Summarising four approaches to job design

	Features	Assumptions about motivation	Job design
Scientific Management	Prescribed standard methods	Pay – piecework	Extreme specialisation Split of planning and doing
Human relations/ job enrichment	Work groups Combination of tasks Some control over planning	Social needs Achievement, growth, responsibility	Less extreme, with some control tasks shifted downwards
Japanese model	JIT, TQM, consensus, lifetime employment, loyalty	Social processes of clan control	Multi-skilling to achieve flexibility
Re-design	Strong leadership from the top Exploitation of IT Abandonment of traditional structures and methods	Emphasis on market discipline and serving the needs of the customer	Process teams Empowerment Multi-dimensional jobs

Exam focus point

Your syllabus specifically mentions the relationship of job design to process design, project management and e-business. You should be aware that these elements of strategic implementation are likely to involve a need for some degree of job redesign. You should bear this in mind when answering questions that deal with those elements.

3 HRM and knowledge work

FAST FORWARD

Knowledge work has become a major part of the economies of developed countries. This has had important effects on the way organisations work and are managed, with a shift away from procedure and control towards a looser, more flexible system based on problem solving and empowerment.

Knowledge brought forward from earlier studies

We discussed organisational learning and knowledge management earlier in this Study Text, when we were considering strategic capability. You should refer back in order to refresh your memory.

Recent years have seen a shift of manufacturing to low-cost sites in developing countries and a consequent decline in the West. As a result, service industries have become far more important to the economies of developed countries. This trend has been accompanied by the recognition of the **knowledge worker** as a vital feature of modern business. This has two important implications:

(a) Knowledge is recognised as a **vital asset** and crucial to business success. Organisations must therefore acquire, organise, manage and exploit knowledge if they are to survive.

(b) This vital asset, knowledge, fundamentally exists in the brains of knowledge workers and is controlled by them. If the organisation is to benefit, its workers must be organised and managed in a way that will **stimulate both learning and creativity**.

These factors have led to a shift away from the classic bureaucratic structure of management and organisation, which was built around the careful planning and control of procedures and operations, to a looser, 'post-modern', 'post-bureaucratic' or 'post-industrial' approach that emphasises information sharing, flexibility and empowerment.

3.1 The move to knowledge work

	From	To
Type of work	Individual	Project teams
Focus	Task performance	Customers, problems, opportunities
Skills and knowledge	Narrow	Specialist but with wide interest
Feedback and results	Rapid	Slow
Employee loyalty	Organisation and career within it	Peers, profession
Contribution to success	Individual support to the wider strategy	A few major successes

3.2 Impact on the organisation

Bratton, quoting Hecksher, suggests that as organisations evolve to take account of these changes, they will display five features:

(a)   **Organisational dialogue and trust** reduces the scope for managerial control and direction and enables a wide range of bottom-up and lateral inputs. This feature depends on the other four.

(b)   **Sharing of information** about the organisation's operations, problems and opportunities.

(c)   **Principle-based management** replaces management based on formal rules and procedure and leads to greater flexibility and adaptation.

(d)   **Communication flows and decision-making** are built around projects and problem-solving rather than hierarchical routine.

(e)   **Peer evaluation** of performance replaces formal credentials and supervisor opinion.

4 Staff development

FAST FORWARD

Human resource development should be seen as an investment in strategic capability since it improves both skills and commitment. It may be approached top-down, in the form of **human capital theory**, or bottom-up through **empowerment**. In the UK, governments encourage rather than enforce HRD efforts, despite concerns about low levels of skills. This voluntarist approach has led to an emphasis on useful, workplace competence-based qualifications.

The traditional personnel management function of training is now supplemented and may be replaced by the wider concept of **human resource development** (HRD).

(a)   The view of training as a **cost** is being replaced with a view of HRD as an **investment in strategic capability**. This view also highlights that **people are a resource**, so HRD plays a crucial role in how those resources are used, managed, controlled and motivated to create competencies in key business processes.

(b)   Investment in **employee learning** and recognition of the **competitive advantage conferred by upgraded skills** triggers the creation of an internal market in such qualities with consequent implications for other HR activities such as recruitment, retention and reward.

(c)   Organisations seeking to benefit from employee loyalty and commitment find that HRD can enable employees to contribute to the **development and success of strategy and operations**.

This **wider vision of HRD** can link to the organisation's strategy in two ways: these correspond to the traditional 'top-down' model of strategy as a controlled response to environmental change and the emergent or 'bottom-up' model.

(a) Under the **top-down** model, the organisation's senior managers are responsible for recognising new, more general and wide-ranging environmental factors that mandate HRD effort. For example, technological developments may lead to the recognition of a skills gap and the need for staff training.

(b) Under the **bottom-up** model, empowered employees recognise individual gaps in skills, knowledge or capability and take steps to resolve them through discussion, co-operation and the development of new methods. An example would be the improvement of a product as a result of customer contact and internal consultation and action.

It is appropriate for organisations to utilise both approaches, though this requires senior management effort to reconcile them and enable them to work in a synergistic fashion, rather than interfering with each other.

A traditional view of the place of HRD in strategic management is that it **responds to imperatives** generated by the strategic management process, whatever form that takes. Some HRD professionals would argue that HRD should be a major component of that process in order to create a learning culture as a basis for more effective strategy. This is not yet a popular approach in the UK.

4.1 Establishing HRD

The prevailing view of HRD in UK commercial organisations is **human capital** theory. This sees investment in HRD as analogous to investment in other assets and judges its value in terms of return on investment. This approach requires clear evidence of probable benefit before investment is made in HRD and restricts developmental activities that have uncertain though possibly important benefits. The extreme case of this view is the drive to reduce training costs and ensure control of work practices through **deskilling** and careful **job design**.

The alternative view is a **developmental humanistic** approach, as discerned by Gold and Smith. This approach features empowerment; lifelong learning and the learning organisation; productivity through a sense of meaningful work; and learning as a way of both coping with change and fulfilling ambitions. Advocates of this approach accept that it is necessary to present its advantages in terms that relate to human capital theory if it is to be adopted.

The benefit of an active commitment to HRD may be considered at three levels:

(a) **The individual's** job prospects and potential income are enhanced by vocational and academic qualifications.

(b) **The organisation** may find that recruitment, adaptation to change, staff turnover and productivity are enhanced by good HRD, but Machin and Vignoles have suggested that any causal relationship that exists may in fact work in the reverse sense; that is, it may just be that profitable and productive firms do more HRD.

(c) At the **national economic and social level**, there is a link between general education and economic growth, but it is difficult to establish one between training and growth.

In general, the UK displays a **voluntarist approach** to HRD, in that the role of government is to encourage rather than to enforce HRD. This contrasts with the **interventionist approach** current in France, under which the government imposes a training levy based on payroll value and uses the funds to reimburse employers that undertake training. This system was tried in the UK by the Labour government of the late 1960s and later abolished because the system inevitably imposed a **deadweight cost of administration** in addition to the cost of any HRD actually undertaken. A company undertaking all of the HRD deemed appropriate would only be reimbursed with 97.5% of the levy it had paid, the balance being consumed by government in administering the scheme.

The dominance of the voluntarist view in the UK has led government to promote HRD within a market-led framework. Research commissioned by the National Skills Task Force indicates that there is a major shortage of technical skills but that employers either fail to recognise this or work around it by concentrating on low skill-content products. Government has responded to this problem with a range of supply-side measures and exhortation. Measures have included infrastructure improvements, including a network of institutions to co-ordinate national initiatives, and the development of a comprehensive national scheme of **competence based qualifications**.

Key term

> **Competencies**, in the sense used here, are 'the required outcomes expected from the performance of a task in a work role, expressed as performance standards with criteria'. *Gold*

Exam focus point

> An article titled 'Competency frameworks' (2009) written by Gareth Owen is available in the technical articles section for P3 on the ACCA website. It would be worth taking the time to study this article.

Competency frameworks are concerned with the behaviour that is relevant to the job, and the effective (or competent) performance of that job.

The emphasis on workplace performance reflects the human capital approach to HRD.

The qualifications themselves are called national vocational qualifications (NVQs) in England and Wales, and Scottish vocational qualifications (SVQs) in Scotland. There has been criticism of the N/SVQ approach because of their emphasis on **outcomes measured against standards** rather than on knowledge and understanding. It has also been suggested that they have simply added to the number of qualifications available rather than rationalising them overall.

4.2.1 Institutions

The UK national structure of institutions concerned with HRD includes the Qualifications and Curriculum Authority, which oversees all standards in both education and training, and a number of Regional Development Agencies and Learning and Skills Councils, which promote and oversee all education and training after the age of 16 years.

4.2.2 Application of competencies

Competency frameworks can be used to provide a more structured approach to recruitment; for managing performance; for providing a benchmark for rewards and promotion; and for training and development.

(a)   **Recruitment**. Competencies can be used as a basis for person specifications, and as a basis for comparing candidates during the selection process. The competencies required to do the job are identified, and then the suitability of various candidates is compared against them.

(b)   **Managing performance**. Competencies can be used to demonstrate the levels of performance and behaviour needed to achieve the business strategy. An organisation will have competencies for its business overall, but these can then be filtered down to individual departments, and ultimately, individual employees. In this way, if each individual achieves their objectives (competencies) the organisation will achieve its objectives as well.

(c)   **Benchmark for rewards and promotion** (appraisal). The comparison of a person's actual performance against their target competencies can be used as the basis of an appraisal system.

(d)   **Training and development**. Competencies can be used to identify the training needs of staff, so that a development plan can be drawn up to meet those needs.

In order to qualify as an ACCA member, you not only have to pass your exams but also have to demonstrate your practical experience. ACCA's Practical Experience Requirements are a framework for recording achievement, allowing you to demonstrate your competence against a number of performance objectives. In this way, the practical experience requirements could be considered as a competence framework.

4.3 Workplace learning

Advocates of HRD suggest that learning is fundamental if the organisation is to cope with environmental change, uncertainty and complexity. HRD practitioners place the following concepts under the umbrella of workplace learning.

- Organisational learning
- Knowledge management
- The learning organisation
- E-Learning

Organisational learning, the learning organisation and knowledge management are dealt with elsewhere in this Study Text. E-learning is an effective way to acquire knowledge and non-manipulation skills using interactive software.

4.4 Succession planning

FAST FORWARD

Succession planning not only provides for continuity of leadership, it also facilitates management development at all levels.

ey term

Succession planning is undertaken in order to ensure continuity in the organisation's leadership. It involves the systematic identification, assessment and development of managerial talent at all levels.

Succession planning should be an integral part of the HR plan and should support the organisation's chosen strategy. The developed plan should also be compatible with any changes that are foreseen in the way the organisation operates. It is likely that strategic objectives will only be obtained if management development proceeds in step with the evolution of the organisation.

4.4.1 Benefits of succession planning

(a) The development of managers at all levels is likely to be improved if it takes place within the context of a succession plan. Such a plan gives focus to management development by suggesting objectives that are directly relevant to the organisation's needs.

(b) Continuity of leadership is more likely, with fewer dislocating changes of approach and policy.

(c) Assessment of managerial talent is improved by the establishment of relevant criteria.

4.4.2 Features of successful succession planning

(a) The plan should focus on future requirements, particularly in terms of strategy and culture.

(b) The plan should be driven by top management. Line management also have important contributions to make. It is important that it is not seen as a HR responsibility.

(c) Management development is as important as assessment and selection.

(d) Assessment should be objective and preferably involve more than one assessor for each manager assessed.

(e) Succession planning will work best if it aims to identify and develop a leadership *cadre* rather than merely to establish a queue for top positions. A pool of talent and ability is a flexible asset for the organisation.

Chapter Roundup

- The study of leadership has produced a wide range of theories; these may be analysed into four main groups:

  - Trait theories
  - Behavioural theories
  - Contingency theories
  - Transformational theories

- Job design is essentially about organising work and that has always been a major role of management. Four approaches are identified.

  - **Scientific Management** is an engineering approach that seeks to apply a single, ideal solution to any given piece of work. It leads to work study, deskilling, efficiency and alienation.

  - **Job enrichment** attempts to overcome the undesirable effects of the Scientific Management approach by making work more meaningful for the worker.

  - The **Japanese model** emphasises enhanced worker responsibility in pursuit of higher quality and reduced waste.

  - **Re-engineering** pursues major improvements in organisational systems while, at the same time, empowering workers to make the best use of their skills and abilities.

  - Managers should be as **humane** as possible when undertaking **job design**.

- Productivity through **work specialisation** leads to mechanisms of close managerial control pull. Together, these forces produce **job dissatisfaction** and **poor motivation**. All job design must attempt to reconcile these forces.

- **Knowledge work** has become a major part of the economies of developed countries. This has had important effects on the way organisations work and are managed, with a shift away from procedure and control towards a looser, more flexible system based on problem solving and empowerment.

- Human resource development should be seen as an investment in strategic capability since it improves both skills and commitment. It may be approached top-down, in the form of **human capital theory**, or bottom-up through **empowerment**. In the UK, governments encourage rather than enforce HRD efforts, despite concerns about low levels of skills. This voluntarist approach has led to an emphasis on useful, workplace competence-based qualifications.

- Succession planning not only provides for continuity of leadership, it also facilitates management development at all levels.

Quick Quiz

1   What are the three desirable psychological states that job enrichment is intended to produce?

2   What elements of the Japanese production model does Bratton identify as influencing the Japanese approach to job design?

3   What effects will the move to knowledge work have on the organisation?

4   How does human capital theory view the cost of HRD?

5   What are competencies?

Answers to Quick Quiz

1   Experience of meaningful work; experience of responsibility for outcomes; knowledge of actual results

2   Flexible manufacturing; quality methods; minimisation of waste

3   Organisational dialogue and trust, which depends on sharing of information; principle-based management rather than procedure-based management; problem-solving and project-based communication-flows; peer evaluation of performance

4   As investment in assets

5   Competencies, in the sense used here, are 'the required outcomes expected from the performance of a task in a work role, expressed as performance standards with criteria'

Now try the question below from the Practice Question Bank

Number	Level	Marks	Time
Q16	Examination	10	18 mins

15: Human resource management | Part H People

Strategic development

16

Strategic development

Topic list	Syllabus reference
1 Intention, emergence and realisation	C3(a)
2 Developing intended strategies	C3(b)
3 Developing emergent strategies	C3(c), (d)
4 Diversity of strategic processes	C3(e)
5 Challenges and implications	C3(e)

Introduction

We have covered a great deal of ground in this Study Text, but nearly all of our
discussion has related to specific ideas that may be used when developing
strategy; that is to say, we have concentrated on tools, models and techniques
that may be used to create answers to specific strategic problems. We have
said very little about the wider processes by which an overall strategy is
designed. This final chapter attempts to round off our consideration of
business strategy by looking at the ways in which strategies come into
existence.

There are two principal classes of strategies: the intended and the emergent.
We will start by contrasting these classes and discussing their relationship.
Then we will look at each in more detail. The final sections of this chapter will
examine some challenges and more general concepts relating to strategy
development.

Study guide

Exam guide

This may seem a rather theoretical chapter at first, but it is important that you realise that in the real world, strategies often emerge rather than develop via some neatly ordered process. Therefore, the material covered here may well appear in many examination case studies. Also, Section 5 has some detail on specific strategic challenges that could be useful in dealing with the kind of complex scenario typical of Section A questions.

However, this final chapter also draws together all the theories and issues we have looked at in this Study Text to describe how business strategies develop.

Remember that the areas shown in the middle row of the rational diagram of the syllabus – business process change, e-business – can help shape an organisation's business strategy, and by discussing emergent strategies, this chapter reminds us of that.

It is important that you have an integrated view of the syllabus when you sit the P3 examination.

1 Intention, emergence and realisation

FAST FORWARD

Realised strategy may emerge from everyday actions and routine decisions, or it may be the result of considered intention. **Intended strategies** may also fail to be realised.

You will recall that in Chapter 1 of this Study Text, we explained the way that JS&W analyse strategy into three main elements: **strategic position**, **strategic choices** and **strategy into action**.

(a) The strategic managers must attempt to **understand** the organisation's strategic position.

(b) Strategic choices are about **scope**, the **direction** and **method** of development and how to achieve **competitive advantage**.

(c) Strategies must be made to **work in practice**. Major issues here include **structuring**, **enabling** and **change**.

This analysis is written in terms of **management**: that is to say, as though strategy is a project that managers work on and bring to completion in a deliberate and logical fashion. Understanding of strategic position informs strategic choice: together they create an **intention**. The next stage, strategy into action is about how we **realise** that intention.

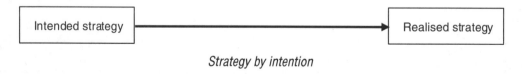

Strategy by intention

BPP
LEARNING MEDIA

In our discussion of the **strategy lenses,** we explained that this represents just one view of strategy and that there are other, equally valuable, views of its nature. These views describe what we may call **emergent strategy**. The essence of this kind of strategy is that it is not the result of any kind of top-down, intended managerial process. This kind of strategy comes about as a largely unintended result of the everyday activities, decisions and processes that take place at all levels of the organisation. Thus, realised strategy can **emerge,** as well as arise from, intention.

We also have to be aware that what managers intend **may not actually be realised**: plans may be unworkable for a variety of reasons, resources may be inadequate, important stakeholders may be obstructive and so on.

You have probably encountered examples in everyday life where an intended strategy is not realised. Think, for example, of the times where organisations have promised 'excellent customer service' or 'first rate service'. Has the service you have actually received matched those promises? 'Excellent customer service' may be the intended plan, but the realised plan often falls short of what is intended.

Our diagrammatic overview thus has to be amended to include these extra possibilities.

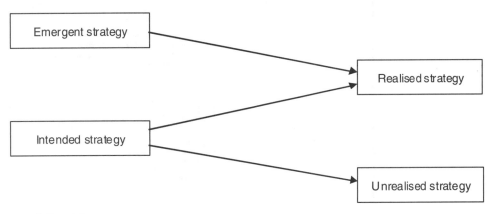

Strategy: a fuller picture

2 Developing intended strategies

FAST FORWARD

Intended strategies are developed in a systematic way, making use of rational procedures and, probably, specialist staff. This approach has advantages associated with system and method, and disadvantages associated with ponderousness and inflexibility. More recently, workshops and project teams have been used to develop intended strategies and strategy consultants have been employed.

The development of intended strategies is associated with **strategic planning systems**. JS&W use the phrase 'systematised, step-by-step, chronological procedures' in their discussion of this idea. Typically, such a system will proceed in a linear fashion, starting from mission and objectives and working through to implementation and the feedback of performance review. Such a system is illustrated on the next page.

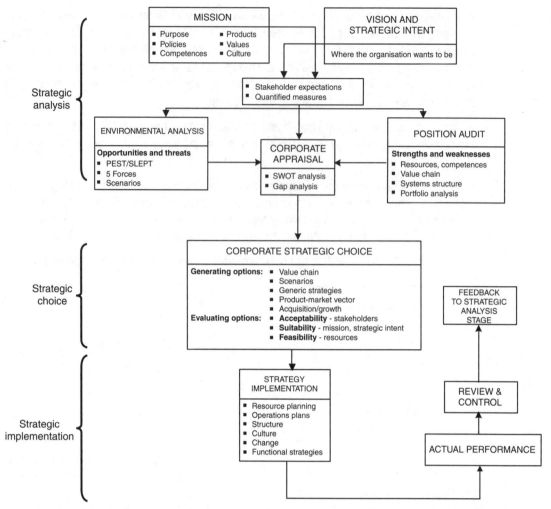

When you look at the detail of this model, you will recognise much that we have discussed in this Study Text. However, for the purposes of our current discussion, the important thing about this diagram is not the way it draws together a number of related ideas, but that **it represents the traditional view of how strategy is actually made**: it is a representation of a **corporate subsystem** that would have staff, managers, offices and interactions with other corporate systems.

The idea that strategy should be made in this way is no longer popular for reasons that will be reviewed later in this section, but it does have its advantages, both for **determining** what the strategy should be and in **implementing** it.

2.1 Advantages of a formal system of strategic planning

Advantages	Comment
Provides a structure	Developing strategy is a complex task, with many variables to take into account. A formal system provides a structure for analysis and planning
Risk management	A full scheme of strategic planning should both identify and help in managing these risks
Stimulation of thought, challenge and questioning	The system of strategic planning provides a structure for discussion and can encourage creativity and challenges to the paradigm
Decision-making	Companies cannot remain static – they have to cope with changes in the environment. The planning process draws attention to the need to change and adapt, not just to 'stand still' and survive

Advantages	Comment
Control	Management control can be better exercised if targets are explicit
Consistency	Plans for a range of business unit activities can be integrated and long-term and short-term objectives can be made consistent with one another. Otherwise, strategies can be rendered ineffective by budgeting systems and performance measures that have no strategic content
Communication	Discussion at the various stages helps to make the reasoning behind strategy clear, while the creation of specific plans prompts appropriate dissemination
Time horizon	Longer-term views can be built in to the system by setting a suitable time horizon for the planning period
Co-ordination	Business unit plans, the use of resources and the activities of different business functions can be co-ordinated and directed towards a common goal
Objectives	Managers are forced to define what they want to achieve
Responsibility and involvement	A plan shows people where they fit in and what they have to do

2.2 Criticisms of formal strategic planning

(a) Making strategic plans is not the same thing as managing strategy, which is the long-term scope and direction of the organisation. The complexity of the model shown above is capable of **distracting managers' attention** from controlling actual progress.

(b) It is also easy to confuse strategic planning and control with **budgetary processes**. There is an obvious relationship between the two, but they are not the same. The latter is a complex but routine activity; the former requires careful consideration of the kind of material dealt with in this Study Text.

(c) The best is the enemy of the good: there is no guarantee that a complex planning system will produce the perfect strategy and too much time and effort can be spent searching for it.

(d) A further problem with a complex and formal system of planning is that the various aspects of analysis that it involves can lead to a simple **acceptance of the current *realised* strategy**.

(e) A **split may develop** between the people responsible for **planning** and those responsible for **implementation**. Line managers may be too busy to take part in the planning process, while planners are unlikely to have the authority required to implement the plans they produce. The result is that planning becomes divorced from operational reality. This division can be reinforced if commercial confidentiality receives too much emphasis and planning is carried on in an atmosphere of secrecy.

(f) Particularly in very large organisations, the planning system may be **too extensive and complex** for even quite senior managers to understand the way it works. This hinders proper input and application.

(g) Very detailed analysis can lead to information overload; this, in turn, can prevent the planners from recognising major strategic issues when they arise.

(h) Over-formal planning systems and over-rigid control can hamper innovative thinking.

Possibly as a result of these problems, the use of formal strategic planning systems has declined markedly and it has been common for more responsibility for strategic decision-making to be devolved to line managers. Planning has become more informal and has tended to concentrate on discussion of key strategic issues and establishing overall strategic scope and direction.

2.3 Workshops and project teams

As formal planning systems have declined in importance, there has been a growth in the use of project teams and workshops to develop aspects of overall strategy. Such groups can be set up at almost any level in the organisation and can be particularly useful for keeping managers at the strategic apex in touch

with current routine operational experience and problems. A wide range of specific purposes may be served using these methods.

(a) A top management group might **set overall strategy** after considering reports from specialists, functions and business units.

(b) **Strategic analysis** could be undertaken by more junior managers who then report upwards.

(c) A cross-hierarchical group might be set up to **challenge current assumptions**.

(d) Similar groups might be formed to **generate new ideas and approaches** to problems.

(e) The planning of **strategic implementation** cannot be done by top management alone. Similarly, **monitoring progress** could be done in workshops.

(f) Consideration of **factors blocking strategic change** could be carried out by a project team.

2.4 Strategy consultants

Strategy consultants have a range of roles to play in strategic management. Some of these are political, such as lending their authority to a new CEO who wishes to bring about change, or symbolic, as when their presence and activity emphasise the importance of a new approach. They can also assist with key aspects of the strategic management process.

(a) **Strategic analysis and options generation** may be an appropriate task for consultants where the situation is confused or there is disagreement among top managers. Consultants may bring a fresh and impartial approach.

(b) Consultants should bring **knowledge and experience** and can be transmitters of best practice between organisations.

(c) Consultants may assist in the process of **strategic decision-making**. However, they should not exercise undue influence: responsibility for strategy should remain with the managers at the strategic apex of the client organisation.

(d) **Strategic change** is a fruitful field for the employment of consultants, especially in such activities as coaching and training.

2.5 Imposed strategy

Powerful external stakeholders may be able to impose a strategy. This is most common in the public sector, where government may make generally applicable regulations that constrain strategic choice, or may take more specific action to force a particular strategy on to an organisation. Privatisation is an example of the way in which governments have imposed strategic change on organisations.

3 Developing emergent strategies

FAST FORWARD

Logical incrementalism develops strategy in small experimental steps. Resource allocation procedures may lead to the emergence of strategy, as may the cultural processes that make up the paradigm. However, an obsolete paradigm will lead to **strategic drift** and the emergence of inappropriate strategic moves. Strategies may emerge from the bargaining and negotiation associated with political activity.

The practices developed during detailed strategic implementation may also be a source of emergent strategies.

Realised strategy can emerge as well as arise from intention. However, this is not a random process: emergent strategies require extensive management if they are to be successful.

3.1 Logical incrementalism

> **Logical incrementalism** is the deliberate development of strategy by experimentation and learning from partial commitments.   *JS&W*

Quinn observed processes typical of logical incrementalism.

(a)   A **generalised view** of a desired future state and rather wide objectives

(b)   Constant **environmental scanning** rather than firm forecasts

(c)   A combination of building a **strong core business** on experience and **experimenting** with possible strategic options

(d)   'Subsystems' consisting of groups of people that experiment with products and markets

(e)   Employment of **formal and informal processes** to draw out patterns of development

Such an approach combines an element of intention with a significant amount of emergence. It allows for constant adjustment and testing of strategy, good quality of environmental information, readiness to change and continuing internal consultation.

3.2 Resource allocation routines

Bower and Burgelman concluded independently that strategy arises as a consequence of **competitive resource allocation** within organisations. Managers at lower and intermediate levels bid for resources for the projects they favour. The basic decision rules and the strategic context are set at the strategic apex, but strategy is determined by resource allocation decisions made at lower levels. JS&W quote the example of Intel, which in the 1980s switched from making memory chips to concentration on microprocessors in this fashion.

3.3 Cultural processes

The structures, assumptions, practices and processes that make up the paradigm and the wider cultural web may be sufficiently influential as to determine strategy, particularly in the shape of strategic responses to environmental changes. Experience of methods that have worked in the past can offer a comforting approach to dealing with new ambiguities and uncertainties. However, making strategy in this way can slow response to environmental change and lead to **strategic drift**.

> **Strategic drift** occurs when strategies progressively fail to address the strategic position of the organisation and performance deteriorates.   *JS&W*

JS&W suggest that **strategic drift** arises because of the tendency to prefer small adjustments to large ones. If performance deteriorates, the first reaction will be to impose tighter control over implementation. If this is ineffective, a new strategy may be developed. However, this will take place within the constraints of the cultural web. By the time the organisation's leaders understand and accept that cultural change is required, it may be too late.

3.4 The Icarus paradox

Miller describes the way in which a once successful paradigm becomes obsolete, referring to the effect as the **Icarus paradox**.

Miller suggests that when companies succeed, their success can lead to a kind of dislocated feedback of the qualities that made them succeed; this distortion then leads to failure.

Miller diagnoses four important aspects of this distortion.

(a)   **Leadership failures** occur when success reinforces top management's preconceptions, makes them over confident, less concerned for the customer's views, conceited and obstinate.

(b) **Cultural domination** by star departments and their ideologies leads to intolerance of other ideas and reduces the capacity for innovative and flexible response.

(c) **Power games and politics** are used by dominant managers and departments to resist change and amplify current strategic thinking.

(d) **Corporate memory**, consisting of processes, habits and reflexes, is substituted for careful thought about new problems.

The interplay of these factors leads to decline, usually along one of four **trajectories**.

(a) **Craftsmen become tinkerers**. Quality-driven engineering firms become obsessed with irrelevant technical detail.

(b) **Builders become imperialists**. Acquisitive, growth driven companies over-expand into areas they cannot manage properly.

(c) **Pioneers become escapists**. Companies whose core competence is technically superb innovation and state-of-the-art products lose focus and waste their resources on grandiose and impractical projects.

(d) **Salesmen become drifters**. Marketing oriented companies with stables of valuable brands become bureaucratic pursuers of sales figures whose market offerings become stale and uninspired.

3.5 Political processes

It is common to view organisations as arenas of political activity: we discussed the political aspects of change management earlier in this Study Text.

Key term

> The **political view** of strategy development is that strategies develop as the outcome of processes of bargaining and negotiation among powerful internal or external interest groups (or stakeholders).

The political view is reasonable, in that powerful executives are likely to defend and seek to extend their power and influence. It is probable that both information flows and strategic analysis will therefore be influenced by political manoeuvres. Existing strategies and potential challengers will become identified with particular factions and the outcome of strategic choice may amount to victory and defeat if compromise is not reached. It is reasonable to view the political processes of negotiation as a kind of emergent or incremental approach to making strategy.

Nevertheless, the political process is equally capable of leading to significant innovation, as powerful managers seek new ideas to enhance their own power.

Exam focus point

> We have said that emergent strategies are to be contrasted with intended strategies in that they come about as a result of the everyday activities decisions and processes that take place at all levels of the organisation. In this context, it is important to remember the relational diagram of your syllabus: process change, quality initiatives and e-business are both the important elements of strategic implementation and sources from which unintended strategies are likely to emerge.

4 Diversity of strategic processes

FAST FORWARD

> There is no single correct way to develop strategy and effective strategies may well result from the simultaneous working of more than one process.

We have examined a wide range of means of arriving at strategy and considered the advantages and disadvantages of each. The picture is complex and somewhat obscure, but we may offer some comments on the idea of strategic method, based, as usual, on JS&W.

(a) There is **no single correct way** to develop a strategy. This is important because it highlights the importance of context. For example, we would expect the way strategies develop in a rapidly changing environment to be different to the way strategies develop in an environment with little change.

(b)   Strategy development is likely to vary at different **times** and in different contexts.

(c)   Different managers will **perceive strategy development differently**. For example, top managers tend to see their strategic work as rational and intended; middle managers may be more aware of the impact of politics.

(d)   It is unlikely that any organisation's strategy is the result of a single process; several are likely to be at work, and this may well produce a more successful outcome than a single approach.

5 Challenges and implications

FAST FORWARD

Organisational learning can form a strong base for the development of strategy, especially when environmental conditions are both complex and dynamic. Simple and static conditions permit a planning approach. Stable but complex environments promote decentralisation of strategic development.

Our discussion above raises some challenges and implications for the management of strategy development.

5.1 Strategic drift

We have discussed the nature of strategic drift already. The tendency to prefer small adjustments can lead to a growing mismatch between strategic posture and strategic reality. Cultural rigidity can also reduce the organisation's ability to innovate and confine it to simply **reacting** to its environment, rather than **seeking to influence** it.

The challenge for strategic managers here is to promote the ability and inclination to challenge received wisdom in a creative and objective way. A strategy-making system that incorporates more than one of the approaches discussed in this chapter is more likely to be successful at this than concentrating on any one in particular.

5.2 The learning organisation

Continuing challenge to assumptions and search for improvement are typical of a **learning organisation**. We have already considered some aspects of organisational learning in our coverage of knowledge management earlier in this Study Text.

Exam focus point

An article titled 'The learning organisation' written by Fearghal McHugh is available in the technical articles section for P3 on the ACCA website. It would be worth taking the time to study this article.

Key term

A **learning organisation** is capable of continual regeneration from the variety of knowledge, experience and skills of individuals within a culture that encourages mutual questioning and challenge around a shared purpose or vision.   *JS&W*

A learning organisation emphasises the **sharing of information and knowledge,** both up and down the normal communication channels, and horizontally, through **social networks** and **interest groups**. It challenges notions of hierarchy and managers are facilitators, rather than controllers. Such an organisation is inherently capable of change. The concept has much in common with that of **logical incrementalism**. The challenge is to combine the advantages of rational planning with the resilience and adaptability provided by the learning approach.

5.3 Uncertainty and complexity

Not only must strategy take account of environmental conditions, the system and methods used in its development must also be appropriate to those conditions. It is usual in this context to analyse an organisation's environment along axes of **complexity** and **change**.

Simple and static environments are amenable to analysis and forecasting based on history and leading indicators and the rational model of strategy is more or less appropriate. However, this approach becomes less useful as environmental conditions become more complex or more dynamic, or both simultaneously.

Organisational design becomes important in environments that are **reasonably stable** but display **significant complexity**. Decentralisation into specialised organisational parts will allow the various aspects of the environment to be dealt with separately as they evolve.

Relatively **simple environments** that are subject to **rapid change** will display **significant uncertainty**. Scenario planning may be a useful technique under these conditions. Extensive and continuous environmental scanning will be required and the creativity and cooperation typical of **logical incrementalism** and the **learning organisation** will be required.

Complex and dynamic environments present the greatest challenge. Decentralisation is also appropriate here, combined with an acceptance at the strategic centre that operation experience and learning present at the periphery represent the organisation's greatest strategic strength.

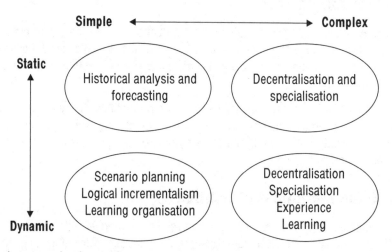

Environment and strategy development

5.4 Managing strategy development

As we have already indicated, the use of more than one approach is likely to be useful when an organisation develops its strategy. Also, the processes it uses are likely to vary with its circumstances. JS&W complete their consideration of the management of strategy development by considering some further, connected points.

(a)   It will be necessary to select different development processes for different purposes in the same organisation. Co-ordination across SBUs will require a rational approach, but within each business unit a different approach, perhaps based on learning may be appropriate, for example.

(b)   Managers responsible for strategy development must therefore take care to ensure that **appropriate processes are used in each separate context**.

(c)   Managers at the **strategic apex** must consider their role, since there are several approaches they can use.

(d)   In divisionalised organisations, it is likely that **different levels will use different strategic processes**, with an emphasis on rational planning at the centre and on experience and learning in the divisions.

(e)   Therefore, managers at different levels must **understand the importance of the roles played at other levels**.

5.5 Reviewing strategy

At the end of this book, it is appropriate to review the subject of strategy as a whole, and we will do so by looking again at the relational diagram of syllabus capabilities.

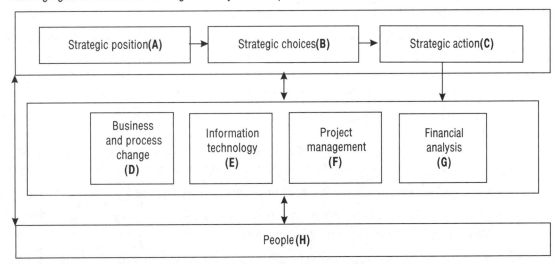

The diagram illustrates the importance of having an overall strategic perspective (position, choice, action) but also highlights the need for all the components of an organisation to fit with, and support, that strategy. The middle and bottom layers of the relational diagram show this.

However, remember the double headed arrow between the top and the middle layers indicates that as well as being **planned** (top-down), strategy can also **emerge** (middle-up) from the operational activities of an organisation.

Effective strategy is both planned and emergent. Good plans are the foundations of any strategy, but the real story lies in how the strategy unfolds, and how the various parts of an organisation react and adapt to what is happening around them.

Chapter Roundup

- **Realised strategy** may emerge from everyday actions and routine decisions, or it may be the result of considered intention. **Intended strategies** may also fail to be realised.

- **Intended strategies** are developed in a systematic way, making use of rational procedures and, probably, specialist staff. This approach has advantages associated with system and method and disadvantages associated with ponderousness and inflexibility. More recently, workshops and project teams have been used to develop intended strategies and strategy consultants have been employed.

- **Logical incrementalism** develops strategy in small experimental steps. Resource allocation procedures may lead to the emergence of strategy, as may the cultural processes that make up the paradigm. However, an obsolete paradigm will lead to **strategic drift** and the emergence of inappropriate strategic moves. Strategies may emerge from the bargaining and negotiation associated with political activity.

  The practices developed during detailed strategic implementation may also be a source of emergent strategies.

- There is no single correct way to develop strategy and effective strategies may well result from the simultaneous working of more than one process.

- Organisational learning can form a strong base for the development of strategy, especially when environmental conditions are both complex and dynamic. Simple and static conditions permit a planning approach. Stable but complex environments promote decentralisation of strategic development.

Quick Quiz

1　The sources of realised strategy may be divided into two categories. What are they?

2　How might intended strategies be developed?

3　Theorists have described several sources of emergent strategies. What are they?

4　What is strategic drift?

5　Can you recommend a single mode of strategy development that will be satisfactory under all conditions?

Answers to Quick quiz

1 Intended strategies and emergent strategies

2 Typically, within planning departments, but more recently, through workshops and project teams and by employing consultants

3 Logical incrementalism, resource allocation routines, cultural processes and political processes

4 Strategic drift occurs when strategies progressively fail to address the strategic position of an organisation, and its performance deteriorates. Strategic drift reflects a preference for minor adjustments rather than clear changes to address performance issues

5 You might try, but would be ill-advised to do so. There is no single way to develop strategy. A strategy must always be appropriate to its context

Now try the question below from the Practice Question Bank

Number	Level	Marks	Time
Q17	Examination	50	90 mins

This question is actually a case study question with an extensive scenario. This brings together many of the themes that you have studied throughout this text book and is included to give you an idea as to the length of question you will be likely to face in the compulsory Section A of your P3 exam.

Practice question and answer bank

1 Bartok Fuel

20 mins

Bartok Fuel is a private company run by two brothers, David and Sean Bartok. The company was founded in the 1960s by their father, Gerald, who started life with a petrol station and car repair workshop. After some years, Gerald expanded by buying a tanker and starting to distribute household fuel to customers. This part of the business has grown successfully and now has some 15 tankers and an annual turnover of $30 million.

In the 1960s, the car repair business included the manufacture of car windscreens. From this grew an element of the business, called Bartok Glass, which now makes sealed glass window units for the construction industry and has a turnover of about $8 million.

During the 1970s and 1980s Gerald had purchased a number of sites from which petrol was sold. These sites are still owned by the company but are now leased to other companies and used for a variety of purposes. The original garage no longer exists, but the company still operates a car dealership and repair workshop in the centre of Erewhon, a large town in the country Oceania. This part of the business started in the 1990s and for some time was fairly profitable, particularly when it was a luxury car dealership run by Gerald's younger son, Sean. However, due to changes in the market place, the luxury car franchise had to be sold and the business now sells budget cars.

The fuel distribution and glass businesses continue to be fairly profitable under the management of the older brother David, but the car business is facing hard times. The car retail business is notoriously cut-throat, with margins as low as 2– 3% and very high targets set by the manufacturers. The car dealership also deals in second hand cars and this area is slightly more profitable. This division now employs about 50 people.

David is the managing director of the company and at a recent board meeting he put forward a number of proposals for improving the profitability of the car dealership and garage. One suggestion is that the site should be sold for its development potential and the car dealership brought to an end.

A further option brought up by David is the potential for entering the emerging market for fuel distribution in the distant country of Arcadia. He has recently met an Arcadian entrepreneur who was visiting Oceania, who is making considerable profits in this area and is looking for investment from a new partner. David is very keen on this option and is trying to push it through.

Required

(a)   Describe the approach to strategy that Bartok Fuel has adopted in the past.
(b)   What factors should the Board consider before making any decisions on the proposals to dispose of the Erewhon site for development and to enter the Arcadian fuel distribution market?

2 National advantage

20 mins

D4D is a politically stable, developing country enjoying a temperate climate and a young, educated population, many of whom are educated to graduate level. Those who have studied at this level have tended to do so abroad, since there are limited opportunities to do so in D4D.

The economy is mixed, based on agriculture and some light manufacturing, but has enjoyed considerable revenue from oil exploration and production which is based offshore in its territorial waters. Some of this revenue is generated by providing services for the oil industry, but the majority comes from a tax on every barrel of oil that the foreign oil companies extract.

The government has used the revenue to keep personal and property taxes low and to support the largely uneconomic local industry. It now recognises that, although politically popular, this decision might not have been in the best long-term interests of the country.

The Finance and Trade Minister of D4D is aware that the oil revenue may only last a further ten years. He wishes to build a competitive advantage over the neighbouring countries. The Prime Minister is sceptical, and has made the observation that 'companies have competitive advantages not countries'.

As a management accountant within the Ministry of Finance and Trade, you have been asked to produce a number of documents, for both the Prime Minister and the Finance and Trade Minister, considering how competitive advantage could be achieved for D4D and examining the possibilities of attracting inward investment from foreign companies.

Required

Using any models you consider appropriate, explain the factors that lead to competitive advantage being present in particular countries.

3 EMS

15 mins

The Environment Management Society (EMS) was established in 1999 by environment practitioners who felt that environmental management and audit should have its own qualification. EMS has its own Board who report to a Council of eight members. Policy is made by the Board and ratified by Council. EMS is registered as a private limited entity.

EMS employs staff to administer its qualification and to provide services to its members. The qualification began as one certificate, developed by the original founding members of the Society. It has since been developed, by members and officers of the EMS, into a four certificate scheme leading to a Diploma. EMS employs a full-time chief examiner who is responsible for setting the certificate examinations which take place monthly in training centres throughout the country. No examinations are currently held in other countries.

If candidates pass all four papers they can undertake an oral Diploma examination. If they pass this oral they are eligible to become members. All examinations are open-book one hour examinations, preceded by 15 minutes' reading time. At a recent meeting, EMS Council rejected the concept of computer-based assessment. They felt that competence in this area was best assessed by written examination answers.

Candidate numbers for the qualification have fallen dramatically in the last two years. The Board of EMS has concluded that this drop reflects the maturing marketplace in the country. Many people who were practitioners in environmental management and audit when the qualification was introduced have now gained their Diploma. The stream of new candidates and hence members is relatively small.

Consequently, the EMS Board has suggested that they should now look to attract international candidates and it has targeted countries where environmental management and audit is becoming more important. It is now formulating a strategy to launch the qualification in India, China and Russia.

However, any strategy has to recognise that both the EMS Board and the Council are very cautious and notably risk averse. EMS is only confident about its technical capability within a restricted definition of environmental management and audit. Attempts to look at complementary qualification areas (such as soil and water conservation) have been swiftly rejected by Council as being non-core areas and therefore outside the scope of their expertise.

Required

Internal development, acquisitions and strategic alliances are three development methods by which an organisation's strategic direction can be pursued. Explain the principles of internal development and discuss how appropriate this development method is to EMS.

(8 marks)

4 Natalia Norman

45 mins

Natalia Norman is a designer and manufacturer of knitwear clothing. She has based her designs on ethnic patterns, inspired by clothing she has seen in Central Asia. She has sourced her products both from these Asian regions – Uzbekistan and Kazakhstan – as well as from small factories in parts of the United Kingdom. Her products, though stylish, are relatively cheap, but her marketing strategy is totally passive. She has a web-site and most of her sales are reactive, responding to orders over the internet. The resultant sales and, in particular, profits have been disappointing and so she has hired a marketing consultant to give her some advice. The following are extracts from the consultant's report.

'Your product, although distinctive, is insufficiently unique. The designs have no patents nor copyright and because the production technology is so simple and inexpensive there are few barriers to entry. Competition is all too prevalent. Your promotion is too general. It focuses on no specific market. By relying on the internet your advertising is rather indiscriminate and you have failed to create a loyal following and your image is diffused with little opportunity for building brand awareness. There is a failure within distribution. Most consumers wish to see, handle or try on products before making a purchase, particularly if the products do not already have a well-established reputation and/or a brand name. In your case the only exposure your products have is via the world-wide web. Your pricing structure is too cost-based. You are able to source your products cheaply but your margins are too low to provide you with the necessary capital to reinvest if the business is to develop profitably in the future.

'You have failed to establish yourself in the market place as a dominant player. Too many of your business decisions are reactive and often too late to have adequate impact. You are following market trends and not attempting to lead them.'

Natalia is naturally disturbed by the criticisms which this report has levelled at her company's operations and has decided that she must be more positive in her actions. In particular she has decided that her marketing efforts must be more focused and she must pursue more proactively her competitive activities.

Required

In order to focus her company's marketing efforts more precisely Natalia has decided to segment the market for knitwear products.

(a)   Suggest potential bases for segmenting this knitwear market and discuss the benefits which a more focused segmentation could bring to the company.   **(15 marks)**

(b)   Evaluate strategies which Natalia might pursue as a market follower to make her knitwear company more competitive.   **(10 marks)**

(Total = 25 marks)

5 Firebridge Tyres Ltd   36 mins

Firebridge Tyres Ltd (FTL) is a wholly owned UK subsidiary of Gonzales Tyre Corporation (GTC) of the USA. FTL manufactures and sells tyres under a number of different brand names.

(a)   Firespeed, offering high product quality, at a price which offers good value for money
(b)   Freeway, a cheap brand, effectively a standard tyre
(c)   Tufload, for lorries and commercial vehicles

FTL has good relationships with car firms and distributors.

GTC is rather less focused; not only does it make tyres and some other components, but it also owns a chain of car service centres specialising in minor maintenance matters such as tyre replacement, exhaust fitting, and wheel balancing.

FTL has experienced a fall in sales revenue, partly as a result of competition from overseas producers, in what is effectively a mature market. Moreover, sales of new cars have not been as high as had been hoped, and consumers are more reluctant than before to part with their money.

FTL's managers have had meetings with GTC's managers as to how to revive the fortunes of the company. FTL would like to export to the US and to Asia. GTC has vetoed this suggestion, as FTL's tyres would compete with GTC's. Instead, GTC suggests that FTL imitate GTC's strategy by running a chain of service stations similar to GTC's service stations in the US. GTC feels that vertical integration would offer profits in its own right and provide a distribution network which would reduce the impact of competition from other tyre manufacturers. GTC has no shortage of cash.

You are a strategic consultant to FTL.

Required

(a)   Discuss the principal factors in the external environment that would influence FTL's strategic choice.   **(6 marks)**

(b)   Describe the barriers to entry that FTL might face if it decided to enter the service centre business.
(6 marks)

(c)   Assess whether FTL's existing strategic capability gives it a good chance of success in the service centre business. **(8 marks)**

(Total = 20 marks)

6 Nadir Products: ethics   36 mins

John Staples is the Finance Director of Nadir Products plc, a company which manufactures and sells bathroom products such as baths, sinks and toilets. These products are sold through a selection of specialist shops and through larger stores. Customers include professional plumbers and also ordinary householders who are renovating their houses themselves. The company operates at the lower end of the market and does not have a strong reputation for service. Sales have been slowly declining whereas those of competitors have been improving. In order to encourage increased sales the Board of Directors have decided to pay senior staff a bonus if certain targets are achieved. The two main targets are based on profit levels and annual sales. Two months before the end of the financial year the Finance Director asks one of his staff to check through the orders and accounts to assess the current situation. He is informed that without a sudden improvement in sales before the year end the important sales targets will not be met and so bonuses will be adversely affected.

The Finance Director has proposed to other senior staff that this shortfall in sales can be corrected by taking one of the following decisions.

1.   A significant discount can be offered to any retail outlet which takes delivery of additional products prior to the end of the financial year.

2.   Scheduled orders due to be delivered at the beginning of the next financial year can be brought forward and billed before the end of this year.

3.   Distributors can be told that there is a risk of price increases in the future and that it will be advisable to order early so as to circumvent this possibility.

The Board is not sure of the implications associated with such decisions.

Required

(a)   As a consultant, prepare a report for the Board of Nadir Products assessing the commercial and ethical implications associated with each of the proposed options mentioned above.   **(8 marks)**

(b)   Assess the significance of the corporate social responsibility model for Nadir Products. **(12 marks)**

(Total = 20 marks)

7 Arragon Antennas   36 mins

Arragon Antennas Ltd is a company based in the country of Dragovia. It designs and manufactures antennas for airborne navigation and communication systems. The industry is characterised by dedication to high technical standards because of the demands of aircraft safety. There are three main parts to the business: design and integration of antennas for new aircraft; aftermarket spares for existing systems; and sub-contract manufacture of other firms' designs.

Design of new installations is highly technical and very time consuming since it depends on extensive tests, including test flying. Globally, there are only three other manufacturers capable of this work.

The aftermarket operation includes spares for Arragon's own products and for antennas the company has designed to replace the other three manufacturers' own proprietary designs. Sales of the latter are somewhat price sensitive, but the aircraft spares market generally is characterised by the high prices charged to captive customers for approved spares.

Demand for subcontracting work tends to be intermittent but forms a profitable supplement to the manufacture of the company's own designs. Nobody in the industry thinks it odd that Arragon should both manufacture for and compete with other firms.

Arragon's market is now being threatened by Wizzomatic Inc, which is a subsidiary of a major armaments group based in the larger country of Erewhon. Wizzomatic is offering a family of standardised antennas derived from its work for the Erewhon government. The antennas offer a substantial price advantage over most proprietary designs and are being promoted as suitable for most applications.

Required

(a)   Assess the strategic options available to Arragon Antennas.
(b)   Suggest an appropriate marketing mix for Arragon Antennas.

8 United Products   36 mins

United Products (UP) was formed 46 years ago by the merger of two large commercial organisations: Bulk Foods and Rowbotham Enterprises. Over the years it has acquired and disposed of several businesses and now has operations in Europe and North America. It has wholly owned subsidiaries operating in flour milling; vineyards; grocery retailing; agricultural machinery manufacturing and distribution; chemicals (particularly fertilisers); publishing; film production; and forestry. It is also involved via joint ventures and partnerships in quarrying, electronics design and clothes retailing.

The company is regarded by investors as fairly safe but dull. Its growth has not kept pace with its competitors and some of its divisions' performance is distinctly poor.

UP is organised into divisions, some of which are product based and some geographically based. Control is devolved to the CEOs of each division, subject to the compilation and submission of detailed monthly performance reports to the corporate HQ in Fazackerley, near Liverpool in the UK. Corporate HQ requires that each division has identifiable managers responsible for production, sales and finance. These managers are frequently visited by senior members of the relevant head office staff. It is corporate policy to promote from within, and all divisional CEOs must have experience of working both at corporate HQ and in at least three divisions.

There has been a history of disputes between HQ and the divisions. Many have complained about the complexity of the monthly reports and the cost of compiling them. Some have said that they find HQ requirements and visits to be disruptive and counter-productive. However, the Corporate CEO, is very concerned about the tendency of the divisions to go their own way.

Required

(a)   Evaluate the way that UP is currently organised.
(b)   Explain the meaning of the term virtual organisation. Assess whether such an approach would be suitable for any of UP's operations.

9 Auto Direct   22 mins

Mark Howe, Managing Director of Auto Direct, is a victim of his own success. Mark has created an innovative way of selling cars to the public which takes advantage of the greater freedom given to independent car distributors to market cars more aggressively within the European Union. This reduces the traditional control and interference of the automobile manufacturers, some of whom own their distributors. He has opened a number of showrooms in the London region and by 2004 Auto Direct had 20 outlets in and around London. The concept is deceptively simple; Mark buys cars from wherever he can source them most cheaply and has access to all of the leading volume car models. He then concentrates on selling the cars to the public, leaving servicing and repair work to other specialist garages. He offers a classic high volume/low margin business model.

Mark now wants to develop this business model onto a national and eventually an international basis. His immediate plans are to grow the number of outlets by 50% each year for the next three years. Such growth will place considerable strain on the existing organisation and staff. Each showroom has its own management team, sales personnel and administration. Currently the 20 showrooms are grouped into a Northern and Southern Sales Division with a small head office team for each division. Auto Direct now employs 250 people.

Required

Using appropriate strategies for managing change provide Mark with a brief report on how he should pursue his proposed growth plans.

(12 marks)

10 BPR and supply chain

15 mins

ABC has a chain of twenty supermarkets. When inventory items reach their re-order level in a supermarket the in-store computerised inventory system informs the stock clerk. The clerk then raises a request daily to the ABC central warehouse for replenishment of inventory via fax or e-mail. If the local warehouse has available stock, it is forwarded to the supermarket within twenty-four hours of receiving the request. If the local warehouse cannot replenish the stock from its inventory holding, it raises a purchase order to one of its suppliers. The supplier delivers the inventory to the warehouse and the warehouse then delivers the required inventory to the supermarkets within the area. The ABC area warehouse staff conduct all business communication with suppliers.

ABC recently contracted an IT consultant to analyse and make recommendations concerning their current supply chain briefly described above. Following the initial investigation the consultant reported.

'To enable an established traditional company like ABC to develop a Virtual Supply Chain system it may be necessary to employ a Business Process Re-engineering (BPR) approach.'

Required

With reference to the above scenario, describe what is meant by a Business Process Re-engineering approach.

11 Fashion retailer

45 mins

Paul Singh operates in the fashion clothing industry, owning 20 retail stores selling mainly to the teenage and youth market. This industry segment, comprising many small firms, each with a few retail stores, has very few large scale competitors. Paul's business has grown at a rapid rate with him acquiring his first store only five years ago. Despite this growth in business there has never been any associated integration of activities. Paul has been too busy growing his company to pay attention to consolidation and efficiency. However, he has now realised that despite this fast expansion his profits have not grown at the same rate as turnover. This part of the fashion business operates with very slim margins. The products are cheap but with the ever changing demand for fashion garments there are few opportunities for individual stores to hold inventory for long periods of time. This has prevented Paul from taking advantage of economies of purchasing.

Each of his stores has tended to be run in isolation. Paul has left his local managers to decide on buying inventory and on merchandising. His view has been that these managers are nearer to the customers and therefore they will know the fashion trends better. This appears to have worked with regard to turnover but he now needs to operate in a more cost-conscious manner. His computing system is being used in a old-fashioned way. It focuses on providing store accounts and is really only used by the small financial team (largely unqualified or still studying) located at the Head Office. Paul has been talking to friends who are operating in similar but non-competitive environments, and they have told him how useful they have found the up-to-date computer-based information systems. Several standard software packages have recommended. However, one person has said that it would be more cost-effective to have a standard package modified to fit Paul's particular business operations.

Required

(a)   Using a suitable model to support your arguments explain how the strategic use of information systems could provide Paul with a competitive edge in this currently fragmented industry.

(12 marks)

(b)   Acting in the role of a consultant, write a report to Paul discussing packages generally and assessing the two software package options that have been suggested.   **(13 marks)**

(Total = 25 marks)

12 Good Sports Ltd   45 mins

Good Sports Limited is an independent sports goods retailer owned and operated by two partners, Alan and Bob, based in the country of Oceania. The sports retailing business in Oceania has undergone a major change over the past ten years. First of all the supply side has been transformed by the emergence of a few global manufacturers of the core sports products, such as training shoes and football shirts. This consolidation has made them increasingly unwilling to provide good service to the independent sportswear retailers too small to buy in sufficiently large quantities. These independent retailers can stock popular global brands, but have to order using the Internet and have no opportunity to meet the manufacturer's sales representatives. Secondly, Oceania's sportswear retailing has undergone significant structural change with the rapid growth of a small number of national retail chains with the buying power to offset the power of the global manufacturers. These retail chains stock a limited range of high volume branded products and charge low prices the independent retailer cannot hope to match.

Good Sports has survived by becoming a specialist niche retailer catering for less popular sports such as cricket, hockey and rugby. They are able to offer the specialist advice and stock the goods that their customers want. In recent years Good Sports has become aware of the growing impact of e-business in general and e-retailing in particular. They employed a specialist website designer and created an online purchasing facility for their customers. The results were less than impressive, with the Internet search engines not picking up the company website. The seasonal nature of Good Sports' business, together with the variations in sizes and colours needed to meet an individual customer's needs, meant that the sales volumes were insufficient to justify the costs of running the site.

Bob, however, is convinced that developing an e-business strategy suited to the needs of the independent sports retailer such as Good Sports will be key to business survival. He has been encouraged by the growing interest of customers in other countries to the service and product range they offer. He is also aware of the need to integrate an e-business strategy with their current marketing, which to date has been limited to the sponsorship of local sports teams and advertisements taken in specialist sports magazines. Above all, he wants to avoid head-on competition with the national retailers and their emphasis on popular branded sportswear sold at retail prices that are below the cost price at which Good Sports can buy the goods.

Required

(a) Provide the partners with a short report on the advantages and disadvantages to Good Sports of developing an e-business strategy and the processes most likely to be affected by such a strategy.

(15 marks)

(b) Good Sports Limited has successfully followed a niche strategy to date.

Assess the extent to which an appropriate e-business strategy could help support such a niche strategy.

(10 marks)

(Total = 25 marks)

13 DRB   45 mins

DRB Electronic Services operates in a high labour cost environment in Western Europe and imports electronic products from the Republic of Korea. It re-brands and re-packages them as DRB products and then sells them to business and domestic customers in the local geographical region. Its only current source of supply is ISAS electronics based in a factory on the outskirts of Seoul, the capital of the Republic of Korea. DRB regularly places orders for ISAS products through the ISAS web-site and pays for them by credit card. As soon as the payment is confirmed ISAS automatically e-mails DRB a confirmation of order, an order reference number and likely shipping date. When the order is actually despatched, ISAS send DRB a notice of despatch e-mail and a container reference number. ISAS currently organises all the shipping of the products. The products are sent in containers and then trans-shipped to EIF, the logistics company used by ISAS to distribute its products. EIF then delivers the products to the DRB factory. Once they arrive, they are quality inspected and products that pass the inspection are re-branded as DRB products (by adding appropriate logos) and packaged in specially fabricated DRB boxes. These products

are then stored ready for sale. All customer sales are from stock. Products that fail the inspection are returned to ISAS.

Currently 60% of sales are made to domestic customers and 40% to business customers. Most domestic customers pick up their products from DRB and set them up themselves. In contrast, most business customers ask DRB to set up the electronic equipment at their offices, for which DRB makes a small charge. DRB currently advertises its products in local and regional newspapers. DRB also has a website which provides product details. Potential customers can enquire about the specification and availability of products through an e-mail facility in the website. DRB then e-mails an appropriate response directly to the person making the enquiry. Payment for products cannot currently be made through the website.

Feedback from existing customers suggests that they particularly value the installation and support offered by the company. The company employs specialist technicians who (for a fee) will install equipment in both homes and offices. They will also come out and troubleshoot problems with equipment that is still under warranty. DRB also offer a helpline and a back to base facility for customers whose products are out of warranty. Feedback from current customers suggests that this support is highly valued. One commented that 'it contrasts favourably with your large customers who offer support through impersonal off-shore call centres and a time-consuming returns policy'. Customers can also pay for technicians to come on-site to sort out problems with out-of-warranty equipment.

DRB now plans to increase their product range and market share. It plans to grow from its current turnover of $5m per annum to $12m per annum in two years time. Dilip Masood, the owner of DRB, believes that DRB must change its business model if it is to achieve this growth. He believes that these changes will also have to tackle problems associated with:

- Missing, or potentially missing shipments. Shipments can only be tracked through contacting the shipment account holder, ISAS, and on occasions they have been reluctant or unable to help. The trans-shipment to EIF has also caused problems and this has usually been identified as the point where goods have been lost. ISAS does not appear to be able to reliably track the relationship between the container shipment and the Waybills used in the EIF system.

- The likely delivery dates of orders, the progress of orders and the progress of shipments is poorly specified and monitored. Hence deliveries are relatively unpredictable and this can cause congestion problems in the delivery bay.

Dilip also recognises that growth will mean that the company has to sell more products outside its region and the technical installation and support so valued by local customers will be difficult to maintain. He is also adamant that DRB will continue to import only fully configured products. It is not interested in importing components and assembling them. DRB also does not wish to build or invest in assembly plants overseas or to commit to a long-term contract with one supplier.

Required

(a) Draw the primary activities of DRB on a value chain. Comment on the significance of each of these activities and the value that they offer to customers. **(9 marks)**

(b) Explain how DRB might re-structure its upstream supply chain to achieve the growth required by DRB and to tackle the problems that Dilip Masood has identified. **(10 marks)**

(c) Explain how DRB might re-structure its downstream supply chain to achieve the growth required. **(6 marks)**

(Total = 25 marks)

14 Project initiation

36 mins

Project management in the ABC company

Dave is the project manager in-charge of a project team installing new software in the ABC Company. The installation is currently three weeks behind schedule, with only seven weeks left before the installation should be complete. Due to the time constraints, Dave has cancelled all project meetings to try and focus his team on meeting the project deadlines. While this action has had some slight improvement in the amount of work being carried out, members of the team have been complaining that they cannot discuss problems easily. Most of the team are professional staff with appropriate project management qualifications.

Over the last week, both of the systems analysts have left to move onto other assignments due to double bookings by the project management company. This did not help the morale of the remaining team members. To try and compensate for the lack of staff, the project manager has asked two other team members with a small amount of systems analysis experience to continue their jobs. To try and impress upon them the seriousness of the situation, Dave also made these members responsible for any mistakes in the analysis documentation.

In the last few days, the working situation in the team has become significantly worse, with many minor quarrels and disagreements breaking out. Dave has chosen to ignore these problems, and simply asked the team to focus on completing the project.

Required

(a) Identify and explain where the ABC Company project is being poorly managed. **(10 marks)**
(b) Explain how the project manager can help resolve these difficulties. **(10 marks)**

(Total = 20 marks)

15 Educational Institution

45 mins

You are a newly-appointed Finance Manager of an Educational Institution that is mainly government-funded, having moved from a similar post in a service company in the private sector. The objective, or mission statement, of this Institution is shown in its publicity material as:

'To achieve recognised standards of excellence in the provision of teaching and research.'

The only financial performance measure evaluated by the government is that the Institution has to remain within cash limits. The cash allocation each year is determined by a range of non-financial measures such as the number of research publications the Institution's staff have achieved and official ratings for teaching quality.

However, almost 20% of total cash generated by the Institution is now from the provision of courses and seminars to private sector companies, using either its own or its customers' facilities. These customers are largely unconcerned about research ratings and teaching quality as they relate more to academic awards such as degrees.

The Head of the Institution aims to increase the percentage of income coming from the private sector to 50% over the next five years. She has asked you to advise on how the management team can evaluate progress towards achieving this aim as well as meeting the objective set by government for the activities it funds.

Required

(a) Discuss the main issues that an Institution such as this has to consider when setting objectives.

Advise on:

(i) Whether a financial objective, or objectives, could or should be determined
(ii) Whether such objective(s) should be made public **(9 marks)**

(b) The following is a list of financial and non-financial performance measures that were in use in your *previous company:*

FINANCIAL	NON-FINANCIAL
Value added	Competitive position
Profitability	Customer satisfaction
Return on investment	Market share

Required

Choose *two of each* type of measure, explain their purpose and advise on how they could be used by the Educational Institution over the next five years to assess how it is meeting the Head of the Institution's aims.

(16 marks)

Note. A report format is NOT required in answering this question.

(Total = 25 marks)

16 Coxford Doors

18 mins

Coxford Doors is a family owned wood products company, specialising in producing doors and windows to be sold directly to house builders. There are currently no sales directly to homeowners who may wish to purchase doors and windows to replace their existing ones. In recent years the industry has become much more competitive. Most of the customers are now large nationwide builders, the industry having gone through a period of consolidation. These customers generally require standardised products in large volume, and they buy on the basis of low prices and guarantees of regular delivery. This has put great pressure on companies such as Coxford Doors. This company is still operating as if it were dealing with the fragmented market of twenty years ago. The family, in seeking uninterrupted growth, has permitted the workforce to have a substantial degree of self-management. This has avoided industrial unrest but there have been disadvantages to this approach. This delegated decision-making has led to delays in manufacturing and problems with quality. There has appeared to be a lack of focus. Consequently the company has lost important contracts and is gradually seeing its sales volume and profits decline.

The family has employed Andrew Smith as the new Managing Director, giving him the responsibility for turning the company around. He has decided that power and control must now return to the centre. The passive style of management pursued in the earlier years is now giving way to a more centralised and autocratic approach. However it is obvious that such a change in management style could create even further problems for the company.

Required

Discuss the benefits and problems which this more centralised style of management might bring to Coxford Doors.

(10 marks)

17 Shirtmaster Group

90 mins

Introduction

Tony Masters, chairman and chief executive of the Shirtmaster Group, is worried. He has recently responded to his senior management team's concerns over the future of the Group by reluctantly agreeing to appoint an external management consultant. The consultant's brief is to fully analyse the performance of the privately owned company, identify key strategic and operational problems and recommend a future strategy for the company. Tony is concerned that the consultant's report will seriously question his role in the company and the growth strategy he is proposing.

Group origins and structure

Tony's father, Howard Masters, set up Shirtmaster in the 1950s in Elmrich, the capital city of the country of Gondour . Howard was a skilled tailor and saw the potential for designing and manufacturing a distinctive range of men's shirts and ties marketed under the 'Shirtmaster' brand. Howard set up a shirt manufacturing company with good access to the employee skills needed to design and make shirts. Howard had recognised the opportunity to make distinctive shirts incorporating innovative design features including the latest man-made fibres. In the 1960s Elmrich was a global fashion centre exploiting the UK's leading position in popular music. Men became much more fashion conscious, and were willing to pay premium prices for clothes with style and flair. Shirtmaster by the 1960s had built up a Gondour-wide network of more than 2,000 small independent clothing retailers. These retailers sold the full range of men's wear including made-to-measure suits, shirts and matching ties, shoes and other clothing accessories. Extensive and expensive TV and cinema advertising supported the Shirtmaster brand.

The Shirtmaster Group is made up of two divisions – the Shirtmaster division which concentrates on the retail shirt business and the Corporate Clothing division which supplies workwear to large industrial and commercial customers. Corporate Clothing has similar origins to Shirtmaster, also being a family owned and managed business and is located in the same town as Shirtmaster. It was set up to supply hardwearing jeans and workwear to the many factory workers in the region. The decline of Gondour manufacturing and allied industries led to profitability problems and in 1990 the Shirtmaster Group acquired it. Tony took over executive responsibility for the Group in 1996 and continues to act as managing director for the Shirtmaster Division.

Shirtmaster division – operations and market environment

By 2008 the Godour market for men's shirts was very different to that of the 1960s and 1970s when Shirtmaster had become one of the best known premium brands. In a mature market most of Shirtmaster's competitors have outsourced the making of their shirts to low cost manufacturers based overseas in Catopia and Europolis. Shirtmaster is virtually alone in maintaining a Gondour manufacturing base. Once a year Tony and the buyer for the division go Eurpolis, visiting cloth manufacturers and buying for stock. This stock, stored in the division's warehouse, gives the ability to create a wide range of shirt designs but creates real problems with excessive stock holdings and outdated stock. Shirtmaster prides itself on its ability to respond to the demands of its small retail customers and the long-term relationships built up with these retailers. Typically, these retailers order in small quantities and want quick delivery. Shirtmaster has to introduce new shirt designs throughout the year, contrasting with the spring and autumn ranges launched by its competitors. This creates real pressure on the small design team available.

The retail side of the shirt business has undergone even more fundamental change. Though the market for branded shirts continues to exist, such shirts are increasingly sold through large departmental stores. There is increasing competition between the shirt makers for the limited shelf space available in the departmental stores. Shopping centres and malls are increasingly dominated by nationwide chains of specialist clothing retailers. They sell to the premium segment of the market and are regarded as the trendsetters for the industry. These chains can develop quickly, often using franchising to achieve rapid growth, and are increasingly international in scope. All of them require their suppliers to make their clothes under the chain's own label brand. Some have moved successfully into selling via catalogues and the Internet. Finally, the Gondour supermarket chains have discovered the profitability of selling nonfood goods. The shirts they sell are aimed at value for money rather than style, sourced wherever they can be made most cheaply and sold under the supermarket's own label. Small independent clothing retailers are declining both in number and market share.

The Shirtmaster division, with its continued over-reliance for its sales on these small independent retailers, is threatened by each of the retail driven changes, having neither the sales volume to compete on price nor the style to compete on fashion.

The Shirtmaster division's international strategy

Tony's answer to these changes is to make the Shirtmaster brand an international one. His initial strategy is to sell to clothing retailers based in the nearby country of Catopolis and, once established, move the brand into the fast growing consumer markets in Europolis. He recognises that the division's current Godour focus means that working with a Catopian partner is a necessity. He has given the sales and marketing manager the job of finding major retailers, distributors or manufacturers with whom they can make a strategic alliance and so help get the Shirtmaster range onto the shelves of Catopian clothing retailers.

Corporate Clothing division – operations and market environment

Corporate Clothing has in recent years implemented a major turnaround in its business as the market for corporate clothing began to grow significantly. Corporate Clothing designs, manufactures and distributes a comprehensive range of workwear for its corporate customers, sourcing much of its range from low

cost foreign suppliers. It supplies the corporate clothing requirements of large customers in the private and public sectors. Major contracts have been gained with banks, airlines, airports and the police, fire and ambulance services.

The Corporate Clothing division supplies the whole range of workwear required and in the sizes needed for each individual employee. Its designers work closely with the buyers in its large customers and the division's sales benefit from the regular introduction of new styles of uniforms and workwear. Corporate employers are increasingly aware of the external image they need to project and the clothes their employees wear are the key to this image. Corporate Clothing has invested heavily in manufacturing and IT systems to ensure that it meets the needs of its demanding customers. It is particularly proud of its computer-aided design and manufacturing (CAD/CAM) systems, which can be linked to its customers and allows designs to be updated and manufacturing alterations to be introduced with its customers' approval. Much of its success can be attributed to the ability to offer a customer service package in which garments are stored by Corporate Clothing and distributed directly to the individual employee in personalized workwear sets as and when required. The Gondour market for corporate workwear was worth £500 million in 2005. Evidence suggests that the demand for corporate workwear is likely to continue to grow.

The Corporate Clothing division also has ambitions to enter the markets for corporate clothing in Catopia and recognises that might be most easily done through using a suitable strategic partner. There is friendly rivalry between the two divisions but each operates largely independently of the other. Over the past 10 years the fortunes of the two divisions have been completely reversed. Corporate Clothing now is a modest profit maker for the group – Shirtmaster is consistently losing money.

Shirtmaster Group – future strategy

Tony is determined to re-establish Shirtmaster as a leading shirt brand in Gondour and successfully launch the brand in Catopia. He sees a strategic alliance with a Catopian partner as the key to achieving this ambition. Though he welcomes the success of the Corporate Clothing division and recognises its potential in Catopia, he remains emotionally and strategically committed to restoring the fortunes of the Shirtmaster division. Unfortunately, his autocratic style of leadership tends to undermine the position of the senior management team at Shirtmaster. He continues to play an active role in both the operational and strategic sides of the business and is both well known and regarded by workers in the Shirtmaster division's factory.

The initial feedback meeting with the management consultant has confirmed the concern that he is not delegating sufficiently. The consultant commented that Tony's influence could be felt throughout the Shirtmaster division. Managers either try to anticipate the decisions they think he would make or, alternatively, not take the decisions until he has given his approval. The end result is a division not able to meet the challenges of an increasingly competitive retail marketplace, and losing both money and market share.

Table 1 – Financial Information on the Shirtmaster Group ($ million)

	2008	2009	2010	2011 Budget	2012 Forecast	2013 Forecast
Total sales	25.0	23.8	21.4	23.5	24.4	26.7
Gondour sales	24.5	23.2	21.0	22.7	23.4	24.7
Overseas sales	0.5	0.6	0.4	0.8	1.0	2.0
Cost of sales	17.7	16.8	15.2	16.3	16.8	17.8
Gross profit	7.3	7.0	6.2	7.2	7.6	8.9
Marketing	1.7	1.5	1.2	1.7	1.9	2.2
Distribution	1.6	1.4	1.2	1.4	1.5	1.9
Administration	1.8	1.8	1.7	1.9	1.9	2.1
Net profit	2.2	2.3	2.1	2.2	2.3	2.7
Shirtmaster division						
Total sales	14.8	12.6	10.3	11.7	12.0	13.5
Gondour sales	14.3	12.0	9.9	10.9	11.0	11.5
Overseas sales	0.5	0.6	0.4	0.8	1.0	2.0
Cost of sales	11.1	9.8	8.2	9.1	9.4	10.1
Gross profit	3.7	2.8	2.1	2.6	2.6	3.4
Marketing	1.5	1.3	1.0	1.5	1.7	2.0
Distribution	1.2	1.0	0.8	0.9	1.0	1.3
Administration	1.3	1.2	1.1	1.2	1.2	1.3
Net profit	(0.3)	(0.7)	(0.8)	(1.0)	(1.3)	(1.2)
Inventory	2.0	2.2	3.0	2.7	2.5	2.0
Employees	100	100	98	98	99	100
Corporate Clothing division						
Total sales	10.2	11.2	11.1	11.8	12.4	13.2
Cost of sales	6.6	7.0	7.0	7.2	7.4	7.7
Gross profit	3.6	4.2	4.1	4.6	5.0	5.5
Marketing	0.2	0.2	0.2	0.2	0.2	0.2
Distribution	0.4	0.4	0.4	0.5	0.5	0.6
Administration	0.5	0.6	0.6	0.7	0.7	0.8
Net profit	2.5	3.0	2.9	3.2	3.6	3.9
Inventory	0.9	1.0	0.8	0.8	0.9	1.0
Employees	84	84	80	79	77	75

Required

(a) Assess the strategic position and performance of the Shirtmaster Group and its divisions over the 2008-2010 period. Your analysis should make use of models where appropriate. **(20 marks)**

(b) Both divisions have recognised the need for a strategic alliance to help them achieve a successful entry into Catopian markets.

Critically evaluate the advantages and disadvantages of the divisions using strategic alliances to develop their respective businesses in Catopia. **(15 marks)**

(c) The Shirtmaster division and Corporate Clothing division, though being part of the same group, operate largely independently of one another.

Assess the costs and benefits of the two divisions continuing to operate independently of one another.

(15 marks)

(Total = 50 marks)

1 Bartok Fuel

> **Top tips.** This is quite a simple question that offers a gentle introduction to the style of the examination. Part (b) is typical of the sort of question that usually forms one of the requirements of the Section A case study, being essentially a critical discussion of possible specific strategies. It is usually pretty clear what the overall worth of the proposals is, but not always. Discuss this sort of thing as rationally as you can, using simple models and pointing out any implications you can discern.

Part (a)

There would appear to be no real evidence of any formal strategic planning in the past. There is no mention of any mission statement or objectives for the company. The company seems to have moved from a garage and workshop into fuel distribution and glass manufacture almost by accident. These developments might have **emerged from patterns of behaviour** rather than any planning process and it could be argued that the company illustrates the emergent strategy model. However, there is also an element of **logical incrementalism** as the business has not strayed far from its origins but has taken small steps into new areas where it already has some knowledge and expertise.

It could also be argued that only a small number of strategic options were ever considered and the options that have been taken in the past have perhaps simply been accepted as satisfactory rather than embraced as ideal. This approach has been termed **bounded rationality** by *Herbert Simon*.

Part (b)

Each of the two strategies being considered requires very different considerations from the board.

If the Erewhon site is sold for its development potential, this will clearly be a boost to the company's cash flow. However, as we have no information about the company's current financial position, we cannot comment as to whether this is an element of the decision to sell. Nevertheless, the board must consider what use can be made of the funds received. It may be that the two options are related in David's mind and the funds from the sale of the Erewhon site are to be earmarked for investment in Arcadia. In any case, the sale should only be considered further if it seems likely that the income can be invested in a way that will **generate a higher return** than the garage business currently achieves.

If the Erewhon site is to be shut down there are also considerable **human resource issues** to be addressed. The division employs 50 people who must either be made redundant or be re-employed in other areas of the business. In either case, the cost of redundancy payments or of retraining must be taken into account. The car dealership appears to be a fairly stand-alone element of the business but it must also be considered whether its closure will have any **knock-on effects** on the other parts of the company.

The proposed expansion into Arcadia is fraught with potential problems. Bartok Fuel has always been an Oceania based business and therefore expansion abroad is a major issue. The results of a **PEST analysis** would be daunting. The company has no experience of doing business in Ardacia and it knows nothing of local business conditions or regulations. Language and culture are likely to present major difficulties.

All this is partially countered by the existence of a partner who knows the market and the culture of Arcadia, but Bartok Fuel will still be making something of a leap in the dark. In fact, they would be **wholly dependent** on the probity, efficiency and goodwill of their partner. It would appear that the company's only real contribution will be to provide risk capital and the brothers must ask themselves if they really see that as their area of expertise – they are not running a bank, after all.

2 National advantage

Porter notes that some nations' industries succeed more than other in terms of international competition. He does not suggest (as the D4D Prime Minister rightly notes) that countries as such are competitive, but that various factors support or inhibit the ability of the industries and firms **within** them to compete successfully on the international stage. Porter's 'diamond' model suggests that the degree of competitive advantage enjoyed by different nations results from the interaction of four basic factors.

Factor conditions

Factor conditions are a country's endowment of inputs to production. This includes **human resources, physical resources, knowledge, capital and infrastructure** (transport, communications etc). D4D appears to benefit from positive basic factor conditions (oil reserves and related revenues, a temperate climate, a young tertiary educated population and political stability) – but there are limitations (eg lack of local education institutions) and risks (eg dwindling oil reserves). D4D does not currently have advanced factors which are necessary to achieve high-order competitive advantages such as their own production technologies.

Demand conditions

The home market determines how firms perceive, interpret and respond to buyer needs. Strong and sophisticated demand encourages **growth, high quality, innovation and economies of scale**: all these build competences for competing more effectively abroad. Given the recent revenue D4D has earned from oil, it is possible that it has not been focusing on demand conditions very closely. If that is the case, then the short-term benefits from oil could potentially be weakening its competitive advantage in the longer term.

Firm strategy, structure and rivalry

Capital markets, ownership structures, attitude to time horizons, degree of **innovation and entrepreneurship** vary from country to country. National cultures have been shown to orient business towards certain industries: in D4D's case, agriculture and light manufacturing.

Meanwhile, **domestic rivalry makes exporting attractive** and keeps firms on their toes, while the opposite is also true: as in D4D's case, lack of domestic rivalry stunts competitive development and encourages firms to rely on the home market. The government could be more pro-active in fostering innovation and entrepreneurship among firms to encourage them to become more successful, but it appears to be happy to support the uneconomic local industry.

Related and supporting industries

Competitive success in one industry is linked to success in related industries, by creating a pool of managerial and technical talent, the exchange of information for organisational/industry learning and benchmarking, and a robust supply market for parts and components.

Clustering

A 'cluster' is a linking of industries through network relationships which are either vertical (within the supply chain) or horizontal (common customers, technology or skills). Porter believes clustering to be a key to national competitive advantage: firms will be more likely to succeed internationally if there is a supporting cluster that supports lower costs, infrastructure development, transfer of expertise and so on.

3 EMS

The decline in the number of people taking the qualification appears to be a reflection of the maturity of the marketplace. The large pool of unqualified environmental managers and auditors that existed when the qualification was launched has now been exploited. There are now fewer candidates taking the examinations and fewer members joining the EMS. The organisation's response to this has been to look for international markets where it can promote the qualifications it currently offers. It hopes to find large pools of unqualified environmental managers and auditors in these markets.

The scenario suggests that EMS currently has relatively limited strategic ambitions. There is no evidence that EMS plans to develop new qualifications outside its current portfolio. Indeed, attempts to look at complementary qualifications (such as soil and water conservation) have been rejected by Council. Hence, expansion into new strategic business markets does not appear to be an option.

Strategy Development

Internal development

Internal development takes place when strategies are developed by building on or developing the organisation's own capabilities. It is often termed organic growth. This is how EMS has operated up to now. The original certificates were developed by the founders of the Society. Since then, additional certificates have been added and the Diploma programme developed at the instigation of members and officers of the Society.

In many ways this type of organic growth is particularly suited to the configuration of the organisation, one where there is a risk-averse and cautious culture. The organic approach spreads cost and risk over time and growth is much easier to control and manage. However, growth can be slow and indeed, as in the case of EMS, may have ceased altogether. Growth is also restricted by the breadth of the organisation's capabilities. For example, EMS has not been able to develop (or indeed even consider developing) any products outside of its fairly restricted product range. Furthermore, although internal development may be a reasonable strategy for developing a home market it maybe an inappropriate strategy for breaking into new market places and territories. This is particularly true when, as it appears in the case of the EMS, internal resources have no previous experience of developing products in overseas markets.

In summary, internal growth has been the method of strategy development at EMS up to now, based on a strategic direction of consolidation and market penetration. There is no evidence that EMS is considering developing new products to arrest the fall in qualification numbers. However, the Board has suggested developing new markets for the current qualification range and India, China and Russia have been identified as potential targets. It seems unlikely that internal development will be an appropriate method of pursuing this strategic direction.

4 Natalia Norman

Part (a)

Top tips. The great advantage of careful market segmentation is that it permits a precise determination of the marketing mix variables. This saves money and allows the firm to make best use of its competences.

However, make sure you apply your knowledge of market segmentation to the specific problems represented by the scenario, rather than simply suggesting generic bases which can be used for market segmentation.

Easy marks. Part (a) is about segmentation methods and is worth fifteen marks overall, which can be expected to break down into seven for suggesting the bases and eight for saying why segmentation is a good idea. Thus we might expect three marks for proposing three bases and saying a little about the relevance of each, with another three (or possibly four) for deeper discussion. Our discussion of each of the bases we have chosen illustrates this approach, progressing from the name of the base through its relevance to its wider implications or applications.

Segmentation would be Natalia's first step towards a more active relationship with her existing and potential customers. If she knew who they were in more detail she could design her market offering in a way that would improve her own **efficiency** while also providing increased **customer satisfaction**.

The simplest form of segmentation is probably **geographical**. Natalia's potential market could be very simply split into domestic and overseas, for instance. Indeed, she probably does this already, in a sense, since she must make appropriate arrangements for the extra complications of shipping to foreign customers. Geographical segmentation would be necessary if Natalia wished to sell in other ways than via the internet, perhaps by issuing catalogues, since the styles of knitwear offered would have to appeal to varying local tastes.

Geographical segmentation becomes much more useful when it is combined with demographic information. This **geo-demographic** segmentation would enable Natalia to target segments defined by such variables as place, age, sex, income and social class. A consideration of these variables might for instance lead her to concentrate her marketing effort on older, affluent people in specific metropolitan areas. This would have immediate implications for design, quality, promotion, price and distribution.

Psychographic segmentation analyses the market according to personality and lifestyle. This might be difficult for Natalia to use, but if she could, perhaps by continuing to employ her marketing consultant, it might offer important advantages in the areas of design and promotion in particular.

A further segmentation variable is customer **behaviour**. This includes such matters as sensitivity to changes in the marketing mix variables, purchase frequency and magnitude and how the product is used. This approach might be useful to Natalia. For example, she might find that some of her designs are frequently bought by women for their menfolk. This might have important implications for design and sizing.

The benefit of accurate market segmentation is that it permits a more precise specification of the marketing mix variables, so that they are shaped to conform to the needs of the target segment or segments.

Product. Different segments will probably require different products. When the size of each segment, its product requirements and their costs are known, it will be possible both to estimate the most profitable segment to attack and to specify fairly precisely the nature of the products needed to do so. Natalia might find, for instance, that she needed to adjust her designs to make her range more recognisable and coherent.

Price. Pricing decisions are fundamental to trade and very difficult to take. It is very easy to set prices too high, so that customers are put off, or too low, so that potential profit is lost. The problem is compounded by the complex messages about quality, exclusivity and value that can be sent by price levels and changes to them. At the moment, Natalia's products are relatively cheap and this is preventing her from generating the funds needed for expansion: she may find that she can charge more for some of her knitwear.

Promotion. Natalia's consultant has identified her promotion efforts as insufficiently focused, which has led to a diffuse image and little brand awareness. Detailed knowledge of the characteristics of her target segments will allow Natalia to develop the accuracy of her promotion. She may find, for example, that a large market exists which is unwilling to use the internet at all and so remains in ignorance of her products.

Place. Natalia's distribution is currently largely via her website. This limits her potential market to those who are both confident in the use of computers and interested in original design knitwear. It is likely that a much larger market could be served through a more traditional approach using prestige clothing outlets. This could be established by careful consideration of the results of the segmentation exercise.

Part (b)

Reactive follower strategy

The **market follower** accepts the status quo and thus **avoids the cost and risk associated with innovation** in product, price or distribution strategy. Such a **me-too** strategy follows closely what the leader does and is based on the leader's approach. This can be both profitable and stable.

However, it is very easy for this strategy to come to depend entirely on charging lower prices. As the follower is unlikely to have the scale economies that accrue to the market leader, this means accepting a much lower level of profit. Given the inimitable style of Natalia's products, this does not seem a strategy she should use.

Another strategy is to **follow at a distance** but not copy the leader too closely. This permits the follower to demonstrate some innovative and original features while still copying other ideas from the leader, thereby saving time and expense on research and development. Such a strategy allows a company to compete in areas where their strengths are valued – in Natalia's case, probably in design.

However, a strategy which may be more appropriate for Natalia to use it to **follow selectively** rather than simply imitating the market leader.

To be consistently successful, the market follower must not simply imitate.

Follow selectively

The follower should **compete in the most appropriate market and product segments**, maintain its **customer base** and ensure that its **turnover grows** in line with the general expansion of the market.

BPP LEARNING MEDIA

Natalia could attempt to do this by exploiting the originality of her designs, thus effectively differentiating her market offering and justifying higher prices. The development of her **brand image** will be a necessary precondition for success with this strategy.

Natalia is unlikely to have sufficient resources to become an overall market leader, but her products seem to be relatively innovative and unique. This is likely to mean she is not merely an imitator, recycling ideas from the leader. Therefore, with appropriate marketing mix strategies supporting the business, Natalia's company could become a **strong niche market player**.

The option of developing a market niche is particularly important where the niche is of a viable size and has growth potential, yet is not seen as threatening to major competitors so as to attract their interest and attention. In this case, if Natalia can **develop the core competences** of design, branding, quality and image they should enable her to develop and expand her business from being merely a low cost supplier of non-branded goods to having a more differentiated product with a brand value of their own.

An important problem for the market follower is that it may constitute an **attractive target** for market challengers seeking growth by acquisition, or indeed for the market leader seeking to extend control over the market.

An agreed takeover may, in due course, be a suitable way for Natalia to realise the equity in her business; however, assuming that she wishes to maintain her independence of operations for the foreseeable future she must control her costs and exploit appropriate opportunities to achieve differentiation. Otherwise, cash flow difficulties may force her to sell out.

5 Firebridge Tyres Ltd

> **Top tips**. This is a fairly straightforward question on the environment and strategic capability. Part (a) may look very wide ranging and therefore rather daunting. This is a good example of the way in which the use of a model (such as PEST) can help you to organise your thoughts. You will see from our answer that a detailed knowledge of the motor industry is not required to answer this question.

Part (a)

Main factors in the external environment

The environment of an organisation is everything outside the boundaries of the organisation. Organisations are by definition open to the environment: it is the source of their inputs; it is the destination of their outputs; and it sets constraints over what the organisation can do. Some argue that the environment is increasingly a source of uncertainty for organisations, and that it is becoming harder to read. The degree of uncertainty it causes results from its complexity and the rate of change.

Hofer and Schendel argue that the very purpose of strategy is to secure some sort of environmental fit. This might be an extreme position, as it implies reaction to the environment rather than activity to shape environmental forces. However, any formal strategic planning process takes the environment into account.

As far as the general environment is concerned, we can analyse PEST and competitive factors.

Political and legal factors

Firebridge Tyres Ltd (FTL) operates in a stable political environment. Agreements between governments have opened up international markets, not only to FTL but to its competitors: however GTC does not want FTL to increase its exports outside Europe. There is no shortage of car service stations, a fragmented industry, so political interference is unlikely. Local government might determine the siting of certain activities. FTL is indirectly affected by government transport policy, if this affects the demand for and use of cars.

Economic factors

In the UK, tyres must be checked annually, as part of the MOT testing process. The overall level of economic activity determines transport use, which influences wear and tear of tyres. However, in times of hardship, people will be less likely to buy the premium brand range preferring to go for the lower cost Freeway range, cheaper overseas tyres, or even retreads. The general level of prosperity also influences

the number of people in the population who use cars; rising incomes and wealth mean rising numbers of cars purchased, hence greater demand for tyres. People will also move to lower cost service options in hard times: FTL does not want a service business lumbered with heavy overheads. The UK market is much smaller than the US: GTC might be unrealistic in assuming that the same formula, which might depend on economies of scale, would work over in the UK.

Social factors

Social factors influence demand indirectly, via political pressure for legislation or changing patterns of demand. For example, governments are more concerned with ecological issues. There are disposal problems with used tyres. This might affect what they are made of. Some can be burnt as fuel, but with landfill taxes increasing, recyclable tyres may be preferred. The proposed service business depends on patterns of car use. It may be that many drivers and will prefer a garage.

Technological factors

Tyres are a fairly mature technology, although there are improvements to be made to increase their grip, their longevity, and their recyclability. Any changes in the plastics and materials industry might be relevant. Also, if cars become lighter, lighter tyres will be needed.

The main factor in the environment is competition, which is impinging directly on FTL.

A number of service chains already exist in the UK, but otherwise the industry is fairly fragmented. Competition on price is important, but also on quality. However, FTL needs to assess how the competition will respond.

The competitive environment can be described using Porter's five forces model (barriers to entry– see below, substitute products, customer bargaining power, supplier bargaining power, competitive rivalry). There are few substitute products, but competitive rivalry is intense. Suppliers have low bargaining power probably.

Part (b)

Barriers to entry discourage new competitors to an industry. If they are low, it is easy to set up shop, but hard to discourage other people from doing so too. The main barriers to entry are described below.

Economies of scale

For some firms, a barrier to entry is the **size of the operation needed to be profitable**. Tyres are high volume, low margin products on the whole, and for most cases, the best way to make money is to manufacture in large quantities. A large plant implies high fixed costs and **a high breakeven point**. There is little evidence that significant economies of scale can be achieved in *servicing*. There are some service chains, but the industry seems fragmented.

Product differentiation

FTL already pursues this strategy by producing different tyres, directed at different segments. In service, differentiation might be achieved on the basis of FTL's **brand name**, and a promise of service quality. Advertising costs might be considerable, however, to build the brand.

Capital requirements

No new factories need to be built, of course, but FTL will have to acquire leases or freeholds of a number of properties in which to set up its service stations. Many of the prime spots might be taken over by petrol stations. Ideally FTL will be positioned near residential areas or near roads, to make them easy to find. The cost of this depends on the size of the operation that GTC is proposing.

Switching costs

Switching costs are minimal; new customers are easy to find, but hard to keep, unless service quality is better.

Distribution

The chain is basically a distribution outlet for FTL's tyres. The importance of choosing the right sites for distributing the service was identified above. Existing service providers know the market, but otherwise they have no special advantages.

Conclusion

Barriers to entry are fairly low. This will make it easy to set up business, but hard to make a profit perhaps, unless some unique lessons can be transferred from GTC, operating in a very different transport infrastructure.

Part (c)

Strategic capability and critical success factors

Strategic capabilities have four essential qualities.

- They produce effects that are valuable to buyers.
- They are **rare**.
- They are **robust** in that they are difficult for competitors to imitate.
- They are **non-substitutable**.

Critical success factors, on the other hand, are product features that are particularly valued by a group of customers. Organisations must get these things right if they are to succeed. Some of these factors relate to physical products, but many depend on internal processes and the basic infrastructure of the business.

FTL is a manufacturing business, producing what is essentially a commodity product, tyres, and making a stab at product differentiation. This competence is not truly distinctive, as there are other tyre manufacturers in the world, but FTL has built up a market presence in Europe. The strategic capabilities that led to this position probably look something like those shown below.

(a) Building a **brand** that consumers recognise, and preventing its erosion by competition
(b) Good commercial relations with the distributors, who are the **strategic customers**
(c) Making **incremental technical innovations** in order to encourage new sales

How do these relate to the proposed service centre business? A key problem is that services are a very different proposition to products. There are several possible resources and competences for the proposed servicing business.

(a) A brand that customers recognise and choose, having realistic and satisfied expectations of what it offers
(b) Well-chosen sites that are easily accessible, offer plenty of parking and are comfortable to wait in.
(c) Well-trained staff who not only know how to change wheels and tyres, and do other repairs but who are able to demonstrate high standards of customer care
(d) To be seen as preferable to the local garage in terms of the processes by which the service is provided

FTL's existing competences, at best, cover brand building. It has no experience in choosing and managing properties or customer service staff: US conditions are different, so a transfer of skills between the US and the UK firm may be hard to achieve. FTL runs a manufacturing business; a service business, based on a variety of intangibles such as staff courtesy, is a different proposition. The required cultures of the two businesses might conflict.

The firm might have to spend a lot of money on training, both technically and in terms of customer care. Also money would have to be spent on building the brand. However, GTC should be able to provide some expertise in building the service aspects.

In short, FTL's current strategic capability is not suited to this plan, given the fragmented nature of the industry. GTC may be able to provide some help, but GTC might end up investing more money and making short term losses, rather than the profits it is looking for.

FTL is in a difficult situation, because its managers are tied by the priorities of the US parent.

6 Nadir Products: ethics

Part (a)

> **Top tips**. While this question clearly has an important ethical slant, it is important to deal with the commercial impact of the proposed courses of action. If you feel your experience has not prepared you to do this, think in terms of stakeholder theory and ask yourself what connected stakeholders like customers are reasonably entitled to expect and how *you* would react to these ploys.
>
> Do not spend more than a minute on dealing with the report form requirement: a suitable heading and, perhaps, numbered paragraphs are all that are required. A short introductory paragraph giving the reason for the report is a good way to get started.

REPORT

To: Board Members, Nadir Products plc
From: A Consultant
Date: December 2001
Subject: Proposed adjustments to turnover reporting

You asked me to comment on the commercial and ethical implications of suggestions that had been made about the value of this year's turnover. There was concern that a current decline in sales will adversely affect the level of bonuses paid to senior staff.

My first comment is that the assumption behind the suggestions appears to be wrong. The aim of the bonus scheme was surely to provide an incentive for senior staff to take appropriate action to improve performance. If performance has not improved, it would be perverse to adjust the numbers so that they receive the bonuses anyway. There is an element of moral hazard here: if the bonuses are in effect guaranteed and not dependent on improved performance, the incentive effect disappears and the scheme might as well be abandoned.

I understand that there is concern that staff will be adversely affected by the downturn in sales value. However, I must point out the questionable nature of the suggestions from an ethical point of view. It is likely that the detailed proposals will create a conflict of interests since each has the potential to disadvantage shareholders. It would be ethically inappropriate to pursue any course of action that reduced shareholder value in order to enrich senior staff.

I will now examine the individual proposals.

Discount for additional sales. A discount is an unexceptional sales promotional device that may be used, for instance, to increase or defend market share or to shift excess inventory. It has a cost, in the form of reduced margin, and it is a matter of commercial judgement to decide whether the benefit is greater than the cost. It may also have the effect of merely bringing sales forward in time, so that later trading periods suffer.

Of the three suggestions, this is the most defensible. However, it is quite *indefensible* if it is undertaken solely in order to boost bonuses, because of the conflict of interest discussed above.

Bringing forward scheduled orders is a form of window dressing. Your auditors will deploy checks on such activities as a matter of course, and may succeed in detecting this. The accounts would then have to be adjusted, since there is no commercial justification for the practice. It can be seen as detrimental to shareholders since the reported profit would be overstated and, while this may have a positive effect on share value in the short term, were it ever discovered, it would bring into question the company's corporate governance. Such a scheme is also likely to irritate customers who may respond by delaying payment and even seeking a new supplier. This would clearly disadvantage the company.

This suggestion is unacceptable on both ethical and practical grounds.

Warning of possible price rises. I take it as read that there are no actual plans to raise prices? If this is the case, to say that such plans exist is untruthful and therefore inappropriate for a company that wishes to maintain high ethical standards. Further, to hide behind a form of words such as 'there *may* be price rises' would be equally dishonest, since the intention would be to create a specific, incorrect impression in customers' minds. When the warning is eventually shown to be spurious, customers' estimation of the company will fall, with an eventual knock-on effect on turnover.

This ploy is comparable to the previous one in its potential effect on shareholders and customers but is even more unethical.

Conclusion. None of the suggestions is acceptable ethically or commercially as a solution to the senior staff bonus problem.

Part (b)

The stakeholder view is that many groups have a stake in what the organisation does. This is particularly important in the business context, where shareholders own the business but employees, customers and government also have particularly strong claims to having their interests considered. It is suggested that modern corporations are so powerful, socially, economically and politically, that unrestrained use of their power will inevitably damage other people's rights. Under this approach, the exercise of corporate social responsibility constrains the corporation to act at all times as a good citizen. Particular emphasis is laid on the preservation of employment and protection of the environment.

Another argument points out that corporations exist within society and are dependent upon it for the resources they use. Some of these resources are obtained by direct contracts with suppliers but others are not, being provided by government expenditure. Examples are such things as transport infrastructure, technical research and education for the workforce. Clearly, Nadir Products contributes to the taxes that pay for these things, but the relationship is rather tenuous and the tax burden can be minimised by careful management. The company can do as much or as little as it cares to in this connection.

Mintzberg suggests that simply viewing organisations as vehicles for shareholder investment is inadequate, since in practice, he says, organisations are rarely controlled effectively by shareholders. Most shareholders are passive investors. We do not know whether or not this is the case with Nadir Products.

Many organisations regard the exercise of corporate social responsibility as valuable in promoting a positive corporate image. The management of Nadir Products therefore may feel that it is appropriate to take an instrumental approach to such matters as sponsorship and charitable giving. Charitable donations and artistic sponsorship are useful media of public relations and can reflect well on the business. They can be regarded as another form of promotion, which like advertising, serves to enhance consumer awareness of the business. It would be necessary for the company to ensure that the recipients of its generosity were appropriate to its operations at the bottom end of the market: grand opera would probably be inappropriate.

The arguments for and against social responsibility are complex ones. However, ultimately they can be traced to different assumptions about society and the relationships between the individuals and organisations within it. It is unlikely to be something that need occupy a great deal of the time of Nadir Products' directors.

7 Arragon Antennas

Part (a)

Top tips. We answer the first part of this question largely in terms of *Porter's* **generic strategies**. This is because of the nature of the scenario. There is mention of price sensitivity, to which cost is related; the market is clearly highly specialised, so the idea of a niche approach is relevant; and finally, the products tend to be highly differentiated.

It would be possible to take a product-market growth vector approach, but that model would not be so appropriate. We are given no information relevant to market penetration; product development is clearly going on anyway; market development and diversification are high-risk strategies for such a specialised company working in such high technology. Generally, *Ansoff's* model is most useful for less specialised companies, particularly those working in consumer products and services.

The possible solution of a reorganisation of the industry, however, could be applied just as easily to an analysis using the product-market model.

Arragon Antennas is under threat from a new entrant that appears likely to enjoy a substantial cost advantage because of high volumes and the prior amortisation of development costs. However, Wizzomatic's products, being standardised, are unlikely to be suitable for many specialised applications.

Wizzomatic appear to be seeking to establish themselves as the cost leaders within the industry, using their cost advantage to build up volume. Cost leaders tend to seek as much product standardisation as possible in order to obtain economies of scale and Wizzomatic seem to have a major advantage here.

It would therefore not be advisable for Arragon to meet the new entrant head on. The price cuts necessary to build the necessary volume would be likely to starve the company of cash, thus prejudicing its new design work. It would find itself in the classic 'stuck in the middle' trap, subject to continuing high costs but unable to raise its prices.

A much safer option for Arragon would be to pursue two specific target market segments.

- The new design market, where they have expertise and a reputation that Wizzomatic cannot challenge with its standardised products
- Those parts of the spares market that require more specialised products than Wizzomatic can supply

The first of these options represents a strategy of differentiation, while the second is a niche strategy.

It is likely that if Wizzomatic succeeds in establishing itself in the market it has chosen, Arragon will see its volumes falling. This need not lead to a fall in turnover if it is able to penetrate its chosen segments more deeply. However, a fall in volume of standard antennas will mean an increase in fully absorbed cost per unit, with a knock-on effect on margin. It may be that Arragon will have to withdraw from the volume part of its business. This will lead to concomitant downsizing of its production capacity unless it succeeds in retaining much of its existing aftermarket business.

To expand its share of the new systems market, Arragon will have to increase its sales effort and its design and test capacity. We have no way of knowing how easy this will be, but we may speculate that the highly skilled staff required will be fairly difficult to find, while the design and test facilities are likely to be quite expensive. Depending on the company's access to investment funds, therefore, this strategy may require a long period of time to implement.

The niche spares market will probably be easier to expand initially, since Arragon is likely to have the manufacturing capacity available, as discussed above. An immediate problem here is likely to be that the other three established players may also be planning a similar strategy.

It is possible that the other three principal suppliers in the industry will also feel the heat of Wizzomatic's arrival. This is all the more likely if they too are unable to meet the challenge head on. It may be that this could be a cue for restructuring the industry, by merger or takeover. The aim would be to accumulate the resources necessary to compete with Wizzomatic rather than ceding dominance in the volume sales segments of the market.

A strategy of consolidation would not be easy to implement. It would probably involve painful rationalisation of several functions, with job losses and other staff upheaval. There would also be a probability of conflict between perceived winners and losers, which would be exacerbated if the rationalisation took the form of takeover rather than merger.

The aim of the consolidation would be for a larger, more efficient company to emerge, retaining the best of the products, people, markets and resources of its parents. A careful strategic analysis would be necessary to ensure that the new strategy built on strengths and avoided weaknesses. It may be, for example, that even a merged company would not dispute the volume market but would aim to dominate the new design market.

Part (b)

> **Top tips**. Arragon Antennas is a manufacturing company, so the basic 4 Ps mix is what is required here. With a question like this, do not dwell too much on background explanations. Cut to the chase and make as many good valid points as you can. You don't need to know anything about aircraft communication systems. But you do need to be generally aware of the differences between consumer and industrial marketing.

Product

The product element of Arragon's marketing mix is relatively simple. A firm's product may be viewed as a solution to a customer's problem. Arragon's products are therefore of two basic types: the newly developed and very high-value added antennas designed for new aircraft; and the standard antennas produced either for use as spares or for supply to other businesses.

Quality is clearly a major issue affecting both types of product, because of the requirements of aircraft safety. The standard antennas must be produced to existing precise specifications, while the new designs must satisfy strict performance requirements before they are released to service.

Packaging is also likely to be important. Spares, in particular, must have a long shelf life and may be transported to any part of the world. The packaging will have to provide substantial protection against climatic variables such as heat and humidity, as well as against impact and abrasion.

Price

We are told that prices in the industry are generally high and that co-operation between suppliers is not unusual. While presumably not engaging in price-fixing, it seems that the small group of suppliers in the industry tend not to compete on price. It is likely that winning contracts for new systems design is likely to depend far more on long-term relationships with customers and proven technical quality. In the spares market, it would seem that Wizzomatic's arrival may shake up the existing rather cosy arrangements, both as far as supplies direct to users and subcontract manufacturing are concerned. So long as variable costs can be covered, Arragon may feel it can cut its prices in these markets in order to maintain its manufacturing capacity in being.

Arragon will have to establish exactly which of Wizzomatic's products are acceptable substitutes for its own and where there are gaps in Wizzomatic's standardised range. Those gaps can then be exploited with higher prices.

Promotion

Arragon's products are complex, expensive and sold to industrial buyers, so the company's main promotional effort is likely to go into personal selling by experienced sales engineers. There is also likely to be attendance at trade fairs and a small amount of reminder advertising in the specialist press. Public relations effort is likely to be minimal and also concentrated on the specialist press.

Distribution

Distribution to aircraft manufacturers is likely to be direct to the end user, without any use of intermediaries. The subcontract work will also go direct to the purchasers. Distribution of aftermarket spares may involve the use of intermediaries, since the products are highly standardised technically and may be sold globally without modification. Since the products are expensive, regional or national intermediaries may be able to provide a service by investment in spares inventories.

8 United Products

Part (a)

> **Top tips**. This is a wide ranging question and, perhaps, therefore, somewhat daunting. Remember that with this type of question there will be a lot of easy marks for explaining the basics. For example, a list of strengths and weaknesses would glean quite a few marks, though not 50%.

In order to score well on this question you must do two slightly different things when you are applying your knowledge to the scenario: use the setting to illustrate your theory; and suggest ways in which the theory might be used to make improvements.

Thus, for example, we say that the internal transfer and promotion from within policy is an example of the way that relatively junior managers can obtain good experience of real business problems. Similarly, we say that the detailed monthly reporting might be over-restrictive in its effects and, on examination, might prove to be unnecessarily expensive.

Notice also that we begin with a comment about the very nature of UP's business, which you might think is a matter over and above the question of its organisation. Don't forget that there is scope in this exam for this sort of digression if you make it relevant to the scenario.

Divisionalisation is a common form of organisation structure in large organisations, especially those that encompass a wide variety of products, technologies and geographical locations. UP seems to qualify under all three of these categories. The form has been found to allow for overall control from the corporate headquarters without drowning it in the detail of micromanagement at long range.

The diversity of the company's operations is itself worthy of comment from a strategic point of view. There is obviously a tradition of having widely different operations and it is possible to discern some potential for synergy, in agriculture and retailing, for instance. However, the organisation is committed to managing a very wide range of technologies and markets and it may be that its lacklustre financial performance is linked to a lack of specialist knowledge among its senior managers. The policy of moving managers from division to division, while generally good for their personal development may actually hamper the progress of the more specialised operations.

It is generally considered that conglomerate diversification only adds value when the expertise of the corporate headquarters is such that its allocation of capital is more effective than would be achieved by a normally efficient capital market. Whether this is the case with United Products must be subject to some doubt. The less profitable divisions are protected from the disciplines of the market by the corporate HQ, while those with good prospects may find themselves starved of funds.

UP clearly displays one disadvantage of the divisional form. There is a tendency for the divisions to be more bureaucratic than they would be as independent organisations in order to service the demands of the corporate HQ's control procedures. UP takes this to an extreme, demanding monthly reports and carrying out frequent functional inspections rather than encouraging a responsive autonomy by the use of simple **key performance indicators**. The probable effect of this is to stifle the creativity and sense of ownership that flow from greater autonomy. This is most likely to be visible in the divisions that operate in complex, unstable environments, such as film-making, publishing and fashion retailing. A side effect is the absorption of an excessive degree of divisional revenue in management charges for HQ and in the divisional bureaucracies themselves.

Another problem of divisionalisation was referred to by *Mintzberg* as the pull to balkanise. This is the natural desire of the division heads for independence from central control. In an organisation like UP, with its rather bureaucratic approach, this might take the form conforming to the letter of the rules but manipulating activities and finances. So long as the reporting parameters fall within set limits, it may be possible to conceal unauthorised ventures for a long time, possibly with unfortunate consequences.

A final comment might be made about the mixture of divisional types: there are both product divisions and geographical divisions. This might be a sensible response to UP's geographical range and variety of products. On the other hand it might be a source of confusion and conflict between geographical and product based managers for control of particular operations. This will be particularly apparent when new markets are entered. The problem may be exacerbated by the management structures put in place for the various joint ventures. Overall, the potential for complexity and confusion is significant.

Part (b)

Top tips. The idea of virtuality has become very fashionable and people tend to use the term rather loosely. The definition we give is academically correct. Be sure that you do not confuse the virtual organisation with *Handy's* concept of the **shamrock organisation**, which is merely an organisation that makes extensive use of self-employed and temporary staff in order to be able to control its labour costs in times of economic slowdown.

The idea of a virtual organisation or cybernetic corporation has attracted considerable attention as the usefulness of IT for communication and control has been exploited. The essence of the virtual organisation is the electronic linking of spatially dispersed components.

Such an organisation is a temporary or permanent collection of geographically dispersed individuals, groups, organisational units (which may or may not belong to the same organisation), or entire organisations that depend on electronic linking in order to complete the production process.

However, an organisation is not a virtual organisation merely because it uses IT extensively and has multiple locations. Many organisations fall into that category.

Also, organisations that make extensive use of temporary and self-employed labour are not necessarily virtual organisations because of that, though they may have some virtual characteristics.

UP almost certainly uses extensive IT systems for its internal communications. It would be surprising if it did not have an internal e mail system and it may well have a corporate intranet. However, it clearly has activities that are very real as opposed to virtual, such as its agricultural, extractive, manufacturing and retailing operations.

Of the activities we are told about, electronic design is perhaps the one most suited to the virtual approach. It may be possible for design engineers to work in isolation, using computer aided design equipment and communicating by e mail. However, where the design work requires a team effort, co-ordination may become a problem.

Publishing may also be a candidate, depending on the nature of what is published. Authors of books are likely to work alone, and editors may be able to do the same, as may their assistants and other specialists such as proof readers and indexers. The transmission of entire texts by electronic means is quite feasible and some specialist books are published by being printed on demand from computer memory.

9 Auto Direct

Top tips. You must think hard about the wording of this question. Superficially, it asks you for a summary of change management strategies in a particular context, which would be a large job to do properly, but offers only twelve marks. The implication is that you must not descend into too much detail about any particular model or approach.

Managing Director, Auto Direct

Report: Change management strategies and methods

The change that you are contemplating, while extensive, is incremental and does not involve the transformation of your organisation. It therefore falls into the category of **adaptation**, which implies that you may proceed step by step and leave your basic assumptions and approach unchanged.

It would be a very worthwhile exercise to consider some of the factors that might affect the success of your programme of change. Chief among these are likely to be the various human factors present in your staff.

Presumably you will include some element of promotion and cross-posting of your existing workforce in order to provide a basis of experience at your new sites, so you should consider the degree of **readiness** (or willingness) of your staff to undertake the development you plan.

You should also consider your company's managerial **capability** and **capacity** in terms of resources to undertake change. The former depends largely on past experience.

While good **project management** of a programme of change is very important, it is the **human aspects of the change management process** that are crucial. This is because change will not happen unless people make it happen. A number of strategies are proposed for dealing with this aspect of change management.

Participation in decision-making is sometimes recommended as a way of improving motivation generally and may be useful in the context of change. It is probably advantageous to involve staff in decisions affecting them, their conditions and their work processes and at least hear what they have to say. However, participation is not a universal panacea and can be very **time consuming**. Also, the normal **management style and culture** of the organisation must be considered. It is probably inappropriate to promote participation exclusively in the context of change if staff are not used to it: their main reaction may be one of suspicious cynicism.

An **autocratic** approach, imposing change by means of **coercion** can work reasonably well in some circumstances, especially where the staff expect nothing else. It has the benefit of saving time and is probably the **best approach in times of crisis**. However, it does have the weakness of ignoring the experience and knowledge that staff may be able to offer.

In any event, **communication** with staff about the proposed change is commonly regarded as an essential process. Ideally, information will be provided as early as possible, explaining why change is necessary and the course that will be followed. Anxiety, particularly over job security, is common during change and a programme of communication and education can go a long way to allay it.

Sometimes neither participation nor coercion can resolve all problems and **negotiation** may be required. This is often the case when the labour force is strongly organised and when there is disagreement between management factions as to the best course to follow.

This has been a brief overview of some approaches to change management. You will no doubt be in a position to decide which are most appropriate to the circumstances of Auto Direct.

10 BPR and supply chain

> **Top tips**. Ensure you revise the features of supply chains in general, and virtual supply chains in particular. Remember at all times that the examiner is interested in your ability to apply your knowledge in a practical setting.

Business Process Re-engineering (BPR) is the fundamental rethinking and radical design of business processes to achieve dramatic improvements in critical contemporary measures of performance, such as cost, quality, service and speed.

In other words, BPR involves significant change in the business rather than minimal or incremental changes to processes. This is essentially different from procedures such as automation where existing processes are simply computerised. Although some improvements in speed may be obtained, the processes are essentially the same. For example, the local warehouse could use EDI to send an order to the supplier, which may be quicker than email. However, the process of sending the order and receiving the goods to the warehouse is the same.

Using BPR, the actual reasons for the business processes being used can be queried, and where necessary replaced with more efficient processes. For example, rather than inventory being ordered from the store via the central warehouse, the supplier could monitor inventory in each store using an extranet. When goods reach re-order level, the supplier is aware of this and can send goods directly to the store. Not only does this provide inventory replenishment much more quickly, it is also more cost effective for the supplier as the central warehouse effectively becomes redundant.

Key features of BPR involve the willingness of the organisation to accept change and the ability to use new technologies to achieve those changes. In the example, ABC may have to clearly explain the benefits to staff from the new systems, to ensure that they are accepted. ABC may also need to obtain additional skills in terms of IT and ability to implement and use those systems. New hardware and software will also certainly be required. The aim of BPR is to provide radical improvements in efficiency and cost savings of up to 90%. Amending the supply chain as noted above will help to these benefits.

11 Fashion retailer

Top tips. Fashion retailing is a fairly specialised job. However, we all have some experience of it from the customer's side of the counter. Don't be afraid to make some educated deductions about, for instance, the need for careful inventory control when a wide range of goods is moving rather quickly.

An organisation's value-creating activities must be mutually supporting.

Part (a)

Paul's business is in the fashion clothing industry with 20 retail stores but little integration between the stores. This part of the fashion industry operates with very slim margins and with profitability not keeping pace with the increase in turnover, Paul realises that he must operate in a more cost-conscious manner. The computer system is currently underused and is operating in a passive manner, simply providing basic information rather than contributing to the business' competitive advantage in any way.

We can use **Porter's value chain model** to consider how the IS function can be applied to help provide Paul with a competitive edge in his business.

Paul's firm will only be as strong as the weakest link in its value chain. The IS investment will be worthwhile if it can be used to reduce costs or to differentiate Paul's business from the others in the industry sector.

Primary activities

Inbound logistics

This relates to the purchasing function and the storage of inventory and distribution to the stores. An IS system can help with inventory control levels, economic ordering and efficient distribution routings.

Operations

IS can be used to monitor the performance of each store with details being provided about profitability, inventory levels, inventory turnover, expense levels, staff absences and so on. IS could also be used to analyse the different consumer demand profile in different locations in order to help each store ensure that it has sufficient inventories of the type of sales made in its store.

Outbound logistics

This element of the chain concerns distribution to customers and is more relevant in a manufacturing industry. In Paul's business there will not be much distribution to customers but the system may be able to produce a customer database to assist with marketing and promotions.

Marketing and sales

Paul could use IS to indicate customer purchasing patterns for different stores and to develop databases for promotions. Internet retailing is a possibility, though it would create a fulfilment problem.

Service

This area of the chain is to do with the provision of service to the customers and it is not likely that IS can be of much use here although it could be used to monitor, control and facilitate transfers between stores.

Support activities

Firm's infrastructure

In this area IS can be used to help with the budgeting, finance and management information in order to improve the Paul's company's performance compared to that of his competitors.

Human resources management

As Paul's organisation is quite small and consists largely of retail sales staff, there will not be many very useful applications of IS in this area however it may be used to make recruitment and appraisals more efficient.

Technology development

It is possible that Paul could make some radical changes, for example, developing the business' e-commerce ability and starting to sell through an online store.

However, if he doesn't want to make such dramatic changes, Paul can still use IS to support process improvements; for example, by enabling the operational changes to the ordering and inventory management processes.

Procurement

This area of support activity is concerned with linking the purchasing system to the sales system. This could be used to automatically update inventory records and indicate when new orders should be placed and could also help to minimise times when excessive inventory is held in a store. It could also consolidate orders to achieve bulk purchase discounts.

Part (b)

To: Paul Singh
From: A Consultant
Date: December 20XX
Subject: Software package options

Introduction

You asked for advice on the use of software packages and, in particular on two specific software package options that have been suggested to you.

- Standard package
- Modified standard package

In general, **standard packages are robust systems** that incorporate wide experience of business procedures and their automation. They can provide immediate benefits in the form of improved methods, records and possibilities for analysis of data. They are, however, based on **standardised modules** and are **not necessarily optimised for any given commercial application**. Claims by vendors that their products can give a competitive edge are questionable: **competitors can easily buy the same product**. The best that can be said is that a standard package should provide an effective way of doing things. Also, such packages force the organisation to adjust itself to the requirements of the software.

Standard packages do, however, offer a number of positive qualities.

(a)   While selection may take some time, **installation** should be rapid and there should be no requirement for extensive testing. However, time would be required for staff training and familiarisation.

(b)   **Quality** should be guaranteed both by the vendor and, except for launch customers, by earlier installation by other customers.

(c)   **Documentation and training** should be immediately available and of high quality since these are important selling points.

(d)   **Maintenance support** should be good and would normally include help desk service and routine software amendments to correct faults as they become apparent.

(e)   Comprehensive **package evaluation** should be possible. This might include use for a trial period and visits to existing installations.

On the other hand, there are problems to note.

(a)   **Property rights** over the software usually reside with the supplier. This has three important potential consequences for the user.

  (i)   The supplier controls future development of the software.

(ii) The supplier controls the support available and may discontinue it, forcing the customer to purchase an upgrade.

(iii) The supplier may sell the product rights to another supplier, perhaps to the prejudice of the customer.

(b) The **financial stability** and survival of the supplier is not guaranteed.

(c) **Inadequate performance** is quite likely: the customer may have to accept restricted functionality or pay for tailored amendments, with accompanying disadvantages discussed below. Further problems may be caused by unwanted standard features: these may cause difficulties in training and implementation.

(d) **Legal redress** for lack of functionality will almost certainly not be available.

(e) **Changing requirements** can erode a package's functionality. Potential purchasers evaluate a package against their current requirements. These may change as time passes or may not have been properly specified in the first place. In either case, the package fails to provide full satisfaction.

Because of the generic nature of standard packages, some clients have them tailored to fit their requirements and their existing systems and procedures. This approach has been recommended to you, but is generally a **mistake**.

- The cost advantage of buying off the shelf is destroyed.
- Introduction is delayed.
- Reliability is reduced.
- New versions of the same software will be useless until they too have been modified.

Generally it is cheaper and more effective to redesign the organisation's processes to fit a standard package than to do the opposite.

12 Good Sports Ltd

Part (a)

> **Top tips.** This question puts e-commerce firmly into a strategic context. IT and the internet pervade the modern business organisation and so it should be possible for you to offer sensible comments upon this basis. The main advantages and disadvantages of an e-business strategy that you put into your answer must be applicable to Good Sports' own business situation. It is not a foregone conclusion that involvement in e-commerce will be unequivocally beneficial. There a several strategic issues to consider – such as the familiar framework of 'suitability, acceptability and feasibility'. Porter's generic strategies are also brought into this question.
>
> **Easy marks.** Depends on how well you know the e-business material in Chapter 11. If you have a good knowledge of e-business you should be able to identify a number of advantages and disadvantages.

REPORT

To: Alan and Bob, Good Sports Limited
From: Strategic consultant
Date: December 20XX
Subject: E – Business strategy

Introduction

Very few businesses can afford to ignore the **potential of the internet** for driving forward strategy and activity. The markets that Good Sports operates in are being affected by the development of e-business. Small enterprises such as this one can gain access to customers on a global scale, which only relatively recently would have been viewed as impossible. In many ways the advantages and disadvantages of e-business can be viewed from the perspective of the customer.

Advantages of an e-business strategy

Through the integration and acceleration of standard business processes via highly sophisticated IT systems (order placing, stock control, dispatch and so on), attention to customer needs, and communication with them, can be much quicker.

Although the internet has a global reach, its benefits are not confined to large organisations. Good Sports can move into a global marketplace.

Websites can provide new channels of communication, linked with customer databases which can be analysed to provide much greater insights into consumer buying behaviour.

Increased quantities of data, and more sophisticated methods of analysing it, mean that greater attention can be paid to customising product offerings to more precisely defined **target customers**.

Disadvantages of an e-business strategy

E-commerce presents completely new problems of management and organisation, not least because it needs the **involvement of specialists**. There may be a lack of in-house expertise.

A detailed cost/benefit analysis should be undertaken. It may even be decided that costs exceed the benefits of setting up the e-business operation.

New technology installed by Good Sports will need to **link up with existing business systems**, so the resources needed (money, time and effort) should not be underestimated.

Processes

For Good Sports, e-business will probably be a **supplement** to its traditional retail operations, with the website forming a supplementary channel for communication and sales. Even so, its development is likely to have wide implications and involve and affect several functions, and so should be managed at the highest level. It is also necessary that it conform to the standard criteria for any strategic choice: suitability, acceptability and feasibility. Precise objectives for this new strategy need to be set. The company will need to go back to basics and ask itself some fundamental questions such as:

- What do customers want to buy from us?
- What business are we in?
- What kind of suppliers might we need?
- What categories of customer do we want to attract and retain?

Assuming that these questions can be answered satisfactorily, new technology can be introduced to connect electronically with employees, customers and suppliers to help drive the strategy forward.

Part (b)

With a **niche strategy**, a firm concentrates its attention on one or more particular secure segments (or niches) of the market, and does not try to serve the entire market. Good Sports has pursued such a strategy, seeking to serve a local market for less popular sports, in a way that insulates it from competition against the major high volume retailers who are concentrating on the more popular sports such as football.

In this way, Good Sports has been able to ensure that it **does not spread itself too thinly** in the market for sporting goods. There is nothing in the scenario to suggest they have reached saturation point in their chosen niche market. The question then needs to be asked whether it makes strategic sense for Good Sports to invest in online transaction capability to continue to serve (and develop) its market.

Bargaining power of customers

It is recognised that one of the key features of e-business is that it brings far greater **price transparency**, with customers being able to shop around for the cheapest deal using the vast information resources available on the internet (either from other companies, or other customers). The **customer has become far more powerful**. There is a theory that customers expect goods and services to be discounted when sold online (and indeed, many are) since they are aware that administrative costs are likely to be lower than in more traditional forms of distribution. Good Sports will need to find out how likely this is to happen with their customers, and whether there are competitors who are offering lower prices on the same range of goods. This should be easy to find out using market research and a search of competitor sites.

Such customer involvement however could provide a mechanism for **increasing customer loyalty**, for example by targeting particular groups and finding out more about their sports activity and spending habits. This can be done via online questionnaires or surveys, and could lead to the identification of new niche markets, currently not served by any competitors, that can be developed (such as new types of sports equipment to be included in the product range; new services).

As indicated in the answer to part (a), Good Sports needs to go back to basics and consider all the costs and benefits that could be associated with offering such enhanced online capability to its chosen niche market.

13 DRB

(a)   A simple value chain of the primary activities of DRB is shown below.

Handling and storing inbound fully configured equipment Quality inspection	Re-branding of products Re-packaging of products	Customer collection Technician delivery and installation	Local advertising Web based enquiries support	On-site technical support Back to base
Inbound logistics	**Operations**	**Outbound Logistics**	**Marketing and sales**	**Service**

Comments about value might include:

Inbound logistics: Excellent quality assurance is required in inbound logistics. This is essential for pre-configured equipment where customers have high expectations of reliability. As well as contributing to customer satisfaction, high quality also reduces service costs.

Operations: This is a relatively small component in the DRB value chain and actually adds little value to the customer. It is also being undertaken in a relatively high cost country. DRB might wish to re-visit the current arrangement.

Outbound logistics: Customer feedback shows that this is greatly valued. Products can be picked up from stock and delivery and installation is provided if required. Most of the company's larger competitors cannot offer this service. However, it is unlikely that this value can be retained when DRB begins to increasingly supply outside the geographical region it is in.

Marketing and sales: This is very low-key at DRB and will have to be developed if the company is to deliver the proposed growth. The limited functionality of the website offers little value to customers.

Service: Customer feedback shows that this is greatly valued. Most of the company's competitors cannot offer this level of service. They offer support from off-shore call centres and a returns policy that is both time consuming to undertake and slow in rectification. However, it is unlikely that this value can be retained when DRB begins to increasingly supply outside the geographical region it is in.

(b)   DRB has already gained efficiencies by procuring products through the supplier's web-site. However, the website has restricted functionality. When DRB places the order it is not informed of the expected delivery date until it receives the confirmation email from ISAS. It is also unable to track the status of their order and so it is only when it receives a despatch email from ISAS that it knows that it is on its way. Because DRB is not the owner of the shipment, it is unable to track the delivery and so the physical arrival of the goods cannot be easily predicted. On occasions where shipments have appeared to have been lost, DRB has had to ask ISAS to track the shipment and report on its status. This has not been very satisfactory and the problem has been exacerbated by having two shippers involved. ISAS has not been able to reliably track the transhipment of goods from their shipper to EIF, the logistics company used to distribute their products in the country. Some shipments have been lost and it is time-consuming to track and follow-up shipments which are causing concern. Finally, because DRB has no long term contract with ISAS, it has to pay when it places the order through a credit card transaction on the ISAS website.

DRB has stated that it wishes to continue importing fully configured products. It is not interested in importing components and assembling them. It also does not wish to build or invest in assembly plants in other countries. However, it may wish to consider the following changes to its upstream supply chain:

- Seek to identify a wider range of suppliers and so trade through other sell-side websites. Clearly there are costs associated with this. Suppliers have to be identified and evaluated and financial and trading arrangements have to be established. However, it removes the risk of single-sourcing and other suppliers may have better systems in place to support order and delivery tracking.

- Seek to identify suppliers who are willing and able to re-brand and package their products with DRB material at the production plant. This should reduce DRB costs as this is currently undertaken in a country where wage rates are high.

- Re-consider the decision not to negotiate long-term contracts with suppliers (including ISAS) and so explore the possibility of more favourable payment terms. DRB has avoided long-term contracts up to now. It may also not be possible to enter into such contracts if DRB begins to trade with a number of suppliers.

- Seek to identify suppliers (including ISAS) who are able to provide information about delivery dates prior to purchase and who are able to provide internet-based order tracking systems to their customers. This should allow much better planning.

- Consider replacing the two supplier shippers with a contracted logistics company which will collect the goods from the supplier and transport the goods directly to DRB. This should reduce physical transhipment problems and allow seamless monitoring of the progress of the order from despatch to arrival. It will also allow DRB to plan for the arrival of goods and to schedule its re-packaging.

DRB might also wish to consider two other procurement models; buy-side and the independent marketplace.

In the buy-side model DRB would use its website to invite potential suppliers to bid for contract requirements posted on the site. This places the onus on suppliers to spend time completing details and making commitments. It should also attract a much wider range of suppliers than would have been possible through DRB searching sell-side sites for potential suppliers. Unfortunately, it is unlikely that DRB is large enough to host such a model. However, it may wish to prototype it to see if it is viable and whether it uncovers potential suppliers who have not been found in sell-side websites searches.

In the independent marketplace model, DRB places its requirements on an intermediary website. These are essentially B2B electronic marketplaces which allow, on the one hand, potential customers to search products being offered by suppliers and, on the other hand, customers to place their requirements and be contacted by potential suppliers. Such marketplaces promise greater supplier choice with reduced costs. They also provide an opportunity for aggregation where smaller organisations (such as DRB) can get together with companies that have the same requirement to place larger orders to gain cheaper prices and better purchasing terms. It is also likely that such marketplaces will increasingly offer algorithms that automatically match customers and suppliers, so reducing the search costs associated with the sell-side model. The independent marketplace model may be a useful approach for DRB. Many of the suppliers participating in these marketplaces are electronics companies.

(c) DRB's downstream supply chain is also very simple at the moment. It has a web-site that shows information about DRB products. Customers can make enquiries about the specification and availability of these products through an e-mail facility. Conventional marketing is undertaken through local advertising and buyers either collect their products or they are delivered and installed by a specialist group of technicians. DRB could tune its downstream supply chain by using many of the approaches mentioned in the previous section. For example:

(i) Developing the website so that it not only shows products but also product availability. Customers would be able to place orders and pay for them securely over the website. The site could be integrated with a logistics system so that orders and deliveries can be tracked by the customer. DRB must recognise that most of its competitors already have such systems. However, DRB will have to put a similar system in place to be able to support its growth plans.

(ii) Participating in independent marketplace websites as a supplier. DRB may also be able to exploit aggregation by combining with other suppliers in consortia to bid for large contracts.

(iii) DRB may also consider participating in B2C marketplaces such as eBay. Many organisations use this as their route to market for commodity products.

DRB may also wish to consider replacing its sales from inventory approach with sales from order. In the current approach, DRB purchases products in advance and re-packages and stores these products before selling them to customers. This leads to very quick order fulfillment but high storage and financing costs. These costs will become greater if the planned growth occurs. DRB may wish to consider offering products on its website at a discount but with specified delivery terms. This would allow the company to supply to order rather than supply from inventory.

14 Project initiation

Top tips. You may find it easier to structure your answer with headings for each problem you identify, and then in two separate paragraphs, answer the two parts of the question. This should ensure that actions to resolve the problem are included in your answer.

Leadership style

(a) The leadership style of the manager is tending to be autocratic; that is team members are being told what to do without the opportunity to discuss the decisions being made. This leadership style tends to be appropriate for staff who need a lot of guidance through a project.

(b) In this situation, most of the staff have professional qualifications, indicating that they are able to think though problems for themselves and monitor their own work effectively. A more appropriate management style would be participative. Dave could discuss the work to be done and then let staff carry out this work. This approach would benefit staff by providing them with more responsibility and benefit Dave by freeing up more time to monitor the overall progress of the project.

Lack of communication

(a) The cancelling of project meetings can have an adverse effect on morale, as well as making communication between the team members more difficult. While it appears that more work will be carried out on the project, if staff feel that they are not being communicated to, or that they cannot discuss problems, then overall work efficiency is likely to suffer.

(b) This problem is easy to resolve; Dave should re-introduce the team meetings and apologise for making the mistake of cancelling them in the first place. This will provide an appropriate channel of communication and help team members realise it was not their fault that the meetings were cancelled.

Lack of project updates

(a) The other problem with cancelling team meetings is that project team members will not be aware of how the project is progressing overall. Team members may not feel motivated to work harder if they perceive that other members are not 'pulling their weight'. The possibility of conflicts within the team suggest that morale and trust may be low, and so motivation may be an issue.

(b) Re-introducing the team meetings will assist communication and help all team members to see how the project is progressing. When all team members can see that everyone is working hard, then this will have a positive impact on morale and the overall amount of work being done.

Accountability for errors

(a) Making team members accountable for errors is acceptable, where those members made mistakes in the first place. However, in this situation, the 'trainee' systems analysts were not responsible for a large percentage of the analysis work as this was carried out by the previous analysts.

(b) Dave should really be grateful that these two team members are attempting to continue this important work, and not place hindrances in their way. An appropriate way of maintaining motivation would be to simply ask for explanation of any errors found; accountability for those errors can be decided later, if necessary.

Conflicts within the team

(a) The number of small disputes within the team indicate that working relationships are not good. These problems will tend to affect overall communication and working efficiency within the team, as members will not feel that they can discuss problems with each other.

(b) In this situation, Dave is wrong to ignore the problem; his team is already behind schedule and trying to hide the problem is more likely to make it worse. Dave must attempt to resolve the conflicts in some way, preferably by meeting and discussing with the team members why the conflicts are arising.

If the problems cannot be resolved, the project will continue to fall behind schedule. The conflicts and the lack of trained analysts may indicate that the project deadlines need to be moved, or the project cancelled until a full working team with good relationships can be used.

15 Educational Institution

> **Top tips.** The key to (a) was recognising the range of requirements that the Institution now has to fulfil – the needs of different stakeholders and the different objectives that should be met. You would have limited the marks you could earn if you had not discussed publicity of objectives. In (b) we have provided answers for all the measures, although you were only asked to discuss a selection. You need to think carefully about what could distort the measures used and how they might prompt action.

Part (a)

(i) **Different stakeholders**

At present the government is the most important **external stakeholder**. However the government will become less important and private sector users more important as the proportion of income derived from private sector courses increases. In addition the Institution will also have to take into account the interests of staff (internal stakeholders) and public sector students.

Links between financing and objectives

The cash limits set by the government relate to the **effectiveness** of the Institution's operations. The limits that the Institution has to meet are determined by what its outputs are in terms of research publications and quality. The Institution will have to take into account the methods of **measuring** these non-financial objectives.

Use of finance

Fulfilling the government's requirements (and therefore obtaining finance) is the most important current objective. However the Institution should also consider how it makes the best use of the finance it obtains, and here financial objectives become important. It should be looking to **minimise costs** as far as possible. The Institution should have the objective of choosing the **most economical** option that does not compromise the achievement of the non-financial objectives. The Institution should also have the objective that the **expenditure** it undertakes produces the **maximum return** in terms of meeting the non-financial objectives.

Level of investment

The Institution also needs to consider how much to spend on **long-term investment** rather than spend its entire budget on short-term requirements. If the Institution does not invest in upgrading facilities, over time teaching and research quality will suffer as the best staff move to other institutions with better facilities, and the Institution fails to fulfil more demanding expectations of quality.

(ii) **Advantages of publicising objectives**

Publicising the above objectives seems unexceptionable, as the Institution will be demonstrating that it is trying to achieve **value for money** from its operations. Likewise publicising an **investment target** will indicate to prospective teachers and students the Institution's recognition that it needs to allocate resources to ensure that it keeps up with changing views on what constitutes **excellence.**

Disadvantages of publicising objectives

The main problem with publicising objectives is that the Institution may be judged on the basis of objectives which it does not have the freedom to set. As well as fulfilling government requirements on effectiveness, the Institution may also need to take into account **other government guidelines**, for example those relating to mix of students. In addition publicising objectives may **highlight conflicts** between serving the needs of the public sector and serving the needs of private sector clients.

Part (b)

Value added

Value added can be defined in financial terms as **sales revenues** less **the cost of running courses** (lecturers' fees, costs of producing material, costs of facilities used). Sales revenue is not however the only measure of the success of an Educational Institution. Better measures may be percentages of students **passing their exams**. For non-exam private sector courses the measure should ideally relate to **enhanced job performance**.

Use of value added

The Institution will undoubtedly pay attention to revenues, but it will also need to measure the benefits students have gained from its courses. Benefits can be measured in a variety of ways; for non-exam courses they could take the form of students demonstrating improved skills or knowledge at the end of the course, for example by giving a presentation. Data about all the **costs directly related** to the courses will also be needed. Sophisticated measures such as **shareholder value added** can be used to measure the impact of **fixed and working capital investment**, and the Institution's **required rate of return**.

Profitability

Profitability can be used to **measure the returns** that the **resources input** are generating, **relative** to the **sales** made. Measured in these terms, profit measures by themselves do not take account of the **investment** used to generate the profits.

Use of profitability

Profits may be distorted by the **accounting policies**, the **method** used for **allocating the costs** of running the Institution or depreciation. Depreciation charges may be particularly problematic if many of the assets have not been purchased on the open market but provided by the government, and have **no resale value**. Provided though that profits are calculated on a **consistent basis** over the five year period, the **trend of profits** should indicate the Institution's progress towards its targets.

Profits should also be used in conjunction with measures of **quality**. If profits have been **increased** by **cutting costs** and running poorer quality courses, in time the increase may be negated by the **fall in turnover** resulting from customers looking elsewhere for higher quality training.

Profitability measures can also influence the **range** and **frequency** of courses run, with the **most profitable** courses being run more often. However past profits may not be the **best indication** of future prospects, and focusing on the performance of individual courses may **not highlight** the **links** between them.

Return on investment

Return on investment is calculated by **dividing profits** by the **value of assets used**.

Use of return on investment

Again the profit figures used may be subject to distortion, but return on investment does at least take into account the **resources needed** to generate profits. However the figures might be distorted by the methods used to **allocate assets**. Provided though the methods used are consistent, return on investment can be used as an indication of changing efficiency levels over time. Its use may however **restrict investment**, as managers seek to keep down levels of capital employed; this may not be in the Institution's best interests as it is trying to expand its courses programme.

Competitive position

There are various measures of competitive position that may be valuable to the Institution. These include the **number and variety of courses** offered by competitors, also the extent to which competitors are introducing **new courses,** the **standard of courses** offered and the **pricing structure** of courses.

Use of competitive position

The Institution can **benchmark** competitors by sending its **staff** on **competitors' courses**, and getting them to report on the standards of teaching, material and facilities. The feedback provided should indicate to the Institution in what areas its **own courses** need to be **improved** to match those offered by competitors. Benchmarking may also highlight **strengths** of the Institution's courses compared with its competitors, and these **strengths** can be **emphasised** in **marketing literature.**

Customer satisfaction

Customer satisfaction is likely to be a key measure for the Institution. If customers are satisfied with the courses provided, they are likely to **book further courses** and also **recommend the courses** to others.

Use of customer satisfaction

The Institution can obtain feedback from customers **by review forms** at the end of every class. These should allow participants to **rank different aspects** of the courses (quality of teaching, quality of material, facilities provided). **Targets** could be set for the marks that should be achieved. These targets could be increased over time, and also improvements made to courses that failed to reach the targets. Alternative methods of assessing how customers' needs have been met include **internal peer reviews**, **quality audits**, and obtaining **feedback** from **private sector participants' employers**.

Another way of measuring satisfaction is to track the **level of bookings** from **previous participants** on Institution courses. In a competitive market, customers will only book again if they are happy with what they have received in the past.

Market share

Market share measures the **percentage share** that an organisation has in the **total market** for a good or service. It measures the **success** of the **sales performance**, **pricing strategy** and **product quality**.

Use of market share

The Institution will need to research who offers similar courses and **ascertain numbers** who go. The courses offered by others need to be tracked over time. In order to achieve its growth targets, it may be better for the Institution to concentrate on expanding courses in areas in which it currently has **low market share**, since there may be potential to attract customers away from competitors. **Market share targets** may be set as **subsidiary targets** to **growth targets**.

16 Coxford Doors

This company seems to have operated more like a soviet than a business. No doubt there has been much job-satisfaction, but the company's ability to compete and add value has deteriorated.

A participatory style of management has been shown in many studies to enhance personal **motivation** and **commitment** to the organisation's mission. This occurs via the process of **internalisation**, whereby the members of the workforce adopt the corporate goal as their personal goal. This can lead to better industrial relations, higher quality and better service. However, there is no conclusive evidence that such an approach necessarily leads to improved overall performance. This is borne out by the situation at Coxford Doors.

Andrew Smith's style of management is likely to bring the focus that has been missing in the past. He will no doubt speed up the decision making process (probably by making most decisions himself) plan effectively and issue clear instructions. Confusion and delay should be reduced and control enhanced. This will improve the business's responsiveness and ability to satisfy customers.

However, Andrew Smith is likely to encounter resistance from a work force used to proceeding according to its own ideas of what is appropriate. Morale and loyalty are both likely to suffer from the loss of autonomy. There is likely to be a lack of co-operation and, possibly, active resistance to the new order. The commercial position might deteriorate further as a result.

Even if there is acceptance that the trading position demands change it is unlikely to be wholehearted. A strong undercurrent of resentment may be created, resurfacing at some time in the future, perhaps when the commercial situation has improved.

Routine changes are harder to sell than **transformational** ones if they are perceived to be unimportant and not survival-based.

Culture change is perhaps hardest of all, especially if it involves basic assumptions. This is certainly the case at Coxford Doors. However, the necessary preconditions for change are in place. Andrew Smith is himself an **outsider**, prepared to challenge and expose, in a visible way, the existing behaviour pattern; his appointment will act as a **trigger**; and **alterations to the power structure** will be an inherent part of his actions.

The unfreeze stage is likely to include extensive **communication** and **consultation processes**, but the objective must be kept in sight; concern for proper treatment of employees must not be allowed to subvert the overall aim.

Change is the second stage of the process and is mainly concerned with introducing the new, desirable behaviours and approaches. This will involve retraining and practice to build up familiarity and experience. Individuals must be encouraged to take ownership of the new ways of doing things. For this to happen they must be shown to work.

Refreeze is the final stage, involving consolidation and reinforcement of the new behaviour. Positive or negative reinforcement may be used, with praise, reward and sanctions applied as necessary.

It will be important for Andrew Smith to retain **control of the process** at all times, since the company's history of participative management will tend to undermine his move towards a firmer style. He must make it clear from the outset that change must take place, while remaining flexible on the detail and the style of its introduction. It would be advisable to aim for an intermediate style of management, in which the workforce retain a voice. Operational control must be improved, but it should not be necessary to move to a completely autocratic way of doing things.

17 Shirtmaster Group

Part (a)

> **Top tips.** Although you are provided with a lot of financial information your focus must be on the *strategic position* of the group and its divisions, rather than on calculations and numbers themselves.
>
> The question is all about gaining an understanding of the key trends, and this includes analysing the separate performances of the two divisions. Your findings are likely to inform your answers to later parts of the question.
>
> **Easy marks.** The figures should indicate to you that the two divisions are performing very differently. If you work through the key features of each division you should be able to identify a number of strengths, weaknesses, opportunities and threats from the material given in the scenario.
>
> **Tutorial note.** We have included all the figures from the question and added in key percentages so that we can then use them in our answer.
>
> You should not replicate all the data in the exam; simply calculate the key percentages, ratios or trends and then use them in your analysis.

	2008	2009	2010	2011 Budget	2012 Forecast	2013 Forecast
Overall Shirtmaster Group:						
Total sales	25.0	23.8	21.4	23.5	24.4	26.7
Gondour sales	24.5	23.2	21.0	22.7	23.4	24.7
Trend in total sales		*– 5%*	*– 10%*	*10%*	*4%*	*9%*
Overseas sales	0.5	0.6	0.4	0.8	1.0	2.0
Cost of sales	17.7	16.8	15.2	16.3	16.8	17.8
Cost of sales %	*71%*	*71%*	*71%*	*69%*	*69%*	*67%*
Gross profit	7.3	7.0	6.2	7.2	7.6	8.9
Gross profit %	*29%*	*29%*	*29%*	*31%*	*31%*	*33%*
Marketing	1.7	1.5	1.2	1.7	1.9	2.2
Distribution	1.6	1.4	1.2	1.4	1.5	1.9
Administration	1.8	1.8	1.7	1.9	1.9	2.1
Other costs %	*20%*	*20%*	*19%*	*21%*	*22%*	*23%*
Net profit	2.2	2.3	2.1	2.2	2.3	2.7
Net profit %	*9%*	*10%*	*10%*	*9%*	*9%*	*10%*
Shirtmaster division:						
Total sales	14.8	12.6	10.3	11.7	12.0	13.5
Gondoir sales	14.3	12.0	9.9	10.9	11.0	11.5
Trend in total sales		*– 15%*	*– 18%*	*14%*	*3%*	*13%*
Overseas sales	0.5	0.6	0.4	0.8	1.0	2.0
Cost of sales	11.1	9.8	8.2	9.1	9.4	10.1
Cost of sales %	*75%*	*78%*	*80%*	*78%*	*78%*	*75%*
Gross profit	3.7	2.8	2.1	2.6	2.6	3.4
Gross profit %	*25%*	*22%*	*20%*	*22%*	*22%*	*25%*
Marketing	1.5	1.3	1.0	1.5	1.7	2.0
Distribution	1.2	1.0	0.8	0.9	1.0	1.3
Administration	1.3	1.2	1.1	1.2	1.2	1.3
Other costs %	*27%*	*28%*	*28%*	*31%*	*33%*	*34%*
Net profit	(0.3)	(0.7)	(0.8)	(1.0)	(1.3)	(1.2)
Net profit %	*–2%*	*–5%*	*–8%*	*–9%*	*–11%*	*–9%*
Inventory	2.0	2.2	3.0	2.7	2.5	2.0
Employees	100	100	98	98	99	100

	2008	2009	2010	2011 Budget	2012 Forecast	2013 Forecast
Corporate Clothing division:						
Total sales	10.2	11.2	11.1	11.8	12.4	13.2
Trend		*12%*	*-1%*	*6%*	*5%*	*6%*
Cost of sales	6.6	7.0	7.0	7.2	7.4	7.7
Cost of sales %	*65%*	*63%*	*63%*	*61%*	*60%*	*58%*
Gross profit	3.6	4.2	4.1	4.6	5.0	5.5
Gross profit %	*35%*	*38%*	*37%*	*39%*	*40%*	*42%*
Marketing	0.2	0.2	0.2	0.2	0.2	0.2
Distribution	0.4	0.4	0.4	0.5	0.5	0.6
Administration	0.5	0.6	0.6	0.7	0.7	0.8
Other costs %	*11%*	*11%*	*11%*	*12%*	*11%*	*12%*
Net profit	2.5	3.0	2.9	3.2	3.6	3.9
Net profit %	*25%*	*27%*	*26%*	*27%*	*29%*	*30%*
Inventory	0.9	1.0	0.8	0.8	0.9	1.0
Employees	84	84	80	79	77	75

The results and forecast for the two divisions indicate that the Shirtmaster Group is a composite of two very different performances by the totally separate divisions. These divisions are operating in very different markets, with very different strategies and very different results. For the group as a whole, sales have declined to 2010 and net margins are struggling to get into double figures.

The Shirtmaster division is **dragging down the performance of the entire group**. The overall group net profit margin of 10% in 2010 masks the fact that the Shirtmasters division suffered a net loss, while Corporate Clothing recorded a net profit margin of 26%.

Using the information from the scenario to consider the Shirtmasters value chain, for example, Tony Masters' strategy of being an integrated shirt manufacturer carrying out all the activities needed to design, manufacture and distribute its shirts is in doubt, because most of its competitors have recognised the commercial sense in **outsourcing production to cheaper and more flexible manufacturers overseas**. There is no competitive advantage in retaining production in the higher cost Gondour, particularly when the company has no other point of differentiation (such as recognised high style or fashion) for its products.

The premium end of the shirt market, its historical focus, has changed since the days of Shirtmasters' earlier success and the division now needs to change to respond to a new **market structure** with **new participants in the value system**.

The figures indicate that Shirtmaster's reliance on small retailers has seen the costs of its support activities (marketing, distribution and administration) take up a huge part of its turnover (19% in 2010, and forecast to rise still further to 23% by 2013).

Trips to buy cloth from foreign suppliers have resulted in **large inventories of expensive cloth**, around a month's worth of sales being held at any one time. Meeting the demands of its many small customers is therefore having a real impact on marketing, manufacturing and distribution costs. High inventory levels will also have an adverse impact on the business's **working capital requirements**.

Making reference to Porter's five competitive forces, the key ones at work are the **rivalry between the shirt makers**, and the increased **buying power of customers** in the industry – the specialist retail outlets and supermarkets. To accommodate these forces, Shirtmasters may have to consider the possibility of making own brand shirts for the supermarkets so that it can expand its market.

The effect of these problems is revealed in selected aspects of performance, when compared to the Corporate Clothing division:

	Shirtmaster division	Corporate Clothing division
Sales growth to 2010	Slowing	Increasing
Gross margin	Lower	Higher and sustained
Sales per employee	Modest	Improving
Marketing etc expenses	Out of control	Acceptable levels
Inventory levels	Too high	More modest
Net margins	Negative	Positive
Market share	Minimal, stagnant	Growing
Product innovation	Nil	Customer focus
Process innovation	Nil	Investment in technology
Customer base	Declining	Growing

The measures above reflect a **balanced scorecard approach** to performance analysis. On all measures, Corporate Clothing is a stronger performer and this must be due to its **focus on the customer**, through its willingness to embrace the realities of its market, invest in appropriate technology and take close note of customer needs. The contrast with Tony's 'pet' division, Shirtmasters, could not be more stark, and should serve to impress upon the senior management of the group the need to give more strategic responsibility to managers possessing the necessary detachment to manage Shirtmasters more effectively.

Part (b)

> **Top tips.** Begin your answer by defining a strategic alliance, and outlining its advantages and disadvantages. We have concentrated upon the suitability of a joint venture for this answer. Apply the advantages and disadvantages to the circumstances of Shirtmakers and Corporate Clothing and use your answers to part (a) to examine the suitability of each company. You should answer large scenario questions in order, as your answers to one part may inform the content of a later part, as is the case here.

Johnson, Scholes and Whittington define a strategic alliance as 'where two or more organisations share resources and activities to pursue a strategy'. Alliances can be particularly attractive to smaller firms such as Shirtmakers, or where expensive new technologies or markets are being developed and the costs can be shared. One particular form of strategic alliance is the joint venture, whereby two or more firms join forces for manufacturing, financial and marketing purposes and each has a share in both the equity and the management of the business.

Particular advantages to Shirtmakers and Corporate Clothing of the pursuit of such an alliance are the following.

(a)   **Share costs**. As the capital outlay is shared, joint ventures can be especially attractive. The joint operation may lead to economies of scale that mean that costs can be reduced.

(b)   **Cut risk.** A joint venture can reduce the risk of government intervention if a local firm is involved.

(c)   Alliances provide **close control** over marketing and other operations, as both companies have a strong interest in ensuring that processes are effective.

(d)   Overseas joint ventures provide **local knowledge**. Alliances are commonly entered into where, as in this scenario, a company is seeking to expand overseas.

(e)   **Synergies.** One firm's production expertise, for example, can be supplemented by the other's marketing and distribution facility. In this way, particular competences can be exploited for the good of the whole alliance.

(f)   **Learning.** Alliances can also be a learning exercise in which each partner tries to learn as much as possible from the other, particularly about local markets.

(g) **Technology.** New technology offers many uncertainties and many opportunities. Such alliances provide funds for expensive research projects, spreading risk.

(h) **The alliance itself can generate innovations** and be a learning exercise for all participants.

(i) The alliance can involve **testing the firm's core competence** in different conditions, which can suggest ways to improve it.

When choosing the type of alliance to pursue, the following factors need to be considered by Shirtmakers and Corporate Clothing.

What benefits are going to be offered by collaboration?

- Which partners should be chosen?
- Is the environment favourable to a partnership?
- What activities and processes will have to be set up?
- Are there any other alliances within the industry?

Johnson, Scholes and Whittington argue that for an alliance to be successful there needs to be a **clear strategic purpose** and **senior management support**; **compatibility** between the partners; time spent defining **clear goals**, governance and other organisational arrangements; and **trust** between the partners that together they can get the job done.

The major disadvantage of joint ventures is that there can be **major conflicts of interest**. Disagreements may arise over profit shares, amounts invested, the management and control of the alliance, and overall strategy. Shirtmakers and Corporate Clothing would need to make sure that such issues are clearly set out and agreed at the beginning to avoid damaging clashes later.

The Shirtmaster and Corporate Clothing divisions have very different experience and business conditions to offer any potential partner. Shirtmaster may struggle to attract a partner with its current product and strategy, particularly its insistence on **retaining manufacture in Gondour** when most competitors now source from cheaper markets in Catopia and Eurpolis. Its dwindling network of low volume small retail customers, and the processes by which it manages its stock and designs would appear to many potential partners and Catopian retailers to be anachronistic. By contrast, the Corporate Clothing division seems to be much more favourable as a potential partner. The market for corporate workwear is growing, and the company employs sophisticated systems coupled with a superior customer service record. This could be repeated in Catopia if the right partner could be found.

Part (c)

> **Top tips.** This is a complex question. The existence of the two divisions largely reflects the origins of the two family businesses, and the divisions have grown and developed separately. Think about the advantages and disadvantages of divisionalisation and how these are currently manifested in the Shirtmasters group. Does divisionalisation make sense for the management of these businesses? Their products may be along the same lines, but their trading conditions and circumstances are very different.

Divisionalisation has some advantages, notably **focusing the attention of subordinate management** on business performance and results. It therefore can provide a good training ground for junior managers in the individual divisions. It also enables proper concentration on particular product-market areas – in this case, shirts and workwear.

Problems can arise, as in this scenario, with the **power of the head office**, and **control of resources**. It appears that Tony Masters has more emotional commitment, and presumably more management time, to devote to Shirtmaster at the expense of Corporate Clothing.

Mintzberg believes there are inherent problems in divisionalisation, many of which are actually those of conglomerate diversification. In the Shirtmaster group, it could be that each business might be better run independently. The different businesses might offer different returns for different risks which shareholders might prefer to **judge independently**.

There does not appear to be any common effort between the divisions, with no sharing of resources apparent from the scenario details. While both are in the clothing market, their respective value systems

run very differently. Information systems are also likely to operate independently. This may be leading to **duplication of effort** and **waste of resources**.

If divisionalisation is to operate effectively, divisional management should be free to use their authority to do what they think is right for their part of the organisation. This is not happening in the Shirtmaster division, and the time has come for Tony Masters to allow his management team to **develop strategy** to drive the company forward, perhaps with the necessity to take some tough decisions that he appears incapable of making. Performance in both divisions needs to be clearly identified and controlled, and resources channelled to those areas showing potential.

Each division must have a potential for growth in its own area of operations. It seems that only Corporate Clothing can satisfy this test in current trading conditions.

Divisions should exist side by side with each other. If they deal with each other, it should be as an arm's length transaction. There should be no insistence on preferential treatment to be given to one particular unit. While there is no suggestion in the scenario that this is happening, Tony Masters' favouring of the Shirtmaster division in more subtle ways is having an effect upon performance.

Using the BCG matrix it is possible to classify the Shirtmaster division as a 'dog' with low market share, in a market with little growth. It needs refreshed management to take it forward and find new markets. The Corporate Clothing division, by contrast, has a small share of a growing market, and this potential also needs to close management.

Index

BPP LEARNING MEDIA

Review Form – Paper P3 Business Analysis (4/15)

Please help us to ensure that the ACCA learning materials we produce remain as accurate and user-friendly as possible. We cannot promise to answer every submission we receive, but we do promise that it will be read and taken into account when we update this Study Text.

Name: _____   Address: _____

_____

_____

How have you used this Study Text?
(Tick one box only)

☐ On its own (book only)

☐ On a BPP in-centre course _____

☐ On a BPP online course

☐ On a course with another college

☐ Other _____

Why did you decide to purchase this Study Text? *(Tick one box only)*

☐ Have used BPP Texts in the past

☐ Recommendation by friend/colleague

☐ Recommendation by a lecturer at college

☐ Saw information on BPP website

☐ Saw advertising

☐ Other _____

During the past six months do you recall seeing/receiving any of the following?
(Tick as many boxes as are relevant)

☐ Our advertisement in *ACCA Student Accountant*

☐ Our advertisement in *Pass*

☐ Our advertisement in *PQ*

☐ Our brochure with a letter through the post

☐ Our website www.bpp.com

Which (if any) aspects of our advertising do you find useful?
(Tick as many boxes as are relevant)

☐ Prices and publication dates of new editions

☐ Information on Text content

☐ Facility to order books off-the-page

☐ None of the above

Which BPP products have you used?

Text	☑	Passcards	☐	Other	☐
Kit	☐	i-Pass	☐		

Your ratings, comments and suggestions would be appreciated on the following areas.

	Very useful	Useful	Not useful
Introductory section	☐	☐	☐
Chapter introductions	☐	☐	☐
Key terms	☐	☐	☐
Quality of explanations	☐	☐	☐
Case studies and other examples	☐	☐	☐
Exam focus points	☐	☐	☐
Questions and answers in each chapter	☐	☐	☐
Fast forwards and chapter roundups	☐	☐	☐
Quick quizzes	☐	☐	☐
Question Bank	☐	☐	☐
Answer Bank	☐	☐	☐
Index	☐	☐	☐

	Excellent	Good	Adequate	Poor
Overall opinion of this Study Text	☐	☐	☐	☐

Do you intend to continue using BPP products?   Yes ☐   No ☐

On the reverse of this page is space for you to write your comments about our Study Text We welcome your feedback.

The BPP Learning Media ACCA Range Manager of this edition can be emailed at:accaqueries@bpp.com

Please return this form to: BPP Learning Media Ltd, FREEPOST, London, W12 8AA

TELL US WHAT YOU THINK

Please note any further comments and suggestions/errors below. For example, was the text accurate, readable, concise, user-friendly and comprehensive?